YOUNG CANADA

DICTIONARY

Third Expanded Edition

Nelson Canada

I(T)P An International Thomson Publishing Company

Toronto • Albany • Bonn • Boston • Cincinnati • Detroit • London • Madrid • Melbourne
Mexico City • New York • Pacific Grove • Paris • San Francisco • Singapore • Tokyo • Washington

I(T)P™
International Thomson Publishing
The ITP logo is a trademark under licence

Published in 1996 by
Nelson Canada,
A division of Thomson Canada Limited
1120 Birchmount Road
Scarborough, Ontario M1K 5G4

Printed and bound in Canada

1 2 3 4 5 6 7 8 9 0 / BP / 4 3 2 1 0 9 8 7 6 5

Canadian Cataloguing in Publication Data

Main entry under title:
Young Canada dictionary

3rd ed.
ISBN 0-17-604741-7

1. English language – Dictionaries, Juvenile.
I. Liebman, Daniel.

PE1628.5.Y68 1995 j423 C95–931530–6

Editorial and Production Team

Editor: Daniel Liebman
Executive Editor: Joe Banel
Project Manager: Lana Kong
Developmental Editor: Alan Simpson
Copy Editor: Susan Wallace-Cox
Senior Production Editor: Deborah Lonergan
Editorial Assistant: Kathleen ffolliott
Composition Team: Elaine Andrews, Zenaida Diores, Nelson Gonzalez
Production Coordinator: Renate McCloy
Art Director: Liz Harasymczuk
Interior Design: Katharine Lapins
Cover Design and Art Direction: Peggy Rhodes
Text Illustrations: Kathryn Adams, Kim La Fave, Sam Sisco
Cover Illustration: Ron Job

Review Panel

The publisher wishes to thank the following educators for their valuable advice given during the development of this edition of the *Young Canada Dictionary*:

Halina Bartley, Elementary Program Consultant, Peterborough County Board of Education, Peterborough, ON
Joyce Billinkoff, Language Arts Support Teacher, Machray School, Winnipeg, MB
Maureen Capotosto, Principal, Gracefield Public School, North York, ON
Mady Davidson, Language Arts Support Teacher, Machray School, Winnipeg, MB
Kevin Grant, Upper Elementary Teacher, Braemore School, Antigonish, NS
Veda Hanninen, Consultant, Early Years/ Formative Years, Sudbury Board of Education, Sudbury, ON
Georgina Hedges, Program Coordinator, Exploits Valley Integrated School Board, Grand Falls-Windsor, NF
Lucy Miller, Consultant, Junior Education, Carleton Roman Catholic School Board, Nepean, ON
William Nugent, Teacher, Andover Elementary School, Perth-Andover, NB
Gladys Rosencrans, Program Consultant, School District No. 41, Burnaby, BC
Norma Sommerville, Teacher, Alexmuir Junior School, Scarborough, ON
Evelyn Steinberg, Principal, Gulfstream School, North York, ON

The *Young Canada Dictionary*

Where do you look

- when you want to find out how to spell a word?
- when you want to know what a word means?
- when you want to know how to pronounce a word?

The answer: in the *Young Canada Dictionary.*

How to Find a Word

What if you want to look up the word **pitcher**? Here are three simple steps for finding this word quickly.

Step 1
Open the dictionary close to where you think your word is located.

Think of it as having two parts: the *front part* and the *back part*. The front part has all the words beginning with **a** to **m**. The back part has all the words beginning with **n** to **z**.

The word **pitcher** will be under the letter **p**. **P** is quite near the beginning of the back part of the dictionary. So open your dictionary a little more than halfway.

Step 2
Look at the guide words at the top of the page.

At the top of the page you will see two words. These are called **guide words**. They guide you to the page that has the word you are looking for.

Guide words look like this in this dictionary:

The guide word on the left tells you the first word on that page. The guide word on the right tells you the last word on that page.

To find the word **pitcher**, look at the guide words at the top of each page until you find those beginning with **p**.

Step 3
Look at the first two letters in the word you are looking for.

You don't have to look through all the words beginning with **p** to find the word **pitcher**. Just look for the first two letters, **p** and **i**. Turn the pages until you find a guide word that starts with **pi**.

pinch ► **plague**

The guide words "pinch" and "plague" show that **pitcher** is somewhere on this page. Look down the columns of **pi** words until you find **pitcher**. You have located your word!

1. Guide words

pinch ▶ plague

2. Entry word

3. Pronunciation

4. Part of speech

11. Word note

5. Definition

fasten things: *a safety pin.* **2.** a piece of jewellery with a clasp, worn on clothing. **3.** one of the bottle-shaped clubs to be knocked down in the game of bowling. —*v.* to fasten with a pin. **pinning. pinned.** (*opp.* **unpin.**)

pinch (pinch) *n.* **1.** a sharp, quick squeeze with the thumb and a finger. **2.** a small amount: *a pinch of salt. pl.* **pinches.** —*v.* to squeeze between the thumb and a finger. **pinching. pinched.**

pine (pīn) *n.* a tall tree with cones and very thin, sharp, green leaves that are called needles: *Pines do not lose their needles in winter.*

pineapple (pīn′ ap′ əl) *n.* a large, sweet, yellow fruit that grows in hot places: *A pineapple has a rough, prickly skin.*

The old English word "pinappel" was first used for what we now call a "pine cone." The fruit we now call **pineapple** got its name because its shape and skin made it look like a large prickly pine cone.

Ping-Pong (ping′ pong′) *n.* a trademark name for table tennis.

pink (pingk) *n.* a very light red colour. —*adj.* having this colour.

pint (pīnt) *n.* a unit for measuring volume, equal to about 0.5 L.

pinto (pin′ tō) *n.* a spotted horse or pony. *pl.* **pintos.**

pioneer (pī′ ə nēr′) *n.* **1.** one of the first people who settle in a new place, preparing the way for others. **2.** someone who is the first to do something.

pipe (pīp) *n.* **1.** a long, metal or plastic tube that carries gas, oil, water, or other substances. **2.** a musical instrument shaped like a tube, such as a flute. **3.** a tube with a small bowl at one end, used for smoking tobacco.

pirate (pī′ rit) *n.* in earlier times, a person who attacked and robbed ships at sea.

pistol (pis′ təl) *n.* a small gun fired with one hand.

pit (pit) *n.* **1.** a deep hole in the ground. **2.** a hard seed or stone in a fruit: *a peach pit.*

pitch (pich) *n.* in baseball, a throw of the ball to the batter. *pl.* **pitches.** —*v.* **1.** to throw: *to pitch a ball.* **2.** to set up: *to pitch a tent.* **pitching. pitched.**

pitcher (pich′ ər) *n.* **1.** a large jug: *a pitcher of milk.* **2.** the baseball player who pitches the ball: *The pitcher struck out the batter.*

pitchfork (pich′ fȯrk′) *n.* a long, large fork, used for tossing hay.

pitchfork

pitiful (pit′ ə fəl) *adj.* deserving pity: *a sick, starved, pitiful animal.* —**pitifully** *adv.*

pity (pit′ ē) *n.* sympathy and sorrow for a person in trouble. —*v.* to feel pity for someone: *Azhar pitied his friend who was in pain.* **pitying. pitied.** he **pities.**

pizza (pēt′ zə) *n.* a flat, round dough covered with tomato sauce, cheese, or other ingredients; it is baked until crusty.

place (plās) *n.* a position, spot, or location: *a place at the table; a place in line; a place in history.* —*v.* to put something in a certain spot: *We placed our shoes by the front door.* **placing. placed.**

take place to happen: *Describe the events that take place in the story.*

plague (plāg) *n.* a dangerous disease that spreads quickly among people.

201

9. Plural form

7. Illustration

10. Related adverb

8. Verb forms

6. Examples

Guide to the *Young Canada Dictionary*

The most important parts of the dictionary are labelled on page 4. Here is an explanation of these different parts.

1. **Guide words:** When you are trying to find a word, the guide words are *the words you look at as you turn the pages.* The guide word on the left tells you the first word on that page. The guide word on the right tells you the last word on that page.

2. **Entry word:** The entry word is the first item in any dictionary entry. It is the word printed in heavy, black letters so that you can find it easily. It gives you the *proper spelling* of the word. If you just want to know how to spell a word, this is sometimes all you need to look at.

   The **entry** is *all the written words that appear with the entry word.* The entry gives you a lot of information about the word, such as:

   - the *pronunciation* of the word
   - the kind of word it is (the *part of speech*)
   - the *definition* of the word
   - the different *verb forms* of verbs
   - the *plural form* of some nouns
   - the *related adverb* for some adjectives.

3. **Pronunciation:** The pronunciation shows you *how to pronounce (say) a word correctly.* The word is written again (in brackets) to help you "sound out" each syllable. You will notice that some special marks are used. For example, a short, straight bar over a vowel (ā) tells you this **a** has a "long" vowel sound—the sound you hear in "fate." "Fat," without the final **e**, has a "short" vowel sound.

   Look at the "Pronunciation Guide" on the last page of this dictionary to see how different letters are pronounced. Then look up **audition**, **knowledge**, **moustache**, and **quay** to see how they are spoken.

4. **Part of speech:** A part of speech is a type of word. The parts of speech mentioned in this dictionary are *article, adjective (adj.), adverb (adv.), conjunction (conj.), interjection (interj.), noun (n.), preposition (prep.),* and *verb (v.).*

   Turn to the last page of this dictionary and you will find all the parts of speech above listed under "Abbreviations."

5. **Definition:** The definition gives you *the meaning of a word.* Sometimes there is more than one meaning. When this happens, the meanings are numbered **1**, **2**, and so on.

   > **pitcher** (pich′ ər) *n.* 1. a large jug: *a pitcher of milk.* 2. the baseball player who pitches the ball.

   Many words can be used as more than one part of speech. For example, the word *wrinkle* can be used as a noun and also as a verb: *A wrinkle* (noun) is *"a crease in cloth or on the skin." To wrinkle* (verb) means *"to become creased."*

6. **Example:** Often, the definition will give an example to make the meaning clearer. The example might be a *complete sentence* or just a *phrase.*

Look at label number 6 on page 4. Two examples are shown. One is a sentence, and one is a phrase. Which is which? How do you know?

7. **Illustration:** Many words in this dictionary have a picture to make the meaning of the word clearer.

8. **Verb forms:** Different forms are shown when the entry word is a verb. The **–ing** ending and the **–ed** ending are always shown at the end of the entry.

Some verbs have special forms, for example: *strike – striking – struck.* Look up **buy**, **catch**, **find**, **seek**, and **steal**, and see how these verbs change.

9. **Plural form:** Many nouns become plural (more than one) just by adding an **s** at the end, for example, **cat** → **cats**. However, making a noun plural is not always this simple. For example, the plural form of **copy** is **copies**, not "copys." When you look up the word **copy**, the plural form is also shown.

Write down what you think the plural form is for each of these nouns: **batch**, **child**, **hero**, **party**, **shelf**. Then check your answers by looking up these words in the dictionary.

10. **Related adverb:** Adding the **–ly** ending to many adjectives turns them into adverbs: brave + ly → bravely. The adverb **bravely** means "in a brave way": *The soldiers fought bravely.*

A related adverb is shown with the adjective, usually at the end of the entry. If an adverb has more or different meanings, it is listed as a separate entry.

From the adjectives *calm, dangerous, glad, quiet,* and *safe,* figure out the meaning of each of these related adverbs: **calmly**, **dangerously**, **gladly**, **quietly**, **safely**. Can you think of sentences where you could use these words?

11. **Word note:** Word notes *give you hints to help you use a word correctly.* Do you know the difference between **accept** and **except**? Look up either of these words to find a word note that tells you how to use them.

Other word notes tell you *the history of some of our words.* Look at label number 11 on page 4. That word note explains the history of the word **pineapple**.

Another kind of word note explains *the difference between words with similar meanings.* Look up **plateau** to find a word note explaining the difference between **plateau**, **plain**, and **prairie**.

a (ə *or* ā) *article* one; any; each: *a glass of water; a day of the week; once a month.*

abacus (ab′ ə kəs) *n.* a rectangular frame with rows of wires holding beads that slide back and forth. Abacuses, which originated in China, are used for doing arithmetic. *pl.* **abacuses.**

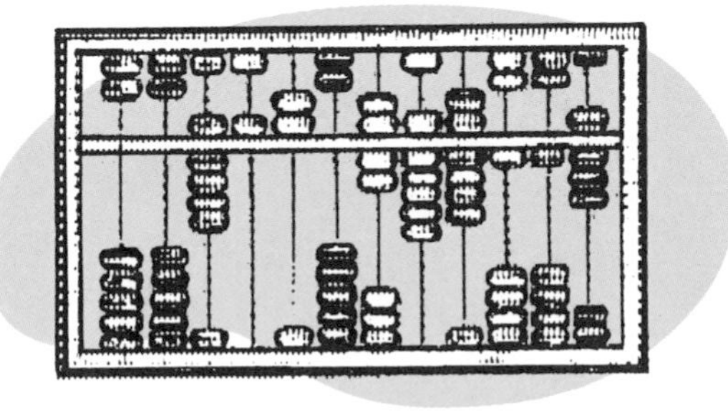

abacus

abandon (ə ban′ dən) *v.* to leave someone or something, and never return: *The sailors abandoned the sinking ship.* **abandoning. abandoned.**

abbreviate (ə brē′ vē āt′) *v.* to shorten something such as a word, a sentence, or a story: *"British Columbia" can be abbreviated by writing "B.C."* **abbreviating. abbreviated.**

abbreviation (ə brē′ vē ā′ shən) *n.* a shortened form of a word: *"Dr." is the abbreviation for "doctor."*

There are many common **abbreviations** we see and use every day. Here are some examples:

"Mr." is short for "Mister."

"RCMP" is short for "Royal Canadian Mounted Police."

"NDP" is short for "New Democratic Party."

abdomen (ab′ də mən *or* ab′ dō mən) *n.* **1.** the belly: *Your abdomen contains your stomach and other organs.* **2.** the rear section of an insect's body.

ability (ə bil′ ə tē) *n.* the power or skill to do something: *A fish has the ability to swim.* *pl.* **abilities.**

able (ā′ bəl) *adj.* having the power or skill to do something: *A bird is able to fly.* (*opp.* **unable.**)

abnormal (ab nȯr′ məl) *adj.* unusual and unexpected: *This warm weather is abnormal for November.* —**abnormally** *adv.*

aboard (ə bȯrd′) *adv.* on or into a ship, plane, bus, or train.

aboriginal (ab′ ə rij′ ə nəl) *n.* one of the original or earliest inhabitants of a land.

about (ə bowt′) *prep.* **1.** close to: *It was about two o'clock.* **2.** to do with: *The movie is about a girls' hockey team.* —*adv.* around: *The boys were running about the field.*

about to just going to: *She was about to go out when the phone rang.*

above (ə buv′) *prep.* higher than: *The picture hangs above the fireplace.* —*adv.* overhead: *Look at the clouds above.*

abroad (ə brod′) *adv.* in another country, usually one across the sea: *Instead of travelling through Canada, we'll go abroad and visit Japan.*

abrupt (ə brupt′) *adj.* **1.** sudden; not expected: *an abrupt end to the song.* **2.** rude, not polite: *an abrupt answer.* —**abruptly** *adv.*

absence (ab′ səns) *n.* being away: *Jan's absence meant that Rehana would have to play first base for her.*

absent (ab′ sənt) *adj.* not there: *I was absent from school.*

absent-minded (ab′ sənt mīn′ dəd) *adj.* forgetful; not paying attention.

absolute (ab′ sə lūt′) *adj.* complete: *May I have absolute silence from everybody in the audience, please!* —**absolutely** *adv.*

absorb (ab zȯrb′ *or* ab sȯrb′) *v.* to take in liquid: *The paper towel quickly absorbed the water.* **absorbing. absorbed.**

absurd (ab zûrd′ *or* ab sûrd′) *adj.* absolutely foolish; beyond belief: *Don't be absurd! Cows don't oink and pigs don't moo.* —**absurdly** *adv.*

abundance (ə bun′ dəns) *n.* a great amount: *My brother has an abundance of energy!*

abundant (ə bun′ dənt) *adj.* **1.** more than enough. **2.** very plentiful: *We have an abundant crop of tomatoes this year.* —**abundantly** *adv.*

abuse (ə būs′) *n.* bad words or treatment: *The stranger shouted abuse at me, calling me unkind names.*

abuse (ə būz′) *v.* to treat a person or thing badly by speaking in a mean way, by causing physical harm, or by not giving the care that is needed: *The dog was shy because it had been abused by its previous owner.* **abusing. abused.**

academic (ak′ ə dem′ ik) *adj.* having to do with school or education: *Your report card shows your academic achievements.* —**academically** *adv.*

Acadian (ə kād′ ē ən) *n.* a person who settled in Acadia, the part of eastern Canada that used to be a French colony: *The Acadians settled in what is now New Brunswick and mainland Nova Scotia.*

accelerate (ak sel′ ər āt′) *v.* to go faster, or to make something go faster: *to accelerate a car.* **accelerating. accelerated.**

accent (ak′ sent) *n.* a person's style of speaking and pronouncing words: *Ian speaks with an English accent.* —*v.* when speaking, to place more stress on some sounds than on others: *In the word "accept," we accent the second syllable.* **accenting. accented.**

accept (ak sept′) *v.* to take something that is offered: *to accept a gift.* **accepting. accepted.**

> Be careful not to mix up **accept** with "except." "Except" means "other than."

acceptable (ak sept′ ə bəl) *adj.* pleasing, or good enough: *The dinner wasn't special, but it was acceptable.* —**acceptably** *adv.*

access (ak′ ses) *n.* an entrance; a way of approach. *pl.* **accesses.** —*v.* to find information stored in a computer: *Can you access your geography homework on the computer?* **accessing. accessed.**

accessible (ak ses′ ə bəl) *adj.* able to be reached: *The island is accessible by boat in the summer and snowmobile in the winter.*

accident (ak′sə dənt) *n.* something harmful or unpleasant that happens suddenly or unexpectedly: *The accident happened when the two cars hit each other.*
by accident not on purpose.

accidental (ak′ sə den′ təl) *adj.* not on purpose: *an accidental fall.* —**accidentally** *adv.*

accommodate (ə kom′ ə dāt′) *v.* to have room for, or to provide with space: *The theatre can accommodate 500 people.* **accommodating. accommodated.**

accompany (ə kum′ pə nē) *v.* to go with: *Our cousin will accompany us to the theatre.* **accompanying. accompanied.** she **accompanies.**

accomplish (ə kom′ plish) *v.* to do or finish: *Nadia can accomplish many tasks in one day.* **accomplishing. accomplished.**

accomplishment (ə kom′ plish mənt) *n.* something that has been accomplished successfully: *Getting perfect marks on a test is an accomplishment.*

according to (ə kȯr′ ding tü) from what someone says: *According to Nick, it is now one o'clock.*

accordion (ə kȯr′ dē ən) *n.* a portable musical instrument with a keyboard.

accordion

account (ə kownt′) *n.* **1.** a record of money spent, owned, or saved: *a bank account.* **2.** a description or an explanation: *The witness gave an account of the accident.*

accumulate (ə kyū′ myə lāt′) *v.* to collect; to pile up: *By the time we returned from our trip, a pile of mail had accumulated.* **accumulating. accumulated.**

accurate (ak′ yə rit) *adj.* free from mistakes; very exact: *My new watch gives accurate time.* —**accurately** *adv.*

accuse (ə kyūz′) *v.* to blame someone: *The detective accused two people of the crime.* **accusing. accused.**

accustomed to (ə cus′ təmd tü) adapted to something: *I am now accustomed to getting up early for my summer job.*

ace (ās) *n.* a playing card with a single heart, spade, diamond, or club in the middle. —*adj.* expert or highly skilled in an activity: *She is an ace fighter pilot.*

ache (āk) *n.* a pain, such as a *headache, toothache,* or *earache.* —*v.* to have a pain. **aching. ached.**

achieve (ə chēv′) *v.* to accomplish something; to be successful: *We achieved our goal of raising $300 for the school trip.* **achieving. achieved.**

achievement (ə chēv′ mənt) *n.* something that you accomplish: *Getting good marks in science is a real achievement for my brother.*

acid (as′ id) *n.* a liquid with a sour, sharp taste. Strong acids cause burns and can eat away at substances such as metals. —*adj.* sharp or sour to the taste: *Lemons have an acid taste.*

acid rain rain that is polluted when acid is released into the atmosphere by industry: *One cause of acid rain is coal smoke that combines with water vapour in the air.*

acknowledge (ak nol′ ij) *v.* **1.** to admit that something is true: *He acknowledged his mistake and then corrected it.* **2.** to state that you have received something: *Did she acknowledge the gift that you sent?* **acknowledging. acknowledged.**

acorn (ā kȯrn) *n.* the nut-like fruit of the oak tree.

acquire (ə kwīr′) *v.* to get something: *to acquire information, to acquire a new piece of jewellery.* **acquiring. acquired.**

acre (ā′ kər) *n.* an area of land, equal to about 4000 m^2.

acrobat (ak′ rə bat′) *n.* a person who can do daring leaps, jumps, and flips, often on a trapeze.

acrobatic (ak′ rə bat′ ik) *adj.* as if performed by an acrobat: *The dancer made an acrobatic leap high into the air and landed very gracefully.*

acronym (ak′ rə nim) *n.* a word made up of the first letters of a group of words: *Scuba is an acronym, formed from the words "self-contained underwater breathing apparatus."*

across (ə kros′) *prep.* to the other side of: *They swam across the river.* —*adv.* on the other side: *They were safely across.*

act (akt) *n.* **1.** a deed; a happening: *an act of bravery.* **2.** a section of a play or an opera: *The school play is in three acts.* **3.** (usually capitalized) a law made by Parliament.
—*v.* **1.** to do something: *That boy needs help. Act now!* **2.** to behave; to pretend: *The two girls acted as if they were ill.* **3.** to take the role of a character in a play. **acting. acted.**

action (ak′ shən) *n.* **1.** a deed; a happening. **2.** movement: *the action of a clock.*

activate (ak′ tə vāt′) *v.* to start something, usually a machine: *Once the burglar alarm is activated, a bell will ring when the door opens.* **activating. activated.**

active (ak′ tiv) *adj.* lively: *Samira is an active person, always doing things.*
—**actively** *adv.*

activity (ak tiv′ ə tē) *n.* movement, action, or something you do at a certain time: *Baseball is my favourite outdoor activity.* *pl.* **activities.**

actor (ak′ tər) *n.* a person who performs in a movie, TV, or stage production.

actress (ak′ trəs) *n.* a female actor.

actual (ak′ chū əl) *adj.* real, not imaginary.
—**actually** *adv.*

acute (ə kyūt′) *adj.* very sharp and severe: *Before his appendix operation, Costas had an acute pain in his abdomen.* —**acutely** *adv.*

acute angle an angle that measures between zero and ninety degrees.

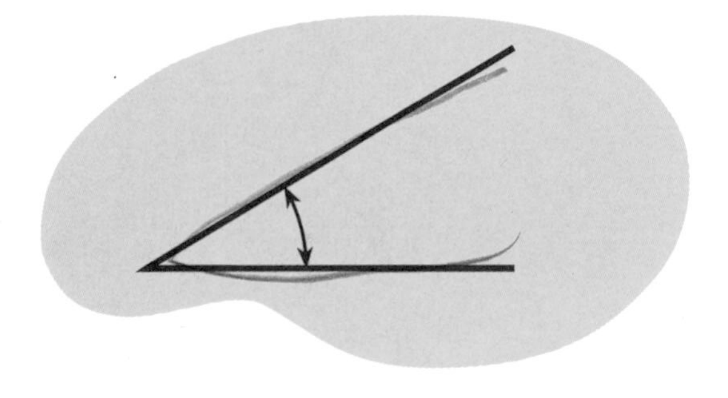

acute angle

ad (ad) *n.* short for **advertisement**.

Adam's apple (ad′ əmz ap′ əl) the lump in the front of the neck, which moves up and down when you swallow.

adapt (ə dapt′) *v.* to change in order to deal with a new situation: *Maria adapted quickly to her new school. She made new friends and joined several clubs.* **adapting. adapted.**

add (ad) *v.* **1.** to put something in, on, or with another thing: *to add milk to tea.*
2. to find the total of two or more numbers: *3 added to 4 equals 7.* **adding. added.**

addict (ad′ ikt) *n.* a person who is not able to stop a harmful habit, such as smoking or drinking alcohol or taking drugs.

addition (ə dish′ ən) *n.* **1.** the adding of one thing to another. **2.** adding numbers or amounts.
in addition also.

additional (ə dish′ ən əl) *adj.* added; extra: *When you go camping, take an additional pair of shoes in case the pair you are wearing becomes wet.* —**additionally** *adv.*

address (ə dres′ *or* ad′ res) *n.* **1.** the house number, street, town, province, and postal code of the location where you live or work.
2. (ə dres′) a speech: *The visitor gave the students a short address.* *pl.* **addresses.**

address (ə dres′) *v.* **1.** to write on a letter or package where it is to go. **2.** to give a speech to a group of people. **addressing. addressed.**

adequate (ad′ ə kwit) *adj.* **1.** enough: *Do you have adequate food for the camping trip?*
2. good enough: *The number of volunteers is adequate.* —**adequately** *adv.*

adhere (ad hēr′) *v.* to stick to something: *The bandage was hard to remove because it adhered so well to my skin.* **adhering. adhered.**

adhesive (ad hē′ siv) *n.* a substance that sticks things together. —*adj.* sticky: *Carefully remove the adhesive tape.*

adjective (aj′ ik tiv) *n.* a describing word (part of speech) that gives information about a noun: *a red rose; an iron gate; a good man.*

adjust (ə just′) *v.* to change something to make it better or more comfortable: *Let's adjust the colour on the TV set.* **adjusting. adjusted.**

admiral (ad′ mə rəl) *n.* the highest officer in the Canadian navy.

admiration (ad′ mə rā′ shən) *n.* a feeling of respect for someone or something: *I have great admiration for that singer.*

admire (ad mīr′) *v.* **1.** to think highly of someone or something. **2.** to look at with pleasure: *We admired the beautiful sunset.* **admiring. admired.**

admission (ad mish′ ən) *n.* **1.** entry: *admission to university.* **2.** the price for being allowed to enter: *Admission to the fair is free.* **3.** a confession: *an admission of guilt.*

admit (ad mit′) *v.* **1.** to let in: *This ticket admits two people.* **2.** to confess: *She had to admit that she was wrong.* **admitting. admitted.**

admittance (ad mit′ əns) *n.* permission to enter: *The notice on the door reads "No admittance."*

adolescence (ad′ ə les′ əns) *n.* the period of growth between childhood and adulthood.

adolescent (ad′ ə les′ ənt) *n.* a teenager.

adopt (ə dopt′) *v.* **1.** to bring up someone else's child legally as your own: *My stepfather adopted me.* **2.** to take and use as your own: *He adopted a Scottish accent and started wearing a kilt.* **adopting. adopted.**

adorable (ə dȯr′ ə bəl) *adj.* cute and lovable.

adore (ə dȯr′) *v.* to love very much. **adoring. adored.**

adult (ə dult′ *or* ad′ ult) *n.* a grown-up person. *—adj.* grown-up, mature.

advance (ad vans′) *n.* a movement forward. *—v.* to move forward. **advancing. advanced.**

advanced (ad vanst′) *adj.* at a higher stage of development: *This class is for advanced dancers, not beginners.*

advantage (ad van′ tij) *n.* a favourable quality or situation that puts you in a better position than others: *Our football players had the advantage of being bigger than those on the other team.* (*opp.* **disadvantage.**)

adventure (ad ven′ chər) *n.* a daring and exciting experience: *I like stories about adventure in the Arctic.*

adventurous (ad ven′ chər əs) *adj.* daring; wanting to have an adventure.

adverb (ad′ vu̇rb) *n.* a describing word (part of speech) that gives information about a verb, an adjective, or another adverb: *He sneezes quite loudly on a very cold day.* The adverbs in this example are *quite, loudly,* and *very.*

advertise (ad′ vər tīz′) *v.* to announce something, usually for sale, in a newspaper or magazine, on TV or radio. **advertising. advertised.**

advertisement (ad′ vər tīz′ mənt *or* ad vu̇r′ tis mənt) *n.* a public announcement in a newspaper or magazine, on TV or radio, about a product or service for sale: *We read the newspaper advertisement for the bikes. Then we went to see what they looked like.*

advice (ad vīs′) *n.* helpful suggestions; guidance: *My parents gave Choy advice on how to get a job.*

advise (ad vīz′) *v.* to give helpful suggestions or guidance. **advising. advised.**

affect (ə fekt′) *v.* to cause a change: *Louise's illness will affect her holiday plans.* **affecting. affected.**

Be careful not to mix up **affect** (a verb) with "effect" (a noun); "effect" means the result of an action.

affection (ə fek′ shən) *n.* fondness or love: *I have great affection for my grandparents.*

affectionate (ə fek′ shən it) *adj.* showing or expressing affection. —**affectionately** *adv.*

afford (ə fȯrd′) *v.* to spare money for something: *I can't afford to buy a new pair of jeans.* **affording. afforded.**

affordable (ə fȯrd′ ə bəl) *adj.* costing an amount of money that someone can pay: *Not only was the bicycle well made, but it was also very affordable to me.*

afraid (ə frād′) *adj.* frightened; full of fear.

African (af′ ri kən) *n.* a person born in or living in Africa. —*adj.* having to do with the continent of Africa.

after (af′ tər) *prep.* **1.** following or behind in place: *2 comes after 1.* **2.** following or later in time: *after dinner.* —*conj.* following the time that: *The class doesn't end until after the bell rings.*

after all in spite of other things that have happened: *After visiting my cousin, we realized that he wasn't mean after all.*

afternoon (af′ tər nün′) *n.* the part of the day between noon and evening.

afterward, afterwards (af′ tər wərd, af′ tər wərdz) *adv.* later.

again (ə gen′ *or* ə gān′) *adv.* once more.

against (ə genst′ *or* ə gānst′) *prep.* **1.** facing: *to walk against the wind.* **2.** touching: *Mario leaned against the fence.* **3.** not in favour of: *I am against cruelty to animals.*

age (āj) *n.* **1.** the number of years a person has lived or a thing has existed: *Yasmin's age is ten years. What is the age of that building?* **2.** a period of life: *middle age.* **3.** a period of history: *the Stone Age.* —*v.* to grow old. **aging. aged.**

agency (ā′ jən sē) *n.* a business that handles a business activity for a person: *We used a real-estate agency to sell our house.* *pl.* **agencies.**

agent (ā′ jənt) *n.* **1.** a person or company who handles a business activity for another person: *A talent agent can help an unknown actor find a good film role.* **2.** a person involved in secret police or government work: *a secret agent.*

aggressive (ə gres′ iv) *adj.* quick to become angry and attack: *The neighbours' dog becomes very aggressive whenever someone walks past their house.* —**aggressively** *adv.*

agile (a′ jīl) *adj.* able to move quickly and easily; nimble: *an agile gymnast.* —**agilely** *adv.*

agitate (aj′ ə tāt′) *v.* to shake up forcefully; to disturb: *Bad news always agitates me.* **agitating. agitated.**

ago (ə gō′) *adj.* gone by; past: *My sister was born seven years ago.*

long ago many years past.

agony (ag′ ə nē) *n.* great pain or suffering.

agree (ə grē′) *v.* **1.** to have the same opinion: *Do you both agree on this matter?* **2.** to say yes; to consent: *Ruth agreed to play baseball.* **agreeing. agreed.**

agreeable (ə grē′ ə bəl) *adj.* pleasing; friendly; easy to get along with: *I enjoy her company because she's so agreeable.* —**agreeably** *adv.*

agreement (ə grē′ mənt) *n.* **1.** the act of agreeing. **2.** an understanding or arrangement between people or nations: *the free-trade agreement.* (*opp.* **disagreement.**)

agriculture (ag′ rə kul′ chər) *n.* farming, especially, the growing of crops.

ahead (ə hed′) *adv.* **1.** forward; in front: *She's a faster runner and went ahead of me.* **2.** in advance: *Let's call ahead for tickets.*

aid (ād) *n.* help; assistance. —*v.* to help. **aiding. aided.**

AIDS (ādz) (acquired immune deficiency syndrome) *n.* a serious disease that destroys the body's ability to fight infection.

aim (ām) *n.* **1.** the pointing of an object at a target. **2.** a goal: *Their aim is to get on the Olympic team.* —*v.* **1.** to point or direct an object at something. **2.** to have a purpose: *Olga and Ryan aim to be the best pair skaters.* **aiming. aimed.**

air (er) *n.* the mixture of gases that fills the space around us; atmosphere: *the air we breathe.* —*v.* **1.** to let fresh air in or through: *to air a room.* **2.** to broadcast a TV or radio program. **airing. aired.**

on the air being broadcast: *The news goes on the air at six o'clock.*

air conditioner (er′ kon dish′ ən ər) a device that cools the air in buildings or cars.

aircraft (er′ kraft) *n.* any flying machine. *pl.* **aircraft.**

airline (er′ līn) *n.* a company that operates airplanes for transporting people and things.

airmail (er′ māl) *n.* mail transported by aircraft.

airplane (er′ plān) *n.* a vehicle that flies through the air and is equipped with wings and jet engines or propellers.

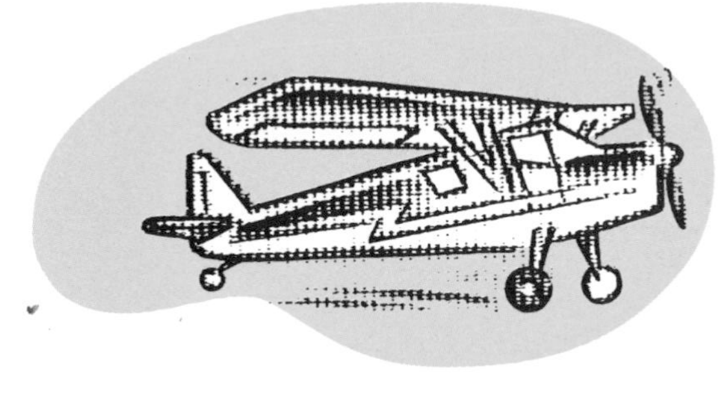

airplane

airport (er′ pôrt) *n.* a place where aircraft land and take off. An airport has runways, a building for the passengers, and places for storing and repairing aircraft.

aisle (īl) *n.* a long, narrow passageway for walking, such as between rows of seats in a theatre, or between shelves in a grocery store.

alarm (ə lärm′) *n.* **1.** fear or sudden fright caused by a feeling of danger: *We watched with alarm as the tornado approached.* **2.** a warning of danger: *The alarm was given when the enemy came near.* **3.** a bell or other signal used as a warning.

album (al′ bəm) *n.* a book with blank pages, used for storing and displaying photos, stamps, cards, or other flat objects.

alcohol (al′ kə hol′) *n.* the colourless liquid in wine, beer, and liquor that causes a person to feel light-headed.

alcoholic (al′ kə hol′ ik) *n.* a person who is addicted to alcohol. —*adj.* made with alcohol, or having to do with alcohol.

ale (āl) *n.* an alcoholic drink made from grain: *Ale is like beer, but heavier.*

alert (ə lûrt′) *adj.* watchful; ready to act quickly: *The swimmers were alert, waiting for the signal to start the race.*

algebra (al′ jə brə) *n.* a branch of mathematics in which letters and symbols are used to represent numbers.

alias (ā′ lē əs) *n.* a false name: *The criminal used an alias. pl.* **aliases.**

alibi (al′ i bī′) *n.* the statement a person makes to prove he or she was somewhere else when a crime was committed. *pl.* **alibis.**

alien (ā′ lē ən) *n.* a person from a different country; a being from another place: *an alien from outer space.* —*adj.* **1.** foreign; from a different country. **2.** strange; unfamiliar.

alike (ə līk′) *adj.* similar: *The sisters are alike in many ways.*

alive (ə līv′) *adj.* **1.** living; not dead. **2.** lively; active.

all (ol) *n.* every one: *All of us are sick.* —*adj.* **1.** the whole of: *Did you eat up all your dinner?* **2.** every one of: *All the runners finished the race.*

all right **1.** correct: *Your test answers are all right.* **2.** adequate, but not excellent: *The cafeteria food is all right.* **3.** yes; very well: *All right, I'll go.* **4.** in good health; not injured: *Were you all right after you fell?*

allergic (ə lůr′ jik) *adj.* having an allergy: *Ben is allergic to cats. He sneezes when they are around.*

allergy (al′ ər jē) *n.* an unpleasant, sometimes life-threatening, physical reaction, such as sneezing or itching, when a person comes in contact with certain foods, animals, plants, or other substances. *pl.* **allergies.**

alley (al′ ē) *n.* a narrow lane between buildings. *pl.* **alleys.**

alligator (al′ ə gā′ tər) *n.* a large reptile, with a long, thick body, short legs, and a snapping jaw with sharp teeth. Alligators have a shorter, wider jaw than crocodiles. They live in rivers and lakes in the southeastern United States and in China.

alligator

allow (ə low′) *v.* to let; to permit: *Our parents will allow us to go to the dance if we finish our homework first.* **allowing. allowed.**

allowance (ə low′ əns) *n.* a regular amount of money given to someone: *My older brother gets a bigger weekly allowance than I do, but I save more than he does.*

ally (al′ ī) *n.* a country or person who helps you in a war or struggle. *pl.* **allies.**

almanac (ol′ mə nak′) *n.* a book published every year that has facts and information on different subjects, such as the weather, holidays, important historical dates, the sun, the moon, and so on. Many almanacs are arranged like calendars.

almond (o′ mənd *or* ol′ mənd) *n.* the oval-shaped nut of the almond tree, which grows in warm places.

almost (ol′ mōst) *adv.* nearly.

alone (ə lōn′) *adj., adv.* with nobody else; with nothing else.

along (ə long′) *prep.* from one end to the other: *We drove along the main street.* —*adv.* **1.** on forward: *Move along!* **2.** in company or as company: *I took my brother along.*

alongside (ə long′ sīd′) *prep., adv.* by the side of.

aloud (ə lowd′) *adv.* loud enough for all to hear: *The teacher read the story aloud to the class.*

alphabet (al′ fə bet′) *n.* the set of letters of a language. In English, the alphabet contains 26 letters, starting with A and ending with Z.

Just as we sometimes call the **alphabet** the "ABCs," the ancient Greeks called it the "ABs." Of course, the Greeks had different names for their letters. They called the letter A "alpha," and the letter B "beta." "AB" was pronounced "alpha-beta" from which we get our word "alphabet"!

alphabetical (al′ fə bet′ ə kəl) *adj.* following the order of the letters of the alphabet: *A dictionary is arranged in alphabetical order.* —**alphabetically** *adv.*

already (ol red′ ē) *adv.* by this time: *Aziza was already there when we arrived.*

also (ol′ sō) *adv.* too; as well: *Should I also ask my sister to play?*

altar (ol′ tər) *n.* a raised place or table, often in a church or a temple, used for religious ceremonies.

alter (ol′ tər) *v.* to change: *Because it was raining, we had to alter our plans to hold a picnic.* **altering. altered.**

alteration (ol′ tər ā′ shən) *n.* a change.

alternate (ol′ tər nit) *adj.* other: *There were no tickets left for the movie, so we made alternate plans.* —**alternately** *adv.*

alternate (ol′ tər nāt′) *v.* to take turns: *We alternated tasks. I washed the dinner dishes on Monday, Wednesday, and Friday, and my brother washed them on the other evenings.* **alternating. alternated.**

alternative (ol tər′ nə tiv) *n.* **1.** a choice between two things: *You have the alternative of taking the bus or the train.* **2.** one of two or more choices: *I like the alternative of taking the bus.*

although (ol THō′) *conj.* even if; even though: *I will go out although there's a blizzard outside.*

altitude (al′ tə tūd *or* al′ ti tyūd) *n.* the height of something above the ground or above sea level: *The plane is flying at an altitude of 3500 m.*

altogether (ol′ tə ge′ THər) *adv.* **1.** wholly; totally: *This answer isn't altogether wrong.* **2.** counted together: *We visited three museums altogether.*

aluminum (ə lū′ mə nəm) *n.* a silver-coloured, light metal, used for making baking foil, soft-drink cans, and so on.

always (ol′ wāz *or* ol′ wiz) *adv.* forever; every time: *I shall always try to be early.*

am (am) *v.* a singular form of the verb **be**, used only with "I" in the present tense: *I am going to sleep.*

a.m. before noon, or between midnight and noon: *I woke up at 7 a.m.*

amateur (am′ ə chər) *n.* a person who does an activity just for pleasure, not professionally for money: *The players on college sports teams are usually amateurs.* —*adj.* done by an amateur: *She's an amateur pianist.*

amaze (ə māz′) *v.* to fill with wonder: *The magician amazed us with her tricks.* **amazing. amazed.**

amazement (ə māz′ mənt) *n.* being amazed; great surprise: *We watched the magician's tricks in amazement.*

ambassador (am bas′ ə dər) *n.* the official appointed by a country's government to represent that country in a foreign land: *Who is Canada's ambassador to the United States?*

amber (am′ bər) *n.* the hardened resin of ancient pine trees, deep gold or brownish in colour. It is often used to make jewellery. —*adj.* having this colour: *Traffic lights are red, green, and amber.*

ambition (am bish′ ən) *n.* a strong desire to be successful at something: *Her ambition is to become an astronaut.*

ambitious (am bish′ əs) *adj.* **1.** having the strong desire to be successful at something: *The ambitious student worked very hard on the project.* **2.** challenging; needing much effort: *The hospital's fundraising goal is ambitious.* —**ambitiously** *adv.*

ambulance (am′ byə ləns) *n.* a large vehicle for carrying ill or injured people to hospital.

ambush (am′ bůsh) *n.* a surprise attack on an enemy from a hiding place. *pl.* **ambushes.** —*v.* to attack an enemy by surprise after lying in wait. **ambushing. ambushed.**

amen (ā′ men *or* o′ men) *n.* a word at the end of a prayer, meaning "so be it."

amid (ə mid′) *prep.* in the middle of; among.

ammunition (am′ yə nish′ ən) *n.* bullets and shells for guns.

among (ə mung′) *prep.* **1.** surrounded by: *We walked among the flowers and trees.* **2.** to each of more than two: *Share the sandwiches among the four of you.*

amount (ə mownt′) *n.* **1.** quantity: *a large amount of sugar.* **2.** sum total: *What is the amount of our bill?* —*v.* to add up to: *The bill amounts to $3.50.* **amounting. amounted.**

amphibian (am fib′ ē ən) *n.* a cold-blooded animal able to live both on land and in water: *Toads and frogs are amphibians.*

amplify (am′ plə fī′) *v.* to make something louder or more powerful: *When Charles spoke into the microphone, his voice was amplified around the hall.* **amplifying. amplified.** it **amplifies.**

amuse (ə myūz) *v.* to make someone laugh or smile; to entertain. **amusing. amused.**

amusement (ə myūz′ mənt) *n.* **1.** entertainment. **2.** enjoyment: *We showed our amusement by laughing at the clown.*

amusing (ə myū′ zing) *adj.* funny; entertaining.

an (an *or* ən) *article* one; any; each. "An" is used in the place of "a" when the next word begins with a vowel: *an apple; an egg; an iceberg; an orange; an uncle.*

analyze, analyse (an′ ə liz′) *v.* to examine carefully, in detail: *The scientist analyzed the formula.* **analyzing. analyzed.**

ancestor (an′ ses tər) *n.* a relative who lived a long time ago.

anchor (ang′ kər) *n.* a heavy object, usually of metal and with hooks, that is attached to a boat with a rope or cable, and dropped into the water to keep the boat in place. —*v.* to hold a boat in place with an anchor. **anchoring. anchored.**

anchor

ancient (ān′ shənt) *adj.* **1.** living or existing long ago: *the ruins of an ancient fort.* **2.** very old: *an ancient tree.*

and (and *or* ənd) *conj.* as well as; plus: *Alex and Kim are friends. 1 and 1 are 2.*

angel (ān′ jəl) *n.* **1.** a heavenly being; a messenger of God. **2.** an affectionate name: *You're such an angel.* —**angelic** *adj.*

anger (ang′ gər) *n.* the feeling of being extremely annoyed or displeased with someone or something.

angle (ang′ gəl) *n.* the space between two straight lines that meet.

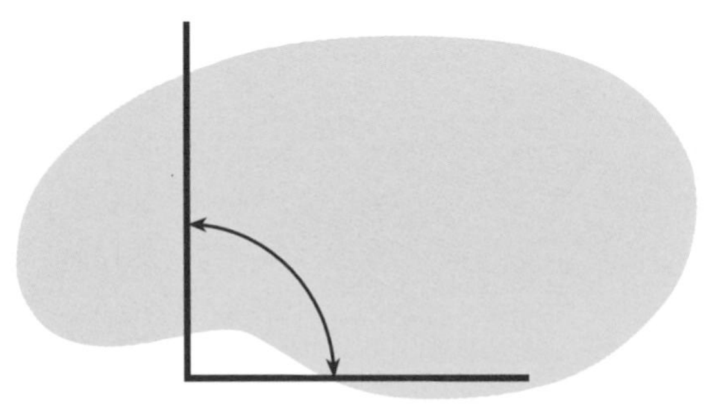

angle

Anglophone (ang′ lə fōn′) *n.* in Canada, a person whose main language is English.

angrily (ang′ grə lē) *adv.* in a bad temper; furiously.

angry (ang′ grē) *adj.* feeling anger; bad-tempered; in a rage: *an angry person; an angrier person; the angriest person of all.*

animal (an′ ə məl) *n.* any living thing that is not a plant. Animals can usually move from place to place and need to eat food and drink water.

animated (an′ ə mā′ təd) *adj.* **1.** lively: *Carmen became animated as she talked about her puppy.* **2.** in film, made up of many drawings that are photographed one after the other so that the objects seem to move: *Animated movies are also known as cartoons.* —**animatedly** *adv.*

animation (an′ ə mā′ shən) *n.* **1.** life; spirit. **2.** animated movies. **3.** the process of making animated movies.

ankle (ang′ kəl) *n.* the joint where the foot meets the leg.

anniversary (an′ ə vůr′ sə rē) *n.* a day that is remembered each year for something important that happened on it: *a wedding anniversary. pl.* **anniversaries.**

announce (ə nowns′) *v.* to let everyone know something: *The principal announced a field trip.* **announcing. announced.**

announcement (ə nowns′ mənt) *n.* a notice or statement that tells people about something.

announcer (ə nown′ sər) *n.* a person who makes announcements or who reads the news on radio or TV.

annoy (ə noi′) *v.* to trouble someone; to bother; to irritate: *He annoyed me by playing his radio loudly.* **annoying. annoyed.**

annoyance (ə noi′ yəns) *n.* **1.** a feeling of being bothered. **2.** something that annoys.

annual (an′ yū əl) *adj.* happening once every year: *Our annual picnic takes place in May.* —**annually** *adv.*

anonymous (ə non′ ə məs) *adj.* **1.** not named: *written by an anonymous person.* **2.** by or from an unknown person: *This is an anonymous letter—nobody signed it.* —**anonymously** *adv.*

another (ə nuTH′ ər) *adj.* **1.** one more: *Have another piece of cake.* **2.** different: *Choose another subject.*

answer (an′ sər) *n.* **1.** a reply to a question, a letter, or an invitation. **2.** the solution to a problem. —*v.* **1.** to reply to a question, a letter, or an invitation. **2.** to solve a problem. **answering. answered.**

ant (ant) *n.* a small, mostly wingless, insect that lives in a large colony in the ground.

antarctic (ant ȧrk′ tik) *adj.* at or near the South Pole.

the Antarctic the south polar region.

anteater (ant′ ē′ tər) *n.* a toothless mammal that feeds mostly on ants and has a long nose and a long, sticky tongue.

anteater

antelope (an′ tə lōp′) *n.* a swift, four-legged mammal that looks like a deer and has horns. Antelopes are found mainly in Africa and Asia but are also sometimes found in the North American plains.

antenna (an ten′ ə) *n.* **1.** one of two feelers on the head of such animals as insects, lobsters, and shrimp. *pl.* **antennae. 2.** a metal wire on a TV, radio, cordless phone, and so on, for receiving signals. *pl.* **antennas.**

anthem (an′ thəm) *n.* a country's official song, performed on many public occasions: *Our national anthem is "O Canada."*

anthology (an thol′ ə jē) *n.* a book containing a collection of stories or poems, written by different authors: *Do you like the anthology of mystery stories we're reading in class? pl.* **anthologies.**

> **anti–** is a prefix meaning "against" or "the opposite of": *A car's anti-lock brake system allows sudden braking without the wheels becoming locked.*

anticipate (an tis′ ə pāt′) *v.* to expect or look forward to: *We anticipate about thirty people at the party.* **anticipating. anticipated.**

antique (an tēk′) *n.* something made long ago and often valuable, such as a piece of furniture: *This chair is an antique.* —*adj.* from long ago; ancient.

antlers (ant′ lərz) *n. pl.* the horns of a male deer, elk, moose, and so on.

antonym (an′ tə nim′) *n.* a word that means the opposite of another word: *The antonym of "hard" is "soft."*

anxious (angk′ shəs) *adj.* **1.** worried; uneasy; fearful. **2.** wanting something, but not being sure whether you will get it: *Jasmine was anxious to be on the baseball team.* —**anxiously** *adv.*

any (en′ ē) *adj.* **1.** one of several: *Visit us any day.* **2.** some: *Do you have any money?*

anybody (en′ ē bud′ ē) *n.* any person.

anyone (en′ ē wun′) *n.* any person.

anything (en′ ē thing′) *n.* **1.** any thing: *Have you anything to do?* **2.** any one thing: *Anything will do for the sale.*

anyway (en′ ē wā′) *adv.* in any case; still: *It was raining, but we held the picnic anyway.*

anywhere (en′ ē wer′) *adv.* in or to any place: *I will go anywhere with you.*

apart (ə pärt′) *adv.* **1.** separate; alone: *The stranger stood apart from the others.* **2.** in pieces: *Mother took the machine apart.*

apartment (ə pärt′ mənt) *n.* a room or several rooms for living in: *Our apartment is on the third floor of this building.*

ape (āp) *n.* a mammal with no tail, that is related to monkeys and humans: *A gorilla is an ape.*

apiece (ə pēs′) *adv.* each; for each: *The books cost five dollars apiece.*

apologetic (ə pol′ ə jet′ ik) *adj.* full of regret; feeling sorry: *The store sent an apologetic letter because they had made an error.* —**apologetically.** *adv.*

apologize (ə pol′ ə jīz′) *v.* to say you are sorry for something: *I apologize for being late.* **apologizing. apologized.**

apology (ə pol′ ə jē) *n.* a statement that says you are sorry: *Please accept my apology for not writing to you before now.* *pl.* **apologies.**

apostrophe (ə pos′ trə fē) *n.* a punctuation mark (') used in contractions (short forms) of words and to show possession: *We're going to a party at Akira's house.* *pl.* **apostrophes.**

apparent (ə per′ ənt) *adj.* easily seen; obvious: *It is apparent from your good mark that you studied hard for the test.*

appeal (ə pēl′) *v.* **1.** to interest greatly: *Hockey appeals to many Canadians.* **2.** to beg for help: *Dimitri appealed for assistance.* **appealing. appealed.**

appear (ə pēr′) *v.* **1.** to come into sight: *The sun appeared from behind a cloud.* (*opp.* **disappear.**) **2.** to seem: *Andrea appears to be tired.* **appearing. appeared.**

appearance (ə pēr′ əns) *n.* **1.** coming into sight: *The appearance of the police made the robbers run.* (*opp.* **disappearance.**) **2.** how someone or something looks: *The appearance of the building made us feel that it wasn't safe.*

appendix (ə pen′ diks) *n.* **1.** extra information at the end of a book. **2.** a small pouch in your abdomen: *Your appendix is attached to the large intestine.* *pl.* **appendixes** or **appendices.**

appetite (ap′ ə tīt′) *n.* enjoyment of or desire for food: *My brother has a good appetite and can eat at any time.*

appetizing (ap′ ə tīz′ ing) *adj.* appealing to the appetite in smell or taste: *The smell of freshly baked bread is appetizing.*

applaud (ə plod′) *v.* to clap hands in approval; to cheer. **applauding. applauded.**

applause (ə ploz′) *n.* the act of clapping hands or cheering in approval.

apple (ap′ əl) *n.* a firm, roundish fruit that is red, green, or yellow in colour.

We not only eat **apples**, we use them in many expressions as well: Adam's apple; the apple of your eye; easy as apple pie. Do you know how to use each of these expressions?

appliance (ə plī′ əns) *n.* a machine used to do work around the house: *An electric mixer, a toaster, and a dishwasher are appliances.*

application (ap′ lə kā′ shən) *n.* **1.** a written form or request to get a job, to become a member of a group, or to get into a university or other school. **2.** a computer program, especially one that can be controlled with a computer mouse.

apply (ə plī′) *v.* **1.** to ask for a job: *I'm going to apply for a job at that fast-food restaurant.* **2.** to put on: *Apply the bandage.* **applying. applied.** she **applies.**

appoint (ə point′) *v.* to select: *The Prime Minister appointed a new Minister of Health.* **appointing. appointed.**

appointment (ə point′ mənt) *n.* **1.** a plan to meet someone at a particular time: *a doctor's appointment.* **2.** the choosing of someone, not through an election: *an appointment of a judge to the Supreme Court of Canada.*

appreciate (ə prē′ shē āt′) *v.* **1.** to value something or someone: *I appreciate having you as a friend.* **2.** to increase in value: *Over the years, the value of our house has appreciated.* **appreciating. appreciated.**

appreciation (ə prē′ shē ā′ shən) *n.* thankfulness: *We showed our appreciation for his help by sending a thank-you note.*

appreciative (ə prē′ shē ə tiv′) *adj.* showing thankfulness: *Our neighbours were appreciative when we helped them find their dog.*

approach (ə prōch′) *n.* **1.** the way to something: *The plane slowed down on its approach to the airport.* **2.** a way of doing things: *She has a useful approach for difficult tasks.* *pl.* **approaches.** —*v.* to come near or nearer to; to move toward: *The stranger quietly approached us.* **approaching. approached.**

appropriate (ə prō′ prē it) *adj.* proper or correct for a particular occasion: *A fancy suit is not appropriate for the picnic.* (*opp.* **inappropriate.**) —**appropriately** *adv.*

approval (ə prū′ vəl) *n.* **1.** agreement; permission: *Britta joined the club with her parents' approval.* **2.** favourable opinion: *The crowd showed its approval for the team's victory by cheering loudly.*

approve (ə prūv′) *v.* to agree to; to give permission: *My parents don't approve of my staying out late on week nights.* **approving. approved.** (*opp.* **disapprove.**)

approximate (a prok′ sə mit) *adj.* almost exact: *The approximate temperature is twenty-three degrees Celsius.*

approximate (a prok′ sə māt′) *v.* to estimate; to try to come close to an amount: *Can you approximate how many people are in the room?* **approximating. approximated.**

approximately (a prok′ sə mit′ lē) *adv.* about: *Approximately 800 people live in our village.*

apricot (ap′ rə kot′ *or* āp′ rə kot) *n.* a soft fruit, orange in colour and like a peach.

April (ā′ prəl) *n.* the fourth month of the year.

April probably comes from the Latin word *aperire,* meaning "to open," because it is in April that the flowers open up.

apron (ā′ prən) *n.* a piece of protective clothing worn over the front part of the body to keep clothes clean when working.

apt (apt) *adj.* **1.** likely to: *David is so forgetful; he is apt to leave behind his umbrella.* **2.** suitable: *That is an apt reply to my question.*

aquarium (ə kwer′ ē əm) *n.* a tank holding live fish and water. *pl.* **aquaria** or **aquariums.**

aquatic (ə kwot′ ik) *adj.* having to do with water: *Swimming is an aquatic sport.*

arch (ärch) *n.* **1.** the curved top of a doorway, tunnel, or bridge. *pl.* **arches. 2.** the curved part of the foot between the heel and toe.

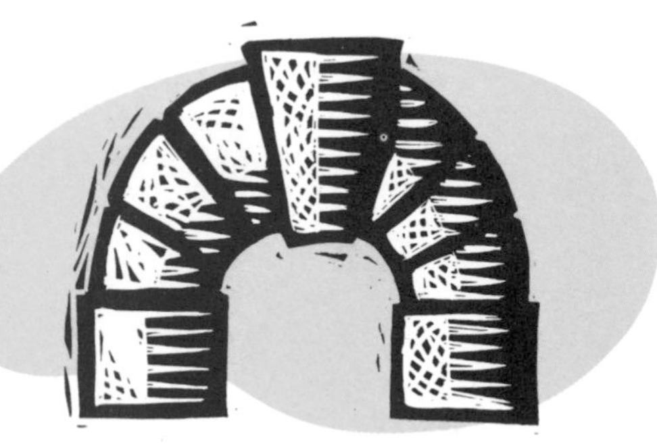

arch

archaeology (är′ kē ol′ ə jē) *n.* the study of people who lived long ago: *Scientists working in archaeology dig up and study what is left of old buildings, tools, and other objects from earlier cultures.*

archery (är′ chər ē) *n.* the use of bows and arrows.

architect (är′ kə tekt′) *n.* a person who designs buildings and draws plans for builders to follow.

architecture (är′ kə tek′ chər) *n.* the design and style of a building: *This building is an example of Victorian architecture.*

arctic (ärk′ tik *or* är′ tik) *adj.* at or near the North Pole.

the Arctic the north polar region.

are (är) *v.* a form of the verb **be** in the present tense, used with "you" and "we" and "they": *You are eating; we are eating; they are eating.*

area (er′ ē ə) *n.* **1.** a space; a region: *the area around the city; the area of our backyard.* **2.** any flat surface. **3.** the measurement of a surface: *The area of British Columbia is 948 596 km^2. pl.* **areas.**

area code the three-digit part of a telephone number used for phoning someone who lives in another region, such as another city, province, or country.

arena (ə rē′ nə) *n.* a large space for public events. *pl.* **arenas.**

aren't (ärnt) a contraction (short form) of **are not**.

argue (är′ gyū) *v.* to disagree with someone, often in a noisy way: *Don't argue with the referee!* **arguing. argued.**

argument (är′ gyə mənt) *n.* **1.** a disagreement with someone, in which you state your opinions strongly; a quarrel. **2.** a reason for or against something: *My argument for buying a new bike is that my old one is falling apart!*

arise (ə rīz′) *v.* to get up. **arising. arose.** I have **arisen** (ə riz′ ən).

arithmetic (ə rith′ mə tik) *n.* a form of mathematics: addition, subtraction, multiplication, and division.

arm (ärm) *n.* **1.** the part of your body from the shoulder to the hand. **2.** any part like an arm: *the arms of a chair. —v.* to supply with weapons: *The soldiers are well armed.* **arming. armed.**

armchair (ärm′cher) *n.* a comfortable chair with cushions and an arm on each side of the seat.

armour, armor (är′mər) *n.* metal clothing worn by soldiers in old times.

arms (ärmz) *n. pl.* **1.** weapons. **2.** a special badge worn by persons of high rank: *a coat of arms.*

army (är′ mē) *n.* **1.** a large group of soldiers trained to fight on land. **2.** a very large number: *an army of insects. pl.* **armies.**

aroma (ə rō′ mə) *n.* a pleasant smell: *The aroma of freshly baked cookies lured us into the kitchen. pl.* **aromas.**

arose (ə rōz′) see **arise**.

around (ə rownd′) *prep., adv.* in a circle; on all sides.

arrange (ə rānj′) *v.* **1.** to set in order: *to arrange books on a shelf.* **2.** to make plans: *to arrange to meet a friend.* **arranging. arranged.**

arrangement (ə rānj′ mənt) *n.* **1.** a group of things put in order: *an arrangement of flowers.* **2.** a plan: *I made an arrangement with my aunt to walk her dog every day.*

arrest (ə rest′) *v.* to legally hold someone and keep him or her in jail: *The police arrested the robber after chasing him down an alley.* **arresting. arrested.**

arrival (ə rīv′ əl) *n.* coming to a place from somewhere else: *They waited for the plane's arrival at the airport.*

arrive (ə rīv′) *v.* **1.** to come: *The time to go has arrived.* **2.** to reach a place after a journey. **arriving. arrived.**

arrow (er′ ō) *n.* a weapon made of a pointed stick with feathers at one end, shot from a bow.

art (ȧrt) *n.* **1.** painting or drawing. **2.** the study of, or the making of, beautiful things, such as painting, music, dancing, and poetry. **3.** skill; craft: *the art of weaving.*

artery (ȧr′ tər ē) *n.* **1.** any of the long tubes in the body that carry blood from the heart to all parts of the body. **2.** a main road. *pl.* **arteries.**

article (ȧr′ ti kəl) *n.* **1.** a particular thing; an item. **2.** a piece of writing in a newspaper or magazine: *We read an article about yesterday's robbery.* **3.** a part of speech: the words "a," "an," and "the" are articles.

artificial (ȧr′ tə fish′ əl) *adj.* **1.** made by humans, not natural. **2.** not real; imitation: *artificial flowers.* —**artificially** *adv.*

artist (ȧr′ tist) *n.* **1.** a painter or sculptor. **2.** any person who makes or does beautiful things: *Dancers, singers, and actors are all artists.*

artistic (ȧr tis′ tik) *adj.* **1.** done by an artist or having the quality of art. **2.** fond of art and beautiful things. —**artistically** *adv.*

as (az *or* əz) *adv.* **1.** for example: *Some dogs, such as spaniels, have long hair.* **2.** the same: *I am as old as my cousin.* —*conj.* **1.** while: *As they were talking, it started to rain.* **2.** in the way that: *We did just as we were told.*

ascend (ə send′) *v.* to go up; to rise; to climb.

ash (ash) *n.* **1.** the greyish, powdery substance left after a fire. **2.** a type of tree, with strong, tough wood often used to make baseball bats. *pl.* **ashes.**

ashamed (ə shāmd′) *adj.* very sorry for something wrong or silly you have done.

ashore (ə shȯr′) *adv.* on or to the shore: *The ship was driven ashore by the storm.*

Asian (ā′ zhən) *n.* a person born in or living in Asia. —*adj.* having to do with the continent of Asia.

aside (ə sīd′) *adv.* on or to one side: *Kay stepped aside to avoid the crowd.*

ask (ask) *v.* to question someone: *We were lost and had to ask the way.* **asking. asked.**

asleep (ə slēp′) *adv.* not awake.

asparagus (əs per′ ə gəs) *n.* a plant, whose young, green stalks are eaten as a vegetable.

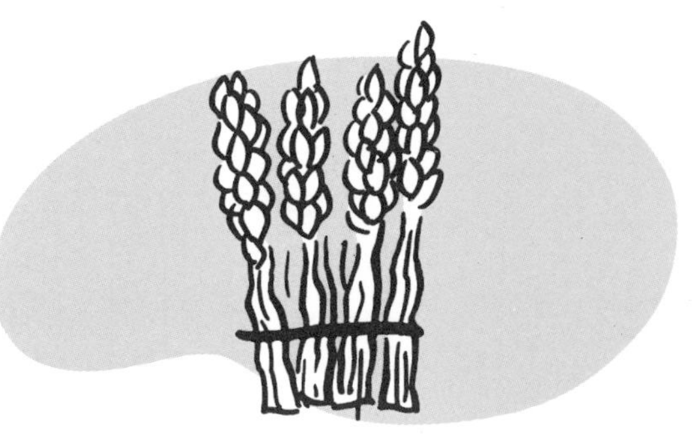

asparagus

aspect (as′ pekt) *n.* one side or one way of looking at something: *Have you considered every aspect of your plan?*

asphalt (as′ folt) *n.* **1.** a black, sticky substance, which is mixed with gravel to pave roads. **2.** a road surface.

ass (as) *n.* **1.** a donkey. **2.** a silly person.

assemble (ə sem′ bəl) *v.* to meet; to gather together: *A crowd assembled around the accident.* **assembling. assembled.**

assembly (ə sem′ blē) *n.* a meeting: *The principal made some announcements at this morning's assembly. pl.* **assemblies.**

assign (ə sīn′) *v.* to give out something to do: *The teacher assigned mathematics for homework.* **assigning. assigned.**

assignment (ə sīn′ mənt) *n.* something given out to be done: a job, project, report, or other work: *Can you help me with my geography assignment?*

assist (ə sist′) *n.* the act of helping another hockey player score a goal. —*v.* to help. **assisting. assisted.**

assistance (ə sis′ təns) *n.* help; aid: *May I give you some assistance?*

assistant (ə sis′ tənt) *n.* someone who serves or helps.

assorted (ə sȯr′ tid) *adj.* of different kinds: *assorted candies.*

assortment (ə sȯrt′ mənt) *n.* a mixture of different kinds: *an assortment of sandwiches.*

assume (ə sūm′) *v.* to believe something is true: *If we assume Ted went looking for us where he saw us last, then he's probably waiting beside the movie theatre.* **assuming. assumed.**

assumption (ə sump′ shən) *n.* a belief that something is true, without having proof that it is.

assure (ə shůr′) *v.* **1.** to make sure: *Winning our last game assured our team of a play-off spot.* **2.** to say positively: *I assure you that I have never lied to you.* **assuring. assured.**

asthma (az′ mə) *n.* a disease that makes it hard to breathe, and causes coughing and wheezing.

astonish (əs ton′ ish) *v.* to surprise greatly; to amaze. **astonishing. astonished.**

astrology (əs trol′ ə jē) *n.* the practice of looking at the position of the stars to predict what will happen in the future.

astronaut (as′ trə not′) *n.* a person who travels to and works in outer space.

astronomer (əs tron′ ə mər) *n.* a person who studies astronomy.

astronomy (əs tron′ ə mē) *n.* the study of the sun, moon, planets, stars, and other heavenly bodies.

at (at) *prep.* **1.** in, by, on, or near: *Fran is at her aunt's house.* **2.** in the direction of: *The child pointed her finger at me.* **3.** for: *I bought two pencils at fifty cents each.* **4.** right on the time of: *Dinner is at six o'clock sharp!*

ate (āt) see **eat**.

athlete (ath′ lēt) *n.* a person who is active or skilled in sports.

athletic (ath let′ ik) *adj.* good at sports.

Atlantic (at lan′ tik) *n.* the ocean extending from North America and South America to Europe and Africa.

the Atlantic Provinces New Brunswick, Newfoundland, Nova Scotia, and Prince Edward Island.

atlas (at′ ləs) *n.* a book of maps. *pl.* **atlases.**

In Roman mythology, Atlas was made to hold up the earth on his shoulders as a punishment for angering the gods. Early books of maps often included a picture of Atlas. Because of this picture, people gradually began calling a book of maps an **atlas**.

atmosphere (at′ məs fēr′) *n.* the air around the earth.

atom (at′ əm) *n.* **1.** the smallest particle of a chemical element that can combine with other substances. **2.** a very small part of anything.

attach (ə tach′) *v.* to join together. **attaching. attached.**

attached to fond of: *My cousin is very attached to her pet kitten.*

attack (ə tak′) *n.* **1.** a fight or a hostile move against someone. **2.** a sudden illness: *a heart attack.* —*v.* to make a hostile move against someone. **attacking. attacked.**

attempt (ə tempt′) *v.* to try to do something: *to attempt to beat a record.* **attempting. attempted.**

attend (ə tend′) *v.* to be present at: *to attend school.* **attending. attended.**

attendance (ə ten′ dəns) *n.* **1.** being present. **2.** the number of people present: *Two hundred people were in attendance at the concert.*

attention (ə ten′ shən) *n.* care and thought; concentration: *Pay attention to what I am saying!*

attentive (ə ten′ təv) *adj.* being thoughtful or caring: *My older sister's boyfriend is very attentive to her.*

attic (at′ ik) *n.* a space or room just under the roof of a house.

attitude (at′ ə tūd *or* at′ ə tyūd) *n.* the way a person thinks, acts, or feels: *a cheerful attitude.*

attorney (ə tůr′ nē) *n.* a lawyer. *pl.* **attorneys.**

attract (ə trakt′) *v.* to pull to itself: *A magnet attracts iron nails.* **attracting. attracted.**

attraction (ə trak′ shən) *n.* something that is liked and attracts people; charm.

attractive (ə trak′ tiv) *adj.* charming; pleasing to the senses: *an attractive boy or girl.* (*opp.* **unattractive.**)

auction (ok′ shən) *n.* a sale in which each item is sold to the person who offers the most money for it.

audience (o′ dē əns) *n.* the people gathered together at a performance or meeting.

audio (o′ dē ō) *n.* the sound part of a TV program or movie.

audio– is a prefix meaning "hearing" or "sound": *an audiotape is used for recording sound.*

audition (o dish′ ən) *n.* a try-out performance in which musicians, dancers, or actors show their skills so that others can judge how good they are. —*v.* to perform at an audition: *I am going to audition for a part in the school play.* **auditioning. auditioned.**

auditorium (o′ də tȯr′ ē əm) *n.* a large room to hold an audience.

August (o′ gəst) *n.* the eighth month of the year.

aunt (ant *or* ȧnt) *n.* **1.** a sister of your father or mother. **2.** the wife of your uncle.

author (o′ thər) *n.* a writer of books.

authority (ə thȯr′ ə tē) *n.* **1.** power over other people: *The police have the authority to arrest criminals.* **2.** an expert: *Rhea is an authority on coins and stamps.* *pl.* **authorities.**

autobiography (o′ tə bī og′ rə fē) *n.* the story of a person's life written by himself or herself. *pl.* **autobiographies.**

autograph (o′ tə graf′) *n.* a person's signature.

automatic (o′ tə mat′ ik) *adj.* working by itself: *An automatic watch needs no winding.* —**automatically** *adv.*

automation (o′ tə mā′ shən) *n.* machinery that runs by itself, without help from people: *Robots are a form of automation.*

automobile (o′ tə mə bēl′) *n.* a motor car.

autumn (o′ təm) *n.* the season after summer, also called **fall**.

available (ə vāl′ ə bəl) *adj.* something that can be obtained: *There are a few seats available for the concert.* (*opp.* **unavailable.**)

avalanche (av′ ə lanch) *n.* a heavy fall of snow and rocks down a mountain side.

avenue (av′ ə nyū′ *or* av′ ə nū′) *n.* a road or street.

average (av′ rij *or* av′ ər ij) *n.* the number found by adding two or more quantities together and dividing the total by the number of quantities: *The average of 1, 2, and 3 is 2 (1 + 2 + 3 = 6 ÷ 3 = 2).* —*adj.* **1.** at a halfway point; medium. **2.** ordinary; not very good or very bad. **3.** like most people: *Rajan is of average weight for his age.*

aviation (ā′ vē ā′ shən) *n.* the study of aircraft and flying.

aviator (ā′ vē ā′ tər) *n.* a pilot of an aircraft.

avoid (ə void′) *v.* to keep clear of; to keep away from: *Let's start our trip early and avoid the traffic.* **avoiding. avoided.**

await (ə wāt′) *v.* to wait for. **awaiting. awaited.**

awake (ə wāk′) *adj.* not asleep.

award (ə wȯrd′) *n.* a prize, honour, or reward. —*v.* to give a prize, honour, or reward. **awarding. awarded.**

aware (ə wer′) *adj.* knowing; alert to: *Lucia was aware of a smell of burning before she saw the fire.* (*opp.* **unaware.**)

away (ə wā′) *adv., adj.* **1.** at a distance **2.** in the opposite direction: *The man walked away.* **3.** absent: *We have been away on holiday.*

awe (o) *n.* a feeling of wonder, respect, or fear about something magnificent or mysterious: *Seeing the Rockies filled us with awe.* —*v.* to fill with awe. **awing. awed.**

awesome (o′ sum′) *adj.* causing awe; amazing: *Seeing the huge eagle swoop so close was an awesome sight.*

awful (o′ fəl) *adj.* very bad: *We are having awful weather!*

awfully (o′ fəl ē) *adv.* very; terribly: *You are awfully brave!*

awhile (ə wīl′) *adv.* for a short time: *Could you stay awhile longer?*

awkward (ok′ wərd) *adj.* **1.** clumsy; not easy to manage: *Opening the door when both hands are full is awkward.* **2.** uncomfortable; embarrassing: *an awkward situation.*

axe (aks) *n.* a sharp tool used to chop wood.

axis (ak′ sis) *n.* a real or imaginary line around which an object turns: *The earth's axis passes through the North and South Poles.* *pl.* **axes** (ak′ sēz).

axle (ak′ səl) *n.* the pole on which a wheel turns.

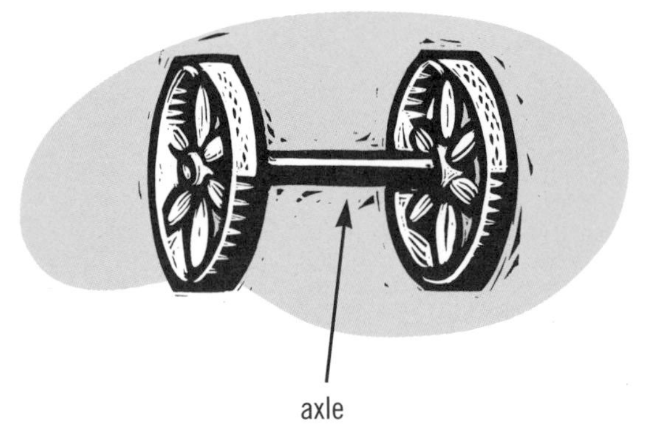

aye (ī) *adv.* yes: *All in favour, say "aye."*

baa (bah) *n.* the cry of a sheep or a goat. *pl.* **baas.**

babble (bab′ əl) *v.* to make noises or talk foolishly. **babbling. babbled.**

baboon (ba būn′) *n.* a large type of monkey that lives mostly in Africa, has a face rather like a dog, and has a short tail.

baboon

baby (bā′ bē) *n.* a very young child; an infant. *pl.* **babies.** —*v.* to treat like a baby: *Stop babying me! I'm old enough to make up my own mind!* **babying. babied.** he **babies.**

babysitter (bā′ bē sit′ ər) *n.* a person who looks after young children when their parents are not home.

bachelor (bach′ ə lər) *n.* a man or woman who is not married.

back (bak) *n.* **1.** the part of your body that is opposite to the front part; the upper part of an animal's body. **2.** the part of anything that is opposite to the front part: *the back of the room.* —*adj.* opposite to front: *the back seat.* —*adv.* **1.** toward the rear; backward: *Step back, please!* **2.** to or in an earlier time or place: *Let's go back to our old school.* **3.** to the place from which something came: *Jean gave the book back.*

back and forth going first one way and then the other way: *The train goes back and forth between Moncton and Saint John.*

back out not to keep a promise: *He backed out when he received another invitation.*

back up **1.** to move slowly backward, especially in a car or truck. **2.** to support something or someone: *Do you have proof to back up your claim?* **3.** to make a copy of something in case the original is lost or destroyed: *I backed up copies of all my computer files on floppy disks.*

backbone (bak′ bōn) *n.* the spine—the line of little bones down the back of your body.

backfire (bak′ fīr′) *v.* **1.** in a car engine, to fire or explode too soon. **2.** to have a plan go wrong: *The surprise birthday party for Ari backfired—he never arrived!* **backfiring. backfired.**

background (bak′ grownd′) *n.* **1.** the part of a picture or scene at the back: *I can see the mountains in the background.* **2.** a surface on which other things are shown: *yellow polka dots on a blue background.* **3.** a person's past education and experience: *Her background as a writer helped her get the job at the newspaper.*

backpack (bak′ pak′) *n.* a large leather, canvas, or nylon bag with two straps for carrying on your back; a knapsack.

backward, backwards (bak′ wərd, bak′ wərdz) *adv.* **1.** toward the back. **2.** with the back first: *Try walking backward!* **3.** in reverse direction: *"Live" spelled backward is "evil."*

backyard (bak′ yȧrd) *n.* a yard behind a house.

bacon (bā′ kən) *n.* the meat from the back and sides of a pig.

bacteria (bak tēr′ ē ə) *n. pl.* very tiny living things that can be seen only under a microscope: *Some bacteria cause disease.*

bad (bad) *adj.* **1.** not good: *a bad dog; bad weather; bad news.* **2.** rotten; decayed: *This banana has gone bad.*

bade (bad *or* bād) see **bid.**

badge (baj) *n.* a special sign worn on your clothes, showing that you have a certain job or belong to a certain group: *a police officer's badge.*

badger (baj′ ər) *n.* a grey, hairy animal of the weasel family that lives in a hole in the ground.

badly (bad′ lē) *adv.* **1.** wrongly; not well: *The paint job was done badly—it's cracking and peeling already.* **2.** very much; greatly: *I badly want to go to the picnic.*

bag (bag) *n.* a sack made of paper, cloth, soft plastic, or leather: *a handbag; a shopping bag.*

bagel (bā′ gəl) *n.* a hard bread roll, shaped like a doughnut.

baggage (bag′ ij) *n.* cases and bags that hold your belongings when you take a trip.

baggy (bag′ ē) *adj.* fitting loosely: *baggy pants; baggier pants; the baggiest pants of all.*

bagpipes (bag′ pīps) *n. pl.* a musical instrument with a bag and pipes.

bagpipes

bail (bāl) *n.* money paid to keep a person who has been arrested out of jail until his or her trial. —*v.* to scoop water out of a boat. **bailing. bailed.**

bait (bāt) *n.* food put on a hook to tempt a fish, or food used to lure an animal into a trap.

bake (bāk) *v.* to cook in an oven, using steady, dry heat. **baking. baked.**

baker (bāk′ ər) *n.* a person who bakes bread and cakes.

bakery (bā′ ker ē) *n.* a place where bread and cakes are baked or sold. *pl.* **bakeries.**

balance (bal′ əns) *n.* **1.** steadiness: *The gymnast kept her balance while performing on the balance beam.* **2.** an instrument for weighing things, used by chemists and other people. —*v.* to keep steady, as when walking on a tightrope. **balancing. balanced.**

balcony (bal′ kə nē) *n.* **1.** a platform built outside the upper floors of a building. **2.** the upper floor of a theatre. *pl.* **balconies.**

bald (bold) *adj.* having no hair on the head.

bale (bāl) *n.* a bundle of hay, cotton, or straw.

ball (bol) *n.* **1.** something round, like a sphere: *a ball of wool.* **2.** a round object used in sports: *a tennis ball.* **3.** a fancy party with dancing.

ballet (ba lā′ *or* bal′ ā) *n.* a form of graceful, athletic dancing that usually tells a story. Ballet involves turns, leaps, poses, and lifts.

balloon (bə lūn′) *n.* an airtight, round bag filled with air or light gas.

ballot (bal′ ət) *n.* a piece of paper on which a secret vote is written: *The ballots were counted to find out who won the election.*

bamboo (bam bū′) *n.* a tall, woody grass that grows in hot climates. The hollow stems are often used for making furniture.

ban (ban) *n.* something that is not allowed: *In this town, there is a ban on owning wild animals.* —*v.* not to allow, or to forbid something: *Dogs are banned from the park.* **banning. banned.**

banana (bə nan′ ə) *n.* a long, curved, soft, white fruit with a thick, yellow skin. *pl.* **bananas.**

band (band) *n.* **1.** a narrow strip used for holding things together: *an elastic band.* **2.** a group of musicians playing together: *a rock band.* **3.** a group of aboriginal people recognized as an official unit in Canada: *the Squamish band.* —*v.* to form a group. **banding. banded.**

bandage (ban′ dij) *n.* a strip of cloth or plastic used to cover a wound. —*v.* to cover a wound with a bandage. **bandaging. bandaged.**

bandit (ban′ dit) *n.* a robber.

bang (bang) *n.* a sudden, loud noise. —*v.* **1.** to make a sudden, loud noise: *Don't bang on the door!* **2.** to hit sharply: *He banged his knee against the table.* **banging. banged.**

bangs (bangz) *n. pl.* a fringe of hair cut and combed straight across the forehead.

banish (ban′ ish) *v.* to force someone to go away or to leave his or her country or home. **banishing. banished.**

banjo (ban′ jō) *n.* a musical instrument of the guitar family; it has a round body and four or five strings, which are plucked. *pl.* **banjos.**

bank (bank) *n.* **1.** a heap of earth or snow. **2.** the side of a river. **3.** a place where money is stored and kept safe: *a piggy bank; a savings bank.*

banner (ban′ ər) *n.* a kind of flag.

banquet (bang′ kwit) *n.* a large feast or dinner party.

bar (bȧr) *n.* **1.** a rod, usually of metal or wood: *the bars of a cage.* **2.** a piece of solid material shaped like a rectangle: *a bar of soap.* **3.** a place where drinks of liquor, beer, or wine are sold. —*v.* to keep out or to forbid: *They barred us from entering the arena without a ticket.* **barring. barred.**

barbecue (bȧr′ bə kyū′) *n.* **1.** an open fireplace for outdoor cooking. **2.** a meal cooked in this way. —*v.* to cook over an open fireplace. **barbecuing. barbecued.**

barber (bȧr bər) *n.* a person whose job it is to cut hair, usually for men and boys.

bare (ber) *adj.* **1.** naked; uncovered. **2.** plain, without trimmings: *the bare truth.* **3.** empty: *a bare room.* —*v.* to uncover; to reveal: *The dog bared its teeth.* **baring. bared.**

barely (ber′ lē) *adv.* hardly: *I barely have enough time to do all my homework.*

bargain (bȧr′ gən) *n.* **1.** something that is bought cheaply and is good value for the money. **2.** an agreement: *We made a bargain that you would wash the dishes next time.* —*v.* to try to get a good buy on something by suggesting the salesperson lower the price. **bargaining. bargained.**

barge (bȧrj) *n.* a flat-bottomed boat used on rivers or canals.

bark (bȧrk) *n.* **1.** the outer covering of a tree trunk or branch. **2.** the short, sharp cry of a dog or a wolf. —*v.* to make the sound of a bark. **barking. barked.**

barn (bȧrn) *n.* a farm building used for sheltering animals or for storing crops or equipment.

barometer (bə rom′ ə tər) *n.* an instrument that measures air pressure. Barometers are used to forecast changes in the weather.

barrel (ber′ əl) *n.* **1.** a large, wooden container, with a flat, round top and bottom, and curved sides. **2.** the tube of a gun.

barren (ber′ ən) *adj.* unable to produce: *No trees or plants could grow in the barren soil.*

barrier (ber′ ē ər) *n.* something that stops you from going farther, such as a railing or fence.

base (bās) *n.* **1.** the lowest part; the bottom. **2.** a part on which something rests or stands. **3.** in baseball, one of the four corners of the diamond.

baseball (bās′ bol) *n.* **1.** a game played with a bat and ball on a field with four bases. **2.** the ball used in this game.

basement (bās′ mənt) *n.* the lowest floor of a building, below or partly below the ground.

bashful (bash′ fəl) *adj.* shy; timid. —**bashfully** *adv.*

basic (bā′ sik) *adj.* simple, but important: *a basic fact.* —**basically** *adv.*

basin (bā′ sən) *n.* a round, shallow bowl, often used to hold water for washing.

basis (bā′ sis) *n.* **1.** a thing that something else is based on; a reason: *What is the basis for your statement that he is such a great actor?* **2.** the way in which something is done: *The letter carrier comes to our house on a daily basis. pl.* **bases** (bā′ sēz).

basket (bas′ kət) *n.* a container usually made of woven straw or twigs.

basketball (bas′ kət bol′) *n.* **1.** a game played with a large ball on a court with two small, raised, basket-shaped nets at either end. **2.** the ball used in this game.

bass (bas) *n.* a North American freshwater fish caught for food or sport. *pl.* **bass.**

bass (bās) *n.* **1.** a male singer who sings in the lowest range. **2.** a double bass: a very large stringed instrument, similar to a violin, that makes deep tones. *pl.* **basses.**

bat (bat) *n.* **1.** a wooden club used in baseball and other games. **2.** a small winged animal that flies at night. —*v.* to use a bat in baseball. **batting. batted.**

bat

batch (batch) *n.* a number of things of the same kind: *We made a batch of cookies for the bake sale. pl.* **batches.**

bath (bath) *n.* the washing of your whole body.

bathe (bāTH) *v.* to take a bath. **bathing. bathed.**

bathing suit (bāTH′ ing sūt) a piece of clothing that you wear when swimming or splashing in water.

bathroom (bath′ rūm) *n.* a room with a washbasin, a toilet, and a bathtub or shower.

bathtub (bath′ tub) *n.* a large tub in which you wash your body.

baton (bə ton′) *n.* **1.** a short, heavy stick passed from runner to runner in relay races. **2.** a thin stick used for conducting by the leader of a band or orchestra.

batter (bat′ ər) *n.* **1.** a mixture of eggs, flour, and milk, beaten together: *pancake batter.* **2.** in baseball, a person who is batting.

battery (bat′ ər ē) *n.* a small, sealed container with chemicals that produce electricity: *This flashlight needs a new battery. pl.* **batteries.**

battle (bat′ əl) *n.* **1.** a fight between two armies in a war. **2.** a hard struggle: *a battle against a storm at sea.* —*v.* to fight; to struggle. **battling. battled.**

battlefield (bat′ əl fēld′) *n.* the place where a battle is fought.

bay (bā) *n.* **1.** a part of an ocean or a lake that fills a curved area of land; an inlet: *Hudson Bay.* **2.** the deep howl of a hunting dog. *pl.* **bays.** —*v.* to howl loudly, as a hunting dog does. **baying. bayed.**

bazaar (bə zär′) *n.* **1.** a sale of different things donated by people, often for the purpose of raising money for charity. **2.** a market in West Asian (Middle Eastern) countries.

be (bē) *v.* **1.** to exist. **2.** to happen; to take place: *When is the party?* **3.** to be located in a particular place: *Where are my glasses?* **4.** to belong to a particular group: *I am Chinese. My uncle is a teacher. Poodles and collies are dogs.* **5.** to have a certain quality: *Roses are red.*

> **Be** is often used as a helping (auxiliary) verb with other verbs: *I'll **be** seeing a movie. **Is** he listening? You **are** talking too much. What **was** she doing?*

beach (bēch) *n.* the shore of an ocean or a lake, either sandy or covered with pebbles. *pl.* **beaches.**

bead (bēd) *n.* a small round piece of wood, glass, plastic, or metal with a hole through it, used to make a necklace or bracelet.

beak (bēk) *n.* the hard, pointed part of a bird's mouth.

beam (bēm) *n.* **1.** a long piece of wood or metal, cut into the shape of a rectangle and used to make buildings. **2.** a ray of light.

bean (bēn) *n.* **1.** a seed from a pod, eaten as a vegetable: *a lima bean; a soy bean.* **2.** the pod itself: *green beans.*

bear (ber) *n.* a large, furry mammal with a short tail: *a polar bear.* —*v.* **1.** to support: *How much weight will the bridge bear?* **2.** to carry: *The mule can bear heavy loads.* **3.** to put up with: *I can't bear the noise.* **4.** to produce: *This tree bears many plums.* **bearing. bore** (bȯr). I have **borne** (bȯrn).

bear

bearable (ber′ ə bəl) *adj.* able to be borne or endured: *My slight headache is bearable.* (*opp.* **unbearable.**)

beard (bērd) *n.* the hair on a man's face.

beast (bēst) *n.* any four-footed animal.

beat (bēt) *n.* a sound, stroke, or blow made again and again: *the beat of the drums.* —*v.* **1.** to hit or pound again and again: *We beat the dirt out of the rug.* **2.** to defeat another person or group: *We beat the other team.* **beating. beat.** I have **beaten.**

beautiful (byū′ tə fu̇l) *adj.* very pleasing to the senses; lovely. —**beautifully** *adv.*

beauty (byū′ tē) *n.* **1.** loveliness. **2.** a lovely thing: *That horse is a beauty!* *pl.* **beauties.**

beaver (bē′ vər) *n.* a rodent with thick fur, a broad tail, and large, gnawing teeth, that moves about in water and on land, and builds dams in rivers.

Beavers (bē′ vərz) *n. pl.* junior members of the Scouts, aged 5 to 7.

because (bē koz′) *conj.* for the reason that; since: *We came inside because it was raining.*

beckon (bek′ ən) *v.* to signal to someone, using your hand, to come toward you. **beckoning. beckoned.**

become (bē kum′) *v.* **1.** to grow or develop into: *My best friend wants to become a doctor.* **2.** to suit: *That dress becomes you.* **becoming. became.** I have **become.**

bed (bed) *n.* **1.** a piece of furniture for sleeping or resting on. **2.** an area of soil in a garden for growing flowers or vegetables. **3.** the bottom of a sea or river.

bedroom (bed′ rūm) *n.* a room to sleep in.

bee (bē) *n.* a winged insect that gathers pollen and nectar from flowers, and has a stinger. Some kinds of bees live together in large colonies, making honey and wax.

beech (bēch) *n.* a tree with smooth, grey bark and strong wood. *pl.* **beech.**

beef (bēf) *n.* meat from cattle.

beehive (bē′ hīv) *n.* a hive or house for bees.

been (bēn *or* bin) *v.* a form of the verb **be** in the past tense; it is always used with "have," "has," or "having": *We have been playing basketball.*

beep (bēp) *n.* a short, high sound like the one made by some horns. —*v.* to make such a sound. **beeping. beeped.**

beer (bēr) *n.* an alcoholic drink made from grain.

beet (bēt) *n.* a plant with a round, dark red root that is eaten as a vegetable.

beetle (bē′ təl) *n.* an insect with a hard, shiny back to protect its wings. Some beetles are very large.

beetle

before (bē fȯr′) *prep.* **1.** in front of or ahead of: *She stood before the shop window.* **2.** earlier than: *I was here before practice started.* —*conj.* earlier than: *Don't leave the table before finishing your meal.*

beg (beg) *v.* **1.** to ask humbly for food or money: *The dog was begging for a bone.* **2.** to ask a favour: *I beg you to forgive me.* **begging. begged.**

beggar (beg′ ər) *n.* a poor person who lives by begging for food or money.

begin (bē gin′) *v.* to start. **beginning. began.** I have **begun.**

beginner (bē gin′ ər) *n.* someone who is just starting to learn or do something.

beginning (bē gin′ ing) *n.* the starting point or first part of something: *The movie's beginning was funnier than the ending.*

behave (bē hāv′) *v.* **1.** to act in a certain way. **2.** to show good or bad manners in front of others: *Behave yourself!* **behaving. behaved.**

behaviour, behavior (bē hāv′ yər) *n.* the way someone or something acts or behaves.

behind (bē hīnd′) *prep.* **1.** at the back of: *Stand behind me.* **2.** later than. **3.** following: *The tortoise was behind the hare.* —*adv.* not on time; late: *I am behind in my work.*

beige (bāzh) *n.* a light brown colour. —*adj.* having this colour.

being (bē′ ing) *n.* **1.** a living creature: *a human being.* **2.** existence; life. —*v.* a form of the verb **be**: *She is being humorous.*

belief (bē lēf′) *n.* an idea you think is true; an opinion: *a belief in the goodness of people.* *pl.* **beliefs.**

believe (bē lēv′) *v.* to think that something is true: *Our team believes that we can win the game.* **believing. believed.**

believe in to have faith in.

bell (bel) *n.* an object shaped like an upside-down cup, which gives a ringing sound when struck.

bellow (bel′ ō) *v.* to roar; to shout in an angry way. **bellowing. bellowed.**

belly (bel′ ē) *n.* the lower part of the front of your body; the abdomen. *pl.* **bellies.**

belong (bē long′) *v.* **1.** to be owned by: *That book belongs to me.* **2.** to be a member of: *Margie belongs to the Science Club.* **belonging. belonged.**

belongings (bē long′ ingz) *n. pl.* the things that a person owns; possessions.

below (bē lō′) *prep.* under; beneath; lower than: *The first floor is below the second floor.* —*adv.* in or to a lower place: *We climbed the mountain and looked at the valley below.*

belt (belt) *n.* a strap worn around your waist, usually made of leather or plastic.

bench (bench) *n.* **1.** a long, wooden seat. **2.** a work table. *pl.* **benches.**

bend (bend) *n.* a curve or turn: *a bend in the road.* —*v.* **1.** to curve something: *to bend a wire.* **2.** to bow or to lean over: *Bend over and touch your toes.* **bending. bent.**

beneath (bē nēth′) *prep.* lower than; under: *I stretched out beneath a tree.*

benefit (ben′ ə fit) *n.* something good; an advantage: *A warm coat is a great benefit on a cold day.* —*v.* to help: *Regular practice would benefit my piano-playing.* **benefiting. benefited.**

berry (ber′ ē) *n.* a small, juicy fruit with many seeds: *a raspberry; a blackberry. pl.* **berries.**

berserk (bůr zůrk′) *adj., adv.* out of control: *In the movie, the robot went berserk and started destroying things.*

beside (bē sīd′) *prep.* by the side of: *The cottage is beside the lake.*

besides (bē sīdz′) *prep.* in addition to: *Besides our class, many other students were at the dance.*

best (best) *adj.* excellent; the very finest: *The blue team is good, the yellow team is better, but the red team is the best.* —*n.* an excellent thing or person: *She's the best in the school.*

bet (bet) *n.* a promise to give something, such as money, to someone if he or she is right and you are wrong: *We made a bet on who would win the Stanley Cup.* —*v.* to gamble that something will happen: *I bet that my team would win.* **betting. bet.**

betray (be trā′) *v.* to give away a secret to an enemy. **betraying. betrayed.**

better (bet′ ər) *adj.* finer; more valuable; of higher quality: *This ring is good, but that one is better. The gold ring is the best of the three.*

between (bē twēn′) *prep.* **1.** in the middle of two things: *I am between my older sister and younger brother in age.* **2.** either one or the other of: *Choose between the two pictures.* **3.** with another person: *Share the cake between both of you.*

beverage (bev′ ər ij) *n.* any liquid for drinking: *Milk and orange juice are beverages.*

beware (bē wer′) *v.* to be on your guard against; to watch out for: *Beware of the growling dog.*

bewilder (bē wil′ dər) *v.* to confuse completely: *I was bewildered when I returned to my room and found everything in a different place.* **bewildering. bewildered.**

beyond (bē yond′) *prep.* **1.** on the other side of; farther on than: *beyond the village.* **2.** too far for; out of range of: *beyond my reach.*

> **bi–** is a prefix that means "two": a "bicycle" has two wheels; to "bisect" means to divide into two sections.

bias (bī′ əs) *n.* a strong like or dislike that makes it difficult for a person to behave fairly; a prejudice: *He has a bias against me, so he always believes you rather than me. pl.* **biases.** —*v.* to show such a like or dislike. **biasing. biased.**

bib (bib) *n.* a small cloth tied around a baby's neck to keep food from soiling the baby's clothes.

biceps (bī′ seps) *n.* the large muscle at the front of the upper arm; it rises up when you bend your elbow. *pl.* **biceps** or **bicepses.**

bicycle (bī′ si kəl) *n.* a two-wheeled vehicle with pedals, handlebars, and a seat.

bid (bid) *n.* an offer of money for something, usually at an auction. —*v.* **1.** to command: *I bid you to stay here.* **2.** to make an offer of money, usually at an auction: *I bid ten dollars for the lamp.* **3.** to say or tell: *He bid me goodbye.* **bidding. bade.** I have **bidden.**

big (big) *adj.* **1.** large; great: *a big cat; a bigger cat; the biggest cat on the street.* **2.** important: *Our big baseball game is on Saturday.*

bike (bīk) *n.* a short name for **bicycle**.

bilingual (bī ling′ gwəl) *adj.* speaking two languages well: *Marie is bilingual: she speaks both French and English.*

bill (bil) *n.* **1.** a written statement showing how much money is owed: *a telephone bill; a restaurant bill.* **2.** paper money: *a five-dollar bill.* **3.** a bird's beak. **4.** a suggestion for a new law. —*v.* to send a bill. **billing. billed.**

billboard (bil′ bȯrd) *n.* a large, outdoor sign for advertisements.

billion (bil′ yən) *n., adj.* one thousand million (1 000 000 000).

bin (bin) *n.* a box or barrel for storing things: *a bread bin; a garbage bin.*

bind (bīnd) *v.* to tie together with thread, string, or rope. **binding. bound.**

binder (bīn′ dər) *n.* **1.** a hard cover with metal rings used to hold loose sheets of papers together. **2.** a farm machine that reaps and binds grain.

binoculars (bə nok′ yə lərz) *n. pl.* two very small telescopes fastened side by side. Binoculars make distant objects appear closer when you look through them with both eyes.

binoculars

bio– is a prefix that means "life." For instance, "biology" is the study of living things.

biography (bī og′ rə phē) *n.* a written history of a person's life. *pl.* **biographies.** —**biographical** *adj.*

biology (bī ol′ ə jē) *n.* the scientific study of plant and animal life. —**biological** *adj.*

birch (bu̇rch) *n.* a tree with smooth bark, often white, which peels off like paper. *pl.* **birch.**

bird (bu̇rd) *n.* a feathered animal that has wings and two legs, and lays eggs. Most birds can fly.

birth (bu̇rth) *n.* **1.** the act of being born: *a baby's birth.* **2.** the start of anything: *the birth of an idea.*

birthday (bu̇rth′ dā) *n.* the day on which a person was born. *pl.* **birthdays.**

biscuit (bis′ kit) *n.* a cracker or a type of cookie.

The word **biscuit** comes from two Latin words which, together, mean "twice-cooked." Originally, a biscuit was simply a piece of bread cooked a second time—something like toast.

bishop (bish′ əp) *n.* **1.** a church official of high rank. **2.** a chess piece that moves in diagonal lines.

bison (bī′ sən) *n.* a wild mammal with a shaggy, dark brown coat, related to cattle. The North American bison is better known as the **buffalo**. *pl.* **bison.**

bit (bit) *n.* **1.** a small piece of something: *Please give me a bit more time to finish my essay.* **2.** a metal part of a horse's bridle, which goes in the horse's mouth and is used to guide the animal. **3.** in computers, a single, basic unit of information. —*v.* see **bite**.

a bit a little; slightly: *I'm feeling a bit sick.*

bite (bīt) *n.* **1.** a piece of food cut off by the teeth; a mouthful: *I took a bite of my apple.* **2.** a sting: *a mosquito bite; the bite of winter.* —*v.* to cut into or off with the teeth. **biting. bit.** I have **bitten.**

bitter (bit′ ər) *adj.* **1.** having a sharp, unpleasant taste. **2.** harsh; cutting: *a bitter wind.* —**bitterly** *adv.*

bizarre (bi zȧr′) *adj.* very strange or weird.

black (blak) *n.* the colour of a car tire; opposite to white. —*adj.* having this colour.

blacken (blak′ ən) *v.* to make or become black. **blackening. blackened.**

black-fly (blak′ flī) *n.* a small, black fly with a painful bite. *pl.* **black-flies.**

blackmail (blak′ māl) *v.* to force someone to give you money by threatening to tell a shameful or embarrassing secret about him or her. **blackmailing. blackmailed.**

blacksmith (blak′ smith) *n.* a person who works with iron and makes shoes for horses.

bladder (blad′ ər) *n.* the bag-like part of the body that stores waste liquid.

blade (blād) *n.* **1.** the flat, cutting part of a knife or sword. **2.** a long, thin leaf: *a blade of grass.*

blame (blām) *n.* responsibility for something bad or wrong: *The new ballplayer took the blame for losing the game.* —*v.* to hold someone or something responsible for something bad: *Don't blame me for your mistake.* **blaming. blamed.**

blank (blangk) *n.* an empty space. —*adj.* without writing or markings; empty: *a blank page; a blank wall; a blank stare.* —**blankly** *adv.*

blanket (blang′ kət) *n.* a bedcover to keep people warm.

blast (blast) *n.* **1.** an explosion. **2.** a loud sound: *a blast of trumpets.* **3.** a gust of air: *a blast of wind.* —*v.* to blow up, usually with explosives. **blasting. blasted.**

blast-off (blast′ of) *n.* the launch of rockets or spaceships into space.

blaze (blāz) *n.* a brightly burning fire.

bleach (blēch) *n.* something that makes an object white by taking out its colour: *laundry bleach.* —*v.* to make clean or white: *We bleached the dirt out of the clothes.* **bleaching. bleached.**

bleachers (blēch′ ərz) *n. pl.* long rows of seats or benches for people to sit on at ballgames.

bleak (blēk) *adj.* dreary; without hope: *His future is bleak because there are no jobs available right now.* —**bleakly** *adv.*

bleat (blēt) *v.* to make a noise like a goat or sheep. **bleating. bleated.**

bleed (blēd) *v.* to lose blood. **bleeding. bled.**

blend (blend) *v.* to mix together well: *Maria blended the paints to make the colour she wanted.* **blending. blended.**

bless (bles) *v.* **1.** to make holy. **2.** to wish well or to grant good fortune: *I hope the farmers are blessed with a good crop.* **blessing. blessed.**

blessing (bles′ ing) *n.* **1.** a short prayer: *Let's say a blessing before the meal.* **2.** good fortune or good wishes: *Your idea has my blessing.*

blew (blū) see **blow.**

blind (blīnd) *adj.* unable to see. —**blindly** *adv.*

blindfold (blīnd′ fōld) *n.* a covering put over a person's eyes to keep him or her from seeing. —*v.* to put a blindfold on someone. **blindfolding. blindfolded.**

blinds (blīndz) *n.* a window shade made of many long, narrow strips of metal, wood, or stiff cloth attached together.

blink (blingk) *v.* to close and open your eyes quickly. **blinking. blinked.**

bliss (blis) *n.* great joy. —**blissful** *adj.*

blister (blis′ tər) *n.* a small, sore swelling under the skin filled with fluid. Blisters are caused by rubbing or burns.

blizzard (bliz′ ərd) *n.* a heavy snowstorm with strong winds.

blob (blob) *n.* a soft drop or lump of something without a definite shape: *a blob of paint.*

block (blok) *n.* **1.** a solid piece of wood, stone, or other hard material: *a block of ice.* **2.** one section of a city street: *The museum is five blocks away.* —*v.* to get in the way of so that others cannot get through: *An overturned truck is blocking the traffic.* **blocking. blocked.**

blond (blond) *adj.* having yellow hair.

blood (blud) *n.* the red liquid pumped around the body by the heart.

bloom (blūm) *n.* a flower or blossom; —*v.* to open up into a flower. **blooming. bloomed.**

blossom (blos′ əm) *n.* a flower, usually of a fruit tree: *an apple blossom.* —*v.* **1.** to open up into a flower. **2.** to develop beautifully: *She blossomed into a star athlete under the new coach.* **blossoming. blossomed.**

blot (blot) *n.* a stain, especially an ink stain.

blouse (blows *or* blowz) *n.* a loose shirt that often has buttons down the front.

blow (blō) *n.* **1.** a hard knock: *a blow with your fist.* **2.** sudden bad luck: *Father's accident was a blow to us all.* —*v.* **1.** to be in motion, as air: *How the wind blows!* **2.** to cause to move by a current of air: *The wind blew my cap away.* **3.** to play a musical instrument, using air from your lungs: *to blow a trumpet.* **blowing. blew.** I have **blown** (blōn).

blow up **1.** to fill up with air: *to blow up a balloon.* **2.** to explode: *They used dynamite to blow up the old building.* **3.** to be very angry: *I lost my temper and blew up at my brother.* **4.** to make a photo larger: *We had our family picture blown up and gave it to our parents.*

blubber (blub′ ər) *n.* the fat of whales and some other sea mammals.

blue (blū) *n.* **1.** the colour of a clear, cloudless sky. **2.** the range of colours between green and purple. —*adj.* **1.** having such a colour. **2.** sad: *The rain is making me feel blue.*

blueberry (blū′ ber′ ē) *n.* a small, round, blue berry. *pl.* **blueberries.**

bluebird (blū′ bùrd) *n.* a small North American bird that has blue feathers on its back.

bluejay (blū′ jā) *n.* a North American bird with a crest on its head and blue feathers.

bluejay

bluff (bluf) *n.* a steep cliff or river bank. —*v.* to fool: *My brother says he can't dance, but I think he's bluffing.* **bluffing. bluffed.**

blunt (blunt) *adj.* **1.** not sharp; dull: *a blunt knife.* **2.** direct and frank, without being very polite: *My cousin was blunt, telling me I was a fool.* —**bluntly** *adv.*

blur (blùr) *v.* to make something less clear to see. **blurring. blurred.**

blurry (blùr′ ē) *adj.* hard to see clearly: *Everything looks blurry because my glasses are so dirty.*

blush (blush) *n.* a redness of the cheeks because of embarrassment or shame. —*v.* to go red in the face because you are embarrassed, excited, or ashamed. **blushing. blushed.**

boar (bôr) *n.* **1.** a wild pig with a coat of dark bristles. **2.** (*fem.* **sow**) a male pig.

board (bôrd) *n.* **1.** a long, flat piece of wood: *a floor board.* **2.** a flat piece of wood or other material used for a special purpose: *a chalk board; a diving board.* **3.** a group of people managing something: *a school board.* **4.** meals paid for in advance: *room and board.* —*v.* **1.** to get on a ship, train, bus, or airplane. **2.** to cover up with boards. **boarding. boarded.**

boarding school a school where students live during the school year.

boast (bōst) *v.* to praise yourself; to brag: *They always boast about how many friends they have.* **boasting. boasted.**

boastful (bōst′ fůl) *adj.* always boasting. —**boastfully** *adj.*

boat (bōt) *n.* an open vessel, used for travelling on water. The body of a boat is hollow, so that it floats on water. It can be made of metal, wood, or other hard materials.

bob (bob) *n.* a short haircut. —*v.* to move quickly up and down: *The cork bobbed on the water.* **bobbing. bobbed.**

bobcat (bob′ kat′) *n.* a small, North American wild cat, with black spots on a brownish coat.

bobcat

bobsled (bob′ sled) *n.* a long racing sled with two sets of runners.

body (bod′ ē) *n.* **1.** the whole physical being of a person, an animal, or a thing. **2.** the main part of a person or an animal, not including the head, limbs, or tail: *Bend your body from the hips.* **3.** a group of people: *the student body.* **4.** a mass of something: *a body of water.* *pl.* **bodies.**

bodyguard (bod′ ē gärd) *n.* someone who protects another person: *the rock star's bodyguard.*

bog (bog) *n.* a soft, wet area of land; a marsh; a swamp.

boil (boil) *n.* a small, painful swelling on the skin. —*v.* **1.** to heat a liquid until it bubbles and starts to change to a gas. **2.** to cook something in boiling water: *to boil an egg.* **boiling. boiled.**

bold (bōld) *adj.* brave and daring: *a bold explorer.* —**boldly** *adv.*

bolt (bōlt) *n.* **1.** a small metal rod, similar to a screw, used to hold things together. A bolt is fastened with a nut. (See **nut** for a picture.) **2.** a sliding metal bar used to fasten a door or gate. **3.** a lightning flash. —*v.* **1.** to fasten with a bolt. **2.** to make a sudden dash: *The startled deer bolted for the woods.* **bolting. bolted.**

bomb (bom) *n.* an explosive weapon, causing great harm and destruction. —*v.* to use such a weapon: *The hijackers tried to bomb the plane.* **bombing. bombed.**

bombard (bom bärd′) *v.* **1.** to attack with bombs. **2.** to pester with words: *Don't bombard me with all your questions!* **bombarding. bombarded.**

bond (bond) *n.* something that ties or binds together: *a bond of affection.*

bone (bōn) *n.* one of the hard, white pieces that make up a skeleton.

bonnet (bon′ ət) *n.* a hat, sometimes worn by babies, with strings that are tied under the chin.

bonus (bō′ nəs) *n.* something extra that is good. *pl.* **bonuses.**

bony (bō′ nē) *adj.* **1.** made of bone. **2.** having bones that stick out; thin: *a bony dog.*

book (bůk) *n.* **1.** a set of printed pages bound together on one side and put between covers for reading: *a library book.* **2.** a set of blank pages for writing: *a notebook.*

bookcase (bůk′ kās) *n.* a piece of furniture with shelves for books.

booklet (bůk′ lət) *n.* a small book, often with a paper cover.

bookworm (bůk′ wûrm) *n.* an informal term for a person who loves to read.

boom (būm) *n.* **1.** a deep, rumbling sound. **2.** sudden, rapid growth. —*v.* **1.** to make a deep, rumbling sound. **2.** to grow rapidly: *Business boomed at the store when the latest fashions arrived.* **booming. boomed.**

boost (būst) *n.* a push or a lift from below: *Give me a boost so that I can climb the tree.* —*v.* to give a boost. **boosting. boosted.**

boot (būt) *n.* a leather, rubber, or plastic covering for the foot and the part of the leg below the knee.

booth (būth) *n.* **1.** a stand for displaying and selling goods. **2.** a small, closed-off space: *a telephone booth.*

border (bȯr′ dər) *n.* **1.** an outside edge or rim: *a flower border around a lawn.* **2.** the line or frontier where two countries meet.

bore (bȯr) *n.* a dull, tiresome person or thing. —*v.* **1.** to drill a hole. **2.** see **bear** (verb). **3.** to tire someone out by dull talk or dull activity. **boring. bored.**

born (bȯrn) *adj.* **1.** brought into life. **2.** having a natural ability: *a born leader.*

borne (bȯrn) see **bear** (verb).

borrow (bȯr′ ō) *v.* to take something from someone for a while, which will be given back later: *My best friend borrowed a pen from me.* **borrowing. borrowed.**

boss (bos) *n.* the person for whom you work. *pl.* **bosses.** —*v.* to give orders to: *My older brother is always trying to boss me around.* **bossing. bossed.**

bossy (bos′ ē) *adj.* fond of telling other people what to do.

both (bōth) *adj., pron.* the two: *Both girls went fishing. They both caught trout.*

bother (boTH′ ər) *n.* a troublesome thing. —*v.* to give trouble to; to annoy: *Flies bothered the people sitting in the park.* **bothering. bothered.**

bottle (bot′ əl) *n.* a container for liquids that has a narrow neck and is closed with a cap. Bottles are made of glass or plastic: *a soft-drink bottle.*

bottom (bot′ əm) *n.* the lowest part: *Ski to the bottom of the hill.*

bough (bow) *n.* a main branch of a tree.

bought (bot) see **buy**.

boulder (bōl′ dər) *n.* a very large, round rock.

boulevard (bůl′ ə vård′) *n.* a broad street.

bounce (bowns) *v.* to hit a surface and spring back off it: *The ball bounced three times.* **bouncing. bounced.**

bound (bownd) *n.* a leap: *With a great bound, the dog jumped over the fence.* —*adj.* heading to: *We are bound for Alberta.* —*v.* **1.** to leap. **2.** see **bind** (verb). **bounding. bounded.**

out of bounds outside the area where you are allowed to walk or play.

boundary (bown′ də rē) *n.* anything marking a limit; a dividing line: *The river was the boundary between the two countries.* *pl.* **boundaries.**

bouquet (bū kā′ *or* bō kā′) *n.* a bunch of flowers.

boutique (bū tēk′) *n.* a small shop, often selling just one kind of item.

bow (bow) *n.* **1.** the front part of a ship. (*opp.* **stern.**) **2.** a bending forward of the body or head, to show respect: *The knight made a bow to the queen.* —*v.* to bend forward to show respect. **bowing. bowed.**

bow (bō) *n.* **1.** a weapon for shooting arrows. **2.** a stick strung with horsehair, for playing a violin or other stringed instrument. **3.** a ribbon tied in loops.

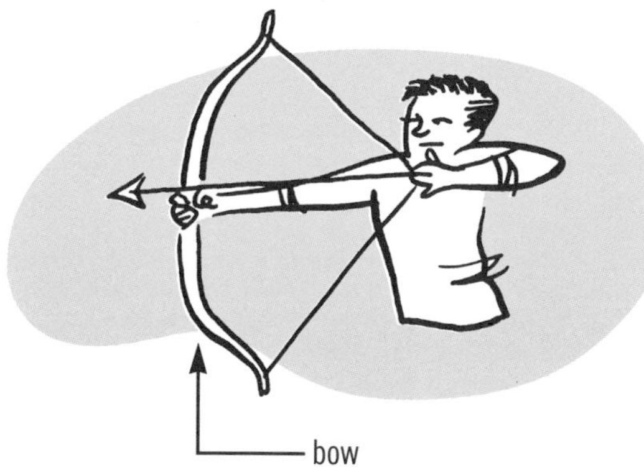

bowl (bōl) *n.* a round, deep dish; a basin. —*v.* to play the game of bowling. **bowling. bowled.**

bowling (bō′ ling) *n.* an indoor game in which a heavy ball is rolled along a wooden lane to try to knock down bottle-shaped pins.

box (boks) *n.* a square or rectangular container, often made of cardboard: *a shoe box; a cereal box. pl.* **boxes.** —*v.* **1.** to fight with the fists as a sport. **2.** to hit someone on the ear with the hand. **boxing. boxed.**

boxing (boks′ ing) *n.* the sport of fighting with the fists, using padded gloves.

boy (boi) *n.* a male child. *pl.* **boys.**

bracelet (brās′ lət) *n.* a band or chain worn as jewellery around the wrist.

braces (brā′ səs) *n. pl.* wires attached to teeth to straighten their position.

bracket (brak′ ət) *n.* **1.** a small shelf or a support for a shelf. **2.** in writing, one of a pair of symbols that are placed around words or numbers. ( ), [ ], and { } are different types of brackets.

brag (brag) *v.* to praise yourself; to boast. **bragging. bragged.**

braid (brād) *n.* a length of braided hair. —*v.* to weave together three or more strands of hair, ribbon, rope, or other material. **braiding. braided.**

Braille (brāl) *n.* a series of raised dots forming the alphabet that blind people can read, using their fingertips.

> An alphabet for the blind was named after Louis **Braille,** a blind man who invented this system of reading.

brain (brān) *n.* the grey mass inside the head of humans and animals; the mind: *The brain enables us to think, feel, learn, and remember.*

brake (brāk) *n.* a part of a vehicle, such as a bicycle, car, or train, that is used for slowing down and stopping. —*v.* to use the brakes. **braking. braked.**

bran (bran) *n.* the outer covering of wheat and other grains.

branch (branch) *n.* **1.** an arm of a tree growing out from the trunk. **2.** a local office or store that is not the main one. *pl.* **branches.**

brand (brand) *n.* **1.** a certain make of a product: *I like this brand of orange juice.* **2.** a mark burned into the skin with hot metal: *Cattle are identified with brands.*

brand-new (brand′ nū′ *or* brand′ nyū) *adj.* completely new and unused: *Our brand-new computer is still in the carton.*

brass (bras) *n.* **1.** a yellow metal, made by mixing melted copper and zinc together. **2.** a musical wind instrument often made of brass, such as the trumpet and the tuba.

brat (brat) *n.* a spoiled child.

brave (brāv) *adj.* fearless; not afraid of pain or danger. —**bravely** *adv.*

bravery (brā′ vər ē) *n.* courage; lack of fear.

bray (brā) *n.* the sound that a donkey makes. —*v.* to make such a sound. **braying. brayed.**

bread (bred) *n.* a food made from flour, yeast, and water, and baked in an oven.

break (brāk) *n.* **1.** a crack; a broken place. **2.** a pause; a rest: *Let's take a break for lunch.* **3.** a chance: *The director gave the young actor a break in a movie.* —*v.* **1.** to crack into pieces: *Don't break the cup!* **2.** to damage something so that it does not work anymore: *I will be angry if you break my watch.* **3.** to disobey: *Don't break the rules!* **4.** to fail to carry out: *You broke your promise!* **breaking. broke.** I have **broken.**

break down **1.** to stop working: *The car broke down on the highway.* **2.** to become upset: *When our cat died, I broke down and cried.* **3.** to divide something into smaller parts: *The math problem is easier to solve if you break it down into several smaller problems.*

break into to enter by force: *Burglars broke into our house.*

break up to bring or come to an end: *The meeting broke up at six o'clock.*

breakfast (brek′ fəst) *n.* the first meal of the day.

breast (brest) *n.* the chest.

breath (breth) *n.* **1.** air taken into and pushed out of the lungs. **2.** a single taking in and pushing out of air: *Take three deep breaths.*

hold your breath to take in a breath and not let it out immediately.

out of breath puffing and panting after running or exercising.

breathe (brēTH) *v.* to take air into the lungs and push it back out. **breathing. breathed.**

breathing (brēTH′ ing) *n.* the activity of taking breaths.

breathless (breth′ ləs) *adj.* **1.** out of breath after running or exercising. **2.** holding your breath out of excitement or fear: *We were breathless after the roller coaster ride.*

breathtaking (breth′ tak′ ing) *adj.* thrilling; awesome: *Niagara Falls is a breathtaking sight.*

breed (brēd) *n.* a particular variety of animal: *Jerseys are a breed of cow, good for producing milk.* —*v.* **1.** to produce young; to reproduce. **2.** to raise animals: *That farmer breeds pigs on her farm.* **breeding. bred.**

breeze (brēz) *n.* a gentle wind. —**breezy** *adj.*

brew (brū) *n.* a drink made by brewing. —*v.* **1.** to make a drink by soaking and boiling: *To brew tea, add boiling water to the leaves or tea bag.* **2.** to make ale or beer. **brewing. brewed.**

bribe (brīb) *n.* money or a gift offered to someone to do something dishonest: *The thief gave the guard a bribe to leave the door unlocked.* —*v.* to offer a bribe. **bribing. bribed.**

brick (brik) *n.* a block of baked clay, used to build walls.

bridal (brī′ dəl) *adj.* having to do with a bride or a wedding: *a bridal gown.*

bride (brīd) *n.* a woman on her wedding day.

bridegroom (brīd′ grūm) *n.* a man on his wedding day.

bridge (brij) *n.* **1.** a road built over a river, a valley, a road, etc. so that people or vehicles can cross over. **2.** a card game for four people. —*v.* to build a bridge or a connection: *How can we bridge the gap between rich and poor?* **bridging. bridged.**

bridge

bridle (brī′ dəl) *n.* the part of a harness that fits on a horse's head. It is made up of the bit, straps, and reins.

brief (brēf) *adj.* short in time: *a brief speech.* —**briefly** *adv.*

bright (brīt) *adj.* **1.** giving off much light; shining: *a bright light.* **2.** vivid; strong: *bright colours.* **3.** intelligent: *That student is very bright and learns quickly.* —**brightly** *adv.*

brighten (brīt′ ən) *v.* to make bright or become bright: *Robert's face brightened when he heard the good news.* **brightening. brightened.**

brilliant (bril′ yənt) *adj.* **1.** shining brightly: *a brilliant diamond.* **2.** very smart: *a brilliant student.* —**brilliantly** *adv.*

brim (brim) *n.* **1.** the edge of a cup or bowl: *Fill my glass to the brim.* **2.** the edge of a hat.

bring (bring) *v.* **1.** to fetch: *Bring me the newspaper.* **2.** to take along: *Did you bring the flashlight?* **bringing. brought.**

bring about to cause to happen.

bring up to raise a child: *They brought up a big family.*

brink (bringk) *n.* the edge of a high place: *We stood on the brink of the cliff.*

brisk (brisk) *adj.* **1.** quick; rapid: *We went for a brisk walk.* **2.** sharp: *The wind is brisk today.* —**briskly** *adv.*

bristle (bris′ əl) *n.* a short, stiff hair: *the bristles of a toothbrush.*

brittle (brit′ əl) *adj.* hard and easily broken: *Be careful—the china is brittle.*

broad (brod) *adj.* **1.** wide. **2.** clear; bright: *broad daylight.*

broadcast (brod′ kast) *n.* a radio or TV program, especially the news. —*v.* to spread news, especially by radio or TV: *The news was broadcast at 10 p.m.* **broadcasting. broadcast.**

broccoli (brok′ ə lē) *n.* a dark green vegetable with stalks and flower buds.

brochure (bro shůr′) *n.* a small pamphlet advertising something: *Before planning our trip, we read lots of travel brochures.*

broil (broil) *v.* to cook something directly under or over heat: *Chicken burns easily when you broil it.* **broiling. broiled.**

broke, broken (brōk, brō′ kən) see **break** (verb).

bronco (brong′ kō) *n.* in western Canada and the western United States, a wild pony or horse. *pl.* **broncos.**

bronze (bronz) *n.* a bright brown metal made by mixing melted copper and tin together. —*adj.* having the colour of bronze.

brooch (brōch) *n.* a decorative pin worn as jewellery. *pl.* **brooches.**

brood (brūd) *n.* **1.** a group of birds all hatched together. **2.** the children of one family. —*v.* to worry about something in a quiet, gloomy way: *The jeweller brooded over the lost ring.* **brooding. brooded.**

brook (brůk) *n.* a small stream.

broom (brūm) *n.* a long-handled brush used for sweeping.

broth (broth) *n.* a thin soup.

brother (bruTH′ ər) *n.* a boy or man who has the same parents as another person.

brother-in-law (bruTH′ ər in lo′) *n.* the brother of a wife or the husband of a sister. *pl.* **brothers-in-law.**

brought (brot) see **bring**.

brow (brow) *n.* the forehead; the part of the face above the eyes.

brown (brown) *n.* the colour of chocolate or soil. —*adj.* having this colour. —*v.* to cook a food until the outside is brown: *I browned the potatoes in the oven.* **browning. browned.**

Brownies (brow′ nēz) *n. pl.* junior members of the Girl Guides, aged 6 to 9.

browse (browz) *v.* **1.** to look casually around a store or library. **2.** to skim a book. **browsing. browsed.**

bruise (brūz) *n.* an injury, caused by a fall or a blow, that breaks the blood vessels under the skin, making the skin look purple.
—*v.* to cause or receive a bruise: *I bruised my knee when I tripped over a rock.* **bruising. bruised.**

brunch (brunch) *n.* a meal eaten in the late morning that combines breakfast and lunch. *pl.* **brunches.**

brunette (brū net′) *adj.* having dark brown hair.

brush (brush) *n.* a tool with bristles for grooming, sweeping, cleaning, and so on: *hair brush; toothbrush; paint brush. pl.* **brushes.**
—*v.* **1.** to use a brush: *Brush your teeth.*
2. to touch lightly: *The cat brushed my leg.* **brushing. brushed.**

Brussels sprouts (brus′ əlz sprowtz) very small, green, cabbage-like vegetables.

brutal (brū′ təl) *adj.* very cruel or harsh: *a brutal ruler of a country; a brutal storm.*
—**brutally** *adv.*

bubble (bub′ əl) *n.* a small, thin balloon of liquid filled with air: *a soap bubble.*

buck (buk) *n.* **1.** (*fem.* **doe**) a male deer, goat, rabbit, or antelope. **2.** (*slang*) a dollar.

bucket (buk′ ət) *n.* a large pail.

buckle (buk′ əl) *n.* a metal clasp on a belt or shoe. —*v.* to fasten with a buckle. **buckling. buckled.** (*opp.* **unbuckle.**)

bud (bud) *n.* **1.** a small swelling on a plant stem that will grow into a leaf, flower, or branch. **2.** a young flower or leaf.

buddy (bud′ ē) *n.* a pal. *pl.* **buddies.**

budge (buj) *v.* to move or change position: *She would not budge from her seat.* **budging. budged.**

budget (buj′ ət) *n.* a plan for spending money carefully. —*v.* to make or use such a plan: *We budgeted our allowance so that we still had money left at the end of the week.* **budgeting. budgeted.**

budgie (buj′ ē) *n.* a small bird, usually kept in a cage, with colourful markings and a chirping voice.

buffalo (buf′ ə lō) *n.* **1.** a large, wild, North American mammal with a shaggy, dark brown coat, related to cattle. (see **bison.**) **2.** a mammal of Africa, India, and Asia, similar to cattle, often called the water buffalo. *pl.* **buffalo.**

water buffalo

buffet (bə fā′) *n.* a meal where people serve themselves from food laid out on a table.

bug (bug) *n.* **1.** any insect or insect-like animal: *Spiders, flies, and ants are bugs.* **2.** a germ: *a flu bug.* **3.** a fault in a machine: *a computer bug.* —*v.* **1.** to annoy someone: *Stop bugging me!* **2.** to hide a small microphone in a room in order to listen secretly to conversations. **bugging. bugged.**

buggy (bug′ ē) *n.* **1.** a light carriage pulled by a horse. **2.** a baby carriage. *pl.* **buggies.**

bugle (byū′ gəl) *n.* a musical instrument like a small trumpet, traditionally used by the military.

build (bild) *v.* to make something by joining parts together; to construct: *to build a factory.* **building. built.**
build up to develop or come together gradually: *Traffic is building up.*

building (bil′ ding) *n.* a structure that is built, usually with four walls and a roof, to hold people, animals, or things.

bulb (bulb) *n.* **1.** a round, underground bud that looks like an onion: *Tulips, lilies, daffodils, and onions all grow from bulbs.* **2.** a bulb-shaped object: *a light bulb; a thermometer bulb.*

A **bulb** used to mean onion. When electricity was invented, the light bulb got its name because it looked like that vegetable.

bulge (bulj) *n.* a swelling. *—v.* to swell outward. **bulging. bulged.**

bulk (bulk) *n.* **1.** great size. **2.** the greatest part or portion: *Three students did the bulk of the work on the class project.*

bulky (bul′ kē) *adj.* large and sometimes a little hard to handle: *a bulky sweater; a bulky package.*

bull (bu̇l) (*fem.* **cow**) *n.* **1.** the adult male of cattle. **2.** the adult male of elephants, whales, seals, and some other large mammals.

bulldozer (bu̇l′ dōz′ ər) *n.* a powerful tractor that digs up and moves earth and rocks.

bullet (bu̇l′ ət) *n.* a rounded piece of metal fired from a rifle or gun.

bulletin (bu̇l′ ə tən) *n.* a brief news announcement: *The TV show was interrupted by a bulletin about the election.*

bulletin board a board made of cork on which messages may be tacked.

bullfrog (bu̇l′ frog) *n.* a large frog that makes a deep croak.

bully (bu̇l′ ē) *n.* someone who frightens or hurts a smaller or weaker person. *pl.* **bullies.** *—v.* to be or act like a bully. **bullying. bullied.**

bump (bump) *n.* **1.** a knock or blow. **2.** a lump or bulge: *Watch that bump in the road!* **3.** a swelling caused by a blow: *a bump on the head.* *—v.* to knock into or against. **bumping. bumped.**

bumper (bum′ pər) *n.* a metal or rubber bar on the front and back of a car that protects the car from bumps.

bun (bun) *n.* **1.** a bread roll, often sweet. **2.** a roll of hair on top or at the back of the head.

bunch (bunch) *n.* a group of things of the same kind, kept together. *pl.* **bunches.**

bundle (bun′ dəl) *n.* a number of things tied or wrapped together: *a bundle of wood.* *—v.* to tie or wrap things together. **bundling. bundled.**

bungalow (bung′ gə lō′) *n.* a small house that is one storey high.

bunk bed (bungk′ bed′) *n.* one or two narrow beds usually built one above the other.

bunny (bun′ ē) *n.* a pet name for a rabbit. *pl.* **bunnies.**

buoy (boi *or* bū′ ē) *n.* a small, floating object, used to guide swimmers or ships away from danger in the water. *pl.* **buoys.**

burden (bu̇r dən) *n.* a heavy load.

bureau (byūr′ ō) *n.* **1.** a desk or chest with drawers. **2.** a department or office: *a travel bureau.*

burglar (bu̇r′ glər) *n.* someone who breaks into a house or other place to steal money or goods.

burglary (bu̇r′ glər ē) *n.* breaking in and stealing. *pl.* **burglaries.**

burial (ber′ ē əl) *n.* placing a dead body in a grave, tomb, or some other resting place.

buried, buries (ber′ ēd, ber′ ēz) see **bury**.

burn (bu̇rn) *n.* **1.** an injury caused by fire, heat, or the sun's rays: *a sunburn.* **2.** a burned place or spot. *—v.* to be on fire; to set on fire. **burning. burned** or **burnt.**

burr (bu̇r) *n.* a prickly seed covering of some plants: *The burrs stuck to our coats as we walked through the woods.*

burrow (bůr′ ō) *n.* a hole in the ground made by an animal and used as its home. —*v.* to make such a hole. **burrowing. burrowed.**

burst (bůrst) *v.* **1.** to break or break apart: *The water pipe burst because of the freezing weather.* **2.** to enter suddenly: *A stranger burst into the room.* **bursting. burst.**

bury (ber′ ē) *v.* **1.** to place a dead body in the ground. **2.** to cover up something in the ground or some other place: *The squirrel buried the nuts under some leaves. He buried his face in his hands.* **burying. buried.** he **buries.**

bus (bus) *n.* a large motor vehicle with seats for many passengers. *pl.* **buses.**

bush (bůsh) *n.* **1.** a woody plant with many branches; a shrub. **2.** the forest: *The lumberjack went into the bush to cut trees.* *pl.* **bushes.**

bushy (bůsh′ ē) *adj.* thick and shaggy like a bush: *a bushy tail; a bushier tail; the bushiest tail of all.*

business (biz′ nis) *n.* **1.** work or job. **2.** a trade, company, shop, or factory: *Mr. and Mrs. Shin have a printing business.* **3.** a matter that you look after and attend to: *It is my business to take care of the dog.*

busy (biz′ ē) *adj.* hard at work; having plenty to do; very active: *Miranda was busy. Michiko was busier. Maya was the busiest of all.* —**busily** *adv.*

but (but) *conj.* though; yet: *I will go, but I do not want to.* —*prep.* except: *Everyone but me saw the movie.*

butcher (bůch′ ər) *n.* a person who cuts up and sells meat.

butler (but′ lər) *n.* the head male servant of a wealthy home.

butt (byūt) *n.* the end of something: *a cigarette butt.* —*v.* to hit hard with the head: *The soccer player butted the ball into the net.* **butting. butted.**

butter (but′ ər) *n.* a solid, yellow fat, separated from milk or cream by churning.

buttercup (but′ ər kup′) *n.* a wildflower with yellow petals in the shape of a cup.

butterfingers (but′ ər fing′ gərz) *n.* a person who is clumsy and drops things.

butterfly (but′ ər flī′) *n.* an insect with large, brightly coloured wings. *pl.* **butterflies.**

butterfly

butterscotch (but′ ər skoch′) *n.* a candy made from butter and brown sugar.

button (but′ ən) *n.* **1.** a round disk of metal or plastic that is sewn onto clothes to fasten them. **2.** a switch: *an elevator button.* —*v.* to close with buttons. **buttoning. buttoned.** (*opp.* **unbutton.**)

buy (bī) *v.* to get something by paying money for it. **buying. bought.** she **buys.**

buzz (buz) *n.* the humming sound made by a fly or bee. *pl.* **buzzes.** —*v.* to make such a sound. **buzzing. buzzed.**

by (bī) *prep.* **1.** at the side of: *He stood by the door.* **2.** through a person's action or effort: *It was painted by me.* **3.** no later than: *Finish your homework by Tuesday.* **4.** through the use of: *We travelled by train.* —*adv.* past: *He walked by.*

by the way off the main topic: *By the way, do you have the time?*

bye (bī) short for **goodbye**.

bystander (bī′ stand′ ər) *n.* a person who stands around watching an event, but does not get involved.

cab (kab) *n.* a car with a driver that carries passengers for a charge: *a taxicab.*

cabbage (kab′ ij) *n.* a vegetable with large, round, pale green leaves.

cabin (kab′ ən) *n.* **1.** a wooden hut. **2.** a small room for passengers on a ship.

cabinet (kab′ ə nət *or* kab′ nət) *n.* **1.** a piece of furniture with shelves or drawers: *a filing cabinet.* **2. Cabinet** a group of ministers of parliament who help the prime minister to govern.

cable (kā′ bəl) *n.* **1.** a strong steel rope: *The ship was tied to the dock with a cable.* **2.** a bundle of wires used to carry electric power, telephone messages, or TV signals.

caboose (kə būs′) *n.* the railway car at the back of a freight train where the crew works, eats, and sleeps.

cackle (kak′ əl) *n.* the screeching noise made by a hen, or a noise like it. —*v.* to make such a sound: *We cackled with laughter.* **cackling. cackled.**

cactus (kak′ təs) *n.* a very prickly plant that grows in the desert. *pl.* **cacti** (kak′ tī) or **cactuses.**

cactus

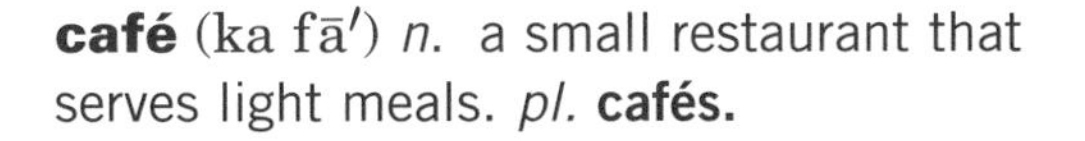

café (ka fā′) *n.* a small restaurant that serves light meals. *pl.* **cafés.**

cafeteria (kaf′ ə tēr′ ē ə) *n.* a restaurant where people serve themselves from counters. *pl.* **cafeterias.**

cage (kāj) *n.* a box with wires or metal bars, used to hold a bird or an animal.

cake (kāk) *n.* **1.** a sweet, baked dessert made from a mixture of flour, butter, sugar, eggs, and other ingredients. Cakes are often covered with icing. **2.** a hard, flat lump: *a cake of soap, a cake of mud.*

calculate (kal′ kyə lāt′) *v.* to find out by adding, subtracting, multiplying, or dividing numbers: *He calculated the total cost of buying groceries for a month.* **calculating. calculated.**

calculator (kal′ kyə lā′ tər) *n.* **1.** a machine that can add, subtract, multiply, divide, and so on. **2.** a person who calculates.

calendar (kal′ ən dər) *n.* a chart showing the days, weeks, and months of the year.

calf (kaf) *n.* **1.** a young cow (male or female). **2.** a young elephant, seal, or whale. **3.** the rounded back part of a person's leg, below the knee. *pl.* **calves.**

call (kol) *n.* **1.** a loud cry: *a call for help.* **2.** the cry of a bird. **3.** the act of telephoning someone. —*v.* **1.** to shout out. **2.** to name: *We called our dog "Tiger."* **3.** to telephone. **4.** to summon: *I'm feeling sick. Call for the doctor!* **calling. called.**

calm (kom) *adj.* **1.** quiet; still; peaceful. **2.** without wind: *a calm day.* **3.** not excited: *A calm police officer directed heavy traffic.* —**calmly** *adv.*

calorie (kal′ ə rē) *n.* a unit that measures the amount of energy produced by food: *There are 80 calories in an apple. pl.* **calories.**

came (kām) see **come.**

camel (kam′ əl) *n.* a desert mammal with one or two humps on its back. Camels store water and fat in their humps.

camel

camera (kam′ ər ə) *n.* a machine used for taking photographs or making movies. A camera has an opening through which an image or picture can be recorded on film. *pl.* **cameras.**

camouflage (kam′ ə flozh) *n.* something that makes a person, creature, or thing seem to be part of the scenery and hard to see: *A polar bear's camouflage is its white coat.* —*v.* to disguise something so that it blends in with the scenery. **camouflaging. camouflaged.**

camp (kamp) *n.* a group of tents or cabins in a park or wilderness area. —*v.* to sleep outdoors in a tent: *We camped for two weeks in the provincial park.* **camping. camped.**

campfire (kamp′ fīr) *n.* an outdoor fire at a camp.

can (kan) *n.* a metal container shaped like a cylinder: *a can of soup.* —*v.* **1.** a helping (auxiliary) verb placed before another verb to mean "be able to": *She can skate very well.* **could** (ku̇d). **2.** to store food or drink in cans or jars. **canning. canned.**

Be careful not to mix up **can** with "may." **Can** means "to be able to"; "may" means "to be allowed" or "to be possible." Can is used for ability, may is used for permission. ***May** I have a glass of water? I **can** drink water.*

Canada goose (kan′ ə də gūs) a large, wild, North American goose.

Canadian (kə nā′ dē ən) *n.* a person born in or living in Canada. —*adj.* having to do with Canada.

canal (kə nal′) *n.* a long, narrow body of water dug across land. Canals are dug to carry boats or to direct the flow of water.

canary (kə ner′ ē) *n.* a yellow songbird, often kept in a cage. *pl.* **canaries.**

cancel (kan′ səl) *v.* to stop something that has been arranged: *The rock band cancelled the concert planned for next month.* **cancelling. cancelled.**

cancer (kan′ sər) *n.* an illness caused by a harmful growth of cells in the body.

candle (kan′ dəl) *n.* a stick of wax with a wick in it that can be burned to give light.

candy (kan′ dē) *n.* a hard or soft sweet piece of food made from sugar, flavouring, and other ingredients. *pl.* **candies.**

cane (kān) *n.* **1.** the hard, springy, or hollow stem of sugar cane or bamboo plants. **2.** a strong stick used for help in walking.

cannibal (kan′ ə bəl) *n.* a person who eats human flesh.

cannon (kan′ ən) *n.* a large, old-fashioned gun on wheels, used to fire iron balls.

cannot (ka′ not) *v.* to be unable to: *We cannot see through the fog.* **could not.**

canoe (kə nū′) *n.* a very light, narrow boat, moved by a paddle.

can't (kant) a contraction (short form) of **cannot**.

cantaloupe (kant′ ə lōp) *n.* a melon with sweet, juicy, orange-coloured flesh.

canter (kan′ tər) *n.* a horse's slow, easy gallop. —*v.* to gallop in such a way. **cantering. cantered.**

canvas (kan′ vəs) *n.* a strong, heavy cloth used to make shoes, tents, and sails.

canyon (kan′ yən) *n.* a deep valley with steep sides.

cap (kap) *n.* **1.** a small, soft hat, often with a peak: *a baseball cap.* **2.** a lid for a bottle. **3.** a very small explosive, used in toy pistols.

capable (kā′ pə bəl) *adj.* able to do something well; skilled: *Yana is a very capable writer.*

cape (kāp) *n.* **1.** a cloak; an overcoat without sleeves. **2.** a point of land sticking out into the water.

capital (kap′ ə təl) *n.* a city where the government of a country, province, or state is located: *Ottawa is Canada's capital.* —*adj.* involving the death penalty: *capital punishment.*

capital letter a big letter: *capital A, B, C.*

capsule (kap′ səl *or* kap′ syūl) *n.* **1.** a small edible container that holds a dose of medicine for swallowing: *a pill capsule.* **2.** the part of a spacecraft where the astronauts are located.

captain (kap′ tən) *n.* **1.** the commander of a ship. **2.** the leader of a sports team or other group.

capture (kap′ chər) *v.* to seize and hold: *to capture a fort.* **capturing. captured.**

car (kȧr) *n.* a motor vehicle with four wheels, a steering wheel, and seats for four or five passengers; an automobile.

caramel (ker′ ə məl *or* kȧr′ məl) *n.* a chewy candy made from browned sugar, butter, and milk.

card (kȧrd) *n.* **1.** a folded piece of stiff paper, carrying a printed message: *a birthday card.* **2.** a small, rectangular piece of cardboard or plastic: *a library card; a credit card.* **3.** one of a set of 52 cards marked with numbers, symbols, and pictures, used to play games.

cardboard (kȧrd′ bȯrd) *n.* thick, stiff paper, used to make boxes and cards.

cardinal (kȧr′ də nəl) *n.* a bright red, North American songbird, with a crest on its head.

care (ker) *n.* worry; trouble; concern: *He sang happily, without a care in the world.* —*v.* to feel concerned about: *I don't care what she says.*

care for **1.** to look after: *May cares for her cat, feeding him every day.* **2.** to like or love. **caring. cared.**

take care to be careful.

career (kə rēr′) *n.* the type of work that a person chooses to do: *a career in teaching.*

careful (ker′ fəl) *adj.* cautious; taking care; attentive: *Always be careful when using matches.* —**carefully** *adv.*

careless (ker′ ləs) *adj.* not taking care. —**carelessly** *adv.*

caretaker (ker′ tāk′ ər) *n.* a person who looks after a building; a janitor.

cargo (kȧr′ gō) *n.* goods carried by ship, truck, or plane; freight. *pl.* **cargoes.**

Caribbean (ker′ ə bē′ ən *or* kə rib′ ē ən) *adj.* having to do with the Caribbean Sea or the Caribbean islands: *Jamaica and Trinidad are Caribbean islands.*

caribou (ker′ ə bū) *n.* a type of reindeer with large antlers that lives in northern Canada. *pl.* **caribou.**

caribou

> The **caribou** gets its name from a Native Canadian word. The Algonquian word *khalibu* means "one who scratches"—a favourite activity of the caribou.

carnation (kȧr nā′ shən) *n.* a round, colourful flower with a spicy smell: *Carnations are often pinned on a suit.*

carnival (kȧr′ nə vəl) *n.* a travelling amusement show with rides, games, and food.

carol (ker′ əl) *n.* a song or hymn of joy.

carpenter (kȧr′ pən tər) *n.* a person who makes and repairs wooden furniture and wooden building parts.

carpet (kȧr′ pət) *n.* a thick, soft, woven covering for floors and stairs.

carriage (ker′ ij) *n.* a vehicle that moves on wheels and is pushed or pulled: *a baby carriage; a horse carriage.*

carrot (ker′ ət) *n.* a plant with a long, orange, crunchy root, eaten as a vegetable.

carry (ker′ ē) *v.* **1.** to take something from one place to another. **2.** to support; to bear: *Can you carry such a heavy load?* **carrying. carried.** she **carries.**

carry out to make happen: *We carried out our plan to hold a school fair.*

cart (kȧrt) *n.* a small, light vehicle that is pulled or pushed by hand or by an animal: *a shopping cart.* —*v.* to move something in a cart, or as if by a cart. **carting. carted.**

carton (kȧr′ tən) *n.* a large cardboard box.

cartoon (kȧr tūn′) *n.* **1.** a funny drawing. **2.** a film made up of many drawings photographed one after the other so that objects appear to move.

cartwheel (kȧrt′ hwēl′) *n.* a sideways somersault, with the arms and legs stretched straight like the spokes of a wheel.

carve (kȧrv) *v.* **1.** to cut wood or stone into a shape. **2.** to cut meat into slices. **carving. carved.**

case (kās) *n.* **1.** a box or container: *a pencil case; a jewel case.* **2.** an example; an instance: *The child has a case of chicken pox.* **3.** a situation or condition: *That's not the case at all!*

in any case whatever happens: *Rain or shine, I'll go in any case.*

in case if it should happen that: *Take your jacket in case it rains.*

cash (kash) *n.* money in the form of coins or bills: *A bank teller handles a lot of cash.* —*v.* to change into cash: *to cash a cheque.* **cashing. cashed.**

cashier (kash ēr′) *n.* a person in charge of handling money, usually in a bank or store.

casserole (kas′ ər ōl′) *n.* a deep dish in which food, such as meat and vegetables, may be cooked and served; the food cooked in a casserole.

cassette (kə set′) *n.* a plastic case containing magnetic tape for recording sounds or images: *an audiocassette.*

cast (kast) *n.* **1.** a stiff bandage, used to protect broken bones while they are mending. **2.** the actors in a play, TV program, or movie. —*v.* **1.** to throw or fling: *Sophie cast her fishing line into the river.* **2.** to choose actors for a play, TV program, or movie. **casting. cast.**

castle (kas′ əl) *n.* the home of a king or queen.

casual (kazh′ ū əl) *adj.* relaxed; not formal: *Can we wear casual clothes to the restaurant, or do we have to dress up?* —**casually** *adv.*

cat (kat) *n.* **1.** a small, furry mammal with sharp claws, whiskers, and pointed ears, kept as a pet. **2.** a member of the cat family: *Lions, tigers, and leopards are wild cats.*

catalogue, catalog (kat′ ə log′) *n.* a list of items, with information about each item: *a catalogue of books in a library; a store catalogue.*

catastrophe (kə tas′ trə fē) *n.* a disaster: *The heavy floods were a catastrophe for the region. pl.* **catastrophes.**

catch (kach) *n.* the act of grasping something: *The football player made a good catch. pl.* **catches.** —*v.* **1.** to grab hold of something that is moving: *to catch a ball.*

2. to wait for or chase something to get hold of it: *to catch a bus; to catch someone in time.* **3.** to be made ill by: *to catch a cold.* **catching. caught** (kot).

catch up to come from behind and reach the place or time where others are: *They are far ahead of us, but if we run we can catch up with them.*

catcher (kach′ ər) *n.* in baseball, the player who stands behind home plate to catch balls thrown by the pitcher.

category (kat′ ə gȯr′ ē) *n.* a group of the same kind of things: *Apples, bananas, and peaches are part of the category "fruit."* *pl.* **categories.**

caterpillar (kat′ ər pil′ ər) *n.* a young butterfly or moth, which looks like a small, hairy, colourful worm.

catfish (kat′ fish′) *n.* a fish that lives in lakes and rivers: *The name of the catfish comes from the long spines around its mouth that look like the whiskers of a cat.* *pl.* **catfish.**

cattle (kat′ əl) *n.* four-legged mammals including cows, bulls, steers, and oxen that are raised to provide milk and meat, and to pull heavy loads.

caught (kot) see **catch** (verb).

cauliflower (ko′ lē flow′ ər) *n.* a vegetable with a large, white head of crunchy flowers.

cause (koz) *n.* **1.** a person or thing that makes something happen; a reason: *Careless smoking was the cause of the fire.* **2.** a worthy goal or organization that people support: *Give money to a good cause.* —*v.* to make something happen: *The heavy rain caused a flood.* **causing. caused.**

caution (ko′ shən) *n.* great care: *Handle the box of eggs with caution.* —*v.* to warn of danger: *The guard cautioned us not to touch the animals in the cage.* **cautioning. cautioned.**

cautious (ko′ shəs) *adj.* careful; watching for possible danger: *a cautious driver.* —**cautiously** *adv.*

cave, cavern (kāv, kav′ ərn) *n.* a large hole in a cliff or hillside.

cavity (kav′ ə tē) *n.* a hollow place: *a cavity in a tooth.* *pl.* **cavities.**

CD an abbreviation for **compact disc.**

cease (sēs) *v.* to stop; to come to an end: *When all talking ceased, the teacher showed the film.* **ceasing. ceased.**

cedar (sē′ dər) *n.* an evergreen tree with spreading branches and fragrant wood.

ceiling (sē′ ling) *n.* the inside top surface of a room, opposite to the floor.

celebrate (sel′ ə brāt′) *v.* to mark or honour an occasion by doing something special: *Let's have a party to celebrate his birthday.* **celebrating. celebrated.**

celebration (sel′ ə brā′ shən) *n.* a happy event in honour of someone or something.

celery (sel′ ər ē) *n.* a vegetable with long, crunchy, pale green stems.

cell (sel) *n.* **1.** a small, basic unit of life: *All animals and plants are made of cells.* **2.** a small room in a prison. **3.** a battery.

cellar (sel′ ər) *n.* **1.** an underground storeroom. **2.** a basement: *We keep our ski and hockey equipment in the basement during the summer.*

cello (chel′ ō) *n.* a stringed instrument, much larger than a violin, that rests on the floor and is held between the player's knees. *pl.* **cellos.**

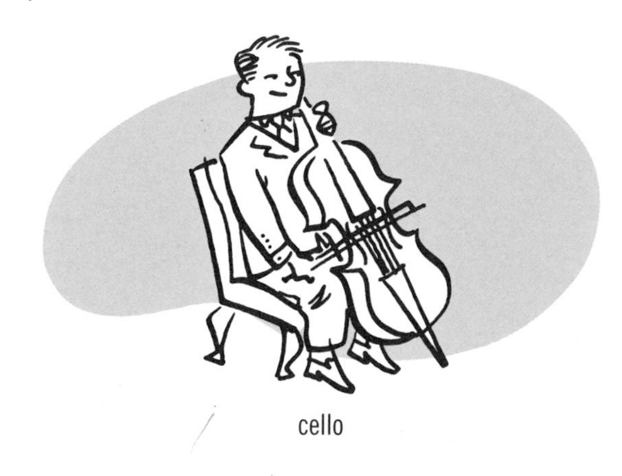

cello

cellular (sel′ yə lər) *adj.* **1.** involving the cells that make up a plant or animal. **2.** involving telephone "cells"—special radio stations that allow a cellular phone to communicate with other telephones.

Celsius (sel′ sē əs) *adj.* a scale for measuring temperature; °C is the symbol. Water freezes at zero degrees Celsius (0°C) and boils at one hundred degrees Celsius (100°C).

cement (sə ment′) *n.* a grey powder used to make concrete. Cement is mixed with water and becomes very hard when it dries.

cemetery (sem′ ə ter′ ē) *n.* a burial ground for the dead. *pl.* **cemeteries.**

census (sen′ səs) *n.* an official counting of all the people who live in a country or a region. *pl.* **censuses.**

cent (sent) *n.* a Canadian or American coin, worth one-hundredth of a dollar.

cent– is a prefix meaning "hundred." Some words using this prefix are "century" (100 years) and "centipede," a creature with so many legs that people imagined there were 100 of them.

centimetre (sen′ tə mē′ tər) *n.* a unit for measuring length; cm is the symbol; 100 cm = 1 m.

centipede (sent′ ə pēd′) *n.* a creeping, wormlike animal with many segments, each with its own pair of legs.

central (sen′ trəl) *adj.* at or near the centre: *Prince George is in central British Columbia.* —**centrally** *adv.*

centre, center (sen′ tər) *n.* **1.** the middle point or spot. **2.** a large or important building: *a shopping centre; a science centre.* **3.** in sports, the position in the middle of the forward line. —*v.* to put in the centre: *Centre the flowers on the table.* **centring. centred.**

century (sen′ chə rē) *n.* one hundred years. *pl.* **centuries.**

ceramics (sə ram′ iks) *n. pl.* pottery, or the art of making pottery. —**ceramic** *adj.*

cereal (sēr′ ē əl) *n.* **1.** the seeds of wheat, rice, corn, oats, and other grains used as food. **2.** breakfast food made from any or several of these grains.

Ceres was the Roman goddess of agriculture. From her name, we get the word **cereal**. Cereals are made from grains such as oats, wheat, and corn. Can you think of others?

ceremony (ser′ ə mō′ nē) *n.* a formal activity to mark a special occasion: *a wedding ceremony. pl.* **ceremonies.**

certain (sůr′ tən) *adj.* **1.** sure; positive: *Are you certain it will snow?* (*opp.* **uncertain.**) **2.** particular: *I am looking in the library for a certain book.*

certainly (sůr′ tən lē) *adv.* surely; without doubt: *We will certainly be there.*

certificate (sůr tif′ ə kit) *n.* an official, written statement that states something is true or has been accomplished: *He passed all his courses and got a certificate in teaching.*

chain (chān) *n.* a row of metal rings or links joined together: *a gold chain.* —*v.* to fasten with a chain: *The dog was chained to the tree.* **chaining. chained.**

chair (cher) *n.* a seat for one person, with a back and legs; a chairperson.

chairperson (cher′ půr′ sən) *n.* a person in charge of a meeting or committee.

chalet (sha′ lā) *n.* a cabin, often built in snowy mountain areas: *a ski chalet.*

chalk (chok) *n.* **1.** a white limestone, seen in some cliffs. **2.** a marking stick, used for writing on chalkboards.

chalkboard (chok′ bȯrd) *n.* a smooth, hard surface used for writing on with chalk.

challenge (chal′ ənj) *n.* a difficult or dangerous task or contest: *Climbing the* *mountain will be a challenge.* —*v.* to dare someone to take part in a contest, game, or other activity: *Esther challenged Peter to a game of checkers.* **challenging. challenged.**

chamber (chām′ bər) *n.* a room.

champion (cham′ pē ən) *n.* the winner of a game or contest.

championship (cham′ pē ən ship′) *n.* the title of champion; first place: *Our school won the track-and-field championship.*

chance (chans) *n.* **1.** luck; accident: *It was only by chance that I found my lost cap.* **2.** an opportunity: *You have a good chance of getting that job.* **3.** a risk: *Don't take a chance by showing up late.*

change (chānj) *n.* **1.** difference: *There is no change in the way the team is playing this year.* **2.** money you get back when you pay too much. —*v.* **1.** to make or become different: *The weather has changed since this morning.* **2.** to put one thing in place of another; exchange: *I changed from sneakers to sandals.* **changing. changed.**

channel (chan′əl) *n.* **1.** a long, narrow body of water that connects two larger bodies of water: *The English Channel is between England and France.* **2.** a band of radio waves used by a TV or radio station.

chant (chant) *v.* **1.** to sing. **2.** to call out or sing over and over: *The crowd chanted between hockey periods.* **chanting. chanted.**

chap (chap) *n.* a boy or man; a fellow: *He's a friendly chap.* —*v.* to crack or become sore because of dryness or cold: *My lips have chapped.* **chapping. chapped.**

chapel (chap′ əl) *n.* a small church.

chapter (chap′ tər) *n.* a section of a book.

character (ker′ ik tər) *n.* **1.** the nature of a person or thing; personality: *My sister has a fine character; she is honest and kind.* **2.** a person in a book, story, movie, or play.

charcoal (chär′ kōl) *n.* a black substance, made of partly burned wood, used in drawing pencils and for cooking food outdoors in a barbecue.

charge (chärj) *n.* **1.** fee: *There is a charge of five dollars to see the school play.* **2.** responsibility; control: *Who is in charge of the office?* **3.** an attack: *The army general led the charge.* —*v.* **1.** to put a price on something. **2.** (for police) to accuse someone of a crime. **3.** to fill with electricity: *to charge batteries.* **4.** to attack. **5.** to buy items with a credit card. **charging. charged.**

chariot (chär′ ē ət) *n.* in ancient times, a two-wheeled vehicle pulled by horses. Chariots were used in battles, races, and ceremonies.

chariot

charity (cher′ ə tē) *n.* **1.** money or help given to people in need. **2.** an organization that helps people in need. *pl.* **charities.**

charm (chärm) *n.* **1.** the power to please and delight: *a child of great charm.* **2.** an object that is supposed to bring good fortune: *a lucky charm.* **3.** a magic spell. —*v.* **1.** to delight someone. **2.** to put under a magic spell. **charming. charmed.**

charming (chärm′ ing) *adj.* delightful; attractive.

charred (chärd) *adj.* scorched; blackened by fire: *charred wood.*

chart (chärt) *n.* **1.** a map, especially one for sailors. **2.** a sheet showing information in the form of a list, table, or diagram. **3.** a graph: *a pie chart.*

charter (chär′ tər) *n.* an official document that lists rights and responsibilities: *a charter of rights.* —*v.* to rent or hire: *The school chartered a bus for the class trip to the museum.* **chartering. chartered.**

chase (chās) *n.* **1.** the act of chasing: *an exciting police chase.* **2.** a hunt. —*v.* **1.** to go after something and try to catch it; to pursue: *The dog chased the fire engine.* **2.** to drive away: *Don't chase the squirrel away.* **chasing. chased.**

chat (chat) *n.* a friendly talk between people. —*v.* to talk in a friendly, informal way. **chatting. chatted.**

château (sha tō′) *n.* the French word for castle. *pl.* **châteaux.**

chatter (chat′ ər) *n.* constant and sometimes silly talk. —*v.* **1.** to talk constantly and foolishly. **2.** to rattle together: *The cold weather makes my teeth chatter.* **chattering. chattered.**

chauffeur (shō fər′) *n.* a person paid to drive a car.

cheap (chēp) *adj.* **1.** inexpensive. **2.** of poor quality: *A cheap toy breaks easily.* —**cheaply** *adv.*

cheat (chēt) *v.* **1.** to act dishonestly: *to cheat on a test.* **2.** to take something from someone dishonestly: *My older sister cheated me out of my allowance.* **cheating. cheated.**

check (chek) *n.* **1.** an examination to make sure everything is right. **2.** something or someone that holds back action: *a hockey check.* **3.** a mark (✓) to show that something is correct. **4.** a restaurant bill. —*v.* **1.** to examine carefully to make sure everything is right or in good condition: *I checked my answers again.* **2.** to stop someone or something; to hold back: *He was angry, but he checked his words.* **checking. checked.**

checkers (chek′ ərz) *n.* a game played by two people, each starting with 12 disks (called checkers) that are moved around a two-coloured board with 64 squares.

check-up (chek′ up) *n.* a complete examination: *a medical check-up; a car check-up.*

cheek (chēk) *n.* the rounded side of your face below each eye.

cheer (chēr) *n.* a shout of encouragement or joy: *a school cheer.* —*v.* to shout encouragement: *They cheered the school team.* **cheering. cheered.**

cheer up to become happier or to make someone happier: *Your letter cheered me up.*

cheerful (chēr′ fəl) *adj.* bright and smiling; happy. —**cheerfully** *adv.*

cheese (chēz) *n.* a solid food made from thickened, sour milk.

cheetah (chē′ tə) *n.* a large, spotted wild cat that has long legs and can run very fast. Cheetahs live in parts of Africa and Asia.

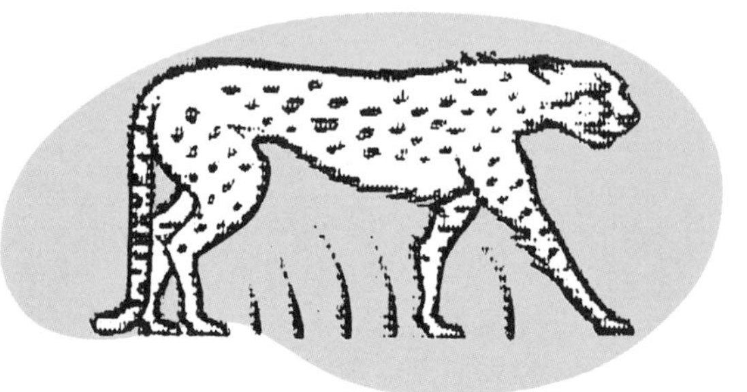

cheetah

chef (shef) *n.* a cook, usually the head cook in a restaurant.

chemical (kem′ ə kəl) *n.* a substance used in chemistry.

chemist (kem′ist) *n.* a person trained in chemistry and who makes substances such as dyes and medicines.

chemistry (kem′ is trē) *n.* the study of what things are made of and how they change when they are mixed together, heated, cooled, and so on.

cheque (chek) *n.* a written order to a bank to pay money from your bank account to someone.

cherry (cher′ ē) *n.* a small, round, red fruit with a hard pit inside. *pl.* **cherries.**

chess (ches) *n.* a game of skill played by two people, each with 16 chess pieces that are moved around a two-coloured board with 64 squares.

chest (chest) *n.* **1.** a strong box with a lid: *a tool chest.* **2.** the upper, front part of your body where your ribs, lungs, and heart are.

chestnut (ches′ nut′) *n.* **1.** the brown nut of the chestnut tree. **2.** a reddish-brown colour. *—adj.* having this colour.

chew (chü) *v.* to grind food with the teeth. **chewing. chewed.**

chick (chik) *n.* a very young bird, especially a young chicken.

chickadee (chik′ ə dē′) *n.* a small, North American bird with a round body, grey feathers, and a dark patch, like a cap, on its head. *pl.* **chickadees.**

chicken (chik′ ən) *n.* **1.** a hen or rooster. **2.** the meat of this bird.

chicken pox (chik′ ən poks) a very contagious disease. Its symptoms are a fever and itchy, red spots all over the body.

chief (chēf) *n.* the leader or head of a group. *—adj.* main; most important: *Her chief wish is to own a bicycle.*

child (chīld) *n.* **1.** a young boy or girl. **2.** a daughter or son: *My uncle has two children.* *pl.* **children.**

childhood (chīld′ hůd) *n.* the condition or the time of being a child: *My mother spent her childhood in Jamaica and came to Canada when she was sixteen.*

chill (chil) *n.* **1.** a cold feeling that causes shivering. **2.** coldness: *an autumn chill.* **3.** a sudden feeling of fear or dread: *Chills went down my spine.* *—v.* **1.** to make cold: *Chill the juice in the fridge.* **2.** to frighten: *The scary story chilled all the children.*

chilly (chil′ ē) *adj.* cold: *a chilly day; a chillier day; the chilliest day of the week.*

chime (chīm) *n.* **1.** a set of bells. **2.** a sound or tune made by a chime or bell. *—v.* **1.** (for bells) to ring. **2.** (for a clock) to strike the hour. **chiming. chimed.**

chimney (chim′ nē) *n.* a long, hollow, upright structure that lets smoke escape from a fireplace or furnace. *pl.* **chimneys.**

chimpanzee (chim′ pan zē′) *n.* a medium-sized African ape with dark hair. Chimpanzees are very intelligent. *pl.* **chimpanzees.**

chin (chin) *n.* the part of the face below the mouth.

china (chī′ nə) *n.* fine, ceramic dishes.

chinook (shi nük′) *n.* **1.** a warm winter wind that blows across parts of Western Canada. **2.** a large Pacific salmon.

chip (chip) *n.* **1.** a small piece that has been cut or broken off: *wood chips; potato chips.* **2.** the place from which this small piece has broken off: *This cup has a chip.* *—v.* to break off a small piece. **chipping. chipped.**

chipmunk (chip′ mungk) *n.* a small, striped rodent, related to the squirrel.

chirp (chürp) *n.* the high, short sound made by some birds and insects: *the chirp of sparrows.* *—v.* to make such a noise. **chirping. chirped.**

chisel (chiz′ əl) *n.* a tool for cutting wood or stone. *—v.* to use such a tool. **chiselling. chiselled.**

chlorine (klör′ ēn *or* klör ēn′) *n.* a greenish-yellow gas, with a sharp, unpleasant smell, which is used to clean water for drinking and for swimming pools.

chocolate (cho′ kə lət *or* chok′ lət) *n.* a dark brown, bitter food made from ground, roasted cacao seeds, or beans. It is sweetened and used to make candy, cakes, and drinks.

choice (chois) *n.* the choosing of something: *It is hard to make a choice because I like so many ice-cream flavours.*

choir (kwīr) *n.* a group of singers.

choke (chōk) *v.* to be unable to breathe because of something blocking the throat; to suffocate: *I nearly choked on a piece of apple.* **choking. choked.**

choose (chūz) *v.* to select or decide: *I chose three games to take along on the trip.* **choosing. chose.** I have **chosen.**

chop (chop) *n.* a small piece of meat joined to a bone: *a pork chop.* —*v.* to cut with sharp blows: *to chop down a tree; to chop up vegetables.* **chopping. chopped.**

chopsticks (chop′ stiks) *n. pl.* a pair of long, narrow sticks, held between the thumb and fingers and used for eating.

chore (chȯr) *n.* a task: *Drying the dishes is one of my daily chores.*

chorus (kȯr′ əs) *n.* **1.** a group of people singing together: *The chorus on the stage sang popular songs.* **2.** the part of a song that is repeated. *pl.* **choruses.**

chrome (krōm) *n.* an expensive, very shiny, silver-coloured metal that does not rust.

chubby (chub′ ē) *adj.* plump; a little overweight: *a chubby baby; a chubbier baby; the chubbiest baby of all.*

chuckle (chuk′ əl) *n.* a quiet laugh. —*v.* to laugh quietly. **chuckling. chuckled.**

chum (chum) *n.* a close friend; a pal.

chunk (chungk) *n.* **1.** a thick piece: *a chunk of meat for the dog.* **2.** a large amount: *Cleaning my room will take quite a chunk of time!*

church (chu̇rch) *n.* a building where people meet for religious worship.

churn (chu̇rn) *n.* a container in which cream is beaten to make butter. —*v.* to beat cream into butter. **churning. churned.**

cigar (si gär′) *n.* a fat roll of tobacco leaves for smoking.

cigarette (sig′ ə ret′) *n.* shredded tobacco rolled in a paper tube, used for smoking.

cinch (sinch) *n.* (*informal*) a sure and easy thing: *Winning the championship was a cinch.*

cinema (sin′ ə mə) *n.* a movie theatre. *pl.* **cinemas.**

cinnamon (sin′ ə mən) *n.* a reddish-brown spice used to flavour sweets and desserts.

circle (su̇r′ kəl) *n.* a perfectly round ring. —*v.* **1.** to move around in a ring: *The cat circled the bird cage.* **2.** to draw a circle around something: *I circled my answer.* **circling. circled.**

circular (su̇r′ kyə lər) *n.* an advertisement or notice sent to a number of people: *Everyone on our street received a circular about the fair.* —*adj.* in the shape of a circle.

circumference (su̇r kum′ fər əns) *n.* the outside edge of a circle.

circumstance (su̇r′ kəm stans′) *n.* a condition or fact that affects something else: *What were the circumstances behind the argument between the two friends?*

circus (su̇r′ kəs) *n.* a travelling show with clowns, acrobats, and sometimes animals. *pl.* **circuses.**

A **circus** includes entertainers performing in a ring. In ancient times, the word "circus" referred to a ring—a "circular" area where great shows were held.

citizen (sit′ ə zən) *n.* a member of a nation, by birth or by choice.

citrus fruits (sit′ rəs frūts) oranges, grapefruits, lemons, and limes.

city (sit′ ē) *n.* a very large and important town, where many people live and work. *pl.* **cities.**

city hall the building where the mayor and the government of a city meet.

civilization (siv′ ə lə zā′ shən) *n.* every aspect of a people's way of life: *the ancient Greek civilization.*

claim (klām) *n.* **1.** a demand to something as a right. **2.** a statement that something is true: *I don't believe his claim that flying saucers exist.* **3.** a prospector's piece of land. —*v.* **1.** to say that you have a right to something or that it belongs to you: *Anna claimed the wallet at the lost and found department.* **2.** to state that something is true: *My sister claims she is the comedian of our family.* **claiming. claimed.**

clam (klam) *n.* a shellfish that lives in beaches. A clam has a soft body inside and a hard shell in two parts that close together tightly.

clammy (klam′ ē) *adj.* damp and cold: *clammy hands.*

clamp (klamp) *n.* a piece of metal equipment that holds parts together firmly. —*v.* to fasten something with or like a clamp. **clamping. clamped.**

clap (klap) *n.* a slapping together of the hands. —*v.* to slap your hands together; to applaud. **clapping. clapped.**

clarinet (kler′ ə net′) *n.* a musical wind instrument, shaped like a tube with a bell-shaped bottom.

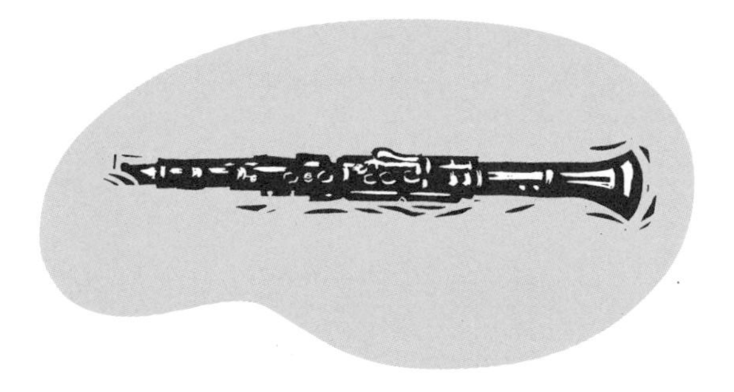

clarinet

clash (klash) *v.* **1.** to hit together or come together with a loud noise. **2.** to disagree strongly or not to match: *Your purple pants clash with your orange shirt.*

clasp (klasp) *n.* a hook used to hold something together: *Her necklace was fastened by a metal clasp.* —*v.* **1.** to fasten something with a clasp. **2.** to hug someone or to give a firm handshake. **clasping. clasped.**

class (klas) *n.* **1.** a group of students who are taught together. **2.** a number of persons, animals, or objects that are alike in certain ways: *The class called "mammals" includes people, apes, bears, and other warm-blooded animals. pl.* **classes.**

classical (klas′ ə kəl) *adj.* having to do with symphonies, operas, and similar music.

classmate (klas′ māt′) *n.* a student who is in the same class as you.

classroom (klas′ rūm′) a room in which school classes are held.

clatter (klat′ ər) *n.* sharp, rattling sounds: *the clatter of dishes.* —*v.* to make such sounds: *The horses' hooves clattered down the road.* **clattering. clattered.**

claw (klo) *n.* the sharp, curved nail of a cat and some other animals and birds. —*v.* to tear at something with claws: *The tiger clawed at the meat.* **clawing. clawed.**

claw

clay (klā) *n.* a smooth, sticky kind of earth, which can be shaped when wet and hardened in a furnace: *Bricks and pottery are made of clay.*

clean (klēn) *adj.* **1.** free of dirt. **2.** neat and tidy. —*v.* to remove dirt. **cleaning. cleaned.**

clear (klēr) *adj.* **1.** bright; cloudless: *a clear sky.* **2.** easily understood: *The speaker had a clear voice.* (*opp.* **unclear.**) —**clearly** *adv.* —*v.* to clean out and tidy: *Al cleared the cupboards.* **clearing. cleared.**

clerk (klůrk) *n.* **1.** a salesperson in a store. **2.** an office worker who looks after files, records, and other papers.

clever (klev′ ər) *adj.* **1.** bright; intelligent; quick. **2.** able to do things well: *She's a clever carpenter.* —**cleverly** *adv.*

click (klik) *n.* a small, sharp sound: *the click of a camera.* —*v.* to make such a sound. **clicking. clicked.**

cliff (klif) *n.* a high, steep or vertical area of rock or earth.

climate (klī′ mət) *n.* the kind of weather that a place usually has.

climb (klīm) *n.* a climbing or going up: *a mountain climb.* —*v.* **1.** to go up stairs, a hill, a tree, and so on. **2.** to rise steeply: *The jet climbed into the sky.* **climbing. climbed.**

cling (kling) *v.* to hold firmly to: *The little raccoon clung to its mother.* **clinging. clung** (klung).

clinic (klin′ ik) *n.* a medical centre where you can see a doctor or dentist for treatment.

clip (klip) *n.* a fastener: *a hair clip; a paper clip.* —*v.* to trim with scissors or shears: *to clip a hedge.* **clipping. clipped.**

clipboard (klip′ bȯrd′) *n.* **1.** a small board with a big clip for holding papers. **2.** an area in a computer's memory where information can be stored for a short time.

cloak (klōk) *n.* a cape.

clock (klok) *n.* an instrument that tells the time.

The word **clock** comes from a Latin word, *clocca,* which means "bell." Early clocks had no hands—they worked by sounding a bell every hour.

clockwise (klok′ wīz′) *adj., adv.* in the direction in which the hands of a clock move. (*opp.* **counterclockwise.**)

clog (klog) *v.* to block up or become blocked up: *Grease clogged the pipe, so that water would not go down the sink.* **clogging. clogged.**

close (klōs) *adj.* **1.** near. **2.** dear: *We are close friends.* **3.** almost equal: *It was a close game, but we won by a point.* —*adv.* near: *The bird flew close to the house.*

close (klōz) *v.* **1.** to cover an opening by moving a door, putting on a lid, and so on; to shut: *Close the door, please!* **2.** to come to an end: *The fair closes on Friday.* **closing. closed.**

closely (klōs′ lē) *adv.* carefully: *Josh examined the photograph closely.*

closet (kloz′ ət) *n.* a small room for storing things such as clothes, sheets, or towels.

cloth (kloth) *n.* **1.** a material made by weaving cotton, wool, silk, nylon, linen, or other fibres together. **2.** a piece of woven material: *a dishcloth.*

clothes (klōTHz) *n.* the garments people wear, such as pants, skirts, shirts, saris, kimonos, or caftans.

clothing (klō′ THing) *n.* clothes.

cloud (klowd) *n.* **1.** a large white or grey mass of tiny water drops, floating high in the sky. **2.** anything like a cloud: *a cloud of smoke.* —*v.* to cover with a cloud. **clouding. clouded.**

cloudy (klowd′ ē) *adj.* covered with clouds: *a cloudy sky; a cloudier sky; the cloudiest sky of all.*

clover (klō′ vər) *n.* a meadow plant with leaves in three or sometimes four parts.

clown (klown) *n.* a circus performer who makes everyone laugh with jokes or tricks. —*v.* to act like a clown. **clowning. clowned.**

club (klub) *n.* **1.** a short, heavy stick used as a weapon. **2.** a long stick with a special head for hitting a ball: *a golf club.* **3.** a group of people who meet to enjoy a hobby or an interest together: *a club for coin collectors.* **4.** a playing card with one or more (♣) marks on it. —*v.* to hit with a club. **clubbing. clubbed.**

cluck (kluk) *v.* to make a noise like a hen. **clucking. clucked.**

clue (klū) *n.* a small object or sign that helps in solving a mystery or answering a riddle: *Fingerprints were the only clue to help the police solve the crime.*

clump (klump) *n.* a small cluster: *a clump of flowers.*

clumsy (klum′ zē) *adj.* awkward in moving about and in doing things: *a clumsy clown; a clumsier one; the clumsiest clown of all.*

clung (klung) see **cling**.

cluster (klus′ tər) *n.* a bunch; a group: *a cluster of grapes.*

clutch (kluch) *n.* a tight hold: *The mouse is in the owl's clutches.* *pl.* **clutches.** —*v.* **1.** to grab. **2.** to hold tightly. **clutching. clutched.**

clutter (klut′ ər) *n.* a mess; things left in an untidy way: *Please clear your clutter before starting the project.* —*v.* to leave things in an untidy way: *The room was cluttered with books and newspapers.* **cluttering. cluttered.**

coach (kōch) *n.* **1.** a large, closed, four-wheeled carriage pulled by horses. **2.** a railway car. **3.** a person who trains a sports team. *pl.* **coaches.** —*v.* to train someone for a sport. **coaching. coached.**

coal (kōl) *n.* a hard, black substance used as fuel.

coarse (kôrs) *adj.* **1.** made up of fairly large parts; not fine: *coarse sand.* **2.** rough; not smooth: *coarse cloth.* —**coarsely** *adv.*

coast (kōst) *n.* the seashore. —*v.* to slide downhill without any power: *The sled coasted down the snowy hill.* **coasting. coasted.**

coat (kōt) *n.* **1.** an outer garment made of heavy or protective material, with buttons or a zipper down the front. **2.** a covering: *a coat of paint.*

coating (kōt′ ing) *n.* a layer covering something: *a coating of icing on a cake.*

coat of arms an emblem or a design that identifies a noble family, a government, or a school: *Long ago, knights had coats of arms on their shields.*

coax (kōks) *v.* to encourage gently, using soft words: *I tried to coax the squirrel to come and take a peanut from my hand.* **coaxing. coaxed.**

cob (kob) *n.* the hard, centre part of an ear of corn to which the kernels are attached.

cobbler (kob′ lər) *n.* someone who mends boots and shoes.

cobra (kō′ brə) *n.* a poisonous snake of Asia and Africa.

cobra

cobweb (kob′ web) *n.* a spider's net, used for catching insects.

cock (kok) (*fem.* **hen**) *n.* a rooster.

cockpit (kok′ pit) *n.* the place in an aircraft where the pilot sits.

cockroach (kok′ rōch) *n.* an insect with a flat, shiny body. Some cockroaches are house pests, found in kitchens. *pl.* **cockroaches.**

cocoa (kō′ kō) *n.* **1.** a brown, chocolate-flavoured powder. **2.** a hot chocolate drink made from this powder.

coconut (kō′ kə nut) *n.* the large nut of the coco palm tree, which grows in hot climates. Coconuts have a hard, brown, hairy husk, a sweet white flesh, and a sweet white liquid called coconut milk.

coconut

> A **coconut** has three dark marks at one end. These marks look something like two eyes and a mouth. That's how the coconut got its name: *coco* is Spanish and Portuguese for "ugly face."

cocoon (kə kūn′) *n.* the silky case spun for protection by some young insects: *The caterpillar spins a cocoon before it changes into a moth or a butterfly.*

cod (kod) *n.* a fish found in the northern Atlantic Ocean. *pl.* **cod.**

code (kōd) *n.* **1.** signs or special words used to write a secret message or to give information. **2.** a set of rules or laws: *the traffic code.*

coffee (ko′ fē) *n.* a hot drink made from the roasted seeds, or beans, of the coffee plant.

coffin (ko′ fin) *n.* the box in which a dead person is buried.

cog (kog) *n.* a wheel with cutouts like teeth along the edge, used in machinery; a gear.

coil (koil) *n.* a wire or rope wound around and around in a spiral. *—v.* to wind around in a spiral. **coiling. coiled.**

coin (koin) *n.* a round piece of metal money.

coincidence (kō in′ sə dəns) *n.* two or more things happening by chance at the same time: *By coincidence, my two favourite movies came out in the same year.*

cold (kōld) *n.* **1.** lack of heat. **2.** an illness that causes sneezing, a runny nose, and coughing. *—adj.* **1.** without warmth; having a low temperature; chilly. **2.** not friendly: *a cold look.*

cold-blooded (kōld′ blud′ əd) *adj.* having a body temperature that becomes colder or warmer when the surrounding temperature goes up or down. Mammals and birds are warm-blooded; fish and reptiles are cold-blooded.

collage (kə lozh′) *n.* a picture made by pasting different materials, such as string, newspaper, and glitter, on a piece of paper.

collapse (kə laps′) *v.* to fall down suddenly, or to break down: *The rickety old barn collapsed in the storm.* **collapsing. collapsed.**

collar (kol′ ər) *n.* **1.** the band around the neck of a shirt, dress, or coat. **2.** a band worn around the neck: *a dog collar.*

collect (kə lekt′) *v.* **1.** to gather in: *to collect taxes; to collect test papers.* **2.** to gather as a hobby: *Shonna collects stamps.* **collecting. collected.**

collection (kə lek′ shən) *n.* a number of things collected together: *a coin collection.*

collector (kə lek′ tər) *n.* a person who collects things as a hobby.

college (kol′ ij) *n.* **1.** a school attended after high school: *a community college.* **2.** a building that is part of a university.

collide (kə līd′) *v.* to bump hard into something; to crash. **colliding. collided.**

collie (kol′ ē) *n.* a large, shaggy dog with a long pointed nose. *pl.* **collies.**

collision (kə lizh′ ən) *n.* a crash when one thing bangs into another.

colon (kō′ lən) *n.* **1.** a punctuation mark (:), used to introduce a list, an example, or sometimes a quotation. **2.** the lower part of the large intestine in the human body.

colonel (kůr′ nəl) *n.* an army officer who commands a regiment.

colony (kol′ ə nē) *n.* **1.** a group of people settling in a new land. **2.** the place where such a group settles. **3.** a group of animals of the same kind, living together: *an ant colony.* *pl.* **colonies.**

colour, color (kul′ ər) *n.* red, blue, and yellow, or any combination of these. —*v.* to give colour to, or change the colour of, something. **colouring. coloured.**

colourful, colorful (kul′ ər fůl) *adj.* full of bright colours.

colourless, colorless (kul′ ər ləs) *adj.* having little or no colour; dull.

colt (kōlt) (*fem.* **filly**) *n.* a young male horse.

column (kol′ əm) *n.* **1.** a narrow, upright building support; a pillar. **2.** a list of numbers or words, one below the other. **3.** a narrow, vertical section of type in a newspaper or magazine.

column

comb (kōm) *n.* **1.** a thin piece of plastic or metal with teeth, used to smooth your hair. **2.** the red crest on a rooster's head. —*v.* to smooth your hair with a comb. **combing. combed.**

combat (kom′ bat) *n.* a battle; a fight.

combination (kom′ bə nā′ shən) *n.* **1.** a combining of things. **2.** something that results from a combining: *Purple is a combination of blue and red.*

combine (kom′ bīn) *n.* a farm machine driven over a field, used to cut grain and separate the seeds from the stalks.

combine (kom bīn′) *v.* to bring, join, or unite together: *We combined flour and water into a paste.* **combining. combined.**

come (kum) *v.* **1.** to move toward you; to approach: *I can hear the train coming.* **2.** to arrive: *On which day will they come?* **3.** to be from: *We came from Nigeria.* **4.** to become: *My dream has come true.* **coming. came.** I have **come.**

come about to happen: *How did your great success come about?*

come across to find by chance: *Michael came across his missing sock when he was looking for a shirt.*

come up to arise; to be mentioned: *During the conversation, the subject of my mom's new car came up.*

comedian (kə mē′ dē ən) *n.* a performer who tells jokes and makes people laugh.

comedy (kom′ ə dē) *n.* a funny play, movie, or program. *pl.* **comedies.**

comet (kom′ it) *n.* a large ball of ice that orbits the sun. When a comet comes near the sun, some of the ice melts to form a long, flowing tail.

comfort (kum′ fərt) *n.* **1.** a relaxed, easy feeling: *We sat in great comfort in front of the fire.* (*opp.* **discomfort.**) **2.** kind words or actions to ease someone's suffering. —*v.* to ease someone's suffering by kind actions or words. **comforting. comforted.**

comfortable (kum′ fər tə bəl) *adj.* at ease. —**comfortably** *adv.*

comic (kom′ ik) *n.* **1.** a comedian. **2.** a comic book. —*adj.* funny: *a comic actor.*

comical (kom′ ə kəl) *adj.* funny; amusing. —**comically** *adv.*

comma (kom′ə) *n.* a punctuation mark (,), used to separate words or a group of words in a sentence. *pl.* **commas.**

command (kə mand′) *n.* **1.** an order. **2.** in a computer program, an action, such as pressing a key, that tells the computer to do something. **3.** to have control over: *The captain has command of the ship.* —*v.* **1.** to order someone to do something. **2.** to have control of: *The captain commands the ship.* **commanding. commanded.**

commando (kə man′ dō) *n.* a unit of troops trained to carry out raids. *pl.* **commandos.**

comment (kom′ ənt) *n.* an opinion or other remark, either spoken or written down. —*v.* to make such a remark: *Father commented that the weather was improving.* **commenting. commented.**

commerce (kom′ ürs) *n.* trade; business; buying and selling.

commercial (kə mür′ shəl) *n.* an advertisement on radio or TV. —*adj.* having to do with commerce. —**commercially** *adv.*

commit (kə mit′) *v.* **1.** to do something, usually wrong: *to commit a crime; to commit an error.* **2.** to promise: *She committed to speaking at the meeting.* **3.** to devote yourself to something. **committing. committed.**

committee (kə mit′ ē) *n.* a small group of people who meet to make rules and plan programs: *The school newspaper committee meets every Monday.*

common (kom′ ən) *adj.* happening or found often or everywhere; not rare: *Daisies are common wildflowers.* (*opp.* **uncommon.**) —**commonly** *adv.*

common sense natural good judgment; an ability to deal with practical things in a sensible way: *When it is freezing outside, wearing a coat is common sense.*

Commonwealth (kom′ ən welth′) *n.* an association of many countries that were once part of the British Empire. Its full name is the Commonwealth of Nations.

commotion (kə mō′ shən) *n.* noisy confusion: *The mouse in the kitchen caused a commotion when we all climbed up on chairs.*

communicate (kə myū′ nə kāt′) *v.* to tell something to others by talking, writing, or using technology. **communicating. communicated.**

communication (kə myū nə kā′ shən) *n.* the passing of information from one person or place to another: *The telephone allows for instant voice communication around the world.*

community (kə myū′ nə tē) *n.* a group of people living in the same neighbourhood or having similar concerns: *the arts community.* *pl.* **communities.**

commute (kə myūt′) *v.* to travel a distance to work or school: *It takes Mom an hour to commute by train to her job.* **commuting. commuted.**

compact (kom′ pakt) *adj.* taking up a small amount of space: *a compact car.*

compact disc a small disc on which a sound recording or other information is stored.

companion (kəm pan′ yən) *n.* a person who spends time with you or goes with you somewhere.

company (kum′ pə nē) *n.* **1.** guests: *We had company over for tea yesterday.* **2.** a business firm. *pl.* **companies.** **3.** companionship: *I like your company when I go shopping.*

compare (kəm per′) *v.* to look at how two or more things are alike or different: *When you compare these two drawings, you see that Gwen's is more colourful than Nadia's.* **comparing. compared.**

comparison (kəm per′ ə sən) *n.* the comparing of things.

compartment (kəm pärt′ mənt) *n.* a separate section: *This jewellery box has five compartments.*

compass (kum′ pəs) *n.* **1.** an instrument that shows direction: *The needle on a compass points to the magnetic North Pole.* **2.** an instrument used for drawing circles or measuring distances. *pl.* **compasses.**

compass

compete (kəm pēt′) *v.* to take part in a contest with other people: *to compete in the Olympic Games.* **competing. competed.**

competition (kom′ pə tish′ ən) *n.* **1.** a race, game, or other contest. **2.** the other contestants: *Our competition was so skillful, we almost lost the game to them.*

competitor (kəm pet′ ə tər) *n.* a person who takes part in a contest or competition.

complain (kəm plān′) *v.* to find fault with something: *She complained that the soup was cold.* **complaining. complained.**

complaint (kəm plānt′) *n.* the finding of fault: *There were several complaints about the food at camp.*

complete (kom plēt′) *adj.* whole; not lacking anything: *a complete box of crayons.* (*opp.* **incomplete.**) —*v.* to finish: *Complete your homework before you go out.* **completing. completed.** —**completely** *adv.*

complexion (kəm plek′ shən) *n.* the appearance of the skin on the face: *a smooth complexion.*

complicated (kom′ plə kāt′ id) *adj.* difficult; not simple: *a complicated problem.*

compose (kəm pōz′) *v.* **1.** to make up or put together: *Canada is composed of ten provinces and two territories.* **2.** to write something, such as a piece of music or a letter. **composing. composed.**

composer (kəm pō′ zər) *n.* a person who writes music.

composition (kom′ pə zish′ ən) *n.* a piece of writing or music.

compost (kom′ pōst) *n.* a mixture of decaying natural substances, such as vegetable peels and dead leaves, used to make fertilizer. —*v.* to make compost. **composting. composted.**

comprehend (kom′ prē hend′) *v.* to understand: *Please speak more slowly so I can comprehend what you are saying.* **comprehending. comprehended.**

comprehension (kom′ pre hen′ shən) *n.* understanding, or the ability to understand something: *This book is beyond my comprehension.*

compromise (kom′ prə mīz′) *n.* an agreement in which each side gives up something so that everybody is satisfied: *We reached a compromise—I watch the TV programs I want on Wednesday, and he watches what he wants on Thursday.* —*v.* to settle a disagreement, with each side giving up something. **compromising. compromised.**

compute (kəm pyūt′) *v.* to figure out; to calculate: *Please compute this sum.* **computing. computed.**

computer (kəm pyū′ tər) *n.* an electronic device that can do math calculations at very fast speeds, store and process information, and control machinery.

conceal (kən sēl′) *v.* to hide; to keep secret. **concealing. concealed.**

conceited (kən sēt′ id) *adj.* having too high an opinion of yourself: *That conceited player thinks he is the best member of the team.*

concentrate (kon′ sən trāt′) *v.* **1.** to give careful attention to one thing only; to focus: *Concentrate on your work.* **2.** to make a mixture stronger: *The canned soup is concentrated, so you need to add water to it.* **concentrating. concentrated.**

concept (kon′ sept) *n.* a general idea: *the concept of time.*

concern (kən sûrn′) *n.* a matter of importance or of interest: *The driver's main concern is safety.* —*v.* to relate to or be important to: *The new rule concerns everyone in the club.* **concerning. concerned.**

concerned (kən sûrnd) *adj.* caring or worried about something: *My parents are concerned about my safety.*

concert (kon′ sərt) *n.* a musical performance by a number of players.

conclude (kən klūd′) *v.* to finish; to end. **concluding. concluded.**

concrete (kon′ krēt) *n.* a hard building material, made from cement, water, and sand or gravel.

condition (kən dish′ ən) *n.* **1.** the state in which something or someone is: *The dog in the animal shelter is in poor condition.* **2.** a requirement: *Father gave us the puppy on the condition that we look after it.*

condominium (kon′ də min′ ē əm) *n.* **1.** an apartment building in which the apartments are owned by the people living in them. **2.** an apartment in such a building.

conduct (kon′ dukt′) *n.* behaviour: *His conduct is always excellent.*

conduct (kən dukt′) *v.* **1.** to lead: *The guide conducted the people through the museum.* **2.** to direct an orchestra or a choir. **conducting. conducted.**

conductor (kən duk′ tər) *n.* **1.** a person who directs an orchestra or a choir. **2.** a person in charge of a train, bus, or streetcar, and who collects the fares.

cone (kōn) *n.* **1.** anything shaped like a clown's hat, circular at one end and coming to a point at the other: *an ice-cream cone.* **2.** the woody fruit of an evergreen tree.

cone

Confederation (kən fed′ ər ā′ shən) *n.* the union in 1867 of several British colonies in North America to create the Dominion of Canada.

conference (kon′ fər əns *or* kon′ frəns) *n.* an important meeting to discuss things: *a science conference.*

confess (kən fes′) *v.* to admit; to say you have done something wrong: *I confessed that I had eaten the last cookie.* **confessing. confessed.**

confession (kən fesh′ ən) *n.* a statement that you have done something wrong.

confidence (kon′ fə dəns) *n.* complete trust in something or someone: *I have confidence that you will win the race tomorrow.*

confident (kon′ fə dənt) *adj.* sure of yourself: *The catcher felt confident that she wouldn't miss the ball.* —**confidently** *adv.*

confuse (kən fyūz′) *v.* **1.** to mix up: *That police officer is pointing in both directions and confusing the people driving the cars.* **2.** to mistake one thing for another: *It's easy to confuse identical twins.* **confusing. confused.**

confusion (kən fyū′ zhən) *n.* a mix-up.

congratulate (kən grach′ ə lāt′) *v.* to express good wishes to someone over his or her success or luck: *The other runners congratulated me when I won the race.* **congratulating. congratulated.**

congratulations (kən grach′ ə lā′ shənz) *n. pl.* an expression meaning "good wishes for your success or fortune."

coniferous (kō nif′ ər əs) *adj.* having pine cones: *Fir trees are coniferous.*

conjunction (kən jungk′ shən) *n.* a word, (a part of speech) such as "and," "or," "but," and "if," used to join together words or groups of words: *In "ham and cheese," the word "and" is a conjunction.*

connect (kə nekt′) *v.* to join or hook up one thing to another. **connecting. connected.** (*opp.* **disconnect.**)

connection (kə nek′ shən) *n.* the joining together of two parts.

conquer (kong′ kər) *v.* to defeat in battle; to overcome: *Medical research has not yet conquered many diseases.* **conquering. conquered.**

conqueror (kong′ kər ər) *n.* someone who conquers; a victor.

conscience (kon′ shəns) *n.* an inner feeling of right and wrong: *My conscience tells me I shouldn't bully my little sister.*

conscious (kon′ shəs) *adj.* **1.** awake and aware of everything around: *The accident victim is conscious.* **2.** aware: *We are late because we weren't conscious of the time.* —**consciously** *adv.*

consent (kən sent′) *v.* to agree to something; to give permission. **consenting. consented.**

consequence (kons′ sə kwens′) *n.* a result: *He tried to walk along the top of the wall and, as a consequence, he fell off.*

conservation (kon′ sər vā′ shən) *n.* the protection and wise use of natural resources.

conserve (kən sürv′) *v.* to use something carefully so as not to waste it; to save: *to conserve water.* **conserving. conserved.**

consider (kən sid′ ər) *v.* to think over: *Consider all the choices before giving your answer.* **considering. considered.**

considerate (kən sid′ ər ət) *adj.* thoughtful of others: *Our neighbours are not considerate; they always play loud music late at night.* (*opp.* **inconsiderate.**)

consist (kən sist′) *v.* (used with **of**) to be made up: *A year consists of twelve months.* **consisting. consisted.**

console (kən sōl′) *v.* to give comfort to someone: *Sunita consoled her brother when his team lost the finals.* **consoling. consoled.**

consonant (kon′ sə nənt) *n.* any letter of the alphabet that is not one of the five vowels (a, e, i, o, u).

constable (kon′ stə bəl) *n.* a police officer.

constant (kon′ stənt) *adj.* **1.** never changing. **2.** happening all the time: *the constant ticking of a clock.* **3.** always present. —**constantly** *adv.*

constellation (kon′ stə lā′ shən) *n.* a group of stars in the sky that form the outline of an object or animal.

constitution (kon′ stə tū′ shən *or* kon′ stə tyū′ shən) *n.* the principles or rules used to govern a country or an organization.

construct (kən strukt′) *v.* to build; to put together: *to construct a model airplane.* **constructing. constructed.**

construction (kən struk′ shən) *n.* **1.** the building of something. **2.** something that is constructed.

consume (kən süm′) *v.* **1.** to eat or drink. **2.** to use up: *A big car consumes more gas than a small car.*

consumer (kən süm′ ər) *n.* someone who buys and uses food, clothes, and other products: *Canadians are heavy consumers of energy.*

contact (kon′ takt) *v.* to get in touch with: *Contact her when you get off the plane.* **contacting. contacted.**

contact lens a small, thin, plastic lens placed on the eye to improve vision. *pl.* **contact lenses.**

contagious (kən tā′ jəs) *adj.* spreading from one person to another: *a contagious disease; contagious laughter.*

contain (kən tān′) *v.* to hold; to have as contents: *This bowl contains peanuts and almonds.* **containing. contained.**

container (kən tān′ ər) *n.* a box, jar, can, and so on, used to hold something.

contaminate (kən tam′ ə nāt′) *v.* to pollute: *The oil slick contaminated the ocean.* **contaminating. contaminated.**

content, contented (kən tent′) *adj.* pleased; satisfied. (*opp.* **discontented.**) —**contentedly** *adv.*

contents (kon′ tents) *n. pl.* the things inside a book or a container: *Towels and sheets were the only contents of the old trunk.*

contest (kon′ test) *n.* a game or race that people try to win.

contestant (kən tes′ tənt) *n.* a person who takes part in a contest: *a contestant on a quiz show.*

continent (kon′ tə nənt) *n.* a very large mass of land: *Europe, Asia, Africa, North America, South America, Australia, and Antarctica are the seven continents of the world.*

continual (kən tin′ yū əl) *adj.* happening again and again; frequent: *There were continual breaks in the lesson.* —**continually** *adv.*

continue (kən tin′ yū) *v.* **1.** to go on without stopping: *It continued raining all day.* **2.** to start again after stopping: *After a break for lunch, the cyclists continued their ride.* **continuing. continued.**

continuous (kən tin′ yū əs) *adj.* going on without a break: *the continuous roar of traffic.* —**continuously** *adv.*

contract (kon′ trakt) *n.* an agreement: *The pitcher signed a contract with the baseball team.*

contract (kən trakt′) *v.* to become smaller; to shrink: *The pupils of your eyes contract in bright light.* **contracting. contracted.**

contraction (kən trak′ shən) *n.* a shortened form of two words: *"Isn't" is a contraction of "is not."*

contrast (kon′ trast) *n.* a great difference: *What a contrast there is in the team's performance from last year. They are ten times better this year.*

contrast (kən trast′) *v.* to compare things in order to show differences. **contrasting. contrasted.**

contribute (kən trib′ yūt) *v.* to pay or give something: *Our family contributed money to the new hospital.* **contributing. contributed.**

control (kən trōl′) *n.* power over something: *The pilot has control of the plane.* —*v.* to be in charge of; to have power over. **controlling. controlled.**

controversial (kon′ trə vůr′ shəl) *adj.* causing strong opinions in favour of or against: *The new statue in the park is controversial; some people like it, while others feel it is a waste of money.*

convenient (kən vēn′ yənt) *adj.* handy; saving trouble: *This shortcut to school is very convenient.* (*opp.* **inconvenient.**)

conversation (kon′ vůr sā′ shən) *n.* a chat.

convert (kən vert′) *v.* to change something into something else: *to convert a cheque into cash.* **converting. converted.**

convict (kon′ vikt) *n.* a criminal in prison.

convict (kən vikt′) *v.* to prove someone is guilty: *The gang was convicted of robbery.* **convicting. convicted.**

convince (kən vins′) *v.* to persuade someone: *Carol convinced me that she was right.* **convincing. convinced.**

coo (kü) *n.* the sound that a pigeon makes. —*v.* to make such a sound. **cooing. cooed.** the dove **coos.**

cook (kůk) *n.* a person who prepares food. —*v.* to prepare food by heating it. **cooking. cooked.**

cookie (kůk′ ē) *n.* a small, sweet cake or biscuit. *pl.* **cookies.**

cool (kül) *adj.* **1.** slightly cold: *The evening air was cool.* **2.** calm, not excited: *The lion tamer was very cool when she walked into the cage.* —*v.* to make something cool or cold. **cooling. cooled.**

coop (küp) *n.* a cage or pen for chickens, rabbits, or other small animals.

cooperate (kō op′ ər āt′) *v.* to work together: *Because everyone cooperated, our group finished the science-fair project on time.* **cooperating. cooperated.**

cooperation (kō op′ ər ā′ shən) *n.* working together for a purpose: *Preparing the project requires the cooperation of all the students in the group.*

cope (kōp) *v.* to be able to handle a hard situation; to manage: *He finds it difficult to cope with both schoolwork and a part-time job.* **coping. coped.**

copier (kop′ ē ər) *n.* a person or machine that copies: *a photocopier.*

copper (kop′ ər) *n.* a shiny, reddish-brown metal, used for wires, pots, and many other things.

copy (kop′ ē) *n.* **1.** anything made to look like something else: *a copy of a famous painting.* **2.** one of a number of books, magazines, or newspapers printed at the same time. *pl.* **copies.** —*v.* **1.** to make a similar thing: *We copied the map from the atlas.* **2.** to imitate: *The baby copies everything her older brother does.* **copying. copied.** she **copies.**

coral (kòr′ əl) *n.* a rock-like substance, usually red, white, or pink, formed from the skeletons of tiny sea creatures: *Coral comes in many shapes and colours. Some kinds are used to make jewellery.*

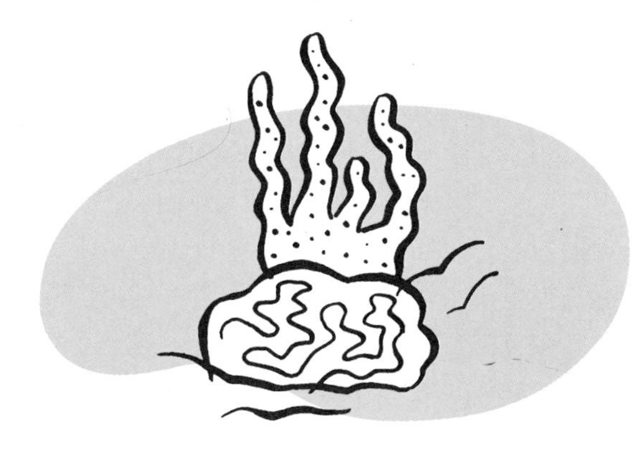

coral

cord (kòrd) *n.* **1.** a thick, strong string. **2.** a wire attached to a telephone or an electrical appliance.

corduroy (kòr′ də roi′) *n.* a strong, cotton material that has velvety ridges.

> Nobody is really sure where the word **corduroy** comes from. One explanation is that it comes from the French words *corde du roi,* which mean "cord of the king." According to this explanation, corduroy was worn by French kings when they went hunting.

corduroys, cords (kòr′ də roiz′, kòrdz) *n. pl.* trousers made of corduroy.

core (kòr) *n.* the centre of a thing: *the core of an apple.*

cork (kòrk) *n.* a plug for a bottle, made from the light bark of the cork oak tree.

corn (kòrn) *n.* **1.** a grain with plump yellow kernels that grow in rows along a cob. **2.** a hard lump on a toe.

corner (kòr′ nər) *n.* the place where two walls, lines, streets, or other surfaces meet.

corny (kòrn′ ē) *adj.* (*slang*) sentimental and silly: *a corny movie.*

corporal (kȯr′ pə rəl) *n.* a soldier higher in rank than a private, lower in rank than a sergeant.

corpse (kȯrps) *n.* a dead body.

correct (kə rekt′) *adj.* without an error. (*opp.* **incorrect.**) —**correctly** *adv.* —*v.* to put right: *Correct your mistakes.* **correcting. corrected.**

correction (kə rek′ shən) *n.* the act of correcting, or something that has been corrected.

correspond (kȯr′ ə spond′) *v.* **1.** to match with: *Your description of the house corresponds with the picture.* **2.** to write letters to: *Do you correspond often with your pen pal?* **corresponding. corresponded.**

corrode (kə rōd′) *v.* to eat away at metal or other substances: *Strong acids corrode metals.* **corroding. corroded.**

cost (kost) *n.* the price: *What is the cost of this toy train?* —*v.* to have a price of; to sell for: *It costs five dollars.* **costing. cost.**

costume (kos′ tyūm) *n.* a clothing outfit worn by an actor in a play or movie.

cot (kot) *n.* a narrow bed that can be folded up and put away.

cottage (kot′ ij) *n.* a small house, usually in the country.

cotton (kot′ ən) *n.* **1.** the soft, fluffy fibres of the cotton plant. **2.** thread or cloth woven from cotton fibres.

cotton

couch (kowch) *n.* a sofa or long seat for three or four people. *pl.* **couches.**

cougar (kū′ gər) *n.* a large, beige-brown wild cat that lives in North and South America: *The cougar hunts deer and other wild animals.*

cough (kof) *n.* the sharp sound made when you clear your throat or your lungs. —*v.* to make such a sound. **coughing. coughed.**

could (kůd) see **can**.

couldn't (kud′ ənt) a contraction (short form) for **could not**.

coulee (kū′ lē) *n.* a dry river bed. *pl.* **coulees.**

council (kown′ səl) *n.* a group of people called together to discuss something: *a town council.*

councillor (kown′ sə lər) *n.* a member of a town or city council.

counsel (kown′ səl) *n.* advice; guidance. —*v.* to give advice to: *My older sister counselled me to try out for the team.* **counselling. counselled.**

counsellor (kown′ sə lər) *n.* someone who gives advice or guidance: *a school counsellor.*

count (kownt) *n.* **1.** the total number counted: *What was the final count of votes in the election?* **2.** in some countries, a member of a noble family. —*v.* **1.** to say numbers in order. **2.** to find the total number of. **3.** to depend on: *We are counting on you to play in the school band.* **counting. counted.**

countdown (kownt′ down′) *n.* the counting backwards of minutes and seconds before a missile or spaceship is launched.

counter (kown′ tər) *n.* a long table in a kitchen, restaurant, bank, or store.

counterclockwise (kown′ tər klock′ wīz) *adj., adv.* in the direction opposite to the direction in which a clock's hands move.

counterfeit (kown′ tər fit′) *adj.* fake; not real: *The gang was arrested for making counterfeit money.* —*v.* to make fake copies.

country (kun′ trē) *n.* **1.** land away from towns, such as farmland and wild areas: *We visited friends at a farm in the country.* **2.** a nation: *North America is made up of two countries: Canada and the United States.* *pl.* **countries.**

county (kown′ tē) *n.* a government district in some countries, provinces, and states. *pl.* **counties.**

couple (kup′ əl) *n.* two; a pair: *I caught a couple of fish.*

coupon (kū′ pon) *n.* a ticket that can be exchanged for a gift or money: *We had a discount coupon for the museum.*

courage (kůr′ əj) *n.* bravery; fearlessness.

courageous (kə rā′ jəs) *adj.* brave; fearless.

course (kȯrs) *n.* **1.** the direction that something takes when it is moving: *the course of a river.* **2.** a series of lessons: *My friends and I took a course in first aid.* **3.** a dish at a meal: *For the main course at dinner, we had chicken.* **4.** an area for a sport or game: *a golf course.*
of course naturally; certainly; yes.

court (kȯrt) *n.* **1.** a place where justice is given: *a court of law.* **2.** a place where certain games are played: *a basketball court.* **3.** a royal palace.

courteous (kůr′ tē əs) *adj.* polite; thoughtful of others. (*opp.* **discourteous.**) —**courteously** *adv.*

courtyard (kȯrt′ yȧrd′) *n.* an open space surrounded by buildings or walls.

cousin (kuz′ ən) *n.* the son or daughter of an aunt or uncle.

cove (kōv) *n.* a small bay.

cover (kuv′ ər) *n.* **1.** something put over another thing to protect or hide it. **2.** a lid. —*v.* to put a cover on something: *We covered the firewood with a waterproof sheet.* **covering. covered.** (*opp.* **uncover.**)

cow (kow) (*masc.* **bull**) *n.* **1.** a full-grown female of cattle. **2.** the female of other large mammals, such as the elephant and moose.

We often use the word **cows** to mean **all** cattle, not just female ones.

coward (kow′ ərd) *n.* someone who lacks courage and runs away from trouble or danger.

cowardice (kow′ ər dis) *n.* a lack of courage.

cowardly (kow′ ərd lē) *adj.* behaving like a coward.

cowboy, cowgirl (kow′ boi, kow′ gůrl) *n.* a person who looks after cattle on a ranch or who rides in a rodeo or stampede.

coyote (kī′ ōt *or* kī ō′ tē) *n.* a wild prairie mammal that looks like a small wolf. *pl.* **coyotes** or **coyote.**

cozy (kō′ zē) see **cosy.**

crab (krab) *n.* a shellfish with a round body, eight legs, and a pair of claws.

crab

crabby (krab′ ē) *adj.* in a cross or grumpy mood: *a crabby child; a crabbier child; the crabbiest child of them all.*

crack (krak) *n.* **1.** a split: *a crack in a cup.* **2.** a sharp sound: *the crack of a whip.* **3.** a try: *I'll have a crack at shooting the ball into the basket.* —*v.* **1.** to split: *to crack a vase.* **2.** to break open: *to crack a nut.* **3.** to make a sharp sound: *to crack a whip.* **cracking. cracked.**
crack up to burst out into laughter.

cracker (krak′ ər) *n.* **1.** a thin, crisp biscuit or wafer. **2.** a small paper roll containing such things as a paper hat and a small toy, used at parties.

crackle (krak′ əl) *n.* a short, snapping, rustling noise: *the crackle of a fire.* —*v.* to make such noises: *The wood crackled in the fire.* **crackling. crackled.**

cradle (krā′ dəl) *n.* a baby's bed which can be rocked back and forth.

craft (kraft) *n.* the art of making things with your hands: *Wood carving, weaving, and pottery are crafts.*

crafty (kraf′ tē) *adj.* sly; cunning: *a crafty fox; a craftier fox; the craftiest fox of all.*

cram (kram) *v.* to stuff: *The monkey crammed the banana into its mouth.* **cramming. crammed.**

cramp (kramp) *n.* a pain from a strained muscle, often in your leg or arm.

cramped (krampt) *adj.* too small and crowded: *a cramped apartment.*

cranberry (kran′ ber′ ē) *n.* a sour, dark-red berry, used for juice and sauces. *pl.* **cranberries.**

crane (krān) *n.* **1.** a big machine with a long arm for lifting and moving heavy weights. **2.** a wading bird with a long beak and long legs.

crash (krash) *n.* **1.** the act of falling, breaking, colliding, or smashing: *a car crash.* **2.** the noise of something colliding or smashing. *pl.* **crashes.** —*v.* **1.** to fall, break, collide, or smash. **2.** (for a computer) to stop working suddenly. **crashing. crashed.**

crate (krāt) *n.* a large wooden case for holding goods.

crater (krā′ tər) *n.* a low place in the ground, shaped like a bowl. The mouth of a volcano is a crater. A meteor or an explosion can form a crater.

crave (krāv) *v.* to want something very much: *I crave a good book to read.* **craving. craved.**

craving (krāv′ ing) *n.* a great longing for something: *He has a craving for chocolate.*

crawl (krol) *n.* **1.** a very slow pace. **2.** an overarm stroke in swimming. —*v.* **1.** to move on hands and knees. **2.** to creep slowly along the ground. **crawling. crawled.**

crayon (krā′ on) *n.* a stick of coloured wax, used for drawing pictures.

crazy (krā′ zē) *adj.* **1.** mentally ill. **2.** silly; foolish; wild.

creak (krēk) *n.* a small, squeaking noise: *the creak of an old door.* —*v.* to make such a noise. **creaking. creaked.**

creaky (krēk′ ē) *adj.* making a creaking noise: *a creaky gate; a creakier gate; the creakiest gate of all.*

cream (krēm) *n.* the fatty, yellowish part of milk. Cream is used to make butter and is added to many other foods.

creamy (krēm′ ē) *adj.* rich and smooth like cream: *a creamy milkshake; a creamier one; the creamiest one of all.*

crease (krēs) *n.* a mark made when paper or cloth is folded and pressed down. —*v.* to make such a fold. **creasing. creased.**

create (krē āt′) *v.* **1.** to make something new: *The inventor created a new kind of engine.* **2.** to cause: *The stranger's odd appearance created a lot of gossip in the town.* **creating. created.**

creation (krē ā′ shən) *n.* **1.** the act of making something completely new: *The creation of each painting takes many hours of work.* **2.** a thing that somebody has made: *This is Lee's latest artistic creation.*

creative (krē ā′ tiv) *adj.* **1.** able to think up and make new things. **2.** imaginative; artistic: *creative writing.*

creature (krē′ chər) *n.* a living thing.

credit (kred′ it) *n.* **1.** honour or praise for something done: *Angela received credit for her work.* **2.** time allowed for the payment of goods: *To buy something on credit means to pay for it at a later date.*

credit card a plastic card that lets you buy things now and pay for them later.

creek (krēk) *n.* a small stream.

creep (krēp) *n.* (*slang*) an unpleasant person. —*v.* to move slowly, carefully, and quietly; to crawl; to tiptoe: *We crept up the stairs.* **creeping. crept.**

the creeps a crawling, tingling feeling you get from something scary or disgusting.

crescent (cres′ ənt) *n.* the thin, curved shape of the moon at certain times of the month.

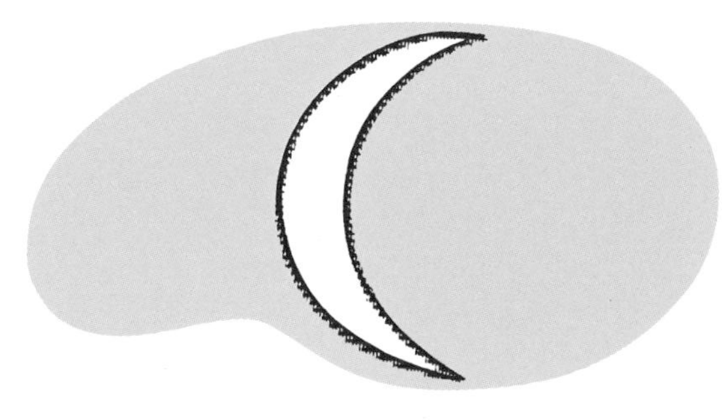

crescent

crest (krest) *n.* **1.** the highest point: *the crest of a hill; the crest of a wave.* **2.** a bunch of feathers on the head of a bird. **3.** an emblem worn on clothing as identification: *a hockey crest; a school crest.*

crew (krū) *n.* the people who work on a ship, plane, train, and so on.

crib (krib) *n.* a baby's bed.

cricket (krik′ ət) *n.* **1.** an insect that looks like a small, black grasshopper. **2.** a game played with a ball and bats on a grass field.

cried, cries (krīd, krīz) see **cry**.

crime (krīm) *n.* the breaking of the law, especially in a serious way: *He committed a crime when he stole the book from the store.*

criminal (krim′ ə nəl) *n.* a person who has committed a crime.

crimson (krim′ zən) *n.* a deep red colour. —*adj.* having this colour.

crippled (krip′ əld) *adj.* unable to move properly because of an injury or disease; disabled.

crisis (krī′ səs) *n.* a time of danger or serious difficulty: *If people use up the world's supply of fuel, we will face an energy crisis. pl.* **crises** (krī′ sēz).

crisp (krisp) *adj.* **1.** dry, hard, and breaking easily, like toast. **2.** fresh and firm: *a crisp apple.* **3.** cool and refreshing: *a crisp autumn day.* **4.** short and sharp: *a crisp answer.* —**crisply** *adv.*

crisscross (kris′ kros′) *v.* to mark with lines that cross each other. **crisscrossing. crisscrossed.**

criticize (krit′ ə sīz′) *v.* **1.** to find fault with: *You are always criticizing me!* **2.** to discuss the good and bad points of something: *We criticize every movie we see.* **criticizing. criticized.**

croak (krōk) *n.* the low, hoarse noise that a frog makes. —*v.* to make such a noise. **croaking. croaked.**

crocodile (krok′ ə dīl′) *n.* a large reptile that has thick, scaly skin, short legs, and a pointed snout. Crocodiles live in rivers and lakes in tropical countries.

crocodile

Crying **"crocodile tears"** means you're just pretending to feel sad about something. People used to think crocodiles cried to get their prey to come closer.

crook (krůk) *n.* (*informal*) a thief.

crooked (krůk′ id) *adj.* twisted; full of bends: *a crooked street.* —**crookedly** *adv.*

crop (krop) *n.* plants grown for food: *Wheat is a major crop grown in the Prairies.*

cross (kros) *n.* **1.** a mark shaped like + or x. **2.** the main symbol for the Christian religion. *pl.* **crosses.** —*adj.* in a bad mood. —*v.* **1.** to go to the other side of: *to cross the road.* **2.** to draw a line through: *I crossed my name off the list.* **crossing. crossed.**

crossing (kros′ ing) *n.* **1.** a place where a person may cross a street. **2.** a place where train tracks cross a road.

crouch (krowch) *v.* to bend low: *Magda crouched to get under the rail.* **crouching. crouched.**

crow (krō) *n.* a big, black bird with a harsh call. —*v.* to make a noise like a rooster, in happiness or in triumph: *The champions crowed over their victory.* **crowing. crowed.**

crow

crowd (krowd) *n.* a large number of people gathered together. —*v.* to gather together in large numbers: *Hundreds of people crowded the store.* **crowding. crowded.**

crowded (krowd′ əd) *adj.* full, or too full, of people or things: *a crowded room.*

crown (krown) *n.* a heavy band made of precious metal and jewels, worn on the head by a king or queen.

cruel (krū′ əl) *adj.* extremely unkind; causing pain and suffering: *a cruel ruler.* —**cruelly** *adv.*

cruelty (krū′ əl tē) *n.* the causing of pain and suffering.

cruise (krūz) *n.* a pleasure trip on a ship.

cruiser (krū′ zər) *n.* a police car.

crumb (krum) *n.* a tiny piece of bread, cake, a cookie, and so on.

crumble (krum′ bəl) *v.* to break into small pieces. **crumbling. crumbled.**

crunch (krunch) *n.* the act or sound of crunching. —*v.* **1.** to grind or crush noisily with the teeth: *I crunched up my apple.* **2.** to make a crunching sound: *the crunch of snow under boots.* **crunching. crunched.**

crush (krush) *n.* **1.** a crowding of people: *There was quite a crush when the big sale started.* **2.** a sudden, brief liking for someone: *a crush on a movie star.* *pl.* **crushes.** —*v.* **1.** to press or squeeze something so hard that it breaks or is badly damaged: *The big tree fell on our house and crushed it.* **2.** to grind up: *to crush rocks.* **crushing. crushed.**

crust (krust) *n.* **1.** a hard outer covering: *a pie crust.* **2.** the solid upper layer of the earth: *the earth's crust.*

crutch (kruch) *n.* a padded, thick stick, used as a support for walking by injured or lame people. *pl.* **crutches.**

cry (krī) *n.* a loud call or shout. *pl.* **cries.** —*v.* **1.** to call out or shout loudly. **2.** to shed tears. **crying. cried.** he **cries.**

crystal (kris′ təl) *n.* **1.** a hard, clear mineral that looks like ice. **2.** a solid substance with a regular shape: *Snow crystals are shaped like stars with six points.*

cub (kub) *n.* a young fox, bear, wolf, lion, tiger, and so on.

cube (kyūb) *n.* a solid object with six square sides, all alike: *a sugar cube.*

Cubs (kubz) *n. pl.* members of the Scouts between the ages of 8 and 10.

cuckoo (kū′ kū) *n.* a grey bird whose call sounds like "cuckoo."

cucumber (kyū′ kum bər) *n.* a long vegetable with a dark green skin and white flesh. It is used in salads or is pickled.

cud (kud) *n.* food that comes back into the mouth from the stomach of a cow, sheep, deer, or other animal, to be chewed again.

cuddle (kud′ əl) *v.* to hug someone. **cuddling. cuddled.**

cue (kyū) *n.* **1.** a hint or clue, especially for actors: *When the clock chimes, that is your cue to go on stage.* **2.** a long, pointed rod used to hit the ball in the game of billiards or pool. *pl.* **cues.**

cuff (kuf) *n.* **1.** the turned-up fold at the bottom of a pant leg. **2.** the end of a sleeve near the wrist.

cultivate (kul′ tə vāt) *v.* to grow crops, or to prepare soil for growing crops. **cultivating. cultivated.**

cultural (kul′ chər əl) *adj.* having to do with culture, especially the arts.

culture (kul′ chər) *n.* the arts, beliefs, customs, and institutions of a group of people: *We are reading about ancient Chinese culture.*

cunning (kun′ ing) *adj.* sly; clever: *a cunning escape.*

cup (kup) *n.* **1.** a small container with a handle, used for drinking. **2.** anything like a cup: *Our team won the sports cup.*

cupboard (kub′ ərd) *n.* a small closet or cabinet with shelves for dishes, food, sheets, or other items.

curb (kůrb) *n.* the concrete edge of a street. —*v.* to hold back; to control: *Curb your appetite.* **curbing. curbed.**

curd (kůrd) *n.* the thick part of sour milk: *Cheese is made from curds.*

cure (kyūr) *n.* a drug or treatment that heals: *Researchers are looking for a cure for cancer.* —*v.* **1.** to heal; to make well: *The medicine cured my sore throat.* **2.** to preserve food by drying, salting, or smoking. **curing. cured.**

curiosity (kyūr′ ē os′ ə tē) *n.* a strong desire to learn or know something.

curious (kyūr′ ē əs) *adj.* **1.** eager to know or learn: *Ivan was curious about what I was hiding behind my back.* **2.** unusual: *It's a curious fact that all the students in my class have freckles.* —**curiously** *adv.*

curl (kůrl) *n.* a coil or ringlet of hair. —*v.* **1.** to roll or coil something into curls. **2.** to play the game of curling. **curling. curled.**

curling (kůrl′ ing) *n.* a game played on ice in which the players slide heavy, round, flat stones toward a target.

curly (kůr′ lē) *adj.* having curls; wavy: *curly hair; curlier hair; the curliest hair of all.*

currency (kůr′ ən sē) *n.* the money of a country: *The yen is the Japanese unit of currency.* *pl.* **currencies.**

current (kůr′ ənt) *n.* **1.** a stream of water or air moving quickly: *Wind is a current of air.* **2.** a flow of electricity along a wire or cable. —*adj.* belonging to the present time: *News is broadcast every day to keep us informed about current events.* —**currently** *adv.*

curry (kůr′ ē) *n.* a dish of meat or vegetables seasoned with curry powder, a yellowish mixture of spices, some of which are hot.

curse (kůrs) *n.* an evil wish: *the sorcerer's curse.* —*v.* **1.** to use bad language; to swear. **2.** to wish evil on someone: *The sorcerer cursed the young prince.* **cursing. cursed.**

cursor (kůr′ sər) *n.* a marker on a computer screen, often a flashing line or bar.

curtain (kůr′ tən) *n.* a large cloth hung in front of a window or a theatre stage.

curtsy (kůrt′ sē) *n.* a bow of respect or thanks, made by placing one foot behind the other and bending the knees deeply: *to curtsy before a dance.*

curve (kůrv) *n.* a smooth bend: *a curve in the road.* —*v.* to cause a curve, or to move in the direction of a curve: *The ball curved downwards.* **curving. curved.**

cushion (kůsh′ ən) *n.* a pillow or pad for a chair or sofa.

custard (kus′ tərd) *n.* a pudding made of eggs, milk, and sugar.

custom (kus′ təm) *n.* **1.** a usual way of doing things; a habit: *It is his custom to eat very little at breakfast.* **2.** a traditional or cultural activity: *Celebrating a holiday with a feast is a custom in many cultures.*

customer (kus′ tə mər) *n.* a person who buys something.

cut (kut) *n.* **1.** an opening made by cutting. **2.** a wound caused by a sharp object: *The cut on my hand was caused by broken glass.* —*v.* **1.** to slash or separate with a knife, scissors, or other sharp object. **2.** to shorten or reduce: *to cut hair; to cut someone's salary.* **cutting. cut.**

cut it out an informal expression that means "Stop doing that!"

cute (kyūt) *adj.* attractive and lovable: *a cute puppy.*

cutlery (kut′ lə rē) *n.* knives, forks, and spoons.

cutting (kūt′ ing) *n.* something cut, such as a stem from a plant. —*adj.* hurtful and mean: *a cutting remark.*

cycle (sī′ kəl) *n.* **1.** a series of events that repeats: *the cycle of the seasons.* **2.** a series of actions happening in a particular order: *the cycle of a washing machine.* —*v.* to ride a bicycle. **cycling. cycled.**

cyclist (sī′ klist) *n.* a person riding a bicycle.

cyclone (sī′ klōn) *n.* a violent windstorm in which the air spins rapidly; a tornado.

cygnet (sig′ nət) *n.* a young swan.

cylinder (sil′ ən dər) *n.* a hollow or solid object that is shaped like a tube. Each end of a cylinder is a circle.

cymbals (sim′ bəlz) *n. pl.* brass plates used by a drummer to make a clashing sound.

cymbals

dab (dab) *n.* a drop or small lump of something: *a dab of paint.* —*v.* to put something on with soft touches: *He dabbed some lotion on his sunburn.* **dabbing. dabbed.**

dad, daddy (dad, dad′ ē) *n.* father. *pl.* **daddies.**

daffodil (daf′ ə dil) *n.* a tall plant with yellow or white flowers shaped like bells.

daffodil

dagger (dag′ ər) *n.* a weapon with a short, pointed blade.

daily (dā′ lē) *adj.* happening or appearing every day: *a daily newspaper.* —*adv.* every day: *The newspaper comes out daily.*

dainty (dān′ tē) *adj.* pretty and delicate: *dainty flowers; daintier flowers; the daintiest flowers in the garden.* —**daintily** *adv.*

dairy (der′ ē) *n.* a place where milk and cream are made into cheese and butter. *pl.* **dairies.**

daisy (dā′ zē) *n.* a small plant with white or pink flowers with a yellow centre. *pl.* **daisies.**

dam (dam) *n.* a wall built to hold back the water of a river, stream, creek, and so on. —*v.* to build a dam.

damage (dam′ ij) *n.* breaking; injury; harm: *The accident caused great damage to the bike.* —*v.* to break, injure, or harm: *He damaged his bike in the accident.* **damaging. damaged.**

damp (damp) *adj.* a bit wet.

dance (dans) *n.* **1.** movement in time to music. **2.** a party where people dance. —*v.* to move the feet and body in time to music. **dancing. danced.**

dancer (dans′ ər) *n.* a person who dances.

dandelion (dan′ də lī′ ən *or* dan′ dē lī′ ən) *n.* a weed with a bright yellow flower.

> Some people think that the leaf of a dandelion looks like a lion's tooth. The French words for lion's tooth are *dent de lion.* This is where the word **dandelion** came from.

dandruff (dan′ drəf) *n.* small white pieces of dead skin that fall from the scalp.

danger (dān′ jər) *n.* something that may cause injury or death: *Fire in a building is a danger to those inside.*

dangerous (dān′ jər əs) *adj.* not safe: *Skating on thin ice is dangerous.* —**dangerously** *adv.*

dangle (dang′ gəl) *v.* to hang or swing loosely: *The keys dangled from the chain.* **dangling. dangled.**

dare (der) *v.* **1.** to risk; to take a chance: *The farmhand dared to walk up to the bull.* **2.** to challenge someone: *I dare you to walk up to that bull.* **daring. dared.**

daredevil (der′ dev′ əl) *n.* a person who takes risks.

dark (därk) *adj.* **1.** without light: *a dark room.* **2.** deep in colour: *a dark blue coat.*

darken (därk′ ən) *v.* to make or become dark. **darkening. darkened.**

darkness (därk′ nəs) *n.* lack of light: *We walked in the darkness without a flashlight.*

darling (där′ ling) *n.* someone very dear to you.

darn (därn) *v.* to mend a hole in cloth: *I'm going to darn the toe of my sock.* **darning. darned.**

dart (därt) *n.* a small arrow thrown by hand at a board. —*v.* to move quickly and suddenly: *When the rabbit saw me, it darted away.* **darting. darted.**

dart

dash (dash) *n.* **1.** a quick rush or race. **2.** a punctuation mark (—), used to show a break or an interruption: *"Look out—the train is coming toward us!"* —*v.* to rush quickly or race: *She dashed after the thief.* **dashing. dashed.**

dashboard (dash′ bôrd′) *n.* the panel in a car that holds the instruments.

data (dā′ tə *or* dat′ ə) *n. pl.* facts; items of information.

database (dā′ tə bās′ *or* da′ tə bās′) *n.* a computer program that stores large amounts of information so that it can be sorted, studied, or presented in new and useful ways: *They entered 2000 names into the mailing list database, and the database put them in alphabetical order.*

date (dāt) *n.* **1.** the day, month, and year of some event: *What is the date of the school dance?* **2.** an appointment: *Let's set a date for visiting the zoo.* **3.** a person you go out with. **4.** the very sweet, brown, sticky fruit of the date palm tree. —*v.* to go out socially with someone. **dating. dated.**

out of date old-fashioned.

up to date in use now; modern.

daughter (do′ tər) *n.* a female child: *My uncle has one daughter.*

daughter-in-law (do′ tər in lo′) *n.* the wife of a son. *pl.* **daughters-in-law.**

dawdle (do′ dəl) *v.* to waste time. **dawdling. dawdled.**

dawn (don) *n.* **1.** sunrise. **2.** the beginning: *the dawn of a new age.*

day (dā) *n.* **1.** the time between sunrise and sunset. **2.** a period of 24 hours, from one midnight to the next. *pl.* **days.**

daydream (dā′ drēm′) *n.* a pleasant imaginary happening or fantasy that comes to mind while you are awake. —*v.* to have a daydream. **daydreaming. daydreamed.**

daylight (dā′ līt′) *n.* sunlight.

daylight-saving time one hour later than standard time: *We switch to daylight-saving time in the spring, so that we have an extra hour of sunlight at the end of the day.*

daytime (dā′ tīm′) *n.* the time between sunrise and sunset.

daze (dāz) *n.* a confused state of mind: *I wandered about in a daze.* —*v.* to confuse; to stun: *I was so dazed when I fell that I forgot where I was.* **dazing. dazed.**

dazzle (daz′ əl) *v.* to hurt the eyes or impress the mind by looking at something very bright or very attractive: *We were dazzled by the fireworks.* **dazzling. dazzled.**

dead (ded) *adj.* **1.** not alive: *a dead body.* **2.** without power: *a dead battery.*

deadline (ded′ līn′) *n.* the time by which work must be done: *Our deadline to finish reading the book is next Monday.*

deadly (ded′ lē) *adj.* causing death: *a deadly poison; a deadlier poison; the deadliest poison of all.*

deaf (def) *adj.* not able to hear well or at all.

deal (dēl) *n.* **1.** a sharing out: *a deal of the cards.* **2.** a bargain: *I got a good deal on the used bike.* **3.** an agreement: *I made a deal with my brother.* —*v.* **1.** to share out playing cards. **2.** to do business by buying or selling: *This store deals in hardware items.* **dealing. dealt** (delt).

a great deal a lot: *When the home team scored a goal, the fans cheered a great deal.*

dealer (dēl′ ər) *n.* **1.** a business person who buys and sells goods. **2.** in a card game, the person who deals out the cards to the other players.

dear (dēr) *n.* a loved or lovable person. —*adj.* **1.** lovable. **2.** a greeting at the beginning of a letter: *Dear Grandma and Grandpa.* **3.** expensive. —**dearly** *adv.*

death (deth) *n.* the end of life.

debate (di bāt′) *n.* a discussion between two people or two groups of people who see different sides of an issue. —*v.* to discuss the reasons for or against something: *Our class debated whether wearing fur is cruel to animals.* **debating. debated.**

debt (det) *n.* something, usually money, that you owe to someone.

decade (dek′ ād) *n.* ten years.

decay (di kā′ *or* dē kā′) *n.* rot, or the process of rotting: *Tooth decay can start in early childhood. pl.* **decays.** —*v.* to rot and waste away. **decaying. decayed.**

deceive (di sēv′) *v.* to mislead; to cheat or trick: *He deceived me when he said he would help me, but didn't.* **deceiving. deceived.**

December (di sem′ bər) *n.* the twelfth month of the year.

In Latin, decem means "ten." So why is our twelfth month called December? It is because the calendar of the ancient Romans began in March and had only ten months.

decent (dē′ sənt) *adj.* proper; good; well-mannered: *decent behaviour.* —**decently** *adv.*

decide (di sīd′) *v.* to make up your mind: *I can't decide whether to wear the brown or the blue pants.* **deciding. decided.**

deciduous (di sij′ ū əs) *adj.* losing leaves once each year: *Maple trees are deciduous.*

decimal (des′ ə məl) *adj.* based on the number 10: *The metric system is a decimal system of measurement.*

decision (di sizh′ ən) *n.* a choice or a judgment that has been decided: *The umpire's decision is that Megan hit a foul ball.*

deck (dek) *n.* **1.** the floor of a ship, especially the upper floor in the open air. **2.** a set of playing cards.

declaration (dek′ lə rā′ shən) *n.* an announcement; a public statement.

declare (di kler′) *v.* to announce; to say something in public: *The sports official declared our team the winner.* **declaring. declared.**

decorate (dek′ ə rāt′) *v.* **1.** to make something look nicer, especially a house or the walls of a room. **2.** to pin a medal or ribbon on someone as an honour. **decorating. decorated.**

decoration (dek′ ə rā′ shən) *n.* **1.** something used to decorate: *Before the birthday party, we put up balloons as decorations.* **2.** a badge, medal, or ribbon awarded as an honour.

decrease (di krēs′) *v.* to become less, smaller, or shorter: *In winter, the length of the day decreases. In summer, it increases.* **decreasing. decreased.**

dedicate (ded′ ə kāt′) *v.* to give yourself or something to a particular cause or purpose: *The wildlife researcher dedicated her life to saving endangered animals. The author dedicated his book to the memory of his father.* **dedicating. dedicated.**

deed (dēd) *n.* **1.** an action. **2.** a great or noble action: *brave deeds.*

deep (dēp) *adj.* **1.** going far down from the top: *a deep well.* **2.** low: *a deep voice.* **3.** not shallow: *She is a deep person.* **4.** intense: *a deep colour.*

deeply (dēp′ lē) *adv.* very much; truly: *The sad movie upset me deeply.*

deer (dēr) *n.* a wild mammal that eats grass and leaves, has hooves, and can run very quickly. A male deer has antlers. *pl.* **deer.**

deer

defeat (di fēt′) *n.* the loss of a game or battle. —*v.* to beat someone in a game or battle. **defeating. defeated.**

defect (dē′ fekt) *n.* a flaw: *The videotape had a defect and wouldn't play in the VCR.*

defence, defense (di fens′ *for 1;* dē′ fens *for 2*) *n.* **1.** a protection against attack: *The wall around the fort was built as a defence.* **2.** a team (or part of a team) that tries to keep the other team from scoring.

defend (di fend′) *v.* to protect; to guard against attack: *The soldiers defended the bridge against the enemy attack.* **defending. defended.**

define (di fīn′) *v.* to explain clearly the meaning of something: *A dictionary defines words.* **defining. defined.**

definite (def′ ə nit) *adj.* clear; sure: *Lai made a definite promise to be home early.*

definitely (def′ ə nit lē) *adv.* certainly; for sure: *It will definitely snow tomorrow.*

definition (def′ ə nish′ ən) *n.* the meaning of a word: *Some words have more than one definition.*

defy (di fī′) *v.* **1.** to refuse to obey: *He defied the rules.* **2.** to dare: *I defy you to prove that the job can't be done.* **defying. defied.** she **defies.**

degree (di grē′) *n.* **1.** a unit for measuring temperature: *Today's temperature will be 20 degrees Celsius (20°C).* **2.** a unit for measuring the angles in a circle: *A circle has three hundred and sixty degrees (360°).* **3.** a course of study in a university or college: *a science degree.* **4.** a certain amount or limit: *She's right, to some degree.*

dejected (di jek′ təd) *adj.* sad: *All of the children were dejected after their cat died.*

delay (di lā′) *n.* a wait; a putting off: *Due to rain, there will be a delay before the tennis match starts.* —*v.* to put off till a later time; to cause to be late: *The plane was delayed an hour because of the storm.* **delaying. delayed.**

delete (di lēt′) *v.* to erase or remove: *Please delete my name from your mailing list.* **deleting. deleted.**

deliberate (di lib′ ər ət) *adj.* planned; on purpose: *Was that goal deliberate, or did the puck land in the net by accident?* —**deliberately** *adv.*

delicate (del′ i kət) *adj.* **1.** finely made: *a delicate handkerchief;* **2.** fragile: *a delicate flower.* **3.** sensitive: *a delicate touch.* **4.** not strong: *delicate health.* —**delicately** *adv.*

delicious (di lish′ əs) *adj.* very pleasing in taste or smell.

delight (di līt′) *n.* great pleasure. —*v.* to please a great deal. **delighting. delighted.**

delightful (di līt′ fəl) *adj.* very pleasing: *We had a delightful time at the picnic.* —**delightfully** *adv.*

delinquent (di ling′ kwənt) *n.* a young person who breaks the law: *a juvenile delinquent.*

deliver (di liv′ ər) *v.* to hand over or distribute something to someone: *to deliver newspapers.* **delivering. delivered.**

deluxe (di luks′) *adj.* very fancy or expensive: *a deluxe restaurant.*

demand (di mand′) *n.* a strong request or need: *Pizza is in great demand at our house.* —*v.* to ask firmly for something as if it is your right. **demanding. demanded.**

democracy (di mok′ rə sē) *n.* a country or group that elects its leaders. *pl.* **democracies.**

democratic (dem′ ə krat′ ik) *adj.* believing in and practising democracy: *We chose our class president in the democratic way by holding a vote.* —**democratically** *adv.*

demolish (di mol′ ish) *v.* to destroy completely: *The fire demolished the wooden building.* **demolishing. demolished.**

demonstrate (dem′ ən strāt′) *v.* to show how something is done: *Our group demonstrated how to use the new computer.* **demonstrating. demonstrated.**

den (den) *n.* **1.** a cave or hole where a wild animal lives. **2.** a small room in a house, often used for reading.

denim (den′ əm) *n.* a heavy blue cloth.

denims (den′ əmz) *n. pl.* jeans or overalls made of denim.

denims

denominator (di nom′ ə nā′ tər) *n.* the number below the line in a fraction: *In 1/2, 2 is the denominator and 1 is the numerator.*

dense (dens) *adj.* tightly packed or very thick: *a dense crowd of people; a dense cloud of smoke.* —**densely** *adv.*

dent (dent) *n.* a small hollow made by a blow or pressure: *A stranger kicked our garbage can and made a dent in it.* —*v.* to make such a hollow. **denting. dented.**

dental (den′ təl) *adj.* having to do with teeth: *I went to the dental clinic to have my teeth examined.*

dentist (den′ tist) *n.* a doctor who takes care of your teeth.

dentures (den′ cherz) *n. pl.* false teeth.

deny (di nī′) *v.* **1.** to say something is not true: *"Do you admit saying that?" "No, I deny it."* **2.** to refuse: *The teacher denied our request to have an all-day picnic.* **denying. denied.** she **denies.**

depart (di pȧrt′) *v.* to go away; to leave: *The train departs from Platform 1.* **departing. departed.**

department (di pȧrt′ mənt) *n.* a separate part of an organization: *a school's science department; a city's fire department.*

department store a large store that has many departments selling different kinds of things.

depend (di pend′) *v.* (used with **on**) **1.** to rely on; to trust: *I depend on you to help me.* **2.** to be a result of: *Whether we go skiing or not depends on the amount of snow that falls.* **depending. depended.**

dependable (di pen′ də bəl) *adj.* reliable: *She's very dependable; she comes in at 8:30 a.m. every day.* (opp. **undependable.**)

deposit (di poz′ it) *n.* **1.** something put in a safe place: *a deposit of money in the bank.* **2.** a partial payment so that something will be held for you: *I gave the store a ten-dollar deposit to hold the shirt for me.* —*v.* **1.** to put down or lay down: *She deposited the garbage bag on the curb.* **2.** to put money into the bank. **depositing. deposited.**

depot (dē′ pō) *n.* a bus or railway station; a warehouse.

depression (di presh′ ən) *n.* **1.** a low or hollow place: *a depression on the old, wooden table.* **2.** an unhappy state of mind: *He suffered from depression when he lost his job and could not find another.* **3.** a period when business is bad and many people are out of work: *an economic depression.*

depth (depth) *n.* how deep something is, measured from top to bottom: *The pool has a depth of four metres at the deep end.*

deputy (dep′ yə tē) *n.* **1.** an assistant: *a deputy police chief.* **2.** in Quebec, a member of the National Assembly. *pl.* **deputies.**

descend (di send′) *v.* **1.** to go down: *The plane is descending onto the runway.* **2.** to climb down: *The climbers descended the mountain.* **descending. descended.**

descendant (di sen′ dənt) *n.* a child, grandchild, great-grandchild, and so on: *My friend Sarah Macdonald says she is a descendant of Canada's first prime minister.*

descent (di sent′) *n.* **1.** a coming down or climbing down: *Our descent from the mountaintop was quite dangerous.* **2.** family origin: *I am of French and Greek descent.*

describe (di scrīb′) *v.* to tell or write about something or someone in detail: *We described our summer holidays.* **describing. described.**

description (di scrip′ shən) *n.* a picture in words about a person, a place, or an event: *Michel's description of his hometown in New Brunswick made me want to go there for a visit.*

desert (dez′ ərt) *n.* a very dry region, often covered with sand or rocks: *Very few plants grow in a desert.*

desert (di zərt′) *v.* to leave behind; to run away from: *Kyle never deserts his friends when they need him.* **deserting. deserted.**

deserve (di zûrv′) *v.* to be worthy of a reward or a punishment: *These cashiers work hard and deserve more pay.* **deserving. deserved.**

design (di zīn′) *n.* **1.** a drawing or an outline used as a guide: *The builder showed us the design of the new house.* **2.** a pattern: *The wallpaper has a design of flowers.* —*v.* to draw a plan of something: *to design a house; to design a dress.* **designing. designed.**

designer (di zīn′ ər) *n.* a person who creates a plan for the way something should look, often by drawing pictures: *A fashion designer creates new styles of clothing.*

desirable (di zīr′ ə bəl) *adj.* worth having; attractive: *The desks near the window of our classroom are the most desirable.*

desire (di zīr′) *n.* a great wish. —*v.* to want very much; to wish for. **desiring. desired.**

desk (desk) *n.* a writing table, usually with drawers for writing supplies.

desk

despair (di sper′) *n.* a feeling of being without hope: *The shipwrecked sailors on the desert island were in deep despair.* —*v.* to give up hope: *The family despaired of ever seeing their lost cat again.* **despairing. despaired.**

desperate (des′ pər it) *adj.* made reckless by despair: *The house was on fire, and the desperate man was ready to jump out of the window.* —**desperately** *adv.*

despise (di spīz′) *v.* to hate very much. **despising. despised.**

despite (di spīt′) *prep.* in spite of: *Despite her hard life, my grandmother still has a cheerful outlook.*

dessert (di zůrt′) *n.* the last, usually sweet, part of a meal, such as fruit, cake, or ice cream.

The French word *desservir* means "to clear the table." After you have cleared away the main-course dishes, it's time for **dessert**.

destination (des′ tə nā′ shən) *n.* the place to which a person or thing is going: *The bus reached its destination ahead of time.*

destroy (di stroi′) *v.* to ruin completely; to wreck: *The hailstorm destroyed all the crops.* **destroying. destroyed.**

destructive (di struk′ tiv) *adj.* causing destruction: *a destructive hurricane.*

destruction (di struk′ shən) *n.* complete ruin; the smashing or breaking of anything.

detach (di tach′) *v.* to separate, often from something larger: *He detached the coupon from the magazine.* **detaching. detached.**

detail (dē′ tāl) *n.* a small or less important part of something larger: *Tell us all the details of your wilderness trip.*

detect (di tekt′) *v.* to discover; to notice: *Betty detected water dripping from the pipe.* **detecting. detected.**

detective (di tek′ tiv) *n.* a person whose job is to solve crimes.

detergent (di tůr′ jənt) *n.* a liquid or powder used for washing dishes or clothes.

deteriorate (dē tēr′ ē ə rāt′) *v.* to make or become worse: *His health is deteriorating, and we don't know if he will ever get better.* **deteriorating. deteriorated.**

determined (di tůr′ mənd) *adj.* with a firmly decided mind: *I was determined to finish my book before the weekend.*

detest (di test′) *v.* to hate very much: *Many people detest spiders.* **detesting. detested.**

develop (di vel′ əp) *v.* **1.** to grow: *Exercise will develop your muscles.* **2.** to change from one form to another: *The roll of film was developed into pictures.* **developing. developed.**

device (di vīs′) *n.* any tool, instrument, or machine that helps you: *A toaster is a device that toasts bread.*

devil (dev′ əl) *n.* **1.** an evil spirit. **2.** a very wicked person.

devote (di vōt′) *v.* to give time to a purpose or a person: *Our neighbours devote a lot of time to gardening.* **devoting. devoted.**

devour (di vowr′) *v.* to eat greedily. **devouring. devoured.**

dew (dū *or* dyū) *n.* small drops of water that form when moisture in the air comes in contact with a cold surface: *Dew appears on grass when it cools down at night.*

diagnosis (di′ əg nō′ səs) *n.* a doctor's judgment of what a patient's illness is: *The doctor gave me her diagnosis: a broken bone.* *pl.* **diagnoses.**

diagonal (dī ag′ ə nəl) *n.* a slanting line, going from one corner of a square or rectangle across to the opposite corner.

diagram (dī′ ə gram′) *n.* a drawing or plan that shows how something works or is made.

dial (dī′ əl *or* dīl) *n.* the face of a clock, a compass, or other device that shows information. —*v.* to make a phone call: *Dial zero for the operator.* **dialing. dialed.**

dial

dialogue (dī′ ə log′) *n.* conversation, usually in a book or a play: *I enjoyed the story because the plot is unusual and the dialogue is familiar. All the characters used words that I could understand.*

dial tone the humming sound that you hear when you lift the receiver from a telephone.

diameter (dī am′ ə tər) *n.* a straight line from one side of a circle to the other, passing through the centre of the circle.

diamond (dī′ mənd) *n.* **1.** a clear, precious stone: *Diamond is the hardest substance known.* **2.** the shape (♦). **3.** a baseball field. **4.** a playing card with one or more diamond shapes on it.

diaper (dī′ pər) *n.* a piece of soft cloth or paper, folded and used as underpants for a baby.

diary (dī′ ə rē) *n.* a small notebook in which you write down what happens each day. *pl.* **diaries.**

dice (dīs) *n. pl.* small cubes, each side marked with one to six dots. Dice are used for playing games. *sing.* **die.**

dictate (dik′ tāt *or* dik tāt′) *v.* **1.** to say words aloud for other people to write down: *The teacher dictated the spelling words.* **2.** to give orders: *The king dictated that all spinning wheels were to be destroyed.* **dictating. dictated.**

dictation (dik tā′ shən) *n.* the saying or reading aloud of words to another person, who writes them down.

dictionary (dik′ shən er′ ē) *n.* a book that lists words in alphabetical order and explains the meaning of each word. *pl.* **dictionaries.**

did (did) see **do.**

didn't (did′ ənt) a contraction (short form) of **did not.**

die (dī) *v.* **1.** to stop living. **2.** (*informal*) to want very much: *I'm dying to hear your story.* **dying. died.** he **dies.**

diet (dī′ ət) *n.* **1.** the food and drink of a person or animal: *What is the diet of a lion?* **2.** special food eaten by a person who is ill, or is trying to lose or gain weight. —*v.* to eat only certain foods because you are trying to lose or gain weight. **dieting. dieted.**

difference (dif′ rəns *or* dif′ ər əns) *n.* **1.** the way in which one thing is unlike another: *Can you tell me the difference between a pen and a pencil?* **2.** the amount left after one number is subtracted from another.

different (dif′ rənt *or* dif′ ər ənt) *adj.* unlike; not the same: *A robin is different from a sparrow.* —**differently** *adv.*

difficult (dif′ ə kult′) *adj.* hard to do or understand: *The test was difficult but we had studied hard for it.*

difficulty (dif′ ə kul′ tē) *n.* something hard to do or understand: *The test presented many difficulties.* *pl.* **difficulties.**

dig (dig) *v.* to make a hole in the ground; to turn over the earth with a shovel. **digging. dug.**

digest (dī jest′) *v.* to process food in the stomach and intestines, so that the body can use it. **digesting. digested.**

digestion (dī jes′ chən) *n.* the process of digesting.

digit (dij′ ət) *n.* **1.** one of the single numbers from 0 to 9: *The number 540 is a three-digit number, and is made of the digits 5, 4, and 0.* **2.** a finger, a thumb, or a toe.

digital (dij′ ə təl) *adj.* providing information in the form of numbers: *A digital clock displays the time as numbers rather than by the movement of hands around a face.*

dignified (dig′ nə fīd′) *adj.* serious and noble: *I tried to answer their silly questions in a dignified way.*

dignity (dig′ nə tē) *n.* a proud and noble quality: *The servant had the dignity of a queen.*

dike (dīk) *n.* a ditch or wall, built to protect against flooding.

dill (dil) *n.* an herb used to make pickles or to season foods.

dilute (dī lūt′) *v.* to make thinner or weaker by adding liquid, especially water: *You dilute canned soup by adding water. You dilute oil paint by adding turpentine.* **diluting. diluted.**

dim (dim) *adj.* not bright or clear: *a dim light; a dimmer light; the dimmest light in the house.* —**dimly** *adv.* —*v.* to make dim or become dim: *to dim lights.* **dimming. dimmed.**

dime (dīm) *n.* a Canadian or U.S. coin worth ten cents.

dimension (di men′ shən *or* dī men′ shən) *n.* a measurement in any one direction: *A sheet of paper has two dimensions—length and width. A book has three dimensions—length, width, and thickness.*

dimple (dim′ pəl) *n.* a small hollow in your flesh, such as in the cheek or chin.

din (din) *n.* a loud, constant noise; a racket: *The vacuum cleaner is making a terrible din!*

dine (dīn) *v.* to eat a meal: *We dined on fresh lobster when we visited New Brunswick.* **dining. dined.**

diner (dī′ nər) *n.* **1.** a person eating a meal. **2.** a small restaurant, usually by a highway.

dinghy (ding′ ē) *n.* a small rowboat. *pl.* **dinghies.**

dingy (din′ jē) *adj.* dull and dirty-looking: *a dingy room; a dingier room; the dingiest room in the house.*

dining room a room where meals are eaten.

dinner (din′ ər) *n.* **1.** the main meal of the day. **2.** a social event that includes dinner: *Awards were given out at our annual hockey dinner.*

dinosaur (dī′ nə sȯr′) *n.* one of many kinds of reptiles that lived millions of years ago: *Some dinosaurs were the largest animals that ever lived on land.*

In ancient Greek, *deinos* means "fearful" and *sauros* means "lizard." Therefore, a **dinosaur** is a fearful lizard.

dinosaur

dip (dip) *v.* **1.** to put something into liquid and quickly lift it out again: *to dip a doughnut into milk.* **2.** to slope downward: *The road dipped into the valley.* **dipping. dipped.**

diploma (di plō′ mə) *n.* a certificate that a student receives when he or she graduates.

diplomat (dip′ lə mat′) *n.* a person who represents his or her country in making agreements with other countries: *My uncle is a diplomat at the Canadian embassy in Italy.*

direct (di rekt′ *or* dī rekt′) *adj.* **1.** in a straight line: *What is the most direct route to school?* **2.** straightforward; honest: *I want a direct answer.* (*opp.* **indirect.**) —*v.* **1.** to guide or control: *The police officer directed traffic.* **2.** to show the way: *Can you direct me to the post office?* **3.** to aim: *The robber directed his gun at the shoppers.* **directing. directed.**

direction (di rek′ shən *or* dī rek′ shən) *n.* the general line that a person or thing faces, points to, or moves toward: *In what direction should we walk: north, south, east, or west?*

directions (di rek′ shənz *or* dī rek′ shənz) *n. pl.* an explanation of how to get to a certain place or how to do something: *the directions for building a model airplane.*

director (di rek′ tər *or* dī rek′ tər) *n.* a person who guides and manages something: *the director of a business.*

directory (di rek′ tər ē) *n.* a list of names and addresses, usually in alphabetical order: *a telephone directory. pl.* **directories.**

dirt (dürt) *n.* **1.** earth; soil. **2.** filth.

dirty (dür′ tē) *adj.* covered with dirt: *Muffin's paws are dirty, but Pooch's are dirtier, and Bandit's paws are the dirtiest of all.*

dis– is a prefix meaning "not" or "the opposite of." "Disagree" means not to agree; "dislike" means not to like; and "disobey" means not to obey.

disabled (dis ā′ bəld) *adj.* not able to do certain things as well as other people, because of a serious, lasting injury or illness.

disagree (dis′ ə grē′) *v.* to fail to agree. **disagreeing. disagreed.**

disappear (dis′ ə pēr′) *v.* to go out of sight; to vanish: *The car disappeared over the hill.* **disappearing. disappeared.**

disappearance (dis′ ə pēr′ əns) *n.* the act of disappearing.

disappoint (dis′ ə point′) *v.* to fail to satisfy or please; to let down: *Our team's loss in the finals disappointed the whole school.* **disappointing. disappointed.**

disappointment (dis′ ə point′ mənt) *n.* someone or something that disappoints: *The boring hockey game was a disappointment.*

disaster (də zas′ tər) *n.* a great misfortune, accident, or tragedy: *The plane crash was a terrible disaster.*

disc (disk) *n.* **1.** a thin, flat, round plate on which a sound recording is stored: *a compact disc.* **2.** see **disk.**

discipline (dis′ ə plin) *n.* **1.** obedient behaviour and training: *The athletes showed discipline during practices for the track meet.* **2.** punishment.

disconnect (dis′ kə nekt′) *v.* to unplug: *The CD player did not work because I had disconnected it.* **disconnecting. disconnected.**

discount (dis′ kownt) *n.* an amount taken off the full price: *During the sale there was a twenty percent discount on the price of cameras.*

discourage (dis kər′ ij) *v.* to try to stop someone from doing something: *We discouraged her from driving in the snow storm.* **discouraging. discouraged.**

discover (dis kuv′ ər) *v.* to see or learn for the very first time; to find out. **discovering. discovered.**

discovery (dis kuv′ ər ē) *n.* the finding of something new: *the discovery of a new star in the sky. pl.* **discoveries.**

discriminate (dis krim′ ə nāt′) *v.* to treat people unfairly because of their colour, sex, religion, age, and so on. **discriminating. discriminated.**

discuss (dis kus′) *v.* to talk about something with other people: *The family discussed plans for the summer holiday.* **discussing. discussed.**

discussion (dis kush′ ən) *n.* a serious talk about something.

disease (də zēz′) *n.* illness; sickness.

disgrace (dis grās′) *n.* a person or thing that brings shame: *This messy room is a disgrace.* —*v.* to cause shame: *Her gambling disgraced the family.* **disgracing. disgraced.**

disgraceful (dis grās′ fəl) *adj.* shameful; rude and shocking.

disguise (dis gīz′) *n.* a change of clothing and appearance so that people will not recognize you. —*v.* to change your appearance so that people will not recognize you. **disguising. disguised.**

disgust (dis gust′) *n.* a feeling of disliking and being sickened by something or someone. —*v.* to feel disgust: *Cruelty to animals disgusts me.* **disgusting. disgusted.**

disgusting (dis gust′ ing) *adj.* unpleasant and sickening: *a disgusting horror movie.*

dish (dish) *n.* **1.** a flat or shallow container for food; a plate. **2.** a kind of food: *My favourite dish is lamb curry.* **3.** an object shaped like a dish: *a satellite dish. pl.* **dishes.**

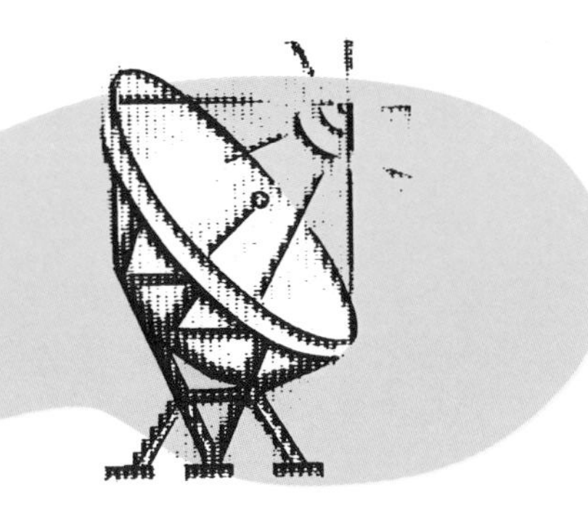

satellite dish

dishonest (dis on′ ist) *adj.* not honest. —**dishonestly** *adv.*

disinfect (dis′ in fekt′) *v.* to destroy harmful germs that may cause disease: *My mother disinfected my cut with rubbing alcohol before she bandaged it.* **disinfecting. disinfected.**

disintegrate (dis in′ tə grāt′) *v.* to break apart into small bits; to crumble: *The old book is disintegrating into dust.* **disintegrating. disintegrated.**

disk, disc (disk) *n.* **1.** a thin, flat, round plate, or anything like it. **2.** a square or round plate used for storing computer data.

disk drive a small machine attached to a computer that reads stored information on disks.

diskette (dis ket′) *n.* a small computer disk.

dislike (dis līk′) *n.* a feeling of not liking. —*v.* not to like: *I dislike chocolate.* **disliking. disliked.**

dismal (diz′ məl) *adj.* dreary: *It was a rainy, dismal day, so we decided to stay indoors.*

dismay (dis mā′) *n.* fear or confusion when you are faced with trouble. —*v.* to become afraid or confused by trouble: *The children were dismayed when their ball broke a window.* **dismaying. dismayed.**

dismiss (dis mis′) *v.* **1.** to send away: *Class dismissed!* **2.** to fire someone from a job: *The company dismissed three workers for stealing.* **dismissing. dismissed.**

disobedient (dis′ ə bē′ dē ənt) *adj.* not obeying.

display (dis plā′) *n.* a show; an exhibition: *a fireworks display. pl.* **displays.** —*v.* to show or exhibit something. **displaying. displayed.**

displease (dis plēz′) *v.* to make unhappy, angry, or annoyed. **displeasing. displeased.**

disposable (dis pōz′ ə bəl) *adj.* designed to be thrown away after use: *disposable diapers.*

dispose (dis pōz′) *v.* to throw out: *Please dispose of the garbage.* **disposing. disposed.**

disqualify (dis kwol′ ə fī′) *v.* **1.** to make unable to do something: *Poor eyesight disqualified him from becoming an aircraft pilot.* **2.** to stop a person from competing in a sports activity: *The swimmer was disqualified because she dove into the water before the race started.* **disqualifying. disqualified.**

dissolve (di zolv′) *v.* to mix something with water or other liquid until it disappears: *to dissolve sugar in coffee.* **dissolving. dissolved.**

distance (dis′ təns) *n.* **1.** the length of space between two places: *The distance between my house and my school is one kilometre.* **2.** a place far away: *Can you see the mountains in the distance?*

distant (dis′ tənt) *adj.* far away: *a distant land.*

distinct (dis tingkt′) *adj.* clear; plain: *There are small but distinct differences between a rabbit and a hare.* —**distinctly** *adv.*

distract (dis trakt′) *v.* to take your mind away from something: *Loud music distracts me when I'm reading.* **distracting. distracted.**

distress (dis tres′) *n.* misery or pain: *The dog with the broken leg was in great distress.* —*v.* to upset someone very much. **distressing. distressed.**

distribute (dis trib′ yūt) *v.* to give out: *The mayor came to our school to distribute the prizes.* **distributing. distributed.**

district (dis′ trikt) *n.* a part of a town, county, or country.

disturb (dis tu̇rb′) *v.* to annoy or interrupt: *Please don't disturb the readers in the library.* **disturbing. disturbed.**

ditch (dich) *n.* a long, narrow hole dug in the ground: *a ditch for draining water away.* *pl.* **ditches.**

dive (dīv) *n.* a downward plunge, usually into water. —*v.* to plunge headfirst into water. **diving. dived** or **dove** (dōv). she has **dived.**

diver (dīv′ ər) *n.* **1.** an athlete who dives for sport. **2.** a person who works underwater, wearing breathing equipment: *After my watch dropped into the deep water, we hired a diver to try to find it.*

diver

divide (di vīd′) *v.* **1.** to separate into parts. **2.** to share out: *We have to divide the pizza among six people.* **3.** in arithmetic, to find out how many times one number contains another number: *8 divided by 2 equals 4.* **dividing. divided.**

divine (də vīn′) *adj.* heavenly: *What a divine hat you're wearing!*

division (di vizh′ ən) *n.* **1.** the dividing of one number by another in arithmetic. **2.** a department: *the history division of a library.*

divorce (di vȯrs′) *n.* the legal ending of a marriage. —*v.* to end a marriage legally. **divorcing. divorced.**

dizzy (diz′ ē) *adj.* having a feeling that you are spinning around and are about to fall: *He felt dizzy after the roller coaster ride; you felt dizzier; and I think I felt dizziest of all.*

do (dū) *v.* **1.** to perform an action: *Do your homework.* **2.** to manage: *How is she doing?* **3.** to work; to have a job. **4.** to finish: *We did our project in time.* **doing. did. done** (dun). he **does** (duz).

> **Do** is often used as a helping (auxiliary) verb with other verbs. It is used for emphasis: *I **do** want to go there.* It is used to ask a question: *Do you want to go?* It is used in negative statements containing the word **not**: *He does not want to go.*

dock (dok) *n.* a platform by the water where a ship can load, unload, or be repaired. —*v.* to bring a boat to a dock. **docking. docked.**

doctor (dok′ tər) *n.* a person who is trained in medicine and is qualified to treat sick people.

document (doc′ yə mənt) *n.* a paper that provides proof or other important information about something: *A birth certificate is a document that proves a person was born in a particular country.*

documentary (doc′ yə ment′ ə rē) *n.* a film that presents actual facts and actual people, not actors. *pl.* **documentaries.**

dodge (doj) *v.* to quickly move out of the way: *I dodged the ball and just missed getting hit by it.* **dodging. dodged.**

doe (dō) (*masc.* **buck**) *n.* a female deer or rabbit.

does (duz) see **do**.

doesn't (duz′ ənt) a contraction (short form) of **does not**.

dog (dog) *n.* an animal, often kept as a pet, that barks and has a good sense of hearing and smell. Dogs are related to wolves.

doll (dol) *n.* a toy that looks like a person.

dollar (dol′ ər) *n.* a unit of money ($1.00) equal to 100 cents in Canada, the United States, and some other countries.

dolphin (dol′ fən) *n.* a sea mammal that looks like a small whale and has a long snout.

dolphin

dome (dōm) *n.* a curved roof shaped like an upside-down bowl.

domestic (də mes′ tik) *adj.* **1.** having to do with home life: *Cooking and cleaning are domestic activities.* **2.** tame, not wild: *Cats and dogs are domestic animals.*

dominate (dom′ ə nāt′) *v.* to control or have power over: *She is the fastest runner; she dominates all her competitors.* **dominating. dominated.**

dominion (də min′ yən) *n.* **1.** rule; control. **2. Dominion** a name given to certain countries: *the Dominion of Canada.*

dominoes (dom′ ə nōz′) *n. pl.* a game played with small, flat, rectangular black tiles with white dots.

donate (dō′ nāt) *v.* to give or contribute: *The whole neighbourhood donated time and money to build the community centre.* **donating. donated.**

donation (dō nā′ shən) *n.* a gift.

done (dun) see **do**.

donkey (dong′ kē) *n.* a mammal that has long ears and looks like a small horse; an ass. *pl.* **donkeys.**

don't (dōnt) a contraction (short form) of **do not**.

donut see **doughnut**.

door (dȯr) *n.* a large, upright panel that opens and closes an entrance to a room or building.

doorway (dȯr′ wā) *n.* an entrance to a building or room.

dose (dōs) *n.* the amount of medicine to be taken at one time.

dot (dot) *n.* a small, round spot. —*v.* to mark with dots. **dotting. dotted.**

double (dub′ əl) *adj.* twice as much or twice as many: *a double scoop of ice cream.* —*v.* to multiply by two. **doubling. doubled.**

doubt (dowt) *n.* an unsure feeling or a suspicion: *I have doubts about going to the game in this bad weather.* —*v.* to be unsure or suspicious about something: *I doubt that she is telling the truth.* **doubting. doubted.**

dough (dō) *n.* a soft, thick mixture of flour, water, and other ingredients: *Dough is baked to make bread, cake, or cookies.*

doughnut, donut (dō′ nut) *n.* a small, round, fried cake with a hole in the centre.

dove (duv) *n.* a kind of pigeon.

dove (dōv) see **dive** (verb).

down (down) *n.* the short, soft, fluffy feathers of a bird. —*prep.* from a higher to a lower place: *They walked down the hill.* —*adv.* at or to a lower place: *Please sit down.*

downhill (down′ hil′) *adv.* toward the bottom of a hill: *We skied downhill.*

downpour (down′ pȯr′) *n.* a heavy rainfall.

downstairs (down′ sterz′) *adv.* down to or on a lower floor.

downtown (down′ town′) *adv.* to the main part of a city: *Let's go downtown to shop in the largest stores.*

downward, downwards (down′ ward, down′ wardz) *adv.* toward a lower place: *The kite drifted downward and landed on the ground.*

doze (dōz) *v.* to sleep lightly; to nap: *The baby dozed in the car.* **dozing. dozed.**

dozen (duz′ ən) *adj.* twelve: *a dozen eggs.*

Dr. (dok′ tər) an abbreviation of **doctor**; always used with a name: *Dr. Young.*

draft, draught (draft) *n.* a breeze blowing in from an open window or door.

drag (drag) *v.* **1.** to pull something heavy along the ground. **2.** to move too slowly: *The boring speech dragged on and on.* **dragging. dragged.**

dragon (drag′ ən) *n.* an imaginary monster: *A dragon looks like a giant lizard and breathes out fire.*

dragon

dragonfly (drag′ ən flī′) *n.* a large insect, often brightly coloured, with a long body and four transparent wings.

drain (drān) *n.* a ditch or large pipe that carries away unwanted water. —*v.* to empty unwanted water. **draining. drained.**

drake (drāk) *n.* a male duck.

drama (dram′ ə) *n.* a stage play, often one that is serious instead of comic. *pl.* **dramas.**

dramatic (drə mat′ ik) *adj.* **1.** having to do with plays. **2.** exciting like a drama: *a dramatic rescue.* —**dramatically** *adv.*

drank (drangk) see **drink.**

drapes, draperies (drāps, drā′ pər ēz) *n. pl.* large curtains that hang in folds.

draught see **draft.**

draw (dro) *n.* **1.** the picking of tickets for a prize: *a lucky draw.* **2.** a game in which neither side wins; a tie. —*v.* **1.** to pull or take out: *He drew the winning ticket from the box.* **2.** to attract: *to draw attention.* **3.** to make a picture on paper with pencil, ink, or crayon. **4.** to move together: *to draw the curtains.* **drawing. drew.** I have **drawn.**

drawbridge (dro′ brij′) *n.* a bridge that can be raised and lowered.

drawer (dròr) *n.* a box that slides in and out of a desk, dresser, and so on.

drawing (dro′ ing) *n.* a picture made with pencil, ink, or crayon.

dread (dred) *n.* a feeling of fear or worry. —*v.* to be afraid of or worried about: *I dread the big test coming up.* **dreading. dreaded.**

dreadful (dred′ fəl) *adj.* terrible; disgusting: *dreadful news; a dreadful accident.* —**dreadfully** *adv.*

dream (drēm) *n.* a picture that comes into your mind while you are asleep. —*v.* to have pictures in your mind while you are asleep. **dreaming. dreamed** or **dreamt** (dremt).

dreary (drēr′ ē) *adj.* dull and gloomy: *a dreary day; a drearier one; the dreariest day of the year.*

drench (drench) *v.* to wet completely. **drenching. drenched.**

dress (dres) *n.* a garment that has a top and skirt in one piece. *pl.* **dresses.** —*v.* to put on clothes. **dressing. dressed.** (*opp.* **undress.**)

dresser (dres′ ər) *n.* a piece of bedroom furniture with drawers for clothes.

dressing (dres′ ing) *n.* **1.** a sauce for salads. **2.** a mixture of bread crumbs, vegetables, and herbs, used to stuff a turkey or chicken. **3.** a bandage on a cut or wound.

drew (drū) see **draw**.

dribble (drib′ əl) *v.* **1.** to drip liquid. **2.** in basketball, to move while bouncing the ball up and down. **dribbling. dribbled.**

dried (drīd) see **dry**.

dries (drīz) see **dry**.

drift (drift) *n.* snow or sand blown into a pile by the wind. —*v.* **1.** to be carried along by the wind: *The boat drifted down the river.* **2.** to be piled up by the wind. **drifting. drifted.**

drill (dril) *n.* **1.** a tool used for making holes. **2.** an activity or exercise done over and over: *a spelling drill.* —*v.* **1.** to make a hole, using a drill. **2.** to teach by having a student do something over and over. **drilling. drilled.**

drink (dringk) *n.* a beverage: *a cold drink.* —*v.* to swallow a liquid. **drinking. drank.** I have **drunk.**

drip (drip) *n.* liquid falling in drops. —*v.* to fall in drops: *Water drips from a leaking tap.* **dripping. dripped.**

drive (drīv) *n.* **1.** a ride in a car: *Let's go for a drive.* **2.** a special effort: *a drive for charity.* —*v.* **1.** to steer and operate a vehicle, especially a car. **2.** to force to go away: *The army drove away the enemy.* **driving. drove.** They have **driven.**

driveway (drīv′ wā′) *n.* a private road that leads from the street to a house or garage. *pl.* **driveways.**

drizzle (driz′ əl) *n.* a fall of light rain. —*v.* to rain lightly. **drizzling. drizzled.**

drone (drōn) *n.* a male bee. —*v.* to make a humming noise, like a bee. **droning. droned.**

droop (drūp) *v.* to hang down loosely; to sag. **drooping. drooped.**

drop (drop) *n.* **1.** a spot of liquid: *a drop of blood.* **2.** a fall or decrease: *a drop in temperature.* —*v.* to fall or let fall: *Don't drop the dish!* **dropping. dropped.**

drought (drowt) *n.* a long period of little or no rain.

drove (drōv) see **drive**.

drown (drown) *v.* **1.** to die by being choked by water. **2.** to cover up sound with a louder sound: *The song on the radio was drowned out by the construction work outside.* **drowning. drowned.**

drug (drug) *n.* a medicine.

drugstore (drug′ stȯr′) *n.* a store where medicines and other things (soap, toothpaste, tissues, and so on) are sold.

drum (drum) *n.* a round musical instrument that makes a sound when tapped with sticks or your hands. —*v.* to beat a drum. **drumming. drummed.**

drum

drumstick (drum′ stik′) *n.* **1.** a stick for beating a drum. **2.** the lower part of a cooked chicken or turkey leg.

drunk (drungk) *adj.* having had too much of an alcoholic drink. —*v.* see **drink**.

dry (drī) *adj.* not wet or damp: *a dry day; a drier day; the driest day of the year.* —*v.* to make or become dry: *to dry dishes.* **drying. dried.** it **dries.**

dryer, drier (drī′ ər) *n.* a machine for drying clothes.

duchess (duch′ əs) *n.* a noblewoman with a rank equal to a duke. *pl.* **duchesses.**

duck (duk) *n.* a water bird with a broad bill, a short body, and webbed feet. —*v.* to lower your head quickly to avoid being hit or seen. **ducking. ducked.**

due (dū *or* dyū) *adj.* **1.** expected: *The train is due at noon.* **2.** owing: *The library book is due today.*

duel (dū′ əl *or* dyū′ əl) *n.* a fight between two people with swords or pistols.

duet (dyū et′) *n.* a piece of music performed by two players or singers.

dug (dug) see **dig**.

dugout (dug′ owt′) *n.* in baseball, a low shelter where the players sit.

duke (dūk *or* dyūk) *n.* a nobleman who ranks below a prince.

dull (dul) *adj.* **1.** not bright: *a dull day.* **2.** not sharp: *a dull knife.* **3.** not interesting: *a dull conversation.* —*v.* to make something less sharp: *to dull a blade.* **dulling. dulled.**

dumb (dum) *adj.* (*informal*) silly or stupid.

dumfound, dumbfound (dum′ fownd′) *v.* to amaze; to stun: *We were dumfounded by the juggler's skill.* **dumfounding. dumfounded.**

dummy (dum′ ē) *n.* a life-size model of a person, used to display clothes in store windows. *pl.* **dummies.**

dump (dump) *n.* a place where garbage is piled up. —*v.* to unload in a pile: *to dump bricks.* **dumping. dumped.**

dune (dūn *or* dyūn) *n.* a hill of sand piled up by the wind.

dungeon (dun′ jən) *n.* an underground prison in a castle.

duplicate (dū′ plə kit *or* dyū′ plə kit) *n.* an exact copy of something: *I'm making a duplicate of my story on the photocopier.*

duplicate (dū′ plə kāt *or* dyū′ plə kāt) *v.* to make an exact copy of something: *We duplicated the photos to give to friends.* **duplicating. duplicated.**

during (dūr′ ing *or* dyūr′ ing) *prep.* **1.** throughout the time of: *He snored during the entire speech.* **2.** at some time in: *Come visit me during the afternoon.*

dusk (dusk) *n.* the time just before it gets dark in the evening.

dust (dust) *n.* fine particles of dirt that float in the air. —*v.* to clean off dust with a cloth or brush: *Wanda and Azhar dusted the furniture.* **dusting. dusted.**

dusty (dus′ tē) *adj.* covered with dust: *a dusty table; a dustier one; the dustiest table of all.*

duty (dū′ tē *or* dyū′ tē) *n.* something a person must or should do: *It is everyone's duty to obey the law.* *pl.* **duties.**

dwarf (dwȯrf) *n.* in fairy tales, a small creature that looks like a human being. *pl.* **dwarfs** or **dwarves.**

dwell (dwel) *v.* **1.** to live in some place: *Sharks dwell in the ocean.* **2.** to think a long time about: *Don't dwell on your problems.* **dwelling. dwelled** or **dwelt.**

dwelling (dwel′ ing) *n.* a house or other place where people live.

dye (dī) *n.* a liquid or powder used to colour things. —*v.* to colour something with a dye: *to dye white shoes black.* **dyeing. dyed.**

dying (dī′ ing) see **die**.

dynamite (dī′ nə mīt′) *n.* an explosive, used for blowing up rocks and other things.

each (ēch) *adj.* every: *Each student brought a book.* —*pron.* every single one: *Each of them read a story aloud.*

each other one another: *When we first met, my best friend and I liked each other right away.*

eager (ē′ gər) *adj.* wanting very much to do or to have something; ready and waiting: *After waiting fifteen minutes, we were eager for the concert to start.* —**eagerly** *adv.*

eagle (ē′ gəl) *n.* a large bird, with a hooked beak, keen eyesight, broad wings, and claws. Eagles hunt small animals and fish.

eagle

ear (ēr) *n.* **1.** the part of the body used for hearing. **2.** the part of a corn plant that contains the corn kernels.

eardrum (ēr′ drum′) *n.* a thin layer of tissue inside the ear that vibrates when sound waves strike it.

early (ůr′ lē) *adj.* happening at or near the beginning: *We took a walk in the early afternoon.* —*adv.* before the usual time: *Paul always arrives early at school, Yoshi arrives even earlier, but Dillon arrives earliest of all.*

earn (ůrn) *v.* **1.** to be paid for working: *Ingrid earns money for raking the leaves.* **2.** to deserve and get: *You all have worked hard and have earned a rest.* **earning. earned.**

earnest (ůr′ nist) *adj.* sincere and serious: *I am earnest when I say I want to help you.* —**earnestly** *adv.*

earphone (ēr′ fōn′) *n.* a device worn over the ears that allows you to listen to a radio, tape player, or CD player without disturbing other people.

earring (ēr′ ring′) *n.* a small piece of jewellery worn on the ear.

earth (ůrth) *n.* **1.** the planet on which we live, which is the third from the sun. **2.** the ground; soil.

earthquake (ůrth′ kwāk′) *n.* a violent shaking of the earth, caused by the movement of melted rock below the earth's surface.

earthworm (ůrth′ wůrm′) *n.* a common, brown worm that lives in soil.

ease (ēz) *n.* comfort; rest; relief: *Mother sat at ease in her armchair.*

easel (ē′ zəl) *n.* a stand on which to rest a painting while you are working on it.

easily (ēz′ ə lē) *adv.* without difficulty: *I can do the magic trick easily.*

east (ēst) *n.* the direction from which the sun rises, opposite to west. —*adv.* to the east: *If you travel east along this road, you will get to the library.*

eastern (ēs′ tərn) *adj.* in or of the east: *Newfoundland is in eastern Canada.*

eastward, eastwards (ēst′ wůrd, ēst′ wūrdz) *adv.* toward or facing the east: *Look eastward to see the sun rising.*

easy (ēz′ ē) *adj.* not difficult: *an easy puzzle; an easier one; the easiest puzzle of all.*

eat (ēt) *v.* **1.** to take food into the mouth, chew it, and swallow it. **2.** to have a meal: *We will eat at six o'clock.* **eating. ate.** I have **eaten.**

eaves (ēvz) *n. pl.* the lower edge of a roof.

eccentric (ek sen′ trik) *adj.* odd; unusual; peculiar: *My eccentric uncle barks like a dog when he gets angry.*

echo (ek′ ō) *n.* a sound that bounces back when you shout at a hill or a large wall. *pl.* **echoes.** —*v.* to make an echo: *The gunshot echoed through the valley.* **echoing. echoed.**

eclipse (ē klips′) *n.* a darkening of the sun or moon: *An eclipse of the sun happens when the moon passes between the sun and the earth. An eclipse of the moon happens when the moon enters the earth's shadow.*

ecology (ē kol′ ə jē) *n.* the study of how living things relate to each other and to their environment. —**ecological** *adj.*

economical (ek′ ə nom′ ə kəl) *adj.* **1.** careful about money; saving money: *A regular airfare is more economical than a first-class fare.* **2.** not wasteful: *An economical engine uses very little gasoline.*

economics (ek′ ə nom′ iks) *n.* the study of how money is made and spent, including the production of goods and services, prices, wages, taxes, and so on.

economize (i kon′ ə mīz′) *v.* to spend money carefully: *We economized by buying chicken when it was on sale.* **economizing. economized.**

economy (ē kon′ ə mē) *n.* the way a country or a region produces goods and services and handles money.

edge (ej) *n.* **1.** a line or place where something ends; a rim or border: *the edge of a table.* **2.** the sharp side of a blade. —*v.* to move little by little: *The car edged into traffic.* **edging. edged.**

on edge nervous; tense.

edgy (ej′ ē) *adj.* tense; irritable.

edible (ed′ ə bəl) *adj.* safe to be eaten: *Most mushrooms are edible, but some kinds are poisonous.* (*opp.* **inedible.**)

edit (ed′ it) *v.* to prepare written or electronic material for publication by correcting mistakes, revising text, checking facts, and so on. **editing. edited.**

edition (i dish′ ən) *n.* **1.** one of the copies of a book, newspaper, or magazine printed at the same time: *Did you see today's edition of the newspaper?* **2.** the form in which a book, newspaper, or magazine is printed: *Do you want the hardcover or paperback edition of this book?*

editor (ed′ ə tər) *n.* a person who checks the writing of other people and prepares it for publication.

educate (ej′ ū kāt′) *v.* to teach or train people. **educating. educated.**

education (ej′ ū kā′ shən) *n.* the learning of knowledge and skills, usually in schools.

educational (ej′ ū kā′ shən əl) *adj.* giving knowledge; instructive.

eel (ēl) *n.* a long, thin fish that looks like a snake.

eel

eerie (ē′ rē) *adj.* weird and mysterious; spooky. —**eerily** *adv.*

effect (i fekt′) *n.* the result of an action or a change: *Medicine has the effect of helping a sick person to get better.*

Be careful not to mix up **effect** (a noun) with "affect" (a verb); "affect" means to cause a change.

effective (i fek′ tiv) *adj.* giving the desired result; successful: *His story is effective because the characters seem so real.* —**effectively** *adv.*

efficient (ə fish′ ənt) *adj.* able to work well, without wasting time, energy, space, or materials: *I find using a computer to write a story is more efficient than writing it by hand. The story looks neater, and I can correct my mistakes before I print it.* —**efficiently** *adv.*

effort (ef′ ərt) *n.* the use of energy or strength to do something; a hard try: *The farmer made a great effort to lift the heavy stone.*

egg (eg) *n.* a round or oval body, in some cases covered with a thin shell, that is laid by a female bird, fish, insect, or reptile. An egg hatches into a young animal.

eggplant (eg′ plant′) *n.* a vegetable that is shaped like a large egg and has a shiny, dark purple skin.

eight (āt) *n., adj.* one more than seven: 8.

eighteen (ā′ tēn′) *n., adj.* ten more than eight: 18.

eighty (ā′ tē) *n., adj.* ten times eight: 80.

either (ē′ THər *or* ī′ THər) *adj., conj.* one or the other of two: *Either Marlene or Matina will be chosen as the new goalie. Either stay at home or come with us.*

> **Either** is used with **or** whenever two choices are being offered: *Either they go or we go.*

elaborate (i lab′ ər it) *adj.* complicated; having many details or parts: *Please don't prepare an elaborate dish for the picnic—just sandwiches will do.* —**elaborately** *adv.*

elastic (i las′ tik) *n.* a rubber band that stretches when pulled and is used to bundle things together. —*adj.* able to go back to its own shape after being stretched or squeezed; springy; flexible.

elated (i lā′ təd) *adj.* thrilled; happy.

elbow (el′ bō) *n.* the joint between your lower arm and upper arm.

elderly (el′ dər lē) *adj.* old in age: *My grandparents are elderly.*

eldest (eld′ əst) *n., adj.* the oldest, usually in a family: *I am the eldest of six children in our family.*

elect (i lekt′) *v.* to choose by voting. **electing. elected.**

election (i lek′ shən) *n.* choosing by a vote.

electric, electrical (i lek′ trik, i lek′ trə kəl) *adj.* having to do with electricity: *an electric lamp; an electrical engineer.* —**electrically** *adv.*

electrician (i lek′ trish′ ən) *n.* a person who installs or fixes electrical equipment.

electricity (i lek′ tris′ ə tē) *n.* a form of energy that flows through wires and can produce light and heat.

electronic (i lek′ tron′ ik *or* ē′ lek tron′ ik) *adj.* having to do with **electrons**, which are very tiny particles of electricity that travel through wires and make certain machines, such as computers, televisions, and radios, work. —**electronically** *adv.*

elegant (el′ ə gənt) *adj.* showing good taste: *an elegant dinner party.*

elementary school (el′ ə mən′ tə rē skūl) a school that begins with kindergarten or grade 1 and goes to grade 6, 7, or 8.

elephant (el′ ə fənt) *n.* a very large, grey mammal of Asia and Africa: *An elephant has large ears, a long trunk, and curved tusks.*

elevate (el′ ə vāt) *v.* to raise; to lift up: *When you hop, you jump with one leg elevated off the ground.* **elevating. elevated.**

elevator (el′ ə vā′ tər) *n.* **1.** a small room that carries people or things up and down in a building. **2.** a building for storing grain.

eleven (i lev′ ən) *n., adj.* one more than ten: 11.

elf (elf) *n.* in folk tales, a small, mischievous fairy. *pl.* **elves.**

eligible (el′ ə jə bəl) *adj.* qualified or suitable for a job, an activity, or a contest: *All students in the class are eligible to enter the writing contest.*

eliminate (i lim′ ə nāt′) *v.* to get rid of: *An air freshener eliminates unpleasant odours in a room.* **eliminating. eliminated.**

elk (elk) *n.* a large deer of North America: *The male elk has broad antlers. pl.* **elk.**

elk

elm (elm) *n.* a tall shade tree with curving branches and hard wood.

else (els) *adj.* **1.** other; different: *I thought I heard you, but it was somebody else.* **2.** in addition: *Who else should come?*
—*adv.* differently: *How else could we have won the game?*

elsewhere (els′ wer′ *or* els′ hwer′) *adv.* in or to some other place: *It's muddy here. Let's go elsewhere.*

embankment (em bank′ mənt) *n.* a mound or wall of earth or stone, usually built to hold back water.

embarrass (em ber′ əs) *v.* to feel shy or ashamed, often because of incorrect or silly behaviour: *I was embarrassed because I was the only one who forgot my friend's birthday.* **embarrassing. embarrassed.**

embarrassment (em ber′ əs mənt) *n.*
1. a feeling of being embarrassed.
2. something that embarrasses.

embassy (em′ bə sē) *n.* the official home and offices of an ambassador. *pl.* **embassies.**

emblem (em′ bləm) *n.* a badge or symbol: *The maple leaf is an emblem of Canada.*

embrace (em brās′) *v.* to hug tightly: *My father embraced my grandmother when she arrived in Canada.* **embracing. embraced.**

embroider (em broi′ dər) *v.* to decorate cloth by sewing fancy designs on it: *I embroidered a cushion with a pattern of flowers.* **embroidering. embroidered.**

embroidery (em broi′ dər ē) *n.* fancy designs sewn on cloth.

embryo (em′ brē ō′) *n.* an animal or plant in the first stages of growth. *pl.* **embryos.**

emerald (em′ ər əld) *n.* a clear, bright green jewel.

emerge (im ůrj) *v.* to come out into view: *The cat emerged from its hiding spot when it smelled food.* **emerging. emerged.**

emergency (i můr′ jən sē) *n.* something serious that happens suddenly and needs attention right away: *A house on fire is an emergency. pl.* **emergencies.**

emigrate (em′ ə grāt′) *v.* to leave the country you were born in and settle in another country. **emigrating. emigrated.**

emotion (i mō′ shən) *n.* a feeling, especially a strong one: *Love, hate, fear, anger, happiness, and sadness are emotions.*

emotional (i mō′ shə nəl) *adj.* **1.** causing strong feelings; moving: *Seeing my cousin for the first time was an emotional experience.* **2.** easily moved: *I get emotional and cry every time I see a sentimental movie.*
—**emotionally** *adv.*

emperor (em′ pər ər) *n.* a man who rules an empire.

emphasis (em′ fə sis) *n.* **1.** special importance given to something to make it stand out: *My teacher puts emphasis on being helpful to others in the class.* **2.** special force given to a word or syllable when speaking: *"Help me," he shouted, with emphasis on the word "me."* *pl.* **emphases.**

emphasize (em′ fə sīz′) *v.* to give special attention to something; to stress: *Linda emphasized that we had to hurry because a storm was coming.* **emphasizing. emphasized.**

empire (em′ pīr) *n.* a group of countries under one ruler.

employ (em ploi′) *v.* to hire someone to work for you. **employing. employed.**

employee (em ploi′ ē *or* em ploi ē′) *n.* someone who is hired to work and receives pay: *A salesperson is a store employee.*

employer (em ploi′ ər) *n.* someone who pays others to work for him or her.

employment (em ploi′ mənt) *n.* work; a job: *My sister is looking for summer employment.*

empress (em′ prəs) *n.* **1.** a woman who rules an empire. **2.** the wife of an emperor. *pl.* **empresses.**

empty (emp′ tē) *adj.* containing nothing: *an empty box.* —*v.* to make or become empty; to pour out: *Please empty the bin.* **emptying. emptied.**

emu (ē′ myū) *n.* a large bird of Australia that can run but cannot fly. It is similar to an ostrich, but smaller. *pl.* **emus.**

emu

enable (en ā′ bəl) *v.* to make able: *The new freezer enables us to store larger amounts of meat.* **enabling. enabled.**

enamel (i nam′ əl) *n.* **1.** the hard, white coating on your teeth. **2.** a smooth, shiny coating for decorating pottery, metal, or other hard surfaces. **3.** a paint that dries to a hard, shiny surface.

enchant (en chant′) *v.* to charm; to put under a magic spell: *The clown's tricks enchanted the children.* **enchanting. enchanted.**

enclose (en klōz′) *v.* **1.** to shut in on all sides; to surround: *The fence encloses the yard.* **2.** to put in a wrapping or envelope: *The money is enclosed with my letter.* **enclosing. enclosed.**

encounter (en kown′ tər) *n.* a chance meeting: *Just as they were leaving the bank, the thieves had an encounter with the police.* —*v.* to meet by chance: *We encountered a moose as we hiked through the park.* **encountering. encountered.**

encourage (en kùr′ əj) *v.* to give someone hope and courage to do something: *The drama teacher encouraged her to audition for the lead role.* **encouraging. encouraged.**

encouragement (en kùr′ əj mənt) *n.* something that encourages a person to try harder: *As an encouragement, the teacher announced he would award a prize for the best essay.*

encyclopedia, encyclopaedia (en sī′ klə pē′ dē ə) *n.* a large book, or set of books, with facts and information on many things. An encyclopedia is arranged in alphabetic order: *We used the encyclopedia often when we were doing our science project.*

end (end) *n.* **1.** the last part; the finish: *the end of the road.* **2.** the part or edge where a thing stops: *the end of our backyard.* —*v.* to finish: *The story ends on the next page.* **ending. ended.**

endangered (en dān′ jərd) *adj.* in danger of disappearing from the earth: *Many kinds of animals are endangered because their habitats are being destroyed.*

ending (end′ ing) *n.* the last part of something: *I like the movie's happy ending.*

endure (en dyūr′ *or* en dūr′) *v.* **1.** to last: *How long will the cold weather endure?* **2.** to stand; to put up with: *How long can we endure this cold weather?* **enduring. endured.**

enemy (en′ ə mē) *n.* a person, group, or country that hates, and tries to harm, another; a foe: *Those two families are bitter enemies.* *pl.* **enemies.**

energetic (en′ ər jet′ ik) *adj.* full of energy: *He is so energetic that he exercises three times a day.* —**energetically** *adv.*

energy (en′ ər jē) *n.* **1.** force and strength: *The runner saved some of her energy for the final few metres of the race.* **2.** power: *Oil, gas, and solar power are forms of energy.* *pl.* **energies.**

engaged (en gājd′) *adj.* promised to marry: *John and Emily were engaged for a year before they were married.*

engagement (en gāj′ mənt) *n.* a promise to marry.

engine (en′ jən) *n.* **1.** any machine that produces power to make things move. **2.** a locomotive: *The engine pulled the train up the hill.*

engine

engineer (en′ jə nēr′) *n.* **1.** a person who is trained in engineering. **2.** the driver of a locomotive.

engineering (en′ jə nēr′ ing) *n.* the designing and building of machines, buildings, roads, and other structures.

English (ing′ glish) *n.* the main language spoken in Great Britain, Canada, the United States, and some other countries. —*adj.* of or from England.

enjoy (en joi′) *v.* to get pleasure from something. **enjoying. enjoyed.**

enjoyable (en joi′ ə bəl) *adj.* giving pleasure: *an enjoyable party.* —**enjoyably** *adv.*

enjoyment (en joi′ mənt) *n.* pleasure: *I get a lot of enjoyment out of going to summer camp.*

enlarge (en larj′) *v.* to make larger: *to enlarge photos.* **enlarging. enlarged.**

enormous (i nôr′ məs) *adj.* very large; huge. —**enormously** *adv.*

enough (i nuf′) *adj.* as much or as many as needed or wanted: *Do you have enough time to go to the store?*

enrol, enroll (en rōl′) *v.* to sign up or register: *Alice and her friends enrolled in summer camp.* **enrolling. enrolled.**

ensure (en shūr′) *v.* to make certain: *Please ensure that you bring a pair of waterproof boots with you because it may rain.* **ensuring. ensured.**

enter (en′ tər) *v.* **1.** to go in. **2.** to join: *Sandy will enter the contest.* **entering. entered.**

entertain (en′ tər tān′) *v.* **1.** to amuse: *The clowns entertained the children.* **2.** to hold a party and have guests: *Tam entertained his friends on his birthday.* **entertaining. entertained.**

entertainment (en′ tər tān′ mənt) *n.* something that entertains you, such as a movie or play.

enthusiasm (en thū′ zē az′ əm) *n.* a strong interest in or excitement over something: *He showed his enthusiasm for the new movie by telling his friends to see it.*

enthusiastic (en thū′ zē as′ tik) *adj.* being strongly interested in or excited about something: *Christina is so enthusiastic about drawing that she always carries paper and pencils.* —**enthusiastically** *adv.*

entire (en tīr′) *adj.* the whole of anything: *The entire crew was saved from drowning.*

entirely (en tīr′ lē) *adv.* totally; completely: *They are entirely happy with all the gifts they received.*

entrance (en′ trəns) *n.* a way in; a doorway: *the entrance to the theatre.*

entrance (en trans′) *v.* to delight; to fill with pleasure: *We were entranced by the beautiful music.* **entrancing. entranced.**

entry (en′ trē) *n.* **1.** a going in; a way in: *The entry to the stage is through the side door.* **2.** a person who takes part in a contest: *There are ten entries in the dance contest.* **3.** a word that is listed in a dictionary: *The next entry in this dictionary is* **envelope**. *pl.* **entries.**

envelope (en′ və lōp *or* on′ və lōp) *n.* a folded and sealed paper cover for a letter.

envious (en′ vē əs) *adj.* feeling envy or jealousy: *He's envious of my new tape player.* —**enviously** *adv.*

environment (en vī′ rən mənt) *n.* all the things that are around people, animals, and plants: *The environment around the factory is not clean.*

environmental (en vī′ rən men′ təl) *adj.* having to do with the environment: *Pollution is an environmental problem.* —**environmentally** *adv.*

envy (en′ vē) *v.* to feel jealous: *He envies his sister because she has a new bike.* **envying. envied.** he **envies.**

epidemic (ep′ ə dem′ ik) *n.* a rapid spreading of a disease in which many people get sick at the same time: *There is a flu epidemic in our school.*

episode (ep′ ə sōd) *n.* **1.** an event. **2.** a part of a story that continues: *I missed the last episode of my favourite TV series.*

equal (ē′ kwəl) *adj.* having the same number or value as something else: *The cat and the pup are equal in size.* —*v.* in mathematics, to be the same as; the symbol is =. **equalling. equalled.**

equation (i kwā′ zhən) *n.* in mathematics, a statement that two quantities are equal: *A simple equation is "4 times 3 equals 6 times 2."*

equator (i kwā′ tər) *n.* an imaginary circle around the middle of the world: *The equator is halfway between the North and South Poles.*

equestrian (i kwes′ trē ən) *n.* a person who rides horses. —*adj.* having to do with horseback riding: *the equestrian events in the Olympics.*

equip (i kwip′) *v.* to provide someone with everything necessary: *to equip a hockey team with uniforms, sticks, and pucks.* **equipping. equipped.**

equipment (i kwip′ mənt) *n.* items you need in order to do certain jobs or play certain sports: *We used new hockey equipment in our first game of the season.*

era (ē′ ra *or* e′ ra) *n.* a particular period of time in history: *Dinosaurs lived during the Mesozoic era.*

erase (i rās′) *v.* to rub out: *Please erase the writing on the board.* **erasing. erased.**

eraser (i rās′ ər) *n.* something used for rubbing out writing: *a pencil eraser; a chalkboard eraser.*

erect (i rekt′) *adj.* standing straight: *The soldier stood erect.* —*v.* to build or construct: *A new school will be erected on this street.* **erecting. erected.**

erode (i rōd′) *v.* to wear away slowly over time: *The ocean waves are eroding the steep hillside.* **eroding. eroded.**

erosion (i rō′ zhən) *n.* the act of eroding: *The erosion of soil can be caused by water or wind.*

errand (er′ ənd) *n.* a small trip made to collect and deliver a message or package.

error (er′ ər) *n.* a mistake.

escalator (es′ kə lā′ tər) *n.* a moving stairway.

escape (es kāp′) *n.* a getting free: *a lucky escape from danger.* —*v.* to get away: *to escape from prison.* **escaping. escaped.**

Escape comes from the Latin words *ex* ("out of") and *cappa* ("cape" or "coat"). The next time you see someone take a coat off, you can say, "Ah, you've escaped!"

escort (es′ kȯrt) *n.* a person or group that goes along with another, often to protect or as a sign of respect: *The winning baseball team was given a police escort at the parade.*

escort (es kȯrt′) *v.* to go with someone as an escort: *Will you escort me to the movies?* **escorting. escorted.**

especially (es pesh′ əl ē) *adv.* most of all: *I like dogs, especially collies.*

essay (es′ ā) *n.* a short piece of writing on a certain subject: *I am writing a two-page essay on acid rain. pl.* **essays.**

essential (ə sen′ shəl) *adj.* necessary and important: *To play the piano well, it is essential to practise every day.*

establish (es tab′ lish) *v.* to set up; to form: *to establish rules; to establish a company.* **establishing. established.**

estate (e stāt′) *n.* **1.** the money and property that a person leaves when he or she dies. **2.** a large house on a large piece of property.

estimate (es′ tə mət) *n.* a guess about the size, amount, or value of something: *My estimate is that the tree is five metres tall.*

estimate (es′ tə māt′) *v.* to guess the size, amount, or value of something: *She estimated that there were a hundred people waiting in line outside.* **estimating. estimated.**

etc. (et set′ ər ə) short for **et cetera**, which means "and other things" or "and so on."

eternal (i tùrn′ əl) *adj.* lasting forever. —**eternally** *adv.*

eternity (i tùrn′ ə tē) *n.* **1.** all of time. **2.** a period of time that seems to go on forever: *The audience waited for an eternity to find out who won the contest. pl.* **eternities.**

ethnic (eth′ nik) *adj.* having to do with the different cultures, languages, and beliefs of different people: *There are many ethnic groups in our province.*

European (yūr′ ə pē′ ən) *n.* a person born in or living in the continent of Europe. —*adj.* having to do with the continent of Europe.

evaporate (i vap′ ə rāt′) *v.* to change from liquid into vapour or gas when heated. **evaporating. evaporated.**

eve (ēv) *n.* **1.** evening. **2.** the day before a holiday: *New Year's eve.*

even (ē′ vən) *adj.* **1.** smooth; level: *an even piece of wood.* **2.** tied: *At the end of the game, the score was even.* **3.** able to be divided by two: *Eight is an even number.* —*adv.* **1.** still; yet: *You will play the piano even better if you practise more.* **2.** although not expected: *Even my youngest brother came to see the play.* —*v.* to make smooth, level, or equal.

get even to take revenge: *I got even for my friend's practical joke by ignoring it.*

evening (ēv′ ning) *n.* **1.** the early part of the night. **2.** the time between day and night.

event (ē vent′) *n.* **1.** a happening: *current events.* **2.** one of the activities in a sports meet: *The high jump was the third event.*

eventually (i ven′ chū ə lē) *adv.* finally; in the end.

ever (ev′ ər) *adv.* at any time: *If you're ever in town, come and see me.*

evergreen (ev′ ər grēn′) *n.* a tree that is always green and does not drop its leaves or needles all at once: *The pine is an evergreen.*

evergreen

every (ev′ rē) *adj.* each: *I pass the house every day.*

every other every second (thing): *Our team practises every other day—on Mondays, Wednesdays, and Fridays.*

everybody (ev′ rē bud′ ē) *pron.* **1.** each person. **2.** all the people: *Is everybody here?*

everyday (ev′ rē dā′) *adj.* happening every day, or likely to happen every day; usual; ordinary: *Eating breakfast is an everyday event.*

everyone (ev′ rē wun′) *pron.* each person; everybody: *Is everyone going to the game?*

everything (ev′ rē thing′) *pron.* **1.** each thing. **2.** all the things: *Everything is ready for the party.*

everywhere (ev′ rē wer′ *or* ev′ rē hwer′) *adv.* in every place: *We looked everywhere for my lost key.*

evidence (ev′ ə dəns) *n.* information that helps prove something: *The evidence gathered by the police showed that two people had committed the crime.*

evident (ev′ ə dənt) *adj.* able or easy to be seen or understood; obvious: *It is evident from your answer that you have not been listening.* —**evidently** *adv.*

evil (ē′ vəl) *adj.* harmful; bad: *an evil deed.*

evolve (i volv′) *v.* to develop in a gradual and natural way: *Over many years, Canada has evolved into a country with many cultures.* **evolving. evolved.**

ewe (yū) (*masc.* **ram**) *n.* a female sheep.

> **ex–** is a prefix that means "past" or "former." An "ex-mayor" no longer serves as mayor.

exact (eg zakt′) *adj.* completely right; correct: *The exact time is two minutes past one.*

exactly (eg zakt′ lē) *adv.* precisely; without mistake: *The clock shows exactly the right time.*

exaggerate (eg zaj′ ər āt′) *v.* to say something is bigger, better, or worse than it really is: *You're exaggerating when you say that dog is as big as a horse!* **exaggerating. exaggerated.**

exam, examination (eg zam′, eg zam′ ə nā′ shən) *n.* **1.** a careful check: *a physical examination.* **2.** a test of knowledge: *a history exam.*

examine (eg zam′ ən) *v.* **1.** to look at closely and carefully. **2.** to test someone's knowledge of a subject. **examining. examined.**

example (eg zam′ pəl) *n.* **1.** a model to be copied: *to set a good example.* **2.** something to use as a sample; a case: *Give me an example of a provincial capital.*

excavate (eks′ kə vāt′) *v.* to dig out from the earth: *Dinosaur fossils were excavated from the ground.* **excavating. excavated.**

exceed (ek sēd′) *v.* to go beyond; to be more or greater than: *The cost of this book exceeds the amount of money I have in my wallet.* **exceeding. exceeded.**

excellent (ek′ sə lənt) *adj.* very, very good.

except (ek sept′) *prep.* other than; leaving out: *Everyone except Joanne went to the fair.*

Be careful not to mix up **except** with "accept"; "accept" means to take something that is offered.

exchange (eks chānj′) *v.* to give one thing in return for another: *Jocelyn exchanged an Australian stamp for an old Canadian one.* **exchanging. exchanged.**

excite (ek sīt′) *v.* to stir up the feelings of: *to excite shoppers by announcing a big sale.* **exciting. excited.**

excited (ek sī′ təd) *adj.* stirred up: *The excited puppy wagged its tail.*

excitement (ek sīt′ mənt) *n.* the condition of being excited: *There was a lot of excitement when the team was introduced.*

exciting (ek sīt′ ing) *adj.* thrilling.

exclaim (eks klām′) *v.* to shout out with excitement. **exclaiming. exclaimed.**

exclamation (eks′ klə mā′ shən) *n.* an excited shout.

exclamation mark a mark (!) put at the end of a sentence to show a strong emotion such as excitement, joy, surprise, or anger: *Hurray! We have won!*

exclude (eks klūd′) *v.* to keep out or leave out: *Don't exclude me from the basketball team just because I am short.* **excluding. excluded.**

excuse (eks kyūs′) *n.* a reason you give for something: *an excuse for being late.*

excuse (eks kyūz′) *v.* to forgive: *Please excuse me for leaving early. I'm in a hurry today.* **excusing. excused.**

execute (ek′ sə kyūt′) *v.* to put someone to death by law. **executing. executed.**

exercise (ek′ sər sīz′) *n.* **1.** something that gives you practice: *an arithmetic exercise.* **2.** an activity for training your body or mind: *Swimming is good exercise.* —*v.* to train the body or mind. **exercising. exercised.**

exhale (eks′ hāl) *v.* to breathe out. **exhaling. exhaled.**

exhaust (eg zost′) *n.* used steam or gas that escapes from an engine. —*v.* to tire out completely: *The long climb exhausted us.* **exhausting. exhausted.**

exhibit (eg zib′ ət) *n.* a public display of things such as school projects, paintings, or old cars. —*v.* to show or display something. **exhibiting. exhibited.**

exhibition (ek′ sə bish′ ən) *n.* **1.** a show; a display: *an exhibition of pictures in an art gallery.* **2.** a large fair: *The Canadian National Exhibition is held in Toronto each summer.*

exist (eg zist′) *v.* **1.** to live: *Rabbits exist on wild plants.* **2.** to be real: *Do you believe that aliens exist?* **existing. existed.**

exit (eg zit′ *or* ek sit′) *n.* a way out: *The exit from the hall was marked with a sign.* —*v.* to leave; to quit: *to exit a room; to exit a computer program.* **exiting. exited.**

exotic (eg zot′ ik) *adj.* rare, unusual, and often from a faraway place: *When we went to Hawaii, we saw exotic birds and flowers.*

expand (eks pand′) *v.* to grow bigger: *Many objects expand when they are heated. They contract when they are cooled down.* **expanding. expanded.**

expect (eks pekt′) *v.* to think something will happen: *I expect to see my brother tomorrow.* **expecting. expected.**

expedition (eks pə dish′ ən) *n.* a journey for some special purpose: *a hiking expedition.*

expel (eks pel′) *v.* **1.** to force out: *to expel air from a tire.* **2.** to dismiss someone from a school or club for bad behaviour. **expelling. expelled.**

expense (eks pens′) *n.* a cost: *What were your expenses on your long trip?*

expensive (eks pen′ siv) *adj.* costing a lot: *an expensive piece of jewellery.* —**expensively** *adv.* (*opp.* **inexpensive.**)

experience (eks pēr′ ē əns) *n.* **1.** skills and knowledge gained by having done things for a long time: *My uncle has experience as a builder.* **2.** what happens to you: *We shared our camp experiences.* —*v.* **1.** to feel. **2.** to have happen to you: *They experienced good weather on their holiday.* **experiencing. experienced.**

experienced (eks pēr′ ē ənst) *adj.* good at something because of practice: *Ms. Fredricks is an experienced carpenter.* (*opp.* **inexperienced.**)

experiment (eks per′ ə mənt) *n.* a test to find what will happen: *a science experiment.* —*v.* to test in order to find out what will happen: *Rajih experimented with several different coloured paints in his art class.* **experimenting. experimented.**

expert (eks′ pùrt) *n.* someone who knows a lot about a subject: *an expert in history.*

expire (eks pīr′) *v.* to come to an end: *Ben renewed his library card just before it expired.* **expiring. expired.**

explain (eks plān′) *v.* to describe the meaning of something: *The coach explained the rules carefully.* **explaining. explained.**

explanation (eks′ plə nā′ shən) *n.* a reason: *The science teacher gave us an explanation of why it gets cold in winter and warm in summer.*

explode (eks plōd′) *v.* to burst into pieces; to blow up. **exploding. exploded.**

explore (eks plȯr′) *v.* **1.** to look around: *to explore an old castle.* **2.** to travel to find out about new lands. **exploring. explored.**

explosion (eks plō′ zhən) *n.* a bursting into pieces; a blowing up.

explosive (eks plō siv) *n.* something that can explode: *Gunpowder is an explosive.* —*adj.* likely to explode.

export (eks′ pȯrt) *n.* a product sent by one country to another: *Wheat is a Canadian export.* —*v.* to send goods out of a country: *Canada exports wheat to many countries.* **exporting. exported.**

expose (eks pōz′) *v.* to uncover or to display something completely: *She rolled up her sleeve and exposed the bruise on her elbow.* **exposing. exposed.**

express (eks pres′) *n.* a fast bus or train that makes only a few stops. *pl.* **expresses.** —*v.* to tell or show through words, actions, or a look on your face: *Jill's smile expressed her happiness at the good news.* **expressing. expressed.**

expression (eks presh′ ən) *n.* **1.** a look on your face: *a worried expression.* **2.** a saying that expresses a thought: *My brother's favourite expression is "We're all in the same boat."*

exquisite (eks kwi′ zət) *adj.* very beautiful: *an exquisite sunset.* —**exquisitely** *adv.*

extend (eks tend′) *v.* **1.** to make larger or longer: *to extend a table.* **2.** to go on: *This road extends past the school.* **extending. extended.**

extension (eks ten′ shən) *n.* **1.** something that is added on: *We are building an extension to our house that will give us three more rooms.* **2.** an extra telephone that is connected to the main line.

extensive (eks ten′ səv) *adj.* covering a large area: *an extensive garden; an extensive shopping list; extensive knowledge.* —**extensively** *adv.*

extent (eks tent′) *n.* a degree; a limit: *I agree with your opinion, to a certain extent but not entirely.*

exterior (eks tēr′ ē ər) *n.* the outside of anything: *The exterior of the boat was painted green.*

exterminate (eks tər′ mə nāt′) *v.* to get rid of by destroying: *to exterminate bugs in the building.* **exterminating. exterminated.**

extinct (eks tingkt′) *adj.* no longer existing: *Dinosaurs have been extinct for millions of years.*

extinguish (eks ting′ gwish) *v.* to put out a flame or fire. **extinguishing. extinguished.**

extra (eks′ trə) *adj.* more than expected; additional: *Do you have an extra pencil that I may borrow? I've lost mine.*

extract (eks trakt′) *v.* to pull out something, often with force: *to extract a tooth.* **extracting. extracted.**

extraordinary (eks trȯr′ də ner′ ē *or* eks′ trə ȯr′ də ner′ ē) *adj.* very unusual. —**extraordinarily** *adv.*

extravagant (eks trav′ ə gənt) *adj.* spending more than you can afford or more than is necessary: *Giving me twenty gifts for my birthday is too extravagant.* —**extravagantly** *adv.*

extreme (eks trēm′) *adj.* **1.** very great: *Take extreme care.* **2.** severe: *extreme cold.*

extremely (eks trēm′ lē) *adv.* very: *My puppy is extremely playful.*

eye (ī) *n.* the part of the body used for seeing.

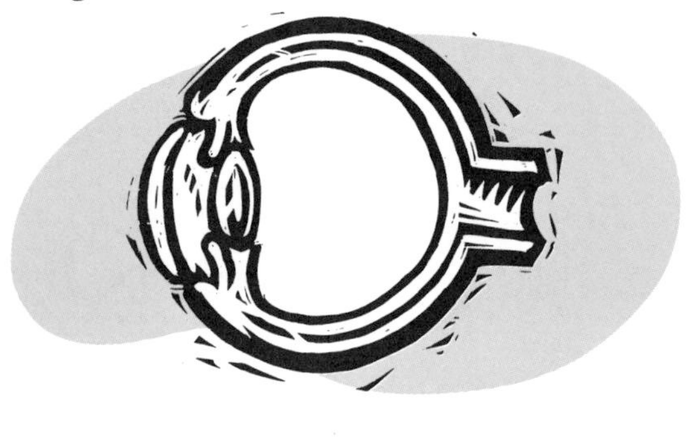

eye

eyebrow (ī′ brow′) *n.* the small ridge of hair over each eye.

eyeglasses (ī′ glas′ əz) *n. pl.* glass or plastic lenses that help you see better.

eyeglasses

eyelash (ī′ lash′) *n.* one of the hairs on the edge of your eyelid. *pl.* **eyelashes.**

eyelid (ī′ lid′) *n.* the flap of skin that covers the eye.

eyesight (ī′ sīt′) *n.* the power to see.

fable (fā′ bəl) *n.* a short story that teaches a lesson.

fabric (fab′ rik) *n.* cloth.

fabulous (fab′ yə ləs) *adj.* amazing; excellent; unbelievable: *The award-winning fireworks display was a fabulous sight.* —**fabulously** *adv.*

face (fās) *n.* **1.** the front of your head. **2.** the front of a clock, building, playing card, and so on. —*v.* to look toward; to have the front toward: *Our house faces a school.* **facing. faced.**

face-off (fās′ of′) *n.* in some sports, the moment when the puck or ball is put into play.

facility (fə sil′ ə tē) *n.* an ability to do something easily: *She has a facility with numbers and can do difficult multiplication in her head. pl.* **facilities.**

facsimile (fak sim′ ə lē) *n.* **1.** an exact copy of something: *This is a facsimile of a letter written hundreds of years ago.* **2.** a fax. *pl.* **facsimiles.**

fact (fakt) *n.* something that is true or real: *After Sophie finished her history project, she checked her facts in the encyclopedia.*

factory (fak′ tə rē *or* fak′ trē) *n.* a building in which things are made, most often with the help of machines. *pl.* **factories.**

fad (fad) *n.* something that suddenly becomes very popular for a short time: *Wrinkled shirts were a fad last year, but nobody wears them now.*

fade (fād) *n.* **1.** to lose colour in sunlight or by washing: *The pants faded because there was bleach in the washing machine.* **2.** to become dim: *The light fades toward evening.* **fading. faded.**

Fahrenheit (fer′ ən hīt′) *adj.* a scale of temperature on which thirty-two degrees is equal to zero degrees Celsius.

Fahrenheit scale and Celsius scale

fail (fāl) *v.* to be unsuccessful; not to do something you try to do. **failing. failed.**

failure (fāl′ yər) *n.* **1.** an unsuccessful try. **2.** the condition of not working properly: *The storm caused a power failure.*

faint (fānt) *adj.* not clearly seen or heard; weak: *a faint light; a faint signature.* —**faintly** *adv.* —*v.* to feel dizzy and pass out: *John fainted after the accident.* **fainting. fainted.**

fair (fer) *n.* a market or show of farm animals or products: *a computer fair.* —*adj.* **1.** light in colour: *fair hair.* **2.** less than good: *This work is only fair.* **3.** honest: *The person was given a fair trial.* (*opp.* **unfair.**) **4.** not raining; clear: *fair weather.*

fairly (fer′ lē) *adv.* **1.** rather; quite: *Although the sun is not out, it's a fairly good day for a picnic.* **2.** in a fair way: *The judge treated the accused people fairly.*

fairy (fer′ ē) *n.* an imaginary small creature with magical powers. *pl.* **fairies.**

faith (fāth) *n.* belief; trust: *Because I have studied hard, I have faith that I will pass the test.*

faithful (fāth′ fəl) *adj.* loyal; able to be trusted: *Daniel is a faithful friend. He always keeps his promises.* (*opp.* **unfaithful.**) —**faithfully** *adv.*

fake (fāk) *adj.* copied; not real: *fake money; fake jewels.*

falcon (fol′ kən *or* fal′ kən) *n.* a kind of hawk that is sometimes used for hunting.

falcon

fall (fol) *n.* **1.** the season after summer; also called "autumn." **2.** a coming down from a higher position: *a bad fall.* —*v.* **1.** to drop from a high place. **2.** to happen: *My birthday falls on a Tuesday this year.* **falling. fell.** they have **fallen.**

falls (folz) *n. pl.* streams of water falling from a high place: *Niagara Falls.*

false (fols) *adj.* **1.** not true: *a false story.* **2.** not real: *false teeth.* —**falsely** *adv.*

fame (fām) *n.* the condition of being well-known: *Some people would rather have fame than fortune.*

familiar (fə mil′ yər) *adj.* common: *Birds are a familiar sight in these woods.* (*opp.* **unfamiliar.**)

family (fam′ ə lē *or* fam′ lē) *n.* **1.** a parent or parents and their children. **2.** close relatives. *pl.* **families.**

famine (fam′ ən) *n.* a great shortage of food, so that many people are starving.

famous (fā′ məs) *adj.* very well-known: *a famous pop singer.*

fan (fan) *n.* **1.** something that makes a cooling breeze: *an electric fan; a paper fan.* **2.** someone who likes and supports a sports team, a singer, an actor, or other person or things. —*v.* to cool with a fan. **fanning. fanned.**

fancy (fan′ sē) *adj.* special; not plain: *a fancy blouse; a fancier one; the fanciest one in the store.*

fang (fang) *n.* **1.** a long, sharp tooth of a dog or wolf. **2.** the poisonous tooth of a snake.

fantastic (fan tas′ tik) *adj.* amazing; unbelievable. —**fantastically** *adv.*

fantasy (fan′ tə sē) *n.* an imaginary thing or event; a daydream. *pl.* **fantasies.**

far (får) *adv.* a long way off; distant: *British Columbia and Newfoundland are far apart.* —*adj.* not near: *the far end of the road.*
so far up to now: *I have not been late for school so far this month.*

faraway (får′ ə wā′) *adj.* being a long distance away: *They lived on a faraway island.*

fare (fer) *n.* the price of a trip on a bus, ship, taxi, train, plane, or subway.

farewell (fer′ wel′) *n.* goodbye: *We said our farewells, then got on the train.*

farm (fårm) *n.* an area of land used to grow crops and raise animals. —*v.* to work on a farm. **farming. farmed.**

farmer (får′ mər) *n.* a person who runs a farm.

farther, farthest (får′ THər, får′ THist) see **far.**

fascinate (fas′ in āt) *v.* to be of great interest; to hold your attention: *These pictures fascinate me. I can't stop looking at them.* **fascinating. fascinated.**

fashion (fash′ ən) *n.* a modern style: *Bright colours are now in fashion.*

fast (fast) *adj.* quick; speedy: *a fast car.* —*adv.* quickly: *Ravi can run fast.* —*v.* to go without food: *Our family fasted for a day.* **fasting. fasted.**

fasten (fas′ ən) *v.* to tie, join, or close: *Please fasten the string around the box.* **fastening. fastened.** (*opp.* **unfasten.**)

fat (fat) *n.* the greasy part of meat. —*adj.* plump: *a fat cat; a fatter cat; the fattest cat on the street.*

fatal (fā′ təl) *adj.* causing death: *Three people died in the fatal boating accident.* —**fatally** *adv.*

father (fo′ THər) *n.* a man who is a parent.

father-in-law (fo′ THər in lo′) *n.* the father of a wife's husband or of a husband's wife. *pl.* **fathers-in-law.**

fatigue (fə tēg′) *n.* a feeling of being very tired: *I felt great fatigue after shovelling the snow off the driveway.* —*v.* to make very tired. **fatiguing. fatigued.**

faucet (fo′ sit) *n.* a device used for turning water on or off; a tap.

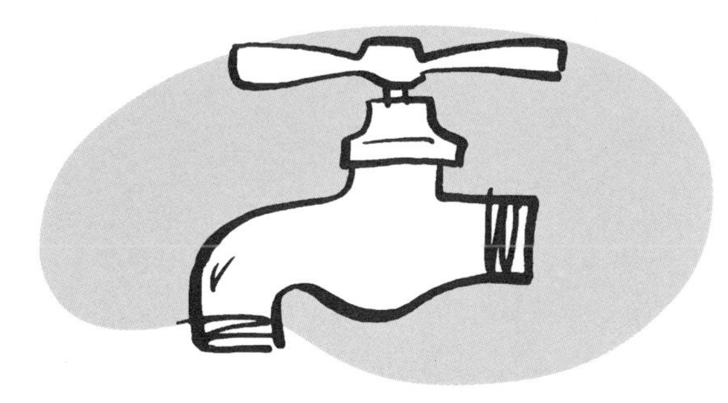

faucet

fault (folt) *n.* something that is wrong; a mistake: *It is my fault that we are late.*

favour, favor (fā′ vər) *n.* a kindness: *Will you do me a favour? Please walk my dog.*

favourite, favorite (fā′ vər it *or* fāv′ rit) *adj.* most liked: *Tennis is my favourite game.*

fawn (fon) *n.* a young deer.

fax (faks) (short for **facsimile**) *n.* **1.** a system that allows documents to be sent over a telephone line. **2.** a document sent over a fax machine. *pl.* **faxes.**

fear (fēr) *n.* a feeling that something dangerous may happen: *a fear of flying in an airplane.* —*v.* to be afraid of: *The farmer's son fears cows.* **fearing. feared.**

The word **fear** comes from **faer**, the Old English word for "danger." Why do we fear something? Because we think it may bring danger.

fearful (fēr′ fəl) *adj.* full of fear. —**fearfully** *adv.*

fearless (fēr′ ləs) *adj.* without fear; sometimes being too brave. —**fearlessly** *adv.*

feast (fēst) *n.* a very large meal, with lots of good things to eat.

feat (fēt) *n.* a deed of great courage or strength: *To walk on a tightrope is a great feat.*

feather (feTH′ ər) *n.* one of the many light, fluffy growths that cover a bird's body.

feature (fē′ chər) *n.* **1.** one of the main parts of your face: your eyes, ears, nose, and so on. **2.** a special part of something: *The nicest feature of the old house is the kitchen.*

February (feb′ yū er′ ē *or* feb′ rū er′ ē) *n.* the second month of the year.

fed (fed) see **feed.**

federal (fed′ ər əl) *adj.* having to do with the government of a country, not of a province or city.

fee (fē) *n.* a charge: *the dentist's fee.*

feeble (fē′ bəl) *adj.* weak; not strong: *After two days with the flu, I felt very feeble.* —**feebly** *adv.*

feed (fēd) *n.* food for animals: *We gave the hens some chicken feed.* —*v.* to give food to: *Please feed the baby.* **feeding. fed.**

feel (fēl) *v.* **1.** to touch: *Simon felt the key in his pocket.* **2.** to be in a mood: *Ruth feels happy because it's her birthday.* **3.** to have an opinion: *I feel this is what we should do.* **feeling. felt.**

feeling (fēl′ ing) *n.* **1.** the sense of touch: *By feeling, we can tell if something is hard, soft, warm, cold, and so on.* **2.** a mood, sense, or emotion: *I have a feeling that I will run well in the race.*

feelings (fēl′ ingz) *n. pl.* a way you feel about yourself, about someone else, or about something: *I hurt my brother's feelings when I said I didn't like his poem.*

feet (fēt) plural of **foot**.

fell (fel) *v.* **1.** see **fall**. **2.** to cut down: *to fell a tree.* **felling. felled.**

fellow (fel′ ō) *n.* a man or boy; a male companion.

felt (felt) *n.* a soft, thick cloth. —*v.* see **feel**.

female (fē′ māl) *n.* **1.** a girl or a woman. **2.** an animal that is, will be, or can be a mother: *A cow is a female. A bull is a male.*

feminine (fem′ ə nən) *adj.* having to do with women and girls: *"She" and "her" are feminine pronouns.*

fence (fens) *n.* a long wall of wooden rails, stones, or wire put around a garden or field. —*v.* to fight with swords. **fencing. fenced.**

fender (fen′ dər) *n.* a metal or plastic guard that protects a car or bicycle wheel.

fern (fürn) *n.* a plant with long, feathery leaves.

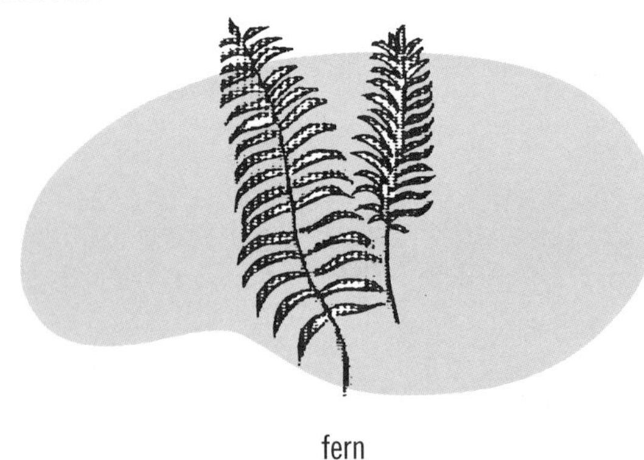

fern

ferocious (fə rō′ shəs) *adj.* fierce; savage: *a ferocious lion.* —**ferociously** *adv.*

Ferris wheel (fer′ əs wēl′) an amusement ride with a large, vertical wheel that rotates and that has seats hanging from its rim.

ferry (fer′ ē) *n.* a boat that carries people, cars, or goods across a body of water. *pl.* **ferries.**

fertile (für′ tīl *or* für′ təl) *adj.* able to produce: *Many vegetables grow in our garden because the soil is so fertile.*

fertilizer (für′ tə līz′ ər) *n.* a substance added to soil, to make it better for growing crops.

festival (fes′ tə vəl) *n.* a celebration of a special occasion, often with music, art, or drama: *Our school held a festival to display the students' art and crafts.*

fetch (fech) *v.* to bring something to a person: *The dog fetched the stick that I threw.* **fetching. fetched.**

fever (fē′ vər) *n.* **1.** a body temperature that is higher than usual. **2.** the common name for some illnesses that give you a high temperature.

few (fyū) *adj.* small in number: *A few students are absent from class today.*

fewer (fyū′ ər) *adj.* a smaller number: *There were fewer boys than girls at the party.*

> **Fewer** or **less**? Use **fewer** for numbers and things that can be counted: *There are fewer cars on the road today.* Use **less** for quantity or size: *There is less rain this morning than there was last night.*

fiancé (fē on′ sā′ *or* fē′ on sā′) *n.* a man who is engaged to marry a woman.

fiancée (fē on′ sā′ *or* fe′ on sā′) *n.* a woman who is engaged to marry a man.

fib (fib) *n.* a small lie that is usually harmless: *I told a fib when I said how much I liked his haircut.* —*v.* to tell such a lie. **fibbing. fibbed.**

fibre, fiber (fī′ bər) *n.* a thread of any kind.

fiction (fik′ shən) *n.* a made-up story: *I like to read about real events, but my favourite stories are fiction.*

fiddle (fid′ əl) *n.* a violin. —*v.* **1.** to play the fiddle. **2.** to fuss over something: *Stop fiddling with your keys!* **fiddling. fiddled.**

field (fēld) *n.* **1.** a piece of land used for crops or for pasture. **2.** a place where sports are played.

fiend (fēnd) *n.* a devil, a monster, or a very cruel person.

fierce (fērs) *adj.* savage; wild. —**fiercely** *adv.*

fifteen (fif′ tēn) *n., adj.* ten more than five: 15.

fifty (fif′ tē) *n., adj.* ten times five: 50.

fig (fig) *n.* a soft, sweet fruit, full of seeds: *Figs grow in warm climates.*

fight (fīt) *n.* a struggle; a quarrel; a battle. —*v.* to struggle or battle against someone or something. **fighting. fought** (fot).

figure (fig′ yər) *n.* **1.** a number symbol: *2, 9, and 74 are figures.* **2.** the shape of someone's body: *We saw the figure of a boy in the distance.*

figure of speech an expression in which words are used in an imaginative way, not according to their exact meaning. "To give a hand" is a figure of speech. It means to clap for someone.

figure out to find an answer or solve a problem by thinking, studying, trying out, and so on: *I figured out how many weeks I would need to save my allowance to buy a new coat.*

figure skate to skate on ice artistically, performing jumps, spins, and other moves. **figure skating. figure skated.**

file (fīl) *n.* **1.** a tool with a rough side: *A file is used for smoothing wood or metal.* **2.** a collection of papers, cards, or computer data arranged in a folder. **3.** a line of people, one behind another: *single file.* —*v.* **1.** to use a file as a tool. **2.** to store information in a file. **filing. filed.**

fill (fil) *v.* to put into a container until there is no more room: *to fill a pail with water.* **filling. filled.**

fillet, filet (fil′ ət, fi lā′) *n.* a piece of fish or meat with the bones removed.

filly (fil′ ē) *n.* (*masc.* **colt**) a young female horse. *pl.* **fillies.**

film (film) *n.* **1.** a roll of thin, light-sensitive material that you put into a camera to take pictures. **2.** a thin layer: *a film of dust on a shelf.*

filthy (fil′ thē) *adj.* very dirty: *filthy hands; filthier hands; the filthiest hands of all.*

fin (fin) *n.* **1.** a short, wing-like part of a fish: *Fins help fish to keep their balance when swimming.* **2.** anything shaped like a fin: *the tail fin of an airplane.*

fin

final (fī′ nəl) *adj.* last; end: *the final part of a story.*

finally (fī′ nəl ē) *adv.* at last: *She finally arrived at the party.*

finals (fī′ nəlz) *n. pl.* the last and most important games in a series.

finance (fī′ nans) *n.* managing money. —*v.* to provide money for something: *My parents financed my summer camp trip.* **financing. financed.**

financial (fī nan′ shəl) *adj.* having to do with money: *the financial section of the newspaper.* —**financially** *adv.*

find (fīnd) *v.* to discover; to locate: *Can you find the data on the computer?* **finding. found** (fownd).

fine (fīn) *n.* money paid as a punishment for breaking a rule: *a fine for returning a library book late.* —*adj.* **1.** sunny: *a fine summer day.* **2.** thin; delicate: *a pen with a fine point.* **3.** very good: *The fishers had a fine catch.* —*adv.* very well: *I feel fine.*

finger (fing′ gər) *n.* one of the five long tips on your hand.

> A **finger** can grasp or pick up something, and that explains how we get this word. Finger comes from the Old English word *fangan,* meaning "to grasp or seize."

fingernail (fing′ gər nāl′) *n.* the thin, hard layer at the end of each finger.

fingerprint (fing′ gər print′) *n.* a mark made by a finger.

finish (fin′ ish) *n.* the end; the last part: *the finish of a race. pl.* **finishes.** —*v.* to complete: *Please finish your breakfast.* **finishing. finished.**

fiord, fjord (fyȯrd) *n.* a long, narrow arm of the sea between steep banks or cliffs: *the fiords of British Columbia.*

fir (fûr) *n.* a tall evergreen tree that has needlelike leaves.

fire (fīr) *n.* the heat, light, and flames from something burning. —*v.* **1.** to shoot with a gun or rifle. **2.** to dismiss from a job: *You're fired!* **firing. fired.**

firecracker (fīr′ krak′ ər) *n.* a small cardboard tube filled with gunpowder.

fire engine a truck that has equipment for putting out fires.

firefighter (fīr′ fī′ tər) *n.* a person trained to put out fires.

fireplace (fīr′ plās′) *n.* a place built in a wall to hold a fire: *A fireplace is found under the chimney.*

fireproof (fīr′ prūf′) *adj.* not able to burn or burn easily.

fireworks (fīr′ wûrks′) *n. pl.* firecrackers, rockets, and other things that give off colourful lights and make a loud noise.

firm (fûrm) *n.* a business: *My mother works for a law firm.* —*adj.* steady and strong: *The soldier marched with firm steps.*

first (fûrst) *adj.* before or ahead of all others: *first prize.* —*adv.* before all others: *Jocelyn came first in the race.*

at first in the beginning: *I tried to explain the rules at first, but then I gave up.*

first aid emergency treatment given to a sick or injured person while he or she is waiting for trained medical workers to arrive.

First Nations the different aboriginal peoples of a country: *The Bella Coola are a First Nation of Canada's west coast.*

fish (fish) *n.* an animal that lives only in water and has gills for breathing, scales, and fins. *pl.* **fish** or **fishes.** —*v.* to catch fish. **fishing. fished.**

fisherman (fish′ ər mən) *n.* a person who catches fish. *pl.* **fishermen.**

> **Fisher** is a better word to use than fisherman, because fishing is done by both women and men.

fist (fist) *n.* a tightly closed hand.

fit (fit) *n.* a sudden attack: *a fit of laughter.* —*adj.* in good condition: *Exercise keeps you fit.* —*v.* to be the right size for something: *The bolt fits into this hole.* **fitting. fit** or **fitted.**

five (fīv) *n., adj.* one more than four: 5.

fix (fiks) *n.* a difficult situation: *The team is in a fix. They need a good pitcher, but they only have good batters. pl.* **fixes.** —*v.* **1.** to repair: *I'll fix the broken bike.* **2.** to fasten: *The camper fixed the flag onto the pole.* **fixing. fixed.**

fizz (fiz) *n.* a bubbling sound. —*v.* to make such a sound. **fizzing. fizzed.**

flabby (flab′ ē) *adj.* weak and limp: *flabby muscles.*

flag (flag) *n.* a piece of cloth with an emblem or decoration on it: *the national flag.*

flake (flāk) *n.* a small, thin chip or piece.

flame (flām) *n.* the glowing, jumping part of a fire. —*v.* to burst into a blaze. **flaming. flamed.**

flammable (flam′ ə bəl) *adj.* easily set on fire.

flannel (flan′ əl) *n.* a soft cloth made of fine wool.

flap (flap) *n.* a piece of paper or other material that is attached on one side only: *the flap on an envelope.* —*v.* to move up and down, or sideways: *A bird flaps its wings.* **flapping. flapped.**

flare (fler) *n.* a very bright blaze of light, which may be used as a signal. —*v.* to blaze up suddenly. **flaring. flared.**

flash (flash) *n.* a sudden light: *a flash of lightning. pl.* **flashes.** —*v.* to shine suddenly: *The car flashed its headlights.* **flashing. flashed.**

flash bulb a light bulb that is attached to a camera: *A flash bulb is used for taking pictures in dim light.*

flashlight (flash′ līt′) *n.* a small light, powered by batteries, that can be carried around easily.

flat (flat) *adj.* level; even: *This field is flat, but that one is flatter. The next field is the flattest of all.*

flatter (flat′ ər) *v.* to say too many nice things to someone. **flattering. flattered.**

flautist (flow′ tist) see **flutist**.

flavour, flavor (flā′ vər) *n.* the taste of something: *This ice cream has a mint flavour.*

flavouring (flā′ vər ing) *n.* a substance used to give a certain flavour: *Vanilla is a flavouring used in many desserts.*

flaw (flo) *n.* a fault or mistake: *This cup has a flaw—it has a chip on the edge.*

flax (flaks) *n.* **1.** a thin plant with small leaves and blue flowers. **2.** the fibres from this plant, which are spun into linen thread.

flea (flē) *n.* a very small, hopping insect without wings.

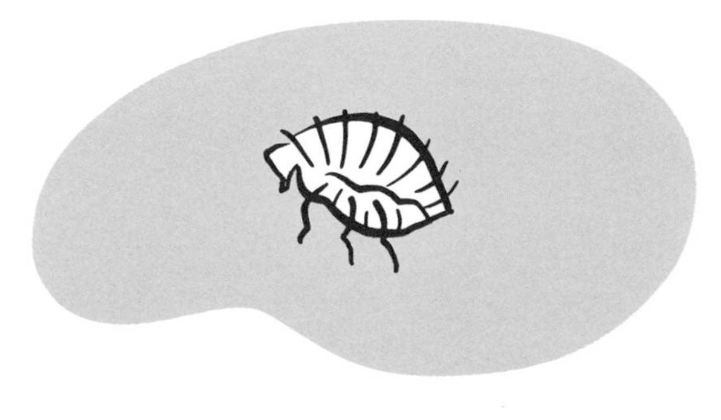

flea

The word **flea** is related to the word "flee." To flee means to run away. A flea is known for hopping away—off one animal and onto the next.

fleck (flek) *n.* a small patch of colour, light, or a substance: *Flecks of old paint are coming off the wooden fence.*

flee (flē) *v.* to run away from trouble or danger. **fleeing. fled.**

fleece (flēs) *n.* the wool of a sheep, especially the amount of wool that has been sheared from the sheep at one time.

fleet (flēt) *n.* a number of ships, planes, or cars in a group.

flesh (flesh) *n.* **1.** the soft part of your body that covers the bones. **2.** the soft part of a fruit or vegetable under the skin or peel.

flew (flū) see **fly**.

flexible (fleks′ ə bəl) *adj.* able to bend; not rigid or stiff: *The wire hanger is flexible, but the wooden one is not.* (*opp.* **inflexible.**) —**flexibly** *adv.*

flick (flik) *v.* to brush lightly with a whip or your finger. **flicking. flicked.**

flicker (flik′ ər) *v.* to shine with an unsteady light: *The candle flame flickered.* **flickering. flickered.**

flies (flīz) see **fly**.

flight (flīt) *n.* **1.** the movement of birds, insects, or aircraft through the air. **2.** an airplane trip. **3.** a set of stairs.

fling (fling) *v.* to throw hard; to hurl: *How far can you fling that stone?* **flinging. flung.**

flint (flint) *n.* a very hard stone that makes a spark when rubbed against steel.

flip (flip) *n.* a quick turning over: *The gymnast did three flips in a row.* —*v.* to turn over quickly: *Flip a coin.* **flipping. flipped.**

flipper (flip′ ər) *n.* **1.** the flat limb of a seal, walrus, or turtle. **2.** a rubber foot covering, shaped rather like a seal's flipper, used by swimmers.

float (flōt) *v.* to rest on water without sinking: *floating soap.* **floating. floated.**

flock (flok) *n.* a group of birds or sheep.

floe (flō) *n.* a mass of floating ice.

flood (flud) *n.* **1.** a great flow of water over a usually dry area: *Heavy rains flooded the town streets.* **2.** anything like this: *A flood of letters came through the mail slot.* —*v.* to become covered with water. **flooding. flooded.**

floor (flȯr) *n.* **1.** the bottom of a room, on which we walk. **2.** a storey of a building: *Toys are located on the fifth floor.*

flop (flop) *n.* a complete failure: *Our play was a flop.* —*v.* **1.** to drop down heavily: *I was so tired, I flopped into an armchair.* **2.** to fail completely: *The new movie flopped.* **flopping. flopped.**

floppy disk (flop′ ē disk) *n.* a small, flat plastic disk used to store computer data.

florist (flȯr′ ist) *n.* a person who sells flowers.

flour (flowr) *n.* the fine, whitish powder made by grinding grain.

flow (flō) *n.* a movement of water or air. —*v.* to move along smoothly in a stream: *The river flowed past our cottage.* **flowing. flowed.**

flower (flow′ ər) *n.* the blossom of a plant.

flower

flown (flōn) see **fly**.

flu (flū) *n.* short for **influenza**, a common illness with fever, aches, sometimes an upset stomach, or other symptoms.

fluffy (fluf′ ē) *adj.* **1.** covered with short hair or fur. **2.** soft and light: *Beat the eggs until they are fluffy.*

fluid (flū′ id) *n.* a substance that flows; a liquid: *Ink, water, and milk are fluids.*

flung (flung) see **fling**.

flurry (flu̇r′ ē) *n.* **1.** a sudden gust of wind. **2.** a sudden excitement: *As soon as we heard that Grandpa would be arriving, our house became a flurry of activity.* **3.** a light fall of snow blown around by the wind. *pl.* **flurries.**

flush (flush) *v.* **1.** to go red with excitement or a fever; to blush. **2.** to wash out with water. **flushing. flushed.**

flute (flūt) *n.* a wind instrument made of wood or metal and shaped like a thin tube.

flutist, flautist (flū′ tist *or* flow′ tist) *n.* a person who plays the flute.

flutter (flut′ ər) *v.* to move back and forth quickly and gently: *The curtains fluttered in the breeze.* **fluttering. fluttered.**

fly (flī) *n.* one of several kinds of small insects with two wings: *a housefly; a blackfly. pl.* **flies.** —*v.* **1.** to move through the air on wings. **2.** to travel by plane. **3.** to make something stay up in the air: *We're going to fly a kite.* **flying. flew.** it **flies.** it has **flown** (flōn).

foal (fōl) *n.* a young horse or donkey.

foam (fōm) *n.* many small white bubbles: *the foam on a wave.* —**foamy** *adj.*

focus (fō′ kəs) *n.* **1.** the condition in which your eyes, a lens, or a camera has the sharpest image. **2.** the main interest: *The new panda is the focus of attention at the zoo. pl.* **focuses** (fō′ kəs′ əz) or **foci** (fō′ kī). —*v.* to get a sharp image by adjusting a camera, a lens, your eyes, and so on. **focusing. focused.**

foe (fō) *n.* an enemy.

fog (fog) *n.* a thick cloud of mist.

foggy (fog′ ē) *adj.* filled with fog: *a foggy day; a foggier day; the foggiest day of the year.*

foil (foil) *n.* a thin sheet of metal: *aluminum foil.*

fold (fōld) *n.* a crease caused by doubling something over. —*v.* to double something over. **folding. folded.** (*opp.* **unfold.**)

folder (fōld′ ər) *n.* **1.** a piece of cardboard that has been folded over and is used to hold papers. **2.** a collection of documents on a computer.

folk (fōk) *n. pl.* people: *city folk; country folk.*

folks (fōks) *n. pl.* relatives: *How are your folks?*

follow (fol′ ō) *v.* **1.** to go after: *to follow a leader.* **2.** to understand: *I don't follow what you are saying.* **following. followed.**

follower (fol′ ō ər) *n.* a person who believes and follows someone else's ideas: *the leader of the gang and his followers.*

fond of (fond uv) liking very much: *She is fond of dogs.*

food (fūd) *n.* what people, animals, and plants eat or take in to keep alive.

fool (fūl) *n.* a silly person. —*v.* to trick someone. **fooling. fooled.**

Fool comes from a Latin word *follis,* which means "leather bag." Some people thought that a fool resembled such a bag—an empty one, full of nothing but air.

foolish (fūl′ ish) *adj.* silly; not wise. —**foolishly** *adv.*

foot (fu̇t) *n.* **1.** the part of the leg on which you stand. **2.** the bottom part: *the foot of a hill.* **3.** a measure of length, equal to about thirty centimetres. *pl.* **feet.**

football (fu̇t′ bol′) *n.* **1.** a game in which an oval-shaped ball is kicked, passed, or carried to the goal. **2.** the large leather ball used in football.

footprint (fu̇t′ print′) *n.* the mark of a foot on soft ground or on a clean floor.

for (fȯr) *prep.* **1.** in return: *I'll give you fifty cents for a lemonade.* **2.** because of: *She was rewarded for her good deed.* **3.** as far as; as long as: *We hiked for ten kilometres. Then we rested for twenty minutes.* **4.** with a purpose: *The tub is for water.*

forbid (fȯr bid′) *v.* to tell someone he or she is not to do something: *I forbid you to go there alone!* **forbidding. forbade** (fȯr bād′) or **forbad** (fȯr bad′). I have **forbidden.**

force (fȯrs) *n.* **1.** power; strength. **2.** a group of people working together: *My aunt is a member of the police force.* —*v.* to make someone do something that he or she does not want to do: *She tried to force her brother to tell his secret.* **forcing. forced.**

forecast (fȯr′ kast′) *n.* a prediction of what the weather will be like: *Tomorrow's weather forecast predicts snow.* **forecasting. forecast.**

forehead (fȯr′ hed′) *n.* the part of your face above the eyes.

foreign (fȯr′ ən) *adj.* having to do with another country, not your own.

forest (fȯr′ əst) *n.* an area covered with many trees.

forestry (fȯr′ əs trē) *n.* the planting of and caring for trees and forests.

forever (fȯr ev′ ər *or* fər ev′ ər) *adj.* always: *I will love you forever.*

forge (fȯrj) *n.* a place where metal is made very hot and then hammered into shape: *a blacksmith's forge.* —*v.* to copy something and pretend it is the real one: *to forge someone's signature.* **forging. forged.**

forget (fər get′) *v.* not to remember: *Matthew forgot to mail the birthday card.* **forgetting. forgot.** she has **forgotten.**

forgetful (fər get′ fəl) *adj.* always or often forgetting something.

forgive (fər giv′) *v.* to pardon or excuse someone: *I forgive you for forgetting my birthday.* **forgiving. forgave.** you have **forgiven.**

fork (fȯrk) *n.* **1.** an eating utensil with prongs, used to pick up food. **2.** a garden tool with prongs, used to lift earth or roots. **3.** a place where a road or river divides.

form (fȯrm) *n.* **1.** a shape: *We shaped the wet sand in the form of a castle.* **2.** a sheet of paper with printed questions and spaces for the answers. —*v.* to make a shape: *to form snow into a ball.* **forming. formed.**

formal (fȯr′ məl) *adj.* **1.** following certain rules; official. **2.** not casual: *It was a formal party. All the guests were wearing their fanciest clothes.* (*opp.* **informal.**) —**formally** *adv.*

former (fȯr′ mər) *adj.* **1.** belonging to the past: *In former times, people travelled by horse.* **2.** the first of two things mentioned: *She enjoys volleyball and baseball, especially the former.*

formula (fȯr′ myə lə) *n.* **1.** a mixture used for feeding babies. **2.** a recipe used to make a product: *a secret formula. pl.* **formulas** or **formulae** (fȯr′ myə lē).

fort (fȯrt) *n.* a strong building made for defence.

forth (fȯrth) *adv.* forward: *The dog paced back and forth.*

fortress (fȯr′ tris) *n.* a fort. *pl.* **fortresses.**

fortunate (fȯr′ chə nət) *adj.* lucky. —**fortunately** *adv.*

fortune (fȯr′ chən) *n.* **1.** wealth; riches: *Our wealthy aunt has promised to leave us a fortune.* **2.** chance; luck: *By good fortune, the tennis court was free when we wanted to play.*

forty (fȯr′ tē) *n., adj.* ten times four: 40.

forward (fȯr′ wərd) *n.* a player on the front line in some sports. —*adj.* in front: *the forward position.* —*adv.* toward the front: *The soldiers marched forward.*

fossil (fos′ əl) *n.* the hardened remains of an ancient animal or plant.

> The Latin word *fossilis* means "dug up," which is how most **fossils** are discovered.

foster parents parents who care for a child as their own, even though the child is not related to them.

foul (fowl) *adj.* **1.** bad; horrible: *foul weather.* **2.** unfair: *foul play.* **3.** outside the limits: *a foul ball.*

fountain (fown′ tən) *n.* a jet of water shooting upward and falling back into a pool.

four (fȯr) *n., adj.* one more than three: 4.

fourteen (fȯr′ tēn) *n., adj.* ten more than four: 14.

fowl (fowl) *n.* a bird that is eaten, such as a chicken or turkey.

fox (foks) *n.* a wild mammal, with pointed ears and a bushy tail, that looks like a small dog. *pl.* **foxes.**

fox

fraction (frak′ shən) *n.* a part of a whole amount: *One-half (1/2) and one-quarter (1/4) are both fractions.*

fracture (frak′ chər) *n.* a break or crack. —*v.* to break or crack: *to fracture a bone.* **fracturing. fractured.**

fragile (fraj′ īl *or* fraj′ əl) *adj.* delicate; easily broken: *This glass vase is fragile.*

fragment (frag′ mənt) *n.* a chip or part of something: *Save the fragments from the broken vase, and we'll try to glue them back together.*

fragrance (frā′ grəns) *n.* a sweet, pleasant smell.

fragrant (frā′ grənt) *adj.* sweet-smelling: *a fragrant rose.*

frail (frāl) *adj.* weak; in delicate health: *a frail old cat.*

frame (frām) *n.* a border of wood or metal around something: *a picture frame; a window frame.* —*v.* to put a frame around. **framing. framed.**

Francophone (frangk′ ə fōn′) *n.* in Canada, a person whose main language is French.

frank (frangk) *adj.* saying what you really think: *I'll tell you my frank opinion.* —**frankly** *adv.*

frantic (fran′ tik) *adj.* wild with excitement: *The dog gave us a frantic welcome.* —**frantically** *adv.*

fraud (frod) *n.* tricking or cheating people out of something: *The store was accused of fraud when it sold used computers as brand-new.*

freckles (frek′ əlz) *n. pl.* light brown spots on the skin.

free (frē) *adj.* **1.** loose, not bound or controlled: *The dog was free to run.* **2.** costing nothing: *The movie is free.* —**freely** *adv.* —*v.* to let go: *She freed the trapped animal.* **freeing. freed.**

freedom (frē′ dəm) *n.* the state of being free.

freeze (frēz) *v.* **1.** to become very cold. **2.** to turn into ice. **freezing. froze** (frōz). it has **frozen** (frō′ zən).

freight (frāt) *n.* the goods carried by a truck, train, ship, or other transport vehicle; cargo.

freighter (frāt′ ər) *n.* a cargo ship.

French (french) *n.* the language spoken in France, Canada, and other countries. —*adj.* belonging to or coming from France.

French fries potatoes that have been cut into strips, then fried in fat.

French horn a large, brass musical instrument that is blown.

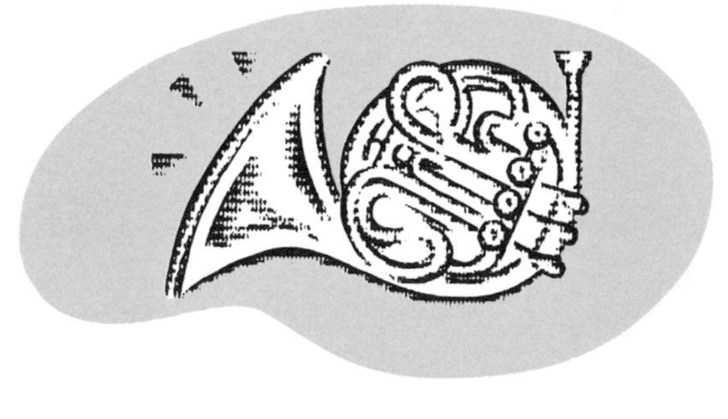

French horn

frenzy (fren′ zē) *n.* wild excitement: *The dog went into a frenzy when it saw the cat.*

frequent (frē′ kwənt) *adj.* happening or appearing often: *My cousin is a frequent visitor. She comes to our house about three times a week.* —**frequently** *adv.*

fresh (fresh) *adj.* **1.** new: *fresh ideas.* **2.** not stale: *fresh bread.* —**freshly** *adv.*

freshwater (fresh′ wo′ tər) *adj.* living in water that is not salty: *Freshwater fish live in lakes and streams.*

Friday (frī′ dā *or* frī′ dē) *n.* the sixth day of the week.

fridge (frij) *n.* a short name for **refrigerator**.

friend (frend) *n.* someone you know well and like.

friendly (frend′ lē) *adj.* like a friend; nice: *a friendly person; a friendlier one; the friendliest one I have ever met.*

friendship (frend′ ship) *n.* a relationship between friends.

fries (frīz) see **fry**.

fright (frīt) *n.* a scare; a fearful shock: *The noise of thunder gave us a fright.*

frighten (frīt′ ən) *v.* to scare someone. **frightening. frightened.**

frightening (frīt′ ning *or* frīt′ ən ing) —*adj.* scary. —**frighteningly** *adv.*

frill (fril) *n.* lace or cloth on the edge of a garment, used as decoration.

fringe (frinj) *n.* a border of many loose threads on the end of a cloth.

frog (frog) *n.* a small amphibian with smooth skin, powerful back legs for jumping, and a deep croak.

frolic (fro′ lik) *v.* to play in a merry way: *The sheep were frolicking in the meadow.* **frolicking. frolicked.**

from (frum *or* from) *prep.* **1.** out of: *Take a card from the deck.* **2.** between: *I played from four to five o'clock.* **3.** beginning at: *Read from the first line.* **4.** because of: *The plant died from the frost.*

front (frunt) *n.* the forward part, not the back: *The engine is at the front of a train.*

frontier (frun tēr′) *n.* **1.** the boundary between two countries. **2.** in earlier times, the part of a country not yet settled.

frost (frost) *n.* powdered ice you see on the ground on a cold day.

frostbite (frost′ bīt′) *n.* an injury caused when one or more parts of the body are exposed to extreme cold.

frosting (frost′ ing) *n.* the sweet layer on the top of a cake, also called **icing**.

frown (frown) *n.* a wrinkling together of the eyebrows. —*v.* to wrinkle your forehead when you are puzzled or angry. **frowning. frowned.**

froze, frozen (frōz, frō′ zən) see **freeze**.

fruit (frūt) *n.* the juicy part of a plant that contains the seeds. Many fruits are sweet and can be eaten: *Apples, plums, bananas, berries, tomatoes, and mangoes are fruits.* *pl.* **fruit** or **fruits.**

fry (frī) *v.* to cook in oil or fat. **frying. fried.** she **fries.**

frying pan a pan with a handle, used to fry food.

fudge (fudj) *n.* a very sweet, soft candy, made with butter, sugar, and a flavouring such as vanilla or chocolate.

fuel (fyū′ əl) *n.* anything that is burned to give heat or energy: *Coal, oil, and wood are fuels.*

> **–ful 1.** a suffix that means "full of." Something "beautiful" is full of beauty.
> **2.** a suffix that means "able to." Something "harmful" is able to harm you.

full (fu̇l) *adj.* filled completely: *The hall is full of people.*

full moon the moon when it appears perfectly round.

fully (fu̇l′ ē) *adj.* completely: *When your leg is fully healed, we will remove the cast.*

fumble (fum′ bəl) *n.* the handling of something in a clumsy way: *We lost the game because of my fumble.* —*v.* to handle something in a clumsy way: *to fumble the ball.* **fumbling. fumbled.**

fumes (fyūmz) *n. pl.* unpleasant gases or smoke from something burning.

fun (fun) *n.* enjoyment; amusement.
make fun of to tease or laugh at someone, sometimes in a hurtful way.

function (fungk′ shən) *n.* **1.** use: *What is the function of this machine?* **2.** a gathering: *There's a function at the theatre to celebrate the opening of the play.* —*v.* to work: *The flash bulb didn't go off. Is the camera functioning properly?* **functioning. functioned.**

fund (fund) *n.* a sum of money collected for a certain purpose: *The town set up a special fund to build a new park.* —*v.* to provide money for something: *My parents are going to fund my university education.* **funding. funded.**

funeral (fyū′ nər əl) *n.* a burial service for a dead person.

fungus (fung′ gəs) *n.* a kind of plant that has no leaves, flowers, or green colour: *Mushrooms, yeast, and moulds are fungi.* *pl.* **fungi** (fung′ gī *or* fun′ jī) or **funguses.**

funnel (fun′ əl) *n.* a tube shaped like a cone: *A funnel is used to pour liquid into a container with a small opening.*

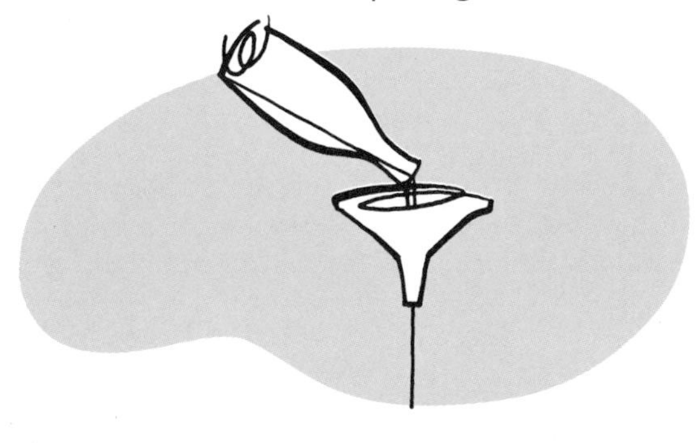

funnel

funny (fun′ ē) *adj.* causing laughter; amusing; comic: *My story was funny. Your story is funnier. Her story is the funniest one I have ever heard.*

fur (fu̇r) *n.* the soft, hairy coat of some animals.

furious (fyū′ rē əs) *adj.* very, very angry: *My brother spilled paint on my favourite shirt, and I was furious!* —**furiously** *adv.*

furnace (fu̇r′ nəs) *n.* **1.** a machine that heats a house or building. **2.** a very hot fire, used to heat water or to melt metals.

furniture (fu̇r′ nə chər) *n.* the objects needed in a room, such as a chair, table, dresser, bed, and lamp.

furrow (fu̇r′ ō) *n.* a long, narrow groove made in the ground by a plough or similar machine. —*v.* to wrinkle: *She furrowed her brow in concentration.* **furrowing. furrowed.**

furry (fu̇r′ ē) *adj.* made of fur or covered with fur: *a furry bunny; a furrier one; the furriest bunny of all.*

further (fu̇r′ ᴛʜər) *adj.* more: *Do you need further help?*

fuss (fus) *n.* bother; excitement: *My dog makes a great fuss when I come home from school.* —*v.* to bother with unimportant things. **fussing. fussed.**

fussy (fus′ ē) *adj.* **1.** making a fuss, usually over something unimportant. **2.** difficult to please: *a fussy baby; a fussier one; the fussiest one in the nursery.*

future (fyū′ chər) *n.* the time that lies ahead; what is still to happen: *I like reading stories about what life will be like in the future.*

fuzz (fuz) *n.* very short, fine hairs or fibres: *the fuzz on a peach.*

fuzzy (fuz′ ē) *adj.* **1.** covered with fuzz. **2.** blurred; not clear: *The photo is fuzzy because you moved when I was taking your picture.*

gable (gā′ bəl) *n.* the triangular wall under a sloping roof.

gadget (gaj′ ət) *n.* a clever device that does something useful: *This gadget is for taking the core out of an apple.*

gain (gān) *n.* an increase. —*v.* **1.** to get; to obtain: *to gain experience.* **2.** to increase: *I gained two kilograms from eating too much on my vacation.* **3.** to catch up to: *That mad bull is gaining on us!* **gaining. gained.**

galaxy (gal′ ək sē) *n.* a very large group of stars. *pl.* **galaxies.**

Our **galaxy** is called the Milky Way.
In Greek, *gala* means "milk."
Our galaxy looks something like
a splash of milk.

gale (gāl) *n.* a very strong wind; a storm.

gallery (gal′ ə rē) *n.* a building or large room for showing paintings, sculptures, and other works of art. *pl.* **galleries.**

gallon (gal′ ən) *n.* a unit of measure for liquids, equal to about 4.5 L.

gallop (gal′ əp) *n.* the fastest run of a horse: *The horse broke into a gallop at the unexpected noise.* —*v.* (for a horse) to run at full speed. **galloping. galloped.**

gamble (gam′ bəl) *n.* a bet or a risk: *We took a gamble that the weather would be fine, and ended up getting soaked in a downpour.* —*v.* **1.** to play a game of chance for money; to bet. **2.** to take a chance; to risk: *The sailors gambled their lives when they crossed the ocean in a tiny boat.* **gambling. gambled.**

game (gām) *n.* **1.** an activity done for fun: *a card game.* **2.** a contest or sport in which the players follow certain rules. **3.** wild birds or animals that are hunted.

gander (gan′ dər) *n.* a male goose.

gang (gang) *n.* a group of people going around together, sometimes for a bad purpose: *a gang of robbers.*

gangster (gang′ stər) *n.* a member of a gang of criminals.

gap (gap) *n.* an opening or space: *There's a gap in my mouth where my tooth fell out.*

garage (gə rozh′ *or* gə roj′) *n.* a building where cars or buses are stored or repaired.

gargle (går′ gəl) *v.* to wash out your mouth and throat by rinsing, but not swallowing. **gargling. gargled.**

garlic (går′ lik) *n.* a strong-smelling plant bulb, used in cooking.

garment (går′ mənt) *n.* any piece of clothing.

garter snake (går′ tər snāk) *n.* a small, harmless, striped snake common in North America.

garter snake

gas (gas) *n.* **1.** a form of matter that expands easily and fills up any container: *Air is made up of various gases, such as oxygen, carbon dioxide, nitrogen, and water vapour.* **2.** a mixture of gases burned as fuel: *Gas is used for heating and cooking.* **3.** short for **gasoline**. *pl.* **gases.**

gash (gash) *n.* a long, deep cut: *a nasty gash on his arm. pl.* **gashes.**

gasp (gasp) *n.* a sudden, deep breath. —*v.* to breathe in suddenly: *The swimmer gasped for air.* **gasping. gasped.**

gate (gāt) *n.* a hinged door in a fence or wall.

gateway (gāt′ wā′) *n.* an opening in a fence or wall that may be closed with a gate.

gather (gaTH′ ər) *v.* **1.** to collect: *to gather flowers.* **2.** to bring or come together: *A crowd gathered around the movie star.* **gathering. gathered.**

gathering (gaTH′ ər ing) *n.* a group of people or animals: *There was a large gathering in front of the town hall today.*

gauge (gāj) *n.* an instrument used for measuring: *The gas gauge showed that the car tank was almost empty.*

gaunt (gont) *adj.* very thin and bony: *gaunt from hunger.*

gauze (goz) *n.* very thin, loosely woven cloth: *Gauze is often used for bandages.*

gaze (gāz) *n.* a long, steady look. —*v.* to look steadily at for a long time: *We gazed at the stars.* **gazing. gazed.**

gear (gēr) *n.* a wheel with teeth around the edge, which fits into the teeth of other wheels; a cog.

gear

geese (gēs) *n.* plural of **goose**.

gem (jem) *n.* a precious stone; a jewel: *Rubies, emeralds, and diamonds are gems.*

gender (jen′ dər) *n.* in grammar, the classifying of certain words as masculine or feminine: *The words "empress" and "queen" have feminine gender.*

general (jen′ ər əl) *n.* an army commander. —*adj.* **1.** for all: *a general rule.* **2.** common; not rare: *What is the general opinion?* **3.** not detailed: *His comments were very general.*
  in general usually.

generally (jen′ ər ə lē) *adv.* **1.** usually: *We generally go to a hockey game once a week.* **2.** in a general way.

generate (jen′ ə rāt) *v.* to create or produce: *to generate electricity.* **generating. generated.**

generation (jen′ ər ā′ shən) *n.* a group of people born around the same time: *My mother and my uncle are of an older generation than my cousins and me.*

generous (jen′ ər əs) *adj.* sharing freely with others; unselfish. —**generously** *adv.*

genie (jē′ nē) *n.* a powerful magician or spirit in fairy tales.

genius (jēn′ yəs) *n.* someone who is extremely smart or talented. *pl.* **geniuses.**

gentle (jen′ təl) *adj.* **1.** soft; low: *a gentle voice.* **2.** mild, not rough: *a gentle breeze.* **3.** kind and soft: *He's such a gentle person.*

gentleman (jen′ təl mən) *n.* a man who has good manners. *pl.* **gentlemen.**

gently (jent′ lē) *adv.* softly; mildly.

genuine (jen′ yū ən) *adj.* real; true; not fake: *This bracelet is made of genuine gold.* —**genuinely** *adv.*

geographic, geographical (jē′ ə graf′ ik, jē′ ə graf′ ə kəl) *adj.* having to do with geography.

geography (jē og′ rə fē) *n.* the study of the world's climate, plants and animals, countries, peoples, industries, and resources.

geology (jē ol′ ə jē) *n.* **1.** the study of the earth's crust, rocks, soil, and minerals. **2.** the type of land, rocks, and minerals found in a region. —**geological** *adj.*

geometry (jē om′ ə trē) *n.* a branch of mathematics that deals with points, lines, angles, shapes, and solids.

gerbil (jür′ bəl) *n.* a small rodent that looks like a mouse and is often kept as a pet.

germ (jürm) *n.* a very tiny living thing that can cause illness and disease.

German shepherd (jür′ mən shep′ ərd) *n.* a large dog, with pointed ears, a black nose, and a brown and black coat.

gesture (jes′ chər) *n.* a movement of the head, hand, arm, or other body part that expresses a feeling or thought: *A hand wave is a gesture.* —*v.* to make such a movement: *They gestured to me to join them.* **gesturing. gestured.**

get (get) *v.* **1.** to gain; to obtain: *Let's get some food to eat.* **2.** to receive: *I got an A on my test.* **3.** to have: *Have you got a tissue?* **4.** to become: *to get cold; to get angry.* **getting. got.** I have **got** or **gotten.**

get along with to be friendly with or work well with.

get away with to do something bad or dishonest without being found out or punished.

get over to become better from an illness.

get together to meet with.

get up **1.** to get out of bed. **2.** to stand up.

ghost (gōst) *n.* the spirit of a dead person, which some people think exists.

giant (jī′ ənt) *n.* an imaginary person of enormous size and strength. —*adj.* huge: *a giant apple.*

gift (gift) *n.* **1.** something given; a present. **2.** a talent: *Ann has a gift for languages: she speaks English, French, and German.*

gigantic (jī gan′ tik) *adj.* enormous in size.

giggle (gig′ əl) *n.* a silly laugh. —*v.* to laugh in a silly way. **giggling. giggled.**

gill (gil) *n.* an opening on either side of a fish's head, used for breathing.

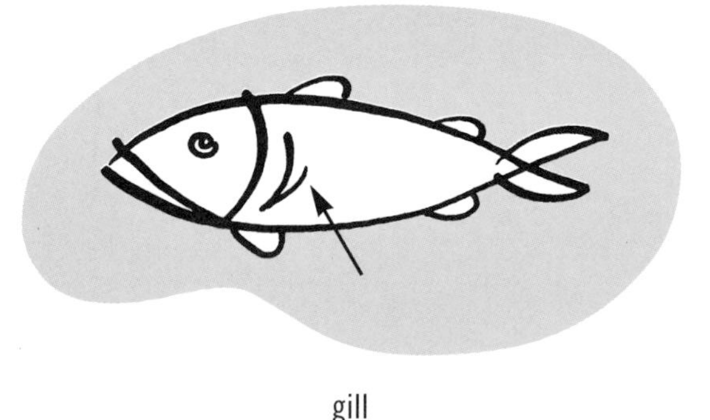

gill

ginger (jin′ jər) *n.* the spicy root of a tropical plant: *Ginger is sometimes ground into a powder that is used for baking.*

gingerbread (jin′ jər bred′) *n.* a cookie or cake flavoured with ginger.

giraffe (jə raf′) *n.* a tall African mammal with a very long neck and a spotted coat.

girl (gürl) *n.* a female child.

Girl Guides an organization for young girls aged nine to twelve that includes nature, volunteer, and leadership activities. **Sparks** and **Brownies** are junior members of the Girl Guides.

give (giv) *v.* **1.** to hand over something: *Please give me the book.* **2.** to hand over as a present: *What are you giving her for her birthday?* **3.** to cause: *Don't give them trouble.* **4.** to say: *Give me an answer.* **giving. gave.** They have **given.**

give in, give up surrender.

glacier (glā′ shər *or* glās′ yər) *n.* a large mass of ice that moves very slowly down a mountainside or along a valley.

glad (glad) *adj.* pleased; happy. —**gladly** *adv.*

gladiator (glad′ ē ā tər) *n.* in ancient Rome, a fighter who was paid to fight other people in an arena to entertain an audience.

glamorous (glam′ ər əs) *adj.* very attractive in a fascinating way: *The children agreed that their parents looked glamorous in evening clothes.* —**glamorously** *adv.*

glamour, glamor (glam′ ər) *n.* great charm: *He loved the excitement and glamour of the city.*

glance (glans) *n.* a quick look. —*v.* to take a quick look. **glancing. glanced.**

gland (gland) *n.* an organ that makes and releases a substance for use in the body: *The liver and the kidneys are glands.*

glare (gler) *n.* a strong, bright light: *the glare of the sun.* —*v.* to stare at someone in an angry way: *She glared at the boy who had rudely interrupted her.* **glaring. glared.**

glass (glas) *n.* **1.** a hard, clear substance, used for making windows, eyeglasses, and containers. **2.** a container used for drinking. *pl.* **glasses.**

glasses (glas′ əz) *n., pl.* short for **eyeglasses**.

gleam (glēm) *n.* a flash of light: *a gleam of sunshine through the clouds.* —*v.* to shine brightly: *I shined the dull teapot until it gleamed.* **gleaming. gleamed.**

glee (glē) *n.* joy; merriment.

glide (glīd) *v.* **1.** to slide smoothly: *The skaters glided over the ice.* **2.** (for an aircraft) to go down slowly without using a motor. **gliding. glided.**

glider (glī′ dər) *n.* a light airplane that has no motor.

glimpse (glimps) *n.* a quick look or view: *As we were hiking, we caught a glimpse of a fox before it dashed into the bushes.* —*v.* to get a quick view of something. **glimpsing. glimpsed.**

glisten (glis′ ən) *v.* to shine; to sparkle: *Dewdrops glisten in the sun.* **glistening. glistened.**

glitter (glit′ ər) *n.* **1.** a sparkling light. **2.** tiny pieces of sparkly material, used for decoration. —*v.* to sparkle or flash: *Diamonds glitter in the light.* **glittering. glittered.**

global (glōb′ əl) *adj.* affecting the whole world: *Pollution is a global problem.* —**globally** *adv.*

globe (glōb) *n.* **1.** a model of the world, in the shape of a ball. **2.** the earth; the world.

gloomy (glū′ mē) *adj.* **1.** dark; dim: *a gloomy cave.* **2.** miserable; sad: *a gloomy person; a gloomier person; the gloomiest person in the room.* —**gloomily** *adv.*

glorious (glȯr′ ē əs) *adj.* splendid: *What a glorious day!*

glory (glo′ rē) *n.* **1.** splendour. **2.** great honour and fame: *Our excellent choir has brought glory to our school for many years.*

glossy (glos′ ē) *adj.* smooth and shiny: *the glossy pages of a magazine.*

glove (gluv) *n.* a covering for your hand, with a separate part for the thumb and each finger.

glow (glō) *n.* a shine from something very hot: *the fire's glow.* —*v.* to give out light or warmth: *The hot coals glowed in the barbecue.* **glowing. glowed.**

glue (glū) *n.* a liquid or paste used to stick things together. —*v.* to stick together with glue. **gluing. glued.**

glum (glum) *adj.* sad or depressed; gloomy: *My sister looked glum—the other children had gone to the movies without her.* —**glumly** *adv.*

gnash (nash) *v.* to grind the teeth together: *The villain gnashed his teeth in anger.* **gnashing. gnashed.**

gnat (nat) *n.* a very small, biting fly.

gnaw (naw) *v.* to chew on: *The dog loves to gnaw on a bone.* **gnawing. gnawed.**

gnome (nōm) *n.* a dwarf in fairy tales.

go (gō) *v.* **1.** to move along: *to go to a place.* **2.** to leave: *to go home.* **3.** to function; to run; to work: *The car won't go.* **4.** to pass: *The time is going very quickly.* **5.** to reach: *How far does that road go?* **going. went.** he **goes.** he has **gone** (gon).

go ahead 1. to go in front. **2.** to start doing: *Go ahead on the project without me.*

go along with to agree with: *Your friends always go along with your ideas.*

go over to look over; to review: *Let's go over the math problem together to see where we made the mistake.*

goal (gōl) *n.* **1.** something you want and work for; an aim: *Her goal is to be an actor.* **2.** in sports such as hockey and soccer, a place where players must put a puck or ball in order to score. **3.** a point scored: *Our hockey team scored three goals.*

goalie, goaltender (gō′ lē, gōl′ ten′ dər) *n.* the player who defends the goal in hockey, lacrosse, and some other sports.

goat (gōt) *n.* a mammal that has straight, often long hair, horns that curve backward, and is raised to provide milk, meat, and sometimes wool.

gobble (gob′ əl) *n.* the sound that a turkey makes. —*v.* to eat something quickly and greedily: *We gobbled up the pizza in minutes.* **gobbling. gobbled.**

goblin (gob′ lən) *n.* a mischievous elf in fairy tales.

god (god) *n.* a being believed to have supernatural powers.

goddess (god′ əs) *n.* a female god. *pl.* **goddesses.**

goggles (gog′ əlz) *n., pl.* tight-fitting glasses worn to protect the eyes: *swimming goggles; safety goggles.*

gold (gōld) *n.* **1.** a precious, deep yellow, shiny metal, used to make coins and jewellery. **2.** the colour of gold. —*adj.* made of gold or having the colour of gold.

golden (gōl′ dən) *adj.* made of gold or looking like gold.

goldfish (gōld′ fish) *n.* a small, orange fish often kept as a pet. *pl.* **goldfish.**

golf (golf) *n.* a game played with clubs and a small ball on a large grass course: *In golf, the players try to hit the ball into holes.*

The game of golf began in Scotland. However, the word **golf** probably comes from a Dutch word, *kolf,* which means a stick or club.

gong (gong) *n.* a round, flat bell that makes a deep ringing sound when struck with a padded hammer.

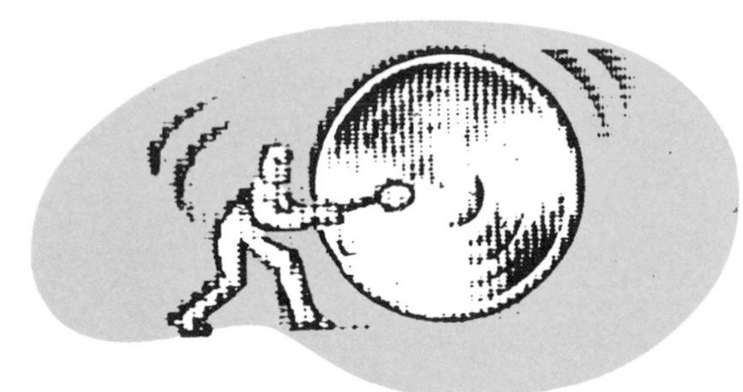

gong

good (gu̇d) *adj.* **1.** high in quality: *a good book; good work.* **2.** right; just: *a good deed.* **3.** decent; honest: *a good person.* **4.** pleasant: *a good time.* **5.** wholesome: *Fruit is good for you.*

for good permanently: *They left the town for good.*

goodbye (gu̇d′ bī′) *n.* an expression you say when leaving someone; farewell.

good-looking (gu̇d′ lu̇k′ ing) *adj.* pleasing to look at; attractive.

goodness (gu̇d′ nəs) *n.* the quality of being good.

goods (gu̇dz) *n., pl.* **1.** belongings: *We packed our goods in boxes before moving.* **2.** wares, products: *What goods are for sale in the market?*

goose (güs) *n.* **1.** a large water bird with a long neck and webbed feet. **2.** a silly person. *pl.* **geese** (gēs).

gopher (gō′ fər) *n.* a large, North American type of squirrel that lives in a hole in the ground: *Gophers are very common in the Prairies.*

gorge (gôrj) *n.* a narrow valley between high cliffs.

gorgeous (gôr′ jəs) *adj.* beautiful; magnificent: *a gorgeous sight.*

gorilla (gə ril′ ə) *n.* the largest and strongest ape: *Gorillas live in Africa.*

gory (gôr′ ē) *adj.* bloody: *a gory injury.*

gossip (gos′ ip) *n.* talk about other people that is not always true and is sometimes unkind. —*v.* to talk about others in such a way. **gossiping. gossiped.**

govern (guv′ ərn) *v.* to rule, control, or manage: *to govern a country.* **governing. governed.**

government (guv′ ərn mənt) *n.* **1.** the act of governing; rule. **2.** the people who govern a country: *The government made some new laws.*

governor (guv′ ər nər) *n.* someone who governs.

Governor General the person who represents the Queen (or King) in Canada.

gown (gown) *n.* a long dress.

grab (grab) *v.* to take hold quickly; to seize; to snatch: *The dog grabbed my hamburger when I turned around.* **grabbing. grabbed.**

grace (grās) *n.* a beautiful manner or movement: *The dancer moved with grace.*

graceful (grās′ fəl) *adj.* beautiful in movement: *a graceful figure skater.* —**gracefully** *adv.*

grade (grād) *n.* **1.** a school year or level: *He is in grade five.* **2.** a mark on a school test, project, and so on, showing how well the student has done. —*v.* to mark a school test, project, or other work. **grading. graded.**

gradual (graj′ ü əl) *adj.* happening little by little: *There has been a gradual improvement in the weather.* —**gradually** *adv.*

graduate (graj′ ü ət) *n.* a person who has completed a school or university course.

graduate (graj′ ü āt) *v.* to finish a school or university course and receive a diploma. **graduating. graduated.**

graduation (graj′ ü ā′ shən) *n.* **1.** the completion of a school or university course. **2.** the ceremony for giving out diplomas to graduates.

grain (grān) *n.* **1.** a type of grass plant whose seeds are used as food: *Corn, wheat, oats, and rice are grains.* **2.** a speck: *grains of dust.* **3.** the marks and lines in wood.

grain elevator a tall building in which grain is stored.

gram (gram) *n.* a unit for measuring mass; g is the symbol. 1000 g = 1 kg.

grammar (gram′ ər) *n.* the rules for using words in language.

granary (gran′ ər ē *or* grān′ ə rē) *n.* a building where grain is stored. *pl.* **granaries.**

grand (grand) *adj.* **1.** large in size: *A grand piano is larger than an upright piano.* **2.** great; splendid: *a grand display of flowers.*

grandchild (grand′ chīld′) *n.* a child of a son or daughter; a granddaughter or grandson. *pl.* **grandchildren.**

grandeur (gran′ jər) *n.* greatness; splendour.

grandfather, granddad, grandpa (grand′ fo′ THər, gran′ dad, grand′ pə) *n.* your mother's father or your father's father.

grandmother, grandma (grand′ muTH′ ər, grand′ mə) *n.* your mother's mother or your father's mother.

grandparent (grand′ per′ ənt) *n.* a grandfather or grandmother.

granite (gran′ ət *or* gran′ it) *n.* a hard rock with flecks of pink, black, grey, and clear minerals, used in buildings, monuments, and other structures.

grant (grant) *v.* to give or allow: *In the story we read, the wizard granted the little girl three wishes.* **granting. granted.**

grape (grāp) *n.* a small, round, juicy fruit that grows in bunches on a vine. Grapes are eaten raw and are also used to make jelly, raisins, and wine.

grapefruit (grāp′ frūt′) *n.* a round citrus fruit, larger than an orange, with a yellow skin and slightly sour taste.

graph (graf) *n.* a chart or diagram showing changes in measurements at different periods of time.

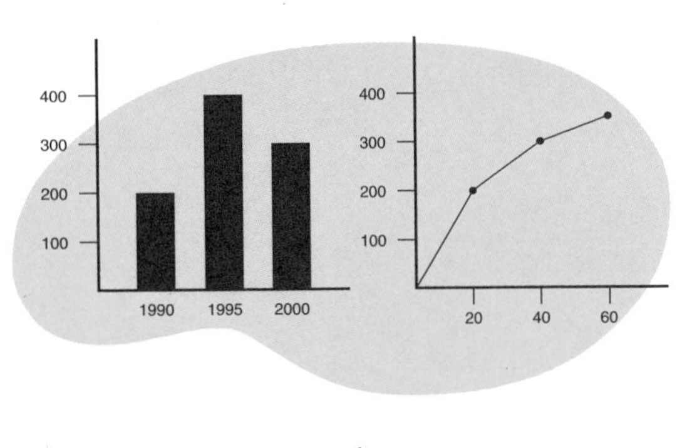

graphs

grasp (grasp) *n.* a firm hold. —*v.* to seize and hold firmly: *The man grasped the railing when he started to fall.* **grasping. grasped.**

grass (gras) *n.* a plant with narrow leaves: *A deep green grass with very short stalks is used in lawns.*

grasshopper (gras′ hop′ ər) *n.* a jumping insect with long back legs.

grate (grāt) *n.* a frame of metal bars for holding wood in a fireplace. —*v.* to shred into pieces by rubbing against a rough surface: *to grate cheese.* **grating. grated.**

grateful (grāt′ fəl) *adj.* thankful: *I am grateful that you helped me with my project.* —**gratefully** *adv.*

grating (grāt′ ing) *n.* a frame of bars that covers an opening.

grave (grāv) *n.* a place where a dead person is buried; a tomb. —*adj.* serious: *Her grave face showed me something was wrong.* —**gravely** *adv.*

gravel (grav′ əl) *n.* loose, small stones, used to cover roads.

graveyard (grāv′ yȧrd′) *n.* a place for burying the dead; a cemetery.

gravity (grav′ ə tē) *n.* the natural force by which the earth or another heavenly body pulls smaller objects toward its centre: *The earth's gravity causes objects to fall to the ground.*

gravy (grā′ vē) *n.* a sauce made from the juices of cooked meats.

gray (grā) see **grey**.

graze (grāz) *v.* to feed on grass: *Cows and sheep are animals that graze.* **grazing. grazed.**

grease (grēs) *n.* **1.** soft animal fat. **2.** thick oil: *car grease.* —*v.* to put grease on something: *Steve greased the baking pan so that the cake wouldn't stick to it.* **greasing. greased.**

greasy (grēs′ ē) *adj.* covered with grease: *a greasy piece of chicken; a greasier one; the greasiest piece of all.*

great (grāt) *adj.* **1.** large: *I paid a great amount of money for this gift.* **2.** important: *The automobile is a great invention.* **3.** extremely good: *a great artist.*

great-grandchild (grāt′ grand′ chīld′) *n.* a child of a grandchild; a great-granddaughter or a great-grandson.

great-grandparent (grāt′ grand′ per′ ənt) *n.* a parent of a grandparent; a great-grandfather or a great-grandmother.

Great Lakes a group of five large lakes in central-eastern North America: *The five Great Lakes are Lake Ontario, Lake Erie, Lake Huron, Lake Michigan, and Lake Superior.*

A quick way to recall the names of the Great Lakes is to think of the word "homes": Huron, Ontario, Michigan, Erie, Superior.

greatly (grāt′ lē) *adv.* very much: *I greatly appreciate your help.*

greed (grēd) *n.* a strong desire to get more than you need of something, such as food or money.

greedy (grēd′ ē) *adj.* wanting more than you need: *a greedy monster; a greedier one; the greediest one in the forest.*

green (grēn) *n.* the colour of grass. *—adj.* having this colour.

greenhouse (grēn′ hows′) *n.* a building made of glass or plastic panes, used for growing plants.

greet (grēt) *v.* to welcome: *The family greeted their friends at the door.* **greeting. greeted.**

greeting (grēt′ ing) *n.* **1.** a welcome. **2.** a message of welcome or good wishes: *A birthday greeting arrived in the mail.*

grey, gray (grā) *n.* a colour made by mixing black and white together: *Grey is the colour of dark clouds. —adj.* having this colour.

greyhound (grā′ hownd′) *n.* a tall, very slender dog that is used for racing.

greyhound

griddle (grid′ əl) *n.* a flat metal plate used for frying pancakes and other foods.

grief (grēf) *n.* deep sorrow due to loss: *I was filled with grief when my friend died.*

grieve (grēv) *v.* to feel very sad due to a loss or serious trouble; to mourn: *The family was grieved to learn of their son's car accident.* **grieving. grieved.**

grill (gril) *n.* a frame of metal bars on which food is placed for cooking over coals or a fire. *—v.* to cook on a grill. **grilling. grilled.**

grim (grim) *adj.* stern; harsh: *a grim look; a grimmer look; the grimmest look of all.* —**grimly** *adv.*

grime (grīm) *n.* dirt that is rubbed in and hard to remove: *We scrubbed the grime off the old floor.*

grin (grin) *n.* a broad smile. *—v.* to smile broadly. **grinning. grinned.**

grind (grīnd) *v.* **1.** to crush to powder: *to grind wheat into flour.* **2.** to rub together: *to grind your teeth.* **grinding. ground.**

grip (grip) *n.* a firm grasp: *She held the fifty-dollar bill in her grip. —v.* to hold firmly: *Don't grip my hand so tightly!* **gripping. gripped.**

grit (grit) *n.* a small bit of stone or sand: *I shook the grit out of my shoe.*

grizzly (griz′ lē) *n.* a large, powerful, North American bear. *pl.* **grizzlies.**

groan (grōn) *n.* a noisy sigh of pain, grief, or disappointment. *—v.* to make a groan. **groaning. groaned.**

grocer (grō′ sər) *n.* a person who sells food, especially fresh fruit and vegetables.

groceries (grō′ sər ēz) *n., pl.* food and household goods sold in a store.

grocery store (grō′ sər ē stȯr) *n.* a store that sells fresh food, canned food, and household goods.

groom (grūm) *n.* **1.** a man on his wedding day. **2.** a person who takes care of horses. *—v.* to make neat and tidy: *to groom a dog's coat.* **grooming. groomed.**

groove (grūv) *n.* a narrow slit or rut cut into plastic, wood, the ground, or other surfaces.

gross (grōs) *n.* twelve dozen (144). —*adj.* **1.** extreme: *a gross error.* **2.** coarse; vulgar: *gross behaviour.*

grotesque (grō tesk′) *adj.* distorted; not natural-looking: *a grotesque mask.*

grouch (growch) *n.* a bad-tempered, complaining person: *You're such a grouch!* *pl.* **grouches.** —**grouchy** *adv.*

ground (grownd) *n.* **1.** the earth's surface on which we walk. **2.** a piece of land for some special purpose: *a campground.*

groundhog (grownd′ hog′) *n.* a large, North American rodent that digs burrows or holes; also called a **woodchuck**.

group (grūp) *n.* a number of people or things that are together: *a group of singers.* —*v.* to arrange into groups: *I grouped my tapes according to the type of music.* **grouping. grouped.**

grouse (grows) *n.* a plump, wild bird that looks a little like a chicken and is often hunted as game. *pl.* **grouse.**

grouse

grove (grōv) *n.* a small group of trees.

grow (grō) *v.* **1.** to become larger naturally; to develop: *Acorns grow into oak trees.* **2.** to plant and raise: *to grow vegetables.* **3.** to increase: *The population grew rapidly.* **4.** to become: *to grow dark.* **growing. grew.** I have **grown.**

grow up to become an adult.

growl (growl) *n.* a deep, low, angry sound, such as made by an angry dog. —*v.* to make such a noise: *The lion growled in its cage.* **growling. growled.**

growth (grōth) *n.* the act of growing.

gruesome (grū′ səm) *adj.* frightening and disgusting: *The end of the scary movie was too gruesome for me.*

grumble (grum′ bəl) *v.* to complain: *My brother grumbles whenever it's his turn to wash dishes.* **grumbling. grumbled.**

grunt (grunt) *n.* a short, low sound that a pig sometimes makes. —*v.* to make such a sound. **grunting. grunted.**

guarantee (ger′ ən tē′) *n.* a promise to fix or replace a product if it breaks down: *The store gave me a two-year guarantee on my bike.* —*v.* to make such a promise: *The store guaranteed the computer for a year.* **guaranteeing. guaranteed.**

guard (gȧrd) *n.* someone who keeps watch and protects: *a security guard.* —*v.* **1.** to keep watch and protect; to defend: *to guard a bank from robbery.* **2.** to keep from escaping: *Guard the prisoners carefully.* **guarding. guarded.**

guardian (gȧr′ dē ən) *n.* a person who has the legal right to take care of someone too young, too old, or too sick to care for himself or herself.

guess (ges) *n.* an opinion about something without being sure of it: *My guess is that it will snow tomorrow.* *pl.* **guesses.** —*v.* **1.** to say what you think is true, without knowing for sure: *The stranger guessed my age correctly.* **2.** to suppose: *It's getting dark; I guess it's time to go.* **guessing. guessed.**

guest (gest) *n.* someone you invite to your home; a visitor.

guidance (gīd′ əns) *n.* direction; help; advice: *My parents gave me guidance on a possible career.* —*adj.* giving guidance: *The guidance counsellor explained different careers.*

guide (gīd) *n.* someone or something that leads or shows the way: *a tour guide.* —*v.* to lead; to show the way. **guiding. guided.**

guide word a word that appears at the top of a page in a dictionary. It tells you the first word or last word on the page: **Guide** *is a guide word on this page.*

guilt (gilt) *n.* **1.** the fact of having done something wrong: *The lawyer proved the criminal's guilt.* **2.** a feeling of shame for having done something wrong: *The student felt guilt over cheating on the test.*

guilty (gil′ tē) *adj.* **1.** having done wrong or committed a crime. **2.** feeling shameful for having done something wrong: *She felt guilty about taking the day off.*

guinea pig (gin′ ē pig) *n.* a small plump rodent with short ears and a short tail, often kept as a pet.

guitar (gi tȧr′) *n.* a musical instrument with a long neck and six strings that are plucked.

The *kithara* was the national instrument of ancient Greece. It had strings that were plucked. In Spain, a similar instrument was called the *guitarra.* In English, this instrument became known as the **guitar**.

gulf (gulf) *n.* a long bay of an ocean or sea that extends far inland: *the Gulf of St. Lawrence.*

gull (gul) *n.* a white bird, with a curved beak and webbed feet, that lives near water.

gulp (gulp) *n.* a large, quick swallow: *She drank the entire glass in three gulps.* —*v.* to swallow quickly without chewing. **gulping. gulped.**

gum (gum) *n.* **1.** a sticky juice from plants and trees. **2.** chewing gum.

gums (gumz) *n., pl.* the pink flesh around your teeth.

gun (gun) *n.* a weapon that shoots bullets or shells through a metal tube or barrel.

gunpowder (gun′ pow′ dər) *n.* a black explosive powder used in fireworks and guns.

guppy (gup′ ē) *n.* a small tropical fish, often kept in an aquarium. *pl.* **guppies.**

gush (gush) *v.* **1.** to pour out suddenly: *Water gushed from the broken pipe.* **2.** to praise in an emotional, excited way: *The family gushed over the new baby.* **gushing. gushed.**

gust (gust) *n.* a strong, sudden blast of wind.

gut (gut) *n.* **1.** the intestine. **2.** *n. pl.* **guts** (*informal*) courage. —*v.* **1.** to remove the inside organs of a fish, chicken, or other animal before cooking. **2.** to destroy the inside of a building: *Fire gutted the house.* **gutting. gutted.**

gutter (gut′ ər) *n.* a channel for carrying off waste water or overflowing water.

guy (gī) *n.* a fellow: *What good guys you are!*

gym, gymnasium (jim, jim nā′ zē əm) *n.* a large room for doing physical exercises and sports.

gymnast (jim′ nəst) *n.* an athlete trained in gymnastics.

gymnastics (jim nas′ tiks) *n., pl.* physical activities, such as stretches, flips, and turns, that develop the muscles.

gypsy (jip′ sē) *n.* a person belonging to a group of wandering people. *pl.* **gypsies.**

ha (ho) *interj.* a word that expresses laughter, triumph, or surprise: *"Ha! Ha! Ha!" they laughed.*

habit (hab′ it) *n.* an activity you do the same way all the time: *They have a habit of waking up very early.*

habitat (hab′ ə tat′) *n.* the type of place where a plant or an animal naturally lives and grows: *The ocean is the whale's habitat. The grasslands of East Africa is the lion's habitat.*

had (had) see **have**.

haddock (had′ ək) *n.* an ocean fish that can be eaten. *pl.* **haddock.**

haddock

hadn't (had′ ənt) a contraction (short form) of **had not**.

haiku (hī′ kū) *n.* a style of poetry that began in Japan: *There are three lines in a haiku. The first line has five syllables, the second has seven, and the third has five. Usually, a haiku focuses on nature.*

hail (hāl) *n.* frozen rain: *Sometimes hailstones can be quite large.*

hair (her) *n.* **1.** one of the fine strands that grow from the skin. **2.** the mass of hairs covering your head or an animal's body.

hairstylist (her′ stī′ list) *n.* a person who takes care of or cuts people's hair.

hairy (her′ ē) *adj.* covered with hair: *a hairy ape; a hairier ape; the hairiest ape of all.*

half (haf) *n.* one of two equal parts that make up a whole. *pl.* **halves** (havz).

half-hearted (haf′ hår′ təd) *adj.* lacking enthusiasm; not really trying: *a half-hearted try.* —**half-heartedly** *adv.*

halfway (haf′ wā) *n.* midway between two points; in the middle.

hall (hol) *n.* **1.** a space leading into a house or building. **2.** a large room for meetings, concerts, parties, or other gatherings. **3.** a building for local government: *a town hall.*

halo (hā′ lō) *n.* **1.** a ring of light around the sun, the moon, or a bright light. **2.** a ring of light around the head, shown in some pictures of angels or holy people. *pl.* **halos.**

halt (holt) *n.* a stopping of something: *The parade came to a halt at the red traffic light.* —*v.* to stop. **halting. halted.**

halve (hav) *v.* **1.** to divide into two equal parts. **2.** to reduce by half: *This recipe is for too many cookies, so we will halve it.* **halving. halved.**

ham (ham) *n.* **1.** salted or smoked meat from a pig's thigh. **2.** an amateur radio operator.

hamburger (ham′ bůr′ gər) *n.* a cooked patty of ground beef, placed in a bun.

hammer (ham′ ər) *n.* a tool used for pounding in nails, shaping metal, or breaking up stone. —*v.* to use a hammer. **hammering. hammered.**

hamper (ham′ pər) *n.* a large basket, often with a cover: *a clothes hamper; a picnic hamper.*

hamster (ham′ stər) *n.* a small rodent with soft fur and a short tail, often kept as a pet.

hand (hand) *n.* **1.** the end of your arm, with a thumb and four fingers. **2.** a pointer on a clock. **3.** a deal of cards: *I won the card game because I had the best hand.* **4.** a member of a ship's crew: *All hands on deck!*

give a hand **1.** to help: *Let's give them a hand with moving the furniture.* **2.** to clap for: *Give a warm hand for our winning team!*

hand down to pass along something, usually from one generation to another: *My grandmother's books were handed down to my father.*

hand in to give to a person in charge: *Hand in your essays.*

hand out to give out: *Hand out the tests to all the pupils.*

hands up an expression meaning "Surrender!"

handbag (hand′ bag′) *n.* a large purse for carrying money and other things.

handcuffs (hand′ kufs′) *n. pl.* a pair of connected metal rings that are locked around a prisoner's wrists.

handcuffs

handicraft (han′ dē kraft′) *n.* an art or craft made by hand: *Handicrafts include weaving, wood carving, and pottery.*

handkerchief (hang′ kər chif *or* hang′ kər chēf′) *n.* a small cloth for wiping your face or nose. *pl.* **handkerchiefs.**

handle (han′ dəl) *n.* the part of a cup, tool, door, or other thing made to be grasped by the hand. —*v.* to touch, hold, or move with your hands: *Handle the glasses carefully.* **handling. handled.**

handlebars (han′ dəl bärz′) *n. pl.* the curved bar at the front of a bicycle, which the rider holds and uses for steering.

handshake (hand′ shāk′) *n.* the clasping of hands between two people as a greeting or to seal a deal.

handsome (han′ səm) *adj.* good-looking.

handwriting (hand′ rī′ ting) *n.* writing done by hand.

handy (han′ dē) *adj.* **1.** clever with your hands: *Mother is handy at house repairs.* **2.** useful to have nearby: *It's handy to keep a flashlight for emergencies.*

hang (hang) *v.* **1.** to fasten something at the top so that it may swing but does not fall: *to hang curtains.* **hanging. hung.** **2.** to put someone to death by hanging him or her from a rope around the neck. **hanging. hanged.**

hang around to stay on in a place: *We hung around the locker room to celebrate our team's victory.*

hang on **1.** to hold tightly: *Hang on to the rope.* **2.** to last; to wait: *Hang on—the fire department will soon be here to help.*

hang up to place a telephone receiver down after you have finished using it.

hangar (hang′ ər) *n.* a large building for aircraft.

hanger (hang′ ər) *n.* a wooden or wire frame on which to hang clothes.

happen (hap′ ən) *v.* to take place; to occur: *The accident happened last night.* **happening. happened.**

happily (hap′ ə lē) *adv.* in a happy way: *We danced happily around the room.*

happiness (hap′ ē nəs) *n.* a state of being happy.

happy (hap′ ē) *adj.* glad; pleased: *Sakira is happy; Abdul is happier; and Zahra is the happiest member of the family today.* (*opp.* **unhappy.**)

harass (har′ əs *or* hə ras′) *v.* to trouble or bother, often by repeated attacks: *The squirrels harassed the birds.* **harassing. harassed.**

harbour, harbor (hȧr′ bər) *n.* a sheltered place along the coast where boats and ships can dock.

hard (hȧrd) *adj.* **1.** firm, not soft: *hard earth.* **2.** difficult: *a hard math problem.* **3.** using much effort: *hard work.*

hard copy the printed copy of work from a computer.

harden (hȧr′ dən) *v.* to make or become solid or hard: *Put the ice cream in the freezer so it will harden.* **hardening. hardened.**

hard hat a metal or plastic helmet used to protect the head of a construction worker, a miner, or other worker.

hardly (hȧrd′ lē) *adv.* barely; only just: *I can hardly reach the top shelf.*
hardly any very few or very little: *There is hardly any bread left.*
hardly ever almost never: *I often write to my friend, but she hardly ever writes back.*

hardship (hȧrd′ ship) *n.* a situation that is hard to bear; difficulty: *When my mother lost her job, our family experienced the hardship of not having enough money.*

hardware (hȧrd′ wer′) *n.* **1.** metal items such as locks, chains, and tools. **2.** a computer and the electrical or mechanical equipment used with it.

hardwood (hȧrd′ wu̇d′) *n.* the wood or timber of a tree that has broad leaves, not needles: *Cherry, oak, and maple trees are hardwoods. Fir trees are softwoods.*

hardy (hȧrd′ ē) *adj.* strong and healthy: *a hardy tree.*

hare (her) *n.* a mammal that looks like a large rabbit with longer ears and longer legs.

harm (hȧrm) *n.* damage; hurt. —*v.* to damage; to hurt. **harming. harmed.**

harmful (hȧrm′ fəl) *adj.* causing harm; not safe: *The berries on that tree are harmful if you eat them.* (*opp.* **harmless.**) —**harmfully** *adv.*

harmonica (hȧr mon′ ə kə) *n.* a small, rectangular, musical instrument, also called a mouth organ. The sound is made by blowing into it.

harmonious (hȧr mō′ nē əs) *adj.* **1.** pleasant to hear: *harmonious sounds.* **2.** friendly; getting along with one another: *a harmonious agreement.* —**harmoniously** *adv.*

harmony (hȧr′ mə nē) *n.* **1.** a pleasing musical sound: *The chorus sang in perfect harmony.* **2.** a feeling of friendship and of usually agreeing on things: *The neighbouring countries live in harmony with each other.*

harness (hȧr′ nəs) *n.* the parts placed on a horse so that a person can ride it: *The harness includes the bridle, saddle, reins, and various straps. pl.* **harnesses.**

harp (hȧrp) *n.* a large musical instrument with many strings that are plucked.

harp

harpoon (hȧr pūn′) *n.* a spear, with a rope fastened to it, used to kill or capture whales and other large sea animals. —*v.* to fire a harpoon. **harpooning. harpooned.**

harsh (hȧrsh) *adj.* **1.** rough; severe: *a harsh winter.* **2.** unkind: *harsh words.* —**harshly** *adv.*

harvest (hȧr′ vəst) *n.* **1.** the gathering of grain, fruit, and other crops at the end of the growing season. **2.** a crop that has been harvested. —*v.* to gather or pick a crop when it is ready. **harvesting. harvested.**

harvester (här′ vəs tər) *n.* a farm machine used to cut and gather crops.

has (haz) see **have**.

hasn't (haz′ ənt) a short form (contraction) of **has not**.

haste (hāst) *n.* a great hurry: *They ran off in haste to catch the bus.*

hasty (hās′ tē) *adj.* acting quickly without thinking: *Don't make a hasty decision before you know all the facts.* —**hastily** *adv.*

hat (hat) *n.* a covering for the head, usually with a brim.

> A **hat trick** means three goals or points scored in one game by one player. In the game of cricket, a player who scored three times in a row used to receive a free hat.

hatch (hatch) *v.* to bring forth baby birds or small fish out of eggs: *The robin's eggs hatched yesterday.* **hatching. hatched.**

hatchet (hach′ it) *n.* a small axe.

hate (hāt) *n.* a strong dislike. —*v.* to dislike very much; to detest. **hating. hated.**

hateful (hāt′ fəl) *adj.* showing or causing hate: *a hateful act.* —**hatefully** *adv.*

hatred (hā′ trəd) *n.* a very strong dislike.

haughty (hot′ ē) *adj.* too proud of yourself and looking down on others. —**haughtily** *adv.*

haul (hol) *v.* to drag; to pull: *The horse hauled the logs along the ground.* **hauling. hauled.**

haunted (hon′ təd) *adj.* believed to be visited by ghosts: *a haunted house.*

have (hav) *v.* **1.** to hold: *Do you have any money on you?* **2.** to own: *They have a large house.* **3.** (used with **to**) must: *We have to go.* **4.** to give birth to: *Our dog had six pups.* **having. had.** she **has.**

> **Have** is often used as a helping (auxiliary) verb with other verbs to show that an action has been completed: *I **have** eaten. You **have** slept.*

haven't (hav′ ənt) a short form (contraction) of **have not**.

hawk (hok) *n.* a bird of prey, with a strong, hooked beak and long, curved claws.

hay (hā) *n.* grass cut and dried as food for animals.

hay fever an allergy caused by pollen of different plants in the air: *Hay fever irritates the nose and throat and can cause sneezing.*

haystack (hā′ stak′) *n.* a large pile of hay.

hazard (haz′ ərd) *n.* a danger or a risk: *This winter's icy roads are a real hazard.*

hazardous (haz′ ər dəs) *adj.* dangerous; risky: *Pollution is hazardous to our health.*

haze (hāz) *n.* slight mist or smoke.

hazel (hā′ zəl) *n.* **1.** a small tree with hazelnuts that can be eaten. **2.** a greenish-brown colour. —*adj.* having this colour.

hazy (hā′ zē) *adj.* misty: *a hazy sky; a hazier sky; the haziest sky of the summer.*

he (hē) *pron.* the male person or animal being talked about. **He** is used as the subject of a verb: *Is Joe coming with us? No, he isn't.*

head (hed) *n.* **1.** the top part of your body. **2.** the top or front of anything: *the head of a parade.* **3.** a leader; the person in charge: *the head of a laboratory.* —*v.* **1.** to lead: *to head a parade.* **2.** to move in a direction: *The train is heading north.* **heading. headed.**

headache (hed′ āk′) *n.* a pain in the head.

headlights (hed′ līts′) *n. pl.* the main front lights of a car, bus, truck, or other vehicle.

headline (hed′ līn′) *n.* the title of a story in a newspaper or magazine.

headphone (hed′ fōn′) *n.* a pair of connected earphones worn on the head.

headquarters (hed′ kwôr′ tərz) *n. pl.* the main office: *police headquarters.*

head start an advantage, often given in a race or other contest: *We gave her a head start by letting her dive first.*

heal (hēl) *v.* to become well again: *My cut healed quickly.* **healing. healed.**

health (helth) *n.* the condition of your body and mind, whether you are well or ill: *If you are well, you enjoy good health.*

healthy (hel′ thē) *adj.* in or causing good health: *Eating lots of vegetables and fruits is a healthy practice.*

hear (hēr) *v.* to receive sounds through the ears. **hearing. heard** (hūrd).

Be careful not to mix up **hear** with "listen." To hear is simply to use your ears. To listen is to pay attention when you hear words or other sounds: *I **hear** noises. I **am listening** to the instructions.*

hearing (hēr′ ing) *n.* one of the five senses—the ability to hear sounds.

heart (härt) *n.* **1.** the muscular organ that pumps blood around the body. **2.** feelings: *My heart tells me that you are a kind person.* **3.** the centre or the most important part: *His office is in the heart of town.* **4.** sympathy; kindness: *That person has no heart; she doesn't care that you are sad.* **5.** a playing card with one or more (♥) marks on it.

by heart from memory: *I know all the words to the song by heart.*

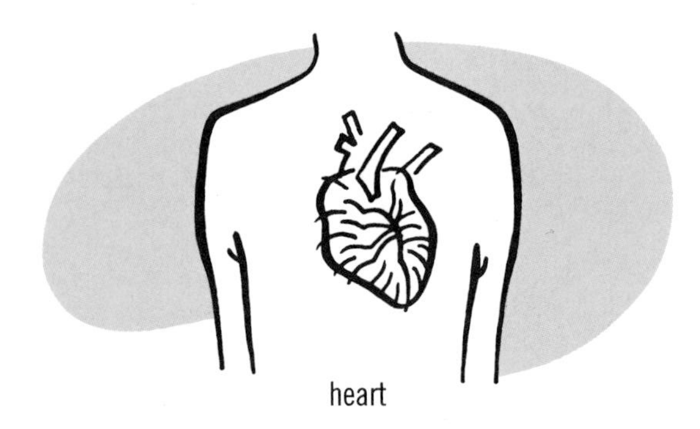

heart

heart attack a sudden illness in which the heart stops working.

heartbreaking (härt′ brā′ king) *adj.* causing great sorrow: *It was heartbreaking to watch the sick baby suffer.*

heartbroken (härt′ brō′ kən) *adj.* crushed with sorrow: *He was heartbroken when his best friend moved to another town.*

hearty (härt′ ē) *adj.* warm and friendly: *a hearty welcome.* —**heartily** *adv.*

heat (hēt) *n.* extreme warmth: *the heat from the sun or from a fire.* —*v.* to make hot; to warm up: *Please heat the water in the kettle.* **heating. heated.**

heated (hēt′ əd) *adj.* excited or angry: *The quiet conversation turned into a heated argument.*

heater (hē′ tər) *n.* a machine used to heat water or to warm the air in a room.

heave (hēv) *v.* to lift up with a great effort: *We heaved the heavy box into the car trunk.* **heaving. heaved.**

heaven (hev′ ən) *n.* **1.** according to some religions, the place where their God lives. **2. the heavens** the sky.

heavy (hev′ ē) *adj.* **1.** weighing a lot; hard to lift or bear: *a heavy load; a heavier one; the heaviest load of all.* **2.** large in amount: *heavy rain.* **3.** strong or thick: *heavy cloth; a heavy fog.* —**heavily** *adv.*

hectare (hek′ ter *or* hek′ tär) *n.* a unit for measuring area; ha is the symbol. 1 ha = 10 000 m^2.

he'd (hēd) a short form (contraction) of **he had** or **he would**.

hedge (hej) *n.* a row of bushes or small trees planted closely together to form a fence.

heel (hēl) *n.* **1.** the back of your foot, under the ankle. **2.** the part of a shoe under the back of your foot.

heifer (hef′ ər) *n.* a young cow.

height (hīt) *n.* how high something is; the distance from bottom to top: *Ali's height is 165 cm.*

heir (er) (*fem.* **heiress**) (er′ əs) *n.* someone who will receive another person's money, property, or title when that person dies: *The eldest prince is heir to the throne.*

held (held) see **hold**.

helicopter (hel′ ə kop′ tər) *n.* an aircraft that has rotating blades on its roof instead of wings: *A helicopter can rise straight up from the ground.*

he'll (hēl) a short form (contraction) of **he will**.

hello (he lō′ *or* hə lō′) *interj.* a greeting.

helmet (hel′ mət) *n.* a hard covering for protecting the head: *a football helmet.*

help (help) *n.* aid; assistance: *Can you give me some help in moving this table?*
—*v.* **1.** to give help. **2.** to give relief: *The medicine helped my cold.* **3.** to avoid: *They can't help laughing at everything.* **helping. helped.**

helpful (help′ fəl) *adj.* giving help; useful: *helpful advice.* —**helpfully** *adv.*

helping (hel′ ping) *n.* a share; a portion: *She asked for a second helping of carrots.*

hem (hem) *n.* the edge of a cloth or garment, turned over and stitched.
—*v.* to sew a hem on the edge of cloth. **hemming. hemmed.**

hemisphere (hem′ ə sfēr′) *n.* one half of the earth's surface: *The earth is divided into hemispheres: northern and southern, and eastern and western.*

hen (hen) *n.* **1.** a female chicken. **2.** the female of some other birds.

her (hůr) **1.** *pron.* the form of **she** that is used as the object of a verb or preposition: *I told her. I showed it to her.* **2.** *adj.* belonging to the girl or woman mentioned: *her books.*

herb (ůrb *or* hůrb) *n.* any plant whose leaves, seeds, or stems are used to flavour food or to make medicines: *Mint and parsley are herbs.*

herd (hůrd) *n.* a group of cattle or other large animals: *a herd of buffalo.*

here (hēr) *adv.* **1.** in or at this place: *Here I am!* **2.** to this place: *Come here!*

heritage (her′ ə təj) *n.* the culture, customs, and traditions handed down from earlier generations: *our country's heritage.*

hero (hē′ rō) *n.* **1.** a person who has done a brave or great deed: *a sports hero.* **2.** the main character of a story or movie. *pl.* **heroes.**

heroic (hi rō′ ik) *adj.* brave and noble: *a heroic deed.* —**heroically** *adv.*

heroism (her′ ō iz′ əm) *n.* great bravery.

heron (her′ ən) *n.* a large wading bird with a long beak, a long neck, and long legs.

heron

hers (hůrz) *pron.* the one belonging to her: *This bicycle is hers.*

herself (hůr self′) *pron.* **1.** her own self or her usual self: *She stopped herself. She's not feeling herself today.* **2.** her self alone: *She flew the airplane by herself.*

> **Herself** is used when the subject and object of a verb are the same: *She talks to herself.* Herself is also used as emphasis: *She told me herself.*

he's (hēz) a short form (contraction) of **he is.**

hesitate (hez′ ə tāt′) *v.* to pause because you are unsure or undecided about something: *I hesitate to ask questions because he looks angry.* **hesitating. hesitated.**

hesitation (hez′ ə tā′ shən) *n.* the act of hesitating.

hey (hā) *interj.* an exclamation used to get someone's attention: *Hey! Can someone please help me?*

hi (hī) *interj.* an informal form of **hello.**

hibernate (hī′ bər nāt′) *v.* to sleep through the winter in a protected place, as bears and some other animals do. **hibernating. hibernated.**

hiccup, hiccough (hik′ up) *n.* a short gasp like a click, sometimes made when you eat or drink too quickly. —*v.* to make a hiccup or hiccups. **hiccupping. hiccupped.**

hide (hīd) *n.* an animal's skin. —*v.* **1.** to put or to keep out of sight: *The dog is hiding behind the garage.* **2.** to keep secret: *to hide facts.* **hiding. hid.** I have **hidden.**

hide-and-seek a game in which you hide and someone tries to find you.

hideous (hid′ ē əs) *adj.* very horrible, ugly, or frightening: *a hideous monster.* —**hideously** *adv.*

high (hī) *adj.* **1.** tall: *a high building; a higher building; the highest building in town.* **2.** located a certain distance above the ground: *How high is the ceiling?* **3.** at a great distance above the ground; not low: *a high roof.* **4.** great in amount or degree: *high taxes.*

highlight (hī′ līt′) *n.* the best or most interesting part of something: *The highlight of the circus was when ten clowns rode together on one bicycle.* —*v.* to emphasize or draw attention to something: *I highlighted the poem by drawing a box around it.* **highlighting. highlighted.**

high-rise (hī′ rīz′) *n.* a tall building with many floors.

high school a school that begins at grade nine or ten and goes to grade twelve.

highway (hī′ wā′) *n.* a main road: *Many highways are designed for cars to travel at high speeds.*

hijack (hī′ jak′) *v.* to take control of a car, a plane, or other vehicle, by force, while someone else is operating it. **hijacking. hijacked.**

hike (hīk) *n.* a long walk. —*v.* to go on such a walk. **hiking. hiked.**

hilarious (hə ler′ ē əs) *adj.* very funny: *a hilarious joke.* —**hilariously** *adv.*

hill (hil) *n.* a raised part of the earth's surface, lower than a mountain.

him (him) *pron.* the form of **he** that is used as the object of a verb or preposition: *I gave him the ball. We started without him.*

himself (him self′) *pron.* **1.** his own self or his usual self: *He dragged himself to the window.* **2.** his self alone: *He climbed the mountain by himself.*

> **Himself** is used when the subject and object of a verb are the same:
> *He cut himself.*
> Himself is also used as emphasis:
> *He himself started the rumour.*

hind (hīnd) *adj.* back; rear: *the hind legs of a donkey.*

hinge (hinj) *n.* a joint on which a door or lid can move back and forth.

hint (hint) *n.* a clue; a small suggestion; a tip: *The gardener gave us some hints on starting a garden.* —*v.* to show by hints: *My sister hinted that she knew where my present was hidden.* **hinting. hinted.**

hip (hip) *n.* the bony part that sticks out on each side of your body between the waist and thigh.

hippo (hip′ ō) *n.* short for **hippopotamus.** *pl.* **hippos.**

hippopotamus (hip′ ə pot′ ə məs) *n.* a large mammal with thick skin, short legs, and a very large mouth. It lives in and near rivers in Africa. *pl.* **hippopotamuses** or **hippopotami** (hip ə pot′ ə mī).

A **hippopotamus** can gallop like a horse on the river bottom, and it spends a lot of time in the water eating plants. Because of where it lives and how it runs, the name of this animal comes from two ancient Greek words—one meaning "river," and the other meaning "horse."

hire (hīr) *v.* to pay someone to do a certain job: *to hire a babysitter.* **hiring. hired.**

his (hiz) *adj.* belonging to the boy or man mentioned: *his jacket.* —*pron.* the one belonging to him: *This jacket is his.*

hiss (his) *n.* a sound like an "s." —*v.* to make such a sound: *Geese and snakes hiss when angry.* **hissing. hissed.** *pl.* **hisses.**

historical (his tôr′ ə kəl) *adj.* having to do with history: *a historical event.*

history (his′ tə rē) *n.* a story or record of events in earlier days. *pl.* **histories.**

hit (hit) *n.* **1.** a blow; a stroke: *a hit on the head.* **2.** something popular: *The new song is a hit.* **3.** in baseball, a stroke by the batter that lets him or her get to at least first base. —*v.* to strike; to knock. **hitting. hit.**

hitch (hich) *v.* to fasten with a rope: *to hitch a horse to a post.* **hitching. hitched.**

to get hitched (*slang*) to get married.

hitchhike (hich′ hīk′) *v.* to travel by getting a free ride in someone else's car. **hitchhiking. hitchhiked.**

HIV (āch′ ī′ vē′) (human immunodeficiency virus) *n.* the virus believed to cause the disease AIDS.

hive (hīv) *n.* **1.** the home of bees. **2.** a large number of bees living together.

hoard (hôrd) *n.* a secret store of goods. —*v.* to store in a secret place: *Squirrels hoard nuts in the ground.* **hoarding. hoarded.**

hoarse (hôrs) *adj.* deep and husky in sound: *My voice is hoarse because I cheered so loudly yesterday.* —**hoarsely** *adv.*

hoax (hōks) *n.* a made-up story or practical joke to trick people. *pl.* **hoaxes.**

hobby (hob′ ē) *n.* an activity that a person does for fun in his or her spare time: *My hobby is making model cars. pl.* **hobbies.**

hockey (hok′ ē) *n.* **1.** a game played on an ice rink with a goal at each end. The players wear ice skates and hit a hard rubber disk, called a puck, with curved sticks that have a blade on the end. **2.** a game played with curved sticks and a small ball on a field.

hoe (hō) *n.* a long-handled tool, with a flat blade, for loosening the soil.

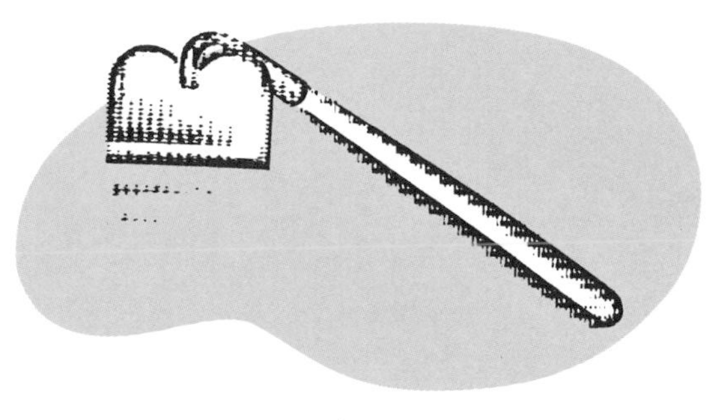

hoe

hog (hog) *n.* a full-grown pig.

hoist (hoist) *v.* to lift up something by ropes: *to hoist a flag.* **hoisting. hoisted.**

hold (hōld) *n.* in a ship, the space below the deck: *Cargo is stored in the hold.* —*v.* **1.** to keep something in your hand: *to hold an umbrella.* **2.** to keep something in a certain place: *He held the baby on his knee.* **3.** to contain: *The bag holds flour.* **4.** to have: *to hold a meeting.* **holding. held.**

hold up **1.** to lift: *to hold up your hand.* **2.** to delay: *Our car was held up by a traffic jam.* **3.** to rob: *The bank was held up by robbers.*

hole (hōl) *n.* **1.** an opening: *I could see through the hole in the wall.* **2.** a pit: *a deep hole in the ground.*

holiday (hol′ ə dā′) *n.* **1.** a day free from work or school: *a public holiday.* **2.** a vacation. *pl.* **holidays.**

hollow (hol′ ō) *n.* a sunken area: *a hollow in the ground.* —*adj.* having an empty space inside; not solid; empty: *a hollow tooth.*

holly (hol′ ē) *n.* a shrub with shiny green leaves and red berries.

holy (hō′ lē) *adj.* sacred; having to do with God or religion.

home (hōm) *n.* **1.** the place where a person lives. **2.** in baseball, the scoring base.

homeland (hōm′ land′) *n.* the country in which you were born or where your home is.

homemaker (hōm′ māk′ ər) *n.* a person who looks after a home and the people living in it.

home run in baseball, a hit that lets the batter get to home base in one trip.

homesick (hōm′ sik′) *adj.* sad because you are away from home and miss it.

homework (hōm′ wu̇rk′) *n.* schoolwork done at home.

homonym (hom′ ə nim′) *n.* a word that has the same pronunciation and the same spelling as another word, but has a different meaning: *Mine (a deep tunnel) and mine (belonging to me) are homonyms.*

homophone (hom′ ə fōn′) *n.* a word that has the same pronunciation as another word, but has a different spelling and meaning: *Some homophones are: pair (two items) and pear (a fruit); bare (naked) and bear (an animal); brake (a car part) and break (to smash).*

honest (on′ ist) *adj.* **1.** truthful; not lying or hiding anything. **2.** fair; not cheating or stealing. **3.** frank: *an honest opinion.* (*opp.* **dishonest.**) —**honestly** *adv.*

honesty (on′ is tē) *n.* the quality of being honest.

honey (hun′ ē) *n.* a very sweet, thick liquid made by bees.

honeymoon (hun′ ē mūn′) *n.* the holiday taken by a newly married couple.

honk (hongk) *n.* the cry that a goose makes, or a similar sound. —*v.* to make such a sound: *to honk a horn.* **honking. honked.**

honour, honor (on′ ər) *n.* **1.** great respect; glory; praise; fame: *We held a party in honour of my grandmother's birthday.* **2.** a title of respect: *The lawyer called the judge "Your Honour."* —*v.* to praise; to treat with respect. **honouring. honoured.**

honourable, honorable (on′ ər ə bəl) *adj.* deserving honour or respect. —**honourably** *adv.*

hood (hu̇d) *n.* **1.** a cloth covering for the head and neck, either separate or part of a jacket or cloak. **2.** the metal cover over a car engine.

hoof (hu̇f *or* hūf) *n.* the hard part covering the foot of a horse, cow, sheep, goat, or pig. *pl.* **hoofs** or **hooves** (hūvs).

hook (hu̇k) *n.* a bent and pointed device made to catch or hold something: *a fish hook; a clothes hook.* —*v.* to catch or fasten with a hook. **hooking. hooked.**

hoop (hūp) *n.* a large, circular band, often made of metal or wood: *The circus performer jumped through the hoop.*

hoot (hūt) *n.* the cry that an owl makes, or a sound similar to it. —*v.* to make such a sound. **hooting. hooted.**

hop (hop) *n.* **1.** a jump on one foot, or with two feet together: *The sparrow hopped toward us.* **2.** a plant whose flowers are used to flavour beer. —*v.* to jump on one foot, or with two feet together. **hopping. hopped.**

hope (hōp) *n.* a feeling that something you wish for will happen: *We have high hopes of winning the championship. They lost hope of* *being rescued.* —*v.* to wish and expect: *We hope our cousins will come for a visit.* **hoping. hoped.**

hopeful (hōp′ fəl) *adj.* full of hope. —**hopefully** *adv.*

hopeless (hōp′ ləs) *adj.* without any hope; without a chance: *It's a hopeless situation—we'll never make the playoffs.* —**hopelessly** *adv.*

horizon (hə rī′ zən) *n.* the line in the distance where the sky seems to meet the land or the water.

horizontal (hȯr′ ə zon′ təl) *adj.* lying flat or level with the ground: *A horizontal line is drawn from left to right. A vertical line is drawn from top to bottom.* —**horizontally** *adv.*

horn (hȯrn) *n.* **1.** the hard, usually pointed part growing on the head of some animals, such as cattle, goats, and sheep. **2.** a musical instrument that you blow. **3.** a warning signal: *a car horn.*

hornet (hȯr′ nət) *n.* a large wasp that stings.

horrible (hȯr′ ə bəl) *adj.* terrible: *When you scrape your nails along a chalkboard, it makes a horrible noise.* —**horribly** *adv.*

horrify (hȯr′ ə fī′) *v.* to upset, shock, or disgust someone: *We were horrified by the terrible news.* **horrifying. horrified.** it **horrifies.**

horror (hȯr′ ər) *n.* great terror, shock or disgust: *They looked in horror at the car crash.*

horse (hȯrs) *n.* a large mammal with a mane, hooves, and a hairy tail. Horses are used for riding and carrying or pulling loads.

horseback (hȯrs′ bak′) *adv.* on the back of a horse: *We will ride horseback through the park.*

horseshoe (hȯrs′ shū) *n.* a U-shaped piece of metal that is nailed to the bottom of a horse's hoof.

horticulture (hȯr′ tə kul′ chər) *n.* the science of growing fruits, flowers, plants, and vegetables.

hose (hōz) *n.* a long, bending tube through which liquid flows: *a garden hose.*

hospital (hos′ pi təl) *n.* a building where sick and injured people are cared for by doctors and nurses.

host (hōst) *n.* a person who entertains or looks after visitors.

hostile (hos′ təl *or* hos′ tīl) *adj.* very unfriendly, rude, and against something: *He was hostile to our ideas and left the meeting before it ended.* —**hostilely** *adv.*

hot (hot) *adj.* **1.** extremely warm; having a lot of heat: *a hot day; a hotter one; the hottest day of the summer.* **2.** easily excited or made angry: *a hot temper.* **3.** causing a burning feeling in the mouth: *hot peppers.*

hot chocolate a drink made by mixing hot milk, sugar, and cocoa powder.

hot dog a wiener in a bun.

hotel (hō tel′) *n.* a building with rooms that travellers pay to stay and sleep in.

hound (hownd) *n.* a hunting dog.

hour (owr) *n.* a length of time equal to sixty minutes; h is the symbol. 1h = 60 min.

hourglass (owr′ glas′) *n.* a simple device for measuring time: *An hourglass has two glass bulbs joined by a very narrow neck. Grains of sand take an hour to pour completely from one bulb to the other.*

house (hows) *n.* a building for people to live in.

House of Commons one of the two parts of the Canadian Parliament. It holds the Members of Parliament, the elected government representatives who meet in Ottawa to make laws.

housework (hows′ wûrk′) *n.* cooking, cleaning, and other work that needs to be done to keep a house in order.

how (how) *adv.* **1.** in what way: *How did you do it?* **2.** to what amount or distance: *How tall are you? How far can you throw?*

however (how ev′ ər) *conj.* yet; nevertheless: *I fixed the clock; however, it has stopped again.*

howl (howl) *n.* a wailing cry: *the howl of a wolf or a dog; a howl of pain.* —*v.* to make such a cry. **howling. howled.**

huddle (hud′ əl) *v.* to press close together: *We huddled together under a blanket in front of the fire.* **huddling. huddled.**

hue (hyū) *n.* a shade; a colour: *all the hues of the rainbow.*

hug (hug) *n.* a close, tight clasp with the arms. —*v.* **1.** to put your arms around and hold close: *Mark hugged his baby sister.* **2.** to keep close to: *The boat hugged the shore.* **hugging. hugged.**

huge (hyūj) *adj.* enormous in size: *An elephant is a huge animal.*

hull (hul) *n.* **1.** the body of a ship. **2.** the leaves at the stem of a strawberry. **3.** the outer covering of certain seeds and fruits. —*v.* to remove a hull from a fruit or seed. **hulling. hulled.**

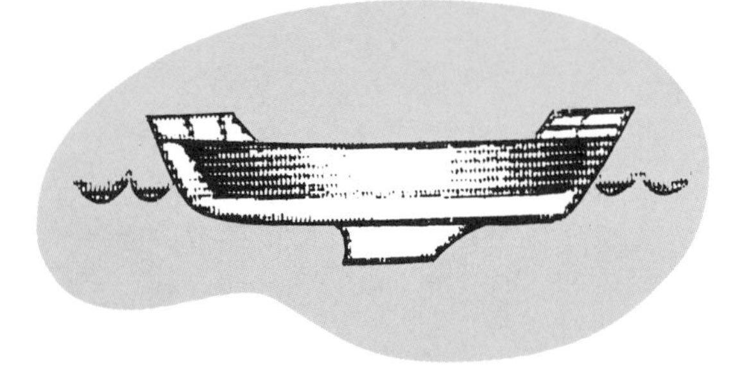

hull

hum (hum) *v.* **1.** to make a noise like a bee. **2.** to make a singing sound with your lips closed: *We hummed a tune as we worked.* **humming. hummed.**

human (hyū′ mən) *n.* a person. —*adj.* having to do with people, not animals: *Speech is a human ability.* —**humanly** *adv.*

humane (hyū mān′) *adj.* kind and merciful: *The Humane Society tries to make sure that animals are treated with kindness.* —**humanely** *adv.*

humanity (hyū ma′ nə tē) *n.* human beings as a group.

humankind (hyū′ mən kīnd′) *n.* human beings as a group; humanity.

humble (hum′ bəl) *adj.* not proud; modest: *She remained humble even after winning first prize.* —**humbly** *adv.*

humid (hyū′ mid) *adj.* moist; damp: *a hot, humid day.*

humidity (hyū mid′ ə tē) *n.* dampness in the air.

humiliate (hyū mi′ lē āt′) *v.* to make someone feel ashamed; to hurt someone's self-respect: *They humiliated me by calling me hurtful names.* **humiliating. humiliated.**

hummingbird (hum′ ing bėrd′) *n.* a tiny, often brightly coloured bird that beats its wings so fast that they make a humming sound.

humorous (hyū′ mər əs) *adj.* funny; amusing: *a humorous story.*

humour, humor (hyū′ mər) *n.* **1.** the quality of being funny or amusing. **2.** the ability to see the funny side of things: *Nadia has a good sense of humour.*

hump (hump) *n.* a large bulge or bump, usually on the back: *a camel's hump.*

hunch (hunch) *n.* (*informal*) a feeling that something will happen: *I have a hunch that we will win tomorrow. pl.* **hunches.**

hundred (hun′ drəd) *n.* ten times ten: 100.

hung (hung) see **hang**.

hunger (hung′ gər) *n.* **1.** a gnawing feeling in the stomach that tells you that you need food. **2.** a strong desire: *a hunger for knowledge.*

hungry (hung′ grē) *adj.* needing food: *a hungry dog; a hungrier dog; the hungriest dog on the street.* —**hungrily** *adv.*

hunk (hunk) *n.* a large piece: *a hunk of cheese.*

hunt (hunt) *n.* the activity of hunting. —*v.* **1.** to chase after an animal in order to catch or kill it: *to hunt ducks.* **2.** to search for: *René hunted everywhere for his cap.* **hunting. hunted.**

hunter (hun′ tər) *n.* a person who hunts.

hurdle (hůr′ dəl) *n.* a barrier for runners or horses to jump over in a race. —*v.* to race over hurdles. **hurdling. hurdled.**

hurl (hůrl) *v.* to throw something with all your strength. **hurling. hurled.**

hurrah, hurray (hə ro′, hə rā′) *interj.* a cheer.

hurricane (hůr′ ə kān′) *n.* a powerful storm with strong winds and heavy rain.

hurry (hůr′ ē) *v.* to move quickly; to rush: *We hurried to get to the cinema before the movie started.* **hurrying. hurried.** she **hurries.**

hurt (hůrt) *n.* something that hurts: *the hurt of losing a friend.* —*v.* to cause pain or harm: *Your speech hurt our cause.* **hurting. hurted.**

hurtful (hůrt′ fəl) *adj.* causing pain or harm. —**hurtfully** *adv.*

husband (huz′ bənd) *n.* a married man.

hush (hush) *v.* to make or become quiet: *The audience hushed when she began speaking.* **hushing. hushed.**

husk (husk) *n.* the dry outer covering of some fruits, vegetables, and seeds: *a corn husk.* —*v.* to remove this covering: *to husk corn.* **husking. husked.**

husky (hus′ kē) *n.* a strong, furry dog, used in very cold regions for pulling sleds. *pl.* **huskies.** —*adj.* **1.** sounding hoarse: *a husky voice.* **2.** big and strong: *a husky lumberjack.*

hut (hut) *n.* a small shed or a cabin.

hydrant (hī′ drənt) *n.* a large water pipe on the street to which fire hoses can be attached.

hydro (hī′ drō) *n.* an informal word often used instead of "hydro-electric power" or "electricity": *The hydro went off when lightning hit the power lines.*

hydro, hydro-electric (hī′ drō, hī′ drō i lek′ trik) *adj.* having to do with electricity produced by water power.

hyena (hī ē′ nə) *n.* a wild, wolf-like animal of Africa and Asia.

hyena

hygiene (hī′ jēn) *n.* the habits for keeping clean, healthy, and free of disease: *Brushing your teeth after every meal is good hygiene.*

hymn (him) *n.* a song of praise.

hyphen (hī′ fən) *n.* a short dash (-), used to separate a word at the end of a line or to join two words into one: *"Up-to-date" is a word with two hyphens. It means "the most modern" or "the latest."*

hypnotize (hip′ nə tīz′) *v.* to put a person into a sleep-like state. **hypnotizing. hypnotized.**

hysterical (his ter′ ə kəl) *adj.* **1.** excited and frightened in an uncontrolled way: *We were hysterical after the earthquake.* **2.** very funny: *a hysterical joke.* —**hysterically** *adv.*

I (ī) *pron.* the person who is speaking or writing. **I** is used as the subject of a verb: *I will walk. I am walking. I walked.*

ice (īs) *n.* frozen water. —*v.* **1.** to cover with ice: *The cold weather made the pond ice over.* **2.** to cover with icing: *to ice a cake.* **icing. iced.**

iceberg (īs′ bûrg′) *n.* a very large mass of ice floating in the sea.

ice cream a frozen dessert made of sweetened, flavoured cream or milk.

ice skate a boot with a metal blade on the bottom, used for gliding on ice.

ice skate

ice-skate (īs′ skāt′) *v.* to skate on ice. **ice-skating. ice-skated.**

ice skater a person who skates on ice.

icicle (ī′ si kəl) *n.* a pointed, hanging stick of ice, formed by dripping water.

icing (ī′ sing) *n.* a mixture of sugar, butter, and flavouring, used to cover cakes.

icon (ī′ kon) *n.* a small picture on a computer screen.

icy (ī′ sē) *adj.* cold as ice: *an icy wind; an icier wind; the iciest wind of the whole winter.*

I'd (īd) a short form (contraction) of **I had** or **I would**.

idea (ī dē′ ə) *n.* **1.** a thought. **2.** an opinion. **3.** a plan: *My friends and I have an idea for how to get rich.*

ideal (ī dī′ əl) *n.* someone or something you think is a model for imitating: *I admire the way you try to live up to your ideals of honesty and kindness.* —*adj.* perfect: *Today is an ideal day for a picnic. It is sunny, mild, and not windy.* —**ideally** *adv.*

identical (ī den′ tə kəl) *adj.* exactly the same: *identical twins.* —**identically** *adv.*

identification (ī den′ tə fə kā′ shən) *n.* a document that proves your identity: *A birth certificate and a driver's licence are two forms of identification.*

identify (ī den′ tə fī′) *v.* to recognize: *I can identify Danielle by her long, red braids.* **identifying. identified.** she **identifies.**

identity (ī den′ tə tē) *n.* who a person is: *The movie star wore a disguise to hide her identity from the photographers. pl.* **identities.**

idiom (id′ ē əm) *n.* an expression whose meaning cannot be understood simply from the words used: *"It's raining cats and dogs" is an idiom that means "it's raining very hard."*

Do you know the meaning of these **idioms**?

- to pull the wool over your eyes
- in hot water
- to cry crocodile tears
- How time flies!
- to put your foot in your mouth
- to cut it out

idiot (id′ ē ət) *n.* a foolish or stupid person.

idiotic (id′ ē ot′ ik) *adj.* foolish or stupid: *idiotic behaviour.*

idle (ī′ dəl) *adj.* **1.** lazy: *an idle person.* **2.** doing nothing: *The machines were idle on* *the public holiday.* —*v.* **1.** to do nothing: *to idle away the time.* **2.** to run a car engine or other motor without putting it to work: *The car idled in the driveway.* **idling. idled.**

idol (ī′ dəl) *n.* **1.** a statue worshipped as a god. **2.** a person you admire and respect very much: *a movie idol.*

if (if) *conj.* **1.** on condition that; supposing that: *I will go if you wish.* **2.** whether: *Let me know if you are going.*

if only I wish that: *If only my family were rich!*

igloo (ig′ lū) *n.* a hut built of blocks of ice and hard snow: *The Inuit used to build igloos to live in when hunting or fishing. pl.* **igloos.**

ignite (ig nīt′) *v.* to set fire to: *to ignite a match.* **igniting. ignited.**

ignorance (ig′ nə rəns) *n.* lack of knowledge or education.

ignorant (ig′ nə rənt) *adj.* knowing little or nothing: *They are ignorant about the dangers of smoking.*

ignore (ig nȯr′) *v.* to pretend not to see or hear; to pay no attention to: *It was difficult to ignore the ringing telephone.* **ignoring. ignored.**

iguana (i gwo′ nə) *n.* a large, green, climbing lizard that lives in Mexico and South America.

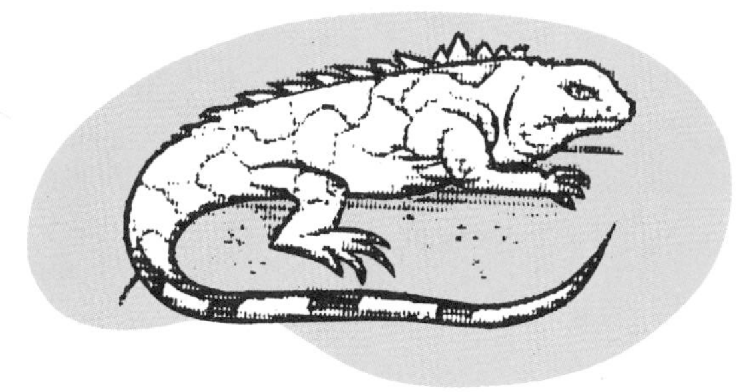

iguana

ill (il) *adj.* **1.** sick; not well: *I felt ill with a headache and a cough.* **2.** bad: *ill fortune.*

I'll (īl) a short form (contraction) of **I will** or **I shall.**

illegal (i lē′ gəl) *adj.* against the law: *It is illegal to drive without a licence.* —**illegally** *adv.*

illiterate (i lit′ ə rət) *adj.* not knowing how to read and write.

illness (il′ nəs) *n.* sickness; poor health.

illusion (i lū′ zhən) *n.* **1.** something that fools the senses: *A magician's tricks are an illusion.* **2.** a mistaken idea: *She has the illusion that everyone is good.*

illustrate (il′ əs trāt′) *v.* to add pictures to: *to illustrate a story in a book.* **illustrating. illustrated.**

illustration (il′ əs trā′ shən) *n.* a picture in a book.

illustrator (il′ əs trā′ tər) *n.* a person who draws pictures for a book.

> **im–** is a prefix meaning "not": "impatient" means not patient; "imperfect" means not perfect.

I'm (īm) a short form (contraction) of **I am.**

image (im′ əj) *n.* **1.** a reflection formed by a mirror, a pool of water, a camera lens, or other shiny surface. **2.** a close or exact likeness of someone or something: *You are the image of your grandfather when he was your age!* **3.** public opinion about someone: *The politician improved her image by visiting factories and schools.*

imaginary (i maj′ ən er′ ē) *adj.* made up; not real: *Many creatures in folk tales, such as dragons and unicorns, are imaginary.*

imagination (i maj′ in ā′ shən) *n.* **1.** the forming of pictures in your mind. **2.** the ability to think up things that don't exist: *Louisa used her imagination to write a story set on a mysterious island.*

imaginative (i maj′ ə nə tiv) *adj.* **1.** showing creative imagination: *What an imaginative story!* **2.** having a strong imagination: *an imaginative child.*

imagine (i maj′ in) *v.* **1.** to picture in your mind. **2.** to suppose or guess: *After our argument, I don't imagine she'll come to my party.* **imagining. imagined.**

imitate (im′ ə tāt′) *v.* to copy or mimic: *A parrot can imitate a person's voice.* **imitating. imitated.**

imitation (im′ ə tā′ shən) *n.* a copy, especially of something valuable: *This is not a real diamond—it is an imitation.*

immediately (i mē′ dē it lē) *adv.* at once: *The house is on fire—leave it immediately!*

immense (i mens′) *adj.* huge; very big: *The immense stadium seats 60 000 people.* —**immensely** *adv.*

immigrant (im′ ə grənt) *n.* a person who comes to a new country to live.

immigrate (im′ ə grāt′) *v.* to come to a new country to live: *to immigrate to Canada.* **immigrating. immigrated.**

immortal (im or′ təl) *adj.* **1.** living forever: *an immortal god.* **2.** lasting forever; never forgotten: *These heroes have become immortal—we will never forget them.*

immune (im yūn′) *adj.* protected from disease: *Vaccinations make us immune to some diseases, such as the measles.*

imp (imp) *n.* in fairy tales, a small, mischievous elf.

impair (im per′) *v.* to damage or weaken: *Drinking alcohol will impair a person's driving ability.* **impairing. impaired.**

impatience (im pā′ shəns) *n.* lack of patience.

impatient (im pā′ shənt) *adj.* not willing to wait: *Don't be so impatient! Your turn will come soon.* —**impatiently** *adv.*

imperial (im pēr′ ē əl) *adj.* having to do with an emperor or empress; royal.

impolite (im′ pə lit′) *adj.* rude; not polite: *It's impolite not to wait your turn.* —**impolitely** *adv.*

import (im′ pȯrt) *n.* a product brought in from a foreign country.

import (im pȯrt′) *v.* to bring in goods from a foreign country: *Canada imports tea from India and China.* **importing. imported.**

importance (im pȯr′ təns) *n.* worth; value: *What is the importance of wealth compared with good health?*

important (im pȯr′ tənt) *adj.* having much meaning, value, or responsibility: *important news; an important person.* (*opp.* **unimportant.**) —**importantly** *adv.*

impossible (im pos′ ə bəl) *adj.* not able to be done or to exist: *It is impossible to be in two places at once.*

imposter (im pos′ tər) *n.* a person pretending to be someone else: *That woman isn't the famous singer—she's an imposter!*

impress (im pres′) *v.* to do something that makes someone remember you: *She impressed me with her passionate speech.* **impressing. impressed.**

improve (im prūv′) *v.* to make or become better: *Ever since I started using a dictionary more often, my spelling has improved.* **improving. improved.**

improvement (im prūv′ mənt) *n.* a better result: *There has been a great improvement in your spelling.*

improvise (im′ prə vīz′) *v.* to make up or do something on the spot, without any preparation: *Our drama teacher asked us to improvise a comedy skit in class today.* **improvising. improvised.**

in (in) *prep.* **1.** inside: *in the house.* **2.** into: *Put it in a box.* **3.** by the end of: *It will be ready in an hour.* **4.** after: *I'll come in a few minutes.* **5.** having: *in pain; in tears.*

in– is a prefix meaning not: "incomplete" means not complete; "inexpensive" means not expensive.

inch (inch) *n.* a unit for measuring length, equal to about 2.54 cm. *pl.* **inches.**

incident (in′ sə dənt) *n.* a happening; an event: *What was the incident that made you so angry at your best friend?*

include (in klūd′) *v.* **1.** to have as part of; to contain; to count in: *This price includes taxes and shipping costs.* **2.** to put in or on: *Include your return address on the envelope.* **including. included.**

income (in′ kum) *n.* the amount of money a person earns from working.

income tax a tax paid on the money you earn from working.

incomplete (in′ kom plēt′) *adj.* not complete: *an incomplete deck of cards.*

incorrect (in′ kə rekt′) *adj.* wrong; not correct: *an incorrect answer.* —**incorrectly** *adv.*

increase (in′ krēs) *n.* a gain; a growth: *a population increase.*

increase (in krēs′) *v.* to make or become greater: *We increased our speed when we got on the highway.* **increasing. increased.**

incredible (in kred′ ə bəl) *adj.* amazing; unbelievable: *The street performer juggled an incredible number of plates at the same time.* —**incredibly** *adv.*

incubator (in′ kyū bā′ tər *or* ing′ kyə bā′ tər) *n.* **1.** a heated box for hatching eggs. **2.** a heated box for protecting babies that are born too early.

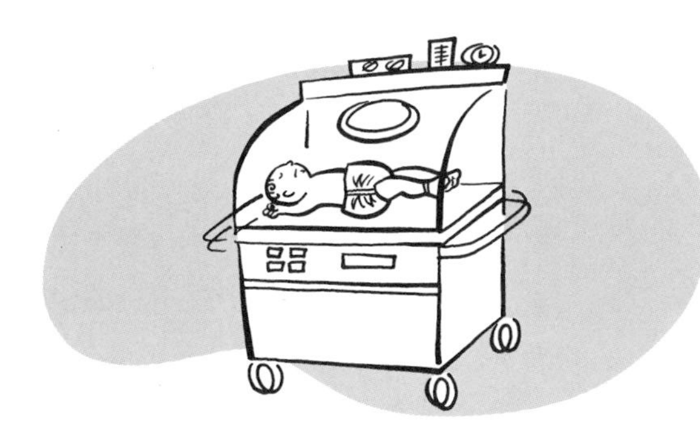

incubator

indeed (in dēd′) *adv.* certainly; truly: *Yes, indeed, I believe you.*

indefinite (in def′ ə nit) *adj.* uncertain; vague: *Our picnic plans will remain indefinite until we hear the weather forecast.* —**indefinitely** *adv.*

indent (in dent′) *v.* to begin the first line of a paragraph farther in from the left margin than the other lines. **indenting. indented.**

independent (in′ də pen′ dənt) *adj.* **1.** not ruled or controlled by another: *an independent country.* **2.** able to look after yourself without help from others: *My older sister has moved away from home and has become independent.*

index (in′ deks) *n.* an alphabetical list at the end of a book: *The index tells you the topics in the book, and the pages on which you can find them. pl.* **indexes** or **indices** (in′ di sēz′).

index finger the finger next to the thumb; also called the **forefinger**.

> Why is the finger next to the thumb called the **index finger**? In Latin, *index* means "indicator"—something used to point at things. We use the index finger to point with.

indicate (in′ də kāt′) *v.* **1.** to point out: *The arrow indicates the direction we should take.* **2.** to show: *Rachel indicated her amusement by laughing out loud.* **indicating. indicated.**

indifferent (in dif′ rənt *or* in dif′ ər ənt) *adj.* not interested: *They were indifferent to our problems.*

indigestion (in′ də jes′ chən) *n.* an uncomfortable feeling in your stomach when you are having difficulty digesting food.

indignant (in dig′ nənt) *adj.* angry at something unfair or mean: *The students were indignant when they heard their school play had been cancelled.*

indirect (in′ di rekt′ *or* in dī rekt′) *adj.* not direct or straight; roundabout: *an indirect route; an indirect way of saying things.* —**indirectly** *adv.*

individual (in′ də vij′ ū əl) *n.* a single person or animal: *Every individual must show his or her ticket.*

indoor (in′ dȯr′) *adj.* done or belonging inside a building: *Basketball is an indoor game.*

indoors (in dȯrz′) *adv.* inside a building: *We spent the rainy morning indoors.*

indulge (in dulj′) *v.* to do something that tempts you: *We indulged ourselves by having a large piece of chocolate cake.* **indulging. indulged.**

industry (in′ dəs trē) *n.* the business of producing goods: *the dairy industry; the car industry. pl.* **industries.**

inedible (in ed′ ə bəl) *adj.* not suitable to be eaten: *These mushrooms are inedible because they are poisonous.*

inexcusable (in′ eks kyūz′ ə bəl) *adj.* not easily excused or forgiven: *inexcusable rudeness.*

inexpensive (in′ iks pen′ siv) *adj.* not expensive; low-priced.

infant (in′ fənt) *n.* a baby or a very young child.

infect (in fekt′) *v.* to cause or to pass on a disease: *The child with chicken pox has infected all the other pupils in the class.* **infecting. infected.**

infection (in fek′ shən) *n.* a disease in the body caused by germs.

inferior (in fēr′ ē ər) *adj.* lower in position or quality: *Her first story is inferior to the wonderful stories she now writes.*

infield (in′ fēld′) *n.* **1.** the area inside a baseball diamond. **2.** in baseball, the positions played by the first, second, and third base players and the shortstop.

infinite (in′ fə nət) *adj.* endless; without limit: *When you look through a telescope, there seems to be an infinite number of stars.* —**infinitely** *adv.*

infirmary (in fůrm′ ə rē) *n.* a place to care for sick people: *the school infirmary. pl.* **infirmaries.**

inflammable (in flam′ ə bəl) *adj.* easily set on fire: *Gasoline is highly inflammable.*

inflate (in flāt′) *v.* **1.** to fill with air or gas: *to inflate balloons.* **2.** to make greater: *to inflate prices.* **inflating. inflated.**

influence (in′ flū əns) *n.* a person or thing that has an effect on another: *She is a good influence on the younger children.* —*v.* to have power over: *The coach's encouragement influenced me to join the team.* **influencing. influenced.**

inform (in fȯrm′) *v.* to give information: *The newscast informed us about the plane crash.* **informing. informed.**

informal (in for′ məl) *adj.* not following strict rules; not formal; casual: *I'm wearing informal clothes to the party—jeans and a T-shirt.* —**informally** *adv.*

information (in′ fər mā′ shən) *n.* facts; knowledge; news: *This travel guide contains useful information about all the places we want to visit.*

ingenious (in jēn′ yəs) *adj.* cleverly and carefully thought out: *Ty has an ingenious idea for getting his parents to their surprise party.*

ingredient (in grē′ dē ənt) *n.* a part of a mixture: *the ingredients for a cake.*

inhabit (in hab′ it) *v.* to live in a place: *The forest is inhabited by deer.* **inhabiting. inhabited.**

inhabitant (in hab′ ə tənt) *n.* a person or animal living in a particular place: *the inhabitants of a village.*

inhale (in′ hāl *or* in hāl′) *v.* to breathe in. **inhaling. inhaled.**

inherit (in her′ it) *v.* to receive money or property from someone who has died: *I inherited a brooch from my grandmother.* **inheriting. inherited.**

inheritance (in her′ ə təns) *n.* something that is inherited: *My grandmother's brooch is my inheritance.*

initial (i nish′ əl) *n.* the first letter of a name: *Robert Louis Stevenson's initials are R.L.S.* —*adj.* happening at the beginning; first: *Our final project was different from our initial plan.*

inject (in jekt′) *v.* to use a special needle to put a liquid medicine into the body. **injecting. injected.**

injection (in jek′ shən) *n.* the injecting of a medicine into the body with a needle; a shot.

injure (in′ jər) *v.* to harm; to hurt: *My sister injured her knee.* **injuring. injured.**

injury (in′ je rē) *n.* harm; a wound: *How bad was her injury? pl.* **injuries.**

ink (ingk) *n.* black or coloured liquid used for writing or printing.

inland (in′ lənd) *adj.* away from the coast: *an inland town.*

inlet (in′ let′ *or* in′ lət) *n.* a narrow strip of water running into land or between islands.

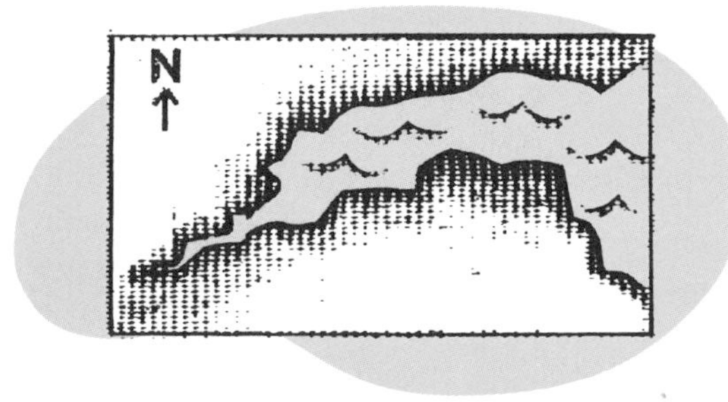

inlet

inn (in) *n.* a small hotel.

inner (in′ ər) *adj.* inside: *the inner walls of a house.*

inning (in′ ing) *n.* in baseball, the period of time when both teams have a turn at bat: *There are usually nine innings in a baseball game.*

innocence (in′ ə səns) *n.* the quality of being free from evil ideas and actions: *the innocence of a small child.*

innocent (in′ ə sənt) *adj.* **1.** not guilty; blameless: *After their arrest, they kept insisting they were innocent of any crime.* **2.** free from evil: *an innocent child.* —**innocently** *adv.*

inquire (in kwīr′) *v.* to ask about something; to try to find something out: *We inquired when the bus would arrive.* **inquiring. inquired.**

inquiry (in kwī′ rē *or* in′ kwə rē) *n.* **1.** a question, or the asking of questions. **2.** an investigation: *The police conducted an inquiry into the murder. pl.* **inquiries.**

insane (in sān′) *adj.* **1.** mentally ill. **2.** crazy; very foolish. —**insanely** *adv.*

insect (in′ sekt) *n.* a small animal such as an ant, bee, or fly. An insect has six legs and three parts to its body. Some insects have wings.

insects

insecure (in′ sə kyūr′) *adj.* lacking confidence; fearful: *He feels insecure in a big crowd.*

insert (in sûrt′) *v.* to put in or to add something: *to insert a coin into a machine; to insert a comma into a sentence.* **inserting. inserted.**

inside (in′ sīd) *adj.* the inner part or side: *The inside of a house has several rooms.* —*adv.* within: *Let's go inside before it snows.*
inside out with the inside facing out: *Your shirt is inside out—the label is on the outside!*

insist (in sist′) *v.* to stick firmly to an idea: *Sheila insisted that she was right.* **insisting. insisted.**

inspect (in spekt′) *v.* to examine carefully to make sure everything is in good condition: *The mechanic inspected the car brakes to make sure they were working properly.* **inspecting. inspected.**

inspector (in spek′ tər) *n.* **1.** a person who inspects and makes sure everything is as it should be: *a restaurant inspector.* **2.** a senior police officer.

inspire (in spīr′) *v.* to encourage others to do something, often by setting an example: *My aunt is a famous painter, and she inspired me to take art classes.* **inspiring. inspired.**

install (in stol′) *v.* to put into place: *to install a new telephone.* **installing. installed.**

instance (in′ stəns) *n.* a particular time something happened; an example: *I can think of many instances when you were angry.*
for instance for example: *There are many types of dog; for instance, there are beagles, German shepherds, and collies.*

instant (in′ stənt) *n.* a brief moment: *He stopped for an instant, then went on talking.* —*adj.* **1.** immediate: *The medicine gave instant relief.* **2.** able to be prepared very quickly: *instant coffee.* —**instantly** *adv.*

instead (in sted′) *adv.* in place of someone, something, or some time: *I can't go to the gym today. I'll go tomorrow instead.*

instinct (in′ stingkt) *n.* a way of feeling or acting that is natural to living creatures from the time of their birth: *Many birds fly south for the winter by instinct.*

institution (in′ stə tū′ shən *or* in′ stə tyū′ shən) *n.* an organization set up to serve or help people: *Hospitals are health institutions. Schools are learning institutions.*

instruct (in strukt′) *v.* to teach; to show someone how to do something. **instructing. instructed.**

instructions (in struk′ shənz) *n. pl.* an explanation of how to do things; directions: *Do you have the instructions for setting up the new videocassette recorder?*

instructor (in struk′ tər) *n.* a teacher.

instrument (in′ strə mənt) *n.* **1.** a tool: *A thermometer is an instrument that measures temperature.* **2.** a device for making music: *Violins, pianos, and flutes are musical instruments.*

insult (in′ sult) *n.* a rude remark intended to hurt someone's pride.

insult (in sult′) *v.* to be rude to someone and hurt his or her pride. **insulting. insulted.**

> The word **insult** comes from a Latin word meaning "to jump upon." When you are insulted, you feel like someone is jumping on you—with their words, not their feet.

integrate (in′ tə grāt′) *v.* to bring parts together into a whole: *The art students integrated all their designs into a single wall display.* **integrating. integrated.**

intellectual (in tə lek′ chū əl) *n.* a person who likes to study and think about ideas: *University professors are usually intellectuals.*

intelligence (in tel′ ə jəns) *n.* the ability to learn and understand and solve problems.

intelligent (in tel′ ə jənt) *adj.* **1.** quick at learning; bright: *an intelligent pupil.* **2.** clever; well-thought-out: *intelligent conversation.* —**intelligently** *adv.*

intend (in tend′) *v.* **1.** to have an aim; to plan: *We intend to play tennis after school.* **2.** to mean: *What did you intend by your remark?* **intending. intended.**

intense (in tens′) *adj.* very strong; extreme: *After six hours of intense studying, I needed a good night's rest.* —**intensely** *adv.*

intention (in ten′ shən) *n.* a purpose; a plan: *It is our intention to go to the cottage on the weekend.*

inter– is a prefix that means "between": an "international" border exists between two nations.

interest (in′ trist *or* in′ tər ist) *n.* **1.** a desire to learn, know, or do something; curiosity: *an interest in sports.* **2.** something that causes such a desire: *Playing chess is one of my interests.* **3.** money that the bank pays you when you have a savings account, or money that you pay the bank if you have a loan. —*v.* to attract attention or curiosity: *Your ideas interest me greatly.* **interesting. interested.**

interesting (in′ tris ting *or* in′ tər əs′ ting) *adj.* attracting and holding your attention: *Our teacher is so interesting that we never get bored in her class.*

interfere (in′ tər fēr′) *v.* **1.** to get in the way of: *Don't interfere with my plans—I know what I'm doing.* **2.** to interrupt: *The party next door lasted all night and interfered with my sleep.* **interfering. interfered.**

interior (in tēr′ ē ər) *n.* the inside: *The interior of the car is clean. The exterior could use a wash.*

interjection (in′ tər jek′ shən) *n.* an exclamation or cry of emotion: *Some interjections are "Oh!" "Ah!" and "Ouch!"*

internal (in tər′ nəl) *adj.* having to do with the inside of something: *The heart is an internal organ of the body.*

international (in′ tər nash′ ən əl) *adj.* between or among nations: *The Olympic Games are an international sports event.* —**internationally** *adv.*

interpret (in tür′ prit) *v.* to explain the meaning of something, often in another language; to translate: *Can you interpret the words of that Russian song?* **interpreting. interpreted.**

interrupt (in′ tə rupt′) *v.* to break into what someone is saying or doing: *Don't interrupt me when I'm talking.* **interrupting. interrupted.**

intersection (in′ tər sek′ shən) *n.* the place where two streets cross: *This busy intersection needs traffic lights to prevent accidents.*

interview (in′ tər vyū′) *n.* a meeting with someone, in which questions are asked: *a job interview.* —*v.* to meet with someone and ask him or her questions: *That news reporter will be interviewing the Prime Minister.* **interviewing. interviewed.**

intestine (in tes′ tən) *n.* the long, curved tube, below the stomach, that helps the body to digest food.

into (in′ tū) *prep.* **1.** to the inside of: *The children went into the stadium.* **2.** to the form of: *The snow changed into rain.*

introduce (in′ trə dūs′ *or* in′ trə dyūs′) *v.* to say the names of people when they meet for the first time: *Ravi, I would like to introduce you to Sandy.* **introducing. introduced.**

introduction (in trə duk′ shən) *n.* **1.** the act of introducing someone. **2.** the opening part of a book.

intrude (in trūd′) *v.* to force your way in without being asked or wanted: *The stranger intruded on our private conversation.* **intruding. intruded.**

Inuit (in′ ū it *or* in′ yū it) *n. pl.* an aboriginal people living in northern Canada and other arctic regions: *Inuit means "people" or "the people." sing.* **Inuk.**

invade (in vād′) *v.* **1.** to attack and enter another country with an army in order to conquer it. **2.** to enter unwanted or by force: *Ants invaded the garden.* **invading. invaded.**

invalid (in′ və lid) *n.* a person who is in poor health and who usually needs help: *The invalid needs to be given his medicine five times a day.*

invasion (in vā′ zhən) *n.* the act of invading.

invent (in vent′) *v.* to think up and make something completely new, especially a machine or a product: *Alexander Graham Bell invented the telephone.* **inventing. invented.**

invention (in ven′ shən) *n.* something that has been invented: *The telephone is an invention.*

inventor (in ven′ tər) *n.* a person who invents something completely new, especially a machine or a product: *Who were the inventors of the personal computer?*

investigate (in ves′ tə gāt′) *v.* to carefully examine and search for an answer to something: *The police are investigating the robbery.* **investigating. investigated.**

investigation (in ves′ tə ga′ shən) *n.* a careful examination or search: *a police investigation.*

invisible (in viz′ ə bəl) *adj.* not able to be seen: *The black cat was invisible in the darkness.*

invitation (in′ və tā′ shən) *n.* a written or spoken offer to someone to come to a special occasion: *a wedding invitation.*

invite (in vīt′) *v.* to ask someone to come somewhere or do something: *We invited her to join us.* **inviting. invited.**

involve (in volv′) *v.* **1.** to be concerned with: *This math problem involves fractions.* **2.** to require: *Becoming an Olympic athlete involves years of training.* **3.** to take part in: *Are you involved in the school concert?* **involving. involved.**

inward, inwards (in′ wərd, in′ wərdz) *adv.* toward the inside or the centre: *Form a circle and face inward.*

iris (ī′ ris) *n.* **1.** the coloured part of your eye. **2.** a tall garden plant with thin leaves and a purple, white, or yellow flower. *pl.* **irises.**

iris

iron (ī′ ərn) *n.* **1.** a strong, grey metal, used for making tools, steel, and so on. **2.** an appliance used to smooth the wrinkles out of clothes. *—adj.* hard like iron: *My mother has an iron will. —v.* to press clothes with an iron. **ironing. ironed.**

irregular (ir reg′ yə lər) *adj.* not following a regular pattern or rule: *The English language has many irregular verbs.*

irresistible (ir′ i sist′ ə bəl) *adj.* too powerful to fight against: *Her laugh was irresistible, and soon the whole group was laughing.* —**irresistibly** *adv.*

irresponsible (ir′ ri spon′ sə bəl) *adj.* not acting in a responsible way: *irresponsible behaviour.* —**irresponsibly** *adv.*

irritable (ir′ ə tə bəl) *adj.* easily irritated or annoyed: *He didn't get enough sleep last night and is irritable today.*

irritate (ir′ ə tāt′) *v.* **1.** to make angry or impatient; to annoy: *The sound of water dripping from a tap irritates me.* **2.** to make sore: *Cigarette smoke irritates my throat.* **irritating. irritated.**

is (iz) *v.* the form of the verb **be** used with "he," "she," "it," or with a person's name: *He is going to sleep. Jean is tall and lean. It is a sunny day.*

–ish is a suffix that means "something like" or "not completely": "yellowish" means something like yellow; a pear is a "roundish" fruit.

island (ī′ lənd) *n.* a piece of land that is completely surrounded by water.

isle (īl) *n.* a small island.

isn't (iz′ ənt) a short form (contraction) of **is not**.

isolated (ī′ sə lā′ təd) *adj.* separated from others: *Our cottage is on an isolated island, far from the mainland.*

issue (ish′ ū) *n.* **1.** an edition of a magazine or newspaper: *Did you see this month's issue of the magazine?* **2.** a subject or problem to be discussed: *The class discussed the issue of air pollution.* —*v.* to send out or publish: *The post office issues stamps.* **issuing. issued.**

it (it) *pron.* the thing, animal, idea, or fact being talked about: *I watched the new TV show and loved it.*

italics (i tal′ əks *or* ī tal′ əks) *n. pl.* slanted letters that are used to set a word or group of words apart from the rest: *This sentence is printed in italics.*

itch (ich) *n.* **1.** a prickly feeling on your skin that makes you want to scratch. **2.** a strong, restless desire: *I have an itch to travel to a foreign country. pl.* **itches.** —*v.* to have or feel an itch. **itching. itched.** it **itches.**

item (ī′ təm) *n.* a separate thing belonging to a larger group: *There are ten items on the shopping list.*

its (its) *adj.* belonging to it: *The cat drank its milk.*

it's (its) a short form (contraction) of **it is**.

Be careful not to mix up **its** with **it's**.
*The dog lost **its** collar.*
***It's** (It is) raining today.*

itself (it self′) *pron.* its own self. **Itself** is used when the subject and object of a verb are the same: *The dog stretched itself out on the rug.*

I've (īv) a short form (contraction) of **I have**.

ivory (īv′ rē *or* ī′ və rē) *n.* **1.** a hard, white substance, like bone, that an elephant's tusks are made of. **2.** a white piano key.
—*adj.* having a creamy or yellowish-white colour, like an elephant's tusk.

ivy (ī′ vē) *n.* a climbing plant, often having shiny green leaves: *ivy-covered walls.*

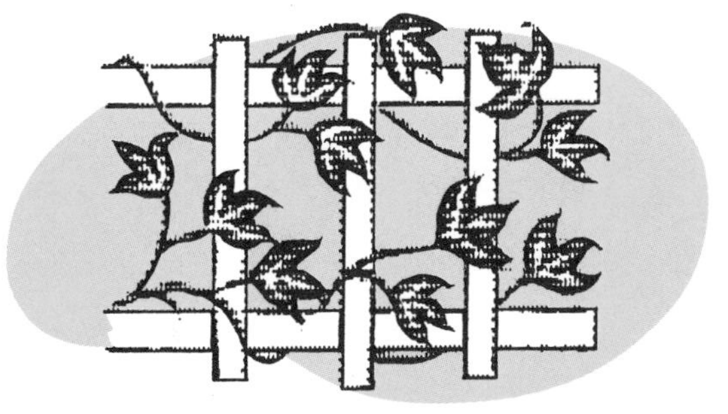

ivy

jab (jab) *v.* to poke or stab: *When I was sewing, I jabbed the needle into my finger by accident.* **jabbing. jabbed.**

jack (jak) *n.* **1.** a device used for raising a heavy object a short distance: *A car jack lifts one corner of a car so that a flat tire can be changed.* **2.** a playing card with a picture of a young man on it.

jacket (jak′ it) *n.* a short coat.

jack-in-the-box (jak′ in ᴛʜə boks′) *n.* a toy figure that springs up suddenly from a box when the top is opened.

jack-o'-lantern (jak′ ə lan′ tərn) *n.* a pumpkin hollowed out and carved into a face for Halloween.

jackpot (jak′ pot′) *n.* the biggest prize of money won in a contest, a lottery, and so on.

jack-rabbit (jak′ rab′ it) *n.* a large hare with very long ears and long back legs.

jack-rabbit

jade (jād) *n.* a hard, precious stone, usually green or white, used in jewellery and carvings.

jagged (jag′ əd) *adj.* having sharp, uneven edges: *I cut my foot on a jagged piece of broken glass.*

jaguar (jag′ wär) *n.* a wild cat of Central and South America that has a spotted coat. It is similar to a leopard, but larger and heavier.

jail (jāl) *n.* a prison, especially a temporary one. —*v.* to lock up in jail. **jailing. jailed.**

jam (jam) *n.* **1.** a bread spread made from fruit boiled with sugar until it is thick. **2.** crowded people or vehicles: *a traffic jam.* —*v.* **1.** to crowd together: *We were jammed in the crowded subway train during rush hour.* **2.** to be stuck: *The window is jammed and won't open.* **jamming. jammed.**

janitor (jan′ ə tər) *n.* the caretaker of a building.

January (jan′ yū er′ ē) *n.* the first month of the year.

jar (jär) *n.* a glass container, with a wide mouth and a lid that can be removed.

jaw (jo) *n.* the upper and lower bones that form the frame of your mouth and hold the teeth: *The lower jaw can move up and down.*

jay (jā) *n.* a bird that chatters noisily and is often brightly coloured. *pl.* **jays.**

jazz (jaz) *n.* a style of music, with strong, unusual rhythms.

jealous (jel′ əs) *adj.* **1.** feeling unhappy and angry because another person has something you want; envious: *She is jealous of her best friend's popularity.* **2.** afraid that someone you love may love somebody else better. —**jealously** *adv.*

jealousy (jel′ ə sē) *n.* a jealous feeling; envy.

jeans (jēnz) *n. pl.* casual pants made of denim or other strong cotton cloth.

In England, "jean" was the name given to a type of tough, cotton cloth. This cloth was first made in Genoa, Italy. So the word **jeans** comes from the name of Genoa.

jeep (jēp) *n.* a powerful car with heavy wheels, used for travelling over bumpy or rough country: *Jeeps were first used in the army.*

jelly (jel′ ē) *n.* a soft yet firm food that is usually made from fruit boiled with sugar. *pl.* **jellies.**

jellyfish (jel′ ē fish′) *n.* a sea animal with a soft, jelly-like body and stinging tentacles. *pl.* **jellyfish.**

jellyfish

jerk (jürk) *n.* a quick, sharp pull or movement. —*v.* to move or pull in jerks: *I jerked the heavy sled along the snow.* **jerking. jerked.**

jester (jest′ ər) *n.* in earlier times, a clown whose job was to amuse kings, queens, and royal guests.

jet (jet) *n.* **1.** a stream of liquid or gas, shot out of a small opening: *The fountain sent up a jet of water.* **2.** a large airplane pushed forward by jets of hot gas.

jet stream a strong wind that blows at a high altitude.

jewel (jū′ əl) *n.* a precious stone, such as a diamond or ruby; a gem.

jewellery, jewelry (jū′ əl rē *or* jūl′ rē) *n.* necklaces, rings, watches, and other ornaments used for decorating the body.

jig (jig) *n.* a lively dance.

jiggle (jig′ əl) *v.* to shake slightly. **jiggling. jiggled.**

jigsaw puzzle (jig′ so puz′ əl) a puzzle of differently shaped cardboard pieces that are fitted together to make a picture.

job (job) *n.* **1.** work that is done for pay; employment: *My cousin has a job in a factory.* **2.** a piece of work; a task: *Inez has the job of sweeping the path.*

jockey (jok′ ē) *n.* a person who rides horses in races. *pl.* **jockeys.**

jog (jog) *v.* to run at a slow, steady pace: *I jogged in the park for an hour.* **jogging. jogged.**

jogger (jog′ ər) *n.* a person who jogs.

join (join) *v.* **1.** to fasten or connect together: *to join hands.* **2.** to become part of a group of people: *to join a team.* **joining. joined.**

joint (joint) *n.* a place where two parts are joined together: *A knuckle is a joint between a finger and the rest of your hand.*

joke (jōk) *n.* something said or done to make people laugh. —*v.* to say or do something as a joke. **joking. joked.**

joker (jōk′ ər) *n.* **1.** a person who tells jokes or plays jokes. **2.** an extra playing card, usually having a picture of a jester.

jolly (jol′ ē) *adj.* merry; full of fun: *a jolly clown; a jollier one; the jolliest clown in the circus.*

jolt (jōlt) *n.* a sudden bump, jerk, or shock. —*v.* **1.** to move in jerks. **2.** to give a sudden shock to: *The bus driver slammed on the brakes and jolted me out of my snooze.* **jolting. jolted.**

jot (jot) *v.* (used with **down**) to make a quick note in writing: *Jot down the phone number before you forget it.* **jotting. jotted.**

journal (jür′ nəl) *n.* **1.** a magazine or newspaper. **2.** a diary.

journalist (jür′ nəl ist) *n.* a person whose job is to write news stories for a newspaper or magazine.

journey (jùr′ nē) *n.* a trip to a distant place, especially over land. *pl.* **journeys.** —*v.* to travel a distance: *We journeyed across Canada.* **journeying. journeyed.**

A French word for "day" is *journée,* and from it we get **journey**. A journey used to mean the distance that a person could travel in one day.

joy (joi) *n.* great happiness or delight.

joyful (joi′ fəl) *adj.* full of joy; glad. —**joyfully** *adv.*

judge (juj) *n.* **1.** a person in charge of a court of law: *A judge passes a sentence when someone is found guilty.* **2.** a person who chooses the winner of a contest. —*v.* **1.** to decide how good something is: *Don't judge a book by its cover.* **2.** to choose the winner of a contest. **judging. judged.**

judgment, judgement (juj′ mənt) *n.* **1.** an opinion or decision. **2.** the ability to judge: *good judgment.*

judo (jū′ dō) *n.* a Japanese form of self-defence and sport, using no weapons.

Judo comes from two Japanese words, *ju* and *do,* which together mean "gentle way." Judo is called a gentle way of fighting because it involves no weapons.

jug (jug) *n.* a container for liquids, with a handle and a spout for pouring.

juggle (jug′ əl) *v.* to toss up several balls or other objects and keep them in the air at the same time. **juggling. juggled.**

juice (jūs) *n.* the liquid in fruits or vegetables, and in meat. —**juicy** *adj.*

July (jū lī′ *or* jə lī′) *n.* the seventh month of the year.

jump (jump) *n.* a leap up off the ground: *a jump over a puddle.* —*v.* to leap up off the ground or over something. **jumping. jumped.**

jumper (jump′ ər) *n.* **1.** a person or animal that jumps. **2.** a sleeveless dress, worn over a blouse.

junction (junk′ shən) *n.* a place where railway lines, rivers, or roads meet or cross.

June (jūn) *n.* the sixth month of the year.

jungle (jung′ gəl) *n.* a tropical area of land thickly covered with trees, bushes, and vines.

junior (jūn′ nyər) *n.* a younger person: *Ann is younger than I am, so she is my junior.* —*adj.* younger or less experienced: *Next year, the junior officer will be a senior officer.*

junk (jungk) *n.* **1.** worthless rubbish. **2.** a Chinese sailing ship, with a flat bottom.

junk

Jupiter (jū′ pə tər) *n.* **1.** in Roman mythology, the ruler of all the gods. **2.** the largest of the nine planets: *Jupiter is the fifth planet from the sun.*

jury (jū′ rē) *n.* a group of people who sit in a court of law to decide if someone is innocent or guilty. *pl.* **juries.**

just (just) *adj.* fair; right: *The jury's decision was a just one.* —*adv.* **1.** barely: *The toddler was just able to reach the chair.* **2.** only; merely: *We were just joking.* **3.** exactly: *This shirt fits me just right.*

justice (jus′ tis) *n.* fairness: *The court expects justice from a jury.*

juvenile (jū′ və nīl *or* jū′ və nəl) *adj.* having to do with young people: *The juvenile section of a library holds children's books.*

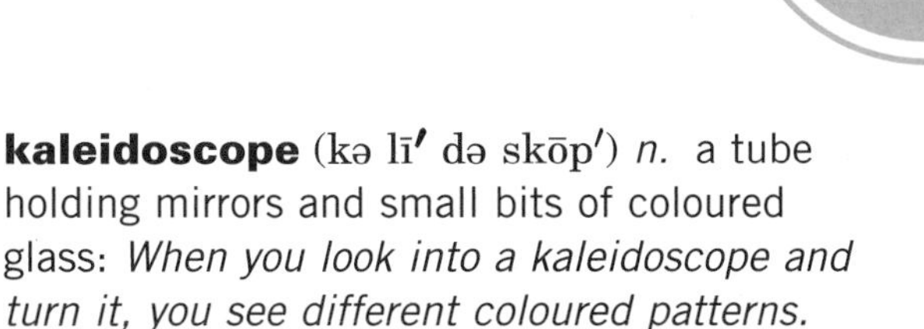

kaleidoscope (kə lī′ də skōp′) *n.* a tube holding mirrors and small bits of coloured glass: *When you look into a kaleidoscope and turn it, you see different coloured patterns.*

kangaroo (kang′ gə rü′) *n.* an Australian mammal, with short front legs, large and strong back legs for jumping, and a pouch for carrying its young. *pl.* **kangaroos.**

karate (kə ro′ tē) *n.* a Japanese form of fighting without weapons. The legs and arms are used to strike blows.

kayak (kī′ ak) *n.* **1.** an Inuit canoe, made of animal skins stretched over a wooden frame. The paddler sits in a hole in the middle. **2.** a similar canoe made of modern materials, used in sports contests.

kayak

keen (kēn) *adj.* **1.** eager; enthusiastic: *Michelle is a keen squash player.* **2.** sharp: *a knife with a keen edge.* —**keenly** *adv.*

keep (kēp) *v.* **1.** to hold or to have: *I will keep the key until it is needed.* **2.** to continue doing something: *to keep walking; to keep still.* **3.** to carry out: *to keep a promise; to keep your word.*

for keeps to keep forever: *If I win this game, I get the prize for keeps.*

keep up to continue: *Keep up the good work!*

keep up with to go as fast as: *Will you be able to keep up with me in the race?*

keg (keg) *n.* a small barrel: *a beer keg.*

kelp (kelp) *n.* a brown seaweed: *Kelp is sometimes eaten as a health food. It is also used as fertilizer.*

kennel (ken′ əl) *n.* **1.** a small shelter for dogs. **2.** a place where dogs are bred or cared for.

kernel (kůr′ nəl) *n.* **1.** the part of a nut inside the shell: *The kernel is the part of a nut that you eat.* **2.** a grain or seed.

ketchup (kech′ əp) *n.* a thick sauce made from tomatoes, onions, sugar, and spices: *Ketchup is put on hamburgers, French fries, and other food as a flavouring.*

The word **ketchup** comes from a Chinese word for a type of fish sauce. In Europe, ketchup was made from fruit, mushrooms, and nuts. Settlers in North America substituted tomatoes, thus creating the ketchup that we use today.

kettle (ket′ əl) *n.* a metal pot with a spout, used for boiling water: *a tea kettle.*

key (kē) *n.* **1.** a small, shaped piece of metal that fits into a lock and opens it. **2.** a black or white part of a piano, or a button on a computer, that is pressed down with the fingers. **3.** a chart that explains the symbols in a map, a dictionary, and so on. **4.** a low island or reef: *the Florida keys.* *pl.* **keys.**

keyboard (kē′ bȯrd′) *n.* a set of keys on a piano, computer, and so on.

keyhole (kē′ hōl′) *n.* the opening in a lock into which a key fits.

khaki (ka′ kē *or* ko′ kē *or* kȧr′ kē) *n.* **1.** a dull yellowish-brown colour. **2.** a strong cloth of this colour, used for soldiers' uniforms. —*adj.* having the colour of khaki.

kick (kik) *n.* a blow with the foot: *The soccer player gave the ball a powerful kick.* —*v.* **1.** to hit with your foot. **2.** to move your feet in swimming. **kicking. kicked.**

kid (kid) *n.* **1.** a young goat. **2.** a child. —*v.* to tease; to joke: *Are you serious, or are you just kidding?* **kidding. kidded.**

kidnap (kid′ nap) *v.* to carry off and hold a person by force. **kidnapping. kidnapped.**

kidney (kid′ nē) *n.* one of two small organs on either side of the body. The kidneys separate waste matter and water from the blood. *pl.* **kidneys.**

kidney bean a dark brown bean shaped like a kidney.

kill (kil) *v.* to cause the death of a person or animal; to slay. **killing. killed.**

kilo- is a prefix meaning "thousand": a "kilogram" is one thousand grams; a "kilometre" is one thousand metres.

kilogram (kil′ ə gram′) *n.* a unit for measuring mass; kg is the symbol. 1 kg = 1000 g.

kilometre (kil′ ə mē′ tər *or* kə lom′ ə tər) *n.* a unit for measuring distance; km is the symbol. 1 km = 1000 m.

kilt (kilt) *n.* a pleated skirt, reaching to the knees, traditionally worn by men in parts of Scotland.

kimono (kə mō′ nə *or* kə mō′ nō) *n.* **1.** a loose robe that has wide sleeves and is tied at the waist with a wide sash. Kimonos are worn by women and men in Japan. **2.** a loose robe worn around the house. *pl.* **kimonos.**

kin (kin) *n.* a person's relatives: *"Next of kin" means the closest living relative or relatives.*

kind (kīnd) *n.* a sort; a type: *There are many kinds of cats.* —*adj.* **1.** helpful and caring: *kind deeds.* **2.** gentle; thoughtful: *kind words.* (opp. **unkind.**)

kindergarten (kin′ dər gär′ tən) *n.* a school or grade for young children that comes before grade one.

The word **kindergarten** comes from two German words: *kinder,* meaning "children," and *garten,* meaning "garden." You might think of a kindergarten as a garden of children!

kindle (kin′ dəl) *v.* to set on fire: *to kindle wood.* **kindling. kindled.**

kindly (kīnd′ lē) *adv.* **1.** in a friendly way: *He acted kindly to his new neighbours.* **2.** please: *Kindly tell me the time.*

kindness (kīnd′ nəs) *n.* kind treatment or a kind act. *pl.* **kindnesses.**

king (king) *n.* **1.** a man who rules a country. **2.** a great leader: *the king of popular music.*

kingdom (king′ dəm) *n.* a country ruled by a king or queen.

kinship (kin′ ship) *n.* **1.** a family relationship. **2.** a bond; a connection: *After playing on the team for a month, I felt a strong kinship with the other players.*

kiosk (kē′ osk) *n.* a small stand or booth where newspapers, candy, or other things are sold.

kiss (kis) *n.* a touch with the lips. *pl.* **kisses.** —*v.* to touch with the lips, as a sign of affection or as a greeting. **kissing. kissed.**

kit (kit) *n.* a set of tools or materials needed to do a certain job: *a tool kit; a first-aid kit.*

kitchen (kich′ ən) *n.* a room where food is prepared and cooked.

kite (kīt) *n.* a light, wooden frame, covered with paper, plastic, or cloth. It is tied to a string and flown in the air on windy days.

kitten (kit′ ən) *n.* a young cat.

kiwi (kē′ wē) *n.* **1.** a small, oval fruit with a light green flesh and a brown, fuzzy skin. **2.** a plump bird of New Zealand that cannot fly and has no tail. *pl.* **kiwis.**

kiwi

knapsack (nap′ sak′) *n.* a large cloth or nylon bag with two straps for carrying it on your back: *A knapsack is often used to carry supplies on a camping trip.*

knead (nēd) *v.* to press, fold, and shape dough or wet clay with your hands. **kneading. kneaded.**

knee (nē) *n.* the joint between the upper and lower part of your leg.

kneecap (nē′ kap′) *n.* the flat bone at the front of your knee.

kneel (nēl) *v.* to go down on your knees. **kneeling. knelt** or **kneeled.**

knew (nyū *or* nū) see **know.**

knife (nīf) *n.* a utensil or tool, used for cutting or spreading. A knife has a metal blade with a sharp edge, fastened to a handle. *pl.* **knives.**

knight (nīt) *n.* a man with the title "Sir": *In earlier times, knights were noblemen who wore armour and fought for their king or queen.*

knit (nit) *v.* to loop yarn into cloth, using long needles: *I'm going to knit a sweater.* **knitting. knitted** or **knit.**

knob (nob) *n.* a round handle for opening a door or a drawer.

knock (nok) *n.* a banging action or blow made with the fist or knuckles: *a knock on the door.* —*v.* to hit with your fist or knuckles: *to knock on a door.* **knocking. knocked.**

knot (not) *n.* **1.** a tight lump made by tying together pieces of rope, string, hair, and so on. **2.** the hard, round area on a tree where a branch grows out. **3.** a unit for measuring speed when navigating ships. —*v.* **1.** to tie a knot: *to knot a string.* **2.** to tangle in knots. **knotting. knotted.**

know (nō) *v.* **1.** to understand: *I know what you mean.* **2.** to have information about: *She knows the answer.* **3.** to be familiar with a person: *I know him.* **4.** to recognize: *I know what that object is.* **5.** to have a skill in: *He knows how to play the piano.* **knowing. knew.** I have **known.**

knowledge (nol′ ij) *n.* understanding; information; education: *She has a great knowledge of history.*

knowledgeable (nol′ ij ə bəl) *adj.* having knowledge; well informed: *Sarah is knowledgeable about science.*

knuckle (nuk′ əl) *n.* a finger joint, especially one between the finger and the rest of the hand.

koala (kō ol′ ə) *n.* a small Australian mammal that is grey and furry, has no tail, and carries its young in a pouch: *Koalas look like teddy bears.*

kung fu (kung fū) *n.* a Chinese form of fighting, using blows and kicks, and sometimes weapons.

lab (lab) short for **laboratory**.

label (lā′ bəl) *n.* a small piece of paper or cloth that is attached to something to mark it: *A label is used to show what something is, who it belongs to, or where it is going.* —*v.* to attach a label to something. **labelling. labelled.**

laboratory (lab′ rə tȯr ē *or* lə bȯr′ ə trē) *n.* a place where scientific work is done. *pl.* **laboratories.**

labour, labor (lā′ bər) *n.* hard work: *After many hours of labour, the workers stopped to have a meal.* —*v.* to work hard; to toil: *We laboured to finish building the scenery for the school play.*

lace (lās) *n.* **1.** delicate material made of fine threads that form a pattern. **2.** a cord or string used to hold something together: *a shoelace.* —*v.* to tie with a lace: *to lace up skates.* **lacing. laced.**

lack (lak) *n.* something that is missing: *The thin animals suffered from a lack of food.* —*v.* to be without something: *They also lacked water.* **lacking. lacked.**

lacquer (lak′ ər) *n.* a shiny substance used as a coating for wood or metal.

lacrosse (lə kros′) *n.* a game in which players use sticks with nets to pass a rubber ball and try to score on the other team.

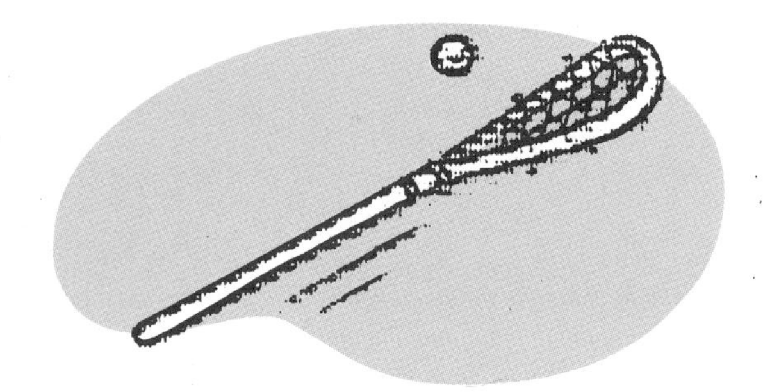

lacrosse stick

Lacrosse was originally played by aboriginal peoples in Canada. There were sometimes hundreds of players on each side. The French settlers changed some rules and gave the game the name by which we know it today. In French, "la crosse" means "the hooked stick."

lad (lad) *n.* a boy or a young man.

ladder (lad′ ər) *n.* a set of steps or rungs fastened between two poles, used for climbing to another level.

ladle (lā′ dəl) *n.* a serving spoon with a long handle, used to serve liquids such as soup.

lady (lā′ dē) *n.* **1.** a woman who has good manners. **2.** a title given to a noblewoman. *pl.* **ladies.**

ladybug (lā′ dē bug′) *n.* a small beetle that is red or orange with black spots.

lag (lag) *v.* to move slowly, falling behind others: *He lagged behind the other hikers.* **lagging. lagged.**

laid (lād) see **lay**.

lake (lāk) *n.* a large body of water with land all around: *Lakes usually have fresh, not salty, water.*

lamb (lam) *n.* a young sheep.

lame (lām) *adj.* not able to walk properly because of a hurt leg. —**lamely** *adv.*

lamp (lamp) *n.* a device that provides light: *a table lamp; a street lamp.*

land (land) *n.* **1.** the solid part of the earth's surface: *land and sea.* **2.** ground; soil: *farmland.* **3.** a country: *Finland is a northern land.* —*v.* to reach land from the sea or air: *The cargo ship landed at Vancouver.* **landing. landed.**

landing (land′ ing) *n.* **1.** the return to land after a voyage or flight: *The space shuttle made a smooth landing.* **2.** a platform between flights of stairs. **3.** a place where boats tie up.

landlord (land′ lȯrd′) *n.* a person who owns a house, an apartment, or other building that he or she rents to someone else.

landscape (land′ skāp′) *n.* **1.** an area of land that has a special appearance; scenery: *The postcard shows a New Brunswick landscape.* **2.** a painting or photograph of scenery.

landslide (land′ slīd′) *n.* a large amount of dirt and rocks that slides down a mountain or hill.

lane (lān) *n.* a narrow road or path.

language (lang′ gwij) *n.* **1.** human speech, spoken or written. **2.** the speech used by the people of a particular country: *the English language; the French language.* **3.** the words and symbols used by a particular group: *computer language; sign language.*

> **Language** comes from the Latin word *lingua,* meaning "tongue." To speak, you use the tongue, as well as the lips and teeth. No wonder we sometimes refer to a language as a "tongue"!

lantern (lan′ tərn) *n.* a glass case with a light inside.

lantern

lap (lap) *n.* **1.** the top of your thighs when you are sitting down: *The cat sat on my lap.* **2.** once around a track: *The race consists of four laps around the field.* —*v.* to drink, using the tongue: *The cat lapped up her milk.*

lapel (lə pel′) *n.* a flap that is folded back against the front, top part of a jacket or coat: *He pinned a flower on the lapel of his jacket.*

laptop (lap′ top′) *n.* a small, light computer that can be used on a person's lap.

large (lȧrj) *adj.* **1.** big in size: *A mountain is a big hill.* **2.** great in amount or number: *a large crowd; a larger crowd; the largest crowd of all.*

larva (lȧr′ və) *n.* the form of an insect after hatching out of an egg. A larva often looks like a short worm: *A caterpillar is the larva of a butterfly. pl.* **larvae** (lȧr′ vē).

laser (lā′ zər) *n.* a device that produces a very powerful and straight beam of light.

lash (lash) *n.* **1.** a swift stroke from a whip. **2.** a hair on an eyelid: *an eyelash.*

lass (las) *n.* a girl or a young woman. *pl.* **lasses.**

lasso (la sū′) *n.* a rope with a loop at the end, used to catch animals. *pl.* **lassos.** —*v.* to catch with a lasso. **lassoing. lassoed.**

last (last) *adj.* **1.** following all the others; at the end; final: *September 30th is the last day of that month.* **2.** the one before: *last night; last week.* **3.** the only one left: *The last one in the game is the winner.* —*v.* to go on; to continue: *The food must last for six days.* **lasting. lasted.**

at last finally: *At last we reached the top of the tower.*

latch (lach) *n.* a part for fastening closed a door or gate. *pl.* **latches.** —*v.* to close with a latch. **latching. latched.**

late (lāt) *adj.* coming or happening after the usual time: *The bus is late today.* —*adv.* after the usual time: *We stayed up late.*

lately (lāt′ lē) *adv.* recently: *How have you been feeling lately?*

later (lāt′ ər) *adv.* in the future: *We'll be going to the movies later this week.*

latest (lāt′ əst) *adj.* the most recent or modern; up-to-date: *My sister has bought the latest model of computer.*

Latin (lat′ ən) *n., adj.* the language of ancient Rome.

latitude (lat′ ə tūd′ *or* lat′ ə tyūd′) *n.* the distance, measured in degrees, north or south of the equator.

latter (lat′ ər) *adj.* the second of two things named: *I enjoy soccer and hockey, especially the latter.*

laugh (laf) *n.* a loud "ha-ha" sound made when you see or hear something funny. —*v.* to make such a sound to show that you are happy or that you find something funny. **laughing. laughed.**

laughter (laf′ tər) *n.* the sound of laughing.

launch (lonch) *n.* the act of sending out a missile or spacecraft: *The launch of the space shuttle is planned for today. pl.* **launches.** —*v.* **1.** to send out or up into the air: *to launch a missile.* **2.** to set a boat on water. **launching. launched.**

laundry (lon′ drē) *n.* **1.** dirty clothes to be washed. **2.** a room where clothes are washed and ironed. *pl.* **laundries.**

lava (lav′ ə) *n.* very hot, melted rock flowing out of a volcano.

law (lo) *n.* a rule made by the government that everyone must obey.

lawn (lon) *n.* an area of cut grass by a house or in a park.

lawn mower (lon mō′ ər) a machine used for cutting the grass in a lawn.

lawyer (loi′ yər *or* lo′ yər) a person who knows the law and is qualified to give people advice about it.

lay (lā) *v.* **1.** to place something down in a resting position: *to lay dishes on a table.* **2.** to produce an egg: *Birds, reptiles, and insects lay eggs.* **laying. laid. 3.** past tense of **lie** (definition 2).

layer (lā′ ər) *n.* one thickness or one coating of something: *I made a cake with three layers.*

laziness (lā′ zē nəs) *n.* the condition of being lazy.

lazy (lā′ zē) *adj.* not willing to work or do much: *a lazy dog; a lazier dog; the laziest dog on the street.* —**lazily** *adv.*

lead (lēd) *n.* the first or most important position: *My brother has the lead in the race.* —*v.* **1.** to show the way by going in front; to guide: *to lead the way.* **2.** to direct: *to lead a group.* **3.** to be at the front: *My brother is leading the race.* **leading. led.**

lead (led) *n.* **1.** a heavy, grey metal, used to make pipes and other objects. **2.** the dark grey part of a pencil that makes marks.

leader (lēd′ ər) *n.* a person who goes in front and shows the way or takes charge: *Martha is the leader of the science club.*

leaf (lēf) *n.* **1.** one of the thin, flat, green parts growing out of the stem of a plant or tree. **2.** a sheet of paper; a page (back and front) in a book. *pl.* **leaves.**

leaflet (lēf′ lət) *n.* a printed sheet of paper, sometimes folded, with information: *We handed out leaflets about the sidewalk sale at the mall.*

league (lēg) *n.* a group of teams that regularly play against one another.

leak (lēk) *n.* a hole or crack through which gas or liquid comes in or escapes: *a leak in the boat.* —*v.* (for a liquid or gas) to enter or escape through a hole or crack: *Gas leaked from the pipe.* **leaking. leaked.**

lean (lēn) *adj.* **1.** thin: *a tall, lean man.* **2.** having little fat: *lean meat.* —*v.* **1.** to rest against: *The ladder is leaning against a wall.* **2.** to slant: *The post leans to one side.* **leaning. leaned.**

leap (lēp) *n.* a jump, especially over something: *The dancer gave a great leap across the stage.* —*v.* to jump: *The dog leaped over the fence.* **leaping. leaped** or **leapt** (lept).

leap year every fourth year, when February has 29 days instead of 28.

How do we know if a year is a **leap year**? If the last two numbers of the year can be evenly divided by four, then it is a leap year. For example, the years 2000 and 2004 are leap years.

learn (lůrn) *n.* **1.** to find out: *to learn the truth.* **2.** to gain knowledge or skill by studying, training, or experience: *Sam is learning how to cook.* **learning. learned** or **learnt** (lůrnt).

learning (lůrn′ ing) *n.* knowledge; education: *a teacher of great learning.*

lease (lēs) *n.* a written agreement that allows a person to rent property for a certain length of time: *a one-year lease on an apartment.* —*v.* to sign such an agreement: *They leased the car for a year.* **leasing. leased.**

leash (lēsh) *n.* a strap or chain for holding a dog. *pl.* **leashes.**

least (lēst) *n.* the smallest amount: *I like football the least of all sports. I like hockey the most.* —*adj.* less than any other: *My least favourite subject is history.*

at least **1.** no fewer or less than: *There were at least thirty people at Zachary's party.* **2.** whatever else happens; in any case: *It's a cloudy day for a picnic, but at least it isn't raining.*

leather (leTH′ ər) *n.* an animal's skin, treated and used to make shoes, gloves, wallets, and other things.

leave (lēv) *v.* **1.** to go out or away from: *Please leave the room.* **2.** to put or let something stay in a certain place: *Leave your shoes in the front hall.* **3.** to let someone be: *Leave her alone for a while.* **leaving. left.**

lecture (lek′ chər) *n.* **1.** a speech; a talk by an expert on a subject: *We went to a science lecture at the museum.* **2.** a scolding: *Our parents gave us a lecture about staying out too late.* —*v.* to give a lecture. **lecturing. lectured.**

led (led) see **lead.**

ledge (lej) *n.* a narrow shelf: *the window ledge.*

leek (lēk) *n.* a vegetable, related to the onion, that has a white bulb topped by long, thick green leaves.

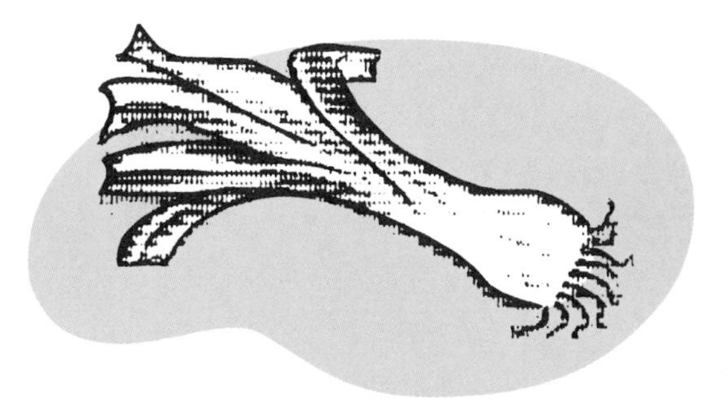

leek

left (left) *n.* the side opposite to right: *When you face north, west is on your left.* —*adj.* on or of the left: *the left hand.* —*adv.* to the left: *Turn left at the corner.* —*v.* see **leave.**

left-handed (left′ hand′ əd) *adj.* using your left hand more easily than you use your right hand: *a left-handed baseball pitcher.*

leftovers (left′ ō′ vərz) *n. pl.* food not finished at one meal and is then served at another meal.

leg (leg) *n.* **1.** one of the limbs on which people and animals stand and walk. **2.** anything like a leg: *a table leg.*

legal (lē′ gəl) *adj.* allowed by the law: *It is not legal to ride a bike on the sidewalk.* (*opp.* **illegal.**) —**legally** *adv.*

legend (lej′ ənd) *n.* a story passed down from long ago that is probably not true or only partly true: *the legend of King Arthur and the Knights of the Round Table.*

legible (lej′ ə bəl) *adj.* clear enough to be read: *legible handwriting.* (*opp.* **illegible.**) —**legibly** *adv.*

legislature (lej′ ə slā′ chər) *n.* a group of people who make laws: *Each province in Canada has its own legislature.*

leisure (lē′ zhər *or* lezh′ ər) *n.* free time away from a job or school: *We enjoyed our leisure by doing puzzles and playing word games.*

lemon (lem′ ən) *n.* a yellow, oval-shaped citrus fruit that has a sour taste.

lemonade (lem′ ən ād′) *n.* a drink made from lemons, water, and sugar.

lend (lend) *v.* to let someone use something of yours for a time: *Will you lend me your bike so I can go to the store?* **lending. lent.**

Be careful not to mix up **lend** and "borrow." You *lend* something *to* someone. You *borrow* something *from* someone.

length (length) *n.* **1.** how long a thing is, measured from one end to the other: *What is the length of a football field?* **2.** the amount of time something lasts: *The length of one day is twenty-four hours.*

lengthy (length′ ē) *adj.* lasting a long time: *This lengthy movie lasts three hours.*

lens (lenz) *n.* a curved piece of glass used in eyeglasses, cameras, and telescopes: *Depending on its shape, a lens makes an object appear closer or farther away.* *pl.* **lenses.**

leopard (lep′ ərd) *n.* a large, wild cat of Africa and Asia. It has a beige coat covered with black spots.

leotard (lē′ ə tärd′) *n.* a tight one-piece body garment worn by dancers and gymnasts. It is like a swimsuit with sleeves.

leprechaun (lep′ rə kon′) *n.* in Irish folk tales, a small, mischievous person.

less (les) *adj.* a smaller amount of; not as much: *I have less money today than I had yesterday.*

Less or fewer? Use *less* for quantity or size: *There is less room in the new arena.* Use *fewer* for numbers and things that can be counted: *There were fewer seats in the old arena.*

lessen (les′ ən) *v.* to make or become less; to decrease: *The pain lessened after I took the pill.* **lessening. lessened.**

lesson (les′ ən) *n.* **1.** something to be learned. **2.** one class period: *a music lesson.*

let (let) *v.* to permit; to allow: *Let me do it.* **letting. let.**

Let is sometimes used as a helping (auxiliary) verb with other verbs to give suggestions or commands: *Let us go to the movies.*

let down to disappoint: *They let us down when they made a promise that they didn't keep.*

let go to release: *Don't let go of the balloon.*

lethal (lē′ thəl) *adj.* causing death: *The poison gas was lethal and the plant died.*

let's (lets) a contraction (short form) of **let us.**

letter (let′ ər) *n.* **1.** one of the symbols of an alphabet: *A, B, and C are letters in the English alphabet.* **2.** a written message put in an envelope and sent to someone.

letter carrier (let′ ər ker′ ē ər) a person who delivers the mail.

lettuce (let′ is) *n.* a green vegetable with large leaves, eaten raw in salads.

level (lev′ əl) *n.* **1.** a height or depth: *What is the level of the water in the swimming pool?* **2.** a grade or rank: *an advanced level of education.* **3.** a storey or floor of a building: *a department store with seven levels.* —*adj.* **1.** flat and even, not sloping:

A pool table has a level surface. **2.** having the same height: *Make the two piles of books level with each other.*

lever (lev′ ər *or* lēv′ ər) *n.* **1.** a tool for lifting heavy objects: *A seesaw is a kind of lever.* **2.** a stick or handle that you pull or push to make a machine work.

liar (lī′ ər) *n.* someone who tells lies.

liberty (lib′ ər tē) *n.* freedom: *The prisoners will have their liberty in five years.*

librarian (lī brer′ ē ən) *n.* a person who is in charge of a library.

library (lī′ brer′ ē) *n.* a room or building where a collection of books, magazines, and so on are kept: *Books may be used inside a library, or they may be borrowed. pl.* **libraries.**

lice (līs) see **louse.**

licence (lī′ səns) *n.* an official document allowing you to keep, use, or do something: *a dog licence; a driver's licence.*

license (lī′ səns) *v.* to allow by law: *A doctor is licensed to treat illnesses.* **licensing. licensed.**

lichen (lī′ kən) *n.* a moss-like plant that spreads over rocks, trees, walls, and on the ground.

lichen

lick (lik) *v.* to wet with your tongue: *to lick a stamp.* **licking. licked.**

licorice (lik′ ə rish *or* lik′ ə ris) *n.* a sweet, strong-tasting black candy.

lid (lid) *n.* **1.** a cover that can be removed: *a box lid.* **2.** an eyelid.

lie (lī) *n.* a false statement. —*v.* **1.** to tell a lie: *The thief lied to the police officer.* **lying. lied.** **2.** to rest in a flat position: *Lie down if you are tired. The book is lying on the table.* **lying. lay.** I have **lain.**

lieutenant (lef ten′ ənt *or* lū ten′ ənt) *n.* an officer, below a captain, in the armed forces.

Lieutenant-Governor (lef ten′ ənt guv′ ər nər) *n.* the official head of a province: *The Lieutenant-Governor of each province is appointed by the Governor General of Canada.*

life (līf) *n.* **1.** the condition of being alive: *People, animals, and plants have life.* **2.** the period of time of being alive: *Grandma has had a long life.* **3.** a human being: *Several lives were lost in the accident. pl.* **lives** (līvz).

lifeboat (līf′ bōt′) *n.* a boat used for rescuing people in the water.

lifeguard (līf′ gärd′) *n.* a person trained to watch over swimmers and rescue them from trouble.

life preserver (līf′ prə zər′ vər) a ring or a jacket that floats in water and is designed to keep people from drowning.

lifestyle (līf′ stīl′) *n.* a way of life: *The lifestyle of my cousins in the city is very different from my lifestyle in the country.*

lifetime (līf′ tīm′) *n.* the period of time of being alive, from birth to death.

lift (lift) *n.* **1.** a ride: *May I have a lift to school?* **2.** something that takes skiers to the top of a hill. —*v.* to raise: *We lifted the heavy box.* **lifting. lifted.**

light (līt) *n.* **1.** brightness from something burning, such as the sun or a lamp. **2.** a device that provides light: *a room light; a flashlight.* —*adj.* **1.** not heavy: *as light as a feather.* —**lightly** *adv.* **2.** not dark: *He is wearing a light blue scarf.* —*v.* **1.** to set fire to: *to light a candle.* **2.** (used with **up**) to make bright. **lighting. lit.**

lightheaded (līt′ hed′ əd) *adj.* feeling dizzy.

lighthearted (līt′ härt′ əd) *adj.* cheerful; without worries. —**lightheartedly** *adv.*

lighthouse (līt′ hows′) *n.* a tower close to a body of water: *A lighthouse has a bright light that warns ships of dangerous rocks.*

lighthouse

lightning (lit′ ning) *n.* a flash of light in the sky, caused by electricity in a thunderstorm.

like (līk) *prep.* **1.** similar to: *The picture I drew looks just like you.* **2.** such as: *The grocer sells fruits like pineapples, kiwis, and mangos.* —*v.* **1.** to be fond of: *I like reading.* **2.** to want: *Would you like something to drink?* **liking. liked.**

likely (līk′ lē) *adj.* probable; to be expected: *It is likely to snow today.* —*adv.* probably.

likeness (līk′ nəs) *n.* **1.** a resemblance or similarity: *I am sometimes confused by the likeness between the two comedians.* **2.** a copy or picture of somebody or something: *My drawing was a perfect likeness of my grandfather.*

likewise (līk′ wīz′) *adv.* **1.** the same: *We watched my father plant the tomatoes and then did likewise.* **2.** also: *Jaad is a fine athlete and likewise an excellent musician.*

lilac (lī′ lək) *n.* **1.** a garden shrub that has purple or white blossoms with a sweet fragrance. **2.** a pale purple colour. —*adj.* having the colour of lilac.

lily (lil′ ē) *n.* a tall garden flower shaped like a trumpet: *Lilies grow from bulbs. pl.* **lilies.**

limb (lim) *n.* **1.** an arm or a leg. **2.** a tree branch.

lime (līm) *n.* **1.** a small, light green citrus fruit with a sour taste. **2.** a white powder made by burning limestone or shells. It is used to improve the soil and to make cement.

limerick (lim′ ər ik) *n.* a kind of humorous verse that has five lines: *In a limerick, the first, second, and fifth lines rhyme with one another. The third and fourth lines are shorter than the others, and they rhyme together.*

limestone (līm′ stōn′) *n.* a rock that is used in building and to make lime powder for cement.

limit (lim′ it) *n.* **1.** a point or line which cannot be passed: *The hills mark the limit of our walk.* **2.** a boundary: *the city limits.* —*v.* to set a limit; to restrict: *I will limit my speech to five minutes.* **limiting. limited.**

limp (limp) *n.* a lame walk, with more weight on one leg than the other. —*adj.* soft and bending easily; not stiff or firm: *Dry, uncooked noodles are hard and brittle; cooked noodles are limp.* —*v.* to walk with a limp. **limping. limped.**

line (līn) *n.* **1.** a long, thin mark: *Connect the dots with a line.* **2.** a row: *a line of people waiting for a bus.* **3.** a cord or rope: *a fishing line.* **4.** a track or route: *a railway line.* —*v.* **1.** to mark with lines. **2.** to put a lining in a piece of clothing. **lining. lined.**

line up **1.** to stand in line. **2.** to put in a line: *Line up the books on the shelf.*

linen (lin′ ən) *n.* **1.** cloth made from fibres of the flax plant. **2.** bedsheets and pillow cases made from linen or from a similar material.

line-up (līn′ up′) *n.* **1.** a row of people waiting for something: *a line-up for concert tickets.* **2.** the players taking part in a game: *The coach announced the line-up of players for Saturday's baseball game.*

linger (ling′ gər) *v.* to stay on, without being in a hurry to leave: *A small group lingered at the party after most people had left.* **lingering. lingered.**

lining (līn′ ing) *n.* a thin layer of material covering the inside of a suit, coat, or dress.

link (lingk) *n.* **1.** one of the connecting rings in a chain. **2.** something that joins or connects: *I feel a link with the country that my parents came from.* —*v.* to join things together: *All of us linked arms to form a circle.* **linking. linked.**

lion (lī′ ən) *n.* a large, wild cat of Africa and southern Asia, with a light brown coat. The males have shaggy manes.

lip (lip) *n.* one of the two pink fleshy edges of your mouth.

lipstick (lip′ stik′) *n.* a wax stick of make-up, used to colour the lips.

liquid (lik′ wid) *n.* a form of matter, such as water, that can be poured.

liquor (lik′ ər) *n.* a strong alcoholic drink.

lisp (lisp) *n.* a slight speech problem, where an "s" sounds like a "th," or an "r" sounds like a "w." —*v.* to speak with a lisp. **lisping. lisped.**

list (list) *n.* a column of names, numbers, words, and so on. —*v.* to arrange names, numbers, words, and so on in a column. **listing. listed.**

listen (lis′ ən) *v.* to hear or try to hear; to pay attention to. **listening. listened.**

literary (lit′ ə rer′ ē) *adj.* having to do with literature or writers: *The literary section of the newspaper includes reviews of new books.*

literate (lit′ ə rət) *adj.* **1.** able to read and write. **2.** educated: *The book club is made up of a literate group of people.* (*opp.* **illiterate.**)

literature (lit′ ər ə chər *or* lit′ rə chər) *n.* creative writing, especially fiction, poetry, and plays: *My brother is studying Canadian literature.*

litre (lē′ tər) *n.* a unit for measuring the volume of liquids; L is the symbol. 1 L = 1000 mL.

litter (lit′ ər) *n.* **1.** a number of animals all born together: *a litter of pigs.* **2.** waste paper and other garbage left lying around. —*v.* to leave such garbage around: *Please don't litter.* **littering. littered.**

little (lit′ əl) *adj.* **1.** small: *The white mouse is little, the brown one is littler, and the grey one is the littlest in the cage.* **2.** not much: *The first jug has little juice in it, the second jug has less, and the third jug has the least of all.*

live (līv) *adj.* **1.** living, not dead. **2.** active; having energy: *a live wire.* —*adv.* showing a TV or radio program as it happens, not taping it to be aired later: *The Stanley Cup game was shown live on TV.*

live (liv) *v.* **1.** to be alive; to have life: *My dog lived to be fifteen years old.* **2.** to dwell: *Fish live in the sea.* **living. lived.**

lively (līv′ lē) *adj.* full of life and pep: *a lively pup; a livelier one; the liveliest pup in the litter.*

liver (liv′ ər) *n.* a large, reddish-brown organ in the body: *The liver is located in the abdomen and helps your body use some of the substances that are in your blood.*

lives (līvz) see **life**.

livestock (līv′ stok′) *n.* horses, cattle, sheep, and other farm animals.

living (liv′ ing) *n.* regular money earned from a job. This money allows people to look after themselves and their families: *She writes newspaper articles for a living.*

living room a large room in a home for general use: *A living room usually has a couch and chairs.*

lizard (liz′ ərd) *n.* a reptile with a long body, a long tail, four short legs, and scales on its skin.

llama (lo′ mə *or* lam′ ə) *n.* a large South American mammal with soft, long wool: *A llama looks like a camel, but it has no hump.*

llama

load (lōd) *n.* a pile of goods to be carried: *a load of hay on a wagon.* —*v.* **1.** to place goods onto or into something: *to load a camera with film.* **2.** to put a bullet into a gun. **loading. loaded.**

loaf (lōf) *n.* **1.** a large, rectangular piece of baked bread that can be cut into slices. **2.** any food made into this shape: *meat loaf. pl.* **loaves.**

loan (lōn) *n.* the lending of money or something else: *The loan from the bank helped us pay for the car.*

lobby (lob′ ē) *n.* a hall or waiting area of a building. *pl.* **lobbies.**

lobster (lob′ stər) *n.* a large shellfish with a narrow body, eight legs, and two large claws.

local (lō′ kəl) *adj.* nearby: *Our local milk store is half a block away.* —**locally** *adv.*

locate (lō′ kāt *or* lō kāt′) *v.* **1.** to find the exact position of someone or something: *I am trying to locate your street on my map.* **2.** to settle somewhere: *The company located the new factory in Halifax.* **locating. located.**

location (lō kā′ shən) *n.* a position or place: *The location of the school is three blocks from my house.*

lock (lok) *n.* **1.** a secure part for closing a door or box, usually needing a key to open it. **2.** a curl of hair. **3.** a section of a river or canal where the water can be raised or lowered: *Locks allow ships to pass to a higher or lower level.* —*v.* to fasten with a lock. **locking. locked.**

locker (lok′ ər) *n.* a small closet that can be locked.

locomotive (lō′ kə mō′ tiv) *n.* the engine of a railway train.

lodge (loj) *n.* a house or an inn, usually in the country.

log (log) *n.* **1.** a sawed piece of a tree trunk or branch: *The early European settlers in Canada made log cabins to live in.* **2.** a diary of a voyage: *A captain keeps a daily log of the activities on a ship.*

logger (log′ ər) *n.* a person whose job is to cut down trees and get them to a sawmill.

logical (loj′ ə kəl) *adj.* able to think in a clear and sensible way: *Lynn's logical mind helps her solve puzzles.* (*opp.* **illogical.**)

> **–logy** is a suffix that means "a science": for instance, "geology" is the scientific study of what the earth is made of (*geo* is Greek for earth).

lone (lōn) *adj.* by itself; single: *We looked at the lone tree on the prairie.*

lonely (lōn′ lē) *adj.* feeling sad because you are by yourself or don't have friends: *a lonely child; a lonelier one; the loneliest child in the school.*

lonesome (lōn′ səm) *adj.* alone or lonely.

long (long) *adj.* **1.** having a great length from end to end; not short: *a long road.* **2.** taking much time: *a long wait.* —*v.* (used with **for** or **to**) to want very much; to wish for: *It was very cold in February, and we longed for summer to come.* **longing. longed.**

longing (long′ ing) *n.* a strong wish for something: *When you are homesick, you have a longing to be home.*

longitude (lonʹ jə tūd *or* lonʹ gə tyūd) *n.* a distance on the earth's surface, east or west of an imaginary line (0° longitude) in Greenwich, England, measured in degrees and marked by lines going from north to south on a map.

look (lu̇k) *n.* a glance or a gaze: *They gave me an angry look. Take a look at this.* —*v.* **1.** to fix your eyes on something; to watch: *Look at that!* **2.** to search for: *I've looked everywhere for my keys.* **3.** to appear: *He looks tired.* **4.** to face: *The house looks east.* **looking. looked.**

look after to take care of.

look down on not to have respect for someone.

look forward to to wait for something with pleasure: *I'm looking forward to my cousin's visit.*

look out to watch out: *Look out! The ball is coming at you!*

look up to to admire and want to be like a particular person: *I look up to my sister because she is kind and generous.*

loom (lūm) *n.* a machine that weaves threads into cloth.

loon (lūn) *n.* a water bird that has a black back covered with white spots. Loons dive for food and have a wailing cry: *Because the Canadian one-dollar coin has a picture of a loon on it, the coin is nicknamed a "loonie."*

loop (lūp) *n.* a ring in a string or rope. —*v.* to make such a ring. **looping. looped.**

loose (lūs) *adj.* **1.** free; not tied up: *The dog is running loose.* **2.** not tightly fastened: *It is easy to untie a loose knot.* **3.** baggy; roomy: *a loose pair of jeans.* —**loosely** *adv.*

loosen (lūsʹ ən) *v.* to make less tight. **loosening. loosened.**

loot (lūt) *n.* things of value stolen by burglars or by soldiers in war. —*v.* to steal goods: *Someone has looted the store.* **looting. looted.**

lopsided (lopʹ sīdʹ əd) *adj.* uneven, with one side lower than the other.

lord (lȯrd) *n.* a title given to a nobleman.

lose (lūz) *v.* **1.** to misplace something so that you cannot find it: *I lost my favourite ring in the woods.* **2.** to be without something that you once had. **3.** to be beaten in a game. **losing. lost** (lost).

loss (los) *n.* something lost: *Our team's loss cost us a place in the finals. pl.* **losses.**

lot (lot) *n.* **1.** a large number or amount: *A lot of birds fly south for the winter.* **2.** a piece of ground: *There is an empty lot next to our school.*

lots (lots) an informal form of **a lot**, meaning many or much.

lottery (lotʹ ə rē) *n.* a gambling game in which many people buy tickets but only a few people win prizes. *pl.* **lotteries.**

loud (lowd) *adj.* noisy. —**loudly** *adv.*

loudspeaker (lowdʹ spēʹ kər) *n.* the part of a stereo, radio, or TV from which the sound comes.

lounge (lownj) *n.* a sitting room with comfortable chairs. —*v.* to sit in a comfortable, easy way. **lounging. lounged.**

louse (lows) *n.* **1.** a very small, biting insect that can live in a person's hair. **2.** (*slang*) a word for a bad or unpleasant person. *pl.* **lice.**

lousy (lowzʹ ē) *adj.* not nice: *lousy weather; lousier weather; the lousiest weather all summer.*

lovable (luvʹ ə bəl) *adj.* easy to love.

love (luv) *n.* **1.** a feeling of deep and strong affection. **2.** in tennis, a score of nothing or zero. —*v.* to like very much; to feel great affection for. **loving. loved.**

lovely (luvʹ lē) *adj.* beautiful; fine; pleasing: *a lovely day; a lovelier one; the loveliest day of the month.*

low (lō) *adj.* **1.** not high or tall: *a low hill; a low number; a low note in music.* **2.** soft; not loud: *He has such a low voice that I can barely hear him.* **3.** not great: *low prices.*

lower (lō′ ər) *adj.* more low: *Prices are lower in this store than in that one.*
—*v.* to take or bring down to a low level: *to lower a flag; to lower your voice.* **lowering. lowered.**

loyal (loi′ əl) *adj.* faithful and true to your family, friends, and country. (*opp.* **disloyal.**) —**loyally** *adv.*

loyalty (loi′ əl tē) *n.* faithfulness: *The dog proved its loyalty when it growled at the stranger. pl.* **loyalties.**

luck (luk) *n.* chance; fortune: *good luck; bad luck.*

luckily (luk′ ə lē) *adv.* thanks to good luck: *Luckily, I found my wool mitt buried in the snow.*

lucky (luk′ ē) *adj.* having good fortune: *a lucky day; a luckier one; my luckiest day ever.* (*opp.* **unlucky.**)

luggage (lug′ ij) *n.* the suitcases and bags that a traveller carries.

lukewarm (lūk′ wȯrm′) *adj.* **1.** not hot and not cold; slightly warm: *lukewarm milk.* **2.** not eager or enthusiastic: *a lukewarm response.*

lullaby (lul′ ə bī′) *n.* a soothing song you sing to put a baby to sleep. *pl.* **lullabies.**

lumber (lum′ bər) *n.* wood cut and prepared for use, such as logs, timber, and boards.

lumberjack (lum′ bər jak′) *n.* a person who cuts down trees.

lump (lump) *n.* **1.** a shapeless mass or piece of something: *a lump of clay.* **2.** a swelling or bump on the skin: *I have a lump on my head from falling off the porch.*

lunar (lū′ nər) *adj.* having to do with the moon: *a lunar eclipse.*

lunch (lunch) *n.* the meal eaten at noon. *pl.* **lunches.**

lung (lung) *n.* one of the two organs inside the chest that fill with air when you breathe in.

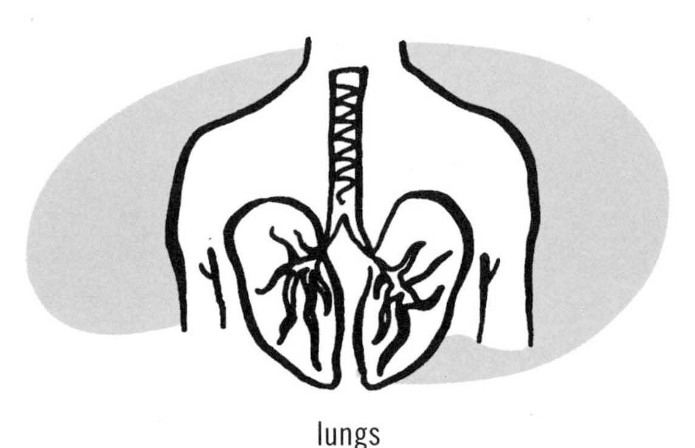

lungs

lure (lūr) *n.* bait: *a lure for fish.* —*v.* to tempt; to attract: *The mouse was lured into the trap by the cheese.* **luring. lured.**

luscious (lush′ əs) *adj.* very delicious: *a luscious cherry pie.*

luxury (luk′ shər ē *or* lug′ zhər ē) *n.* something expensive and enjoyable, which you can't really afford or don't really need: *Our neighbours have the luxury of going on expensive vacation trips. pl.* **luxuries.**

> **–ly** is a suffix that is added to many adjectives to turn them into adverbs. *He is a quiet baby. The baby crawls quietly.* In these sentences, *quiet* is an adjective and *quietly* is an adverb.

lynx (lingks) *n.* a medium-sized wild cat, with pointed ears, a short tail, and large paws.

lynx

lyrics (lir′ iks) *n. pl.* the words of a song.

ma, mama (mo *or* ma, mo′ mə) *n.* mother.

macaroni (mak′ ə ro′ nē) *n.* a food made of flour paste, shaped into small, hollow tubes. Macaroni is often eaten with a cheese or tomato sauce.

machine (mə shēn′) *n.* a device that does a particular job. A machine has moving parts and often runs on electricity: *a sewing machine; a washing machine.*

machinery (mə shēn′ ər ē) *n.* **1.** engines and machines. **2.** the working parts of a machine.

mackerel (mak′ ər əl) *n.* a silvery fish that lives in the ocean. *pl.* **mackerel.**

mad (mad) *adj.* **1.** mentally ill; crazy. **2.** very angry: *a mad crowd; a madder crowd; the maddest crowd of all.* —**madly** *adv.*

made (mād) see **make** (verb).

magazine (mag′ ə zēn′) *n.* a thin book with a soft cover that comes out regularly and has articles, stories, pictures, and advertisements: *A magazine is usually published weekly or monthly.*

magic (maj′ ik) *n.* **1.** a mysterious power: *The magic of the baby's smile made everyone feel happy.* **2.** clever tricks that make impossible things seem to happen: *Magic made a rabbit appear out of the hat.*

magical (maj′ ə kəl) *adj.* mysterious and wonderful; happening as if by magic. —**magically** *adv.*

magician (mə jish′ ən) *n.* a person who can do magic tricks.

magnet (mag′ nət) *n.* a piece of iron or steel that has the power to attract pieces of iron and some other metals toward it.

magnetic (mag net′ ik) *adj.* having the power of a magnet. —**magnetically** *adv.*

magnetism (mag′ nə tiz′ əm) *n.* **1.** the power to attract iron and some other metals. **2.** the power to attract or charm others.

magnificent (mag nif′ ə sənt) *adj.* **1.** splendid; grand: *a magnificent palace.* **2.** excellent: *a magnificent performance.* —**magnificently** *adv.*

magnify (mag′ nə fī′) *v.* to make something look larger: *A microscope magnifies very small objects that are hard to see with the naked eye.* **magnifying. magnified.** it **magnifies.**

magnifying glass a lens that makes things look bigger than they really are.

maid (mād) *n.* a female servant in a house or hotel.

mail (māl) *n.* letters, cards, packages, and anything else sent through the post office. —*v.* to send letters, parcels, and so on, by mail. **mailing. mailed.**

mailbox (māl′ boks′) *n.* **1.** a box in which to put the mail you are sending. **2.** a box in which the mail you receive is placed. *pl.* **mailboxes.**

mail carrier (māl ker′ ē ər) *n.* a person who carries and delivers mail.

main (mān) *adj.* chief; most important; largest: *a main road.*

mainland (mān′ land′ *or* mān′ lənd′) *n.* the main or largest part of a continent or other large land area: *Islands are not part of the mainland.*

mainly (mān′ lē) *adv.* mostly; chiefly.

maintain (mān tān′) *v.* **1.** to keep or continue in the same way: *to maintain speed.* **2.** to keep something in good condition: *I maintain my bike by keeping the tires inflated.* **maintaining. maintained.**

maintenance (mān′ tə nəns) *n.* the activity of repairing something, or of keeping it working properly: *We had to do some maintenance on our car because it wasn't running very well.*

maize (māz) *n.* a kind of corn.

majestic (mə jes′ tək) *adj.* grand or noble like a king or queen. —**majestically** *adv.*

Majesty (maj′ əs tē) *n.* a title for a king, queen, emperor, or empress: *Your Majesty; His Majesty; Her Majesty. pl.* **Majesties.**

major (mā′ jər) *n.* an army officer with a rank above a captain. —*adj.* **1.** important; large: *a major road.* **2.** the most important or the largest: *The baseball player moved from the minor league to the major league.*

majority (mə jȯr′ ə tē) *n.* the larger group (more than half), or the largest group: *The majority of my friends walk to school. pl.* **majorities.** (*opp.* **minority.**)

make (māk) *n.* a kind or brand: *What make is your family's car?* —*v.* **1.** to form; to create: *I made a cake.* **2.** to cause to be or to happen: *Jokes make me laugh.* **3.** to force: *My brother made me tell him my secret.* **4.** to earn: *How much money does she make?* **making. made.**

make believe to pretend.

make do to manage; to get by: *The fridge is empty, so we will have to make do with canned foods.*

make up **1.** to invent: *to make up a story.* **2.** to become friends again: *to make up after an argument.*

make-up (māk′ up) *n.* powder, lipstick, and other cosmetics put on the body, especially the face: *It takes the clown an hour to put her make-up on before the parade.*

male (māl) *n.* **1.** a boy or a man. **2.** an animal that is, will be, or can be a father: *A bull is a male. A cow is a female.*

mall (mol) *n.* a large building made up of many stores, usually with a parking lot outside: *We went to the mall to buy all the supplies we needed for our trip.*

mallard (mal′ ərd) *n.* a common wild duck: *Male mallards have shiny green heads and a white ring around the neck.*

mallard

malt (molt) *n.* grain, usually barley, that is used to make beer.

mammal (mam′ əl) *n.* an animal that is warm-blooded, has a backbone, and usually has some hair or fur; the females have glands that can produce milk to feed their babies: *Humans, whales, dogs, cats, and horses are mammals.*

mammoth (mam′ əth) *n.* an extinct kind of elephant with shaggy hair. —*adj.* huge; enormous: *a mammoth whale.*

man (man) *n.* an adult male human being. *pl.* **men.**

manage (man′ ij) *v.* **1.** to take charge of; to look after; to control: *to manage a store.* **2.** to be able to do something: *Can you manage to carry this heavy box?* **managing. managed.**

manager (man′ ij ər) *n.* a person in charge of a business, a sports team, and so on.

mane (mān) *n.* the long, shaggy hair on the neck of some animals, such as horses and male lions.

mango (mang′ ō) *n.* a sweet, juicy fruit with orange flesh and shaped like a small football: *Mangoes come from Mexico, India, and other warm places. pl.* **mangoes** or **mangos.**

maniac (mā′ nē ak′) *n.* a wild, crazy person.

manicure (man′ ə kyūr′) *n.* a treatment for the hands, in which the skin is softened and the fingernails are trimmed and polished.

manner (man′ ər) *n.* **1.** a way of doing something. **2.** a way of acting or behaving: *I noticed the boys were acting in a strange manner before they ran away from home.*

manners (man′ ərz) *n. pl.* the way people behave toward others: *good manners; bad manners.*

manufacture (man′ yə fak′ chər) *v.* to produce something in large numbers and by machinery, usually in a factory. **manufacturing. manufactured.**

manure (mə nyūr′) *n.* solid animal waste: *Manure is often mixed with straw and spread on soil to make plants grow better.*

manuscript (man′ yə skript′) *n.* a written or typed composition before it is published.

many (men′ ē) *adj.* a great number of: *Many Canadians live on farms. More Canadians live in towns. Most Canadians live in cities.*

map (map) *n.* **1.** a drawing of the earth's surface or of part of it, showing countries, oceans, cities, and other information. **2.** any drawing that shows you how to get to a place.

maple (mā′ pəl) *n.* a tree with broad leaves and wood that is used to make furniture and from which we get maple syrup.

maple leaf the leaf of the maple tree, chosen as an emblem of Canada. *pl.* **maple leaves.**

maple syrup a sweet, thick liquid made from the sap of a sugar maple tree.

marathon (mar′ ə thon′) *n.* **1.** a long-distance race: *An official marathon covers a distance of 26 miles, 385 yards (42 km).* **2.** any long, difficult contest or task: *a dance marathon.*

marble (mȧr′ bəl) *n.* **1.** a hard stone used in making statues and buildings. **2.** a small glass ball used in the game of marbles.

march (mȧrch) *n.* **1.** the regular rhythm of soldiers walking in step with one another. **2.** a piece of music for people to march to. *pl.* **marches.** —*v.* to walk in step with others, as soldiers do. **marching. marched.**

March (mȧrch) *n.* the third month of the year.

mare (mer) (*masc.* **stallion**) *n.* a female horse.

margarine (mȧr′ jər in) *n.* a bread spread made of vegetable oil, often used instead of butter.

margin (mȧr′ jən) *n.* space left at the top, bottom, and sides of written or printed pages.

marigold (mer′ ə gōld′) *n.* a plant that has strong-smelling orange, red, or yellow flowers.

marina (mə rē′ nə) *n.* a place along the waterfront where boats may be docked.

marine (mə rēn′) *adj.* having to do with ships or the sea: *The store at the harbour sells anchors and other marine supplies.*

marionette (mer′ ē ə net′) *n.* a doll that can be made to move when strings attached to it are pulled.

marionette

maritime (mer′ ə tīm′) *adj.* **1.** having to do with the sea. **2.** on or near the ocean: *Halifax and Victoria are maritime cities.*

Maritime Provinces New Brunswick, Nova Scotia, and Prince Edward Island. Also called **the Maritimes**. The Atlantic Provinces include the Maritime Provinces and Newfoundland.

mark (märk) *n.* **1.** a stain, line, scratch, and so on, left on a surface: *dirty shoe marks on a floor.* **2.** a score on a test or a grade on a report card: *a high mark on a history test.* —*v.* **1.** to make a mark on something. **2.** to grade a test. **marking. marked.**

marker (märk′ ər) *n.* a pen with a soft tip, used for marking: *The children used different coloured markers to write on their posters.*

market (mär′ kət) *n.* a place where people meet to buy and sell things: *a farmer's market.*

marketplace (mär′ kət plās′) *n.* an open place where a market is held.

marmalade (mär′ mə lād′) *n.* a jam made of sharp-tasting fruit, such as oranges or lemons, and usually eaten on toast.

maroon (mə rūn′) *n.* a dark red colour. —*adj.* having this colour. —*v.* to leave a person behind on a deserted island or coast, sometimes as a punishment. **marooning. marooned.**

marriage (mer′ ij) *n.* **1.** a wedding. **2.** living together as partners.

marrow (mer′ ō) *n.* the soft material in the centre of bones.

marry (mer′ ē) *v.* to become husband and wife. **marrying. married.** she **marries.**

Mars (märz) *n.* **1.** in Roman mythology, the god of war. **2.** one of the planets of our solar system: *Mars is the fourth planet from the sun.*

marsh (märsh) *n.* an area of soft, very wet ground, containing wildlife and grasses; a swamp. *pl.* **marshes.**

marshmallow (märsh′ mel′ ō) *n.* a kind of candy that is white, soft, and spongy.

martial arts (mär′ shəl ärts) *n. pl.* methods of fighting or defending yourself without weapons, such as kung fu and karate.

marvellous, marvelous (mär′ vəl əs) *adj.* wonderful. —**marvellously** *adv.*

mascot (mas′ kot) *n.* an animal, person, or thing supposed to bring good luck: *Our team's mascot is a bear.*

masculine (mas′ kyə lən) *adj.* having to do with men and boys: *"He" and "him" are masculine pronouns.*

mash (mash) *v.* to crush into a soft mass: *to mash potatoes.* **mashing. mashed.**

mask (mask) *n.* a covering over the face, worn as a disguise or as protection.

masquerade (mas′ kə rād′) *n.* a party where people wear masks and costumes to disguise themselves. —*v.* to appear in a disguise, or to pretend to be someone you are not. **masquerading. masqueraded.**

mass (mas) *n.* **1.** a great lump or quantity. **2.** a large amount or number: *A mass of people were at the concert.* **3.** a measure of the amount of matter an object contains: *The box has a mass of 20 kg. pl.* **masses.**

massacre (mas′ ə kər) *n.* a bloody killing of a large number of people or animals. —*v.* to kill in such a way. **massacring. massacred.**

massage (mə soj′) *n.* the rubbing of the body, often the back and shoulders, to relax a person's muscles. —*v.* to give a massage. **massaging. massaged.**

mast (mast) *n.* a tall pole that holds up sails on a ship.

master (mas′ tər) *n.* **1.** a person who has control over people, animals, or things: *I am the dog's master.* **2.** a person who has great skill in something: *That famous painting was painted by a great master and is now worth a lot of money.*

masterpiece (mas′ tər pēs′) *n.* a great work of art, often the artist's best work.

mat (mat) *n.* **1.** a small rug to wipe your feet on. **2.** a cushion used in gymnastics. **3.** a tangled mass. —*v.* to become tangled: *The dog's hair is badly matted.* **matting. matted.**

match (mach) *n.* **1.** a small stick of wood or cardboard with a tip that flames up when struck. **2.** a game between sides: *a tennis match. pl.* **matches.** —*v.* to be or to look the same: *Your socks don't match. One is blue and the other is green.* **matching. matched.**

mate (māt) *n.* **1.** a companion. **2.** one of a pair: *Where is the mate to the blue sock?* —*v.* to bring together as a pair. **mating. mated.**

material (mə tēr′ ē əl) *n.* **1.** cloth. **2.** what something is made of or used for; a substance: *My sweater is made of a woolly material. Paper is a material for writing on.*

maternal (mə tûr′ nəl) *adj.* like a mother, or having to do with a mother: *My mom's brother is my maternal uncle.* —**maternally** *adv.*

mathematician (math′ ə mə tish′ ən) *n.* a person who is skilled in mathematics.

mathematics (math′ ə mat′ iks) *n. pl.* the study of numbers, shapes, and measurement, often called **math** for short.

matinée (mat ən ā′) *n.* an afternoon performance of a play, movie, or concert.

matter (mat′ ər) *n.* **1.** something you are concerned about: *Our family's health is a serious matter.* **2.** a problem; something that is wrong: *What is the matter with the cat?* **3.** what something is made of. —*v.* to be of importance; to make a difference: *Does it really matter if you have an apple instead of an orange?* **mattering. mattered.**

mattress (mat′ rəs) *n.* the thick, soft part of a bed. *pl.* **mattresses.**

mature (mə chūr′ *or* mə tyūr′) *v.* to develop fully or to ripen: *The calf matured into a cow.* —*adj.* **1.** fully developed: *An adult is a mature human being.* **2.** acting grown-up: *Although he is young, Vince can make mature decisions.* (*opp.* **immature.**) —**maturely** *adv.*

maximum (mak′ sə məm) *adj.* the greatest amount allowed or possible: *The maximum number of people allowed in the auditorium is 350.* (*opp.* **minimum.**)

may (mā) *v.* a helping (auxiliary) verb used before another verb to mean: **1.** "to be allowed": *She may go if she wants to.* **2.** "to be possible": *She may be able to do it if she tries hard.* **might.**

> Be careful not to mix up **may** with "can." May means "to be allowed to," "to ask for or grant permission," or "to be possible." Can means "to be able to." ***May** I have a glass of water? I **can** drink water.*

May (mā) *n.* the fifth month of the year.

maybe (mā′ bē) *adv.* perhaps: *Maybe it will snow this afternoon.*

mayonnaise (mā′ yə nāz′) *n.* a thick, creamy salad dressing made mainly of eggs and oil.

mayor (mā′ ər) *n.* the head of a city, town, or village government.

maze (māz) *n.* a confusing network of winding paths through which it is difficult to find the way.

maze

me (mē) *pron.* the form of the word "I" that is used as the object of a verb or preposition: *Leave me alone. Give it to me.*

meadow (med′ ō) *n.* a grassy field in the country.

meal (mēl) *n.* **1.** food eaten each day at a certain time: *Breakfast, lunch, and dinner are meals.* **2.** grain that is ground into a powder: *cornmeal.*

mean (mēn) *adj.* unkind: *a mean goblin; a meaner goblin; the meanest goblin of all.* —*v.* **1.** to have in mind; to intend: *I mean to go when I am ready.* **2.** to have a specific definition or sense: *"To touch" means "to feel."* **meaning. meant** (ment).

meaning (mēn′ ing) *n.* **1.** what someone has in mind when he or she says or writes something. **2.** the sense of a word.

meaningful (mēn′ ing fu̇l) *adj.* full of meaning or importance: *Your kind words were very meaningful.* —**meaningfully** *adv.*

meantime (mēn′ tīm′) *n.* the time between two events: *We are going on a holiday in a few days; in the meantime, I need to pack.*

meanwhile (mēn′ wīl′ *or* mēn′ hwīl′) *adv.* during the time between two events: *The next game after this one is on Tuesday; meanwhile, we will have to practise very hard.*

measles (mē′ zəlz) *n.* a contagious disease that causes a rash and fever.

measure (mezh′ ər) *n.* the size or amount of something: *a large measure of land; a small measure of sugar.* —*v.* to find the size or amount of something: *to measure the length and width of a room.* **measuring. measured.**

measurement (mezh′ ər mənt) *n.* **1.** the size or amount found by measuring: *The measurements of the room are eight by five metres.* **2.** a system of measuring: *In Canada we use the metric system of measurement.*

meat (mēt) *n.* the flesh of animals, such as cows and pigs, that is used as food.

mechanic (mə kan′ ik) *n.* a person who is skilled in repairing and using machinery.

mechanical (mə kan′ ə kəl) *adj.* having to do with a machine: *The engineer fixed the mechanical problems.* —**mechanically** *adv.*

medal (med′ əl) *n.* a flat piece of metal given as a prize or reward: *Many medals are shaped like coins.*

media (mē′ dē yə) *n. pl.* the forms of communication that can reach large numbers of people: *The media include newspapers, magazines, television, and radio.* *sing.* **medium.**

medical (med′ ə kəl) *adj.* having to do with doctors and medicine: *Doctors are trained at medical school.* —**medically** *adv.*

medicine (med′ ə sin) *n.* a liquid, pill, or other substance taken for an illness or a pain.

medium (mē′ dē əm) *adj.* **1.** average; in the middle: *Medium height is between the shortest and the tallest.* **2.** see **media**.

meet (mēt) *n.* a sports competition: *a swim meet.* —*v.* to come face to face with; to come together: *We'll meet at my house.* **meeting. met.**

meeting (mēt′ ing) *n.* a coming together or gathering of people to talk or to listen to someone.

mellow (mel′ ō) *adj.* **1.** ripe and sweet. **2.** rich and full: *mellow coffee; a mellow voice.* **3.** softer and wiser with age: *Since retiring from her job, my grandmother has become more mellow.* —**mellowly** *adv.*

melody (mel′ ə dē) *n.* a tune that is easy to hum or sing. *pl.* **melodies.**

melon (mel′ ən) *n.* a large, sweet, and juicy fruit that has a rind: *A cantaloupe is one kind of melon.*

melt (melt) *v.* to change from a solid to a liquid: *Snow and butter both melt under a hot sun.* **melting. melted.**

member (mem′ bər) *n.* a person who belongs to a club or group: *Jackie is a member of the Girl Guides.*

Member of Parliament the title given to each representative elected to the House of Commons of the federal parliament.

Member of Provincial Parliament the title given to each representative elected to the provincial legislature of Ontario.

Member of the House of Assembly the title given to each representative elected to the provincial legislatures of Nova Scotia and Newfoundland.

Member of the Legislative Assembly the title given to each representative elected to the provincial legislatures of British Columbia, Alberta, Saskatchewan, Manitoba, New Brunswick, Prince Edward Island, and the Northwest Territories.

Member of the Legislative Council the title given to each representative elected to the legislature of the Yukon.

Member of the National Assembly the title given to each representative elected to the provincial legislature of Quebec.

memo (mem′ ō) (short for **memorandum**) *n.* a brief note sent to someone, often as a reminder. *pl.* **memos.**

memorize (mem′ ə rīz′) *v.* to learn by heart: *It took me only a day to memorize my lines in the play.* **memorizing. memorized.**

memory (mem′ ə rē) *n.* **1.** the power of remembering things: *a good memory.* **2.** something you remember: *I have happy memories of my holiday.* **3.** the place in a computer where information is kept. *pl.* **memories.**

men (men) plural of **man**.

menacing (men′ ə sing) *adj.* threatening: *The angry dog looks menacing.* —**menacingly** *adv.*

mend (mend) *v.* to fix something that is broken or torn. **mending. mended.**

> **–ment** is a suffix meaning "the result of" or "the condition of." Adding -ment to a verb turns it into a noun. For example, a "disagreement" is a quarrel (the result of disagreeing); "amazement" is great surprise (the condition of being amazed).

mental (men′ təl) *adj.* having to do with your mind. —**mentally** *adv.*

mention (men′ shən) *v.* to make a remark about something. **mentioning. mentioned.**

menu (men′ yū) *n.* **1.** a list of the foods and drinks that a restaurant serves. **2.** a list of choices displayed on a computer screen. *pl.* **menus.**

meow (mē yow′) *n.* the sound that a cat makes. —*v.* to make such a sound. **meowing. meowed.**

merchandise (mür′ chən dīs′ *or* mür′ chən dīz′) *n.* goods that are bought and sold: *Our corner store sells a variety of merchandise.*

merchant (mür′ chənt) *n.* a person who sells goods.

Mercury (mer′ kyə rē) *n.* **1.** in Roman mythology, the messenger of the gods. **2.** one of the planets of our solar system: *Mercury is the planet closest to the sun.*

mercy (mür′ sē) *n.* kind treatment given to a person who has done wrong.

merely (mēr′ lē) *adv.* simply; only: *I merely asked a question. What's all the fuss?*

merit (mer′ it) *n.* anything worthy of praise or reward; goodness, value, or worth: *Eli's idea has great merit.*

mermaid, merman (mür′ mād′, mür′ man′) *n.* an imaginary creature that looks like a woman or man from the waist up, but has a fish tail instead of legs.

merry (mer′ ē) *adj.* laughing; happy; full of fun: *a merry party; a merrier party; the merriest party of all.* —**merrily** *adv.*

merry-go-round (mer′ ē gō rownd′) *n.* an amusement ride that has large toy animals on which people sit while the platform turns.

mess (mes) *n.* **1.** a dirty or untidy group of things. **2.** a difficult situation: *How did we get into this mess? pl.* **messes.** —*v.* to make untidy: *to mess up a room.* **messing. messed.**

message (mes′ ij) *n.* written or spoken words passed from one person to another.

messenger (mes′ ən jər) *n.* a person who takes a message from one person to another.

messy (mes′ ē) *adj.* untidy: *a messy room; a messier one; the messiest room of all.* —**messily** *adv.*

met (met) see **meet** (verb).

metal (met′ əl) *n.* a hard and shiny material that can be melted, beaten, or shaped to make things such as coins, wire, pipes, cooking utensils, jewellery, and so on. Iron, steel, copper, lead, brass, and gold are some metals.

metallic (mə tal′ ək) *adj.* having to do with a metal, or being like a metal: *The door was painted a metallic shade of grey.*

metaphor (met′ ə fòr′) *n.* a description that suggests one thing is like another. A metaphor does not use the word "like" or "as": *"My sister is a clown" is a metaphor. "She's as funny as a clown" is a simile.*

meteor (mē′ tē ər) *n.* a large rock that falls from space toward earth: *Shooting stars are meteors that burn up before reaching the ground.*

meter (mē′ tər) *n.* a machine that measures amounts and times: *A gas meter measures how much natural gas is used in a house each day.*

method (meth′ əd) *n.* a way of doing something: *Watch my method of sewing before you try to make an apron yourself.*

metre (mē′ tər) *n.* a unit for measuring length; m is the symbol. 1 m = 100 cm.

metric system (met′ rik sis′ təm) a system of measurement based on the number 10.

metropolitan (met′ rə pol′ ə tən) *adj.* having to do with a city, usually a large city: *The metropolitan area of a city includes the downtown area and the suburbs.*

mice (mīs) plural of **mouse**.

> **micro–** is a prefix meaning "very small": a "microscope" is used for looking at tiny things; a "microchip" is a very small, thin chip inside a computer.

microphone (mī′ krə fōn′) *n.* a device that sends sounds over a distance, or makes them much louder.

microscope (mī′ krə skōp′) *n.* an instrument with lenses, used to make tiny things look large.

microscope

microwave oven (mī′ krō wāv′ uv′ ən) *n.* a type of oven that uses **microwaves**, a kind of wave that can heat food very quickly.

> **mid–** is a prefix meaning "middle": "midday" means the middle of the day; "midnight" means halfway through the night.

middle (mid′ əl) *n.* the halfway point between two things: *I'll stand in the middle, between Paula and Shamun. —adj.* halfway between: *I am the middle person.*

middle age the time when an adult is neither young nor old.

midget (mij′ it) *n.* someone or something much smaller than average size.

midnight (mid′ nīt′) *n.* twelve o'clock at night, written as 12 a.m.; the middle of the night.

midway (mid′ wā′) *n.* the part of a fair where there are rides and games. *pl.* **midways.** *—adj.* halfway; in the middle.

might (mīt) *n.* power; strength: *They used all their might to lift the piano.* *—v.* past tense of **may**.

mighty (mīt′ ē) *adj.* powerful; very strong: *a mighty hero; a mightier hero; the mightiest one of all.* *—***mightily** *adv.*

migrate (mī′ grāt *or* mī grāt′) *v.* to move to another place or country: *Some birds migrate to warmer regions in winter.* **migrating. migrated.**

mild (mīld) *adj.* **1.** gentle: *a mild breeze.* **2.** not strong: *Some soft cheeses have a mild taste.* **3.** neither hot nor cold; medium: *a mild day.* *—***mildly** *adv.*

mile (mīl) *n.* a measure of distance on land equal to about 1.61 km.

military (mil′ ə ter′ ē) *adj.* having to do with an army or war: *military equipment.*

milk (milk) *n.* the white liquid that female mammals produce to feed their young: *Many people use cow's milk for drinking and cooking.* *—v.* to get milk from an animal: *to milk a cow.* **milking. milked.**

milk shake (milk′ shāk′) *n.* a drink made of milk, flavoured syrup, and ice cream, shaken or mixed well.

Milky Way (milk′ ē wā) a broad band of light, made up of numerous stars, that stretches across the sky at night: *Our solar system is located in the Milky Way galaxy.*

mill (mil) *n.* **1.** a building where machines grind grain into flour. **2.** a machine used for grinding or crushing. **3.** a factory where cloth or other goods are made. *—v.* to grind: *to mill grain into flour.* **milling. milled.**

miller (mil′ ər) *n.* a person who works in or runs a flour mill.

milligram (mil′ ə gram′) *n.* a unit for measuring mass; mg is the symbol. 1000 mg = 1 g.

millilitre (mil′ ə lē′ tər) *n.* a unit for measuring liquid; mL is the symbol. 1000 mL = 1 L.

millimetre (mil′ ə mē′ tər) *n.* a unit for measuring length; mm is the symbol. 1000 mm = 1 m.

million (mil′ yən) *n., adj.* a thousand thousands: 1 000 000.

millionaire (mil′ yən er′) *n.* a rich person who has at least a million dollars.

mime (mīm) *n.* an actor who uses gestures but does not speak. *—v.* to act out a story using gestures but no words. **miming. mimed.**

mimic (mim′ ək) *n.* a person who imitates how another person talks, looks, or acts. *—v.* to imitate or copy how another sounds, looks, or acts, sometimes to make fun of them: *Our parrot mimics my whistling.* **mimicking. mimicked.**

mind (mīnd) *n.* **1.** the part of a person that thinks, feels, and remembers. **2.** intelligence: *She has a keen mind.* *—v.* **1.** to look after; to take care of: *I will mind the baby for you.* **2.** to feel bad about; to dislike: *Do you mind doing me a favour?* **minding. minded.**

keep in mind remember.

make up your mind make a decision.

mine (mīn) *n.* **1.** a deep tunnel dug in the earth so that minerals, such as coal, gold, or diamonds, can be taken out. **2.** a bomb in the ground or the sea that explodes when something comes near it or touches it. *—pron.* the one belonging to me: *This book is mine.*

miner (mī′ nər) *n.* a person who works in a mine.

mineral (min′ ər əl) *n.* anything dug out from the earth, such as coal, gold, or diamonds.

mini- is a prefix meaning "very small" or "very short": a "mini-bus" is a small bus; a "miniskirt" is a very short skirt.

miniature (min′ ē ə chər *or* min′ ə chər) *adj.* very small: *A miniature village was displayed in the museum.*

minimum (min′ ə mum) *adj.* the smallest amount allowed or needed: *I need a minimum of eight hours' sleep.* (*opp.* **maximum.**)

mining (mī′ ning) *n.* the digging of minerals out of mines: *gold mining.*

minister (min′ is tər) *n.* **1.** a church official who performs religious ceremonies. **2.** the head of a government department: *the minister of finance.*

mink (mingk) *n.* a mammal very like a weasel, whose fur is used to make coats and other garments.

mink

minnow (min′ ō) *n.* a very small, freshwater fish.

minor (mī′ nər) *n.* a young person who, under the law, is not considered an adult. —*adj.* smaller or less important; not major: *the minor league.*

minority (mə nôr′ ə tē) *n.* the smaller group (less than half), or the smallest group: *Ten children walk to school and five take a bus. I am in the minority who go by bus. pl.* **minorities.** (*opp.* **majority.**)

mint (mint) *n.* **1.** a plant with a strong scent; its leaves are used as a flavouring. **2.** a place where paper money and coins are made.

minus (mī′ nəs) *prep.* less; subtracting; the symbol is –: *Nine minus seven equals two (9 – 7 = 2).*

minute (min′ it) *n.* a measure of time equal to sixty seconds; min is the symbol: *There are sixty minutes in an hour.*

minute (min ūt′ *or* mī nyūt′) *adj.* very small; tiny: *a minute bit of dirt.*

miracle (mir′ ə kəl) *n.* a marvellous and unexpected happening: *It is a miracle that no one was hurt in the accident.*

mirage (mə rahzh′) *n.* something you think you see, but which is not really there; something that does not exist.

mirror (mir′ ər) *n.* a piece of glass with a shiny metal coating on the back: *When you look in a mirror, you see your image.*

mis– is a prefix meaning "bad," "badly," or "wrong": to "misbehave" means to behave badly; to "misspell" a word is to spell it the wrong way.

misbehave (mis′ bē hāv′) *v.* to behave badly. **misbehaving. misbehaved.**

mischief (mis′ chif) *n.* bad or silly behaviour that annoys someone.

mischievous (mis′ chə vəs) *adj.* full of mischief. —**mischievously** *adv.*

miser (mī′ zər) *n.* a greedy person who saves up money and will not spend it.

miserable (miz′ ər ə bəl) *adj.* **1.** unhappy; sad. **2.** poor; bad: *miserable weather.* **3.** ill. —**miserably** *adv.*

misery (miz′ ər ē) *n.* **1.** great unhappiness. **2.** bad conditions: *The homeless people lived in misery. pl.* **miseries.**

misfortune (mis fôr′ chən) *n.* bad luck: *It was her misfortune to lose her job when the factory shut down.*

mislead (mis lēd′) *v.* to give someone the wrong information on purpose. **misleading. misled.**

misplace (mis plās′) *v.* to lose: *I have misplaced my glasses. Will you help me find them?* **misplacing. misplaced.**

Miss (mis) a title sometimes put in front of the name of an unmarried woman or girl: *Miss Grimaldi is my teacher.*

miss (mis) *n.* something that you fail to hit: *She had more hits than misses. pl.* **misses.** —*v.* **1.** to fail to catch, find, reach, hit, see, or hear something: *The batter missed the ball.* **2.** to be lonely for someone who is away from you: *I miss my parents.* **missing. missed.**

missile (mis′ əl) *n.* **1.** something that is fired or thrown, such as a bullet or dart. **2.** a self-propelled rocket.

missing (mis′ ing) *adj.* not in the usual place; lost or gone: *One of the playing cards is missing.*

mission (mish′ ən) *n.* a special job or task: *a rescue mission.*

misspell (mis spel′) *v.* to spell a word the wrong way. **misspelling. misspelled.**

mist (mist) *n.* a thin fog in the air.

mistake (mis tāk′) *n.* something that is wrong; an error: *a spelling mistake.* —*v.* to make an error: *It is sometimes easy to mistake plastic for glass.* **mistaking. mistook.** he is **mistaken.**

misty (mīs′ tē) *adj.* covered in mist: *a misty evening by the lake; a mistier evening; the mistiest evening of all.*

misunderstand (mis′ un dər stand′) *v.* not to understand. **misunderstanding. misunderstood.**

mitt (mit) *n.* **1.** a padded baseball glove used to protect the hand of the person catching the ball. **2.** a mitten.

mittens (mit′ ənz) *n. pl.* gloves that cover four fingers together and the thumb separately.

mix (miks) *v.* to stir together: *to mix paints.* **mixing. mixed.**

mix up **1.** to stir and shake up. **2.** to mistake one thing for another: *I always mix up the names of the two sisters.*

mixture (miks′ chər) *n.* two or more things mixed together.

moan (mōn) *n.* a low groaning sound, often showing pain. —*v.* to make such a sound. **moaning. moaned.**

moat (mōt) *n.* a deep ditch dug around a castle or town and filled with water, used as a defence against enemies.

moat

mob (mob) *n.* a wild, uncontrolled crowd of people.

moccasin (mok′ ə sən) *n.* a soft leather shoe that was originally made and worn by aboriginal peoples in North America.

moccasin

mock (mok) *v.* to make fun of someone. **mocking. mocked.**

model (mod′ əl) *n.* **1.** a small copy: *a model airplane.* **2.** a person who poses for an artist or photographer. **3.** a person who sets a good example: *Ms. Todd is a model of what a police officer should be.* **4.** a style or design: *the latest model of a car.* —*v.* **1.** to make a model. **2.** to pose for an artist or photographer. **modelling. modelled.**

modem (mō′ dəm) *n.* a device that allows you to transmit computer data over distances.

moderate (mod′ ə rət) *adj.* in between; not extreme—not too high and not too low, not too hot and not too cold, not too much and not too little: *moderate prices; a moderate climate.* —**moderately** *adv.*

modern (mod′ ərn) *adj.* up-to-date; having to do with the present time or the very recent past: *modern history.*

modest (mod′ əst) *adj.* **1.** not proud; not bragging about yourself: *He was too modest to admit that he had won the poetry prize.* **2.** simple: *a modest house; a modest lifestyle.* (*opp.* **immodest.**) —**modestly** *adv.*

moist (moist) *adj.* slightly wet; damp.

moisture (mois′ chər) *n.* dampness.

molasses (mə las′ əs) *n.* a dark, thick, sticky liquid made from sugar cane.

mold (mōld) see **mould.**

mole (mōl) *n.* **1.** a small, furry animal that makes tunnels under the ground, leaving molehills on top. **2.** a small, dark brown spot on a person's skin.

molecule (mol′ ə kyūl) *n.* the smallest part into which any substance can be divided without a chemical change taking place: *Depending on the substance, a molecule may be one atom, or it may be a group of atoms arranged in a specific way.*

mollusc, mollusk (mol′ əsk) *n.* a kind of animal that has a soft body, usually covered by a hard shell: *Some molluscs are clams, mussels, oysters, and snails.*

mom, mommy (mum *or* mom, mu′ mē *or* mo′ mē) *n.* mother.

moment (mō′ mənt) *n.* an instant of time.

monarch (mon′ ərk) *n.* a royal ruler, such as a king, queen, or emperor.

monarchy (mon′ ər kē) *n.* a form of government that is headed by a monarch. *pl.* **monarchies.**

Monday (mun′ dā) *n.* the second day of the week.

> The second day of the week is named for the moon. The word **Monday** comes from an old English word meaning "moon's day." This is true in other languages also. For example, the French word for moon is *lune,* and the French name for Monday is *lundi.*

money (mun′ ē) *n.* coins and paper bills, used to pay for things: *I am saving as much money as I can for my vacation.*

mongrel (mong′ grəl) *n.* a dog of mixed breed: *Our dog is a mongrel. It is half German shepherd and half collie.*

monitor (mon′ ə tər) *n.* **1.** a pupil who does a special job for the teacher. **2.** a video screen that shows computer information.

monk (mungk) *n.* a religious man who gives up everything that he owns and lives a simple life by himself or with other monks.

monkey (mung′ kē) *n.* a mammal that lives in the trees in countries that have a hot climate: *Monkeys have long tails, long arms and legs, and hands for grasping.* *pl.* **monkeys.**

monotonous (mə not′ ə nəs) *adj.* unchanging and boring: *The monotonous ticking of the clock made me feel sleepy.* —**monotonously** *adv.*

monster (mon′ stər) *n.* a strange and frightening imaginary creature.

month (munth) *n.* one of the twelve parts of the year.

monthly (munth′ lē) *adj.* coming out or happening every month: *a monthly magazine.* —*adv.* once a month: *The magazine comes out monthly.*

monument (mon′ yə mənt) *n.* a statue or building put up in memory of someone or some event.

moo (mū) *n.* the long, low sound that a cow makes. —*v.* to make such a sound. **mooing. mooed.**

mood (mūd) *n.* the way that you feel at a certain time: *My brother was in a good mood last night. He kept laughing and smiling.*

moody (mūd′ ē) *adj.* changing moods often: *He is moody—happy one minute and sad the next. She is moodier than he is and I am the moodiest of all.* —**moodily** *adv.*

moon (mūn) *n.* the large, bright, white object that shines in the sky at night: *The moon goes around the earth once every 29 1/2 days.*

moonlight (mūn′ līt′) *n.* the light of the moon: *In the moonlight, we could see the shapes of the trees.*

moor (mūr) *n.* in Britain, a wild, open, grassy region. —*v.* to fasten a boat or ship in place, using a rope, a chain, or an anchor. **mooring. moored.**

moose (mūs) *n.* a large mammal with hooves, related to the deer; it lives in the forests of Canada and the northern United States. *pl.* **moose.**

moose

mop (mop) *n.* a sponge or pieces of cloth attached to the end of a long handle and used for cleaning. —*v.* to clean with a mop. **mopping. mopped.**

moral (mȯr′ əl) *n.* a lesson to be learned, often from a story or fable.

morals (mȯr′ əlz) *n. pl.* beliefs about what is right and wrong behaviour.

more (mȯr) *adj.* **1.** additional; extra: *I need more time.* **2.** greater in number, amount, or extent: *She is more athletic than I am.* —*adv.* again: *Please read the story once more.*

more or less not exactly; approximately: *I can more or less understand you, but try to speak more clearly.*

morning (mȯr′ ning) *n.* the time between midnight and noon.

morsel (mȯr′ səl) *n.* a small amount of something to eat: *This chicken wing is a tasty morsel.*

mortal (mȯr′ təl) *n.* a human being. —*adj.* **1.** not living forever: *All living creatures are mortal.* **2.** causing death: *The soldier received a mortal wound.* —**mortally** *adv.*

mosaic (mō zā′ ik) *n.* a picture or design made by fitting together small bits of coloured glass, stone, or tile.

mosque (mosk) *n.* a building for religious worship.

mosque

mosquito (mə skē′ tō) *n.* a small, two-winged insect. The females bite humans and animals, causing small, red, itchy swellings. *pl.* **mosquitoes.**

moss (mos) *n.* a small, low, green plant that grows like a soft covering on damp trees and stones.

most (mōst) *adj.* the greatest number, amount, or quantity: *Most dogs like bones.* —*adv.* the greatest or the best: *Which sport do you like the most?*

motel (mō tel′) *n.* a hotel whose rooms can usually be reached directly from its parking lot.

moth (moth) *n.* an insect that looks like a plain butterfly, but flies mostly at night. *pl.* **moths** (moTHz).

mother (muTH′ ər) *n.* a female parent.

mother-in-law (moTH′ ər in lo′) *n.* the mother of a wife's husband or of a husband's wife. *pl.* **mothers-in-law.**

motion (mō′ shən) *n.* movement: *The whistle sounded, and the train went into motion.*

motion picture a series of pictures that are projected on a screen so quickly that things in the pictures appear to be moving; a movie.

motivate (mō′ tə vāt′) *v.* to make someone want to do something: *After watching the ice-skaters on TV, Kate was motivated to take skating lessons.* **motivating. motivated.**

motive (mō′ təv) *n.* a reason for doing something: *What was the thief's motive for robbing the bank?*

motor (mō′ tər) *n.* the part of a machine that provides the power for making the machine run.

motorboat (mō′ tər bōt′) *n.* a boat that is propelled or run by a motor.

motorcycle (mō′ tər sī′ kəl) *n.* a two-wheeled vehicle powered by a motor.

motorist (mō′ tər ist) *n.* a person who drives or rides in a car.

motto (mot′ ō) *n.* a saying that provides wise advice for a person or group: *My motto is "never say never." pl.* **mottoes.**

mould, mold (mōld) *n.* **1.** a hollow form used to shape a soft substance before it hardens: *a candy mould.* **2.** a fuzzy or woolly growth of fungus, sometimes seen growing on old bread or other food. —*v.* to make or form into a shape. **moulding. moulded.**

mound (mownd) *n.* a heap, like a small hill, of earth, stones, or other material.

mount (mownt) *n.* **1.** a mountain: *Mount Everest.* **2.** a horse for riding. —*v.* to climb onto: *to mount a horse.* **mounting. mounted.**

mountain (mown′ tən) *n.* a very high hill.

mountainous (mown′ tə nəs) *adj.* full of mountains: *Switzerland is a mountainous country.*

Mountie (mown′ tē) *n.* a member of the Royal Canadian Mounted Police. *pl.* **Mounties.**

mourn (mȯrn) *v.* to feel very sorry and sad because someone has died or gone far away; to grieve. **mourning. mourned.**

mouse (mows) *n.* **1.** a small, furry rodent with a pointed nose and a long tail. **2.** a small device that is moved around on a desk by hand, controlling the movement of a point on a computer screen. *pl.* **mice.**

moustache, mustache (məs tash′) *n.* the hair that grows between a man's top lip and nose.

mouth (mowth) *n.* **1.** the opening in your face through which you eat and speak. **2.** any opening like this: *the mouth of a cave. pl.* **mouths** (mowTHz).

mouthful (mowth′ fu̇l) *n.* the amount that your mouth can hold: *I took a mouthful of cereal. pl.* **mouthfuls.**

movable (mūv′ ə bəl) *adj.* able to be moved or carried from one place to another.

move (mūv) *n.* **1.** a movement: *The cat made a quick move when it saw the mouse.* **2.** in a game, a player's turn: *It's your move.* **3.** the act of moving to a new home. —*v.* **1.** to change the position of something: *to move your arms up and down.* **2.** to go to a new home: *Our family is moving from Calgary to Ottawa.* **moving. moved.**

movement (mūv′ mənt) *n.* the act of moving; a change in position or place.

movie (mūv′ ē) *n.* a motion picture.

mow (mō) *v.* to cut grass or grain with a lawn mower or other cutting machine. **mowing. mowed.** she has **mown** or **mowed.**

Mr. (mis′ tər) short for **Mister**, a title put in front of a man's name.

Mrs. (mis′ iz) a title put in front of a married woman's name.

Ms. (miz) a title put in front of a woman's name.

much (much) *adj.* great in amount or extent: *much money; more money; the most money of all.* —*adv.* a great deal: *You sing much better than I do.*

mucus (myū′ kəs) *n.* a slippery substance that coats and protects the inside of the nose, mouth, and throat.

mud (mud) *n.* soft, wet soil or dirt.

muddy (mud′ ē) *adj.* full of mud or covered with mud: *muddy boots; muddier boots; the muddiest boots in the house.*

muffin (muf′ ən) *n.* a small, round, sweetened bread, baked in cups.

muffler (muf′ lər) *n.* **1.** a thick, woollen scarf. **2.** something that helps to silence noises: *a car muffler.*

mug (mug) *n.* a large heavy cup for drinking.

mukluks (muk′ luks) *n. pl.* high, waterproof boots, often made of sealskin, worn by the Inuit and other people.

mule (myūl) *n.* a mammal that is half donkey and half horse.

multicultural (mul′ tē kul′ chər əl) *adj.* having many different cultures in one place, or having to do with many different cultures: *Canada is a multicultural country.*

multiple (mul′ tə pəl) *n.* a number that is produced when two other numbers are multiplied together: *6 is a multiple of 2 and 3.* —*adj.* **1.** having several parts: *a multiple choice test.* **2.** many: *She always has multiple ideas.*

multiplication (mul′ tə plə kā′ shən) *n.* **1.** the act of adding a number to itself a certain number of times. **2.** the process of multiplying two or more numbers.

multiply (mul′ tə pli′) *v.* to make a number larger by a certain number of times: *When 3 is multiplied by 4, the result is 12.* **multiplying. multiplied.** she **multiplies.**

mumble (mum′ bəl) *v.* to speak low and unclearly. **mumbling. mumbled.**

mummy (mum′ ē) *n.* in ancient times, a dead body treated with chemicals and wrapped in cloths so that it would not decay: *Many mummies have been found in ancient Egyptian tombs. pl.* **mummies.**

mumps (mumps) *n.* a contagious illness that causes your face and neck to swell up, making it hard to swallow.

munch (munch) *v.* to chew in a noisy way. **munching. munched.**

municipal (myū nis′ ə pəl) *adj.* belonging to a town or city: *The mayor is the head of the municipal government.*

mural (myūr′ əl) *n.* a large picture painted on a long roll of paper or on a wall.

murder (mėr′ dər) *n.* the unlawful killing of a human being. —*v.* to kill someone unlawfully. **murdering. murdered.**

murmur (mėr′ mər) *n.* the sound of words spoken softly. —*v.* to speak very softly: *The pupil murmured an answer that the teacher could not hear.* **murmuring. murmured.**

muscle (mus′ əl) *n.* one of the parts of your body that can be tightened or loosened, making the body move: *Muscles are made up of strong fibres that look like cords.*

muscular (mus′ kyə lər) *adj.* having strong, well-developed muscles: *a muscular body.*

museum (myū zē′ əm) *n.* a building in which interesting science, art, or cultural objects are displayed.

mush (mush) *n.* a substance that is half liquid, half solid: *I mashed the bananas into mush.*

mushroom (mush′ rūm) *n.* a fungus, shaped like a small umbrella: *Most mushrooms can be eaten, but some are poisonous.*

music (myū′ zik) *n.* a series of pleasant sounds or tones, made by singing or by playing an instrument.

musical (myū′ zə kəl) *n.* a play with songs. —*adj.* having to do with music. —**musically** *adv.*

musician (myū zish′ ən) *n.* a person who performs or composes music.

muskeg (mus′ keg) *n.* a large area of swamp or marsh: *Vast areas of muskeg are found in northern Canada.*

musk-ox (musk′ oks′) *n.* a large hoofed mammal that lives in northern Canada: *The musk-ox has a thick, shaggy coat and large horns.*

musk-ox

muskrat (musk′ rat) *n.* a North American water mammal that looks like a large rat.

mussel (mus′ əl) *n.* a shellfish, similar to a clam, but with a longer, narrow, black shell.

must (must) *v.* a helping (auxiliary) verb used before other verbs to mean "to have to": *I must go to the grocery store before it closes.*

mustache (məs tash′) see **moustache**.

mustard (mus′ tərd) *n.* a spicy, yellow sauce eaten with hot dogs and other foods.

mute (myūt) *adj.* unable to speak. —*v.* to silence something: *He muted the TV so that we could hear each other talk.* **muting. muted.** —**mutely** *adv.*

mutter (mut′ ər) *v.* to speak or grumble in a low voice. **muttering. muttered.**

muzzle (muz′ əl) *n.* **1.** the jaws and nose of an animal. **2.** leather straps put over an animal's mouth to keep it from biting. **3.** the open end of a gun barrel. —*v.* to put a muzzle on an animal. **muzzling. muzzled.**

my (mī) *adj.* belonging to me: *These are my boots, not yours.*

myself (mī self′) *pron.* my own self; my usual self; I alone.

> **Myself** is used when the subject and object of a verb are the same: *I cut myself.*

mysterious (mis tēr′ ē əs) *adj.* **1.** strange. **2.** secret; unknown; hard to understand. —**mysteriously** *adv.*

mystery (mis′ tər ē) *n.* **1.** something strange, not known, or not understood: *Who stole all the baseballs is a mystery.* **2.** a story about a crime: *a murder mystery.* *pl.* **mysteries.**

myth (mith) *n.* a very old, traditional story about how the world and other things were created.

mythology (mə thol′ ə jē) *n.* a collection of myths.

nab (nab) *v.* to catch: *The police nabbed the robbers after a chase.* **nabbing. nabbed.**

nacho (noch′ ō) *n.* a small, flat, corn chip, originally made and eaten in Mexico: *Nachos are often covered with melted cheese and refried beans. pl.* **nachos.**

nag (nag) *n.* **1.** an old and tired horse. **2.** a person who is always finding fault and complaining. —*v.* to keep on scolding and finding fault. **nagging. nagged.**

nail (nāl) *n.* **1.** the thin, hard layer at the end of a finger or toe. **2.** a small metal spike, pointed at one end and flat at the other. —*v.* to hammer a nail into something. **nailing. nailed.**

naive (nī ēv′) *adj.* innocent; having little experience: *He is naive to think that all people are good.* —**naively** *adv.*

naked (nā′ kid) *adj.* bare; without clothes.

name (nām) *n.* what a person or thing is called. —*v.* to give a name to a baby, a pet, or some other thing. **naming. named.**

nap (nap) *n.* a short sleep. —*v.* to take a short sleep. **napping. napped.**

napkin (nap′ kin) *n.* a piece of cloth or paper used at meals for wiping your hands and mouth and for protecting your clothes.

narcissus (när sis′ əs) *n.* a plant that has a sweet-smelling white or yellow flower, similar to a daffodil. *pl.* **narcissuses** or **narcissi** (när sis′ ī).

narrate (ner′ āt) *v.* to tell a story. **narrating. narrated.**

narrator (ner ā′ tər) *n.* a person who tells a story.

narrow (ner′ ō) *adj.* **1.** not wide; thin; slender: *a narrow road.* **2.** not by much: *I had a narrow escape—the car just missed hitting me.* **3.** not open to new ideas or people: *They have narrow minds.* —**narrowly** *adv.* —*v.* to become less wide: *The highway narrows outside the city.* **narrowing. narrowed.**

nasty (nas′ tē) *adj.* **1.** unpleasant; mean: *a nasty monster; a nastier monster; the nastiest monster in the story.* **2.** harmful or serious: *a nasty cut.* —**nastily** *adv.*

nation (nā′ shən) *n.* **1.** a country. **2.** the people of a country.

national (nash′ ə nəl) *adj.* belonging to a nation: *A national anthem is the special song of a nation.* —**nationally** *adv.*

nationality (nash′ ə nal′ ə tē) *n.* the fact of being a citizen of a nation: *My nationality is Canadian.*

native (nā′ tiv) *n.* **1.** someone born in a certain place or country: *Paul is a native of Australia.* **2.** **Native** one of the original inhabitants of North America; an aboriginal. —*adj.* **1.** coming from or having to do with a certain place or country: *Paul is a native Australian.* **2.** **Native** belonging to a group of people who were the first to live in North America.

natural (nach′ ər əl) *adj.* **1.** produced by nature; not made by people: *Wood is a natural material.* **2.** having to do with nature. **3.** able to do something well without much training: *She is a natural swimmer.*

naturally (nach′ ə rəl ē) *adv.* **1.** in a natural way. **2.** easily, without training: *She swims naturally.* **3.** in nature; by nature: *Does the plant grow that way naturally, or did you trim it?* **4.** certainly; of course: *Naturally, I will look after your dog when you go away.*

natural resources land, trees, minerals, and other useful substances found in nature: *This country exports many natural resources, such as lumber, fish, and coal.*

nature (nā′ chər) *n.* **1.** the outdoor world and its plants and animals: *We go camping because we all enjoy nature.* **2.** the character or behaviour of a person or creature: *Our dog has a very gentle nature.*

naughty (no′ tē) *adj.* badly behaved; disobedient: *a naughty child; a naughtier child; the naughtiest child in the class.*

nautical (not′ ə kəl) *adj.* having to do with ships and sailors.

naval (nā′ vəl) *adj.* having to do with the navy: *a naval officer.*

navel (nā′ vəl) *n.* the small round dent on your belly; also called the **belly button**.

navigate (nav′ ə gāt′) *v.* to guide or to plan the route of a ship or aircraft. **navigating. navigated.**

navigator (nav′ ə gā′ tər) *n.* a person who guides a ship or aircraft.

navy (nā′ vē) *n.* a country's warships and their crew. *pl.* **navies.**

navy blue a very dark blue colour.

near (nēr) *prep.* close to; not far from: *My best friend lives near me.*

nearby (nēr′ bī′) *adv.* close: *My best friend lives nearby.*

nearly (nēr′ lē) *adv.* almost: *It is nearly twelve o'clock.*

near-sighted (nēr′ sīt′ əd) *adj.* seeing close objects clearly, but not objects at a distance: *I'm near-sighted; I don't need glasses when I read, but I do need them when I go to the movies.*

neat (nēt) *adj.* **1.** clean and tidy: *a neat desk; a neat worker.* **2.** (*slang*) interesting; clever: *What a neat idea!* —**neatly** *adv.*

necessary (nes′ ə ser ē) *adj.* needed; required.

necessity (nə ses′ ə tē) *n.* something you cannot do without: *Food is a necessity of life.* *pl.* **necessities.**

neck (nek) *n.* **1.** the part of the body that joins the head to the shoulders. **2.** a narrow part like a neck: *the neck of a bottle.*

necklace (nek′ ləs) *n.* a string of beads or a chain worn around the neck.

necklace

nectar (nek′ tər) *n.* a sweet liquid in flowers: *Nectar attracts insects and birds.*

nectarine (nek tə rēn′) *n.* a round, juicy fruit that is like a peach, but does not have a fuzzy skin.

need (nēd) *n.* something that is lacking and is required: *The dog has a need for attention.* —*v.* to require something: *People need food and water to live.* **needing. needed.**

needle (nē′ dəl) *n.* **1.** a tool that is like a pin, with a point at one end and a hole or "eye" at the other end for thread: *A needle is used for sewing.* **2.** an object having this general shape: *a knitting needle.*

needy (nēd′ ē) *adj.* being in need; poor: *I volunteer my time to a food bank that provides food for needy families.*

negative (neg′ ə tiv) *n.* a photographic picture on film, in which the light areas and dark areas are reversed: *Photographs are made from negatives.* —*adj.* **1.** saying "no": *When we asked for a dog, our parents gave us a negative answer.* **2.** seeing the bad or sad side of things. **3.** in a blood test or other medical test, showing that what a person is being tested for is not present. —**negatively** *adv.*

neglect (nə glekt′) *v.* **1.** to give little attention to someone or something. **2.** to fail to do something. **neglecting. neglected.**

negotiate (nə gō′ shē āt′) *v.* to work on an agreement with someone: *They wanted to negotiate a better price.* **negotiating. negotiated.**

neigh (nā) *n.* the sound that a horse makes. —*v.* to make such a sound. **neighing. neighed.**

neighbour, neighbor (nā′ bər) *n.* someone who lives next to or near you.

neighbourhood, neighborhood (nā′ bər hu̇d′) *n.* the area in which you live.

neither (nē′ THər *or* nī′ THər) *adj.* not one or the other: *Neither David nor Kwan skates.*

> **Neither** is followed by "nor":
> *Neither Donald nor Donna is here.*
> "Either" is followed by "or":
> *Either Judy or I will be there.*

nephew (nef′ yū) *n.* the son of a brother or sister: *My cousin André is my mother's nephew.*

Neptune (nep′ tūn *or* nep′ tyūn) *n.* **1.** in Roman mythology, the god of the sea. **2.** one of the planets of our solar system: *Neptune is the eighth planet from the sun.*

nerve (nu̇rve) *n.* **1.** one of the fibres in the body that carries feelings and messages to the brain. **2.** courage; boldness: *Lee has plenty of nerve when she plays hockey.*

nervous (nu̇r′ vəs) *adj.* **1.** anxious; tense: *I'm nervous about my audition tomorrow.* **2.** easily excited or upset: *My nervous dog hides whenever someone rings the bell.* —**nervously** *adv.*

> **–ness** is a suffix that means "the state of being." Adding –ness to certain adjectives turns them into nouns:
> "thickness" is the state of being thick;
> "kindness" is the state of being kind.

nest (nest) *n.* a home of twigs, straw, grass, mud, and other materials, made by birds and other creatures.

nest

net (net) *n.* a material made of string or wire that is woven loosely to leave large spaces. A net is often used to catch something without damaging it: *a fishing net.*

network (net′ wu̇rk′) *n.* a group of lines, routes, or other things that may be located far from each other, but are connected together: *A TV network connects different channels in different locations so that all of the channels can show the same program at the same time.*

never (nev′ ər) *adv.* not ever: *I have never flown on a plane.*

never mind it doesn't matter; forget it.

new (nū *or* nyū) *adj.* **1.** not old; never used before: *These new scissors are shiny and very sharp.* **2.** not seen or known before: *Zack thought of a new idea for our project.* **3.** modern; up-to-date.

news (nūz *or* nyūz) *n.* information about what has just happened: *I received a letter with news about my cousin. We watched the TV news after dinner.*

newspaper (nūz′ pā′ pər *or* nyūz′ pā′ pər) *n.* a daily or weekly paper with news stories, pictures, advertisements, and so on.

next (nekst) *adj.* **1.** the nearest: *the next house.* **2.** coming right after; following: *next week.* —*adv.* in the nearest time or place: *She will sing next.*

next to beside: *Who was the boy sitting next to you?*

nibble (nib′ əl) *n.* a small bite or piece of food. —*v.* to eat food in small bites. **nibbling. nibbled.**

nice (nīs) *adj.* **1.** good; pleasant: *It's a nice day—warm and sunny.* **2.** friendly and kind: *He's a nice person who is always willing to help.* —**nicely** *adv.*

nick (nik) *n.* a cut or scratch in the surface of something.

in the nick of time just in time: *We ran and caught the bus in the nick of time.*

nickel (nik′ əl) *n.* **1.** a hard, silvery-white metal. **2.** a five-cent coin in Canada and the United States.

nickname (nik′ nām′) *n.* a short form of your name, or a name given to you in fun: *My name is Elizabeth; my nickname is Liz.*

niece (nēs) *n.* the daughter of a brother or sister: *My sister's daughter is my niece.*

nifty (nif′ tē) (*slang*) *adj.* handy; clever: *a nifty gadget.*

night (nīt) *n.* the time when it is dark, between sunset and sunrise.

nightgown (nīt′ gown′) *n.* a comfortable gown that is worn for sleeping.

nightingale (nīt′ in gāl′) *n.* a small, reddish-brown bird that sings sweetly, often at night.

nightly (nīt′ lē) *adv.* every night: *The stars come out nightly.* —*adj.* coming out or happening every night: *a nightly news program.*

nightmare (nit′ mēr′) *n.* **1.** a scary dream. **2.** an event so horrible that it seems like a bad dream: *The afternoon of the car crash was a nightmare.*

nimble (nim′ bəl) *adj.* moving quickly and lightly: *a pianist's nimble fingers.* —**nimbly** *adv.*

nine (nīn) *n., adj.* one more than eight: 9.

nineteen (nīn′ tēn′) *n., adj.* ten more than nine: 19.

ninety (nīn′ tē) *n., adj.* ten times nine: 90.

nip (nip) *n.* a small bite or pinch: *The horse gave me a playful nip.* —*v.* to give a small bite or pinch: *The puppies played and nipped each other.* **nipping. nipped.**

no (nō) *adv.* the opposite of yes. A person says "No," to deny, refuse, or disagree: *"Can you swim?" "No, I can't."* —*adj.* not any: *My piggy bank has no money in it.*

no., No. an abbreviation for **number**.

noble (nō′ bəl) *n.* someone born into a family of high social rank or title. —*adj.* **1.** splendid; great: *a noble deed.* **2.** having a high rank or title: *a noble family.* —**nobly** *adv.*

nobody (nō′ bud′ ē) *pron.* no one; no person: *Nobody came to our party.*

nod (nod) *n.* a quick bend of the head. —*v.* to bend your head up and down quickly to mean "yes." **nodding. nodded.**

noise (noiz) *n.* a sound, often loud or unpleasant.

noisy (noiz′ ē) *adj.* making a lot of noise: *a noisy party; a noisier party; the noisiest party of the year.* —**noisily** *adv.*

nominate (nom′ ə nāt) *v.* to name (suggest) someone as a candidate to run for a position in government, a club, a student council, and so on. **nominating. nominated.**

non– is a prefix meaning "no" or "not": "nonsense" is something that makes no sense; a "non-stop" train does not stop along its route.

none (nun) *pron.* not one; not any: *None of my three cats is awake.*

nonfiction (non′ fik′ shən) *n.* works of literature that are based on fact: *A novel is usually a work of fiction, but a book about history is usually nonfiction.*

nonprofit (non′ prof′ ət) *adj.* not making a profit for yourself: *Charities are nonprofit groups. They raise money to help other people or animals.*

nonrenewable (non′ rə nū′ ə bəl *or* non′ re nyū′ ə bəl) *adj.* not able to be replaced after being used up: *Oil is a nonrenewable source of energy. Solar energy from the sun is a renewable source.*

nonsense (non′ sens) *n.* foolish talk or actions.

nonstop (non′ stop′) *adj.* travelling without a single stop: *This nonstop flight goes directly from Regina to Montreal.* —*adv.* without stopping: *My brother can talk nonstop.*

noodle (nūd′ əl) *n.* a food made of flour and water, shaped in a long strip and boiled or fried.

nook (nu̇k) *n.* a quiet little corner.

noon (nūn) *n.* twelve o'clock in the daytime, written as 12 p.m.; the middle of the day.

no one (nō wun) *pron.* nobody; no person: *No one is home at my friend's house.*

noose (nūs) *n.* a loop of rope with a knot that tightens when pulled: *The cowboy caught the calf by throwing a noose around its neck.*

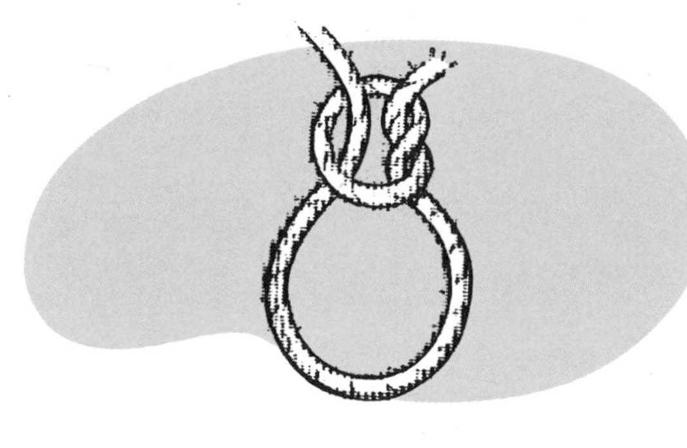

noose

nor (nȯr) *conj.* and not; used after **neither**: *Neither my dog nor my cat can do any tricks.*

normal (nȯr′ məl) *adj.* ordinary; usual; as expected: *Today was a normal day; nothing special happened.*

normally (nȯr′ mə lē) *adv.* usually: *I normally walk to school, but I decided to take the bus today.*

north (nȯrth) *n.* the direction to your left as you face the sunrise; opposite to south.

North American (nȯrth ə mer′ i kən) a person born in or living in Canada, the United States, Mexico, or Central America. —*adj.* having to do with the continent of North America.

northeast (nȯrth′ ēst′) *n.* the direction that is halfway between north and east.

northern (nȯr′ THərn) *adj.* in or of the north: *Canada is a northern country.*

Northern Lights glowing bands of light that appear in the sky at night in northern regions.

North Pole the most northern point of the earth.

northward, northwards (nȯrth′ wərd, nȯrth′ wərdz) *adv.* toward or facing the north.

northwest (north′ west′) *n.* the direction that is halfway between north and west.

nose (nōz) *n.* the part of your face that sticks out above your mouth: *The nose has two nostrils or holes through which you smell and breathe.*

nosedive (nōz′ dīv′) *n.* a sharp dive by an aircraft, head (nose) first. —*v.* (for an aircraft) to make such a dive. **nosediving. nosedived.**

nostril (nos′ trəl) *n.* one of the two openings in your nose.

nosy, nosey (nō′ zē) *adj.* too curious about other people's business; always prying: *a nosy neighbour; a nosier one; the nosiest one on the street.* —**nosily** *adv.*

not (not) *adv.* a word meaning "in no way" or "the opposite of." It is used to make negative statements: *"Are you happy?" "No, I am not."*

notch (notch) *n.* **1.** a small triangular cut; a nick: *The stranded sailor marked the days by cutting notches in a piece of wood.* **2.** a hole in a belt. **3.** a small amount: *Her confidence went up a notch after she won the award.* *pl.* **notches.**

note (nōt) *n.* **1.** words written down as a reminder: *I wrote notes on what the teacher was saying.* **2.** a short written message. **3.** a musical tone, or a symbol for it when writing music. **4.** notice: *Take note of what she is saying.* —*v.* to notice closely; to pay attention to: *Note all the colours in the picture.* **noting. noted.**

notebook (nōt′ bu̇k′) *n.* a book with blank pages on which to write.

noted (nō′ təd) *adj.* worthy of being noticed; famous: *She is a noted scientist.*

nothing (nuth′ ing) *n.* **1.** not anything: *He told me nothing.* **2.** in arithmetic, zero: 0.

notice (nō′ tis) *n.* a written or printed announcement or poster: *The notice says, "Keep off the grass."* —*v.* to see and pay attention; to note: *Did you notice that I got my hair cut?* **noticing. noticed.**

noticeable (no′ tə sə bəl) *adj.* easily seen: *The dent on the car is quite noticeable.* —**noticeably** *adv.*

notify (nō′ tə fī′) *v.* to let someone know; to send a note: *The librarian notified me that my book was overdue.* **notifying. notified.** he **notifies.**

notion (nō′ shən) *n.* an idea or belief, sometimes one that is confused or wrong: *Where did you get the notion that pandas are bears?*

nougat (nū′ gət *or* nū′ go′) *n.* a white, soft, chewy candy.

noun (nown) *n.* a word used as the name of a person, place, thing, quality, condition, event, and so on: *"Alicia," "Neil," "cat," "honesty," "football," and "Canada" are nouns.*

nourish (nu̇r′ ish) *v.* to provide the food that is needed for healthy growth: *Nourished by its mother's milk, the baby whale soon doubled in size.* **nourishing. nourished.**

nourishing (nu̇r′ ish ing) *adj.* good for your health; nutritious: *a nourishing meal.*

novel (nov′ əl) *n.* a long story, in book form, usually about made-up people and events.

November (nō vem′ bər) *n.* the eleventh month of the year.

now (now) *adv.* **1.** at the present time. **2.** at once: *I need your help now!*

now and then once in a while: *Now and then, I listen to a different radio station.*

nowadays (now′ ə dāz′) *adv.* in the present time; in these days: *Nowadays, people don't dress up as much as they used to.*

nowhere (nō′ wer′ *or* nō′ hwer′) *adv.* in no place; not anywhere: *She was nowhere to be seen.*

nozzle (noz′ əl) *n.* a metal spout at the end of a hose or pipe through which liquids or gases pass: *As she adjusted the nozzle on the hose, the water changed from a long stream to a wide spray.*

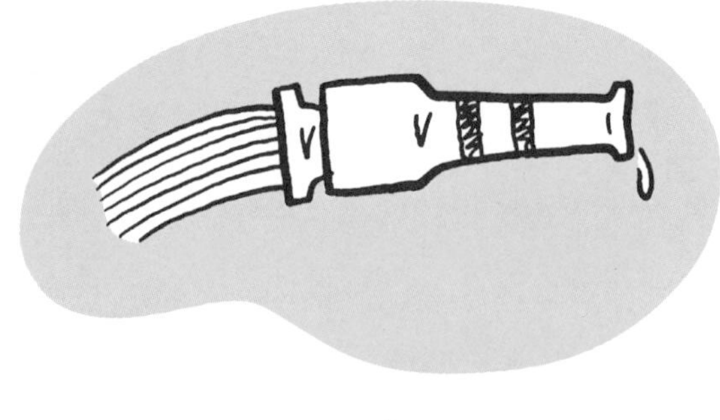

nozzle

nuclear energy (nū′ klē ər en′ ər jē *or* nyū′ klē ər en′ ər jē) energy that is found in the nucleus of an atom: *Nuclear energy is used to make bombs, to produce electric power, and to treat some diseases.*

nucleus (nū′ klē əs *or* nyū′ klē əs) *n.*
1. the tiny central core of an atom.
2. the tiny centre of a plant or animal cell.
pl. **nuclei** (nū′ klē ī).

nude (nūd *or* nyūd) *adj.* bare; naked; without clothes.

nudge (nuj) *n.* a gentle push with your elbow to attract a person's attention.
—*v.* to give a nudge. **nudging. nudged.**

nugget (nug′ it) *n.* a rough lump of metal, usually gold.

nuisance (nū′ səns *or* nyū′ səns) *n.* something that is annoying to people, or someone who bothers other people.

numb (num) *adj.* without any feeling: *My fingers were numb with cold.*

number (num′ bər) *n.* **1.** a word or symbol used to count: *Seven (7), two hundred (200), and five thousand (5000) are numbers.*
2. several: *I have a number of questions.*
3. the total: *What is the number of students in the class?* —*v.* **1.** to mark with a number: *Number the pages.* **2.** to add up to: *The audience numbered more than 500.*
numbering. numbered.

numeral (nū′ mə rəl *or* nyū′ mə rəl) *n.* a written symbol that stands for a number: *The numerals 6 and 5 make up the number 65. In Roman numerals, the number 27 is written as XXVII.*

numerator (nū′ mər ā′ tər *or* nyū′ mər ā′ tər) *n.* the number above the line in a fraction: *In 3/4, 3 is the numerator and 4 is the denominator.*

numerical (nū mər′ ə kəl *or* nyū mer′ ə kəl) *adj.* having to do with numbers: *The numbers 1, 2, 3, 4, 5 are written in numerical order.* —**numerically** *adv.*

numerous (nū′ mər əs *or* nyū′ mər əs) *adj.* very many: *Do you have time to answer my numerous questions?*

nun (nun) *n.* a religious woman who lives her life helping others.

nurse (nùrs) *n.* a person who is trained to care for the sick, the old, or the very young.
—*v.* to care for such people. **nursing. nursed.**

nursery (nùr′ sə rē) *n.* **1.** a room or a building for very young children **2.** a place where young plants are looked after.
pl. **nurseries.**

nut (nut) *n.* **1.** a dry fruit or seed with a hard shell: *A walnut, an almond, and a chestnut are three kinds of nuts.* **2.** a small piece of metal with a hole in the centre: *A nut screws onto a bolt.* **3.** (*slang*) a silly person.

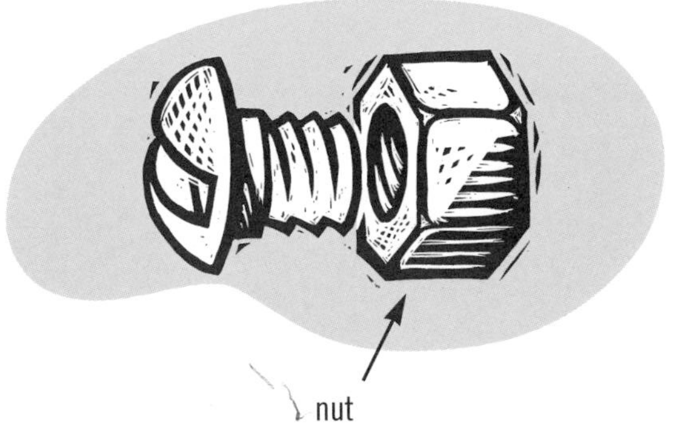

nutrition (nū trish′ ən *or* nyū trish′ ən) *n.* **1.** food. **2.** the process by which plants and animals take in and use food substances: *Eating the right foods leads to good nutrition.*

nutritious (nū trish′ əs *or* nyū trish′ əs) *adj.* good for your health; nourishing: *This cereal is delicious and nutritious.*

nylon (nī′ lon) *n.* an artificial fabric that is very strong and light. —*adj.* made of nylon: *a nylon jacket.*

nylons (nī′ lonz) *n.* thin tights made of nylon.

oak (ōk) *n.* a tree having nuts called acorns; its hard wood is often used to make furniture.

oar (ȯr) *n.* a long pole with a flat blade at one end, used for rowing boats.

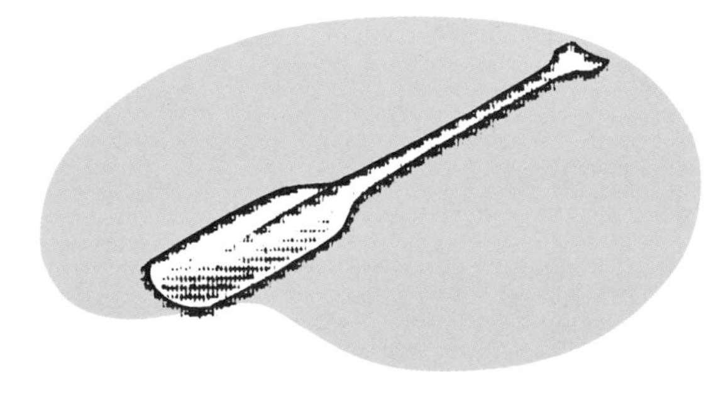

oar

oath (ōth) *n.* a very serious promise to tell the truth or to do something. *pl.* **oaths.**

oatmeal (ōt′ mēl′) *n.* a cooked cereal that is made from rolled or ground oats.

oats (ōts) *n. pl.* a grain, used for cereal and as feed for animals.

obedience (ō bē′ dē əns) *n.* the act of doing as you are told. (*opp.* **disobedience.**)

obedient (ō bē′ dē ənt) *adj.* doing as you are told. (*opp.* **disobedient.**) —**obediently** *adv.*

obese (ō bēs′) *adj.* very fat, in an unhealthy way.

obey (ō bā′) *v.* to do as you are told: *We obeyed the teacher's request to line up at the door.* **obeying. obeyed.** he **obeys.** (*opp.* **disobey.**)

object (ob′ jekt) *n.* **1.** a thing you can see and touch. **2.** an aim: *Her object in life is to be a doctor like her mother.* **3.** in grammar, the word or words that receive the action of a verb or that follow a preposition: *I closed the window. You walked past my brother and me.* The objects in these two sentences are *window* and *my brother and me.*

object (əb jekt′) *v.* to disagree with; to complain against: *I object to being treated like a child by my parents.* **objecting. objected.**

oblige (ə blīj′) *v.* to have to do something: *If I want to pass the test, I am obliged to study for it.* **obliging. obliged.**

oblong (ob′ long) *adj.* longer than wide: *an oblong table.*

obnoxious (əb nok′ shəs) *adj.* extremely unpleasant: *obnoxious behaviour.* —**obnoxiously** *adv.*

observant (əb zu̇r′ vənt) *adj.* quick to notice; watching carefully. (*opp.* **unobservant.**) —**observantly** *adv.*

observation (ob zər vā′ shən) *n.* the act of watching, especially watching carefully: *The patient is under observation at the hospital.*

observatory (əb zu̇r′ və tȯr′ ē) *n.* a building where there are telescopes for studying the stars. *pl.* **observatories.**

observe (əb zu̇rv′) *v.* **1.** to watch carefully; to study: *I observed every move she made.* **2.** to celebrate: *We observe Canada Day by setting off fireworks.* **3.** to follow; to obey: *Observe the rules of the game.* **observing. observed.**

obsession (əb sesh′ ən) *n.* something that you can't stop thinking about: *My cat has an obsession with birds; she watches them all the time.*

obstacle (ob′ stə kəl) *n.* something that is in the way: *The fallen tree was an obstacle on the nature trail.*

obstruct (əb strukt′) *v.* to get in the way of: *The construction on the road is obstructing traffic.*

obtain (əb tān′) *v.* to get something through

effort: *Marga obtained the tickets after waiting in line for hours.* **obtaining. obtained.**

obvious (ob′ vē əs) *adj.* easy to see or understand; clear; plain: *It is obvious that I have longer hair than you do.* —**obviously** *adv.*

occasion (ə kā′ zhən) *n.* an important event: *My grandparents' fortieth anniversary was a great occasion.*

occasional (ə kā′ zhən əl) *adj.* happening now and then: *There were occasional flashes of lightning.* —**occasionally** *adv.*

occupy (ok′ yə pī′) *v.* **1.** to fill or take up space. **2.** to live in: *A family of four occupies that apartment.* **3.** to fill up time: *Reading occupies most of my spare time.* **4.** to be busy: *The coach is occupied with getting the team ready for the big game.* **occupying. occupied.** it **occupies.**

occur (ə kûr′) *v.* to take place; to happen: *New Year's Day occurs on a Monday next year.* **occurring. occurred.**

occur to to come to mind: *Did it occur to you to tell them we would be late?*

occurrence (ə kər′ əns) *n.* an event: *How would you describe the strange occurrence we saw yesterday?*

ocean (ō′ shən) *n.* one of five very large, salty bodies of water: *the Atlantic, Pacific, Indian, Arctic, and Antarctic Oceans.*

o'clock (ə klok′) short for "of the clock" (according to the clock): *It is two o'clock.*

The ancient Greek word for eight was *okto.* This is where we get **oct–** and **octo–**, meaning "eight." An "octopus" has eight arms. An "octet" is a group of eight musicians.

octave (ok′ tiv) *n.* a series of eight notes in a musical scale: *Do, re, mi, fa, sol, la, ti, do make up an octave.*

October (ok tō′ bər) *n.* the tenth month of the year.

octopus (ok′ tə pu̇s) *n.* a cold-blooded animal that lives in the ocean and has a soft, roundish body and eight tentacles. *pl.* **octopuses** or **octopi** (ok′ tə pī).

octopus

odd (od) *adj.* **1.** not even in number; not able to be divided exactly by 2: *5, 7, and 9 are odd numbers.* **2.** not making a matched pair: *odd socks.* **3.** strange; unusual: *a very odd story.* —**oddly** *adv.*

odds and ends things left over.

odds (odz) *n.* the chances of something happening, expressed as numbers: *"The odds are fifty-fifty that it will rain tomorrow" means "There is a fifty percent chance of rain."*

odour, odor (ō′ dər) *n.* a smell, usually an unpleasant one.

of (uv *or* ov) *prep.* **1.** made from: *a stack of wood.* **2.** belonging to: *a member of the family.* **3.** holding: *a shaker of salt.* **4.** having: *a person of honour.* **5.** about: *I've heard of it.*

off (of) *prep.* away from; not on; not touching: *She pushed the bucket off the roof.* —*adv.* **1.** away: *He ran off.* **2.** not on: *Please take off your coat.*

offence, offense (ə fens′ *or* ō fens′) *n.* **1.** a crime; a breaking of the rules: *Is it an offence to ride a bicycle on the sidewalk?* **2.** an attacking group of players: *Our hockey team has a powerful offence.*

offend (ə fend′ *or* ō fend′) *v.* to hurt someone's feelings: *I tried to help without offending him.* **offending. offended.**

offer (of′ ər) *n.* **1.** a price suggested by a person who wants to buy something: *What is their offer for this house?* **2.** a proposal: *an offer of marriage.* —*v.* to present or hold out something to be taken or refused: *to offer help.* **offering. offered.**

office (of′ is) *n.* **1.** a place where a person works: *a dentist's office.* **2.** an important government position: *the office of Mayor.*

officer (of′ ə sər) *n.* **1.** a person who holds a position of power or responsibility: *a police officer.* **2.** a person in command in the armed forces: *A captain is an officer.*

official (ə fish′ əl *or* ō fish′ əl) *n.* an officer: *an official from the hockey league.* —*adj.* having power granted by a group: *the official rules of the game.* (*opp.* **unofficial.**) —**officially** *adv.*

offshore (of′ shȯr′) *adj.* away from land, on or toward the water: *an offshore oil rig.*

offspring (of′ spring′) *n.* the living young produced by humans, animals, or plants: *Mice breed quickly and have many offspring.*

offstage (of′ stāj′) *n.* the area at the sides of and behind a stage, which the audience cannot see.

often (of′ ən *or* of′ tən) *adv.* many times; frequently.

ogre (ō′ gər) *n.* in fairy tales, a monster that eats people.

oh (ō) *interj.* **1.** a word used to express happiness, surprise, bad luck, and so on: *Oh, no!* **2.** a word used when talking to someone before saying his or her name: *Oh, Émil, what are you doing on the weekend?*

oil (oil) *n.* a thick, greasy liquid that floats on water and does not mix with it. —*v.* to put oil on or in something. **oiling. oiled.**

oink (oink) *n.* the sound that a pig makes when it is excited. —*v.* to make such a sound. **oinking. oinked.**

ointment (oint′ mənt) *n.* a type of medicine that is rubbed onto the skin.

okay, O.K. (ō′ kā′) *adj., adv.* all right; yes; correct; approved: *Do you feel okay? O.K., I'll help you.*

Some people think that **O.K.** is the abbreviation of "oll korrect." But what does "oll korrect" mean? It used to be a joking way of writing "all correct."

old (ōld) *adj.* **1.** having existed or lived for a long time: *an old tree; an older tree; the oldest tree in the forest.* **2.** having lived for a certain length of time: *Our cat is six years old.* **3.** belonging to the past: *days of old.*

old age the time when an adult is old.

old-fashioned (ōld′ fash′ ənd) *adj.* no longer used; out-of-date; not modern.

olive (ol′ iv) *n.* a small, oily fruit that is not sweet: *Olives grow on evergreen trees in warm places.*

Olympic Games, Olympics (ō lim′ pik gāmz′, ō lim′ piks) *n. pl.* a group of many different athletic contests held every four years in a different country: *summer Olympics; winter Olympics.*

omelette (om′ lət) *n.* a dish of eggs that have been beaten, cooked in a frying pan, and folded over: *An omelette may be plain, or cooked with cheese, mushrooms, or other ingredients.*

omit (ō mit′) *v.* to leave out or to leave undone: *You omitted an important number in your math answer.* **omitting. omitted.**

on (on) *prep.* **1.** resting on top of: *The pencil is on the desk.* **2.** covering: *to put on clothes.* **3.** during: *on Monday.* **4.** in the state of: *on fire; on sale.* **5.** about: *a book on sports.* —*adv.* **1.** further: *Let's go on.* **2.** not off: *Please turn the light on.*

once (wuns) *adv.* **1.** one time: *I have worn these shoes only once.* **2.** in the past: *Horses once were the main form of transportation.*
all at once suddenly: *All at once, lightning struck the tree.*

at once now; right away: *If you don't leave at once, you'll be late.*

once and for all finally: *Let's make a decision, once and for all.*

once in a while now and then.

one (wun) *n.* **1.** the first whole number after zero: 1. **2.** a single person or thing: *How does one get on the team? I want that one.* —*adj.* single: *There was only one person in the room.*

one by one one after another: *One by one, we took a turn at bat.*

oneself (wun self′) *pron.* one's own self: *It isn't always easy to admit the truth to oneself.*

one-way (wun′ wā′) *adj.* moving, or allowing movement, in one direction only: *a one-way street.*

onion (un′ yən) *n.* a round, strong-smelling plant bulb that is used as a vegetable.

onion

only (ōn′ lē) *adj.* single; sole: *an only child in a family.* —*adv.* **1.** just; merely: *I won only one game of cards.* **2.** and no more: *Only five people came to the party.* —*conj.* **1.** but; except that: *He wanted to go, only he had a bad cold.* **2.** on the condition that: *I'll go only if you go, too.*

onto (on′ tü) *prep.* to a position on: *She threw the ball onto the roof.*

onward, onwards (on′ wərd, on′ wərdz) *adv.* further on: *The soldiers marched onward.*

ooze (üz) *v.* to leak; to flow slowly: *Oil oozed out through the crack in the jar.* **oozing. oozed.**

open (ō′ pən) *adj.* **1.** not closed; in a position that allows movement in and out: *an open door.* **2.** wide and clear: *the open sky.* **3.** willing to accept new ideas: *an open mind.* —*v.* **1.** to unfasten: *Please open the gate.* **2.** to start: *The new movie opens tomorrow.* **opening. opened.**

opening (ō′ pən ing) *n.* **1.** a gap; a space: *an opening in the fence.* **2.** a beginning: *The opening of the baseball season is tomorrow.*

opera (op′ ər ə) *n.* a play set to music, with the performers singing their parts.

operate (op′ ər āt′) *v.* **1.** to work; to run: *to operate a machine.* **2.** to perform surgery: *The doctor operated on me to remove my tonsils.* **operating. operated.**

operation (op′ ər ā′ shən) *n.* **1.** the working of a machine. **2.** a medical treatment, in which a surgeon opens up the body to repair part of it.

operator (op′ ər ā′ tər) *n.* a person who operates a machine: *a telephone operator; a computer operator.*

opinion (ə pin′ yən *or* ō pin′ yən) *n.* what you think or believe; a judgment: *It is my opinion that a cat is a better pet than a dog.*

opponent (ə pō′ nənt) *n.* someone you fight against or play against in a game.

opportunity (op′ ər tü′ nə tē) *n.* a chance: *Tomorrow I will have an opportunity to try out for the team. pl.* **opportunities.**

oppose (ə pōz′) *v.* to fight or argue against: *The people of the town opposed the opening of a new garbage dump.* **opposing. opposed.**

opposite (op′ ə zit) *n.* someone or something that is completely different from another: *The opposite of "up" is "down."* —*prep.* across from: *Our house is opposite the school.* —*adj.* **1.** completely different: *We are going in opposite directions: you are turning left, while I am turning right.* **2.** across: *the opposite side of the street.*

Opposition Party, the Opposition (op′ ə zish′ ən pȧr′ tē) the political party that opposes the party in power. The Opposition has the second largest number of elected members in the government: *Members of the Opposition argue with the government's plans.*

optician (op tish′ ən) *n.* a person who makes or sells eyeglasses and contact lenses.

optometrist (op tom′ ə trist) *n.* a person trained to test your eyesight to see if you need glasses or contact lenses.

or (ȯr) *conj.* a word used to show a choice or a difference: *Is the answer true or false?*

oral (ȯr′ əl) *adj.* spoken, not written: *an oral report.* —**orally** *adv.*

orange (ȯr′ inj) *n.* **1.** a reddish-yellow citrus fruit, with a rough peel. **2.** the reddish-yellow colour of an orange. *—adj.* **1.** having the colour of an orange. **2.** having the flavour of an orange: *orange sherbet.*

orangutan (ō rang′ ů tan′) *n.* a large ape with long arms and shaggy, reddish hair: *Orangutans live on islands in Southern Asia.*

orangutan

orbit (ȯr′ bit) *n.* the path in which a satellite, planet, or other body moves around another body in space: *The earth makes an orbit around the sun once a year.* *—v.* to move in an orbit: *The moon orbits the earth.* **orbiting. orbited.**

orchard (ȯr′ chůrd) *n.* a group of growing fruit trees.

orchestra (ȯr′ kəs trə) *n.* a large group of musicians playing together on different instruments.

orchid (ȯr′ kid) *n.* a plant that has beautiful and colourful flowers, often white or purple.

ordeal (ȯr dēl′) *n.* a painful or difficult experience: *It was an ordeal to hike back to town after our car broke down.*

order (ȯr′ dər) *n.* **1.** tidiness; everything in its proper place: *Wendy always keeps her books in order.* **2.** a command: *The general gave the order to move on.* **3.** a request: *Please give your food order to the waiter.* **4.** a pattern in which one thing follows another: *The words in a dictionary are arranged in alphabetical order.* *—v.* to command or request: *I ordered spaghetti at the restaurant.* **ordering. ordered.**

in order to for the purpose of; so that: *In order to get on the team, Marika had to practise every day.*

out of order broken; not working: *I couldn't call you because our telephone was out of order.*

orderly (ȯr′ dər lē) *adj.* tidy; neat; in order: *The desks were lined up in orderly rows.*

ordinary (ȯr′ də ner′ ē) *adj.* usual; not special; average: *Yesterday was an ordinary day. Nothing unusual happened at all.* —**ordinarily** *adv.*

ore (ȯr) *n.* rock or earth, containing a valuable metal, such as iron or gold.

organ (ȯr′ gən) *n.* **1.** a musical instrument with two or more keyboards, foot pedals, and a set of pipes of different lengths, which makes sounds as air is blown through each pipe. **2.** a part of an animal or plant that does a certain job: *The ear is the organ of hearing.*

organic (ȯr gan′ ək) *adj.* **1.** produced by a living thing: *Bone is an organic substance.* **2.** made from foods that are grown naturally, without the use of artificial chemicals. —**organically** *adv.*

organization (ȯr′ gən ə zā′ shən) *n.* **1.** a group of people who work together for a purpose: *Our organization collects old newspapers for recycling.* **2.** the planning and arranging of an activity: *The organization of the school dance takes a lot of work.*

organize (ȯr′ gən īz′) *v.* **1.** to plan and arrange something: *to organize a party.* **2.** to put in order: *I organized my CD collection.* **organizing. organized.**

origin (ȯr′ ə jən) *n.* the beginning, history, or source of something: *Many words have interesting origins.*

original (ə rij′ ə nəl) *adj.* **1.** completely new; not copied: *This story is original. I made it up myself.* **2.** not like any other: *He has an original way of dressing.* (*opp.* **unoriginal.**)

originally (ə rij′ ə nəl ē) *adv.* first; at the beginning: *That oak tree was originally an acorn.*

oriole (ȯr′ ē ōl) *n.* a songbird with black and orange feathers.

ornament (ȯr′ nə mənt) *n.* an object that is used to add beauty or for decoration.

orphan (ȯr′ fən) *n.* a child whose parents are dead.

orphanage (ȯr′ fən ij) *n.* a home for orphans.

ostrich (os′ trich) *n.* a very large bird found in Africa that has a long neck and long legs: *An ostrich can run fast, but it cannot fly. It is the largest bird known.*

ostrich

other (uTH′ ər) *pron.* different or additional ones: *Are there any others?* —*adj.* **1.** different: *You like these books, but I like other ones.* **2.** opposite; across: *She lives on the other side of the street.* **3.** left; remaining: *I have no other chores to do.* **4.** additional: *Are there any other choices?*

the other day recently: *I ran into an old friend the other day.*

otherwise (oTH′ ər wīz′) *conj.* or else: *Don't spend all your money now; otherwise you will have none left for the movie.*

otter (ot′ ər) *n.* a water mammal that has shiny brown fur and eats fish: *Otters have webbed feet and belong to the weasel family.*

ouch, ow (owch, ow) *interj.* a cry of sudden pain: *Ouch! I've bumped my toe!*

ought (ot) *v.* a helping (auxiliary) verb used before another verb to mean "should" or "have a duty": *We ought to help out the less fortunate.*

ounce (owns) *n.* a unit for measuring mass or weight, equal to about 28 g.

our (owr) *adj.* belonging to us: *We painted our house.*

ours (owrz) *pron.* the one belonging to us: *The house is ours.*

ourselves (owr selvz′) *pron. pl.* our selves alone. "Ourselves" is used when the subject and object of a verb are the same: *We helped ourselves to the food.*

out (owt) *adv.* **1.** away; outside, not in: *She went out.* **2.** to or at an end: *Time is running out.* —*adj.* **1.** not burning: *The fire is out.* **2.** being seen or known: *The flowers come out in springtime. Their secret is out.* —*prep.* through to the outside: *The baby threw the ring out the window.*

out of bounds outside the boundaries or limits.

out-of-date old-fashioned; not modern.

out of work not having a job.

out– is a prefix that means "more than," "better than," or "outside of": to "outnumber" means to be greater in number; to "outfight" means to fight better than the other person; the "outdoors" is outside your door.

outboard (owt′ bȯrd′) *n.* a type of motor that attaches to the back of a boat, rather than being built inside it.

outdoor (owt′ dȯr′) *adj.* in the open air; not inside a building: *outdoor sports.*

outdoors (owt′ dȯrz′) *adj.* into the open air: *Let's go outdoors to play.*

outer (owt′ ər) *adj.* on the outside; farther out: *Open the outer door, but leave the inner door closed.*

outer space space beyond the earth's atmosphere.

outfield (owt′ fēld′) *n.* **1.** in baseball, the playing area outside the diamond. **2.** the positions played by the right, centre, and left fielders.

outfit (owt′ fit′) *n.* a complete set of clothes: *Everyone at the party liked my new outfit.* —*v.* to provide with a set of clothes or equipment: *The campers were outfitted with sleeping bags and knapsacks.* **outfitting. outfitted.**

outgoing (owt′ gō′ ing) *adj.* friendly and not shy: *My sister is an outgoing person and has many friends.*

outing (owt′ ing) *n.* a trip for pleasure: *The family went on an outing to the park.*

outlaw (owt′ lo′) *n.* a criminal.

outlet (owt′ lət) *n.* **1.** a way out; an opening. **2.** a place on a wall for putting in an electrical plug.

outline (owt′ līn′) *n.* **1.** in drawing, a line showing the shape of an object. **2.** a short plan; a rough draft: *an outline of a story.*

outport (owt′ pȯrt′) *n.* in Newfoundland, a small harbour or fishing village.

outside (owt′ sīd′) *n.* the outer part or side: *the outside of a shed.* —*adv.* outdoors: *Let's go outside.*

outstanding (owt′ stan′ ding) *adj.* **1.** excellent: *I saw an outstanding movie.* **2.** not paid: *Your bill is still outstanding. Please pay what you owe as soon as possible.*

outward, outwards (owt′ wərd, owt′ wərdz) *adv.* toward the outside or away from: *The window opens outward.*

outwit (owt′ wit′) *v.* to defeat someone by being more clever: *The detective outwitted the criminal and caught him as he was leaving town.*

oval (ō′ vəl) *adj.* having a shape like an egg or a stretched circle.

oven (uv′ ən) *n.* a space in a stove, used for baking and roasting.

over (ō′ vər) *prep.* **1.** above: *The plane flew over our heads.* **2.** on top of: *Put the blanket over the baby.* **3.** more than: *over a dollar.* **4.** above and across: *Jump over the fence.* —*adj.* finished: *The movie is over.* —*adv.* **1.** to a different place: *Come over to my house.* **2.** again: *Do the job over.*
over with finished: *Get the job over with.*

overalls (ō′ vər olz′) *n. pl.* a pair of loose pants with a top, and straps that go over the shoulders.

overboard (ō′ vər bȯrd′) *adv.* over a ship's side: *The wave swept the crate overboard.*

overcast (ō′ vər kast′) *adj.* completely covered with clouds: *a dark, overcast day.*

overcoat (ō′ vər kōt′) *n.* a long, warm coat, worn in cold weather.

overcome (ō′ vər kum′) *v.* to conquer: *She overcame her fear and dived off the high diving board.* **overcoming. overcame.** I have **overcome.**

overdue (ō′ vər dū′ *or* ō′ vər dyū′) *adj.* later than the time allowed: *My library book is overdue and must be returned.*

overflow (ō′ vər flō′) *v.* to spill over; to flood: *Turn off the water! The tub is overflowing.* **overflowing. overflowed.**

overhead (ō′ vər hed′) *adv.* high above, over your head: *Birds fly overhead.*

overhear (ō′ vər hēr′) *v.* to hear something that you are not meant to hear: *I overheard Marian invite Yoshio to a surprise party for me.* **overhearing. overheard** (ō′ vər hərd′).

overjoyed (ō′ vər joid′) *adj.* more than happy: *I was overjoyed when I won the contest.*

overlap (ō′ vər lap′) *v.* to place over something so that it is partly covered up. **overlapping. overlapped.**

overlook (ō′ vər lu̇k′) *v.* **1.** to miss seeing something: *Don't overlook your spelling mistakes.* **2.** to forgive a mistake or bad behaviour: *The coach decided to overlook our team's single loss so far this season.* **overlooking. overlooked.**

overnight (ō′ vər nīt′) *adj.* during the night or lasting for a night: *We took an overnight train to Calgary.* —*adv.* until the night is over: *I had to stay overnight at my friend's house when the snowstorm hit.*

overpass (ō′ vər pas′) *n.* a bridge that allows one road to cross over another one.

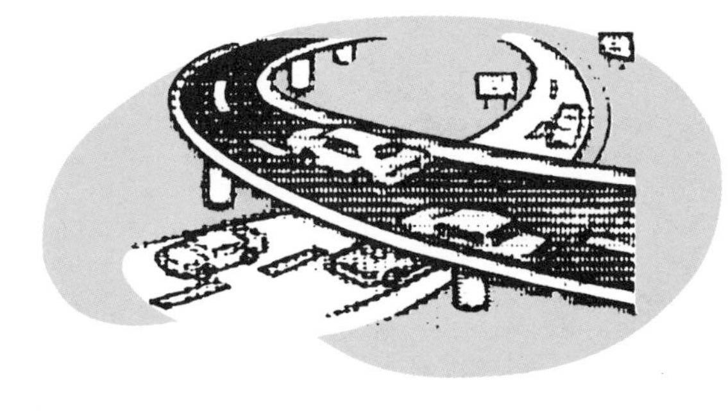

overpass

overseas (ō′ vər sēz′) *adv.* across the sea: *My aunt lives overseas in England.*

overshoes (ō′ vər shūz′) *n. pl.* rubber or plastic shoes worn over regular shoes to protect them from rain or snow.

overtake (ō′ vər tāk′) *v.* to catch up to someone and pass him or her: *Another runner overtook me just before the finish line.* **overtaking. overtook** (ō′ vər tu̇k′).

overtime (o′ vər tīm′) *n.* extra time: *The game was tied, so it went into overtime.*

overwhelm (o′ vər hwelm′ *or* ō′ vər welm′) *v.* to have too much or an unusual amount of something: *I was overwhelmed with joy at winning first prize.* **overwhelming. overwhelmed.**

ow (ow) *interj.* see **ouch**.

owe (ō) *v.* to be in debt: *I will pay you the money I owe.* **owing. owed.**

owl (owl) *n.* a bird with a large head, big eyes, and a hooked beak: *Owls have keen eyesight and hunt at night.*

own (ōn) *adj.* belonging to: *his own place; my own story; their own business.* —*v.* to have; to possess: *They own three TV sets.* **owning. owned.**

on your own responsible for yourself; not relying on others: *My older brother has moved away from home and is on his own.*

owner (ōn′ ər) *n.* a person who owns something.

ox (oks) *n.* a kind of bull, used for pulling carts or for eating as meat. *pl.* **oxen.**

oxygen (ok′ sə jən) *n.* a gas that has no colour or smell: *Animals and plants need oxygen to live. It is part of the air we breathe.*

oyster (ois′ tər) *n.* a flat, round shellfish: *Some kinds of oysters produce pearls, while others are eaten as food.*

ozone (ō′ zōn) *n.* a type of oxygen gas that is found high in the atmosphere and that absorbs ultraviolet rays from the sun.

Pp

pa, papa (po *or* pa, po′ pə *or* pa′ pa) *n.* father.

pace (pās) *n.* the speed of walking: *A turtle moves at a slow pace.* —*v.* to walk back and forth: *She paced the room.* **pacing. paced.**

Pacific (pə sif′ ik) *n.* the ocean separating North America and South America from Asia and Australia.

pack (pak) *n.* **1.** a bundle of things wrapped together for carrying: *He made a pack of clothes to carry on his back.* **2.** a group of animals: *a pack of wolves.* —*v.* **1.** to put in a bundle, or to put clothes into a case. (*opp.* **unpack.**) **2.** to crowd together: *The room is packed with people.* **packing. packed.**

package (pak′ ij) *n.* a thing or things wrapped up or put in a box or bag; a parcel: *a birthday package; a package of cookies.*

pad (pad) *n.* **1.** a cushion. **2.** a number of sheets of paper glued together on one edge for writing or drawing on.

paddle (pad′ əl) *n.* **1.** a short oar used to move a canoe. **2.** a small round board with a handle, used to hit the ball in table tennis. —*v.* to move a canoe with a paddle. **paddling. paddled.**

page (pāj) *n.* **1.** one side of a sheet of paper. **2.** a person who does errands. **3.** a messenger at the House of Commons, the Senate, or a provincial legislature.

paid (pād) see **pay** (verb).

pail (pāl) *n.* a small bucket with a handle.

pain (pān) *n.* an ache; a feeling of being hurt; suffering.

painful (pān′ fəl) *adj.* **1.** hurting. **2.** giving pain or suffering: *a painful injury.* —**painfully** *adv.*

paint (pānt) *n.* a coloured liquid used to cover and protect or decorate a surface. —*v.* **1.** to cover with paint. **2.** to make a picture with paint. **painting. painted.**

painter (pān′ tər) *n.* **1.** a person who paints walls or other surfaces. **2.** a person who paints pictures; an artist.

painting (pān′ ting) *n.* a picture created with the use of paint.

pair (per) *n.* two things of a kind that go together: *a pair of socks; a pair of gloves.*

pajamas see **pyjamas**.

palace (pal′ is) *n.* the home of a king, queen, or other ruler, usually very large and beautiful.

palate (pal′ ət) *n.* the roof of your mouth.

pale (pāl) *adj.* **1.** lacking colour: *He looks pale because he is feeling sick.* **2.** light in colour: *Beige is a pale brown.*

palette (pal′ ət) *n.* a board used by an artist to hold and mix paints.

palm (pom) *n.* **1.** the inside of your hand, between the wrist and fingers. **2.** a type of tree, found in warm places, with a long trunk and large, fan-shaped leaves at the very top.

palm

pamper (pam′ pər) *v.* to spoil people or pets, giving them whatever they want and treating them almost like babies. **pampering. pampered.**

pamphlet (pam′ flət) *n.* a thin booklet with a paper cover.

pan (pan) *n.* **1.** a metal dish. **2.** a heavy metal dish with a handle, used to cook food. —*v.* to wash sand or ore in a pan in search of gold. **panning. panned.**

pancake (pan′ kāk′) *n.* a flat, round cake made of batter that is fried on a griddle.

panda (pan′ də) *n.* a large, gentle, black and white mammal that looks like a bear and lives in and around China: *Pandas feed on bamboo shoots and leaves.*

pane (pān) *n.* a sheet of glass in a window frame.

panel (pan′ əl) *n.* **1.** a flat section of a door or wall. **2.** a group of people taking part in a discussion or judging a contest. —*v.* to put panels of wood on a wall. **panelling. panelled.**

panic (pan′ ik) *n.* a sudden fear that makes people or animals want to run away. —*v.* to feel panic: *The horses panicked when they saw the fire.* **panicking. panicked.**

pansy (pan′ zē) *n.* a small, short flower with petals of two different colours. *pl.* **pansies.**

pant (pant) *v.* to gasp for breath: *All the runners were panting.* **panting. panted.**

panther (pan′ thər) *n.* a large wild cat such as a cougar, a black leopard, or a jaguar.

paper (pā′ pər) *n.* a thin, smooth material used for writing and printing on, for wrapping things, for covering walls, and other purposes.

paperback (pā′ pər bak′) *n.* a book, often an inexpensive one, with a flexible cover rather than a stiff, hard cover.

papier-mâché (pā′ pər mə shā′) *n.* paper strips soaked in a flour and water paste and used for modelling: *Papier-mâché is very hard when dry.*

parachute (per′ ə shūt′) *n.* a very large sheet, shaped like an umbrella: *A parachute is strapped to someone's back so that he or she can jump out of an airplane and float safely to the ground.* —*v.* to jump from an airplane wearing a parachute. **parachuting. parachuted.**

parade (pə rād′) *n.* a march or procession in honour of a special occasion. —*v.* **1.** to march in a parade. **2.** to show off: *They paraded their new toys in front of the other children.* **parading. paraded.**

paradise (per′ ə dīs′) *n.* a place of great happiness and beauty; heaven.

> **Paradise** originally was a Persian word for a closed-in place. Then it came to mean a closed-in park for kings and queens. Finally, the word came to mean heaven or any place of great happiness and beauty.

paragraph (per′ ə graf′) *n.* a group of sentences that focus on a single idea. A paragraph begins on a new line, and the first word is usually indented.

paralyze, paralyse (per′ ə līz′) *v.* to make a person unable to move or feel: *paralyzed by an injury; paralyzed by fear.* **paralyzing. paralyzed.**

parcel (pår′ səl) *n.* a package.

pardon (pår′ dən) *n.* forgiveness: *I beg your pardon.* —*v.* to forgive; to excuse: *Pardon me for being late.* **pardoning. pardoned.**

parent (per′ ənt) *n.* a mother or father.

park (pårk) *n.* **1.** a piece of land with trees, lawns, flowers, paths, and so on, for people to visit for recreation. **2.** a wilderness area protected by the government and used by campers, hikers, and others. —*v.* to leave a car in a place when it is not being used: *We parked the car by the side of the road and walked down to the river.* **parking. parked.**

parka (pär′ kə) *n.* a warm fur or cloth jacket with a hood, first worn by the Inuit.

parka

parking lot a piece of land set aside for cars to park on.

parliament (pär′ lə mənt) *n.* in some countries, a group of people elected or chosen to make laws: *The Canadian Parliament is made up of the House of Commons and the Senate.*

parlour, parlor (pär′ lər) *n.* an old-fashioned name for a living room or sitting room.

parrot (per′ ət) *n.* a brightly coloured, tropical bird that has a hooked beak and can mimic human speech.

parsley (pärs′ lē) *n.* a plant with small, curly leaves that are used to flavour foods.

part (pärt) *n.* **1.** a section or piece of a whole: *Leah and Braham ate part of the cake.* **2.** a role in a play or movie: *I am auditioning for the part of the villain.* **3.** a side: *I took Ryan's part in the argument.* —*v.* **1.** to separate or divide into parts: *to part your hair.* **2.** to leave someone: *to part company.* **parting. parted.**

part with to give up; to let go: *The baby does not want to part with his teddy.*

take part in to join in; to be involved in.

partial (pär′ shəl) *adj.* **1.** not complete: *He received only partial payment because he did not finish the job.* **2.** fond of something: *I'm partial to ice cream.*

partially (pär′ shəl ē) *adv.* partly: *My homework is only partially completed.*

participant (pär tis′ ə pənt) *n.* someone who takes part in a contest, game, or sport; someone who shares or participates.

participate (pär tis′ ə pāt′) *v.* to take part in an activity.

participation (pär tis′ ə pā′ shən) *n.* the act of taking part in an activity.

particle (pär′ tə kəl) *n.* a very small bit; a speck: *a particle of dirt.*

particular (pər tik′ yə lər) *adj.* **1.** specific: *I'm looking for a particular book in the library.* **2.** special: *Terry is a particular friend of mine.* **3.** hard to please; picky: *My brother is very particular about what he wears.*

particularly (pər tik′ yə lər lē) *adv.* especially: *I like sports, particularly tennis and soccer.*

partly (pärt′ lē) *adv.* in part; not completely: *The story is partly true, but I made up the ending.*

partner (pärt′ nər) *n.* **1.** one of two people joined in an activity: *a dance partner; a business partner.* **2.** a steady companion.

part of speech a type of word, such as a verb, noun, pronoun, adjective, adverb, preposition, and so on: *Different parts of speech have different uses in a sentence.* *pl.* **parts of speech.**

partridge (pär′ trij) *n.* a plump, wild bird often hunted as game.

party (pär′ tē) *n.* **1.** a gathering of people for fun or celebration: *a birthday party.* **2.** a political organization: *the Conservative Party; the Liberal Party; the New Democratic Party; the Reform Party.* *pl.* **parties.**

pass (pas) *n.* **1.** a narrow road or way through mountains. **2.** a ticket allowing you to enter a place or a special event: *a free pass to the museum.* *pl.* **passes.** —*v.* **1.** to go past: *We passed a traffic accident on the road.* **2.** to hand over: *Please pass the salt.*

The hockey player passed the puck to her teammate. **3.** to complete a test or a course of study successfully: *They passed the test.* **passing. passed.**

pass out **1.** to hand out: *Please pass out the papers.* **2.** to faint.

passage (pas′ ij) *n.* **1.** a way through. **2.** a few sentences or paragraphs in a book: *Please read the passage at the top of the page.*

passenger (pas′ ən jər) *n.* a traveller in a ship, airplane, car, or other vehicle, who is not the driver or a crew member.

passion (pash′ ən) *n.* a very strong feeling or emotion, such as love, hatred, or anger: *I hate racial prejudice with a passion.*

passionate (pash′ ən ət) *adj.* **1.** feeling very strongly about someone or something: *We are passionate about our volunteer work.* **2.** showing strong emotion or feeling: *a passionate speech.* —**passionately** *adv.*

passport (pas′ pȯrt) *n.* a document that you must have to travel to a foreign country.

password (pas′ wûrd′) *n.* a secret word that lets you enter a place or use private computer files.

past (past) *n.* time gone by: *In the past, people travelled by horse.* —*adj.* gone by; ended: *It has rained a lot during the past month.* —*prep.* **1.** beyond; passing by: *I cycled past my school.* **2.** after, in time: *It is quarter past three.*

Be careful not to mix up **past** with "passed"; "passed" is used only as a verb.

past tense in grammar, the past tense is a form of a verb used to describe an action that has already happened: *When I woke up yesterday, the first thing I saw was a birthday present next to the bed.* In this example, "woke" and "saw" are the past tenses of the verbs "to wake" and "to see."

pasta (pas′ tə) *n.* a food that is made out of flour paste: *Noodles, spaghetti, and macaroni are three kinds of pasta.*

paste (pāst) *n.* a thick mixture used to stick things together. —*v.* to use this mixture: *We pasted wallpaper on the wall.* **pasting. pasted.**

pastel (pas tel′) *n.* **1.** a kind of crayon, used for colouring and drawing. **2.** a soft, pale colour. —*adj.* having a soft, pale colour.

pasteurize (pas′ chər īz′) *v.* to heat milk enough to kill germs. **pasteurizing. pasteurized.**

pastry (pās′ trē) *n.* a dough crust used for pies, tarts, and other baked goods. *pl.* **pastries.**

pasture (pas′ chůr) *n.* grassland for cattle or other animals to feed on.

pat (pat) *n.* a gentle tap: *a pat on the shoulder.* —*v.* to tap gently with your hand: *Sachi patted the friendly dog.* **patting. patted.**

patch (pach) *n.* **1.** a small piece of cloth that covers a hole: *Father sewed a patch on my jeans.* **2.** a small area: *a vegetable patch.* *pl.* **patches.** —*v.* to mend with a patch: *I patched the holes in the knees of my jeans.* **patching. patched.**

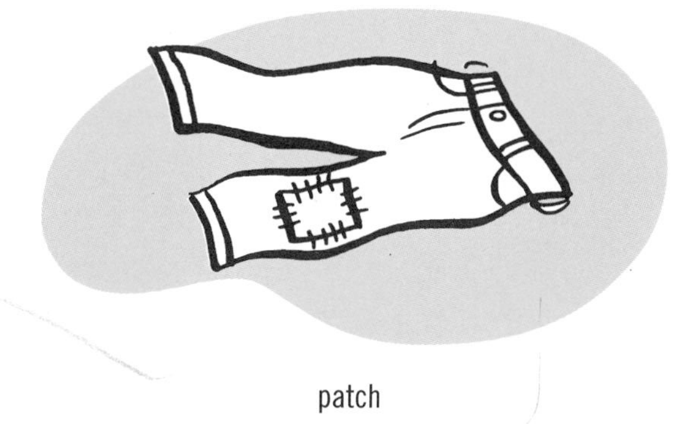

patch

path (path) *n.* a narrow lane or trail.

pathetic (pə thet′ ək) *adj.* causing you to feel sorry for someone or something: *The sick old cat was a pathetic sight.* —**pathetically** *adv.*

patience (pā′ shəns) *n.* the ability to wait calmly without complaining. (*opp.* **impatience.**)

patient (pā′ shənt) *n.* a person who is being treated by a doctor or dentist. —*adj.* calmly waiting without complaining: *Be patient! Our guests will be here soon.* (*opp.* **impatient.**) —**patiently** *adv.*

patio (pat′ ē ō) *n.* an outdoor, paved area next to a house: *We ate our lunch on the patio. pl.* **patios.**

patrol (pə trōl′) *n.* **1.** one part of a Boy Scout troop or a Girl Guide company. **2.** a small group of soldiers or police officers who are on guard. —*v.* to walk around an area, guarding it. **patrolling. patrolled.**

pattern (pat′ ərn) *n.* **1.** a model to be copied: *a paper pattern for a dress.* **2.** a design that repeats: *a pattern of roses on a dress.*

pause (poz) *n.* a short break or rest: *We took a pause in our hike.* —*v.* to stop what you are doing for a short time: *The runner paused for breath.* **pausing. paused.**

pave (pāv) *v.* to cover a street, driveway, or sidewalk with a flat surface of tar or cement. **paving. paved.**

pavement (pāv′ mənt) *n.* a paved area.

paw (po) *n.* the foot of a four-footed animal that has claws.

pay (pā) *n.* the money received for work done: *After two weeks, she was given her pay.* —*v.* **1.** to give money in return for goods or for work done. **2.** to be punished for something: *You'll pay for your mistake one day!* **paying. paid.** she **pays.**

pea (pē) *n.* a round, green seed that grows in a pod and is used for food.

peace (pēs) *n.* **1.** a calm, quiet time. **2.** a time when there is no war.

peaceful (pēs′ fəl) *adj.* quiet and calm. —**peacefully** *adv.*

peach (pēch) *n.* a round, sweet, juicy fruit that has yellow-pinkish flesh, a fuzzy skin, and a large pit. *pl.* **peaches.**

peacock (pē′ kok) *n.* a large male bird with beautiful green, blue, and gold tail feathers that can be spread out like a fan: *A peacock is the male peafowl, and a peahen is the female peafowl.*

peak (pēk) *n.* **1.** a mountain top. **2.** the front part of a cap that sticks out.

peanut (pē′ nut′) *n.* a nut-like seed that grows underground in a yellowish pod or shell and is eaten as food.

peanut butter a bread spread made from crushed peanuts.

pear (per) *n.* a sweet juicy fruit, round at the bottom and smaller near the stem end.

pearl (pürl) *n.* a gem, usually round and white, found in some oyster shells: *Pearls are used to make jewellery.*

peasant (pez′ ənt) *n.* a farm worker in some countries.

pebble (peb′ əl) *n.* a small, round stone.

pecan (pē′ kan *or* pē kon′) *n.* the nut of the pecan tree: *A pecan nut grows in a reddish, oval shell and is often used in pies.*

peculiar (pə kyūl′ yər) *adj.* odd, unusual, or different: *My cat is peculiar—he's scared of mice!* —**peculiarly** *adv.*

pedal (ped′ əl) *n.* the part on which you place your foot in order to move a vehicle or work a machine: *a bicycle pedal.* —*v.* to make a bicycle move by using the pedals. **pedalling. pedalled.**

pedestrian (pə des′ trē ən) *n.* a person who travels on foot: *The pedestrian crossed the street when the traffic light turned red.*

peek (pēk) *n.* a quick, sometimes secret, look: *a peek through a hole in the door.* —*v.* to take a quick look. **peeking. peeked.**

peel (pēl) *n.* the skin or rind of a fruit or vegetable: *a potato peel; an orange peel.* —*v.* to take off the outer skin of something: *Please peel the orange.* **peeling. peeled.**

peep (pēp) *n.* **1.** a quick, secret look; a peek. **2.** a short, high sound made by a young bird or chicken. —*v.* **1.** to take a quick, secret look at something. **2.** to make the sound of a peep. **peeping. peeped.**

peer (pēr) *v.* to look at closely or in a searching way: *She peered at the tiny writing on the page.* **peering. peered.**

peewee (pē′ wē) *n.* **1.** a very small person or thing. **2.** in sports, a player between the ages of eight and twelve years.

peg (peg) *n.* a small metal or wooden pin: *a clothes peg.*

pelican (pel′ ə kən) *n.* a large water bird that has a big pouch under its long beak: *A pelican can hold fish in its pouch.*

pelican

pellet (pel′ it) *n.* a tiny ball: *The ice pellets stung my face.*

pelt (pelt) *n.* the skin of an animal, with the fur still on it: *Long ago in Canada, beaver pelts were traded like money.* —*v.* to throw or pound: *The rain pelted the roof during the storm.* **pelting. pelted.**

pen (pen) *n.* **1.** a writing tool that holds ink. **2.** an enclosed space for keeping animals: *a pigpen.*

A writing **pen** gets its name from a Latin word meaning "feather." That's because the stem of a feather dipped in ink was an early kind of pen.

penalty (pen′ əl tē) *n.* a punishment for a crime or for breaking a rule: *The basketball player got a penalty for knocking over another player. pl.* **penalties.**

pencil (pen′ səl) *n.* a tool for writing or drawing: *Most types of pencils make marks that can be erased easily with a rubber eraser.*

penguin (peng′ gwin) *n.* a black and white sea bird found near the South Pole: *The penguin is the only bird that can swim but cannot fly.*

peninsula (pən in′ sə lə) *n.* a piece of land with water on three sides: *The country of Italy is a peninsula.*

pennant (pen′ ənt) *n.* **1.** a flag or banner, often long and pointed, used as a signal or a decoration. **2.** in sports, a flag or trophy given to the champions.

penny (pen′ ē) *n.* a coin worth one cent. *pl.* **pennies.**

people (pē′ pəl) *n.* **1.** persons; men, women, boys, and girls. **2.** the persons of a nation: *the Canadian people.*

pepper (pep′ ər) *n.* **1.** a hot-tasting, black or white powder used to add flavour to food. **2.** a green, red, or yellow vegetable that is eaten cooked or raw: *A pepper can be either mild-tasting or hot.*

peppermint (pep′ ər mint′) *n.* a plant with a strong scent; its leaves are used to flavour candies, medicines, and toothpastes: *Peppermint creates a cool feeling in the mouth.*

per (pûr) *prep.* for each; to each: *Give out one chocolate bar per person.*

per cent, percent (pûr sent′) *n.* parts of a hundred; the symbol is %: *Three per cent (3%) means 3 out of every 100.*

perch (pûrch) *n.* **1.** a type of small fish: *Some perch live in rivers and lakes; others live in the ocean. pl.* **perch. 2.** a stick or a twig that a bird can rest on.

percussion instrument (pûr kush′ ən in′ strə mənt) a musical instrument, such as cymbals or a drum, played by striking.

perfect (pûr′ fikt) *adj.* without anything wrong; so good that it cannot be better: *A perfect score is 100%.* (*opp.* **imperfect.**)

perform (pûr fôrm′) *v.* **1.** to act, play music, dance, or do some other activity in front of an audience: *They will perform the class play.* **2.** to carry out or to do: *to perform a chore.* **performing. performed.**

performance (pûr fôr′ məns) *n.* **1.** a show in front of an audience: *We saw a performance by dancers.* **2.** the carrying out of an action: *The team's performance was excellent.*

performer (pûr fôr′ mər) *n.* a person who entertains by performing.

perfume (pûr′ fūm *or* pûr fūm′) *n.* a sweet-smelling liquid made from the oil of flowers and herbs: *You apply perfume to your skin.*

perhaps (pûr haps′) *adv.* possibly; it may be: *Kara isn't at school today; perhaps she's not feeling well.*

peril (per′ əl) *n.* great danger or harm: *People's lives were in peril when the earthquake struck.*

period (pēr′ ē əd) *n.* **1.** a length of time: *a period of thirty minutes; a period in a hockey game.* **2.** a dot (.) that marks the end of a sentence.

periodical (pēr′ ē od′ ə kəl) *n.* a magazine or other publication that comes out at regular times.

perish (per′ əsh) *v.* to die, to be ruined, or to be destroyed: *We must leave the burning building or we will perish.* **perishing. perished.**

perk (pûrk) *v.* **1.** to raise sharply: *The dogs perked up their ears.* **2.** to become more lively: *He perked up after hearing the good news.* **perking. perked.**

permafrost (pûr′ mə frost′) *n.* ground that is always frozen: *The Far North contains permafrost.*

permanent (pûr′ mə nənt) *adj.* lasting forever or for a very long time: *Jane has all her permanent teeth.* —**permanently** *adv.*

permission (pûr mish′ ən) *n.* words that allow someone to do something: *We were given permission to go home early because of the snowstorm.*

permit (pûr′ mit) *n.* a written form that gives you permission to do something: *a fishing permit.*

permit (pûr mit′) *v.* to allow; to let: *Dogs are not permitted on the grass.* **permitting. permitted.**

perpendicular (pûr′ pən dik′ yə lər) *adj.* at right angles to a surface, especially the ground: *A skyscraper is perpendicular to the ground.*

perplexed (pûr plekst′) *adj.* puzzled: *I was perplexed by the dog's strange behaviour.*

persist (pûr sist′) *v.* **1.** not to give up; to keep trying: *He persisted in trying to get on the team.* **2.** to last: *The heat wave persisted for days.* **persisting. persisted.**

person (pûr′ sən) *n.* a human being.

personal (pûr′ sən əl) *adj.* private; your own: *You may not read this letter because it's personal.* (*opp.* **impersonal.**)

personality (pûr′ sə nal′ ə tē) *n.* **1.** all the qualities that make one person different from another: *The new student has a friendly, outgoing personality.* **2.** a well-known person: *a TV personality.* *pl.* **personalities.**

personally (pûr′ sən əl ē) *adv.* **1.** as far as you are concerned: *Personally, I'd rather stay at home.* **2.** in person; without the help of others: *She took care of the shopping personally.*

perspiration (pûr′ spə rā′ shən) *n.* salty moisture given off through your skin; sweat.

perspire (pûr spīr′) *v.* to sweat. **perspiring. perspired.**

persuade (pu̇r swād′) *v.* to talk to someone and get him or her to agree to something you want the person to do or say: *My best friend persuaded me to go to the movies with him.* **persuading. persuaded.**

pest (pest) *n.* **1.** something that causes trouble or destruction: *The vegetables in the garden are being eaten by insect pests.* **2.** an annoying person.

pester (pes′ tər) *v.* to annoy or bother. **pestering. pestered.**

pesticide (pest′ ə sīd′) *n.* a poison that kills pests that are harmful to plants or animals.

pet (pet) *n.* an animal that you take care of and treat with affection. —*v.* to pat gently: *to pet a dog.* **petting. petted.**

petal (pet′ əl) *n.* one of the coloured parts of a flower.

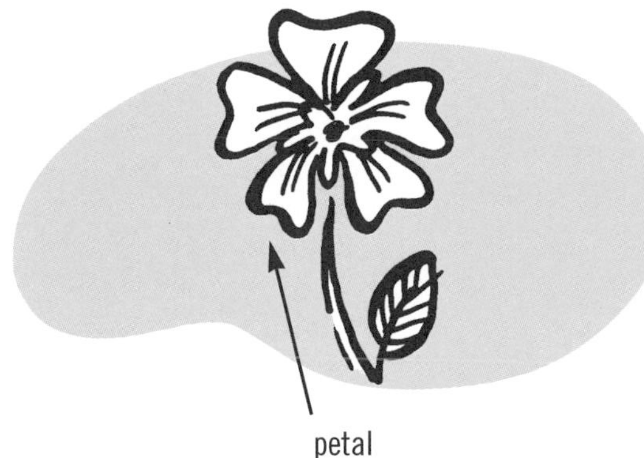

petroleum (pə trō′ lē əm) *n.* an oil that burns quickly and is used to make many products, including gasoline.

pew (pyū) *n.* a long, hard bench used for sitting in a church.

phantom (fan′ təm) *n.* a ghost.

pharmacist (fär′ mə sist) *n.* a person who is licensed to sell medicines and drugs.

pharmacy (fär′ mə sē) *n.* a drugstore. *pl.* **pharmacies.**

phase (fāz) *n.* a stage of growth: *The baby is in the phase of learning how to walk.*

pheasant (fez′ ənt) *n.* a large, wild bird with long, brightly coloured tail feathers.

phenomenal (fə nom′ ə nəl) *adj.* awesome; incredible; extraordinary: *The view from the top of the skyscraper was phenomenal.*

phobia (fō′ bē yə) *n.* a strong, unreasonable fear of something: *I have a phobia about snakes.*

phone (fōn) *n.* short for **telephone**. —*v.* to make a telephone call. **phoning. phoned.**

phony (fō′ nē) *n.* someone who is not what he or she pretends to be; a fake. —*adj.* fake; not real: *We couldn't tell the phony diamond from the real one.*

photo (fō′ tō) short for **photograph**.

photocopy (fō′ tə kop′ ē) *n.* a kind of photograph of printed material taken by a machine called a **photocopier**. *pl.* **photocopies.** —*v.* to make a photocopy: *We photocopied the program for tonight's concert.* **photocopying. photocopied.** she **photocopies.**

photograph (fō′ tə graf′) *n.* a picture taken with a camera.

photographer (fə tog′ rə fər) *n.* **1.** a person whose job is to take photographs. **2.** any person who takes photographs.

phrase (frāz) *n.* a group of words that are used together but do not make a complete sentence: *"Along the way" and "ready or not" are two phrases.*

physical (fiz′ ə kəl) *n.* a medical check-up. —*adj.* **1.** having to do with your body: *Physical exercise is the movement of your body.* **2.** solid or material: *physical objects.* —**physically** *adv.*

physician (fə zish′ ən) *n.* a doctor.

physics (fiz′ iks) *n.* the study of physical matter and energy, and the things that affect them: *Physics deals with light, movement, sound, heat, electricity, and force.*

pianist (pē′ ə nist *or* pē an′ ist) *n.* a person who plays the piano.

piano (pē an′ ō) *n.* a large musical instrument with black and white keys. *pl.* **pianos.**

piano

pick (pik) *n.* a pointed tool used for breaking up hard ground. —*v.* **1.** to choose: *Ingrid picked the dress she wanted to wear.* **2.** to gather with your fingers: *to pick berries.* **picking. picked.**

pick on to tease or bully: *Don't pick on your little brother!*

pick up **1.** to lift: *to pick up a carton.* **2.** to go faster: *The car picked up speed.* **3.** to receive: *to pick up some interesting information.*

pickerel (pik′ ər əl) *n.* a type of large fish that lives in fresh water. *pl.* **pickerel** or **pickerels.**

pickle (pik′ əl) *n.* **1.** the salty water or vinegar in which certain foods are preserved. **2.** a cucumber preserved in pickle. —*v.* to place vegetables or other foods in pickle to preserve them. **pickling. pickled.**

picnic (pik′ nik) *n.* an outdoor meal. —*v.* to have a picnic: *We picnicked in the park.* **picnicking. picnicked.**

picture (pik′ chər) *n.* a drawing, painting, or photograph. —*v.* **1.** to draw or paint a picture. **2.** to imagine: *Close your eyes and picture yourself in a different country.* **picturing. pictured.**

picturesque (pik′ chər esk′) *adj.* beautiful enough to be in a picture: *The mountain scenery is so picturesque.* —**picturesquely** *adv.*

pie (pī) *n.* a round, baked pastry filled with fruit or meat.

piece (pēs) *n.* **1.** a bit or part separated or broken from a whole: *The dish is broken into pieces.* **2.** a part of a whole, complete in itself: *a piece of meat.* **3.** a work of music, writing, or art.

pier (pēr) *n.* a platform that stretches out into the water: *We tied our boat to the pier.*

pierce (pērs) *v.* to stab and make a hole in: *They had their ears pierced yesterday.* **piercing. pierced.**

pig (pig) *n.* a farm animal with a low, heavy body, a large snout, short legs, and hooves: *Pigs are raised for food.*

pigeon (pij′ ən) *n.* a medium-sized bird, often grey in colour: *Pigeons are found in many cities and towns. Some are trained to carry messages.*

pile (pīl) *n.* a number of things, lying one on top of another: *a pile of clean, folded clothes.* —*v.* to stack up: *to pile used newspapers.* **piling. piled.**

pilgrim (pil′ grəm) *n.* **1.** a person who travels, often by walking, to a holy place. **2. Pilgrim** an early American settler from England.

pill (pil) *n.* a small tablet or ball of medicine to be swallowed.

pillar (pil′ ər) *n.* a large post that supports part of a building.

pillow (pil′ ō) *n.* a cloth bag stuffed with feathers or other soft matter on which to rest your head, or for decoration.

pilot (pī′ lət) *n.* **1.** a person who flies an aircraft or spacecraft. **2.** a person who steers a ship into port.

pimple (pim′ pəl) *n.* a small swelling on the skin.

pin (pin) *n.* **1.** a small, straight piece of wire with a sharp point on one end, used to fasten things: *a safety pin.* **2.** a piece of jewellery with a clasp, worn on clothing. **3.** one of the bottle-shaped clubs to be knocked down in the game of bowling. —*v.* to fasten with a pin. **pinning. pinned.** (*opp.* **unpin.**)

pinch (pinch) *n.* **1.** a sharp, quick squeeze with the thumb and a finger. **2.** a small amount: *a pinch of salt. pl.* **pinches.** —*v.* to squeeze between the thumb and a finger. **pinching. pinched.**

pine (pīn) *n.* a tall tree with cones and very thin, sharp, green leaves that are called needles: *Pines do not lose their needles in winter.*

pineapple (pīn′ ap′ əl) *n.* a large, sweet, yellow fruit that grows in hot places: *A pineapple has a rough, prickly skin.*

The old English word "pinappel" was first used for what we now call a "pine cone." The fruit we now call **pineapple** got its name because its shape and skin made it look like a large prickly pine cone.

Ping-Pong (ping′ pong′) *n.* a trademark name for table tennis.

pink (pingk) *n.* a very light red colour. —*adj.* having this colour.

pint (pīnt) *n.* a unit for measuring volume, equal to about 0.5 L.

pinto (pin′ tō) *n.* a spotted horse or pony. *pl.* **pintos.**

pioneer (pī′ ə nēr′) *n.* **1.** one of the first people who settle in a new place, preparing the way for others. **2.** someone who is the first to do something.

pipe (pīp) *n.* **1.** a long, metal or plastic tube that carries gas, oil, water, or other substances. **2.** a musical instrument shaped like a tube, such as a flute. **3.** a tube with a small bowl at one end, used for smoking tobacco.

pirate (pī′ rit) *n.* in earlier times, a person who attacked and robbed ships at sea.

pistol (pis′ təl) *n.* a small gun fired with one hand.

pit (pit) *n.* **1.** a deep hole in the ground. **2.** a hard seed or stone in a fruit: *a peach pit.*

pitch (pich) *n.* in baseball, a throw of the ball to the batter. *pl.* **pitches.** —*v.* **1.** to throw: *to pitch a ball.* **2.** to set up: *to pitch a tent.* **pitching. pitched.**

pitcher (pich′ ər) *n.* **1.** a large jug: *a pitcher of milk.* **2.** the baseball player who pitches the ball: *The pitcher struck out the batter.*

pitchfork (pich′ fȯrk′) *n.* a long, large fork, used for tossing hay.

pitchfork

pitiful (pit′ ə fəl) *adj.* deserving pity: *a sick, starved, pitiful animal.* —**pitifully** *adv.*

pity (pit′ ē) *n.* sympathy and sorrow for a person in trouble. —*v.* to feel pity for someone: *Azhar pitied his friend who was in pain.* **pitying. pitied.** he **pities.**

pizza (pēt′ zə) *n.* a flat, round dough covered with tomato sauce, cheese, or other ingredients; it is baked until crusty.

place (plās) *n.* a position, spot, or location: *a place at the table; a place in line; a place in history.* —*v.* to put something in a certain spot: *We placed our shoes by the front door.* **placing. placed.**

take place to happen: *Describe the events that take place in the story.*

plague (plāg) *n.* a dangerous disease that spreads quickly among people.

plaid (plad) *n.* **1.** a pattern made of stripes of different colours and widths, crossing each other at right angles. **2.** a cloth woven or printed with such a pattern.

plain (plān) *n.* a large area of flat or almost flat land without trees; a prairie. *—adj.* **1.** clear; easy to see or understand: *It is plain from your sneezing and coughing that you are not well.* **2.** simple; not fancy: *a plain dress without a pattern.* —**plainly** *adv.*

plan (plan) *n.* an outline or idea of something to be done: *We made plans for a holiday.* *—v.* to think about and make arrangements for an event or activity: *We planned our picnic for the first Sunday in July.* **planning. planned.**

plane (plān) *n.* **1.** a tool used for smoothing wood. **2.** a completely flat surface. **3.** short for **airplane**.

planet (plan′ it) *n.* one of the nine very large bodies that moves around the sun: *Mercury, Venus, Earth, Mars, Jupiter, Saturn, Uranus, Neptune, and Pluto are planets.*

planetarium (plan′ ə ter′ ē əm) *n.* a building with displays of the stars, sun, planets, and moon.

plank (plangk) *n.* a long, flat piece of wood.

plant (plant) *n.* **1.** any living thing that is not an animal. Most plants make their own food and cannot move around, as animals do: *Plants include trees, shrubs, flowers, grasses, mosses, and fungi.* **2.** a factory: *a steel plant.* *—v.* to put seeds in the earth to grow. **planting. planted.**

plastic (plas′ tik) *n.* a material that, when heated, can be moulded into different shapes. There are many different kinds of plastic. *—adj.* made of plastic.

plate (plāt) *n.* **1.** a round, almost flat dish for food: *a dinner plate.* **2.** in baseball, the home base.

plateau (pla tō′) *n.* a raised area of flat land. *pl.* **plateaus.**

Plateau, plain, and prairie are all words describing flat or almost flat lands. Plain and prairie mean the same thing. A plateau is a flat area raised above the surrounding land or found in the mountains.

platform (plat′ fôrm) *n.* a raised, level surface: *a railway platform.*

platter (plat′ ər) *n.* a large, heavy plate used for serving food.

play (plā) *n.* **1.** an activity done for fun or pleasure: *Recess is the time for play.* **2.** a stage drama, with actors playing parts. **3.** an action in a game: *She made a terrific play and saved the game.* *pl.* **plays.** *—v.* **1.** to have fun: *Let's play a game.* **2.** to take part in sports. **3.** to act or pretend: *to play a hero.* **4.** to perform on a musical instrument: *to play the drums.* **playing. played.** he **plays.**

player (plā′ ər) *n.* a person who plays or performs: *a hockey player.*

playful (plā′ fəl) *adj.* full of fun: *a playful kitten.* —**playfully** *adv.*

playground (plā′ grownd′) *n.* an outdoor area in which to play: *The children were climbing the monkey bars in the playground.*

playoff (plā′ of′) *n.* **1.** an extra game, played to break a tie. **2. playoffs** a series of games played to decide a championship.

plaza (plaz′ ə) *n.* **1.** a shopping centre. **2.** a public square in a city or town.

plead (plēd) *v.* to beg for something: *We pleaded with our parents to let us go to the concert.* **pleading. pleaded.**

pleasant (plez′ ənt) *adj.* nice; friendly; pleasing: *Raju is a pleasant person.* (*opp.* **unpleasant.**) —**pleasantly** *adv.*

please (plēz) *v.* **1.** to give pleasure: *Our gift pleased him.* (*opp.* **displease.**) **2.** to choose; to wish to do: *Do as you* *please.* **3.** a polite word used when you ask for something: *Please pass the salt.* **pleasing. pleased.**

pleasure (plezh′ ər) *n.* enjoyment; a feeling of satisfaction. (*opp.* **displeasure.**)

pledge (plej) *n.* a solemn promise: *The Scouts made a pledge to clean up the park.* —*v.* to make a solemn promise: *My father pledged twenty dollars to help find a cure for cancer.* **pledging. pledged.**

plenty (plen′ tē) *n.* a full supply; as much or more than is needed: *There is plenty of food.* —**plentiful** *adj.*

pliers (plī′ ərz) *n. pl.* a hinged tool used to bend or cut wire or to hold objects.

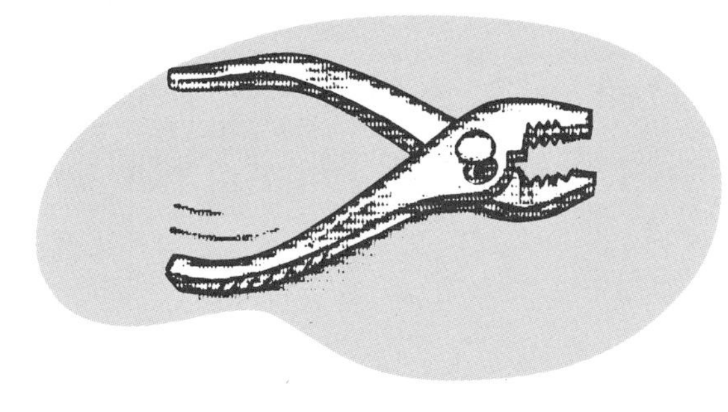

pliers

plod (plod) *v.* to walk or work slowly and heavily: *The tired horse plodded along.* **plodding. plodded.**

plop (plop) *n.* the sound of a small object falling into water without a splash: *The pebble fell into the water with a plop.* —*v.* to allow yourself or something to fall heavily: *I plopped myself down on the ground to rest.* **plopping. plopped.**

plot (plot) *n.* **1.** a small piece of ground: *a vegetable plot.* **2.** the events that make up a story: *The movie's plot is about a burglar who is caught by a smart detective.* **3.** a secret plan; a scheme: *a plot to rob a bank.* —*v.* to make secret plans. **plotting. plotted.**

plough, plow (plow) *n.* **1.** a machine used for turning over the soil: *The farmer ploughed the fields to get the soil ready for spring planting.* **2.** a machine used for clearing away snow: *The city crew spent all night ploughing snow from the roads.* —*v.* **1.** to turn over the soil. **2.** to clear away snow. **ploughing. ploughed.**

pluck (pluk) *v.* **1.** to pull at: *to pluck the guitar strings.* **2.** to pull all the feathers off: *to pluck a chicken.* **plucking. plucked.**

plug (plug) *n.* **1.** a piece of solid material that fills a hole. **2.** a piece of electrical equipment at the end of a cord: *When a plug is placed into an outlet, it makes an electrical connection.* —*v.* **1.** to fill a hole with a plug. **2.** to fit an electrical plug into an outlet: *Plug in the electric kettle and boil the water for tea.* **plugging. plugged.** (*opp.* **unplug.**)

plum (plum) *n.* a soft, edible fruit that is purple, red, green, or yellow in colour.

plumber (plum′ ər) *n.* a person whose job is to work with the pipes and water systems of buildings: *The plumber came to fix our tap when it began to leak.*

plump (plump) *adj.* round and fat.

plunge (plunj) *v.* to dive; to throw yourself into: *The swimmers plunged into the icy water and got right back out again.* **plunging. plunged.**

plural (plu̇r′ əl) *n.* more than one: *"Toys," "cherries," "children," and "mice" are the plurals of "toy," "cherry," "child," and "mouse."*

plus (plus) *n.* something extra that is good; a bonus: *Having my best friend live next door is a plus. pl.* **pluses.** —*prep.* added to; the symbol is +: *3 plus 2 equals 5 (3 + 2 = 5).* —*adj.* better than: *He got B+ on his history project.*

Pluto (plū′ tō) *n.* **1.** in Roman mythology, the god of the underworld. **2.** one of the planets of our solar system: *Pluto is the farthest planet from the sun.*

plywood (plī′ wu̇d′) *n.* a strong board made by gluing together thin layers of wood.

p.m. the time from noon to midnight: *I went to bed at 10 p.m.*

pneumonia (nū mon′ yə *or* nyū mon′ yə) *n.* a disease that affects the lungs and makes breathing difficult.

poach (pōch) *v.* **1.** to cook an egg, without the shell, in boiling water. **2.** to hunt or fish on someone's land without permission. **poaching. poached.**

pocket (pok′ ət) *n.* a small bag sewn into or onto clothes and used to hold things: *He put his hands in his coat pockets to keep them warm.*

pocket money a small amount of money used for personal needs: *Mom gave me some pocket money when I left for camp.*

pod (pod) *n.* a long part of some plants that holds seeds inside: *a pea pod.*

poem (pō′ əm) *n.* an imaginative piece of writing, usually short; its lines often have a rhythm and sometimes a rhyme.

poet (pō′ ət) *n.* a person who writes poems.

poetic (pō et′ ik) *adj.* **1.** having to do with poetry. **2.** beautiful in the way a poem is: *Joel wrote a poetic description of the landscape in his essay about his trip out west.* (*opp.* **unpoetic.**) —**poetically** *adv.*

poetry (pō′ ə trē) *n.* poems: *a book of poetry.*

point (point) *n.* **1.** a small mark or dot. **2.** a sharp end: *the point of a pin.* **3.** the main idea: *What is the point of the story?* **4.** a particular spot or moment: *I gave up at that point.* **5.** a score in a game: *We won by three points.* —*v.* **1.** to show the direction of a place: *to point the way with your finger.* **2.** to aim: *to point a gun.* **pointing. pointed.**

pointer (poin′ tər) *n.* **1.** a stick used for pointing at a chalkboard, map, poster, chart, and so on. **2.** a dog that can be trained to help hunters by pointing its nose at birds that it finds by smell.

point of view the way a person sees or thinks about something; an opinion: *You and I have very different points of view. You liked the movie, but I hated it.*

poison (poi′ zən) *n.* a substance that can injure or kill a living creature when taken into the body. —*v.* to harm or kill with such a substance. **poisoning. poisoned.**

poison ivy a plant that, when touched, causes people to break out in a red, itchy rash.

poison ivy

poisonous (poi′ zən əs) *adj.* full of poison: *A poisonous snake passes venom into your body with its bite.* (*opp.* **nonpoisonous.**)

poke (pōk) *n.* a jab or light punch: *a poke in the ribs.* —*v.* to jab or punch lightly. **poking. poked.**

poke fun at to tease; to joke about.

poker (pōk′ ər) *n.* **1.** a metal rod used for stirring a fire. **2.** a card game.

polar (pō′ lər) *adj.* having to do with the North or South Pole, or both.

polar bear a large, white bear that lives in arctic regions.

pole (pōl) *n.* **1.** a long, thin, rounded piece of wood or metal: *a flagpole.* **2.** either of the two ends of a magnet. **3. Pole** the North or South Pole.

police (pə lēs′) *n. pl.* the group of people trained to keep law and order.

police force a group of police who work in a town or city.

police officer a member of the police force.

polio (pō′ lē ō′) *n.* a serious illness that can cause fever, headaches, and muscles to be paralyzed.

polish (pol′ ish) *n.* a shiny quality, or a substance that gives this quality: *furniture polish; shoe polish. pl.* **polishes.** —*v.* to make something smooth and shiny by rubbing it: *I spent Saturday morning washing and polishing my parents' car.* **polishing. polished.** she **polishes.**

polite (pə līt′) *adj.* showing good manners; courteous: *She was very polite to the visitors.* (*opp.* **impolite.**) —**politely** *adv.*

political (pə lit′ ə kəl) *adj.* involving politics or the government: *a political party.*

politician (pol′ ə tish′ ən) *n.* a person running for, or elected to, an important government position.

politics (pol′ ə tiks) *n. pl.* **1.** the activities of the government: *My parents often talk about politics.* **2.** the job of holding public office: *She would like to have a career in politics.*

polka (pōl′ kə) *n.* **1.** a lively dance for two people. **2.** the music to which you dance the polka.

polka dot a round dot that is repeated over and over to make a pattern on cloth.

pollen (pol′ ən) *n.* a yellowish powder in the centre of flowers.

pollinate (pol′ ə nāt′) *v.* to spread pollen from one flower to another: *Bees pollinate many flowers.* **pollinating. pollinated.**

polliwog (pol′ ē wog′) *n.* a tadpole; a young frog or toad.

pollute (pə lūt′) *v.* to make the air, land, or water dirty. **polluting. polluted.**

pollution (pə lū′ shən) *n.* harmful waste substances in the air, land, or water.

pond (pond) *n.* a very small body of still water that is surrounded by land.

pony (pō′ nē) *n.* a type of small horse. *pl.* **ponies.**

poodle (pū′ dəl) *n.* a dog with very curly hair: *Some poodles are large; others are very small.*

pool (pūl) *n.* **1.** a body of still water, such as a pond. **2.** a large tank, filled with water, used for swimming. **3.** a game played on a very smooth table with six pockets on the sides. Players use long sticks to hit the balls into the pockets. **4.** a group of people sharing something: *a car pool.* —*v.* to share in an activity: *We pooled our money to buy a portable CD player.* **pooling. pooled.**

poor (pūr) *adj.* **1.** having very little money. **2.** not good: *poor health; poor weather.* —**poorly** *adv.*

pop (pop) *n.* **1.** a sudden, small bang. **2.** a fizzy soft drink. —*adj.* (*slang*) short for **popular**: *pop music.* —*v.* **1.** to burst with a pop: *The balloon popped.* **2.** to move suddenly: *to pop out of bed.* **popping. popped.**

popcorn (pop′ kȯrn′) *n.* a kind of corn whose kernels burst open and puff out when heated.

poplar (pop′ lər) *n.* a tree with soft wood, that grows very quickly.

poppy (pop′ ē) *n.* a wild or garden plant with brightly coloured flowers. *pl.* **poppies.**

popular (pop′ yə lər) *adj.* liked by a lot of people: *a popular movie star; a popular song.* (*opp.* **unpopular.**) —**popularly** *adv.*

population (pop′ yə lā′ shən) *n.* the number of people living in a place such as a city, province, or country: *The population of my town is about 30 000.*

porch (pȯrch) *n.* a covered entrance to a building: *My neighbours sit out on their porch in hot summer weather.* *pl.* **porches.**

porcupine (pȯr′ kyə pīn′) *n.* a large rodent that has sharp quills on its back and tail.

porcupine

Porcupine comes from two Latin words *porcus,* meaning "pig," and *spina,* meaning "thorn." A porcupine looks a bit like a thorny pig.

pore (pȯr) *n.* a tiny opening in your skin. —*v.* to examine something very carefully: *to pore over the scores on the sports page of the newspaper.* **poring. pored.**

pork (pȯrk) *n.* meat from a pig.

porpoise (pȯr′ pəs) *n.* a warm-blooded mammal that lives in the ocean, is very intelligent, and looks like a dolphin or a small whale.

porridge (pȯr′ ij) *n.* a breakfast food made by boiling oatmeal or other cereals in water.

port (pȯrt) *n.* **1.** a harbour, or a town with a harbour. **2.** the left side of a ship as you face the front or bow. (*opp.* **starboard.**)

portable (pȯr′ tə bəl) *adj.* light enough to be carried easily: *a portable TV set.*

portage (pȯr tozh′) *n.* the carrying of canoes, boats, and goods over land from one body of water to another. —*v.* to carry such items between bodies of water. **portaging. portaged.**

portion (pȯr′ shən) *n.* a part; a helping: *I took a small portion of potatoes.*

portrait (pȯr′ trət) *n.* a picture of someone, usually of the head and shoulders.

portray (pȯr trā′) *v.* to show, in words, in a picture, or by acting, what someone or something is like: *I like the way your story portrays the character of the boy.* **portraying. portrayed.**

pose (pōz) *n.* a position of the body: *Hold that pose until I take your picture!* —*v.* **1.** to hold a position for a picture: *Our family posed for the photograph.* **2.** to put forward: *to pose a question.* **3.** to pretend: *The robber posed as a police officer.* **posing. posed.**

position (pə zish′ ən) *n.* **1.** the place where someone or something is: *the position of my desk; my position on the team.* **2.** a job: *My mother has taken a new position at work.*

positive (poz′ ə tiv) *adj.* **1.** completely sure: *I am positive that my best friend's birthday is October 21st.* **2.** saying "yes": *Our parents gave us a positive answer when we asked for a dog.* **3.** seeing the good side of things: *My writing partner wrote positive comments on my report.* **4.** in a blood test or other medical test, showing that what a person is being tested for is present.

possess (pə zes′) *v.* to have; to own: *Our family possesses two cars.* **possessing. possessed.**

possession (pə zesh′ ən) *n.* **1.** the fact of owning something. **2.** something owned: *I keep my valuable possessions in a safe.*

possessive (pə zes′ əv) *adj.* **1.** wanting to hold onto everything you own: *He is very possessive—he won't even let me borrow one of his pencils.* **2.** in grammar, showing that something belongs to someone or something; the possessive is often formed by adding an apostrophe and an "s": *In the sentence "This is the cat's toy," "cat's" is a possessive noun.*

possibility (pos′ ə bil′ ə tē) *n.* the fact or condition of being possible; a chance of happening: *There is a good possibility that it will snow today. pl.* **possibilities.**

possible (pos′ ə bəl) *adj.* **1.** able to exist, to happen, or to be done: *It is possible that our team will win.* **2.** may be true: *She's not here yet; it's possible that she got lost.* (*opp.* **impossible.**)

possibly (pos′ ə blē) *adv.* **1.** maybe; perhaps: *Possibly, he lost his way.* **2.** in any possible way; at all: *I can't possibly help you.*

post (pōst) *n.* **1.** a pole: *a metal post.* **2.** the sending or delivery of mail. **3.** a station or settled place: *a trading post.* —*v.* **1.** to stick on a wall or board: *to post a notice.* **2.** to send letters and packages by mail. **posting. posted.**

postage (pōs′ tij) *n.* stamps that show the charge for sending a piece of mail.

postcard (pōst′ kärd′) *n.* a card that can be mailed without an envelope.

poster (pōs′ tər) *n.* a large sign or picture put up on a board or wall.

post office a place where mail is received and sorted, and where you can buy stamps.

postpone (pōs pōn′ *or* pōst pōn′) *v.* to delay until later: *We postponed our visit until next week.* **postponing. postponed.**

posture (pos′ chər) *n.* the way in which a person stands: *Good posture helps you develop a straight spine.*

pot (pot) *n.* a deep, usually round container: *a flower pot; a cooking pot.*

potato (pə tā′ tō) *n.* a roundish vegetable with usually white flesh that grows underground: *Potatoes can be baked, boiled, fried, or made into chips. pl.* **potatoes.**

potter (pot′ ər) *n.* a person who makes pottery.

pottery (pot′ ər ē) *n.* bowls, cups, flower pots, and other objects made of baked clay.

pouch (powch) *n.* a small bag or pocket in which to hold or carry things: *A female kangaroo carries her young in her pouch. pl.* **pouches.**

poultry (pōl′ trē) *n.* chickens, turkeys, geese, ducks, and other birds raised for their meat and often for eggs.

pounce (powns) *v.* to swoop down on or to leap on: *The cat pounced on the mouse.* **pouncing. pounced.**

pound (pownd) *n.* **1.** a unit for measuring mass or weight, equal to about 0.5 kg. **2.** a unit of money used in Britain and some other countries. **3.** a place where stray animals are kept. —*v.* **1.** to hammer or smash: *to pound corn into meal.* **2.** to beat heavily or to throb: *My heart pounded with fear as the stranger pounded on the door.* **pounding. pounded.**

pour (pȯr) *v.* **1.** to let liquid flow: *Please pour the milk.* **2.** to flow: *The milk poured all over the table.* **pouring. poured.**

poverty (pov′ ər tē) *n.* the state of being very poor.

powder (pow′ dər) *n.* something crushed into very tiny bits: *talcum powder.*

power (pow′ ər) *n.* **1.** strength; force. **2.** energy: *electrical power.* **3.** the ability to control others: *a cruel king with power over his people.* —*v.* to supply with power: *A car is powered by gasoline.* **powering. powered.**

powerful (pow′ ər fəl) *adj.* having great power or strength: *a powerful wind.* —**powerfully** *adv.*

powerless (pow′ ər lis) *adj.* helpless; without the power or ability to do something: *Our team was powerless against the champions.*

practical (prak′ tə kəl) *adj.* able to be done: *a practical plan.* (*opp.* **impractical.**)

practically (prak′ tik lē) *adv.* almost; nearly: *It is practically time for bed.*

practice (prak′ tis) *n.* an action done many times, so that you become better at it.

practise (prak′ tis) *v.* to do an action many times in order to become better at it: *Ray practises the piano every day.* **practising. practised.**

prairie (prer′ ē) *n.* a large area of flat or rolling land with grass, but few or no trees.

Prairie Provinces Alberta, Saskatchewan, and Manitoba. The flat, treeless area that stretches across these provinces is called **the Prairies.**

praise (prāz) *n.* words saying that someone or something is very good. —*v.* to say how good someone or something is: *Everyone praised Zoe for rescuing the drowning pup.* **praising. praised.**

prance (prans) *v.* **1.** (for a horse) to rise up and walk on its hind legs. **2.** to move in a playful way, like a horse prancing. **prancing. pranced.**

prank (prangk) *n.* a trick played on someone.

pray (prā) *v.* to speak to in worship; to ask for help or guidance. **praying. prayed.**

prayer (prer) *n.* **1.** words used in praying. **2.** the act of praying.

praying mantis (prā′ ing man′ təs) *n.* a winged insect that has a long, green body and eats grasshoppers and other insects: *A praying mantis doubles up its front legs, making them look like hands clasped in prayer. pl.* **praying mantis** or **praying mantises.**

praying mantis

pre- is a prefix meaning "before": to "preheat" an oven means to heat it up before food is placed in it; a "pre-game practice" is held before the game starts.

preach (prēch) *v.* **1.** to speak on a religious subject. **2.** to give advice, sometimes too much: *The coach is always preaching to the team to practise more.* **preaching. preached.**

precaution (pri ko′ shən) *n.* an action taken in advance to avoid a possible danger or a possible mistake: *Although it may not rain, bringing an umbrella is a wise precaution.*

precious (presh′ əs) *adj.* very valuable: *Jewels are precious stones.*

precipitation (prē sip′ ə tā′ shən) *n.* rain or snow.

precise (prē sīs′) *adj.* exact; accurate: *What is the precise location of the car accident?* (*opp.* **imprecise.**)

precisely (prē sīs′ lē) *adv.* exactly: *The time is precisely four minutes to one.*

predator (pred′ ə tər) *n.* an animal that hunts and kills other animals for food: *All wild cats are predators.*

predict (prē dikt′) *v.* to say in advance what will or may happen: *The weather office predicts rain for tomorrow.* **predicting. predicted.**

prediction (pri dik′ shən) *n.* an announcement in advance of what may happen: *My friends have different predictions about which team will win.*

preface (pref′ əs) *n.* a short message found at the beginning of some books.

prefer (prē fûr′) *v.* to like one thing more than another: *I prefer apples to pears.* **preferring. preferred.**

preferable (pref′ rə bəl *or* pref′ ər ə bəl) *adj.* more desirable. —**preferably** *adv.*

preference (pref′ rəns *or* pref′ ər əns) *n.* something that you prefer; your choice: *My preference is to go out rather than to stay in.*

prefix (prē′ fiks) *n.* letters added at the beginning of a word to change its meaning: *When you put the prefix "dis" in front of* *the word "appear," you get "disappear."* *pl.* **prefixes.**

pregnant (preg′ nənt) *adj.* having a baby developing inside the body.

prehistoric (prē′ his tôr′ ik) *adj.* living or existing a very long time ago, before history was written down. —**prehistorically** *adv.*

prejudice (prej′ ə dis) *n.* an opinion, usually bad, about someone or something, made without having enough information or knowledge.

premier (prē′ mēr *or* prē′ myər) *n.* in Canada, the head of a provincial government.

We get the word **premier** from the Latin word *primus,* meaning "first." A premier is the first (highest) minister of a province. Other words coming from *primus* are "prime," meaning first-rate and "primary," meaning first in importance.

preparation (prep′ ə rā′ shən) *n.* the act of getting ready: *We are making preparations for our holiday.*

prepare (pri per′) *v.* **1.** to get ready: *We need to prepare for our recital.* **2.** to put together from separate parts: *We are preparing dinner.* **preparing. prepared.**

preposition (prep′ ə zish′ ən) *n.* a word that shows the relationship of time or place between one noun or pronoun and another: *The ball went through the window and landed under the table.* The prepositions in this sentence are *through* and *under.*

prescribe (pri skrīb′) *v.* (for a doctor) to give an order for treatment. **prescribing. prescribed.**

prescription (pri skrip′ shən) *n.* a doctor's written order for medicine.

present (prez′ ənt) *n.* **1.** a gift to someone. **2.** the time now, not the past or the future. —*adj.* attending, not absent: *How many people were present at the game?*

present (pri zent′) *v.* **1.** to give a prize or gift to someone: *The captain presented her teammates with T-shirts.* **2.** to put on a performance: *to present a play.* **presenting. presented.**

present tense in grammar, the present tense is a form of a verb used to describe an action or a state that is happening right now: *I have the money. He is busy. It is raining.*

preserve (pri zûrv′) *v.* to keep from harm; to keep safe. **preserving. preserved.**

president (prez′ ə dənt) *n.* **1.** the chief officer of a club, class, company, bank, university, and so on. **2.** the head of certain governments: *the President of the United States.*

press (pres) *n.* **1.** a machine used for printing. **2.** the people who report the news in newspapers and magazines. *pl.* **presses.** —*v.* **1.** to push or squeeze: *to press a button.* **2.** to use an iron to smooth wrinkles out of clothes. **pressing. pressed.**

pressure (presh′ ər) *n.* a force or steady push against something.

pretend (prē tend′) *v.* **1.** to make believe: *Let's pretend we are on the moon.* **2.** to claim that something is true, when it is not: *She pretends to be rich, but she isn't.* **pretending. pretended.**

pretty (prit′ ē) *adj.* nice-looking or attractive in a dainty way: *a pretty ring; a prettier one; the prettiest ring on my finger.*

pretzel (pret′ səl) *n.* a hard, salted, twisted cracker, often shaped like a knot.

pretzel

prevent (pri vent′) *v.* to stop something from happening, or to stop someone from doing something: *He held onto his little brother to prevent him from falling.* **preventing. prevented.**

previous (prē′ vē əs) *adj.* earlier; the one before: *We went by bus on Tuesday, but we walked on the previous day.*

prey (prā) *n.* the animal that is hunted for food by another animal: *Rabbits are the main prey of foxes.* —*v.* to hunt another animal for food: *The lion preyed on the zebra.* **preying. preyed.**

price (prīs) *n.* the cost of buying something: *I went into the store to ask the price of the bicycle in the window.*

priceless (prīs′ ləs) *adj.* beyond any price; so valuable that it cannot be bought: *The paintings in the museum are priceless.*

prick (prik) *n.* a small hole made by a sharp point. —*v.* to stab with a sharp point: *I pricked my finger with the needle while I was sewing.* **pricking. pricked.**

prickle (prik′ əl) *n.* a tingling or stinging feeling: *The boys felt prickles of fear when they heard the strange noise coming from the attic.* —**prickly** *adj.*

pride (prīd) *n.* **1.** a feeling of pleasure because of something you own or have done: *We take pride in our work.* **2.** a high opinion of yourself: *His pride keeps him from saying that he is wrong.* —*v.* to rate highly; to take pride in or believe in yourself: *The baker prides herself on her prize-winning pies.* **priding. prided.**

pried, pries (prīd, prīz) see **pry**.

priest (prēst) *n.* a church official who performs religious ceremonies.

primary (prī′ mer′ ē *or* prī′ mə rē) *adj.* first in time or importance: *A primary school is often the first school that a child attends.*

prime (prīm) *adj.* first in importance.

Prime Minister the chief government minister of some countries, including Canada.

prince (prins) *n.* the son of a king or queen.

princess (prin′ sis *or* prin′ səs) *n.* **1.** the daughter of a king or queen. **2.** the wife of a prince. *pl.* **princesses.**

principal (prin′ sə pəl) *n.* the head of a school. —*adj.* highest in importance or interest: *My principal interests are reading, swimming, and doing volunteer work at our local hospital.* —**principally** *adv.*

principle (prin′ sə pəl) *n.* **1.** an important rule, law, or belief: *a scientific principle.* **2.** a rule of conduct: *"Honesty is the best policy" is a famous principle.*

print (print) *n.* **1.** words written or stamped on a surface. **2.** books, magazines, and newspapers. **3.** a mark pressed on the ground by your foot (a footprint), or on paper by an inky finger (a fingerprint). **4.** a pattern on cloth. —*v.* **1.** to write in separate, not connected, letters: *Please print your name.* **2.** to stamp words on paper with a machine: *to print a book.* **3.** to stamp a design on a surface. **printing. printed.**

printer (prin′ tər) *n.* **1.** a person whose job is to print books, newspapers, magazines, or other material. **2.** a machine that prints words on paper.

prison (priz′ ən) *n.* a secure building where criminals are held.

prisoner (priz′ ən ər) *n.* a person held in prison or captured in war.

privacy (prī′ və sē) *n.* being alone: *I like privacy when I talk on the phone.*

private (prī′ vət) *n.* a soldier in the army who is not an officer. —*adj.* not to be shared with others: *This room is private. Please knock before you come in.* —**privately** *adv.*

privilege (priv′ ə lij) *n.* a special favour or right: *I have the privilege of going first because I am the youngest in the family.*

prize (prīz) *n.* a reward for doing well or for winning a contest: *I won a prize for writing the best story.*

probable (prob′ ə bəl) *adj.* likely to happen or to be true: *It is probable that we will win the game, but it is not completely certain.* (*opp.* **improbable.**)

> Be careful not to mix up **probable** and "possible." Use *probable* if there is a good chance of something happening: *The heavy, dark clouds show rain is probable.* Use *possible* if there is only a slight chance of something happening: *The few, white clouds in the sky show rain is possible, but not probable.*

probably (prob′ ə blē) *adv.* very likely: *We will probably go swimming tomorrow.*

problem (prob′ ləm) *n.* a question or situation that is difficult to solve: *Pollution is a problem around the world.*

procedure (prə sē′ jər) *n.* the proper way of doing something, usually involving a series of steps: *What is the procedure for correctly operating this machinery?*

proceed (prə sēd′ *or* prō sēd′) *v.* to move forward; to go ahead: *Let's proceed with our plan.* **proceeding. proceeded.**

process (prō′ ses *or* pro′ ses) *n.* **1.** the steps or actions for doing or making something: *a process for manufacturing computers.* **2.** the state of being worked on: *The house is in the process of being built.* *pl.* **processes.** —*v.* to prepare in a special way: *We process fruits to make them into jams.* **processing. processed.**

procession (prō sesh′ ən) *n.* a large number of people marching or riding, as in a parade.

proclaim (prō klām′) *v.* to announce in an official way: *The king proclaimed a holiday in honour of his birthday.* **proclaiming. proclaimed.**

produce (prō′ dūs *or* pro dyūs) *n.* vegetables and fruit sold in food stores.

produce (prə dūs′ *or* prə dyūs′) *v.* **1.** to show: *We produced our tickets at the entrance gate.* **2.** to make or manufacture: *The factory produces cars.* **producing. produced.**

product (prod′ əkt) *n.* **1.** anything that is made or created: *Milk is a dairy product.* **2.** the result of multiplying two or more numbers: *When 3 is multiplied by 4, the product is 12.*

production (prə duk′ shən) *n.* the act of creating or manufacturing: *The production of cars is an important industry.*

profession (prə fesh′ ən) *n.* a job requiring special education, such as that of a doctor, lawyer, nurse, accountant, or engineer.

professional (prə fesh′ ən əl) *n.* a person who has a profession. —*adj.* **1.** doing as a job what others do for fun: *a professional musician.* **2.** doing a job that requires special education: *A doctor is a professional person.* —**professionally** *adv.*

professor (prə fes′ ər) *n.* a teacher having high rank in a college or university.

profile (prō′ fīl) *n.* a side view, usually of a person's face: *The Queen's profile is on Canadian coins.*

profile

profit (prof′ it) *n.* the money gained by selling something for more than you paid for it.

profitable (prof′ it ə bəl) *adj.* **1.** making money. **2.** worthwhile: *I spent a profitable day at the library.* —**profitably** *adv.*

program, programme (prō′ gram) *n.* **1.** a written outline of the things to be seen or heard at a concert, play, and so on. **2.** a performance or show: *a TV program.* **3.** a series of instructions for a computer, written in a special computer language. —*v.* to give a machine, usually a computer, instructions so that it can perform a certain task: *I programmed the videocassette recorder to tape a TV show at 7:30 p.m.* **programming. programmed.**

progress (prō′ grəs *or* prog′ res) *n.* a movement forward or an improvement: *The students show progress in spelling.*

progress (prə gres′) *v.* to move forward, to go ahead, or to show improvement. **progressing. progressed.**

prohibit (prō hib′ ət) *v.* to forbid, often by law. **prohibiting. prohibited.**

project (prō′ jekt *or* proj′ ekt) *n.* a plan or activity to be done: *Our project is to collect different leaves.*

project (prə jekt′) *v.* **1.** to throw forward: *Irene projected the pictures on a screen.* **2.** to stick out: *The roof projects beyond the walls of the house.* **projecting. projected.**

projector (prō jek′ tər) *n.* a machine used to show slides or pictures on a screen.

promise (prom′ is) *n.* **1.** words saying that you are sure to do something: *I made a promise that I would walk the dog.* **2.** a reason for hope: *Your story shows promise.* —*v.* to say that you will be sure to do something: *Thomas promised to return Sakina's book.* **promising. promised.**

promote (prə mōt′) *v.* **1.** to give a higher position to: *The club's vice-president was promoted to president.* **2.** to help in the growth or change of something: *Sugar promotes tooth decay.* **promoting. promoted.**

promotion (prə mō′ shən) *n.* a better job or a higher position: *My mother was given a promotion because of her excellent work.*

prompt (prompt) *adj.* **1.** on time: *Be prompt for dinner.* **2.** quick; done at once: *I received a prompt reply to my letter.* —**promptly** *adv.*

prong (prong) *n.* a sharp spike, especially one of the spikes on a fork.

pronoun (prō′ nown) *n.* a word used in place of a noun to refer to a person, place, or thing. Some other pronouns are *I, you, she, her, him, they, who, what,* and *this.*

pronounce (prə nowns′) *n.* **1.** to say aloud the sound of a word: *The word "photo" is pronounced "foe-toe."* **2.** to say something is so: *The minister said "I now pronounce you husband and wife."* **pronouncing. pronounced.**

pronunciation (prə nun′ sē ā′ shən) *n.* the way you say a word.

proof (prūf) *n.* something that shows beyond a doubt that a thing is true: *The footprints are proof that someone was here.*

-proof is a suffix that means "protected against": "waterproof" means not letting water pass through; "fireproof" means not able to be burned.

proofread (prūf′ rēd′) *v.* to read carefully to make sure there are no mistakes: *I will proofread my story and make any corrections before I put it in my writing folder.* **proofreading. proofread** (prūf′ red).

prop (prop) *n.* **1.** a support: *The sagging plant needs a prop to hold it up.* **2.** an object needed for a play: *Simone is in charge of props for our school play. She must find a pillow, an old bike, and an armchair.* —*v.* to support with a prop: *Prop up the plant with a stick.* **propping. propped.**

propel (prə pəl′) *v.* to drive forward: *to propel a plane.* **propelling. propelled.**

propeller (prə pel′ ər) *n.* a device with blades that spin, driving forward a ship, boat, or plane.

proper (prop′ ər) *adj.* correct or suitable: *This is the proper way to make a cake.* —**properly** *adv.*

proper name, proper noun in grammar, the name of a particular person or place; the first letter is usually a capital: *Rosalind, Mr. Hui, and Montreal are all proper names.*

property (prop′ ər tē) *n.* anything a person owns, especially a building or land: *This property is for sale. pl.* **properties.**

prophet (prof′ ət) *n.* a person who tells what will happen in the future.

proportion (prə pôr′ shən) *n.* the amount of something compared with the total: *A large proportion of the students at our school own bicycles.*

proposal (prə pō′ zəl) *n.* **1.** a suggested plan: *Our written proposal explained how we would run the craft show.* **2.** an offer of marriage.

propose (prə pōz′) *v.* **1.** to suggest a plan or activity: *Claude proposed that we take a class trip.* **2.** to ask someone to marry you. **proposing. proposed.**

prose (prōz) *n.* writing or speech that is not in the form of a poem.

prospect (pros′ pekt) *n.* something expected or looked forward to: *I don't relish the prospect of going to the dentist tomorrow.* —*v.* to look for valuable minerals: *From 1897 to 1904, many miners went to the Yukon to prospect for gold.* **prospecting. prospected.**

protect (prə tekt′) *v.* to defend from harm; to guard: *Our dog protects our house when we are not home.* **protecting. protected.**

protection (prə tek′ shən) *n.* defence; shelter: *An umbrella provides protection from the rain.*

protest (prə test′) *v.* to speak against: *The citizens protested against the smoke from the factory.* **protesting. protested.**

proud (prowd) *adj.* **1.** pleased about something you own or have done: *The team was proud of winning the series.* **2.** having too high an opinion of yourself; conceited: *Our proud relatives think they are better than everyone else.* —**proudly** *adv.*

prove (prūv) *v.* **1.** to show beyond a doubt that something is true. **2.** to be found to be: *My sister proved to be a good tennis player.* **proving. proved.** I have **proven.**

proverb (prov′ ərb) *n.* a popular saying that gives advice: *"You can't teach an old dog new tricks" is a proverb.*

provide (prə vīd′) *v.* to supply what is needed: *The camp provided us with food to take on the long hike.* **providing. provided.**

provided, providing (prə vīd′ id, prə vīd′ ing) *conj.* if; on the condition that: *We'll go to the game, provided we finish our homework on time.*

province (prov′ əns) *n.* one of the main, large parts of some countries, such as Canada: *Canada has ten provinces and two territories.*

provincial (prə vin′ shəl) *adj.* having to do with provinces or a province.

prow (prow) *n.* the pointed, front part of a ship.

prow

prowl (prowl) *v.* to move around silently, often looking for something to eat or steal: *The fox prowled around the chicken coop looking for a way to get inside.* **prowling. prowled.**

prune (prūn) *n.* a dried plum: *We put prunes and raisins into our fruitcake.* —*v.* to cut short the unwanted branches of a tree or bush: *I pruned the lilac bush because it was getting too big.* **pruning. pruned.**

pry (prī) *v.* **1.** to search curiously; to be nosy: *He is always prying into my private business.* **2.** to lift up with force: *Can you pry the lid off the paint can?* **prying. pried.** she **pries.**

P.S. short for **postscript**, used at the end of a letter to introduce another message:
Yours truly,
Sean
P.S. Did you find my cap?

psychiatrist (sī kī′ yə trist *or* si kī′ yə trist) *n.* a doctor who treats emotional problems or mental illness.

psychology (sī kol′ ə jē) *n.* the scientific study of how the mind works and how people behave.

puberty (pyū′ bər tē) *n.* the age when boys and girls develop the physical features of adults.

public (pub′ lik) *adj.* open to or belonging to everyone: *a public park.* —**publicly** *adv.*

publish (pub′ lish) *v.* **1.** to prepare and print a book, newspaper, or magazine for sale. **2.** to make information available to everyone: *The results of the writing competition were published in the newspaper.* **publishing. published.**

puck (puk) *n.* a black, hard rubber disk used in hockey.

pudding (pu̇d′ ing) *n.* a soft, sweet dessert: *chocolate pudding.*

puddle (pud′ əl) *n.* a small pool of water.

puff (puf) *n.* a quick blow of breath, smoke, or wind. —*v.* **1.** to blow out smoke, steam, or air. **2.** to swell up. **puffing. puffed.**

puffin (puf′ ən) *n.* a sea bird that has a large head, a thick, brightly coloured bill, and black and white feathers.

pull (pu̇l) *v.* **1.** to grasp something and draw it toward you: *She pulled the cork out of the bottle.* **2.** to move something by holding onto it and using energy: *The horse slowly pulled the heavy wagon up the steep hill.* **pulling. pulled.**

pulley (pu̇l′ ē) *n.* a wheel with a groove around its rim: *Pulleys are attached to ropes and used to lift heavy objects. pl.* **pulleys.**

pulley

pullover (pu̇l′ ō′ vər) *n.* a sweater you put on by pulling it down over your head.

pulp (pulp) *n.* **1.** the soft, juicy part of fruits. **2.** damp, ground-up wood mixed with chemicals and used to make paper.

pulse (puls) *n.* the regular beat caused by the pumping of your heart: *Your pulse can be felt on your wrist and shows how fast your heart is beating.*

puma (pyū′ mə) *n.* another name for a cougar.

pump (pump) *n.* a machine that forces a liquid or a gas into or out of something: *a gasoline pump.* —*v.* to use such a machine: *I pumped air into my bicycle tires.* **pumping. pumped.**

pumpkin (pump′ kin) *n.* a large, roundish, orange fruit, used for pies, for animal feed, and for making jack-o'-lanterns at Halloween: *We carved a scary face in our big pumpkin.*

pun (pun) *n.* a humorous use of a word that suggests two different meanings; for example: *What is the definition of a farmer? (Someone who is outstanding in his or her field.)*

punch (punch) *n.* **1.** a quick hit with the fist. **2.** a tool used to make holes in paper. **3.** a drink made of a mixture of liquids such as fruit juices. *pl.* **punches.** —*v.* **1.** to hit with the fist. **2.** to make a hole in: *I punched a new hole in the leather belt.* **punching. punched.**

punctual (punk′ chū əl) *adj.* arriving on time: *Jacob is always punctual; he never keeps me waiting.* —**punctually** *adv.*

punctuation (pungk′ chū ā′ shən) *n.* the use of periods, commas, and other marks in writing: *Punctuation helps to make the meaning of a sentence clear.*

punctuation marks marks used in writing to help make the meaning clear: *Some punctuation marks are commas, periods, quotation marks, and question marks.*

puncture (punk′ chər) *n.* a hole made by a sharp object: *a puncture in a tire.* —*v.* to make such a hole: *A nail punctured the tire.* **puncturing. punctured.**

punish (pun′ ish) *v.* to make someone suffer for something bad or wrong he or she has done. **punishing. punished.**

punishment (pun′ ish mənt) *n.* the penalty a person must suffer for doing something bad or wrong.

puny (pyū′ nē) *adj.* small and weak.

pup, puppy (pup, pup′ ē) *n.* a young dog. *pl.* **pups** or **puppies.**

pupa (pyū′ pə) *n.* the stage of growth between the larva and the adult in many insects: *A pupa is protected by a cocoon or similar covering. pl.* **pupae.**

pupil (pyū′ pəl) *n.* **1.** a person who is learning in school. **2.** the opening in the centre of your eye.

puppet (pup′ ət) *n.* a doll that can be moved and made to perform, usually on a stage.

puppeteer (pup′ ə tēr′) *n.* a person who makes or works puppets.

purchase (pər′ chəs) *n.* something bought. —*v.* to buy something: *I purchased a warm scarf before winter arrived.* **purchasing. purchased.**

pure (pyūr) *adj.* **1.** very clean: *pure water for drinking.* **2.** not mixed with other things: *pure gold.* (*opp.* **impure.**)

purple (půr′ pəl) *n.* a colour made by mixing blue and red. —*adj.* having this colour.

purpose (půr′ pəs) *n.* the reason for doing something: *The purpose of my visit is to ask for your help.*

on purpose meaning to do something: *Did you spill the water on purpose, or was it an accident?*

purr (půr) *n.* the sound that a happy cat makes. —*v.* to make such a sound. **purring. purred.**

purse (půrs) *n.* a small bag of cloth or leather in which money, keys, and other items are carried.

The word **purse** comes from the old Greek word *byrsa,* meaning "animal skin." A purse used to be a small bag made from animal skin, used for holding money.

pursue (půr sū′) *v.* **1.** to follow or chase in order to capture: *The police officer pursued the thief.* **2.** to aim and work for: *My aunt is pursuing a career in law.* **pursuing. pursued.**

push (půsh) *n.* a gentle shove. *pl.* **pushes.** —*v.* to move something by pressing against it: *to push open a door.* **pushing. pushed.**

puss, pussycat (pu̇s, pu̇s′ ē kat) *n.* a cat.

put (pu̇t) *v.* to place something somewhere: *Put the plate on the table.* **putting. put.**

put off to delay until later: *We put off our visit until our uncle felt better.*

put up with to endure; to make the best of: *I can't put up with the loud noise any longer!*

putt (put) *n.* in golf, a gentle strike of the ball. —*v.* to strike a golf ball gently, aiming to get it in or near the hole. **putting. putted.**

putty (put′ ē) *n.* a soft, greyish mixture used for holding glass in a window frame and for filling in cracks.

puzzle (puz′ əl) *n.* a question that is hard to answer, or a problem that you work out for fun: *a jigsaw puzzle, a crossword puzzle.* —*v.* to confuse and make you think hard to try to find an answer: *This complicated math problem puzzles me.* **puzzling. puzzled.**

pyjamas, pajamas (pə jam′ əz *or* pə jom′ əz) *n. pl.* a buttoned shirt and pants, worn for sleeping.

pyramid (pēr′ ə mid) *n.* a structure that has a square base and four sides, shaped like triangles, that meet in a point at the top.

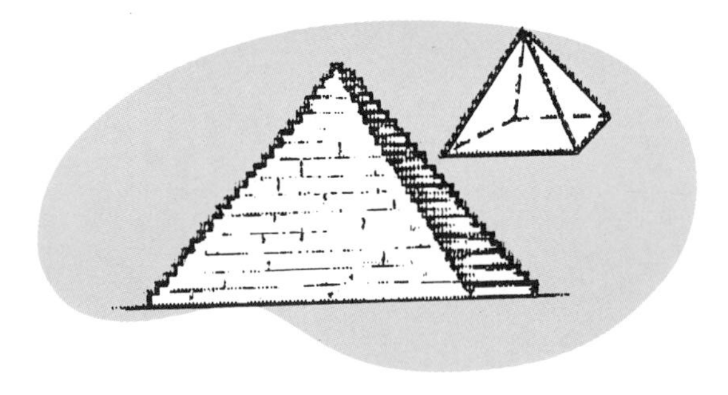

pyramid

python (pī′ thon) *n.* a large, nonpoisonous snake of Africa, Asia, and Australia. It catches its prey by squeezing tightly around it.

quack (kwak) *n.* the sound made by a duck. —*v.* to make such a sound. **quacking. quacked.**

quadruped (kwod′ rə ped′) *n.* a mammal that has four feet: *Horses, sheep, and dogs are quadrupeds.*

quadruple (kwod rū′ pəl) *v.* to multiply by four: *When you quadruple 6, you get 24.* **quadrupling. quadrupled.**

quadruplet (kwod rū′ plət) *n.* one of four children born at the same time to the same mother.

quail (kwāl) *n.* a medium-sized wild bird with a plump body: *Some people like to eat quail. pl.* **quail** or **quails.** —*v.* to shrink in fear: *The mouse quailed before the cat.* **quailing. quailed.**

quail

quaint (kwānt) *adj.* old-fashioned in a pleasant, interesting, or unusual way: *My grandparents live in a quaint little cottage.*

quake (kwāk) *n.* a shaking of the earth; an earthquake. —*v.* to shake; to tremble: *The children quaked with fear in the dark house.* **quaking. quaked.**

qualification (kwol′ ə fə kā′ shən) *n.* training, skills, and experience needed for a job or a certain kind of work: *What are your qualifications for the job as carpenter?*

qualify (kwol′ i fī) *v.* to meet all the requirements for entering a contest or for doing a certain job: *Does she qualify for the race?* (*opp.* **disqualify.**) **qualifying. qualified.** he **qualifies.**

quality (kwol′ ə tē) *n.* **1.** how good or bad a thing is: *This fruit is of poor quality.* **2.** something special that makes a person or animal or thing what it is; a feature: *Two qualities of fur are its softness and warmth. pl.* **qualities.**

quantity (kwon′ tə tē) *n.* an amount: *This recipe calls for a quantity of two cups of flour. pl.* **quantities.**

quarantine (kwȯr′ ən tēn′) *n.* a length of time when a person or animal infected with an illness is kept apart from others, so that the disease does not spread. —*v.* to put a person or animal in quarantine. **quarantining. quarantined.**

quarrel (kwȯr′ əl) *n.* an angry argument. —*v.* to disagree and argue, using angry words. **quarrelling. quarrelled.**

quarry (kwȯr′ ē) *n.* a place where stone for buildings is dug out of the ground or cut into shape. *pl.* **quarries.**

quart (kwȯrt) *n.* a unit for measuring liquid, equal to a little more than one litre.

quarter (kwȯr′ tər) *n.* **1.** one of four equal parts; one fourth: *Divide the orange into quarters.* **2.** a coin worth twenty-five cents in Canada and the United States. **3.** fifteen minutes: *a quarter of an hour.* **4. quarters** a place to stay or live: *living quarters.* —*v.* to divide into quarters: *to quarter an apple.* **quartering. quartered.**

quarterback (kwȯr′ tər bak′) *n.* the football player who calls the signals for the team.

quarterly (kwôr′ tər lē) *adj.* appearing or happening four times a year: *a quarterly meeting.* —*adv.* four times a year: *The magazine comes out quarterly.*

quartz (kwôrtz) *n.* a hard mineral: *Some types of quartz are clear, while other types have brilliant colours.*

quaver (kwā′ vər) *v.* to speak with a trembling voice: *I was so nervous, I could only quaver the answer.* **quavering. quavered.**

quay (kē) *n.* a place where ships can load and unload: *We went down to the quay to catch the ferry to the island. pl.* **quays.**

queen (kwēn) *n.* **1.** a woman who rules a country. **2.** a king's wife. **3.** a great leader: *She is the queen of country music.* **4.** a large female that lays eggs in a bee or ant colony.

queer (kwēr) *adj.* strange; unusual. —**queerly** *adv.*

quench (kwench) *v.* **1.** to satisfy thirst. **2.** to put out a fire with water. **quenching. quenched.**

query (kwēr′ ē) *n.* a question. *pl.* **queries.** —*v.* to question. **querying. queried.**

quest (kwest) *n.* a serious search: *The explorers set out on a quest for gold.*

question (kwes′ chən) *n.* something asked: *Do you have any questions before the test begins?* —*v.* to ask in order to get information. **questioning. questioned.**

no question no doubt: *There's no question she's the best.*

out of the question impossible; not even to be thought of: *My older sister wanted to buy a motorcycle, but my parents said it was out of the question.*

question mark the punctuation mark (?) put at the end of a sentence that asks a question.

questionable (kwes′ chən ə bəl) *adj.* doubtful; able to be questioned as not true or not right: *His skills as a driver are questionable.* (*opp.* **unquestionable.**)

questionnaire (kwes′ chən er′) *n.* a printed list of questions with spaces where the answers can be written: *Questionnaires are often used to find out what a large number of people think about a certain subject.*

quibble (kwib′ əl) *v.* to argue about something that is not important: *The children quibbled over who was going to sit in the front seat of the car.* **quibbling. quibbled.**

quiche (kēsh) *n.* a pie shell filled with a mixture of eggs, milk, and cheese, and then baked.

quick (kwik) *adj.* **1.** fast, speedy: *a quick train.* **2.** prompt: *I got a quick reply to my letter.* **3.** easily angered or excited: *He has a quick temper.* **4.** able to learn quickly; bright: *a quick child.* —**quickly** *adv.*

quicksand (kwik′ sand′) *n.* loose, wet sand into which a person or an animal can sink.

quiet (kwī′ ət) *n.* silence; stillness; peace: *the quiet of night.* —*adj.* **1.** silent; not loud: *Be quiet!* **2.** still; peaceful. —**quietly** *adv.*

quill (kwil) *n.* **1.** a large, stiff, hollow feather: *Quills were once used as writing pens.* **2.** one of the stiff, sharp hairs on a porcupine.

quilt (kwilt) *n.* a thick, padded bed covering, made of many squares of fabric sewn together. —*v.* to make a quilt. **quilting. quilted.**

quintuple (kwin tup′ əl) *v.* to multiply by five: *When you quintuple 8, you get 40.* **quintupling. quintupled.**

quintuplet (kwin tup′ lət) *n.* one of five children born at the same time to the same mother.

quit (kwit) *v.* **1.** to stop: *to quit smoking.* **2.** to give up: *My sister quit her job because she wasn't earning enough money.* **quitting. quit.**

quite (kwīt) *adv.* **1.** completely: *I'm not quite finished.* **2.** rather; fairly: *October can be quite cold.* **3.** very: *February is quite cold.* **4.** really: *This is quite a surprise!*

quite a few quite a large number or amount.

quiver (kwiv′ ər) *n.* a case to hold arrows. —*v.* to shake; to tremble: *The dog quivered with fear during the storm.* **quivering. quivered.**

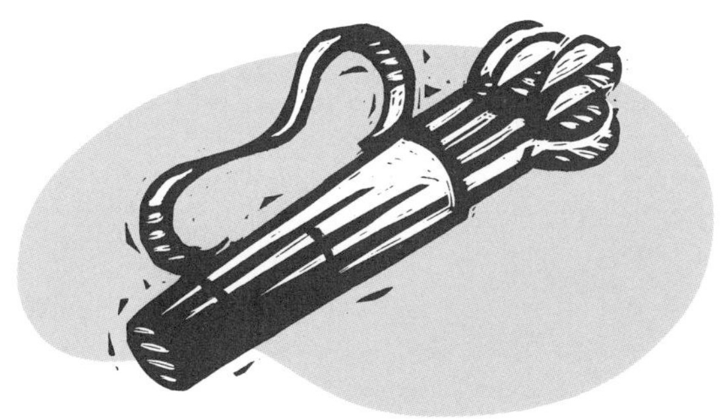

quiver

quiz (kwiz) *n.* a short test. *pl.* **quizzes.** —*v.* **1.** to give a quiz. **2.** to question: *We quizzed her about her holiday.* **quizzing. quizzed.**

Some people think that the word **quiz** comes from a bet made in Dublin, Ireland, in 1780. A man made a bet that he could invent a new word. During the night, he wrote "quiz" on walls all over the city. The next morning, everyone was using this new word—and quizzing one another about what it meant.

quotation (kwō tā′ shən) *n.* **1.** the words someone speaks, repeated exactly by another person. **2.** a short passage from a speech, a book, a poem, and so on. *I write down quotations from my favourite poems.*

quotation marks the punctuation marks ("...") put at the beginning and end of a quote.

quote (kwōt) *n.* a quotation. —*v.* to repeat the exact words that are spoken, or written, by someone. **quoting. quoted.**

quotient (kwō′ shənt) *n.* the number found when one number is divided into another: *When 2 is divided into 8, the quotient is 4.*

rabbi (rab′ ī) *n.* a Jewish religious teacher. *pl.* **rabbis.**

rabbit (rab′ it) *n.* a small, furry mammal with long ears and powerful hind legs for hopping: *Rabbits live in holes they dig in the ground.*

rabid (rab′ id) *adj.* affected by rabies.

rabies (rā′ bēz) *n.* a very serious disease that some animals get. People can get rabies if bitten by an animal that has this disease.

raccoon (ra kūn′) *n.* a small, greyish-brown mammal with dark patches around its eyes; its bushy tail is ringed with bands of dark fur.

The Algonquin name for **raccoon** is *arathcone,* meaning "one that scratches with its hands." A raccoon is very handy with its front paws. Over the years, *arathcone* became "raccoon."

race (rās) *n.* **1.** a contest to see who can move the fastest. **2.** a group of people sharing similar physical features, such as skin colour. —*v.* to go very fast. **racing. raced.**

racial (rāsh′ əl) *adj.* having to do with race: *racial prejudice.* —**racially** *adv.*

racism (rā′ siz əm) *n.* bad treatment of people of other races because you think you are better than they are: *Racism is a form of prejudice.*

rack (rak) *n.* a frame with bars for hanging things: *a towel rack.*

racket (rak′ ət) *n.* loud noise: *Don't make such a racket! You will wake the baby.*

race track an area of land, usually oval-shaped, on which races are held.

racquet, racket (rak′ ət) *n.* a handle and frame with a net of strings, used in tennis and other games.

racquet

radar (rā′ dȧr) *n.* a system that uses **radio waves** to help identify and find an object, usually a ship, an airplane, or a speeding car.

radiate (rā′ dē āt′) *v.* **1.** to give off rays of heat or light. **2.** to spread out from the centre, the way that the sun's rays do: *Roads radiate from the park in the middle of town.* **radiating. radiated.**

radiation (rā dē ā′ shən) *n.* rays of heat or energy.

radiator (rā′ dē ā′ tər) *n.* **1.** a heating device used to warm a room. **2.** the part of a car that keeps the engine cool.

radio (rā′ dē ō′) *n.* **1.** a way of sending and receiving sounds by electric waves. **2.** a machine for sending or receiving such sounds. *pl.* **radios.** —*v.* to send a message by radio: *When our boat broke down, we radioed for help.* **radioing. radioed.** she **radios.**

radioactive (rā′ dē ō ak′ tiv) *adj.* giving off energy in the form of certain kinds of rays. —**radioactively** *adv.*

radish (rad′ ish) *n.* a small, red-skinned vegetable, used in salads. *pl.* **radishes.**

radius (rā′ dē əs) *n.* a straight line going from the centre of a circle or sphere to its outer edge. *pl.* **radii** (rā′ dē ī) or **radiuses.**

raffle (raf′ əl) *n.* a type of lottery in which many people buy tickets for a chance to win a prize. —*v.* to hold such a lottery: *to raffle off a TV.* **raffling. raffled.**

raft (raft) *n.* a platform of logs or planks fastened together for floating on water.

raft

rafter (raf′ tər) *n.* one of the beams that holds up a roof.

rag (rag) *n.* a piece of torn, old cloth, usually used for cleaning: *I tore up my old shirts to use as rags for cleaning the car.*

rage (rāj) *n.* great anger: *He left the room in a rage.*

ragged (rag′ əd) *adj.* having an uneven, untidy edge: *Straighten the ragged edge with a pair of scissors.*

raid (rād) *n.* a sudden attack: *an enemy raid.* —*v.* to attack suddenly. **raiding. raided.**

rail (rāl) *n.* **1.** a long, narrow bar made of metal or wood: *a fence rail; a rail on a railway track.* **2.** railway: *Do you like to travel by rail?*

railway, railroad (rāl′ wā′, rāl′ rōd′) *n.* **1.** a track of parallel steel rails on which trains run. **2.** a transportation system using trains for carrying people, animals, and goods. *pl.* **railways.**

rain (rān) *n.* water falling in drops from clouds. —*v.* (for water) to fall in drops from clouds. **raining. rained.**

rainbow (rān′ bō′) *n.* an arch of colours in the sky: *A rainbow appears when the sun shines through rain or mist.*

raincoat (rān′ kōt′) *n.* a waterproof coat used for protection against rain.

rainfall (rān′ fol′) *n.* the official amount of rain, hail, sleet, or snow falling on an area over a certain period of time: *The city's rainfall this month was fifteen centimetres.*

rainy (rān′ ē) *adj.* having much rain: *a rainy day; a rainier day; the rainiest day of the month.*

raise (rāz) *n.* an increase of something, usually money: *Mom got a pay raise.* —*v.* **1.** to lift up: *to raise a window.* **2.** to grow: *The farmer raises corn.* **3.** to bring up: *to raise a family.* **4.** to increase in amount: *to raise prices.* **5.** to make louder: *Don't raise your voice!* **6.** to collect: *to raise money.* **raising. raised.**

raisin (rā′ zən) *n.* a small, dried grape, used in cakes, cookies, and cereals, or eaten on its own.

rake (rāk) *n.* a garden tool that has a row of spikes attached to one end of a long handle. —*v.* to gather with a rake: *We raked the leaves into a pile.* **raking. raked.**

rally (ral′ ē) *n.* a meeting or gathering: *a Brownie rally.* *pl.* **rallies.**

ram (ram) (*fem.* **ewe**) *n.* a male sheep. —*v.* **1.** to crash into: *In the chase, one car rammed another.* **2.** to push or force down or in: *We rammed the tent pegs into the ground.* **ramming. rammed.**

ramble (ram′ bəl) *v.* **1.** to walk in a wandering way: *We rambled through the forest.* **2.** to talk or write in a way that confuses people: *Don't ramble on. Just talk about one thing at a time.* **rambling. rambled.**

ramp (ramp) *n.* a short, sloping road connecting different levels: *a highway ramp.*

ran (ran) see **run** (verb).

ranch (ranch) *n.* a large farm on which animals, usually cattle, horses, or sheep, are raised. *pl.* **ranches.**

random (ran′ dəm) *adj.* not planned; by chance: *It was a random shot that scored the final goal.* —**randomly** *adv.*

rang (rang) see **ring** (verb).

range (rānj) *n.* **1.** a line; a row: *a range of hills.* **2.** land for cattle, sheep, or horses to roam on and graze. **3.** a stove for cooking. **4.** the distance between certain limits; extent: *a wide range of prices.* —*v.* **1.** to roam; to wander: *The cattle ranged over the hills.* **2.** to vary between certain limits: *The prices range from a quarter to a dollar.* **ranging. ranged.**

ranger (rān′ jər) *n.* a person whose job is to look after a large area of forest.

rank (rangk) *n.* a position; a level: *His mother holds the rank of captain in the army.*

ransom (ran′ səm) *n.* money paid to free someone who has been taken prisoner or kidnapped.

rap (rap) *n.* a quick, sharp tap. —*v.* to tap sharply: *to rap at the door.* **rapping. rapped.**

rapid (rap′ id) *adj.* very fast. —**rapidly** *adv.*

rapids (rap′ idz) *n. pl.* a part of a river where the water moves very fast, often over rocks.

rapturous (rap′ chər əs) *adj.* overcome with joy: *He was rapturous when his dog was found.*

rare (rer) *adj.* **1.** not happening often: *Winning five games in a row is rare for our team.* **2.** not often found: *Sally found a rare flower in the woods.* **3.** meat that is not cooked very much so that the inside is still red: *a rare steak.* —**rarely** *adv.*

rascal (ras′ kəl) *n.* a mischievous person: *That rascal got into the hidden cookies.*

rash (rash) *n.* small, itchy spots that can break out on your skin. *pl.* **rashes.**

rasp (rasp) *n.* a harsh, grating sound, such as the sound of a file scraping against wood. —*v.* to make such a sound. **rasping. rasped.**

raspberry (raz′ ber′ ē) *n.* a small, red, juicy fruit that grows on bushes. *pl.* **raspberries.**

rat (rat) *n.* a rodent that looks like a large mouse with a long, naked tail.

rate (rāt) *n.* **1.** speed: *The car went at a fast rate.* **2.** a price; an amount: *What is the rate of pay for that job?* —*v.* **1.** to put a value on: *Would you rate the movie as good?* **2.** to have a certain rank: *Vicky rates high as a ball player.* **rating. rated.**

rather (raTH′ ər) *adv.* **1.** more willingly: *I would much rather eat fish than meat.* **2.** to a certain extent; fairly; quite: *I felt rather cold standing outside with only a light sweater on.*

rating (rāt′ ing) *n.* a grade or level: *The movie has a rating of three stars, which means it is very good, but not excellent.*

ratio (rā′ shē o′) *n.* the relationship of two or more amounts: *There are twelve chairs and three tables. The ratio of chairs to tables is four to one, which means there are four times as many chairs as tables. pl.* **ratios.**

ration (rash′ ən *or* rāsh′ ən) *n.* a share or portion: *On our camping trip, we had a daily ration of juice.* —*v.* to give out a share or portion: *We rationed the bread on our camping trip because there was not much left.* **rationing. rationed.**

rational (rash′ ən əl) *adj.* able to think in a sensible, reasonable way: *Your arguments are not rational and it is difficult to understand your point.* —**rationally** *adv.*

rattle (rat′ əl) *n.* **1.** the sound made by shaking a lot of hard things together: *We could hear the rattle of the dishes in the cupboard when the train went by.* **2.** a baby's toy that makes this sound. —*v.* to make such a sound. **rattling. rattled.**

rattlesnake (rat′ əl snāk′) *n.* a poisonous snake that makes a rattling sound with its tail: *The snake shakes the end of its tail to make special joints rattle together.*

rattlesnake

rave (rāv) *v.* to talk excitedly, especially about something you are very pleased about: *Everyone is raving about her excellent performance in the play.* **raving. raved.**

raven (rāv′ ən) *n.* a large, black bird that looks like a crow.

ravine (rə vēn′) *n.* a long, deep, narrow valley.

ravioli (rav′ ē ō′ lē) *n. pl.* small envelopes of pasta that contain meat or cheese and are served with a sauce.

raw (ro) *adj.* **1.** not cooked. **2.** having the skin scraped off; sore. **3.** very cold.

rawhide (ro′ hīd′) *n.* the skin of cattle before it has been tanned.

raw material a material before it is used to make a product: *The raw materials for making steel are iron and carbon.*

ray (rā) *n.* a thin stream of light: *A ray of sunshine shone through the clouds.* *pl.* **rays.**

razor (rā′ zər) *n.* a sharp instrument used for shaving off hair.

RCMP an abbreviation of **Royal Canadian Mounted Police**.

re– is a prefix meaning: **1.** "again." To "reopen" means to open again. **2.** "back." To "repay" means to pay back.

reach (rēch) *n.* the distance to which you can stretch your arm: *The ball is beyond my reach.* —*v.* **1.** to stretch out and touch or get: *Can you reach the cereal on the top shelf?* **2.** to arrive at: *They reached the city in the morning.* **3.** to contact: *You can reach me by phone next week.* **reaching. reached.**

react (rē akt′) *v.* to do or say something in response to something that has happened or been said: *I reacted with a happy shout when I heard you were coming to visit.* **reacting. reacted.**

reaction (rē ak′ shən) *n.* the way a person responds to something that has been done or said.

read (rēd) *v.* to look at written words and symbols and understand their meaning. **reading. read** (red).

readable (rēd′ ə bəl) *adj.* **1.** easy or interesting to read: *This is such a readable story, I can't put the book down.* **2.** able to be read: *readable handwriting.*

reader (rēd′ ər) *n.* a person who reads.

ready (red′ ē) *adj.* prepared; willing. —*v.* to prepare for something: *We readied ourselves for the final game.* **readying. readied.** —**readily** *adv.*

real (rēl) *adj.* **1.** true; not imaginary: *This is a real story; I didn't make it up.* **2.** genuine; not artificial: *These are real pearls.*

real estate a piece of land and the buildings or houses, trees, fences, and other things on it.

realistic (rē′ ə lis′ tik) *adj.* **1.** looking like the real thing: *The silk flowers looked so realistic that I watered them.* **2.** seeing life as it really is; not having impossible dreams: *a realistic person.* **3.** reasonable; practical: *My parents wanted a realistic idea of how long it would take me to clean up my room.* (*opp.* **unrealistic.**) —**realistically** *adv.*

reality (rē al′ ə tē) *n.* a fact; a truth; something that is real: *Our dream of owning a house finally became a reality.* *pl.* **realities.**

realize (rē′ əl īz′) *v.* to understand clearly; to be fully aware: *I didn't realize that I was so early.* **realizing. realized.**

really (rē′ lē *or* rē′ ə lē) *adv.* **1.** truly: *I really mean what I say!* **2.** very: *She is really helpful.*

reap (rēp) *v.* to cut or harvest grain or other crops. **reaping. reaped.**

reappear (rē ə pēr′) *v.* to appear again or to come back: *Just when we thought she had gone, she reappeared to get her umbrella.* **reappearing. reappeared.**

rear (rēr) *n.* the back part: *the rear of a train.* —*v.* **1.** to bring up: *to rear children.* **2.** to lift up: *The horse reared its head.* **rearing. reared.**

reason (rē′ zən) *n.* an explanation: *What is your reason for being late?* —*v.* to argue sensibly: *I tried to reason with them, but they would not listen.* **reasoning. reasoned.**

reasonable (rē′ zən ə bəl) *adj.* **1.** sensible; fair: *a reasonable person.* **2.** not expensive: *a reasonable price.* (*opp.* **unreasonable.**)

reasonably (rē′ zən ə blē) *adv.* quite; fairly: *I think I did reasonably well on the test.*

reassure (rē′ ə shūr′) *v.* to make someone feel confident or sure; to remove someone's doubts or fears: *We reassured him that he would be welcome at the meeting.* **reassuring. reassured.**

rebel (reb′ əl) *n.* a person who fights against the people in charge and refuses to obey orders.

rebel (ri bel′) *v.* to refuse to follow orders. **rebelling. rebelled.**

rebellion (ri bel′ yən) *n.* a fight against your own government or against people in authority.

rebound (rē′ bownd) *v.* to spring back or bounce back, the way that a ball does: *The hockey puck rebounded off the boards.* **rebounding. rebounded.**

recall (ri kol′) *v.* **1.** to remember: *I can't recall his name.* **2.** to call someone or something back: *The car company recalled a thousand cars because of a fault in an engine part.* **recalling. recalled.**

receipt (ri sēt′) *n.* a printed note that shows you have paid for something.

receive (ri sēv′) *v.* **1.** to take what is given or sent to you: *We received many presents.* **2.** to welcome visitors: *We received our new neighbours into our home.* **receiving. received.**

receiver (ri sē′ vər) *n.* **1.** the part of a telephone that you put to your ear. **2.** a person or thing that receives something: *a football receiver; a radio receiver.*

recent (rē′ sənt) *adj.* **1.** made, happened, or done a short while ago: *The news tells us about recent events.* **2.** up-to-date; modern: *a recent discovery.* —**recently** *adv.*

reception (ri sep′ shən) *n.* **1.** the way in which someone or something is accepted or welcomed: *We got a warm reception when we visited our grandparents.* **2.** a formal party: *a wedding reception.* **3.** the quality of the signal received on a TV or radio: *The violent storm is intefering with the TV's reception.*

receptionist (ri sep′ shə nist) *n.* a person whose job is to greet people in an office: *The doctor's receptionist asked for my health card.*

recess (ri′ ses) *n.* a short rest or play period. *pl.* **recesses.**

recession (ri sesh′ ən) *n.* a period when business activity slows down.

recipe (res′ ə pē) *n.* directions on how to make something to eat or drink.

> In Latin, the word **recipe** means "take." When following a recipe, you "take" different ingredients and combine them.

recital (ri cī′ təl) *n.* a performance, usually one given by a singer, musician, or dancer.

recite (ri sīt′) *v.* to tell a story or a poem from memory. **reciting. recited.**

reckless (rek′ ləs) *adj.* being careless and risking danger: *Reckless driving causes many accidents.* —**recklessly** *adv.*

recognition (rek′ əg nish′ ən) *n.* **1.** the act of recognizing. **2.** attention; praise: *The scientist received recognition for her research.*

recognize (rek′ əg nīz′) *v.* to know again: *I almost didn't recognize my uncle because he now has a moustache.* **recognizing. recognized.**

recommend (rek′ ə mend′) *v.* **1.** to speak in favour of someone or something: *I can recommend this movie. It is very good.* **2.** to suggest: *I recommend that you try another store.* **recommending. recommended.**

recommendation (rek′ ə men dā′ shən) *n.* a favourable suggestion: *I went to see the movie on my friend's recommendation.*

record (rek′ ərd) *n.* **1.** a written account or diary: *When we have a meeting, we keep a record of everything that is said.* **2.** the best performance in a contest or race: *She holds the world record for the 100-m dash.* **3.** a flat disk that produces sound when played on a record player.

record (ri kȯrd′) *v.* **1.** to write down facts: *He recorded the amount of money he spent.* **2.** to put sounds on a tape or compact disc: *Music is recorded in a special room called a recording studio.* **recording. recorded.**

recorder (ri kȯr′ dər) *n.* **1.** a musical wind instrument that resembles a flute with a mouthpiece and is usually made of wood. **2.** a machine that records sounds on a tape.

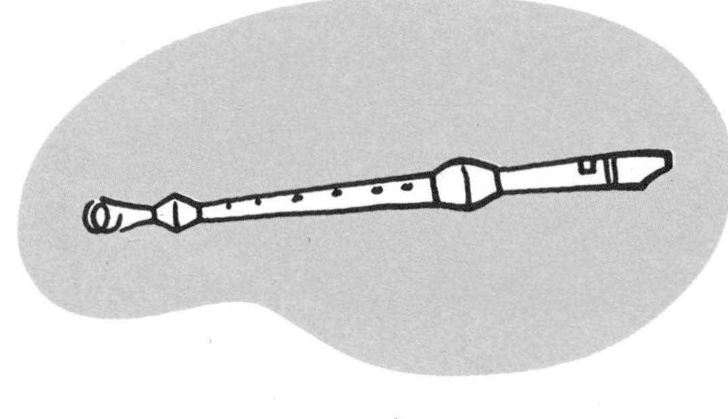

recorder

recover (ri kuv′ ər) *v.* **1.** to get well after an illness. **2.** to get something back: *The police recovered the stolen car within a week.* **recovering. recovered.**

recovery (ri kuv′ ər ē) *n.* **1.** the process of getting well after an illness: *We wish you a speedy recovery.* **2.** getting back something that was lost, stolen, or sent away. *pl.* **recoveries.**

recreation (rek′ rē ā′ shən) *n.* things done for amusement and relaxation, such as games and hobbies. —**recreational** *adj.*

recruit (ri krūt′) *n.* a new member of the army, navy, police force, or other group.

rectangle (rek′ tang′ gəl) *n.* a flat four-sided figure with four right angles: *Two opposite sides of a rectangle are longer than the other two.* —**rectangular** *adj.*

recuperate (ri kū′ pər āt′) *v.* to recover from an illness. **recuperating. recuperated.**

recur (ri kėr′) *v.* to happen again: *I have a dream that recurs about once a month.* **recurring. recurred.**

recycle (rē sī′ kəl) *v.* to put to use again: *Old newspapers are recycled into new paper for printing.* **recycling. recycled.**

red (red) *n.* the colour of blood or rubies. —*adj.* having such a colour.

reduce (ri dūs′) *v.* to make smaller or less; to decrease: *They are on a diet to reduce their weight.* **reducing. reduced.**

reduction (ri duk′ shən) *n.* the amount by which something is made smaller: *There is a fifty per cent reduction in the price of all the shirts.*

reed (rēd) *n.* a tall grass that grows at the edge of water.

reef (rēf) *n.* a ridge of rock, sand, or coral just beneath the surface of the sea.

reel (rēl) *n.* **1.** a spool-like frame used for winding thread, film, fishing line, rope, and so on. **2.** a lively dance.

refer (ri fėr′) *v.* **1.** to send or direct a person elsewhere for help or information: *I needed to label the oceans on my map, so the librarian referred me to an atlas.* **2.** to turn to for help or information: *The speaker referred to her notes.* **referring. referred.**

referee (ref′ ər ē′) *n.* a person in charge of a game or contest: *A referee makes sure that the rules are obeyed and settles any arguments between teams.*

reference (ref′ ər əns) *n.* **1.** something used for information: *A dictionary is a book of reference.* **2.** attention drawn to something: *The speaker made a reference to a recent news story.* **3.** a statement about a person's ability: *My brother has good references from the people he worked for.*

in reference to about; concerning.

refine (ri fīn′) *v.* to make something more pure: *Petroleum is refined to make fuel for heating and gasoline.* **refining. refined.**

reflect (ri flekt′) *v.* **1.** to give back an image or light, as a mirror or clear water does. **2.** to give back heat or sound from a surface. **reflecting. reflected.**

reflection (ri flek′ shən) *n.* something reflected, such as an image, light, heat, or sound: *An echo is a reflection of sound.*

reflex (rē′ fleks) *n.* an automatic reaction of your body to something: *The doctor tested my reflexes by tapping my knee. pl.* **reflexes.**

refresh (ri fresh′) *v.* to make fresh again or to provide new strength: *Refresh yourself by taking a nap.* **refreshing. refreshed.**

refreshments (ri fresh′ mənts) *n. pl.* things to eat or drink.

refrigerate (ri frij′ ər āt′) *v.* to keep cool by putting inside a refrigerator: *Please refrigerate the bacon as soon as you get home.* **refrigerating. refrigerated.**

The prefix **re–**, meaning "again," and the Latin word *frigus,* meaning "cold," give us the word refrigerate.

refrigerator (ri frij′ ər ā′ tər) *n.* a machine that keeps stored food cold.

refuge (ref′ yūj) *n.* shelter: *As the storm moved in, we took refuge in a shed.*

refugee (ref yū jē′) *n.* a person who has fled from one place to another to find safety or protection.

refund (rē′ fund) *n.* money paid back: *The new pen did not work, so I asked for a refund.*

refund (ri fund′) *v.* to pay back money: *The store manager refunded our money because the radio we had purchased did not work.* **refunding. refunded.**

refusal (ri fyūz′ əl) *n.* the act of refusing: *I was hurt by my friend's refusal of my gift.*

refuse (ref′ yūs) *n.* garbage.

refuse (ri′ fyūz) *v.* **1.** to say "no" to; to reject; to turn down: *She refused our help.* **2.** not to do something: *The thieves refused to tell the police where they had hidden the stolen jewels.* **3.** to deny: *Our parents refused our request to stay up past midnight.* **refusing. refused.**

regard (ri gärd′) *n.* respect; admiration: *I have a great regard for Tamar.* —*v.* **1.** to think of: *I regard Tamar highly.* **2.** to look at: *The two lions regarded each other before the smaller one backed down.* **regarding. regarded.**

regardless (ri gärd′ ləs) *adv.* in spite of; ignoring: *Regardless of the cold weather, many people waited in line to see the movie.*

regiment (rej′ ə mənt) *n.* a large unit of soldiers commanded by a colonel.

region (rē′ jən) *n.* a large area of land: *The Arctic region is the area around the North Pole.*

regional (rē′ jə nəl) *adj.* having to do with a region: *The regional winners competed at the national skating finals.* —**regionally** *adv.*

register (rej′ is tər) *n.* **1.** a book or machine that keeps a record of certain items: *a cash register.* **2.** a written list of names and other information: *The register of visitors is at the main desk.* —*v.* to sign in or up: *We registered at the hotel desk before going to our room.* **registering. registered.**

registration (rej′ ə strā′ shən) *n.* the act of registering: *Registration for camp begins in March.*

regret (ri gret′) *n.* a feeling of being sorry: *She felt regret over losing her ring.* —*v.* to be sorry about something: *I regret having hurt another player by accident during the game.* **regretting. regretted.**

regular (reg′ yə lər) *adj.* **1.** even; steady: *the regular ticking of a clock.* **2.** usual: *My regular way of getting to school is to take a bus.* **3.** happening again and again at the same time: *the regular appearance of day and night.* (*opp.* **irregular.**) —**regularly** *adv.*

regulation (reg′ yə lā′ shən) *n.* a rule: *It is against the regulations to park on that street.*

rehearsal (ri hûr′ səl) *n.* a practice to get ready for a performance: *The band had many rehearsals before the concert.*

rehearse (ri hûrs′) *v.* to practise in order to get ready for a performance. **rehearsing. rehearsed.**

reign (rān) *n.* the period of time that a king or queen rules: *His reign on the throne lasted ten years.* —*v.* to rule, as king or queen: *The queen reigned for many years.* **reigning. reigned.**

reindeer (rān′ dēr′) *n.* a large deer that has antlers and lives in northern regions. *pl.* **reindeer.**

reinforce (rē′ in fôrs′) *v.* to make something stronger: *The builders reinforced the wall with a steel beam.* **reinforcing. reinforced.**

reins (rānz) *n. pl.* leather straps attached to a horse's bridle, used to control and guide the horse: *She picked up the reins and led the horse to the barn.*

reins

reject (ri jekt′) *v.* to refuse to accept something, usually because it is not good enough: *My plan was rejected because it didn't completely solve the problem.* **rejecting. rejected.**

rejoice (ri jois′) *v.* to show how pleased or happy you are: *We rejoiced when we won the hockey finals.* **rejoicing. rejoiced.**

relate (ri lāt′) *v.* to tell; to describe: *The sailor related many adventures to the children.* **relating. related.**

related (ri lā′ təd) *adj.* **1.** connected in some way: *These books are related. They are both about tigers.* **2.** belonging to the same family: *Cousins are related to each other.* (opp. **unrelated.**)

relation (ri lā′ shən) *n.* **1.** a connection between things: *There's a relation between the amount of time I practise the piano and how well I play it.* **2.** a relative: *We saw many of our relations at the family picnic.*

relationship (ri la′ shən ship′) *n.* **1.** how two or more things are related: *What is your relationship to Justin? He is my cousin.* **2.** a romance: *My sister has a steady relationship with her boyfriend.*

relative (rel′ ə tiv) *n.* a person who belongs to the same family as someone else: *I have lots of relatives. I have two brothers, two sisters, my parents, four uncles, five aunts, and twelve cousins.*

relax (ri laks′) *v.* **1.** to become less tense: *Relax—it's only a rehearsal.* **2.** to take a rest and enjoy yourself: *We relaxed during the long weekend.* **relaxing. relaxed.** he **relaxes.**

relaxation (rē′ lak sā′ shən) *n.* the act of taking it easy.

relay (ri lā′ *or* rē′ lā) *v.* to take and pass along: *The messenger relayed the information.* **relaying. relayed.**

relay race a race in which each team member goes only a certain distance, and then another team member takes over for the next part of the race.

release (ri lēs′) *n.* **1.** the act of freeing: *the release of the prisoner.* **2.** the time when a movie, book, CD, and so on is first available to the public: *The release of the new comedy will take place in the summer.* —*v.* **1.** to let go: *Release your hold on the rope.* **2.** to set free: *We released the raccoon into the forest.* **3.** to make a new movie, book, CD, and so on available to the public. **releasing. released.**

reliable (ri lī′ ə bəl) *adj.* able to be trusted; dependable: *She is a reliable girl. She will finish her jobs on time.* (*opp.* **unreliable.**) —**reliably** *adv.*

relief (ri lēf′) *n.* freedom from worry, trouble, or pain: *It was a relief to hear that nobody was hurt in the accident.*

relieve (ri lēv′) *v.* **1.** to ease or end worry or pain: *The medicine relieved Michael's headache.* **2.** to take over a duty from someone: *The day nurse relieved the night nurse at 7:00 a.m.* **relieving. relieved.**

religion (ri lij′ ən) *n.* the worship of and belief in a god or gods.

religious (ri lij′ əs) *adj.* having to do with religion: *a religious service.* —**religiously** *adv.*

relish (rel′ ish) *n.* a pickled mixture of chopped vegetables or fruits. *pl.* **relishes.** —*v.* to enjoy or like: *My friends relished the idea of a picnic.* **relishing. relished.** she **relishes.**

reluctant (rə luk′ tənt) *adj.* not wanting to do something: *I was reluctant to touch her pet toad.* —**reluctantly** *adv.*

rely (ri lī′) (used with **on**) *v.* to depend on; to trust: *We rely on you to show us the way.* **relying. relied.** she **relies.**

remain (ri mān′) *v.* **1.** to stay behind: *After the party we remained at our friend's house.* **2.** to be left over: *All that remains from the party is one piece of cake.* **3.** to stay: *Sarah moved to a new city, but we remained good friends.* **remaining. remained.**

remainder (ri mān′ dər) *n.* **1.** what is left over: *We will divide the remainder of the cake.* **2.** the number left over when a number cannot be divided evenly.

remark (ri märk′) *n.* a short statement: *Marc made a nice remark about my new haircut.* —*v.* to say a few words: *My teammate remarked that she felt tired.* **remarking. remarked.**

remarkable (ri mär′ kə bəl) *adj.* special; surprising; worth talking about: *It is remarkable that the lost dog found its way home from so far away.* —**remarkably** *adv.*

remedy (rem′ ə dē) *n.* something that makes you feel better; a cure for an illness: *a remedy for a cold.* *pl.* **remedies.**

remember (ri mem′ bər) *v.* **1.** to bring back to mind: *Do you remember when we went to the zoo?* **2.** to keep in mind: *Remember to take a pen to school.* **remembering. remembered.**

remind (ri mīnd′) *v.* to help someone remember: *I reminded her about the picnic.* **reminding. reminded.**

reminder (ri mīn′ dər) *n.* a few words or a note to someone, to help him or her to remember: *Maria sent René a reminder about the party.*

reminisce (rem′ ə nis′) *v.* to remember pleasant things that happened: *Alicia and Mario reminisced about the fun they had at summer camp.* **reminiscing. reminisced.**

remote (ri mōt′) *adj.* far away: *Our cottage is in a remote part of the province.*

remote control a device that allows a machine, such as a TV or a camera, to be controlled from a distance.

removal (ri mūv′ əl) *n.* the process of removing something: *garbage removal.*

remove (ri mūv′) *v.* to take away or to take off: *I removed my coat and gloves.* **removing. removed.**

renew (ri nu′ *or* ri nyū′) *v.* to borrow or get for another period of time: *to renew a book; to renew a driver's licence.* **renewing. renewed.**

renewable (ri′ nū′ ə bəl *or* ri′ nyū′ ə bəl) *adj.* able to be replaced: *Trees are a renewable resource, but gold is not.* (*opp.* **nonrenewable.**)

rent (rent) *n.* money paid for the use of an apartment, house, or something else you do not own. —*v.* to pay for the use of something: *My parents rented a car on their holiday.* **renting. rented.**

repair (ri per′) *n.* the fixing of something broken or torn: *Our car is at the garage for repairs.* —*v.* to fix something broken or torn. **repairing. repaired.**

repay (ri pā′) *v.* to return money to the person who lent it. **repaying. repaid.**

repeat (ri pēt′) *v.* to say or do something again: *I repeated his directions to make sure I understood them.* **repeating. repeated.**

repetition (rep′ ə tish′ ən) *n.* the repeating of something.

replace (ri plās′) *v.* **1.** to take the place of: *When Sue moved away, Jan replaced her on the team.* **2.** to put back: *He replaced the book on the shelf.* **replacing. replaced.**

reply (ri plī′) *n.* an answer: *Nick sent a reply to our invitation. pl.* **replies.** —*v.* to answer: *"Did you go to the party?" Lisa asked. "No, I did not," Sonya replied.* **replying. replied.** he **replies.**

report (ri pȯrt′) *n.* a written or spoken account of facts or information: *a book report.* —*v.* to give an account of facts, especially news: *The journalist reported a serious fire at City Hall.* **reporting. reported.**

reporter (ri pȯr′ tər) *n.* a person whose job is to collect news for a newspaper, magazine, or radio or TV show.

represent (rep′ ri zent′) *v.* **1.** to stand for; to be a symbol of: *Our flag represents Canada.* **2.** to act for or speak for: *Your member of parliament represents your community in Ottawa.* **representing. represented.**

representative (rep′ ri zen′ tə tiv) *n.* a person who is chosen to act or speak for others.

reproach (ri prōch′) *n.* blame. —*v.* to blame someone: *He reproached me for forgetting my promise.* **reproaching. reproached.**

reproduce (rē′ prə dūs′ *or* rē′ prə dyūs′) *v.* **1.** to imitate or copy: *An electronic keyboard can reproduce the sound of drums.* **2.** to bear young. **reproducing. reproduced.**

reproduction (rē′ prə duk′ shən) *n.* **1.** a copy: *The poster on the wall is a reproduction of a famous painting.* **2.** the process of producing new plants or animals.

reptile (rep′ tīl) *n.* a cold-blooded animal that has a scaly skin and creeps or crawls: *Snakes, turtles, lizards, and crocodiles are reptiles. Many reptiles warm themselves by sitting out in the sunlight.*

reptile

republic (ri pub′ lik) *n.* a nation that is headed by a president: *The citizens of a republic elect a president to run their government.*

reputation (rep′ yə tā′ shən) *n.* what people think and say of you: *The coach has the reputation of being honest and fair.*

request (ri kwest′) *n.* something asked for: *My request for a new computer game was turned down by my parents.* —*v.* to ask for something: *I requested permission to leave school early because I had a doctor's appointment.* **requesting. requested.**

require (ri kwīr′) *v.* **1.** to need: *The teacher required more chalk and sent a student to get some.* **2.** to order: *All students are required to attend.* **requiring. required.**

requirement (ri kwīr′ mənt) *n.* something that is needed or demanded.

rerun (rē′ run′) *n.* a TV or radio program that is repeated.

rescue (res′ kyū) *n.* the saving from danger or harm: *The cat was in the tree, and the firefighters came to the rescue.* —*v.* to save from danger or harm: *The firefighters rescued three people from the burning house.* **rescuing. rescued.**

research (ri sürch′ *or* rē′ sürch) *n.* the searching and finding of information or facts: *I have to do research on pioneer life for my project.* —*v.* to search carefully for information or facts: *The news reporter researched every detail of the story.* **researching. researched.**

resemblance (ri zem′ bləns) *n.* a similar appearance: *There is a great resemblance between my brother and me.*

resemble (ri zem′ bəl) *v.* to look like: *Simone resembles her sister, and sometimes people call her by the wrong name.* **resembling. resembled.**

resent (ri zent′) *v.* to feel angry and hurt: *I resent your telling me what to do!* **resenting. resented.**

reservation (rez′ ər vā′ shən) *n.* an arrangement made ahead of time for something to be kept for you: *We made a reservation for dinner at the restaurant.*

reserve (ri zürv′) *n.* land set aside for a special purpose: *a Native reserve.* —*v.* to arrange ahead of time for something to be kept for you: *Before we left for our trip, we reserved a room at the motel.* **reserving. reserved.**

reservoir (rez′ ər vwär′ *or* rez′ ər vwôr′) *n.* a large tank or pond where water is collected and stored for later use.

residence (rez′ i dəns) *n.* a place where a person lives; a home.

resident (rez′ ə dənt) *n.* a person who lives in a certain place: *Jared is a resident of Saskatoon.*

resign (ri zīn′) *v.* to give up a job or position: *My brother resigned from his job because we are moving.* **resigning. resigned.**

resignation (res′ əg nā′ shən) *n.* the giving up of a job: *The boss asked for her resignation.*

resigned (ri zīnd′) *adj.* accepting a situation without fighting it: *Our team is resigned to being near the bottom of the league.*

resist (ri zist′) *v.* to fight or struggle against: *The robber resisted the police officer.* **resisting. resisted.**

resolve (ri zolv′) *v.* to make a decision, often an important one: *I resolve to spend more time studying.* **resolving. resolved.**

resort (ri zôrt′) *n.* **1.** a holiday place. **2.** something or someone you turn to for help: *I will go to the dentist as a last resort, if nothing else relieves my toothache.* —*v.* (used with **to**) to turn to something when nothing else helps: *Even if you resort to tears, I won't change my decision.* **resorting. resorted.**

resource (ri zôrs′) *n.* **1.** a supply of something useful that will meet a need:

Canada has many natural resources, such as minerals, fish, and lumber. **2.** a person or thing that gives help or information.

resourceful (ri zôrs′ fəl) *adj.* quick or clever at finding a way around a difficulty: *They were resourceful—they made what they couldn't buy.*

respect (ri spekt′) *n.* a good opinion of someone or something: *My grandmother is a kind person. I have a lot of respect for her.* (*opp.* **disrespect.**) —*v.* to admire; to have a good opinion of someone or something: *I respect your ideas.* **respecting. respected.**

respectful (ri spekt′ fəl) *adj.* showing respect: *The children were very respectful to their older relatives.* (*opp.* **disrespectful.**) —**respectfully** *adv.*

respiration (res′ pə rā′ shən) *n.* breathing: *Artificial respiration means making a person breathe again by forcing air into and out of the lungs.*

respond (ri spond′) *v.* to answer; to reply. **responding. responded.**

response (ri spons′) *n.* an answer; a reply: *Your response to the question is right.*

responsibility (ri spon′ sə bil′ ə tē) *n.* **1.** the condition of being responsible: *I accept the responsibility for my mistake.* **2.** a duty: *It is her responsibility to walk the dog every afternoon. pl.* **responsibilities.**

responsible (ri spon′ sə bəl) *adj.* **1.** in charge: *The director is responsible for telling the actors what to do.* **2.** being the main cause: *What was responsible for the fire?* **3.** able to be trusted: *Kurt is a responsible boy. He will water your plants while you're away.* (*opp.* **irresponsible.**) —**responsibly** *adv.*

rest (rest) *n.* **1.** relaxation; being still and quiet: *After we hiked five kilometres, we sat down and had a rest.* **2.** what is left: *You can have the rest of the pie.* **3.** in music, a period of silence. —*v.* to stop activity and to relax or have a nap. **resting. rested.**

restaurant (res′ tə ront *or* res′ tront) *n.* a place where you buy and eat a meal.

restless (rest′ ləs) *adj.* not able to be still and quiet: *The movie was very long and my little brother became restless.* —**restlessly** *adv.*

restore (ri stôr′) *v.* to bring something back to the place or to the way it used to be: *After the stolen trophy was found, it was restored to the cabinet where it belonged.* **restoring. restored.**

restrain (ri strān′) *v.* to hold something or someone back: *It was difficult to restrain my dog from chasing the neighbours' cat.* **restraining. restrained.**

restrict (ri strikt′) *v.* to allow only certain people to do something or go somewhere: *Entrance to the museum's warehouse was restricted to the museum's staff.* **restricting. restricted.**

result (ri zult′) *n.* **1.** the final score or sum: *The result of adding 5 and 4 is 9.* **2.** something that happens because of something else: *Her broken arm was the result of a bad fall.* —*v.* to be a result of something: *Cavities often result from eating lots of sugar.* **resulting. resulted.**

resume (ri zūm′) *v.* to return to an activity after having stopped for a while: *After dinner, my sister and I resumed our chess game.* **resuming. resumed.**

retain (ri tān′) *v.* to hold onto; to keep: *Be sure to retain the store receipt in case you decide to return the skates.* **retaining. retained.**

retire (ri tīr′) *v.* to give up work, usually when you reach a certain age: *When he turned 65 last year, my grandfather retired from his job.* **retiring. retired.**

retreat (ri trēt′) *v.* to move back, such as from an enemy: *The tired soldiers retreated from the battlefield.* **retreating. retreated.**

retrieve (ri trēv′) *v.* to find and bring back: *My brother retrieved my lost watch.* **retrieving. retrieved.**

retriever (ri trēv′ ər) *n.* one of several kinds of dogs that can be trained to find and bring back things.

retriever

return (ri tûrn′) *n.* a coming or going back: *Let's get together on your return from camp.* —*v.* **1.** to come or go back: *to return home.* **2.** to give back. **returning. returned.**

reunion (rē yūn′ yən) *n.* a coming together again of a group of people: *a family reunion.*

reuse (rē yūz′) *v.* to use something again: *We reused the jam jars by filling them with nails and screws.* **reusing. reused.**

reveal (ri vēl′) *v.* to make known: *Don't reveal my secret.* **revealing. revealed.**

revenge (ri venj′) *n.* something done to get even with someone because he or she has harmed you: *After the clerk insulted her, she got revenge by not buying the jeans.*

reverse (ri vûrs′) *n.* **1.** the opposite: *He did the reverse of what I said. I told him to turn left, but he turned right instead.* **2.** the position of gears that makes a car move backward instead of forward. —*v.* to make something go in the opposite way: *When you reverse the spelling of "nap," you get "pan."* **reversing. reversed.**

review (ri vyū′) *n.* **1.** a written or spoken account of how good or bad a book, play, movie, or other work is. **2.** a careful checking of something. —*v.* **1.** to give a written or spoken account: *I reviewed the movie for the class.* **2.** to go over something carefully; to check: *Bill reviewed his answers on the test.* **reviewing. reviewed.**

revive (ri vīv′) *v.* to bring someone back to life or to a conscious state: *They revived the drowning man by giving him artificial respiration.* **reviving. revived.**

revolt (ri vōlt′) *n.* a refusal to obey orders; a rebellion. —*v.* to rebel. **revolting. revolted.**

revolution (rev′ ə lū′ shən) *n.* **1.** the overthrow of the system of government in a country: *Often, a revolution involves fighting between people who support different sides.* **2.** a movement in a circle around something: *the revolution of the moon around the earth.*

revolve (ri volv′) *v.* to move in a circle around something: *The earth revolves around the sun.* **revolving. revolved.**

revolver (ri vol′ vər) *n.* a pistol that can be fired several times without having to be loaded again.

reward (ri wȯrd′) *n.* money or a prize given for something done. —*v.* to give a reward: *We rewarded the girl who found our dog.* **rewarding. rewarded.**

rewind (rē wīnd′) *v.* to reverse the winding of a spool of recording tape or film. **rewinding. rewound.**

rewrite (rē rīt′) *v.* to write something again, often to correct earlier mistakes. **rewriting. rewrote.** she has **rewritten.**

rhino (rī′ nō) short for **rhinoceros**.

rhinoceros (rī nos′ ər əs) *n.* a large, thick-skinned mammal of Africa and Asia with one or two horns on its snout. *pl.* **rhinoceroses.**

rhinoceros

rhubarb (rū′ bärb) *n.* a plant with large leaves and reddish, sour-tasting stalks that can be cooked and eaten.

rhyme (rīm) *n.* a word having the same last sound as another: *"Cat" is a rhyme for "bat." "Able" is a rhyme for "table."* —*v.* to have the same last sound as another word: *"Boy" rhymes with "toy."* **rhyming. rhymed.**

rhythm (riTH′ əm) *n.* a regular beat or flow of sounds or movements: *the rhythm of drumbeats.*

rib (rib) *n.* one of the long, narrow bones that curve around your chest, protecting the lungs and other organs in your chest.

ribbon (rib′ ən) *n.* a narrow strip of material, such as silk, velvet, or satin: *a hair ribbon.*

rice (rīs) *n.* a cereal grass that grows in warm, wet regions. The seeds of this plant are used for food.

rich (rich) *adj.* **1.** having a lot of wealth: *a rich person.* **2.** having a lot of sugar or fat: *a rich dessert.* **3.** producing a lot; fertile: *rich soil.*

rid (rid) *v.* to remove or to get free of something that is not wanted: *to rid a garden of weeds.* **ridding. rid** or **ridded.**

get rid of to remove or to get free from, something unwanted.

riddle (rid′ əl) *n.* a puzzling question, such as: *What goes up when the rain falls down? (An umbrella.)*

ride (rīd) *n.* **1.** a trip in a vehicle, or on an animal. **2.** a large machine with seats, such as a merry-go-round or a Ferris wheel, that people ride on for fun. —*v.* to travel in a vehicle or on an animal's back. **riding. rode.** I have **ridden.**

ridge (rij) *n.* **1.** a raised strip: *The bicycle tires made ridges in the sand.* **2.** a raised strip of land. **3.** a range: *a ridge of hills.*

ridiculous (ri dik′ yə ləs) *adj.* very silly or foolish. —**ridiculously** *adv.*

riding (rīd′ ing) *n.* an area in Canada represented by a member of parliament or a member of a provincial legislature.

rifle (rī′ fəl) *n.* a long gun that is fired from the shoulder.

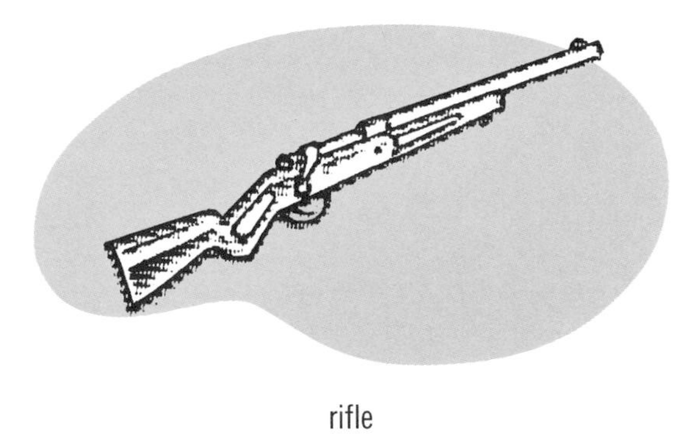

rifle

rig (rig) *n.* the arrangement of the masts, sails, and other equipment of a boat or ship. —*v.* **1.** to equip a boat or ship so that it is ready for use. **2.** to change prices, votes, or other things in an unfair way: *They rigged the election by destroying many ballots.* **rigging. rigged.**

right (rīt) *n.* **1.** the side opposite to left. **2.** what is good, fair, and honourable; the opposite of wrong. **3.** a claim: *Everyone has a right to vote in the class election.* —*adj.* **1.** on the side opposite to left: *When you look at a map of Canada, Alberta is on the right side of British Columbia.* **2.** true; correct: *Your answers are right.* **3.** fair and honourable: *We want to do the right thing.* —*adv.* at or toward the right side.

right away immediately, without delay.

right angle an angle of ninety degrees: *The side and the top or bottom of a sheet of paper are at right angles to each other.*

right-handed (rīt′ han′ did) *adj.* using your right hand more easily than you use your left hand: *a right-handed batter.*

rigid (rij′ id) *adj.* stiff; hard to bend: *a rigid piece of cardboard.* —**rigidly** *adv.*

rim (rim) *n.* the outer edge or border of something, such as a cup, bowl, wheel, glass, or swimming pool.

rind (rīnd) *n.* a thick outer covering: *Oranges, watermelons, and lemons have rinds.*

ring (ring) *n.* **1.** a circle: *The children formed a ring.* **2.** a metal band worn on your finger: *a gold ring.* **3.** the sound of a bell: *I hear a ring at the door.* —*v.* to make a bell ring, or to make a sound like a bell. **ringing. rang.** it has **rung.**

rink (ringk) *n.* **1.** a large, smooth sheet of ice, used by hockey players and other skaters. **2.** a smooth sheet of ice used in the game of curling. **3.** a smooth floor used for roller-skating.

rinse (rins) *v.* to use clean, clear water to wash away soap or dirt. **rinsing. rinsed.**

riot (rī′ ət) *n.* violent and noisy behaviour by a group of people. **2.** something or someone who is very funny: *The new movie is a riot.* —*v.* to move or act, in a group, in a violent and noisy way: *After the close game, the hockey fans rioted and did a lot of damage.* **rioting. rioted.**

rip (rip) *n.* a torn place: *a rip in your pants.* —*v.* to tear roughly and quickly: *to rip open an envelope.* **ripping. ripped.**

ripe (rīp) *adj.* fully developed and ready for eating: *That tomato is finally ripe; it has turned from green to red.* (*opp.* **unripe.**)

ripen (rīp′ ən) *v.* to make or become ripe: *Tomatoes ripen quickly if you leave them in a sunny place.* **ripening. ripened.**

ripple (rip′ əl) *n.* a tiny wave on smooth water.

rise (rīz) *v.* **1.** to get up: *My mother rises very early each morning.* **2.** to move up: *The sun rises in the east.* **3.** to slope upward: *The road rises from the village.* **rising. rose.** it has **risen.**

risk (risk) *n.* the chance of harm or of losing something; danger: *She took a big risk by petting the growling dog.* —*v.* to take a risk: *Firefighters sometimes risk their lives.* **risking. risked.**

risky (ris′ kē) *adj.* full of risk: *a risky move; a riskier one; the riskiest move of all.*

rival (rī′ vəl) *n.* a person or group that competes with another.

river (riv′ ər) *n.* a large stream of water that flows into another river, an ocean, a bay, or a lake.

River and **rival** are based on the same Latin word *rivalis.* The original meaning of rival was someone who competed with you for water from the same river.

rivet (riv′ ət) *n.* a metal pin or bolt, used to fasten pieces of wood or metal together.

roam (rōm) *v.* to wander; to move about without a purpose. **roaming. roamed.**

roar (rȯr) *n.* a loud deep sound made by a lion, heavy traffic, the waves of the sea, and so on. —*v.* to make a roar. **roaring. roared.**

roast (rōst) *n.* **1.** a large piece of meat that is cooked in an oven. **2.** an outdoor meal where food is cooked over an open fire: *a wiener roast.* —*v.* to cook in an oven or over a fire: *to roast chicken.* **roasting. roasted.**

rob (rob) *v.* to steal by force. **robbing. robbed.**

robber (rob′ ər) *n.* a thief who steals by force: *Two robbers with guns held up the bank.*

robbery (rob′ ər ē) *n.* stealing by force: *a bank robbery. pl.* **robberies.**

robe (rōb) *n.* a long, loose outer garment.

robe

robin (rob′ in) *n.* a bird with a reddish breast.

robot (rō′ bot) *n.* a machine that does a task humans do, such as picking up, moving, and welding parts in a factory.

Did you know that when traffic lights were first used, they were known as **robots**?

rock (rok) *n.* **1.** a large piece of stone. **2.** a kind of popular music. —*v.* to move gently back and forth: *to rock in a rocking chair.* **rocking. rocked.**

rocket (rok′ ət) *n.* **1.** a long, tube-shaped machine that is launched into the air or into space by a strong jet of gases. **2.** a firework that goes high up in the air when lit.

rocky (rok′ ē) *adj.* bumpy, or full of rocks: *a rocky road; a rockier road; the rockiest road in the country.*

Rocky Mountains, the Rockies a range of mountains that extends through western Canada and the western United States.

rod (rod) *n.* a thin, straight stick of wood or metal: *a fishing rod.*

rode (rōd) see **ride** (verb).

rodent (rō′ dənt) *n.* a small or medium-sized mammal that has sharp teeth for gnawing: *Rats, mice, rabbits, squirrels, and beavers are rodents.*

rodeo (rō′ dē ō *or* rō dā′ ō) *n.* a contest of skill in riding horses, roping cattle, and other such events: *The Calgary Stampede is the world's biggest rodeo. pl.* **rodeos.**

rogue (rōg) *n.* a dishonest or mischievous person; a rascal.

role (rōl) *n.* a part played by an actor: *In our school play, I have the role of Alexander Graham Bell.*

roll (rōl) *n.* **1.** something flat that is rolled up: *a roll of wrapping paper.* **2.** a round, small bread or pastry: *a hamburger roll.* —*v.* **1.** to turn over and over: *The ball rolled down the stairs.* **2.** to wrap around itself: *to roll up a carpet.* **3.** to sway from side to side: *The ship rolled in the rough sea.* **rolling. rolled.**

roller (rōl′ ər) *n.* a cylinder that can roll, and may be used to shape something: *a paint roller; a hair roller.*

roller coaster (rōl′ ər kōs′ tər) a railway ride at an amusement park or fair: *A roller coaster has steep drops and sharp, fast turns.*

roller-skate (rōl′ ər skāt′) *n.* a skate that has small wheels on the bottom.

roller skate *v.* to skate on roller-skates. **roller-skating. roller-skated.**

Roman (rō′ mən) *n., adj.* **1.** having to do with modern Rome, the capital of Italy. **2.** having to do with ancient Rome, where Latin was spoken.

Roman numerals are letters of the alphabet that were used by the ancient Romans as a system of numbering. Some Roman numerals are **I** (1), **II** (2), **IV** (4), **V** (5), **VI** (6), **X** (10), **L** (50), **C** (100), **D** (500), and **M** (1000).

romance (rō′ mans *or* rō mans′) *n.* **1.** love. **2.** a love story.

romantic (rō man′ tik) *adj.* having to do with romance: *a romantic movie.* (*opp.* **unromantic.**) —**romantically** *adv.*

roof (rūf) *n.* **1.** the top covering of a building. **2.** something that resembles the roof of a building in its purpose or shape: *the roof of a car. pl.* **roofs.**

rookie (ru̇k′ ē) *n.* a person who is new to a group and has no experience.

room (rūm) *n.* **1.** one of the spaces inside a building, enclosed by walls: *a bathroom; a dining room.* **2.** space: *There is plenty of room on the bus.*

roommate (rūm′ māt′) *n.* a person who shares living space with you.

roomy (rūm′ ē) *adj.* full of room or space: *a roomy tent; a roomier tent; the roomiest tent in the camp.*

rooster (rūs′ tər) *n.* a male chicken.

root (rūt) *n.* **1.** the part of a plant that grows downward into the soil. **2.** a word from which other words are made: *"Hair" is the root word of "hairy."*

root for to cheer for: *The fans rooted for the home team.*

rope (rōp) *n.* a long, thick cord made of fibres twisted together. —*v.* to tie with a rope: *We roped the packages together.* **roping. roped.**

rose (rōz) *n.* a sweet-smelling flower that grows on a bush and usually has stems with thorns. —*v.* see **rise**.

rot (rot) *v.* to go bad; to decay. **rotting. rotted.**

rotate (rō tāt′ *or* rō′ tāt) *v.* **1.** to turn around in circles: *The earth rotates on its axis.* **2.** to take turns: *We rotated our crops by planting beets where the beans had been.* **rotating. rotated.**

rotation (rō tā′ shən) *n.* the turning around in a circle: *the rotation of a bicycle wheel.*

rotten (rot′ ən) *adj.* going bad or gone bad: *rotten eggs; rotten apples.*

rough (ruf) *adj.* **1.** not smooth: *rough ground.* **2.** stormy: *a rough sea.*

roughly (ruf′ lē) *adv.* **1.** in a rough way: *Don't treat the dog roughly.* **2.** approximately: *Roughly forty people were at the wedding reception.*

round (rownd) *n.* **1.** a period in a sport such as boxing. **2.** a short song sung by several people, each singer beginning at a different time. —*adj.* **1.** in the shape of a circle: *a round ring.* **2.** in the shape of a sphere: *a round apple.* —*v.* to make a turn: *I rounded the corner.* **rounding. rounded.**

roundabout (rownd′ ə bowt′) *adj.* not a direct way: *The roundabout route to school takes an extra ten minutes but we don't have to walk on the highway.*

round trip a trip to somewhere and back again: *We made a round trip to Calgary and back to Edmonton in two days.*

route (rūt) *n.* **1.** a way of getting to a place: *a short route to school.* **2.** an area regularly covered by a salesperson: *a newspaper route.*

routine (rū tēn′) *n.* a regular way of doing things: *Doing homework is part of my daily routine.* —*adj.* regular: *Drying the dishes is one of my routine jobs.* —**routinely** *adv.*

row (rō) *n.* a line of people or things: *a row of chairs.* —*v.* to make a boat move by using oars: *We had to row the motor boat back to the dock when we ran out of gas.* **rowing. rowed.**

rowboat (rō′ bōt′) *n.* a small boat that is moved with oars: *We are planning to use a rowboat when we go fishing.*

rowboat

royal (roi′ əl) *adj.* having to do with kings or queens or their families: *a royal palace.* —**royally** *adv.*

Royal Canadian Mounted Police, RCMP the federal police force of Canada: *In all provinces except Quebec and Ontario, the Royal Canadian Mounted Police also act as provincial police.*

royalty (roi′ əl tē) *n.* a royal person or royal persons.

rub (rub) *v.* **1.** to move one thing back and forth against another: *If your hands get cold, rubbing them together will help warm them.* **2.** to wipe: *Marguerite rubbed her shoes on the mat.* **rubbing. rubbed.**
rub out to erase.

rubber (rub′ ər) *n.* **1.** springy, elastic material used to make tires, tubes, and other things. **2.** a small piece of rubber used as an eraser. **3.** a low overshoe made of rubber.

rubber band an elastic band, used for holding things together.

rubbish (rub′ ish) *n.* garbage: *Please throw out all the bags of rubbish.*

ruby (rū′ bē) *n.* a clear, red jewel. *pl.* **rubies.**

rudder (rud′ ər) *n.* a flat, movable piece of wood or metal that is attached to the back of a ship or aircraft and is used for steering.

rude (rūd) *adj.* bad-mannered; not polite. —**rudely** *adv.*

ruffle (ruf′ əl) *n.* a strip of wavy cloth or lace attached to a piece of clothing, a curtain, and so on.

rug (rug) *n.* a heavy cloth floor covering, similar to a carpet.

rugged (rug′ əd) *adj.* **1.** uneven, stony, and hilly: *rugged countryside.* **2.** healthy and strong: *a rugged farmer.* **3.** harsh; difficult: *a rugged winter.*

ruin (rū′ in) *n.* an old building that has fallen to pieces or is falling down: *Ruins of many ancient buildings are found in Greece and Italy.* —*v.* to spoil; to make useless: *The heavy frost ruined the fruit crop.* **ruining. ruined.**

rule (rūl) *n.* an order that must be obeyed: *It is a school rule that bicycles are not allowed in the playground.* —*v.* to control or govern: *to rule a country.* **ruling. ruled.**
as a rule usually; generally: *As a rule, we go to the supermarket on Friday or Saturday.*

ruler (rū′ lər) *n.* **1.** a person who controls or governs, especially a king or queen. **2.** a strip of wood, plastic, or metal, marked with centimetres or other units of length: *A ruler is used for measuring and for drawing straight lines.*

ruling (rû′ ling) *n.* a decision made by someone in charge: *The referee made a ruling in our favour.*

rumble (rum′ bəl) *n.* a deep, rolling sound: *the rumble of thunder.* —*v.* to make such a sound: *The train rumbled in the distance.* **rumbling. rumbled.**

rummage (rum′ ij) *v.* to search thoroughly through something by moving its contents around: *We rummaged through the old chest looking for clothes we could wear to the Hallowe'en party.* **rummaging. rummaged.**

rumour, rumor (ru′ mər) *n.* a story or information, which may not be true, passed around from one person to another.

run (run) *n.* **1.** the act of running: *I go for a run every morning.* **2.** a tear in a stocking. **3.** a point scored in baseball or cricket. —*v.* **1.** to move quickly on your feet: *She ran to catch the bus.* **2.** to be in charge of: *My aunt runs a gas station.* **3.** to work: *A subway runs on electricity.* **4.** to compete in a race or an election: *He is running for mayor.* **5.** to extend or continue: *The play ran for three weeks.* **6.** to send out a fluid: *My nose is running because I have a cold.* **running. ran.** I have **run.**
run into to meet by chance: *I ran into my cousin at the hockey game.*
run out of to have none left: *We ran out of bread.*
run over to ride or drive over: *I ran over some broken glass with my bicycle and got a flat tire.*

runaway (run′ ə wā′) *n.* a person or animal that runs away. *pl.* **runaways.**

rung (rung) *n.* one of the steps of a ladder. —*v.* see **ring** (verb).

runner (run′ ər) *n.* **1.** the long, narrow part on which a sled or an ice skate slides. **2.** a person who runs. **3.** an athletic shoe designed for running.

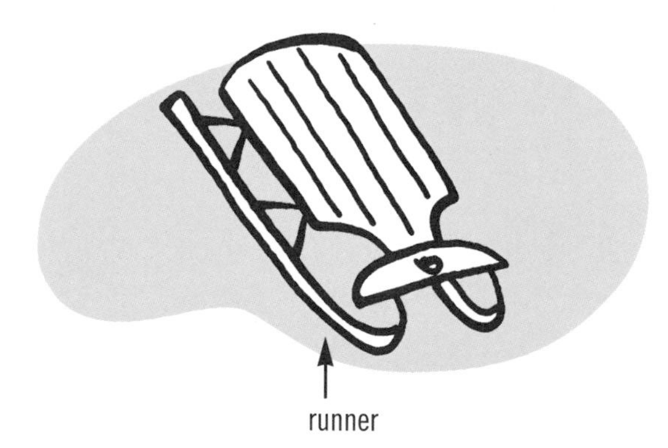

runner-up (run′ ər up′) *n.* the person who finishes in second or third place in a race or contest. *pl.* **runners-up.**

runt (runt) *n.* the smallest and weakest animal born in a litter.

runway (run′ wā′) *n.* a wide, long concrete path for airplanes to take off from and land on. *pl.* **runways.**

rural (rūr′ əl) *adj.* having to do with the country, not the city: *Many students in my school were born in rural areas.*

rush (rush) *n.* **1.** a sudden or hurried movement: *I'm in a rush to catch the bus.* **2.** a tall, grass-like plant that has a hollow stem and grows in marshes. *pl.* **rushes.** —*v.* to hurry about; to move fast or too fast: *Don't rush through your meal.* **rushing. rushed.**

rush hour a time of day when most people are travelling to or from work.

rust (rust) *n.* a reddish-brown coating that forms on some metals, such as iron: *Rust is caused by wetness.* —*v.* to become coated with rust: *The key has rusted and no longer fits in the lock.* **rusting. rusted.**

rustic (rus′ tik) *adj.* having to do with the country or country life: *rustic furniture.*

rustle (rus′ əl) *n.* a soft, crackling sound: *the rustle of leaves in wind.* —*v.* to make this sound. **rustling. rustled.**

rusty (rus′ tē) *adj.* covered with rust: *a rusty nail; a rustier nail; the rustiest nail in the box.*

rut (rut) *n.* a deep groove made by a wheel.
in a rut trapped in a routine: *I'm in a rut—every day seems to be the same.*

rutabaga (rū′ tə bā′ gə) *n.* a turnip with a thick skin and pale yellow, edible flesh.

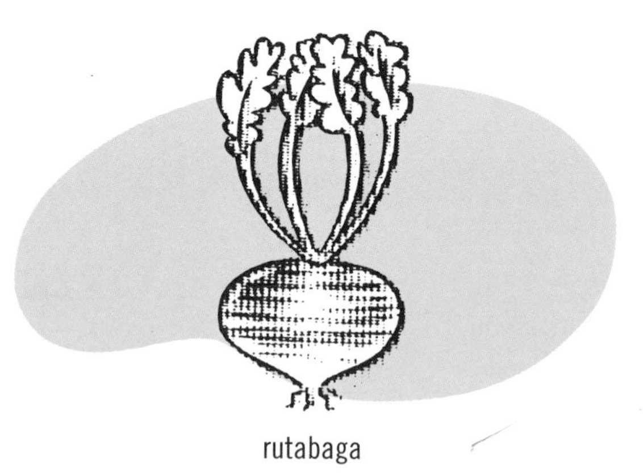

ruthless (ruth′ lis) *adj.* having no pity; without mercy; cruel. —**ruthlessly** adv.

rye (rī) *n.* a grass plant, grown like wheat, used for making flour and as feed for animals.

sabbath (sab′ əth) *n.* a day of rest and worship.

sabre, saber (sā′ bər) *n.* a heavy sword with a cutting edge along one side of the blade.

sabre

sack (sak) *n.* a large bag made of strong cloth: *a sack for potatoes.*

sacred (sā′ krid) *adj.* holy; having to do with God or a god: *sacred music; a sacred place of worship.*

sacrifice (sak′ rə fīs′) *n.* something you value that you give up: *Giving up the hockey tickets was a great sacrifice.* —*v.* to give up something you value. **sacrificing. sacrificed.**

sad (sad) *adj.* unhappy; full of sorrow or grief; low; depressed: *sad news; sadder news; the saddest news of all.* —**sadly** *adv.*

saddle (sad′ əl) *n.* a padded, leather seat for a rider of a horse or other animal. —*v.* to put a saddle on a horse or other animal: *We will saddle the horses and go on a trail ride.* **saddling. saddled.**

The word **saddle** sounds very much like *sattel,* the German word for "sit." This, of course, is what you do on a saddle, so the connection between the words is clear.

safari (sə fȧr′ ē) *n.* a long trip, usually in Africa, often to photograph wildlife and sometimes to hunt animals. *pl.* **safaris.**

safe (sāf) *n.* a strong, metal box in which valuable things are locked. —*adj.* **1.** free from danger or harm: *I feel safe now that I'm off the thin ice.* **2.** careful: *My sister is a safe driver.* **3.** all right: *It's a fine day, so it's safe not to bring an umbrella.* **4.** in baseball, reaching a base safely. (*opp.* **unsafe.**) —**safely** *adv.*

safety (sāf′ tē) *n.* freedom from harm or danger; the state of being safe: *The workers wore hard hats for their own safety.*

sag (sag) *v.* to curve low in the middle: *The old mattress sags.* **sagging. sagged.**

said (sed) see **say**.

sail (sāl) *n.* a large sheet of canvas or cloth attached to a boat or ship: *A sail catches the wind and makes the boat move.* —*v.* to travel in a sailboat or a ship: *We sailed across the bay.* **sailing. sailed.**

sailboat (sāl′ bōt′) *n.* a boat that is moved by the wind blowing against its sail or sails.

sailor (sā′ lər) *n.* a member of a ship's crew.

saint (sānt) *n.* a person who has lived a very holy life.

sake (sāk) *n.* a benefit or a cause: *I went on the errand for your sake, because you are not well.*

salad (sal′ əd) *n.* a mixture of raw or cold cooked vegetables, sometimes with cold meat, fish, cheese, or eggs.

salamander (sal′ ə man′ dər) *n.* an amphibian that looks like a small lizard.

salami (sə lȧ′ mē) *n.* a spicy kind of sausage.

salary (sal′ ə rē) *n.* money paid to someone on a regular basis for work done. *pl.* **salaries.**

sale (sāl) *n.* **1.** the selling of something: *the sale of meat by a butcher.* **2.** the selling of goods at prices lower than usual: *The store has a sale on shoes.*

for sale offered for money: *Our neighbours' house is for sale.*

on sale offered at a reduced price: *I can afford to buy that sweater now because it is on sale.*

salesperson (sālz′ pur′ sən) *n.* a person whose job is selling things.

saliva (sə lī′ və) *n.* the liquid in your mouth: *Saliva helps you to chew and digest foods.*

salmon (sam′ ən) *n.* a large, silvery fish with pink flesh, used for food. *pl.* **salmon.**

salon (sə lon′ *or* sal′ on′) *n.* **1.** a large room for receiving and entertaining guests. **2.** a business selling goods related to art or fashion.

salt (solt) *n.* small, white crystals used to flavour food: *Salt is found in the earth and in sea water.*

The expression "worth your salt" means "you've earned your money," and comes from the fact that ancient Roman soldiers were paid with **salt**, not money. In their day, salt was considered precious. This was because salt was the only thing that kept meat from becoming spoiled.

salute (sə lūt′) *n.* a formal gesture of respect given by raising your right hand to your brow or by firing guns or cannons. —*v.* to give a salute: *The soldiers saluted the general.* **saluting. saluted.**

salvage (sal′ vij) *n.* **1.** the rescuing of a wrecked ship or cargo on it. **2.** anything saved or rescued for use. —*v.* to save or rescue something after a fire or other damage: *The fire at the library was minor, so the firefighters were able to salvage most of the books.*

same (sām) *adj.* **1.** exactly alike, not different: *Identical twins look the same.* **2.** unchanged: *I had not seen him for a year, but he looks just the same.*

sample (sam′ pəl) *n.* a small piece of something that shows you what the rest is like. —*v.* to taste: *He sampled the stew.* **sampling. sampled.**

sand (sand) *n.* tiny grains of earth or rock.

sandal (san′ dəl) *n.* a light, open shoe fastened to the foot by straps.

sandal

sandbar (sand′ bär′) *n.* a bar of sand formed near the shore in a body of water.

sandpaper (sand′ pā′ pər) *n.* a heavy paper that has sand glued to one side: *Sandpaper is used for smoothing and cleaning wood.*

sandwich (sand′ wich) *n.* two slices of bread with butter, meat, jam, or some other food in between. *pl.* **sandwiches.**

sandy (san′ dē) *adj.* **1.** having a light brown or beige colour. **2.** filled with sand: *a sandy beach; a sandier beach; the sandiest beach in the province.*

sane (sān) *adj.* **1.** in your right mind; not mentally ill. **2.** sensible: *What a sane plan!* (*opp.* **insane.**) —**sanely** *adv.*

sang (sang) see **sing**.

sanitary (san′ ə ter′ ē) *adj.* **1.** free of germs and dirt: *a sanitary operating room.* **2.** clean and good for health: *Washing your hands before eating is a sanitary practice.* (*opp.* **unsanitary.**)

sank (sangk) see **sink** (verb).

sap (sap) *n.* the liquid inside plants and trees: *Sap carries water and food through a tree.*

sapphire (saf′ īr) *n.* a blue, clear jewel.

sarcastic (sär kas′ tik) *adj.* using words that mean the opposite of what you want to say, often in an unkind or hurtful way: *My friend was being sarcastic when he said my painting was a masterpiece; I know he hated it.* —**sarcastically** *adv.*

sardine (sär dēn′) *n.* a small, silvery fish used for food, often salted and put in cans.

sari (sä′ rē) *n.* a long piece of light fabric, draped around the body to form a dress. Saris are worn by women in India, Pakistan, and other countries. *pl.* **saris.**

sari

sash (sash) *n.* **1.** a wide ribbon, worn around the waist. **2.** the frame that holds a pane of glass in a window or door. *pl.* **sashes.**

Sasquatch (sas′ kwoch) *n.* a large, hairy, human-like creature said to live in the Rockies: *The Sasquatch is also known as* **Bigfoot**.

sat (sat) see **sit**.

satellite (sat′ ə līt′) *n.* **1.** a smaller body moving in orbit around a larger one: *The moon is a satellite of the earth.* **2.** an artificial object sent into orbit around the earth: *a communications satellite.*

satellite dish a large, saucer-shaped receiver used to pick up TV and radio signals.

satin (sat′ ən) *n.* a smooth cloth that is shiny on one side and dull on the other.

satisfaction (sat′ is fak′ shən) *n.* pleasure; enjoyment: *I get a lot of satisfaction from creating the best science project I can possibly do.*

satisfactory (sat′ is fak′ tə rē) *adj.* good enough to meet the requirements: *The student's work is satisfactory, but not excellent.* (*opp.* **unsatisfactory.**) —**satisfactorily** *adv.*

satisfy (sat′ is fī′) *v.* **1.** to please: *My pitching doesn't satisfy me. I'll have to practise more.* **2.** to fill: *After three helpings, my hunger was satisfied.* (*opp.* **dissatisfy.**) **satisfying. satisfied.** it **satisfies.**

saturate (sach′ ə rāt′) *v.* to soak completely: *My clothes were completely saturated during the rainstorm.* **saturating. saturated.**

Saturday (sat′ ər dā′ *or* sat′ ər dē) *n.* the seventh day of the week.

Saturn (sat′ ərn) *n.* one of the planets of our solar system: *Saturn is the sixth planet from the sun.*

sauce (sos) *n.* a liquid or creamy mixture served with food to make it taste better.

saucer (so′ sər) *n.* a small, round dish on which a teacup is placed.

sausage (so′ sij) *n.* chopped meat that is mixed with spices and stuffed into a thin case shaped like a tube.

savage (sav′ ij) *adj.* wild and fierce: *The savage wind made it difficult to walk.* —**savagely** *adv.*

save (sāv) *n.* a goalie's act of preventing a score by the other team: *What a great save!* —*v.* **1.** to free someone from danger or harm: *They saved my life.* **2.** to keep something for later use: *to save money; to save computer data.* **3.** to avoid waste: *Let's take a shortcut to save time.* **saving. saved.**

savings (sā′ vingz) *n. pl.* money that has been saved: *My savings from babysitting are in the bank and I'm going to buy a computer when I have enough money.*

savour, savor (sā′ vər) *n.* a pleasing taste or smell. —*v.* to enjoy the taste of a food or a drink: *to savour ice cream.* **savouring. savoured.**

saw (so) *n.* a tool that has a blade with sharp, pointed teeth along one edge. —*v.* **1.** see **see**. **2.** to cut with a saw: *to saw wood.* **sawing. sawed.** I have **sawed** or **sawn.**

sawdust (so′ dust′) *n.* powdered wood produced in sawing.

sawmill (so′ mil′) *n.* a place where logs are cut into wooden planks.

saxophone (sak′ sə fōn′) *n.* a musical instrument with a curved, metal body and played by blowing into a mouthpiece and pushing down the keys.

Adolphe Sax invented the **saxophone** in 1840. He named it by adding the Greek word *phone,* which means "sound," to his own last name.

say (sā) *v.* **1.** to speak; to tell. **2.** to judge: *It's hard to say who is right and who is wrong.* **saying. said.** he **says** (sez).

saying (sā′ ing) *n.* wise words that are often repeated: *"Haste makes waste" is a wise saying.*

scab (skab) *n.* a crust that forms over a wound when it is healing.

scald (skold) *n.* a burn from very hot liquid or steam. —*v.* to burn with very hot liquid or steam. **scalding. scalded.**

scale (skāl) *n.* **1.** a piece of equipment used to measure mass or weight. **2.** one of many thin flakes on the skin of a fish or reptile. **3.** a series of musical notes. **4.** a series of marks along a line, used for measuring. **5.** the size of a map compared with the actual size of the real place shown. —*v.* to climb: *The lizard scaled the wall.* **scaling. scaled.**

scale

scallop (skol′ əp or skal′ əp) *n.* a sea animal with a fan-shaped shell that has ridges: *Scallops are eaten as food.*

scalp (skalp) *n.* the skin and hair covering the top and back of your head.

scan (skan) *v.* to look over quickly: *He scanned the computer screen for a word.* **scanning. scanned.**

scamper (skam′ pər) *v.* to move quickly or playfully: *The squirrels scampered in the park.* **scampering. scampered.**

scar (skȧr) *n.* **1.** a mark left on your skin after a cut or a burn has healed. **2.** any mark like this. —*v.* to mark with a scar: *The car's paint was scarred where a tree branch had scraped it.* **scarring. scarred.**

scarce (skers) *adj.* less than enough; rare: *When there was a shortage of wheat, flour became scarce.*

scarcely (skers′ lē) *adv.* hardly; barely; only just: *Joshua scarcely touched his supper.*

scare (sker) *n.* a frightening experience: *He had a scare when the window started rattling.* —*v.* to frighten: *The sudden burst of thunder scared the dog.* **scaring. scared.**

scarecrow (sker′ krō′) *n.* a figure filled with straw and dressed like a person; it is set up in a field to frighten birds away from crops.

scarf (skärf) *n.* a piece of cloth worn around the neck or head. *pl.* **scarfs** or **scarves.**

scarlet (skär′ lit) *n.* a very bright red colour. *—adj.* having this colour.

scary (sker′ ē) *adj.* causing a scare: *a scary story; a scarier one; the scariest one of all.*

scatter (skat′ ər) *v.* to throw, fall, or move in all directions: *We scattered seeds on the field.* **scattering. scattered.**

scavenger (skav′ ən jər) *n.* **1.** an animal, such as a vulture, that feeds on decaying things. **2.** a person who looks for and collects things that have been thrown away.

scavenger hunt a game in which the players search for items on a list, often following clues. The first person to come back with all the items wins.

scene (sēn) *n.* **1.** a view or a picture: *a pretty scene by the river.* **2.** a short section of a play or movie: *The actors practised the second scene.* **3.** a place where something happened: *This is the scene of the crime.*

scenery (sē′ nə rē) *n.* **1.** what you see when you look outside; landscape: *The scenery near my cottage is beautiful.* **2.** a painted background for a stage, which shows the setting of the play.

scenic (sē′ nik) *adj.* having to do with natural, beautiful scenery: *We sent our cousins a postcard that showed the scenic beauty of the Rockies.*

scent (sent) *n.* **1.** a smell: *I like the scent of roses.* **2.** a perfume.

sceptical, skeptical (skep′ tə kəl) *adj.* having doubt about whether something is really true: *I'm sceptical about whether her diamond ring is real because she paid so little for it.* **—sceptically** *adv.*

schedule (skej′ ūl *or* shej′ ūl) *n.* a list of events, with dates and times: *a TV schedule.* *—v.* **1.** to make a schedule. **2.** to make an appointment: *The teacher scheduled our play for next month.* **scheduling. scheduled.**

scheme (skēm) *n.* a secret plan, often to do something bad; a plot: *The gang came up with a scheme for robbing the bank.* *—v.* to plan secretly; to plot. **scheming. schemed.**

scholar (skol′ ər) *n.* an educated person who has a lot of knowledge.

scholarship (skol′ ər ship′) *n.* a grant of money or other aid given to students to help them continue their studies.

school (skūl) *n.* **1.** a place where people are taught. **2.** a large group of fish swimming together.

schooner (skū′ nər) *n.* a sailing ship that has two or more masts on it.

schooner

science (sī′ əns) *n.* knowledge of some part of nature, based on careful study and experiments: *Biology and chemistry are sciences.*

science fiction an imaginary story that is usually set in the future or in another world and is based on elements of science.

scientific (sī′ ən tif′ ik) *adj.* having to do with science: *a scientific discovery.* **—scientifically** *adv.*

scientist (sī′ ən tist) *n.* a person who studies a science.

scissors (siz′ ərz) *n. pl.* a tool with two sharp blades, used for cutting.

scold (skōld) *v.* to say angry words to someone after he or she has done something to anger or annoy you: *My father scolded the dog for digging in the garden.* **scolding. scolded.**

scoop (skūp) *n.* **1.** a small shovel, sometimes used for lifting food: *a scoop for flour.* **2.** a deep, heavy spoon used for serving ice cream. —*v.* to take up or out with a scoop. **scooping. scooped.**

scooter (skū′ tər) *n.* **1.** a child's toy that has a raised steering handle and a foot board: *One foot rests on the board of the scooter, and the other foot pushes it.* **2.** a low-powered motor vehicle that has two small wheels, a steering handle, and a seat.

scope (skōp) *n.* **1.** the range of subjects that are affected by something: *You don't realize the scope of the problem.* **2.** a person's ability: *I cannot build a treehouse on my own; it is beyond my scope.*

scorch (skȯrch) *v.* to burn slightly; to singe: *I scorched my shirt with the iron.* **scorching. scorched.**

score (skȯr) *n.* **1.** the number of runs, points, or goals made in a game: *The score was two to one.* **2.** the total of all the points on a test: *What was your score?* —*v.* **1.** to make a goal, a run, or a point in a game. **2.** to mark a test and add up all the points. **scoring. scored.**

scorn (skȯrn) *n.* a feeling that someone or something is worthless: *The team had nothing but scorn for the cheater.*

scorpion (skȯr′ pē ən) *n.* an animal, related to the spider, that has a long tail: *Scorpions can give a poisonous sting.*

scorpion

scour (skowr) *v.* **1.** to rub hard; to scrub: *I scoured the tub clean.* **2.** to search thoroughly: *The volunteers scoured the hills for the missing boy.* **scouring. scoured.**

scout (skowt) *n.* a person sent ahead to hunt for information or for new opportunities: *a baseball scout.* —*v.* to hunt around and explore: *We scouted around the provincial park for a campsite near the water.* **scouting. scouted.**

Scouts **1.** an organization for young people that includes Beavers, Cubs, Scouts, and programs for older members. **2.** a program for young people, ages 11-14, that includes camping and community service activities.

scowl (skowl) *n.* an angry look, with your eyebrows creased and your mouth tight. —*v.* to make a scowl when you are in a bad temper. **scowling. scowled.**

scramble (skram′ bəl) *n.* a quick climb over a rough area. —*v.* **1.** to beat or mix up: *We scrambled eggs for breakfast.* **2.** to climb or crawl, using the hands and feet: *The children scrambled for the ball.* **scrambling. scrambled.**

scrap (skrap) *n.* a small piece, often torn or left over: *scraps of food; a scrap of paper.* —*v.* to get rid of or throw away: *That idea won't work; let's scrap it.* **scrapping. scrapped.**

scrapbook (skrap′ bu̇k′) *n.* a book of blank pages in which to paste photos, letters, and other things you want to remember.

scrape (skrāp) *n.* a mark on a surface, made by scratching: *I got a scrape on my arm after I fell.* —*v.* **1.** to scratch or rub. **2.** to clean off dirt, using something hard or sharp: *He scraped the mud off his shoes.* **scraping. scraped.**

scratch (skrach) *n.* a mark or a small cut left by something sharp: *The cat's claw made a scratch on my arm. pl.* **scratches.** —*v.* **1.** to make a mark or a small cut with something sharp: *My cat scratched me with her claws.* **2.** to run your fingernails over an itchy part of your skin: *to scratch a mosquito bite.* **scratching. scratched.**

scrawny (skro′ nē) *adj.* thin, weak, and looking sick: *a scrawny cat; a scrawnier one; the scrawniest cat on the street.*

scream (skrēm) *n.* a high, shrill cry, in fear or excitement. —*v.* **1.** to make such a cry. **2.** to speak very loudly: *She had to scream her instructions in order to be heard over the loud music.* **screaming. screamed.**

screech (skrēch) *n.* a high, shrill noise: *the screech of brakes. pl.* **screeches.** —*v.* to make such a noise: *He screeched and ducked when a bat flew at him.* **screeching. screeched.**

screen (skrēn) *n.* **1.** the surface on which a TV picture, a movie, or a computer image is seen. **2.** a covering of fine wires that crisscross and are set in a frame: *A screen is put on a window or door to let in air, but to keep out bugs.*

screw (skrū) *n.* a kind of nail with spiral grooves. —*v.* to fix in place by using a twisting movement: *to screw a bottle cap.* **screwing. screwed.** (*opp.* **unscrew.**)

screwdriver (skrū′ drīv′ ər) *n.* a tool used for turning screws.

scribble (skrib′ əl) *n.* careless, messy writing: *I can't read your scribble.* —*v.* to write or draw in a quick or careless way. **scribbling. scribbled.**

script (skript) *n.* **1.** writing in which the letters are joined together. **2.** the written words of a play, movie, or TV or radio program: *The actors received a copy of the movie script.*

scroll (skrōl) *n.* a roll of paper or parchment with writing on it. —*v.* to make words or pictures on a computer screen move up, down, or across, so that you can view another part of the document. **scrolling. scrolled.**

scrub (skrub) *v.* to clean by rubbing hard: *I scrubbed the floor clean.* **scrubbing. scrubbed.**

scrumptious (skrump′ shəs) *adj.* (*informal*) very delicious: *a scrumptious dessert.*

scuba (skū′ bə) *n.* equipment used for breathing while swimming underwater: *Scuba divers use a mouthpiece that is joined by hoses to a tank of air.*

> **Scuba** is actually an acronym —a word formed from the first letters of a group of words. Look up "acronym" in this dictionary to find the words from which scuba comes.

scuff (skuf) *v.* to scratch up the surface of something: *I scuffed one of my new shoes when I kicked the stone step.* **scuffing. scuffed.**

sculptor (skulp′ tər) *n.* a person who makes sculptures.

sculpture (skulp′ chər) *n.* a statue carved out of wood or stone, or shaped out of clay, metal, or some other hard material.

scurry (skůr′ ē) *v.* to hurry along: *The rabbit scurried under the bushes when it heard my approaching footsteps.* **scurrying. scurried.** it **scurries.**

scythe (sīTH) *n.* a long handle with a large curved blade at the end: *A scythe is used for cutting grass and crops by hand.*

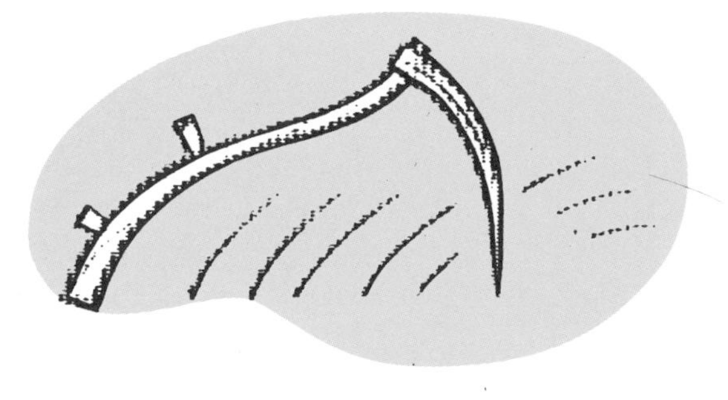

scythe

sea (sē) *n.* **1.** the great body of salt water that covers almost three-fourths of the earth's surface. **2.** any body of salt water smaller than an ocean: *the Mediterranean Sea.*

sea gull a grey and white bird that lives near a large body of water.

seal (sēl) *n.* a mammal that lives in and by the sea: *Seals have flippers instead of feet and a thick layer of fat under the skin.* —*v.* to close very tightly, often by using something sticky: *to seal an envelope; to seal a jam jar with wax.* **sealing. sealed.**

sea lion a large-eared seal that lives in the Pacific Ocean.

seam (sēm) *n.* the line where two pieces of cloth or paper are joined together.

search (sûrch) *n.* the act of looking for someone or something: *The search lasted four days. pl.* **searches.** —*v.* to look everywhere for something: *Kelly searched the house for her pet hamster.* **searching. searched.**

searchlight (sûrch′ līt) *n.* a special light that gives off a powerful beam: *Lighthouses and airport control towers use searchlights.*

sea shell the shell of a sea animal, such as an oyster or a clam.

seashore (sē′ shôr′) *n.* the land along the edge of the sea.

seasick (sē′ sik′) *adj.* on a boat, feeling dizzy and sick to your stomach when the water is rough.

season (sē′ zən) *n.* **1.** one of the four periods of the year: spring, summer, autumn, winter. **2.** a special time for something: *the football season.* —*v.* to add salt, pepper, or other flavourings to food. **seasoning. seasoned.**

seat (sēt) *n.* something to sit on, such as a chair or bench. —*v.* **1.** to give someone a seat: *The smaller children were seated in the front row.* **2.** to have seats for: *The arena seats a thousand people.* **seating. seated.**

seat belt a strong strap that holds a person in the seat of a car or airplane in case of a bump or crash.

seaway (sē′ wā′) *n.* a passage to the sea: *The St. Lawrence Seaway leads from the Great Lakes to the Atlantic Ocean. pl.* **seaways.**

seaweed (sē′ wēd′) *n.* a green or brown plant that grows in the sea or ocean.

secluded (si klūd′ id) *adj.* isolated; shut off from others; private: *a secluded beach.*

second (sek′ ənd) *n.* **1.** a very small measure of time: s is the symbol: *There are sixty seconds in a minute.* **2.** a person or thing next after the first or the best: *He is the second person to get a perfect score.* —*adj.* being next after the first or the best: *She came in second place in the gymnastics competition.*

secondary (sek′ ən der′ ē) *adj.* **1.** coming second: *secondary school.* **2.** of less importance: *The coach tells us that first we should enjoy playing the game; winning is secondary.*

secondary school a school attended after elementary, middle, or junior high school.

second-hand (sek′ ənd hand′) *adj.* used by someone else before you: *My parents bought a second-hand computer.*

secrecy (sē′ krə sē) *n.* the condition of being secret: *Secrecy was needed so that our parents would not learn about their surprise anniversary party.*

secret (sē′ krit) *n.* some news that you keep to yourself or just one or two friends: *Gene shared the secret with his brother.* —*adj.* known to only a few: *a secret cave.* —**secretly** *adv.*

secretary (sek′ rə ter′ ē) *n.* a person who writes letters and keeps records for another person, a company, or a club. *pl.* **secretaries.**

secretive (sē′ krə tiv) *adj.* not open; hiding your thoughts or actions: *What are they up to? Why are they being so secretive?* —**secretively** *adv.*

section (sek′ shən) *n.* a part of a whole: *A section of the roof is leaking.*

secure (si kyūr′) *adj.* **1.** safe; protected: *My money is secure in the bank.* **2.** sure; confident: *I don't feel secure that I know my* *part in the play yet.* **3.** firmly fastened: *Tie the box with a secure knot.* (*opp.* **insecure.**) —**securely** *adv.*

security (si kyūr′ ə tē) *n.* safety; protection: *The guards provided security for the rock star.*

see (sē) *v.* **1.** to look at with the eyes; to view with the aid of light: *In a completely dark room, you cannot see.* **2.** to understand: *I see what you mean.* **3.** to meet with: *We saw our grandparents yesterday.* **seeing. saw.** They have **seen.**

seed (sēd) *n.* the part of a plant from which a new plant can grow; a grain, nut, or bean.

seedling (sēd′ ling) *n.* a young plant grown from a seed.

seeing-eye dog a dog trained to guide a blind person.

seek (sēk) *v.* to look for; to search for: *The police are seeking two people who committed the robbery.* **seeking. sought** (sot).

seem (sēm) *v.* to look like; to appear to be: *The baby seems to be asleep; her eyes are closed and she is breathing peacefully.* **seeming. seemed.**

seen (sēn) see **see.**

seep (sēp) *v.* to trickle or leak: *Water is seeping into the basement from cracks in the walls.* **seeping. seeped.**

seesaw (sē′ so′) *n.* a long board that is set on a support in the middle, used by children for play: *One child sits on each end of a seesaw, making it go up and down.*

seesaw

segment (seg′ mənt) *n.* one of the parts or sections into which something has been divided.

seize (sēz) *v.* **1.** to take hold of suddenly; to grab: *She seized the cup before it smashed on the floor.* **2.** to capture: *The police seized the wanted criminals.* **seizing. seized.**

seldom (sel′ dəm) *adv.* rarely; not often: *We seldom see my uncle because he lives in another city.*

select (si lekt′) *v.* to choose carefully: *Yoshiko selected two large, ripe pears at the grocery store.* **selecting. selected.**

selection (si lek′ shən) *n.* **1.** a choice: *Which selection of music are you playing?* **2.** a collection of things from which to choose: *There is a good selection of books in the library.*

self– is a prefix that means "of yourself" or "by yourself." If you feel "self-conscious," you are very aware of yourself and how you may appear to others. "Self-esteem" is a good feeling about yourself.

self-confident (self′ kon′ fə dənt) *adj.* feeling sure of yourself and your abilities; not embarrassed. —**self-confidently** *adv.*

self-conscious (self′ kon′ shəs) *adj.* shy or embarrassed about yourself in front of other people; worrying what others think of you: *He feels self-conscious in front of strangers and doesn't talk very much.* —**self-consciously** *adv.*

self-defence, self-defense (self′ di fens′) *n.* the act of defending yourself against an attacker: *Karate is a form of self-defence.*

self-employed (self′ em ploid′) *adj.* working for yourself, not for someone else: *My dad is a self-employed carpenter.*

self-esteem (self′ əs tēm′) *n.* confidence in yourself.

selfish (sel′ fish) *adj.* thinking and caring only about yourself: *A selfish person often doesn't like to share something he or she has with other people.* (*opp.* **unselfish.**) —**selfishly** *adv.*

selfless (self′ lis) *adj.* thinking more of others than of yourself; not selfish. —**selflessly** *adv.*

self-service (self′ sûr′ vis) *adj.* having customers serve themselves: *A self-service restaurant has no waiters.*

sell (sel) *v.* to hand over something for sale in return for money. **selling. sold.**

semester (sə mes′ tər) *n.* a long division of a school year, usually half the year: *the fall semester; the spring semester.*

semi– is a prefix meaning **1.** "half." A "semicircle" is half of a circle. **2.** "partly" or "almost." "Semi-finals" are "almost final" games.

semicircle (sem′ ē sûr′ kəl) *n.* a half-circle.

semicolon (sem′ ē kō′ lən) *n.* a punctuation mark (;) that separates the parts of a long complicated sentence or list: *Gino raised his hand and looked toward the teacher; he knew the answer to the question.*

semi-finals (sem′ ē fī′ nəlz) *n. pl.* games that are played to decide who plays in the finals.

Senate (sen′ it) *n.* one of the two parts of the Canadian Parliament; the other part is the House of Commons: *Members of the Senate are appointed by the Governor General.*

Senator (sen′ ə tər) *n.* a member of the Senate.

send (send) *v.* **1.** to make something or someone go somewhere: *to send a letter by mail.* **2.** to ask for something or someone to come to you: *Send for help—the house is on fire!* **sending. sent.**

senior (sēn′ yər) *n.* **1.** an older person: *I am older than Vanessa, so I am her senior.* **2.** an adult who is 65 years old or more. —*adj.* **1.** older **2.** more experienced or at a higher level: *The youngest age allowed in the senior skating tournament is 16.*

sensation (sen sā′ shən) *n.* **1.** a feeling: *I had a sensation of cold when I walked into the room.* **2.** great excitement: *Our team's unexpected win caused a sensation.*

sensational (sen sā′ shən əl) *adj.* exciting: *a sensational story in the newspaper.*

sense (sens) *n.* **1.** the wisdom to know what is best to say or do: *She has a lot of common sense.* **2.** meaning: *Explain the sense of this word.* **3.** one of the five ways we get to know the world: *The five senses are sight, hearing, touch, smell, and taste.* —*v.* to feel; to be aware: *I sense that you are angry.* **sensing. sensed.**

sensible (sen′ sə bəl) *adj.* full of good sense: *It is sensible to count your change after buying something.* —**sensibly** *adv.*

sensitive (sen′ sə tiv) *adj.* **1.** sensing intensely: *A dog's hearing is much more sensitive than a human's.* **2.** quick to feel: *An artist is very sensitive to colours and shapes.* **3.** easily upset or hurt: *My cousin is a very sensitive child. He cries if anyone speaks roughly to him.* (*opp.* **insensitive.**) —**sensitively** *adv.*

sensitivity (sen′ sə tiv′ ə tē) *n.* the quality of being careful not to upset the feelings of others: *The doctor showed great sensitivity when she talked to the parents of the child in the hospital.*

sent (sent) see **send**.

sentence (sen′ təns) *n.* **1.** a group of words that make a complete statement or thought: *A sentence starts with a capital letter and ends with a period, question mark, or exclamation mark.* **2.** a punishment given in a court of law: *The thief was given a sentence of two years in prison.* —*v.* to punish someone with a sentence: *The judge sentenced the criminal to fourteen years in prison.* **sentencing. sentenced.**

sentimental (sen′ tə men′ təl) *adj.* showing or having tender and gentle feelings. —**sentimentally** *adv.*

separate (sep′ ə rit) *adj.* apart from others; not together: *This pile of books is separate from that pile.* —**separately** *adv.*

separate (sep′ ə rāt′) *v.* to divide; to set apart: *We separated the ripe tomatoes from the unripe ones.* **separating. separated.**

separation (sep′ ə rā′ shən) *n.* **1.** a division. **2.** a time apart.

September (sep tem′ bər) *n.* the ninth month of the year.

sequel (sē′ kwəl) *n.* a play, movie, or book that follows another and includes many of the same characters.

sequence (sē′ kwəns) *n.* a number of things happening one after the other: *Monday, Tuesday, and Wednesday follow each other in sequence.*

sequin (sē′ kwin) *n.* a small, sparkly disk sewn onto clothes as decoration: *a gown covered in sequins.*

serene (sə rēn′) *adj.* calm and peaceful: *We walked along the coast, enjoying the sunset and the serene waters of the bay.* —**serenely** *adv.*

sergeant (sär′ jənt) *n.* **1.** a police officer in rank above a constable. **2.** in the army, a soldier who is next in rank above a corporal.

series (sēr′ ēz) *n.* a number of similar things coming one after the other: *We started the hockey season with a series of winning games. pl.* **series.**

serious (sēr′ ē əs) *adj.* **1.** important and needing attention: *We were given a serious warning about running across busy streets.* **2.** very bad: *She had a serious illness.* —**seriously** *adv.*

sermon (sûr′ mən) *n.* a public talk on religious matters.

serpent (sûr′ pənt) *n.* a large snake.

servant (sûr′ vənt) *n.* a person who is paid to work in someone else's house.

serve (sûrv) *n.* in tennis and other games, the hitting of the ball to put it into play: *It's your serve.* —*v.* **1.** to work for someone or something: *A police officer serves the people.* **2.** to prepare and offer food to other people. **3.** in tennis and other games, to put a ball into play. **serving. served.**

service (sûr′ vis) *n.* **1.** a helpful act: *My mother did us a service by driving us to school, on her way to work.* **2.** duty performed in a country's armed forces. **3.** a religious meeting or ceremony. —*v.* to fix or to make ready: *The mechanic serviced our car.* **servicing. serviced.**

service station a place where gasoline is sold and cars are repaired.

serviette (sûr′ vē et′) *n.* a piece of soft paper or cloth, used to protect clothes and to wipe the mouth and hands while eating.

serving (sûr′ ving) *n.* a helping of food.

session (sesh′ ən) *n.* a period for an activity or a meeting: *a recording session.*

set (set) *n.* **1.** a group of things that go together: *a set of golf clubs.* **2.** a machine for receiving TV signals: *a TV set.* **3.** in mathematics, a group of numbers between two brackets: *(1, 2, 3, 4) is a set of numbers.* **4.** a place where a movie or TV show is filmed. —*v.* **1.** to put things in place: *Please set the table for breakfast.* **2.** (for the sun) to go down in the evening: *When does the sun set tonight?* **3.** to begin: *We set out on our trip in the morning.* **4.** to become hard or firm: *The jelly has not set.* **setting. set.**

set aside **1.** to put to one side. **2.** to save for later use: *Jenna set aside two evenings to work on her project.*

set off **1.** to begin a trip: *We set off for a trip through the Rockies.* **2.** to cause something to burn or explode: *to set off a firecracker.*

set out to start: *I set out to go to the store, but ended up at the park instead.*

setback (set′ bak′) *n.* something that halts or reverses your plans: *Our team was improving, but we suffered a setback when our best player was injured.*

setter (set′ ər) *n.* one of several types of dog that can be trained to use its sense of smell for hunting game.

setting (set′ ing) *n.* the place and time in which a story, play, or movie is set: *A small French-Canadian town in the 1950s is the setting for the story.*

settle (set′ əl) *v.* **1.** to get comfortable and stay in one place: *Grandma settled in her chair and went to sleep.* **2.** to decide something: *We settled on having a dog.* **3.** to make a new home: *People from many countries have settled in Canada.* **settling. settled.**

settle down to become calm and quiet: *The audience settled down when the pianist walked on stage.*

settler (set′ lər) *n.* a person who makes a home in a new area: *The first European settlers in Canada experienced many difficulties.*

seven (sev′ ən) *n., adj.* one more than six: 7.

seventeen (sev′ ən tēn′) *n., adj.* ten more than seven: 17.

seventy (sev′ ən tē) *n., adj.* ten times seven: 70.

several (sev′ ər əl *or* sev′ rəl) *adj.* more than two or three, but not many; a few.

severe (sə vēr′) *adj.* harsh; serious: *It was a severe winter. I have a severe cold.* —**severely** *adv.*

sew (sō) *v.* to stitch with a needle and thread. **sewing. sewed.** I have **sewn** or **sewed.**

sewage (sū′ ij) *n.* waste matter that is carried off by sewers and drains.

sewer (sū′ ər) *n.* an underground drain pipe that carries away water and waste matter from buildings.

sewer (sō′ ər) *n.* a person who sews.

sewing machine a machine used for sewing clothes and other things.

sewn (sōn) see **sew**.

sex (seks) *n.* **1.** the condition of being male or female: *A girl belongs to the female sex. A boy belongs to the male sex.* **2.** the physical act by which humans and animals reproduce. *pl.* **sexes.**

shabby (shab′ ē) *adj.* old and worn: *shabby clothes; shabbier clothes; the shabbiest clothes in the closet.*

shack (shak) *n.* a roughly built wooden hut.

shade (shād) *n.* **1.** a dark area sheltered from sunlight: *We sat in the shade of a large tree.* **2.** the lightness or darkness of a colour: *I used several different shades of blue in my painting of the sea.* **3.** something that partly or completely blocks out strong light: *a window shade; a lamp shade.* —**shady** *adj.*

shadow (shad′ ō) *n.* a patch of darkness caused by something standing in the way of a light.

shady (shā′ dē) *adj.* **1.** covered by shade: *a shady yard; a shadier yard; the shadiest yard on the street.* **2.** providing shade: *a shady tree.* **3.** dishonest: *a shady character in a story.*

shaft (shaft) *n.* **1.** a long handle, as on a rake or a golf club. **2.** a long passage leading down into a mine. **3.** a beam: *a shaft of sunlight.*

shaggy (shag′ ē) *adj.* having long, thick, rough hair: *a shaggy dog; a shaggier dog; the shaggiest one in the kennel.*

shake (shāk) *n.* **1.** the act of shaking: *a handshake.* **2.** a drink made by shaking the ingredients: *a milkshake.* —*v.* **1.** to move from side to side or up and down in quick, short movements: *The fierce wind made all the trees shake.* **2.** to tremble: *I am shaking with cold.* **3.** to greet someone by clasping hands: *He shook my hand.* **shaking. shook.** I have **shaken.**

shaky (shā′ kē) *adj.* **1.** not steady or sturdy: *a shaky chair; a shakier chair; the shakiest chair of them all.* **2.** shaking. **3.** not able to be trusted: *a shaky business deal.*

shall (shal *or* shəl) *v.* a helping (auxiliary) verb placed before another verb to show: **1.** a future action or event: *You shall go to school tomorrow.* **2.** an intention: *I shall join the club.* **3.** a question, asking what to do: *Shall we eat? Where shall we go?*

shallow (shal′ ō) *adj.* not deep.

shamble (sham′ bəl) *v.* to walk slowly while dragging your feet; to shuffle. **shambling. shambled.** he **shambles.**

shame (shām) *n.* **1.** a feeling of being sorry and embarrassed because you have done something wrong: *He felt shame because he had not helped his friend.* **2.** something to feel sorry about: *What a shame he lost his job!*

shameful (shām′ ful) *adj.* deserving shame: *Your behaviour was shameful.* —**shamefully** *adv.*

shampoo (sham pü′) *n.* a liquid soap for washing hair or rugs. *pl.* **shampoos.** —*v.* to wash your hair or a rug. **shampooing. shampooed.**

shamrock (sham′ rok) *n.* a plant with small, bright green leaves that are in three parts.

shape (shāp) *n.* **1.** the outline or form of anything: *A baseball field has a diamond shape.* **2.** condition: *The swimmer is in good shape.* —*v.* to form or make: *She shaped the clay into a beautiful piece of sculpture.* **shaping. shaped.**

shapeless (shāp′ lis) *adj.* without a definite form or shape. —**shapelessly** *adv.*

share (sher) *n.* a part or portion given to one person: *We each had an equal share of the blueberries.* —*v.* **1.** to divide out: *We shared the cake.* **2.** to use together: *The boys shared a bedroom.* **sharing. shared.**

shark (shärk) *n.* a large ocean fish that has a large jaw and many sharp teeth: *Most sharks eat flesh or other animal matter.*

shark

sharp (shärp) *adj.* **1.** with an edge or point that can easily make a cut: *a sharp knife.* **2.** with a point: *a sharp pencil.* **3.** sudden: *a sharp bend in the road.* **4.** quick to understand or notice something; keen: *sharp eyes.* **5.** sour or strong tasting: *sharp cheese.* **6.** harsh; cutting: *Her answer to my silly question was sharp.* —**sharply** *adv.*

sharpen (shär′ pən) *v.* to make sharp: *I sharpened my pencil in the morning.* **sharpening. sharpened.**

shatter (shat′ ər) *v.* to break suddenly into small pieces; to smash: *The ball shattered the window.* **shattering. shattered.**

shave (shāv) *n.* **1.** the cutting off of hair with a razor: *Dad has a shave every morning.* **2.** a narrow escape: *We had a close shave when the car started to skid.* —*v.* to cut off hair with a razor. **shaving. shaved.**

shaver (shā′ vər) *n.* an electric razor.

shawl (shol) *n.* a piece of cloth worn around the shoulders.

she (shē) *pron.* the female person or animal being talked about. **She** is used as the subject of a verb: *Katya said that she would make sandwiches for the picnic.*

sheaf (shēf) *n.* **1.** a bundle of cut stalks of wheat or other cereal plants after harvesting. **2.** any bundle of alike things: *a sheaf of paper.* *pl.* **sheaves.**

shear (shēr) *v.* to cut with shears: *The farmer sheared the sheep's wool.* **shearing. sheared.** I have **shorn** or **sheared.**

shears (shērz) *n. pl.* **1.** a pair of large, heavy scissors for trimming a hedge. **2.** an electric cutting tool for shearing hair or sheep.

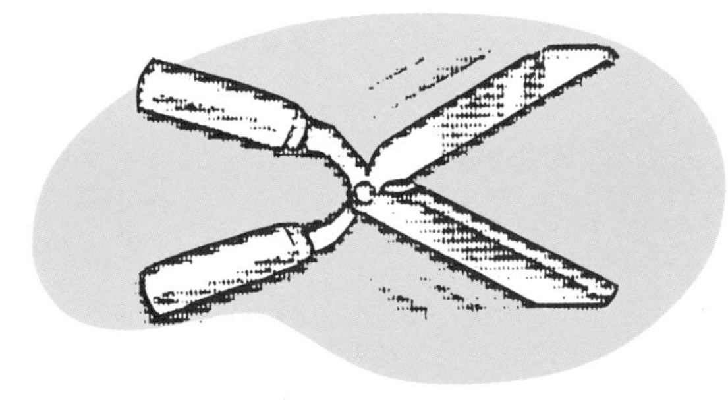

shears

shed (shed) *n.* a hut for storing tools or materials: *a garden shed.* —*v.* **1.** to let fall: *to shed tears.* **2.** to lose or drop: *Many trees shed their leaves in the fall.* **shedding. shed.**

she'd (shēd) a contraction (short form) of **she had** or **she would.**

sheen (shēn) *n.* shininess; brightness.

sheep (shēp) *n.* a mammal that has a thick, usually white, coat of wool: *Sheep are raised for wool and meat. pl.* **sheep.**

sheer (shēr) *adj.* **1.** very thin, allowing you to see partly through: *sheer curtains.* **2.** steep: *There is a sheer drop from the edge of the cliff.*

sheet (shēt) *n.* **1.** a large piece of thin cloth used to cover a bed. **2.** a single piece of paper. **3.** a large, flat piece of anything: *a sheet of ice.*

shelf (shelf) *n.* a horizontal board fastened to a wall, in a cupboard, and so on for putting things on. *pl.* **shelves.**

shell (shel) *n.* **1.** a thin, hard covering: *Eggs, nuts, beetles, and many sea animals have shells.* **2.** a large bullet that explodes when it hits something. —*v.* to take out of a shell: *We shelled all the nuts.* **shelling. shelled.**

she'll (shēl) a contraction (short form) of **she will.**

shellfish (shel′ fish′) *n.* a water animal that has a shell: *Oysters, crabs, and lobsters are shellfish. pl.* **shellfish.**

shelter (shel′ tər) *n.* a place that gives protection or cover: *When it started to rain, we found shelter in an old shed.* —*v.* to protect; to cover: *The tent sheltered us from the rain.* **sheltering. sheltered.**

shelves (shelvz) see **shelf.**

shepherd (shep′ ərd) *n.* a person who looks after sheep.

sherbet (shür′ bət) *n.* a frozen dessert made of fruit juice and sugar.

sheriff (sher′ if) *n.* in Canada, a law officer who carries out certain orders of the court.

she's (shēz) a contraction (short form) of **she is** or **she has.**

shield (shēld) *n.* **1.** a piece of armour, like a large, metal sheet, once carried by knights and soldiers as protection in battle. **2.** anything that protects: *An umbrella is a shield against the rain.* —*v.* to protect. **shielding. shielded.**

shift (shift) *n.* **1.** a slight movement or change: *a shift in the wind.* **2.** a group of workers, or the time that they work: *My mother is on the night shift at the factory.* —*v.* to make a shift: *to shift in your seat.* **shifting. shifted.**

shimmer (shim′ ər) *v.* to shine with a faint, gleaming light: *The lake shimmered in the moonlight.* **shimmering. shimmered.**

shin (shin) *n.* the front of your leg between the knee and the ankle.

shine (shīn) *n.* a brightness: *I gave the car a brilliant shine with car wax.* —*v.* **1.** to give out light: *The light shone in my eyes.* **shining. shone.** **2.** to polish: *She shined her shoes.* **shining. shined.** —**shiny** *adj.*

shingle (shing′ gəl) *n.* **1.** a piece of wood or other material used to cover a roof. **2.** a small sign, sometimes hung outside a doctor's or lawyer's office.

shiny (shī′ nē) *adj.* bright; gleaming: *a shiny floor; a shinier floor; the shiniest floor in the house.*

ship (ship) *n.* **1.** a large boat. **2.** an airplane or spaceship. —*v.* to send by ship, bus, train, or plane: *We shipped presents to my brother in Japan.* **shipping. shipped.**

—**ship** is a suffix used to form words that mean "a condition of": "friendship" is the condition of being a friend. Some other words with this suffix are "hardship" and "ownership."

shipment (ship′ mənt) *n.* goods sent at one time to a place or person.

shipwreck (ship′ rek′) *n.* a ship that is damaged or wrecked; the destruction or loss of a ship.

shirt (shůrt) *n.* a piece of clothing for the upper body: *A dress shirt has a collar and sleeves, and it buttons up at the front. A casual shirt, like a T-shirt, does not have buttons and is pulled over the head.*

shiver (shiv′ ər) *n.* a shaking motion caused by fear or cold. —*v.* to shake with fear or cold: *We shivered in the cold house.* **shivering. shivered.**

shoal (shōl) *n.* **1.** a shallow spot in a river, ocean, or lake: *Fishing is usually good near a shoal.* **2.** a large number; a crowd: *A shoal of dolphins swam past our boat.*

shock (shok) *n.* **1.** a sudden fright or surprise: *The loud bang gave me a great shock.* **2.** a sharp feeling caused by electricity: *Olga felt a shock when she touched a door handle after rubbing her feet on the carpet.* —*v.* to cause a sudden fright or surprise: *The news that there was a fire on our street while I was on holiday shocked me.* **shocking. shocked.**

shoe (shū) *n.* **1.** an outer covering for your foot, usually made with a thick sole and an upper part of cloth or leather. **2.** a u-shaped piece of metal nailed to a horse's hoof to protect it.

shoelace (shū′ lās′) *n.* the cord or string that ties up a shoe.

shone (shon) see **shine**.

shook (shůk) see **shake**.

shoot (shūt) *n.* a new or young plant. —*v.* **1.** to aim an object at a target: *to shoot a bullet; to shoot a basketball.* **2.** to move or cause to move fast: *to shoot a puck toward the goal.* **3.** to come up from the ground; to grow: *The corn is shooting up from the soil.* **shooting. shot.**

shooting star a meteor that looks like a star shooting through the sky.

shop (shop) *n.* a building where things are sold or repaired. —*v.* to buy from stores. **shopping. shopped.**

shoplift (shop′ lift′) *v.* to steal something secretly from a store: *Many stores have hidden cameras to see if anyone is shoplifting.* **shoplifting. shoplifted.**

shopping centre a group of many stores in one place, often with a parking lot.

shore (shȯr) *n.* land at the edge of an ocean, lake, or large river.

shorn (shȯrn) see **shear**.

short (shȯrt) *adj.* **1.** not measuring much from end to end; not long: *a short coat; a short trip.* **2.** not tall: *I am short for my age.* **3.** having too little of something: *She is short of money today.*

shortage (shȯr′ tij) *n.* an amount that is not enough: *There was a shortage of coins at the bank.*

shortcut (shȯrt′ kut′) *n.* a quicker way of getting somewhere or doing something.

shorten (shȯr′ tən) *v.* to make shorter: *My skirt needs to be shortened.* **shortening. shortened.**

shortly (shôrt′ lē) *adv.* soon; in a little while: *The game will begin shortly.*

shorts (shôrts) *n. pl.* short pants.

shortstop (shôrt′ stop′) *n.* the baseball player whose position is between second and third base.

shot (shot) *n.* **1.** the firing of a gun: *I heard a loud shot.* **2.** an aimed throw or stroke in some games: *We took some practice shots before the game.* **3.** an injection of medicine with a needle: *a flu shot.* **4.** a try: *I'll give it a shot.* —*v.* see **shoot**.

shotgun (shot′gun′) a rifle.

should (shu̇d) *v.* a helping (auxiliary) verb placed before another verb to mean "have a duty" or "ought to": *I should be doing my work, but I'm not.*

shoulder (shōl′ dər) *n.* **1.** the part of your body between the neck and the arm. **2.** the side of a road, often unpaved, that is not travelled on.

shouldn't (shu̇d′ ənt) a short form (contraction) of **should not**.

shout (showt) *n.* a loud call or cry: *a shout of joy.* —*v.* to call loudly, or to talk with your voice raised. **shouting. shouted.**

shove (shuv) *n.* a hard, rough push: *Please give the boat a shove into the lake.* —*v.* to push hard and roughly: *We shoved the chairs to one side to make room for a dance floor.* **shoving. shoved.**

shovel (shuv′ əl) *n.* a tool with a long handle and a broad, curved blade, used for digging snow or earth. —*v.* to use a shovel: *We shovelled the snow off the driveway.* **shovelling. shovelled.**

show (shō) *n.* a performance, program, or display: *a TV show; an art show.* —*v.* **1.** to let something be seen; to display: *Show me your new shoes.* **2.** to guide or lead: *Lena showed the way.* **3.** to explain using words or actions: *Show me how to do it.* **showing. showed.** I have **shown.**

show off to draw attention to yourself: *She likes to show off how rich her family is by wearing a lot of expensive jewellery.*

shower (show′ ər) *n.* **1.** a gentle fall of rain. **2.** a wash of your body under a spray of water. **3.** a party where gifts are brought in honour of someone: *a baby shower.* —*v.* to wash your body under a spray of water. **showering. showered.**

shown (shōn) see **show**.

show-off a person who draws attention to himself or herself in a showy way.

shrank (shrangk) see **shrink**.

shred (shred) *n.* a tiny strip or scrap of something. —*v.* to cut into small strips: *Please shred the cabbage and the carrots for the salad.* **shredding. shredded** or **shred.**

shrewd (shrūd) *adj.* clever in judging a person's character or a situation: *She has a shrewd sense of knowing which people she can trust.* —**shrewdly** *adv.*

shriek (shrēk) *n.* a very high scream. —*v.* to give a shriek: *to shriek with pain; to shriek with laughter.* **shrieking. shrieked.**

shrill (shril) *adj.* sounding very high and loud: *I was woken up very early by the shrill cry of a bird.* —**shrilly** *adv.*

shrimp (shrimp) *n.* a small, greyish, edible shellfish that turns pink when cooked. *pl.* **shrimp.**

shrimp

shrine (shrīn) *n.* a religious place associated with a holy person.

shrink (shringk) *v.* to become smaller: *Some kinds of cloth shrink when washed in hot water.* **shrinking. shrank.** it has **shrunk.**

shrivel (shriv′ əl) *v.* to dry up and wrinkle or curl up: *I forgot to water the plant, and now its leaves have shrivelled up.* **shrivelling. shrivelled.**

shrub (shrub) *n.* a bush.

shrug (shrug) *n.* an up and down movement of your shoulders. —*v.* to move your shoulders quickly up and then down, in a way that means "I don't know" or "I don't care." **shrugging. shrugged.**

shrunk (shrungk) see **shrink**.

shudder (shud′ ər) *n.* a sudden shiver caused by fear or cold. —*v.* to shiver suddenly. **shuddering. shuddered.**

shuffle (shuf′ əl) *v.* **1.** to mix up cards or other things. **2.** to walk slowly without lifting your feet; to drag your feet. **shuffling. shuffled.**

shut (shut) *adj.* closed: *The window was locked shut.* —*v.* to move a door or lid to close an opening: *Please shut the gate.* **shutting. shut.**

shut out **1.** to leave out: *My sister shut us out of her plans, saying we were too young.* **2.** in baseball and other sports, to prevent the other team from scoring.

shut up an impolite way of saying "Be quiet!"

shutter (shut′ ər) *n.* **1.** a movable wooden cover for a window. **2.** the part of a camera that opens and closes in front of the roll of film, so that a photo can be taken.

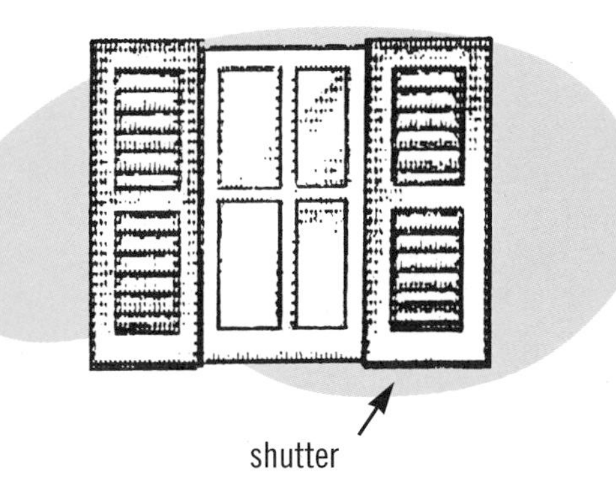

shuttle (shut′ əl) *n.* a vehicle designed to go back and forth: *a space shuttle.*

shy (shī) *adj.* afraid to speak to or to meet people; timid. —**shyly** *adv.*

sick (sik) *adj.* **1.** ill; not well. **2.** wanting to vomit. **3.** tired; disgusted: *I'm sick of hearing about their trip!* —**sickly** *adv.*

sicken (sik′ ən) *v.* to become or cause to become sick or upset: *We were sickened by the pictures of the plane crash.* **sickening. sickened.**

sickness (sik′ nis) *n.* illness; poor health: *There has been a lot of sickness in the class.* *pl.* **sicknesses.**

side (sīd) *n.* **1.** a line or surface that forms part of the boundary around something: *A cube has six sides.* **2.** a surface that is not the front, back, top, or bottom: *Put your bike by the side of the house.* **3.** the part or edge on the left or right, top or bottom: *I like to sleep mainly on my left side. The school is on the north side of the street.* **4.** a team of players: *Which side will win?* **5.** an opinion: *Whose side of the argument do you agree with?*

sideburns (sīd′ bûrnz) *n. pl.* hair grown down the sides of the face, in front of the ears.

sidewalk (sīd′ wok′) *n.* a path for walking on at the side of a street: *Sidewalks are usually paved.*

sideways (sīd′ wāz′) *adv.* **1.** to one side: *Don't look backward or forward; look sideways.* **2.** with one side to the front: *The door is almost shut, but I can squeeze through the opening sideways.*

sidle (sīd′ əl) *v.* to move sideways, especially in a shy or secretive way: *The lonely boy sidled up to a group of popular students.*

siege (sēj) *n.* the surrounding of a town or fort in order to stop supplies from getting in and to force the people to surrender.

sieve (siv) *n.* a fine metal or plastic net that lets only liquids and tiny pieces pass through: *Shaking flour through a sieve removes the lumps.*

sift (sift) *v.* to use a sieve to separate a powder from unwanted lumps or stones. **sifting. sifted.**

sigh (sī) *n.* a deep, long breath out to show that you are tired, unhappy, relieved, and so on. —*v.* to give a sigh. **sighing. sighed.**

sight (sīt) *n.* **1.** one of the five senses—the ability to see. **2.** something that is seen: *The sunset was a wonderful sight.*

sign (sīn) *n.* **1.** a board with words or symbols on it to give information: *a stop sign.* **2.** a body gesture that communicates: *When she nodded her head, it was a sign to start singing.* **3.** anything that points out or represents something else; a symbol: *Is your sneeze a sign of a cold?* —*v.* **1.** to write your name. **2.** to communicate, using hand or body gestures. **signing. signed.**

signal (sig′ nəl) *n.* a message sent by movement, sound, or light: *The police officer gave a signal for the traffic to stop.* —*v.* to send a signal: *She signalled for the race to begin by blowing a whistle.* **signalling. signalled.**

signature (sig′ nə chər) *n.* your name written by yourself.

significance (sig nif′ ə kəns) *n.* the importance or meaning of something: *What is the significance of that story?*

significant (sig nif′ ə kənt) *adj.* having special meaning or importance: *A significant day in the baby's life was when she took her first step.* —**significantly** *adv.*

silence (sī′ ləns) *n.* the absence of sound.

silent (sī′ lənt) *adj.* not making any sound. —**silently** *adv.*

silhouette (sil′ ū et′) *n.* a shadow or outline visible against a lighter background: *We saw the silhouette of a man on the hill.*

silk (silk) *n.* a shiny, smooth cloth made from the cocoons of silkworms.

silky (sil′ kē) *adj.* soft or smooth like silk: *a silky shirt; a silkier shirt; the silkiest shirt in the store.*

sill (sil) *n.* a ledge below a window or door.

silly (sil′ ē) *adj.* not sensible; foolish: *a silly joke; a sillier joke; the silliest joke told.*

silo (sī′ lō) *n.* a tall, round tower that is used to store farm crops. *pl.* **silos.**

silt (silt) *n.* sand or other bits of earth, carried by water to the bottom of a lake, a river, or an ocean.

silver (sil′ vər) *n.* **1.** a precious, shiny, white-grey metal, used for jewellery, cutlery, coins, and so on. **2.** the colour of silver. —*adj.* having this colour.

similar (sim′ ə lər) *adj.* nearly the same; alike: *The sisters look similar, except one has curly hair and the other has straight hair.* —**similarly** *adv.*

similarity (sim′ ə ler′ ə tē) *n.* a resemblance; a likeness: *What are the similarities between a rabbit and a hare?* *pl.* **similarities.**

simile (sim′ ē lē) *n.* a comparison that uses the word "like" or "as."

Some **similes** are: "This bread is hard as a rock"; "The clouds are like fat sheep"; "I'm busy as a bee." Can you think of some more?

simmer (sim′ ər) *v.* to cook at a heat that is just less than boiling. **simmering. simmered.**

simple (sim′ pəl) *adj.* **1.** easy: *These math problems are very simple.* **2.** plain: *This design is very simple.*

simply (sim′ plē) *adv.* **1.** in a simple way. **2.** just; only: *I simply wanted to help.* **3.** absolutely: *I feel simply wonderful today.*

simultaneously (sī′ məl tā′ nē əs lē) *adv.* at the same time: *It's very difficult to watch TV and listen to the radio simultaneously.*

sin (sin) *n.* a wrong or bad deed: *It is a sin to steal.* —*v.* to do wrong: *He sinned when he stole the coat.* **sinning. sinned.**

since (sins) *adv.* from a past time until now: *I have been away since Monday.* —*conj.* because: *Since you ask, I will tell you the secret.*

ever since since the time that: *I have liked you ever since I first met you.*

sincere (sin sēr′) *adj.* honest and true: *Antonio is a sincere boy. He always means what he says.* (*opp.* **insincere.**)

sincerely (sin sēr′ lē) *adv.* truly: *Maria ended her letter, "Sincerely yours."*

sincerity (sin ser′ ə tē) *n.* honesty; the condition of meaning what you do and say.

sinful (sin′ fu̇l) *adj.* full of sin; wicked. —**sinfully** *adv.*

sing (sing) *v.* to make music with your voice, using sounds and words. **singing. sang.** I have **sung.**

singe (sinj) *v.* to burn slightly, especially near the ends: *Don't hold the match so close to your hair—you may singe it.* **singeing. singed.**

singer (sing′ ər) *n.* a person who sings.

single (sing′ gəl) *adj.* **1.** one only: *A single cookie was left in the bag.* **2.** unmarried: *a single woman or man.* **3.** for one only: *a single bed.* —*v.* (used with **out**) to pick out from others: *The coach singled me out as the best catcher.* **singling. singled.**

single file a single line of people: *The students walked into the school in single file.*

single-handed (sing′ gəl han′ did) *adj.* by yourself; without help: *She built that boat single-handed.*

singular (sing′ gyə lər) *adj.* referring to one only: *"Dog" is a singular noun; "dogs" is plural.*

sink (singk) *n.* a basin with a tap, used for washing. —*v.* to go under water: *The ship hit an iceberg and sank.* **sinking. sank.** it has **sunk.**

sip (sip) *n.* a small swallow: *Amun took a sip of water.* —*v.* to drink in small amounts: *Grandma sips her tea.* **sipping. sipped.**

Sir (sûr) *n.* **1.** a title given by a king or queen: *Sir John A. Macdonald was Canada's first prime minister.* **2. sir** a polite name to use when speaking to a man: *May I help you off with your coat, sir?*

siren (sī′ rən) *n.* an alarm on a vehicle that makes a loud, wailing noise as a warning: *a siren on a police car or ambulance.*

sister (sis′ tər) *n.* a woman or girl who has the same parents as another person.

sister-in-law (sis′ tər in lo′) the sister of a husband or the wife of a brother. *pl.* **sisters-in-law.**

sit (sit) *v.* to rest on your bottom on a chair or other surface. **sitting. sat.**

site (sīt) *n.* the place where something was built or will be built; the location or scene of something.

sitter (sit′ ər) *n.* a babysitter.

situation (sich′ ū a′ shən) *n.* a state or condition at a certain time: *It was a difficult situation when I played against my sister in hockey.*

six (siks) *n., adj.* one more than five: 6.

sixteen (siks′ tēn′) *n., adj.* ten more than six: 16.

sixty (siks′ tē) *n., adj.* ten times six: 60.

size (sīz) *n.* the amount of space a thing fills up; how large or small a thing is: *What size shoe do you wear?*

sizzle (siz′ əl) *n.* the hissing noise produced by liquid or food hitting a hot metal surface. —*v.* to make such a noise: *The bacon sizzled in the frying pan.* **sizzling. sizzled.**

skate (skāt) *n.* **1.** a boot with a metal blade fastened at the bottom, used to glide on ice. **2.** a similar shoe that has wheels for rolling over the ground. —*v.* to glide along on skates. **skating. skated.**

skateboard (skāt′ bȯrd′) *n.* a narrow board with wheels on the bottom, which is used for moving over the ground while you balance on it. —*v.* to ride a skateboard. **skateboarding. skateboarded.**

skater (skā′ tər) *n.* a person who skates.

skeleton (skel′ ə tən) *n.* the set of bones in a body.

sketch (skech) *n.* a quick drawing. *pl.* **sketches.** —*v.* to make a quick drawing. **sketching. sketched.**

ski (skē) *n.* one of two long, narrow pieces of wood, metal, or plastic that curve up at the front: *Skis are used for downhill skiing, cross-country skiing, or waterskiing. pl.* **skis.** —*v.* to travel on skis: *I skied all the way down the hill.* **skiing. skied.** she **skis.**

skid (skid) *n.* a sudden, uncontrolled slide on something slippery or very smooth. —*v.* to slip on a wet or icy surface. **skidding. skidded.**

skier (skē′ yər) *n.* a person who skis.

skill (skil) *n.* the power or ability to do something well: *Vasiliki shows skill at painting pictures of people.*

skillful, skilful (skil′ fəl) *adj.* being skilled at an activity: *She is such a skillful carpenter that she built the cupboard faster than all the others.* —**skillfully** *adv.*

skim (skim) *v.* **1.** to remove something floating on top of a liquid: *The cook skimmed the fat from the gravy.* **2.** to glide: *The boat skimmed over the lake.* **3.** to read very quickly, without looking at every word: *Al skimmed the book.* **skimming. skimmed.**

skim milk milk from which the cream has been removed.

skin (skin) *n.* the outer covering of humans, animals, and some fruits and vegetables. —*v.* to remove the skin of an animal or of some fruits or vegetables. **skinning. skinned.**

skin diver a person who swims under water for long periods of time: *A skin diver wears flippers, a face mask, and an oxygen tank.*

skink (skingk) *n.* a type of small lizard that has a long smooth body and short legs.

skinny (skin′ ē) *adj.* very thin: *a skinny child; a skinnier child; the skinniest child in my family.*

skip (skip) *v.* **1.** to jump lightly from one leg to the other, often over a rope. **2.** to leave out a part: *I skipped two questions on the test because I didn't have enough time.* **skipping. skipped.**

skipper (skip′ ər) *n.* **1.** a captain of a ship. **2.** a person who skips.

skirt (sku̇rt) *n.* a garment that hangs down from the waist, mostly worn by women and girls.

skit (skit) *n.* a short, humorous play that is usually made up quickly and performed by a group of people.

skull (skul) *n.* the bony part of your head: *The skull protects the brain.*

skunk (skungk) *n.* a furry, black mammal with a white stripe and a bushy tail: *A skunk sprays a bad-smelling liquid when it is frightened or attacked.*

sky (skī) *n.* the space above the earth where you can see the sun, moon, stars, and clouds. *pl.* **skies.**

sky diving a sport where a person jumps out of an airplane and floats to the ground, wearing a parachute.

sky diving

skyline (skī′ līn′) *n.* the outline of buildings against the sky: *As we drove toward Vancouver, we saw the city's skyline.*

skyscraper (skī′ skrā′ pər) *n.* a very tall building.

slab (slab) *n.* a flat, thick piece: *a slab of stone; a slab of meat.*

slack (slak) *adj.* **1.** loose, not tight: *a slack rope.* **2.** careless or slow: *a slack worker.*

slacks (slaks) *n. pl.* casual pants.

slain (slān) see **slay**.

slam (slam) *n.* a hard bang. —*v.* to bang hard: *The angry man slammed the door when he left.* **slamming. slammed.**

slang (slang) *n.* an informal word or expression that is often used in conversation, but is not used in writing.

slant (slant) *n.* a direction that is not straight up and down; a tilt; an angle: *The poster is hanging at a slant.* —*v.* to tilt. **slanting. slanted.**

slap (slap) *n.* a hit, usually with an open hand. —*v.* to hit with the open hand. **slapping. slapped.**

slash (slash) *n.* a long cut made by a sharp object: *a slash in a tire. pl.* **slashes.** —*v.* to make a slash. **slashing. slashed.**

slaughter (slo′ tər) *n.* the killing of animals for food. —*v.* to kill animals for food. **slaughtering. slaughtered.**

slave (slāv) *n.* a person who is owned by another person.

slavery (slā′ və rē *or* slāv′ rē) *n.* the condition of being a slave, or the practice of owning slaves.

slay (slā) *v.* to kill. **slaying. slayed** or **slew.** I have **slain.**

sled (sled) *n.* a wooden frame on metal runners; it is used to carry people or things over snow.

sleek (slēk) *adj.* smooth and shiny: *Many seals have sleek coats.*

sleep (slēp) *n.* a state of rest for people and animals, in which the eyes are closed and the body does not respond to things happening around it: *Humans need about eight hours of sleep a night.* —*v.* to rest completely with closed eyes. **sleeping. slept.**

sleeping bag a large, soft, padded bag, used for sleeping while camping.

sleepy (slē′ pē) *adj.* feeling tired and wanting to sleep: *a sleepy baby; a sleepier baby; the sleepiest baby of all.*

sleet (slēt) *n.* a mixture of rain and snow or hail.

sleeve (slēv) *n.* the part of a garment that covers your arm.

sleigh (slā) *n.* a sled.

slender (slen′ dər) *adj.* **1.** thin; narrow: *a slender branch on a tree.* **2.** small in amount or size: *Our chances of winning are slender because our best player is sick.*

slept (slept) see **sleep**.

slew (slū) see **slay**.

slice (slīs) *n.* a thin piece or wedge cut from something: *a slice of bacon; a slice of apple pie.* —*v.* to cut slices: *Josh sliced the cheese.* **slicing. sliced.**

slick (slik) *adj.* **1.** smooth and shiny: *slick, wet hair.* **2.** too smooth and clever: *She seems nice, but I don't trust her slick way of talking.* —**slickly** *adv.*

slide (slīd) *n.* **1.** a smooth, sloping surface for sliding on: *The children had fun going down the slide.* **2.** a small piece of film with a picture that can be enlarged by a projector and shown on a screen. **3.** a small, thin piece of glass, on which tiny objects can be placed and looked at under a microscope. —*v.* to glide smoothly over a surface: *The boys slid on the ice.* **sliding. slid** (slid).

slight (slīt) *adj.* not large or very important: *Helen has a slight cold. We have a slight chance of winning if our best player returns to the game.* —**slightly** *adv.*

slim (slim) *adj.* slender; thin: *a slim dancer; a slimmer dancer; the slimmest dancer on the stage.*

slime (slīm) *n.* soft, sticky mud, or something like it.

slimy (slī′ mē) *adj.* **1.** covered with slime: *a slimy mess; a slimier mess; the slimiest mess I've ever seen.* **2.** dirty or disgusting: *What a slimy trick they played on us!*

sling (sling) *n.* **1.** a loop of cloth hanging from the neck, used to support an injured arm. **2.** a strip of leather used to throw stones.

sling

slip (slip) *n.* **1.** a loose, silky garment worn under a dress or skirt. **2.** a small piece of paper: *I wrote Oskar's address on a slip of paper.* **3.** a quick fall or slide. —*v.* **1.** to slide suddenly, losing your balance. **2.** to move quietly: *Gail slipped into her seat.* **slipping. slipped.**

slip your mind to forget something: *I'm sorry I forgot to return your book; it slipped my mind.*

slipper (slip′ ər) *n.* a soft shoe that you wear around the house.

slippery (slip′ ər ē) *adj.* **1.** having a smooth or wet surface that makes it easy to slip: *slippery ice.* **2.** tricky and not able to be trusted: *a slippery character.*

slit (slit) *n.* a long cut or narrow opening. —*v.* to make such a cut: *Elizabeth slit open the envelope with a knife and took out the letter inside.* **slitting. slit.**

slither (sliтн′ ər) *v.* to slide along the ground, as a snake does: *The snake slithered silently toward the mouse.* **slithering. slithered.**

sliver (sliv′ ər) *n.* **1.** a very thin piece: *Please give me a sliver of pie.* **2.** a splinter of wood: *I had a sliver in my finger.*

slogan (slō′ gən) *n.* a catchy phrase used by a company to describe itself or its products in advertisements.

sloop (slūp) *n.* a type of sailboat that has one mast.

slope (slōp) *n.* a line, surface, or piece of land that slants: *a ski slope.* —*v.* to tilt; to be higher at one end than at the other. **sloping. sloped.**

sloppy (slop′ ē) *adj.* **1.** wet or slushy. **2.** messy or careless: *a sloppy dresser; a sloppier dresser; the sloppiest dresser of all.*

slot (slot) *n.* a slit or narrow opening: *Pedro put some coins in the slot of the vending machine to get some milk.*

slouch (slowch) *v.* to walk with your shoulders drooping. **slouching. slouched.**

slough (slū) *n.* **1.** a body of fresh water on the Prairies, formed by rain or melting snow. **2.** a deep mud hole. **3.** a swampy place near a stream or near an ocean inlet.

slough (sluf) *n.* the old skin shed by a snake or other reptile. —*v.* **1.** to shed; to come off:

The snake sloughed its skin. **2.** to get rid of; cast off: *The hiker was glad to slough off her backpack at the end of the trip.* **sloughing. sloughed.**

slow (slō) *adj.* not fast; not doing something quickly: *a slow worker.* **2.** moving at less than normal speed: *a slow train.* —**slowly** *adv.* —*v.* to move more slowly: *The driver slowed down when she reached the bridge.* **slowing. slowed.**

slug (slug) *n.* **1.** a small, slow-moving animal, like a snail, but without a shell. **2.** a piece of lead that is fired from a gun. —*v.* to hit hard: *Alicia slugged the ball out of the stadium.* **slugging. slugged.**

sluice (slūs) *n.* a gate and a channel for water: *A sluice is used to control the flow of water of a river, lake, or canal.*

slum (slum) *n.* a poor and crowded part of a city.

slumber (slum′ bər) *n.* sleep.

slump (slump) *n.* a heavy or sudden fall or loss: *Our team is having a mid-season slump.* —*v.* to fall or drop heavily: *The dog slumped in the grass after its long run.* **slumping. slumped.**

slush (slush) *n.* partly melted snow.

sly (slī) *adj.* tricky; doing things in a secretive way. —**slyly** *adv.*

smack (smak) *n.* **1.** a hard hit with the open hand. **2.** a sharp, slapping noise. —*v.* **1.** to hit with the open hand. **2.** to make a sharp noise: *I smacked my lips hungrily.* **smacking. smacked.**

small (smol) *adj.* little; not big: *a small toy; a smaller toy; the smallest toy of all.*

smart (smärt) *adj.* **1.** quick to understand or learn; intelligent: *a smart girl or boy.* **2.** neat and well-dressed: *The scouts look smart in their new uniforms.* —**smartly** *adv.* —*v.* to feel a stinging pain: *My eyes smart when I am near smoke.* **smarting. smarted.**

smash (smash) *n.* **1.** a violent breaking into pieces: *First I hit the ball, then I heard the smash of glass.* **2.** a great success: *Our play is a smash; the audience loved it.* *pl.* **smashes.** —*v.* to break violently into pieces: *The ball smashed the glass.* **smashing. smashed.**

smear (smēr) *n.* a mark left by rubbing something wet or greasy over a surface: *a smear of grease.* —*v.* to rub on, sometimes sloppily: *We smeared peanut butter on bread.* **smearing. smeared.**

smell (smel) *n.* **1.** a scent: *the smell of burning wood.* **2.** one of the five senses—the ability to smell, using the nose. —*v.* **1.** to use your nose to be aware of scents: *I smell bread baking.* **2.** to give off a bad smell: *The garbage smells.* **smelling. smelled** or **smelt.**

> Different words are used for different types of **smells**. A "scent" can be any kind of smell, but more often it is a sweet smell. A "fragrance" is sweet. An "odour" is usually unpleasant. An "aroma" often describes the smell of something being baked or cooked.

smelly (smel′ ē) *adj.* having a bad smell: *smelly garbage; smellier garbage; the smelliest garbage of all.*

smile (smīl) *n.* a turning up of the corners of your mouth to show you are happy, friendly, or amused. —*v.* to make a smile. **smiling. smiled.**

smog (smog) *n.* visible air pollution.

> The word **smog** comes from taking the first two letters of the word smoke and joining them to the last two letters of the word fog. Smog does look like a smoky fog!

smoke (smōk) *n.* a dark cloud from something burning. —*v.* **1.** to give off smoke: *The fireplace is smoking.* **2.** to draw in and breathe out smoke from tobacco. **smoking. smoked.**

smoky (smōk′ ē) *adj.* filled with smoke: *a smoky room; a smokier room; the smokiest room in the house.*

smooth (smūTH) *adj.* even and flat, not rough or bumpy: *a smooth table top.* —**smoothly** *adv.* —*v.* to make even and flat: *Pam smoothed the wooden bowl with sandpaper.* **smoothing. smoothed.**

smother (smuTH′ ər) *v.* **1.** to stop someone breathing by covering the mouth and nose. **2.** to cover thickly all over: *Chet smothered his hamburger with ketchup.* **smothering. smothered.**

smoulder, smolder (smōl′ dər) *v.* to burn slowly without a flame, but with a lot of smoke. **smouldering. smouldered.**

smudge (smuj) *n.* a dirty mark; a smear. —*v.* to smear something: *Please don't smudge my drawing with your dirty fingers.* **smudging. smudged.**

smuggle (smug′ əl) *v.* to take goods into or out of a country secretly, against the law. **smuggling. smuggled.**

smuggler (smug′ lər) *n.* a person who smuggles.

snack (snak) *n.* a small amount of food that is eaten between meals. —*v.* to eat a light amount of food: *I snacked on an apple.* **snacking. snacked.**

snail (snāl) *n.* a small, slow-moving animal with a soft body and a shell on its back: *Snails are found on land and in water.*

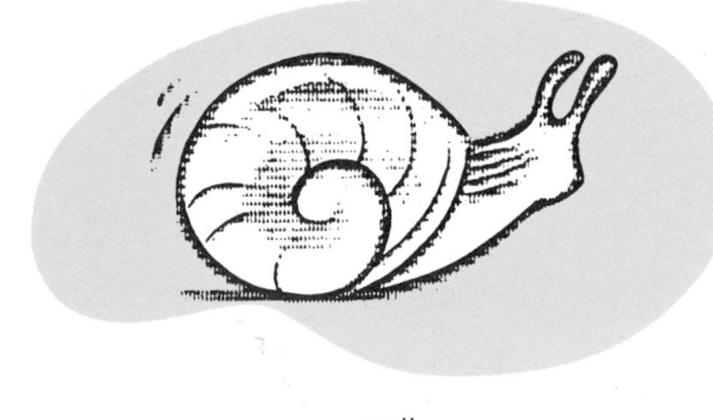

snail

snake (snāk) *n.* a long, narrow reptile that has a scaly skin and no legs: *A snake glides over the ground on its body. Some snakes are poisonous.*

snap (snap) *n.* a sudden sharp sound or break: *He broke the pencil with a snap.* —*v.* **1.** to make a sudden sharp sound: *She snapped her fingers.* **2.** to break suddenly: *The branch snapped.* **3.** to take a photograph. **snapping. snapped.**

snapshot (snap′ shot′) *n.* an informal photograph taken with a small camera.

snare (sner) *n.* a trap with a noose, used to catch animals. —*v.* **1.** to trap with a snare. **2.** to trap: *The police snared the burglar as he was leaving.* **snaring. snared.**

snarl (snärl) *n.* a low, growling sound. —*v.* to make such a sound: *The dog snarled at the stranger.* **snarling. snarled.**

snatch (snach) *v.* to grab something and quickly try to get away: *A thief snatched my knapsack, but luckily a police officer caught him.* **snatching. snatched.**

sneak (snēk) *v.* to move, trying not to be seen or heard: *We had to sneak into the house to prepare for the surprise party.* **sneaking. sneaked.**

sneakers (snē′ kərs) *n. pl.* running shoes.

sneaky (snē′ kē) *adj.* tricky; not honest: *a sneaky trick.*

sneer (snēr) *n.* a curling down of the lip to show hatred or scorn. —*v.* to give a sneer: *Don't sneer until you have heard the whole story.* **sneering. sneered.**

sneeze (snēz) *n.* a sudden, noisy blowing-out of air from your mouth and nose: *A sneeze is a reaction to something irritating your nose or a cold.* —*v.* to make a sneeze. **sneezing. sneezed.**

sniff (snif) *n.* a sudden small breath taken in, often to smell something: *The dog gave the bone a sniff.* —*v.* to take a sniff: *We sniffed the roses in the garden.* **sniffing. sniffed.**

snip (snip) *n.* **1.** a small cut with scissors. **2.** a small piece cut off. —*v.* to make a small cut with scissors: *When I finished sewing, I snipped off the extra thread.* **snipping. snipped.**

snob (snob) *n.* a person who acts like he or she is better than other people.

snoop (snūp) *v.* to pry secretly into things that are not your business; to spy. **snooping. snooped.**

snooze (snūz) *n.* a nap. —*v.* to take a nap. **snoozing. snoozed.**

snore (snȯr) *v.* to breathe noisily while you are asleep. **snoring. snored.**

snorkel (snȯr′ kəl) *n.* a tube for breathing while swimming just beneath the surface of the water. —*v.* to swim underwater, using a snorkel: *We went snorkelling in the Great Barrier Reef.* **snorkelling. snorkelled.**

snort (snȯrt) *n.* a short sound made by forcing the breath out through the nose: *She gave a snort of disgust.* —*v.* to make such a sound: *The horse snorted in fear.* **snorting. snorted.**

snout (snowt) *n.* the part of an animal's head that includes the nose, mouth, and jaws: *a pig's snout.*

snow (snō) *n.* soft, white ice crystals that fall from clouds in cold weather. —*v.* to fall as snow: *It snowed on New Year's Day.* **snowing. snowed.** —**snowy** *adj.*

snowball (snō′ bol′) *n.* a ball made of tightly packed snow.

snowblower (snō′ blō′ ər) *n.* a machine that clears snow by blowing it to one side.

snowbound (snō′ bownd′) *adj.* forced to stay in one place because of heavy snow.

snowdrift (snō′ drift′) *n.* a heap of deep snow.

snowflake (snō′ flāk′) *n.* a single crystal of snow.

snowmobile (snō′ mə bēl′) *n.* a vehicle with a motor and runners, used for travelling over snow.

snowmobile

snowplough, snowplow (sno′ plow′) *n.* a machine with a large shovel, used to clear snow to the side of a road.

snowshoes (snō′ shūz′) *n. pl.* wooden frames shaped something like tennis racquets and crisscrossed with leather strips; they are strapped to the boots and used for walking over deep snow.

snowy (snō′ ē) *adj.* having to do with or covered with snow: *a snowy day; a snowier day; the snowiest day of the winter.*

snug (snug) *adj.* warm and cosy: *The quilt made me feel snug on the cold winter morning.* —**snugly** *adv.*

so (sō) *adv.* **1.** to such a degree: *Don't cry so much.* **2.** very: *I am so glad.* **3.** also; too: *Are you going to the game? So am I.* —*conj.* **1.** therefore; as a result: *We missed the bus, so we had to walk.* **2.** in order that: *Come closer so that I can tell you a secret.*

soak (sōk) *v.* **1.** to make completely wet: *The rain soaked us to the skin.* **2.** to put or to stay in liquid for a long time: *to soak a soiled shirt; to soak in the bathtub.* **soaking. soaked.**

soap (sōp) *n.* a substance made of fat and lye, used with water for washing.

soapstone (sōp′ stōn′) *n.* a soft, greenish-grey stone that can be carved: *Inuit sculptors are known for soapstone carvings.*

soar (sȯr) *v.* to rise high in the sky: *The eagle soared into the sky.* **soaring. soared.**

sob (sob) *n.* a crying sound, made with short breaths. —*v.* to cry with short gasps or breaths. **sobbing. sobbed.**

sober (sō′ bər) *adj.* **1.** serious: *Everyone at the funeral was in a very sober mood.* **2.** not drunk: *A person should not drive a car unless he or she is sober.*

soccer (sok′ ər) *n.* a game played by two teams of eleven players each: *In soccer, players try to move a round ball into a goal, using their feet and sometimes their chest or forehead.*

sociable (sō′ shə bəl) *adj.* friendly; liking to be with other people. —**sociably** *adv.*

social (sō′ shəl) *adj.* having to do with people, the groups they form, and how they get along together: *Social studies include history and geography.* —**socially** *adv.*

society (sə sī′ ə tē) *n.* **1.** human beings living together in a group. **2.** people who join together because they have the same interest; an organization: *The Humane Society is a group that cares for badly treated or lost animals. pl.* **societies.**

sock (sok) *n.* a short cloth covering for the foot, worn with shoes. —*v.* to punch. **socking. socked.**

socket (sok′ it) *n.* an opening into which something fits: *Screw the light bulb into the socket.*

sod (sod) *n.* a layer of earth with grass growing on it.

soda (sō′ də) *n.* a sweet, fizzy drink, sometimes made with ice cream.

soda pop a soft drink.

sofa (sō′ fə) *n.* a long, soft seat with arms, a back, and cushions, for two or more people.

soft (soft) *adj.* **1.** not hard or firm: *a soft pillow.* **2.** low; not loud: *a soft voice.* **3.** gentle: *a soft touch.* —**softly** *adv.*

soft drink a sweet, fizzy cold drink, made with fruit or other flavours.

software (soft′ wer′) any type of computer program.

soggy (sog′ ē) *adj.* wet, heavy, and soft: *soggy ground; soggier ground; the soggiest ground on the field.*

soil (soil) *n.* the top, loosened layer of earth in which plants grow. —*v.* to make or become dirty. **soiling. soiled.**

solar (sō′ lər) *adj.* having to do with, or coming from, the sun.

solar system the sun and all the planets, moons, comets, and other heavenly bodies that orbit it.

sold (sōld) see **sell.**

soldier (sōl′ jər) *n.* a person who is part of an army and is trained to fight in war.

sole (sōl) *n.* **1.** the bottom of a foot, sock, or shoe. *pl.* **soles. 2.** a kind of flat fish that lives in the ocean. *pl.* **sole.** —*adj.* single; only one: *She was the sole witness to the car crash.*

solemn (sol′ əm) *adj.* very serious: *They made a solemn promise not to tell the secret.* —**solemnly** *adv.*

solid (sol′ id) *n.* a form of matter that is not a liquid or a gas: *A solid is usually hard and keeps its own shape.* —*adj.* firm right through, not hollow: *a bar of solid iron.* —**solidly** *adv.*

solitary (sol′ ə ter′ ē) *adj.* **1.** single: *Not a solitary person lives in that old house.* **2.** being alone: *a solitary life.*

solo (sō′ lō) *n.* a music performance by a single player or singer. *pl.* **solos.** —*adj.* singing, playing an instrument, or doing something else alone: *The pilot flew a solo flight across Canada.*

solution (sə lū′ shən) *n.* **1.** the answer to a problem, puzzle, or mystery: *Do you know the solution to the math question?* **2.** a mixture made of a solid dissolved in a liquid.

solve (solv) *v.* to find the answer to a problem, puzzle, or mystery: *The detective solved the crime.* **solving. solved.**

some (sum) *adj.* **1.** a few: *We gathered some berries.* **2.** an amount of: *We ate some pie.* **3.** one or the other: *We shall find some way out of the forest.* —*pron.* a certain person, thing, or amount: *Do you have any money? Yes, I have some.*

somebody (sum′ bud′ ē) *pron.* some person: *Will somebody please help me carry this heavy box?*

somehow (sum′ how′) *adv.* in a way not known: *We shall finish the job somehow.*

someone (sum′ wun′) *pron.* some person: *Someone stole my bike.*

somersault (sum′ ər solt′) *n.* the act of rolling the body in a complete circle, heels over head. —*v.* to turn a somersault. **somersaulting. somersaulted.**

something (sum′ thing) *pron.* a thing not named or known: *I have something in my eye.*

sometime (sum′ tīm′) *adv.* at a future time that is not definitely known: *My sister hopes to find a job sometime soon.*

sometimes (sum′ tīmz′) *adv.* once in a while; now and then: *We sometimes visit each other.*

somewhat (sum′ wot′ *or* sum′ hwot′) *adv.* a little: *You look somewhat unhappy. Is anything wrong?*

somewhere (sum′ wer′ *or* sum′ hwer′) *adv.* in a place not known or named: *I left my key somewhere.*

son (sun) *n.* a male child: *My aunt and uncle have two sons.*

sonic (son′ ik) *adj.* having to do with sound or the speed of sound in air.

son-in-law (sun′ in lo′) *n.* the husband of a daughter. *pl.* **sons-in-law.**

song (song) *n.* **1.** words that are sung. **2.** the musical sounds of a bird.

soon (sūn) *adv.* **1.** in a short time: *Curtis ran and was soon at school.* **2.** early: *Are you going so soon?*

soot (su̇t) *n.* black powder that comes from smoke.

soothe (sūTH) *v.* to comfort and calm someone: *Dad soothed the little boy and told him not to worry.* **soothing. soothed.**

sophisticated (sə fis′ tə kāt′ id) *adj.* **1.** having knowledge of the world through experience. **2.** very complicated and usually better: *More sophisticated computers are being invented all the time.*

sore (sȯr) *n.* a painful spot on the skin, such as a bump or a bruise. —*adj.* painful; tender: *a sore foot.*

sorrow (sȯr′ ō) *n.* sadness; grief.

sorrowful (sȯr′ ō fəl *or* sȯr′ ə fəl) *adj.* feeling sorrow. —**sorrowfully** *adv.*

sorry (sȯr′ ē) *adj.* feeling unhappy about something that has happened, or something you have done: *I'm sorry I hurt you.*

sort (sȯrt) *n.* a kind: *There are all sorts of flowers in the garden.* —*v.* to put things in groups of the same kind: *Jimmy sorted his stamps by country.* **sorting. sorted.**

sought (sot) see **seek.**

soul (sōl) *n.* the spirit—the part of you made up by your personality, emotions, thoughts, and beliefs.

sound (sownd) *n.* a vibration that travels through air or water and is heard by the ears; a noise: *I can hear the sound of drums.* —*adj.* deep: *a sound sleep.* —**soundly** *adv.* —*v.* to make sound: *The music sounds lovely.* **sounding. sounded.**

soundproof (sownd′ prūf′) *adj.* able to keep sound out: *a soundproof room.*

soup (sūp) *n.* a liquid food made by boiling meat, vegetables, grains, and so on in water.

sour (sowr) *adj.* **1.** having the kind of sharp taste that lemons and vinegar have. **2.** spoiled.

source (sôrs) *n.* the place where something has come from: *the source of a river; the source of a rumour.*

south (sowth) *n.* the direction to your right as you face the sunrise; opposite to north.

South American (sowth ə mer′ ə kən) a person born or living in South America. —*adj.* having to do with the continent of South America.

South Pole the most southern point of the earth.

southeast (sowth′ ēst′) *n.* the direction that is halfway between south and east.

southern (suTH′ ərn) *adj.* in or of the south: *the southern part of the United States.*

southward, southwards (sowth′ wərd, sowth′ werdz) *adv.* toward or facing the south: *The traffic moved southward.*

southwest (sowth′ west′) *n.* the direction that is halfway between south and west.

souvenir (sū′ və nēr′) *n.* something you keep to remind you of a certain place, time, event, and so on.

sovereignty (sov′ rən tē) *n.* the power of an independent nation, with complete control over its affairs.

sow (sow) (*masc.* **boar**) *n.* a female pig.

sow (sō) *v.* to plant seeds: *The farmer sowed corn seeds in the field.* **sowing. sowed.**

soybean (soi′ bēn′) *n.* a light brown bean, rich in oil, and sometimes used as a meat substitute.

soy sauce a salty, dark brown sauce made from soybeans and used to flavour rice, noodles, and other foods.

space (spās) *n.* **1.** the unlimited area around us that holds the earth and the entire universe: *We can see distant stars that exist in outer space.* **2.** the distance between things: *a space of two metres.* **3.** an empty place or spot: *We found a parking space just around the corner.*

spacecraft (spās′ kraft′) *n.* any vehicle that can travel into space: *The space shuttle is a spacecraft. pl.* **spacecraft.**

spacecraft

spaceship (spās′ ship′) *n.* a vehicle that travels into space.

spacious (spā′ shəs) *adj.* having a large amount of space; roomy.

spade (spād) *n.* **1.** a garden tool used for digging; it has a long handle and a pointed and curved blade. **2.** a playing card with one or more (♠) marks on it.

spaghetti (spə get′ ē) *n. pl.* long thin sticks of dried pasta, that become soft when boiled in water: *Spaghetti is often served with a tomato and meat sauce.*

> **Spaghetti** comes from the Italian word *spagetta,* which means "strings."

span (span) *n.* the length from end to end, or the distance between two objects: *the span of a bridge.* —*v.* to extend or stretch across something: *The bridge spanned the river.* **spanning. spanned.**

spandex (span′ deks) *n.* an elastic fabric used to make clothing that fits tightly but is also stretchy.

spaniel (span′ yəl) *n.* a medium-sized dog with long hair, drooping ears, and short legs.

spank (spangk) *n.* a smack with the open hand. —*v.* to give a spank. **spanking. spanked.**

spare (sper) *adj.* extra or left over; not being used: *a spare tire.* —*v.* **1.** to give away something you can do without: *Can you spare a quarter?* **2.** to show mercy to: *"Please spare my life," the prisoner begged.* **sparing. spared.**

spareribs (sper′ ribz′) *n. pl.* the ribs of an animal, usually a pig, that are trimmed, cooked, and served with a sauce.

spark (spärk) *n.* **1.** a speck of something burning: *The burning wood threw up sparks.* **2.** a tiny electric flash: *Sparks came from the wire.*

sparkle (spär′ kəl) *n.* a gleam; a glitter: *He had a sparkle in his eyes.* —*adj.* **sparkly.** —*v.* to glitter or twinkle: *The jewels sparkled in the light.* **sparkling. sparkled.**

sparkler (spär′ klər) *n.* **1.** a thing or a person that sparkles. **2.** a firework that burns slowly and sends off a shower of sparks.

sparrow (spar′ ō *or* sper′ ō) *n.* a small bird with brown, grey, and white feathers: *The sparrows ate the seeds in the bird feeder.*

sparse (spärs) *adj.* thinly scattered; not crowded: *Our play was not popular; the audience was sparse.* —**sparsely** *adv.*

spat (spat) see **spit**.

spatter (spat′ ər) *v.* **1.** to scatter or fall in small drops. **2.** to splash with liquid or mud. **spattering. spattered.**

spatula (spach′ ə lə) *n.* a utensil that has a broad, flat blade, used for lifting foods out of a pan or for blending: *We used a spatula to lift the eggs out of the frying pan.* *pl.* **spatulas.**

speak (spēk) *v.* to say words. **speaking. spoke.** I have **spoken.**

speaker (spē′ kər) *n.* **1.** a person who is speaking or giving a speech. **2.** an electrical device used for making sounds louder: *My parents bought new speakers for the stereo.*

spear (spēr) *n.* a weapon with a long handle and a sharp point. —*v.* to stab something with a spear or any other sharp utensil: *I speared a piece of potato with my fork.* **spearing. speared.**

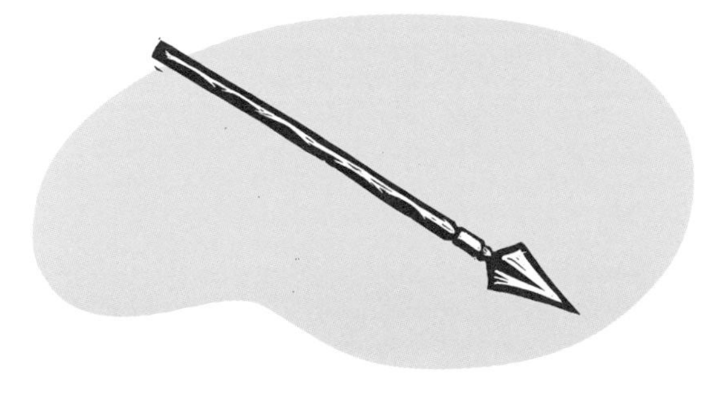

spear

special (spesh′ əl) *adj.* **1.** different from the usual or ordinary: *I have some special news to tell you.* **2.** outstanding; unique: *My best friend is a special person because he is always willing to help others.* —**specially** *adv.*

specialty (spesh′ əl tē) *n.* **1.** something that a person is very good at doing: *Painting flowers is the artist's specialty.* **2.** a special product: *A thin-crust pizza is this restaurant's specialty.* *pl.* **specialties.**

species (spē′ sēz *or* spē′ shēz) *n.* a group of living things that are of the same general kind: *There are many species of dogs.* *pl.* **species.**

specific (spə sif′ ik) *adj.* particular; not general: *Ian likes a specific brand of soup, but I can't remember which one it is.* —**specifically** *adv.*

speck (spek) *n.* a tiny bit or spot: *Sima had a speck of dirt in her eye.*

spectacles (spek′ tə kəlz) *n. pl.* eyeglasses.

spectacular (spek tak′ yə lər) *adj.* making a showy and unusual display: *spectacular fireworks.* —**spectacularly** *adv.*

spectator (spek′ tā tər *or* spek tā′ tər) *n.* a person watching a game, sport, or show.

spectrum (spek′ trəm) *n.* the band of colours that is formed when light is broken up into parts, such as when light passes through water drops: *A rainbow contains all the colours of the spectrum.*

speculate (spek′ yə lāt) *v.* to wonder; to guess: *The police officers speculated about who could have stolen the car.*

sped (sped) see **speed**.

speech (spēch) *n.* **1.** the power of speaking. **2.** a talk given to some people or an audience. *Before the game, the goalie gave a speech to the team. pl.* **speeches.**

speechless (spēch′ lis) *adj.* unable to speak right away because you are so excited or upset about something: *When she won the award, the athlete was speechless.*

speed (spēd) *n.* how quickly something moves or happens: *The car went at a slow speed.* —*v.* to move quickly: *The car sped down the road.* **speeding. sped.**

speedometer (spē dom′ ə tər *or* spi dom′ ə tər) *n.* an instrument that shows the speed of a vehicle.

spell (spel) *n.* **1.** in fairy tales, magic words spoken to cause something to happen: *The witch's spell changed the prince into a frog.* **2.** a period of time: *The spell of wet weather helped the plants grow.* —*v.* to write or say the letters of a word, in the correct order. **spelling. spelled** or **spelt.**

spelling (spel′ ing) *n.* **1.** the way a word is spelled. **2.** the saying or writing of the correct letters in a word: *His favourite subject is spelling.*

spend (spend) *v.* **1.** to pay out money: *I spent five dollars on a present.* **2.** to use time: *We spent an hour swimming.* **spending. spent.**

sphere (sfēr) *n.* any object shaped like a ball; a round solid figure.

spice (spīs) *n.* a part of certain plants used to flavour food: *Ginger, nutmeg, and cinnamon are spices.* —*v.* to add spice to food: *Mark spiced the pizza with pepper.* **spicing. spiced.**

spicy (spī′ sē) *adj.* having the strong taste of spices: *a spicy meal; a spicier meal; the spiciest meal I've ever eaten.*

spider (spī′ dər) *n.* a small animal, similar to an insect, that has eight legs, a body divided into two parts, and no wings: *Many types of spiders spin webs to catch flying insects.*

Most **spiders** spin webs, and this is where their name comes from. Spider comes from the old English word *spithra,* meaning "spinner."

spied, spies (spīd, spīz) see **spy**.

spike (spīk) *n.* a long, sharp nail.

spill (spil) *n.* something that has been spilled. —*v.* to let a liquid fall where it shouldn't, or to fill a container too full so that extra liquid flows out. **spilling. spilled** or **spilt.**

spin (spin) *n.* a quick turn all the way around: *a spin of a wheel.* —*v.* **1.** to turn in circles very quickly; to rotate. **2.** to make thread. **3.** (for a spider) to create a web. **spinning. spun.**

spinach (spin′ ich) *n.* a dark green, leafy vegetable, often used in salads.

spine (spīn) *n.* **1.** a long set of small bones that fit together down the middle of the back; backbone. **2.** a spike or sharp-pointed growth on a plant or animal: *A cactus plant and a porcupine have spines.*

spiral (spī′ rəl) *n.* a curve that winds upward or downward, and often gets smaller or larger: *The staircase went around in a spiral.*

spiral

spirit (spir′ it) *n.* **1.** a person or animal's soul. **2.** a ghost.

spiritual (spir′ i chū əl) *adj.* having to do with the spirit: *Many religions focus on spiritual matters.* —**spiritually** *adv.*

spit (spit) *n.* **1.** a rod on which meat is turned and roasted. **2.** a narrow piece of land that juts into the water. —*v.* to shoot saliva or something else out of your mouth: *We spat the watermelon seeds into the grass.* **spitting. spat.**

spite (spīt) *n.* a wish to hurt someone by cruel behaviour: *My cousin broke his brother's toy out of spite.*

in spite of even though there is: *We went on the hike in spite of the bad weather.*

splash (splash) *n.* the noise made when something heavy falls into water. *pl.* **splashes.** —*v.* to throw liquid about: *The children splashed in the pool.* **splashing. splashed.**

splendid (splen′ did) *adj.* magnificent; grand: *The princess lived in a splendid castle.* —**splendidly** *adv.*

splendour, splendor (splen′ dər) *n.* great beauty or luxury: *The splendour of the palace took our breath away.*

splint (splint) *n.* a piece of wood that is used to hold a broken bone in place.

splinter (splin′ tər) *n.* a thin, sharp piece of wood, metal, or glass; a sliver: *Toni had a splinter of wood in her thumb.* —*v.* to break into splinters: *The glass splintered as it hit the floor.* **splintering. splintered.**

split (split) *n.* a long, thin break or opening; a crack: *There's a split in my pants.* —*v.* **1.** to crack open from end to end: *The bolt of lightning split the tree in half.* **2.** to divide or share in half: *My friend and I split the last piece of pizza.* **splitting. split.**

spoil (spoil) *v.* **1.** to damage or ruin something, or to make it less good: *The frost spoiled some of the fruit crop.* **2.** to go bad: *Milk spoils if left too long in a warm place.* **3.** to make someone selfish by never saying "no" and letting the person have his or her own way: *to spoil a child.* **spoiling. spoiled** or **spoilt.**

spoke (spōk) *n.* one of the thin rods that connect the rim of a wheel to the centre. —*v.* see **speak.**

sponge (spunj) *n.* **1.** an ocean animal that lives attached to rocks. **2.** this animal's light, soft skeleton, with many holes, that soaks up water: *A sponge is used for bathing and cleaning.* **3.** an artificial washing or cleaning sponge.

sponsor (spon′ sər) *n.* a person or an organization that supports or pays for something. —*v.* to support or pay for: *I am sponsoring Alison in the marathon run.* **sponsoring. sponsored.**

spontaneous (spon tā′ nē əs) *adj.* done in a natural way, without planning: *The children gave the babysitter a spontaneous hug when he left.* —**spontaneously** *adv.*

spook (spūk) *n.* (*informal*) a ghost. —*v.* to frighten or startle: *A loud noise spooked the horse.* **spooking. spooked.**

spooky (spūk′ ē) *adj.* frightening in an eerie or a ghostly way: *a spooky house; a spookier house; the spookiest house of all.*

spool (spūl) *n.* a small cylinder on which to wind thread, film, fishing line, wire, and so on.

spoon (spūn) *n.* a small, shallow bowl at the end of a handle, used for stirring, serving, or eating food.

sport (spȯrt) *n.* **1.** a game involving physical activity and skill, often involving teams of players: *Some sports are football, hockey, and golf.* **2.** a person who plays a sport honestly and takes a loss without getting angry: *a good sport.*

spot (spot) *n.* **1.** a small mark of a different colour: *A leopard has black spots on its yellow coat.* **2.** a stain: *There's a spot on your shirt.* **3.** a particular place: *This is the spot where I saw the deer.* —*v.* to see and pick out: *Lorraine spotted an owl in the tree.* **spotting. spotted.**

spotlight (spot′ līt′) *n.* a bright light shining on one spot, as on a stage.
in the spotlight to be the focus of attention.

spout (spowt) *n.* the narrow part of a container through which a liquid flows: *the spout of a kettle.* —*v.* to shoot out a liquid through a narrow opening: *The whale spouted water when it surfaced beside the ship.* **spouting. spouted.**

sprain (sprān) *n.* an injury caused by twisting a muscle or joint in your body. —*v.* to twist a muscle or joint: *to sprain an ankle.* **spraining. sprained.**

sprang (sprang) see **spring**.

sprawl (sprol) *v.* to sit or lie with arms and legs spread out carelessly: *Jack sprawled across the couch to watch television.* **sprawling. sprawled.**

spray (sprā) *n.* liquid flying or blowing in tiny drops. —*v.* to scatter tiny drops of liquid: *Yasmin sprayed paint on the wooden chair.* **spraying. sprayed.**

spread (spred) *n.* a covering for a surface: *a woollen spread for the bed; a cheese spread for a sandwich.* —*v.* **1.** to stretch out: *The eagle spread its wings.* **2.** to lay out all over a surface, or to cover a surface: *to spread butter on bread.* **spreading. spread.**

spring (spring) *n.* **1.** the season after winter. **2.** a place where water flows out of the ground. **3.** a metal spiral that goes back into shape after it has been pressed or stretched. —*v.* to jump up suddenly: *Darren sprang out of bed when the alarm rang.* **springing. sprang.** it has **sprung.**

sprinkle (spring′ kəl) *n.* a light scattering of powder or drops of liquid: *a sprinkle of rain.* —*v.* to scatter powder or drops of liquid: *Dessa sprinkled salt on her food.* **sprinkling. sprinkled.**

sprinkler (spring′ klər) *n.* a device for sprinkling water: *a sprinkler for the lawn; an automatic sprinkler to put out fires.*

sprint (sprint) *v.* to run very quickly for a short distance. **sprinting. sprinted.**

sprout (sprowt) *n.* a new growth on a plant. —*v.* to begin to grow: *The bean seeds are sprouting in the water.* **sprouting. sprouted.**

spruce (sprūs) *n.* an evergreen tree, with leaves that look like green needles, and cones.

sprung (sprung) see **spring**.

spun (spun) see **spin**.

spur (spu̇r) *n.* a small, spiked wheel on the heel of the rider of a horse, which is used to urge the horse to go faster.

spur

spurt (spu̇rt) a sudden gush or squirt of a liquid. —*v.* to gush or squirt suddenly: *Paint spurted out of the tube.* **spurting. spurted.**

spy (spī) *n.* someone who tries secretly to find out things about a person, a government or business, or another country. *pl.* **spies.** —*v.* **1.** to watch secretly. **2.** to catch sight of: *Sasha spied a rabbit in the field.* **spying. spied.** he **spies.**

squad (skwod) *n.* a small group of people working together: *a police squad.*

squander (skwon′ dər) *v.* to spend foolishly; to waste: *Don't squander your money on such an expensive video game.* **squandering. squandered.**

square (skwer) *n.* **1.** a flat shape with four right sides and four equal angles. **2.** a four-sided open space in a city or town. —*adj.* having the shape of a square.

squash (skwosh) *n.* **1.** any of several vegetables that grow on vines along the ground. *pl.* **squash. 2.** a game somewhat like tennis, played with a hollow rubber ball. —*v.* to squeeze or crush. **squashing. squashed.**

squat (skwot) *v.* to rest on your heels, with the knees fully bent. **squatting. squatted.**

squeak (skwēk) *n.* a short, high sound. —*v.* to make this sound: *The mouse sqeaked in its cage.* **squeaking. squeaked.**

squeaky (skwē′ kē) *adj.* making a high, mouse-like noise: *The squeaky door needs oil.*

squeal (skwēl) *n.* a long, high cry. —*v.* to make this sound: *The pig squealed when its foot got caught in the fence.* **squealing. squealed.**

squeeze (skwēz) *n.* a firm pressing of something: *Give the lemons a good squeeze.* —*v.* **1.** to press something hard: *Squeeze the lemons to get all of the juice out.* **2.** to crowd into a small space. **squeezing. squeezed.**

squint (skwint) *n.* to look at something with your eyes partly closed: *The sun shining on the snow made me squint.* **squinting. squinted.**

squirm (skwûrm) *v.* to wriggle, often uncomfortably: *The worm squirmed on the hook.* **squirming. squirmed.**

squirrel (skwûr′ əl) *n.* a small rodent with a long, fluffy tail: *Squirrels eat nuts and live in trees.*

squirt (skwûrt) *n.* a jet of liquid in a fine stream. —*v.* to shoot liquid in a fine stream: *Juice squirted out when I bit into the tomato.* **squirting. squirted.**

St. (strēt *or* sānt *or* strāt) short for **street** or **saint** or **strait.**

stab (stab) *n.* a wound made with a pointed object. —*v.* to wound someone with a pointed object. **stabbing. stabbed.**

stable (stā′ bəl) *n.* a building in which horses are kept.

stack (stak) *n.* a large pile: *a stack of bricks; a haystack.* —*v.* to pile up: *We stacked the empty boxes in the corner.* **stacking. stacked.**

stadium (stā′ dē əm) *n.* a large, open sports ground, with rows of seats all around.

staff (staf) *n.* **1.** a long stick or pole: *the staff of a flag.* **2.** a group of people who work together: *a hospital staff.*

stag (stag) *n.* an adult male deer, usually one that has antlers.

stage (stāj) *n.* **1.** a raised platform in a theatre, used for performances. **2.** a point, level, or step a person has reached: *I've reached the stage of rewriting the first draft of my story.* —*v.* to present a play: *Our school staged a spring performance.* **staging. staged.**

stagecoach (stāj′ kōch′) *n.* a large, closed coach, pulled by horses: *Stagecoaches were once used for carrying people and mail.* *pl.* **stagecoaches.**

stagger (stag′ ər) *n.* an unsteady, swaying walk. —*v.* to walk in a swaying, unsteady way: *I felt dizzy after riding the merry-go-round and staggered to a bench.* **staggering. staggered.**

stain (stān) *n.* a dirty or coloured spot: *My gym shorts are covered with grass stains.* —*v.* to soil. **staining. stained.**

staircase (ster′ kās′) *n.* a set of steps with a handrail.

stairs (sterz) *n. pl.* a set of steps leading from one floor of a building to another.

stake (stāk) *n.* **1.** a thick post, pointed at one end and hammered into the ground. **2. stakes** money or something else of value being risked in a gamble.

at stake being risked: *With one game left and the teams tied, the championship is at stake.*

stale (stāl) *adj.* old; not fresh: *stale bread.*

stalk (stok) *n.* a stem of a flower or plant. —*v.* to hunt quietly, keeping out of sight. **stalking. stalked.**

stall (stol) *n.* **1.** the space for one cow or one horse in a barn or stable. **2.** a place for displaying things at a market or fair.
—*v.* **1.** to stop running because there isn't enough power: *The car stalls on very cold mornings.* **2.** to put off: *I stalled for ten minutes before getting out of bed this morning.* **stalling. stalled.**

stall

stallion (stal′ yən) (*fem.* **mare**) *n.* an adult male horse.

stammer (stam′ ər) *v.* when speaking, to repeat the same sound before being able to finish the word: *I stammered when I first made a speech in front of the class.* **stammering. stammered.**

stamp (stamp) *n.* **1.** a small piece of paper that is stuck to letters and packages showing the mailing charge. **2.** a tool that presses a design on a surface. —*v.* **1.** to stick a stamp on a letter or package. **2.** to press a design on a surface, using a stamp. **3.** to bang your foot heavily on the ground. **stamping. stamped.**

stampede (stam pēd′) *n.* **1.** a sudden rush of confused animals or people. **2.** a rodeo, often with other amusements, at a fair: *the Calgary Stampede.* —*v.* to rush madly in confusion: *The buffalo stampeded when they heard the hunter's shot.* **stampeding. stampeded.**

stand (stand) *n.* a piece of furniture on which to rest things. —*v.* **1.** to be on your feet or to rise to your feet. **2.** to bear; to put up with: *I can't stand the pain any longer.* **3.** (used with **for**) to mean; to represent: *B.C. stands for British Columbia.* **standing. stood.**

stand out to be noticeable, especially in a good way: *He won a prize because his project stands out from the others.*

standard (stan′ dərd) *n.* a model or level for comparing people or things, or for measuring how good they are: *You must meet a high standard to enter the public speaking competition.*

stank (stangk) see **stink**.

stanza (stan′ zə) *n.* a group of lines in a poem: *We are reading a poem that has four stanzas.*

staple (stā′ pəl) *n.* **1.** a small, thin piece of wire, shaped like a square U, whose two ends are pressed flat to hold papers together. **2.** a main food product or other product: *Rice is a staple in the diet of many Asian countries.* —*v.* to fasten with a staple. **stapling. stapled.**

stapler (stā′ plər) *n.* a tool used to staple together paper, cloth, or other materials.

star (stȧr) *n.* **1.** a heavenly body that looks like a speck of light in the night sky: *A star gives off bright light and heat. The sun is a star.* **2.** an outstanding actor, singer, sports player, or other famous person. **3.** a large part in a play, movie, or program. —*v.* to have a large part in a play, movie, or program: *My favourite actor is starring in a new movie.* **starring. starred.**

starboard (stȧr′ bərd) *n.* the right side of a ship looking towards the bow. (*opp.* **port.**)

starch (stȧrch) *n.* **1.** a powder or liquid used to make clothes stiff. **2.** a white, tasteless substance that is found in potatoes and other foods.

stardom (stȧr′ dəm) *n.* the condition of being a star actor, singer, sports player, or other famous performer.

stare (ster) *v.* to watch someone or something for a long time with a steady look. **staring. stared.**

starfish (stȧr′ fish′) *n.* a sea creature that has a flat body shaped like a star. *pl.* **starfish.**

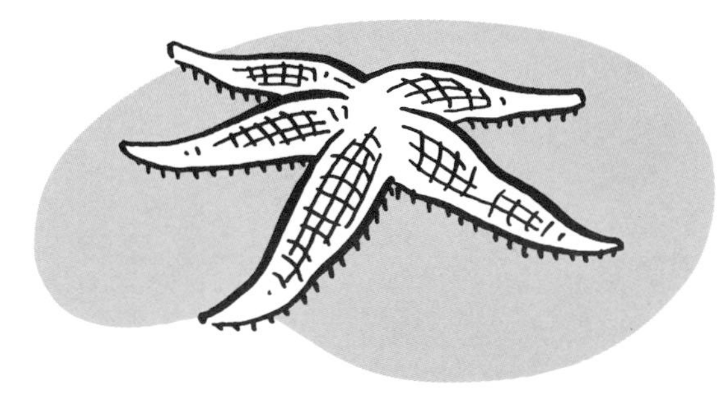

starfish

starry (stȧr′ ē) *adj.* full of stars or shiny like a star: *a starry sky; a starrier sky; the starriest sky of the week.*

start (stȧrt) *n.* **1.** a beginning: *That race had a good start.* **2.** a sudden movement of surprise or fear: *Dan gave a start when he saw the bear.* —*v.* **1.** to begin: *Isabel started to sing.* **2.** to move suddenly in surprise or fear. **starting. started.**

startle (stȧr′ təl) *v.* to suddenly surprise or frighten someone and make him or her jump. **startling. startled.**

starve (stȧrv) *v.* to become weak or die from a lack of food. **starving. starved.**

state (stāt) *n.* **1.** the condition of a person or thing: *My old clothes are in a bad state.* **2.** one of the large parts of the United States and some other countries. —*v.* to say or put into words in a formal way: *The sign states that pets are not allowed in the park.* **stating. stated.**

statement (stāt′ mənt) *n.* a sentence that expresses a fact or an opinion: *During our class debate, I made a statement explaining why I am a vegetarian.*

static (stat′ ik) *n.* electricity in the air that causes a crackling sound on radios and TV sets.

station (stā′ shən) *n.* **1.** a stopping place along a route: *a railway station.* **2.** a building used for a certain purpose: *a police station.*

stationary (stā′ shən er′ ē) *adj.* not moving, or fixed in one place: *A stationary bicycle stays in one place, and is used for exercising.*

stationery (sta′ shən er′ ē) *n.* writing paper and envelopes.

statue (stach′ ū) *n.* a figure of a person or animal that is made of clay, stone, metal, or some other solid material.

stay (stā) *v.* **1.** to remain behind: *Father stayed at home while we went out.* **2.** to live somewhere for a short time: *We stayed at a country cottage for the night.* **3.** to keep on being: *We stayed friends after she moved to another province.* **staying. stayed.**

steady (sted′ ē) *adj.* **1.** firm, not wobbling: *I made sure the ladder was steady before I climbed up to the roof.* **2.** not changing: *a steady fall of rain.* (*opp.* **unsteady.**) —**steadily** *adv.*

steak (stāk) *n.* a slice of meat or fish for cooking.

steal (stēl) *v.* to take something that is not yours and keep it. **stealing. stole.** I have **stolen.**

steam (stēm) *n.* water in the form of gas or vapour: *Boiling water gives off steam.* —*v.* **1.** to give off steam. **2.** to cook with steam. **steaming. steamed.**

steamboat (stēm′ bōt′) *n.* a boat driven forward by an engine that is powered by steam.

steel (stēl) *n.* a tough, strong metal, made from iron and carbon.

steep (stēp) *adj.* having a very sharp slope. —**steeply** *adv.*

steeple (stē′ pəl) *n.* a high tower on top of a church roof.

steer (stēr) *n.* a young bull. —*v.* to guide a ship or vehicle in the direction you want to go. **steering. steered.**

stem (stem) *n.* the main part of a plant; the long, thin part of a plant that holds up a leaf, flower, or fruit.

stench (stench) *n.* an extremely unpleasant smell: *There is quite a stench coming from the garbage room.*

stencil (sten′ səl) *n.* a thin sheet of material in which letters and patterns are cut. —*v.* to use a stencil to outline letters or patterns. **stencilling. stencilled.**

step (step) *n.* **1.** a movement made by lifting your foot and putting it down in a new place: *She took ten steps forward.* **2.** a part of a staircase on which you walk. **3.** a point or a level in a process: *What is the next step for building the airplane model?* —*v.* to take a step: *She stepped forward and made her speech.* **stepping. stepped.**

stepchild (step′ chīld′) *n.* a child of a person's husband or wife by an earlier marriage.

stepparent (step′ per′ ənt) *n.* someone whom your father or mother marries after the death or divorce of your other natural parent: *a stepmother; a stepfather.*

stereo (ster′ ē ō′) *n.* a set of machines, including two or more speakers, for listening to recorded music. *pl.* **stereos.**

sterile (ster′ īl *or* ster′ əl) *adj.* free from germs.

sterilize (ster′ ə līz′) *v.* to make sterile. **sterilizing. sterilized.**

stern (stůrn) *n.* the back part of a ship. (*opp.* **bow.**) —*adj.* strict or harsh: *We were given a stern warning not to lie again.* —**sternly** *adv.*

stew (stū or styū) *n.* meat and vegetables cooked gently together in water.

steward (stū′ ərd *or* styū′ ərd) *n.* a person in charge of food and other services on an airplane, train, or ship.

stick (stik) *n.* **1.** a thin, long piece of wood. **2.** a thin piece of anything: *a stick of chalk.* **3.** a shaped piece of wood: *a hockey stick.* —*v.* to fasten firmly, often with tape or glue: *I stuck up posters about the school play.* **sticking. stuck.**

stick out to be a little apart from the others or to stand out: *My red running shoes stick out from all the white ones.*

sticky (stik′ ē) *adj.* able to stick to something: *sticky glue; stickier glue; the stickiest glue on the shelf.*

stiff (stif) *adj.* not easy to bend or move: *My fingers are stiff with cold.* —**stiffly** *adv.*

stifle (stī′ fəl) *v.* **1.** to cut the air off, making it difficult to breathe. **2.** to stop; to hold back: *We stifled our giggles in the library.* **stifling. stifled.**

still (stil) *adj.* quiet and with no movement: *a still pond.* —*adv.* **1.** not moving: *Sit still!* **2.** now as before: *He is still in bed.* **3.** yet: *I'm still not sure.*

stilts (stilts) *n. pl.* two poles, each with a step part way up, for walking high above the ground.

stimulate (stim′ yə lāt′) *v.* **1.** to excite: *The story stimulated my imagination.* **stimulating. stimulated.**

sting (sting) *n.* a biting pain, such as from an insect bite or sting. —*v.* **1.** for an insect or thorn to prick the skin: *Tricia was stung by a wasp.* **2.** to hurt like a sting: *The smoke made my eyes sting.* **stinging. stung.**

stinger (sting′ ər) *n.* the pointed tail of wasps and other insects.

stingy (stin′ jē) *adj.* not willing to spend money or to share; not generous: *a stingy person; a stingier one; the stingiest person I ever met.*

stink (stingk) *n.* a bad smell. —*v.* to smell bad. **stinking. stank** or **stunk.**

stir (stůr) *v.* **1.** to mix together two or more substances by moving them around with a spoon: *Dad stirred sugar into his tea.* **2.** to start to move: *The baby stirs early every morning.* **stirring. stirred.**

stirrups (stůr′ əps) *n. pl.* a rider's footrests hanging from each side of a horse's saddle.

stitch (stich) *n.* **1.** in sewing and knitting, a loop of thread made with a needle. **2.** a loop of sterile thread used by doctors to hold skin together after a bad cut or an operation. —*v.* to join with stitches. **stitching. stitched.**

stock (stok) *n.* **1.** a supply of things kept to be used or sold: *The store has a large stock of soups.* **2.** broth from cooked meat, fish, or vegetables. —*v.* to keep a supply: *We stocked our cottage with firewood.* **stocking. stocked.**

stocking (stok′ ing) *n.* a long, thin, close-fitting covering for your foot and leg, reaching to the upper thigh.

stole, stolen (stōl, stō′ lən) see **steal**.

stomach (stum′ ək) *n.* the muscular organ in your body where food goes after you have swallowed it.

stone (stōn) *n.* **1.** a small piece of rock. **2.** a jewel: *a precious stone.* **3.** the hard seed of some fruits: *a peach stone; a cherry stone.*

stood (stůd) see **stand**.

stool (stūl) *n.* a small seat with no back or arms.

stool

stoop (stūp) *n.* a bent-over position: *to walk with a stoop.* —*v.* to bend forward and downward: *Lai stooped to pick up the coin.* **stooping. stooped.**

stop (stop) *n.* **1.** the ending of movement: *Don't stand until the plane has come to a full stop.* **2.** a place where a bus or train halts for passengers: *a bus stop.* —*v.* to end movement or another action: *The referee stopped the game because of the fight.* **stopping. stopped.**

storage (stȯr′ ij) *n.* a place for keeping or storing things: *We used the old trunk as storage for our costumes.*

store (stȯr) *n.* a shop where goods are sold: *a grocery store.* —*v.* to save and put away for later use: *Maria stored her friends' addresses in the computer.* **storing. stored.**

storey, story (stȯr′ ē) *n.* a level, from floor to ceiling, of a building, including all the rooms on that level: *Our house is three storeys high. pl.* **storeys, stories.**

stork (stȯrk) *n.* a wading bird with a long beak, a long neck, and long legs.

storm (stȯrm) *n.* bad weather with heavy rain or snow, strong winds, and sometimes thunder. —**stormy** *adj.*

stormy (stȯr′ mē) *adj.* **1.** rough; having to do with a storm: *stormy weather.* **2.** very emotional or even violent: *They have a stormy relationship.*

story (stȯr′ ē) *n.* **1.** a description of imaginary characters and what happens to them. **2.** a description of real people and what happened to them: *a news story. pl.* **stories.**

stout (stowt) *adj.* **1.** big and strong. **2.** fat.

stove (stōv) *n.* a kitchen appliance, used for heating and cooking food.

stowaway (stō′ ə wā′) *n.* a person who hides in a ship or airplane in order to travel for free. *pl.* **stowaways.**

straight (strāt) *adj.* not bent or curved: *Can you walk in a straight line?* —*adv.* **1.** in a way or position that is not bent or curved: *Stand up straight!* **2.** without delay: *We went straight home after school.*

straighten (strāt′ ən) *v.* to make straight or neat: *to straighten your room.* **straightening. straightened.**

straightforward (strāt′ fôr′ wərd) *adj.* honest and frank, not tricky: *I want a straightforward answer to my question.* —**straightforwardly** *adv.*

strain (strān) *n.* an injury caused by too much effort. —*v.* **1.** to stretch, pull, push, or use much effort: *The horse strained to pull the heavy plough.* **2.** to separate a liquid from solid bits, using a sieve: *to strain the seeds out of fresh orange juice.* **straining. strained.**

strait (strāt) *n.* a narrow channel between two large bodies of water.

strand (strand) *n.* a single hair or thread: *A rope is made of many strands of thread twisted together.* —*v.* to leave in a helpless way: *The sailors were stranded on a lonely island.* **stranding. stranded.**

strange (strānj) *adj.* **1.** unusual; peculiar: *I had a strange feeling when I walked into the old house.* **2.** not known to you: *a strange bird; a strange place.* —**strangely** *adv.*

stranger (strān′ jər) *n.* someone you do not know: *A stranger asked me the way to the bus stop.*

strangle (strang′ gəl) *v.* to kill by squeezing the throat; to choke. **strangling. strangled.**

strap (strap) *n.* a strip of leather or cloth, used to hold something in place. —*v.* to fasten with a strap: *Strap on your seat belt.* **strapping. strapped.**

strategy (strat′ ə jē) *n.* a plan for fighting a war or doing some other activity: *We easily won the game because our new strategy surprised the other team. pl.* **strategies.**

straw (stro) *n.* **1.** the dried, yellow stalks of wheat or other cereals. **2.** a thin, plastic tube used for sucking up a drink.

strawberry (stro′ ber′ ē) *n.* the juicy red, edible fruit of a plant that grows close to the ground. *pl.* **strawberries.**

stray (strā) *n.* a lost animal or child. —*adj.* lost: *We found a stray animal in the park.* —*v.* to wander about and get lost: *Tina's dog strayed from home.* **straying. strayed.**

streak (strēk) *n.* a stripe: *a streak of paint.* —*v.* **1.** to mark with streaks. **2.** to move very fast: *A jet streaked across the sky.* **streaking. streaked.**

stream (strēm) *n.* **1.** a small river. **2.** a flow of people or things moving along: *A steady stream of cars drove into the park on the holiday weekend.* —*v.* to flow or move steadily: *People streamed out of the stadium after the game.* **streaming. streamed.**

streamline (strēm′ līn′) *v.* to build or make something in a shape that lets water or air flow smoothly around it.

street (strēt) *n.* a road with buildings on both sides: *We stood at the edge of the street to watch the parade.*

streetcar (strēt′ kär′) *n.* a passenger vehicle that travels on rails on the street and is powered by electricity.

strength (strength) *n.* the quality of being strong; power: *Even after swimming across the lake, the dog had the strength to keep on going.*

strengthen (streng′ thən) *v.* to make or become stronger: *Regular exercise helps to strengthen your muscles.* **strengthening. strengthened.**

stress (stres) *n.* pressure; strain: *The foot bridge almost collapsed under the stress of the heavy snow.* —*v.* to give importance to something: *We stress the first syllable when we say the word "birthday." The doctor stressed that I needed more rest if I wanted to get better soon.* **stressing. stressed.**

stretch (strech) *v.* **1.** to make something longer by pulling the ends in opposite directions: *Chan stretched the piece of elastic to fit over the box but it broke and went flying across the room.* **2.** to reach: *Verna stretched out her hand for the book.* **3.** to extend: *This road stretches to the next town.* **stretching. stretched.**

stretcher (strech′ ər) *n.* a frame of poles covered with material, used for carrying a sick or wounded person.

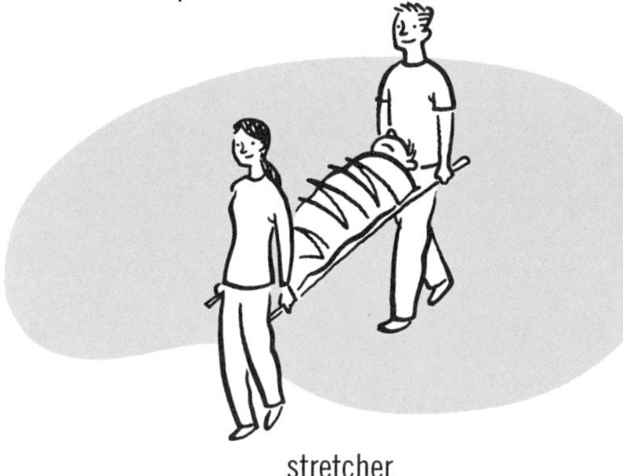

stretcher

strict (strikt) *adj.* following, or making others follow, a rule very carefully; stern. —**strictly** *adv.*

strike (strīk) *n.* **1.** a stopping of work: *The factory workers went on strike for better pay.* **2.** a pitch in baseball that counts against the batter. —*v.* **1.** to hit with a lot of force: *Don't strike the dog.* **2.** to stop work: *The workers are striking for more pay.* **3.** to give the time by sounding bells: *The clock struck three.* **4.** to crash into: *The car struck a lamp post.* **5.** to find a valuable mineral in the ground: *to strike gold.* **striking. struck.**

strike out **1.** in baseball, to pitch three strikes to a batter. **2.** to put a line through a written word, showing that it should be taken out.

string (string) *n.* **1.** a thin cord made of threads twisted together, used for tying things. **2.** a series of objects attached to a string or wire: *a string of lights.* **3.** a cord or wire on a musical instrument. —*v.* to put on a string: *to string beads to make a necklace.* **stringing. strung.**

stringed instruments musical instruments that have strings and are played with a bow or with the fingers: *Some stringed instruments are the violin, harp, guitar, and cello.*

strip (strip) *n.* a long, narrow piece of anything: *a strip of cloth.* —*v.* to take off: *to strip wallpaper from a wall.* **stripping. stripped.**

stripe (strīp) *n.* a long, narrow streak of colour: *an umbrella with red and white stripes.*

stroke (strōk) *n.* **1.** a hard hit or blow: *a stroke of a tennis racquet.* **2.** a swimming movement: *Fernando swims the back stroke well.* **3.** a mark made by a pen, crayon, or brush: *With a few strokes she drew a picture of a car.* **4.** a sudden illness that can paralyze the body. —*v.* to rub gently: *to stroke a cat.* **stroking. stroked.**

stroll (strōl) *n.* a slow, quiet walk. —*v.* to walk slowly and easily: *We strolled in the park.* **strolling. strolled.**

stroller (strō′ lər) *n.* a small, chair-like carriage in which very small children are placed and pushed along.

strong (strong) *adj.* powerful; having strength; not weak.

struck (struk) see **strike**.

structure (struk′ chər) *n.* anything that is built out of parts, especially something large: *A bridge, house, tower, or building is a structure.*

struggle (strug′ əl) *n.* a great effort or fight: *a struggle against an enemy.* —*v.* to make a great effort or to fight with force: *I struggled with the math problem.* **struggling. struggled.**

strung (strung) see **string**.

stub (stub) *n.* a short piece that is left: *the stub of an old pencil.* —*v.* to bang your toe into something hard. **stubbing. stubbed.**

stubborn (stub′ ərn) *adj.* not changing your mind or giving in easily: *Janet is being stubborn about not going to the picnic, even though all her friends are going.* —**stubbornly** *adv.*

stuck (stuk) see **stick**.

student (stū′ dənt *or* styū′ dənt) *n.* a person who is learning things, usually at school: *Each student wrote a story about the hockey player.*

studio (stū′ dē ō′ *or* styū′ dē ō′) *n.* **1.** a place where an artist or photographer works. **2.** a place where movies are filmed, or where radio or TV programs are made. *pl.* **studios.**

studious (stū′ dē əs *or* styū′ dē əs) *adj.* interested in learning and studying: *He is a studious boy and spends many hours in the library.* —**studiously** *adv.*

study (stud′ ē) *n.* **1.** a subject that you learn about: *Efra is interested in the study of dinosaurs.* **2.** a room used to read or think in. *pl.* **studies.** —*v.* **1.** to try to learn: *Jennifer is studying for the history test.* **2.** to examine carefully: *The scouts studied the map to find their way.* **studying. studied.** she **studies.**

stuff (stuf) *n.* **1.** the material that a thing is made of: *What is this sticky stuff?* **2.** a thing or things, often useless: *There is a lot of old stuff in the basement.* —*v.* to pack full: *to stuff a suitcase with clothes.* **stuffing. stuffed.**

stuffing (stuf′ ing) *n.* **1.** padding in a pillow or cushion. **2.** a mixture of bread crumbs, herbs, and other ingredients that is stuffed into a chicken or turkey before it is cooked.

stuffy (stuf′ ē) *adj.* not having fresh air: *a stuffy room; a stuffier room; the stuffiest room in the house.*

stumble (stum′ bəl) *v.* to trip over something and nearly fall. **stumbling. stumbled.**

stump (stump) *n.* the part of a tree trunk left in the ground after the tree has been cut down. —*v.* to puzzle or confuse: *That question has stumped the experts.* **stumping. stumped.**

stun (stun) *v.* **1.** to knock unconscious, or nearly so. **2.** to give someone shocking or very surprising news: *We were stunned to hear about my uncle's sudden death.* **stunning. stunned.**

stung (stung) see **sting.**

stunk (stungk) see **stink.**

stunt (stunt) *n.* a daring or risky act that attracts attention: *a martial-arts stunt in an adventure movie.* —*v.* to slow down the growth of something: *Lack of light stunted the growth of these plants.* **stunting. stunted.**

stupid (stū′ pid *or* styū′ pid) *adj.* **1.** not showing good sense; silly: *a stupid trick.* **2.** slow in understanding. —**stupidly** *adv.*

sturdy (stůr′ dē) *adj.* strong and healthy: *a sturdy tree; a sturdier one; the sturdiest tree in the yard.*

sty (stī) *n.* **1.** a closed-in pen for pigs. **2.** a swelling on the edge of the eyelid. *pl.* **sties.**

style (stīl) *n.* **1.** a way of doing something: *I like her athletic, yet graceful style of skating.* **2.** a way of dressing; fashion: *This type of shirt is in the latest style.* —*v.* to arrange hair by curling or straightening it; pinning it up; cutting, brushing, or combing it; and so on.

> **sub–** is a prefix meaning "below" or "under"; "sub-zero" means that the temperature is below zero; a "subway" is an underground way.

subdivision (sub′ də vizh′ ən) *n.* an area of land divided into many parts on which houses are built: *I can see the new subdivision from my bedroom window.*

subdue (səb dū′ *or* səb dyū′) *v.* to overcome or to soften: *I subdued his sadness by telling him a funny story.* **subduing. subdued.**

subject (sub′ jikt) *n.* **1.** something thought about, talked or written about, or studied: *In our class today, we discussed the subject of air pollution.* **2.** a person who is under the control of another: *a subject of the queen.* **3.** in grammar, the person or thing that comes before a verb and carries out the action: *Nadia has gone to school. The party will take place next week.* The subjects in these sentences are *Nadia* and *The party.*

sublime (sə blīm′) *adj.* excellent; wonderful: *a sublime dessert.*

submarine (sub′ mə rēn′) *n.* a ship that can travel under water.

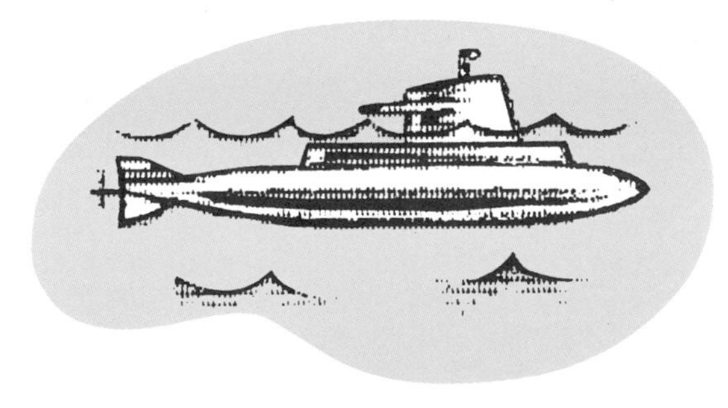

submarine

submerge (səb mürj′) *v.* to go beneath the surface of a liquid: *The children submerged the shells in the goldfish bowl.* **submerging. submerged.**

submit (səb mit′) *v.* to give in or to surrender: *Submit your reports after class. After she asked me twice, I submitted to her request.* **submitting. submitted.**

subscription (səb skrip′ shən) *n.* a promise to take and pay for a magazine, a newspaper, concert tickets, and so on for a certain length of time: *I have a subscription to a nature magazine for one year.*

substance (sub′ stəns) *n.* any material; what a thing is made of.

substitute (sub′ stə tūt′ *or* sub′ stə tyūt′) *n.* someone or something that takes the place of another: *a sugar substitute.* —*v.* to put someone or something in place of another: *The coach substituted a new pitcher when a left-handed batter came up to bat.* **substituting. substituted.**

subtle (sut′ əl) *adj.* not obvious; fine; faint: *There is a subtle difference in these two shades of green paint.* —**subtly** *adv.*

subtract (səb trakt′) *v.* to take away one number from a greater number: *Subtract 5 from 7, and 2 is left.* **subtracting. subtracted.**

subtraction (səb trak′ shən) *n.* the taking away of one number from a greater one.

suburb (sub′ ürb) *n.* an area of houses just outside or near a city.

suburban (sə bür′ bən) *adj.* having to do with the suburbs, not the city or the country.

subway (sub′ wā′) *n.* **1.** an underground passage. **2.** an electric railway that travels underground. *pl.* **subways.**

succeed (sək sēd′) *v.* **1.** to manage to do what you set out to do: *Ali succeeded in finishing the marathon.* **2.** to follow and take the place of somebody: *Ellen succeeded Stefan as president of the club.* **succeeding. succeeded.**

success (sək ses′) *n.* **1.** a person or thing that succeeds in what was tried; a wonderful result or achievement: *My first cake was a disaster, but the next one was a great success.* **2.** fame or wealth: *Her success as a singer has not changed her.*

successful (sək ses′ fəl) *adj.* having success: *He was successful in qualifying for the final race.* (*opp.* **unsuccessful.**) —**successfully** *adv.*

such (such) *adj.* so much, so great, so good, so bad, and so on: *I had such fun. They have had such bad luck.*

such as **1.** of the same kind: *flowers such as these.* **2.** for example; like: *She likes strong colours, such as purple, turquoise, and lime green.*

suck (suk) *v.* **1.** to roll something around in your mouth, but not chew it: *to suck a mint.* **2.** to draw something into your mouth: *to suck soda pop through a straw.* **sucking. sucked.**

suction (suk′ shən) *n.* the act of sucking liquid, gas, or solids out of or into a space.

sudden (sud′ ən) *adj.* quick; not expected; without any warning: *a sudden storm; a sudden recovery from an illness.* —**suddenly** *adv.*

suds (sudz) *n. pl.* soapy water with bubbles on top.

sue (sū) *v.* to use the law when you feel you have been unfairly treated: *The hockey player is suing the team for firing him.* **suing. sued.**

suede (swād) *n.* soft leather with a surface that feels like velvet, not smooth.

suffer (suf′ ər) *v.* to feel pain, discomfort from an illness, or sorrow: *Janet is suffering from a bad cold.* **suffering. suffered.**

sufficient (sə fish′ ənt) *adj.* enough: *I have sufficient money for my trip.* (*opp.* **insufficient.**) —**sufficiently** *adv.*

suffix (suf′ iks) *n.* letters put at the end of a word to change its meaning or to form a new word: *When you put the suffix "–proof" at the end of the word "water," you get "waterproof." pl.* **suffixes.**

suffocate (suf′ ə kāt′) *v.* to choke; to keep from breathing: *We were nearly suffocated by the smoke.* **suffocating. suffocated.**

sugar (shůg′ ər) *n.* sweet crystals or powder used in desserts, cakes, candies, drinks, and other foods: *Sugar comes mostly from sugar beets and sugar cane.*

suggest (səg jest′ *or* sə jest′) *v.* to offer an idea to other people: *Terri suggested that we all play ball.* **suggesting. suggested.**

suggestion (səg jes′ chən *or* sə jəs′ chən) *n.* an idea, plan, or advice offered to other people.

suicide (sū′ ə sīd′) *n.* the planned taking of one's own life.

suit (sūt) *n.* **1.** a set of clothes to be worn together: *A man's suit has a jacket and trousers.* **2.** any of the four types of playing cards in a deck: *The four suits are clubs, diamonds, hearts, and spades.* —*v.* to be right for: *That dress suits you.* **suiting. suited.**

suitable (sūt′ ə bəl) *adj.* right for a situation or person: *I need a suitable outfit to wear to the wedding.* —**suitably** *adv.*

suitcase (sūt′ kās′) *n.* a large, flat, rectangular bag for carrying clothes when you travel.

sulk (sulk) *v.* to act angry in a quiet way because you are unhappy about something: *My brother is sulking in his room because I didn't like his present.* **sulking. sulked.**

sulky (sul′ kē) *adj.* silent and in a bad temper. —**sulkily** *adv.*

sullen (sul′ ən) *adj.* gloomy and not talking to others because you are bitter or angry: *The sullen child sat in the far corner of the room.*

sum (sum) *n.* **1.** a certain amount: *a sum of money.* **2.** the total amount when you add numbers or things together: *The sum of two and three is five.*

summarize (sum′ ə rīz′) *v.* to write or tell something in a few words: *Summarize the movie's plot in three sentences.*

summary (sum′ ə rē) *n.* a short report or description, giving the main points: *In your book report, write a summary of the plot. pl.* **summaries.**

summer (sum′ ər) *n.* the season after spring; the warmest season of the year: *Every summer I go to visit my grandparents.*

summit (sum′ it) *n.* the top; the highest point: *the summit of a mountain.*

summon (sum′ ən) *v.* to order to come: *The king summoned his doctor to the royal court.*

sun (sun) *n.* the very bright star in the sky during the day; it gives off heat and light.

sunburn (sun′ bůrn′) *n.* a red, sore area of your skin that has been burned by the rays of the sun.

sundae (sun′ dā *or* sun′ dē) *n.* ice cream served with a candy sauce, nuts, cherries, and whipped cream.

Sunday (sun′ dā *or* sun′ dē) *n.* the first day of the week.

sundial (sun′ dī′ əl *or* sun′ dīl′) *n.* an instrument that shows the time by the position of the sun's shadow on its face.

sunflower (sun′ flow′ ər) *n.* a large yellow flower that grows on a tall plant: *Sunflower seeds can be eaten and are also used for cooking oil.*

sunflower

sung (sung) see **sing**.

sunglasses (sun′ glas′ əz) *n. pl.* coloured or tinted eyeglasses that help protect your eyes from sunlight.

sunk (sungk) see **sink**.

sunlight (sun′ līt′) *n.* the light shining from the sun.

sunny (sun′ ē) *adj.* bright with sunshine; not cloudy: *a sunny day; a sunnier day; the sunniest day yet.*

sunrise (sun′ rīz′) *n.* the time when the sun appears to come up.

sunset (sun′ set′) *n.* the time when the sun appears to go down.

sunshine (sun′ shīn′) *n.* the light shining from the sun.

super (sū′ pər) *adj.* (*slang*) **1.** very large. **2.** excellent.

> **super**– is a prefix meaning "great," "above," or "more"; a "supermarket" is larger than a regular market or grocery store, and it carries a lot of food products.

superb (sū pėrb′) *adj.* excellent; of very high quality. —**superbly** *adv.*

superintendent (sū′ pər in ten′ dənt) *n.* **1.** a person in charge; a person who directs or manages: *superintendent of schools.* **2.** a person who looks after an apartment or office building.

superior (sə pēr′ ē ər) *adj.* **1.** better than: *These apples are superior to those.* **2.** higher in rank: *A general is superior to a captain.*

supermarket (sū′ pər mär′ kit) *n.* a very large store that sells food and household goods: *Shoppers serve themselves in a supermarket.*

supernatural (sū′ pər nach′ ə rəl *or* sū′ pər nach′ rəl) *adj.* not part of the natural world; having to do with spirits or unexplained events. —**supernaturally** *adv.*

supersonic (sū′ pər son′ ik) *adj.* travelling faster than the speed of sound: *a supersonic jet.*

superstition (sū′ pər stish′ ən) *n.* a belief that something can cause good luck or bad luck: *It is a superstition that walking under a ladder brings bad luck.*

superstitious (sū′ pər stish′ əs) *adj.* having superstitions.

supervise (sū′ pər vīz′) *v.* to manage and direct other people or an activity: *The teacher supervised the children in the playground.* **supervising. supervised.**

supervisor (sū′ pər vī′ zər) *n.* a person who manages and directs others.

supper (sup′ ər) *n.* the last meal of the day; the evening meal.

supply (sə plī′) *n.* a quantity of things kept ready to be used or sold: *The market has a large supply of peaches this week.* *pl.* **supplies.** —*v.* to provide: *The butcher supplies us with good cuts of meat.* **supplying. supplied.** she **supplies.**

support (sə pôrt′) *n.* **1.** something that holds up something else. **2.** help or encouragement: *The hospital needs the support of our community.* —*v.* **1.** to hold up; to bear: *The elevator can support no more than ten people.* **2.** to help; to encourage: *We support the local football team.* **supporting. supported.**

suppose (sə pōz′) *v.* **1.** to imagine; to pretend: *Let's suppose we are on a spaceship.* **2.** to think something is likely to happen; to guess: *I suppose he'll bring it later.* **supposing. supposed.**

suppress (sə pres′) *v.* **1.** to put an end to by force: *That country suppresses free speech.* **2.** to hold back: *to suppress a laugh.* **suppressing. suppressed.**

supreme (sū prēm′ *or* sə prēm′) *adj.* the highest or the best. —**supremely** *adv.*

sure (shūr) *adj.* **1.** certain: *John is sure he met you before.* **2.** confident: *to be sure of yourself.* —**surely** *adv.*

surf (sürf) *n.* waves breaking on the seashore.

surface (sür′ fəs) *n.* the outside or top part of anything: *the surface of the moon; the surface of a table.* —*v.* to rise to the surface: *The diver surfaced after a few seconds.* **surfacing. surfaced.**

surfing (sürf′ ing) *n.* the sport of riding a board on a wave toward the shore.

surgeon (sür′ jən) *n.* a doctor who performs operations.

surgery (sür′ jər ē) *n.* the treatment of illness and injury by operating on the body.

surname (sür′ nām′) *n.* a person's family name: *Chong is the surname of Wayne Michael Chong.*

surprise (sər prīz′ *or* sə prīz′) *n.* something unexpected or sudden: *My cousin's gift was a surprise.* —*v.* to do something that someone does not expect: *We surprised Maria with our visit.* **surprising. surprised.**

surrender (sə ren′ dər) *n.* the act of giving up. —*v.* to give up: *Surrender your tickets at the door.* **surrendering. surrendered.**

surround (sə round′) *v.* to be on all sides around something: *Trees surround the farm.* **surrounding. surrounded.**

surroundings (sə rown′ dingz) *n. pl.* the things that are around you; your environment: *When I work, I like my surroundings to be bright, cheerful, and neat.*

survey (sür′ vā) *n.* **1.** a general view of something. **2.** a map or plan of an area. **3.** a collection of information to show what people think about something: *We took a survey to see if people wanted a new road.* *pl.* **surveys.**

survey (sər vā′) *v.* to take or make a survey. **surveying. surveyed.**

survive (sər vīv′) *v.* to remain alive: *The shrubs survived the cold of last winter.* **surviving. survived.**

survivor (sər vī′ vər) *n.* a person who survives an accident, illness, injury, or hardship.

suspect (sus′ pekt) *n.* someone who is thought to be guilty of a crime, although there is little or no proof.

suspect (səs pekt′) *v.* **1.** to imagine: *I didn't suspect they would plan a surprise party.* **2.** to think someone is guilty without having proof: *She suspects that I took her watch.* **suspecting. suspected.**

suspend (səs pənd′) *v.* **1.** to hang something so that it can swing. **2.** to keep out for a time as punishment: *to be suspended from school.* **suspending. suspended.**

suspense (səs pens′) *n.* the condition of being uncertain, worried, or afraid that something might happen: *I was in suspense until the very end of the book.*

suspicion (sə spish′ ən) *n.* a feeling that something is wrong or that someone is guilty: *I have a suspicion that they cheated on the test.*

suspicious (sə spish′ əs) *adj.* feeling that something is wrong; not trusting: *My neighbour is suspicious of people she doesn't know well.* —**suspiciously** *adv.*

swallow (swol′ ō) *n.* a small bird that can fly very fast: *Swallows have pointed wings and a pointed tail.* —*v.* to pass food or liquid down your throat. **swallowing. swallowed.**

swallow

swam (swam) see **swim**.

swamp (swomp) *n.* an area of soft, very wet ground. —*v.* **1.** to cover with water: *Water swamped the boat.* **2.** to overwhelm: *I'm swamped with work.* **swamping. swamped.**

swan (swon) *n.* a large, graceful water bird that is usually white and has a long neck.

swap (swop) *n.* an exchange of one thing for another: *Avtar likes my stamp collection, and I like his baseball cards, so we decided to do a swap.* —*v.* to exchange one thing for another. **swapping. swapped.**

swarm (swȯrm) *n.* **1.** a large group of insects: *a swarm of bees.* **2.** a large group of people or animals. —*v.* to form a swarm. **swarming. swarmed.**

> **Swarm** comes from the old English word *swearm,* which meant a group of bees.

sway (swā) *v.* to swing from side to side. **swaying. swayed.**

swear (swer) *v.* **1.** to make a promise or to take an oath: *In the court of law, the witness swore to tell the truth.* **2.** to use bad language. **swearing. swore.** they have **sworn.**

sweat (swet) *n.* the salty moisture that forms on your skin when you are very hot or ill. —*v.* to give off this moisture. **sweating. sweated.**

sweater (swet′ ər) *n.* a knitted garment worn over the upper part of your body to keep you warm.

sweatshirt (swet′ shu̇rt′) *n.* a heavy, warm shirt, pulled over the head, often worn for outdoor sports.

sweep (swēp) *n.* the act of sweeping: *Give the kitchen a quick sweep.* —*v.* to clean the floor or ground with a brush or broom. **sweeping. swept.**

sweet (swēt) *n.* a candy. —*adj.* **1.** tasting like sugar. **2.** pleasant to smell: *a sweet flower.* **3.** pleasant to hear: *a sweet voice.* **4.** nice; lovable: *a sweet person.* —**sweetly** *adv.*

sweeten (swē′ tən) *v.* to make sweet: *I sweetened the lemonade with honey.* **sweetening. sweetened.**

swell (swel) *adj.* (*slang*) good: *That's swell.* —*v.* to grow bigger; to bulge: *My sprained ankle has swelled so much that I can't put on my shoe.* **swelling. swelled.** it has **swollen** or **swelled.**

swept (swept) see **sweep**.

swerve (swu̇rv) *v.* to change direction quickly: *Joan swerved on her bicycle to avoid the little boy.* **swerving. swerved.**

swift (swift) *adj.* fast; speedy; quick: *a swift automobile.* —**swiftly** *adv.*

swim (swim) *n.* the act of swimming. —*v.* to move through water using your arms and legs. **swimming. swam.** I have **swum.**

swimmer (swim′ ər) *n.* a person who swims.

swindle (swin′ dəl) *v.* to cheat someone out of money or property: *He realized he had been swindled when the "gold" watch turned green.* **swindling. swindled.**

swine (swīn) *n.* a pig. *pl.* **swine.**

swing (swing) *n.* a seat hanging on ropes or chains on which a child swings. —*v.* **1.** to move back and forth: *to swing on a rope.* **2.** to turn quickly: *The driver swung around the corner.* **swinging. swung.**

swirl (swûrl) *v.* to spin around and around: *The leaves swirled in the wind.* **swirling. swirled.**

switch (swich) *n.* a small knob or button used to turn something on or off: *a switch for the light. pl.* **switches.** —*v.* **1.** to change from one thing to another: *Last year I switched from violin lessons to piano lessons.* **2.** to turn on or off with a switch. **switching. switched.**

swollen (swō′ lən) see **swell**.

sword (sȯrd) *n.* a long steel blade with a handle, used as a weapon.

swore, sworn (swȯr, swȯrn) see **swear**.

swum (swum) see **swim**.

swung (swung) see **swing**.

syllable (sil′ ə bəl) *n.* a separate sound in a word, usually containing a vowel sound: *The word "dictionary" has four syllables.*

symbol (sim′ bəl) *n.* something that stands for or represents something else: *A lion is a symbol of courage. Red is the symbol for "stop" or "danger."*

sympathetic (sim′ pə thet′ ik) *adj.* understanding the pain or sorrow of others: *When our cat died, my best friend was very kind and sympathetic.* —**sympathetically** *adv.*

sympathy (sim′ pə thē) *n.* a feeling of being sorry for someone who is ill, sad, or in trouble. *pl.* **sympathies.**

symphony (sim′ fə nē) *n.* a long piece of music written for an orchestra. *pl.* **symphonies.**

symptom (simp′ təm) *n.* a sign of illness or of something else wrong: *Sneezing is often a symptom of an allergy.*

synagogue (sin′ ə gog′) *n.* a building for religious worship and teaching.

syndrome (sin′ drōm) *n.* a group of symptoms that indicate a disease or an illness.

synonym (sin′ ə nim′) *n.* a word that has the same or almost the same meaning as another word: *Two synonyms for "happy" are "glad" and "joyful."*

synthesizer (sin′ thə sīz′ ər) *n.* an electronic musical instrument that imitates many different musical sounds.

synthetic (sin thet′ ik) *adj.* made by humans, not by nature: *Plastic is a synthetic product. Wood is natural.* —**synthetically** *adv.*

syrup (su̇r′ əp *or* sir′ əp) *n.* a thick, sweet, sticky liquid: *I like lots of syrup on my pancakes.*

system (sis′ təm) *n.* **1.** a number of things that form a whole or work together: *the solar system; the railway system.* **2.** a way of doing things: *My father has his own system for doing the laundry.*

Tt

tab (tab) *n.* **1.** the small metal loop that you pull to open a can. **2.** a restaurant bill. **3.** on a computer or typewriter, a marker that can be set: *Tabs allow you to create columns of words or numbers.*

table (tā′ bəl) *n.* **1.** a piece of furniture with a flat top and legs: *You eat your meals at a table.* **2.** a list of numbers or information: *a multiplication table.*

tablecloth (tā′ bəl kloth′) *n.* a cloth that covers a table.

tablespoon (tā′ bəl spūn′) *n.* **1.** a large spoon used for eating and serving food. **2.** a unit of measurement used in cooking: *A tablespoon equals 15 mL.*

tablet (tab′ lət) *n.* a small, flat piece of medicine that is swallowed; a pill.

table tennis a game played on a table with a net at the middle. The players use small, wooden paddles to hit a hollow, plastic ball over the net: *Another name for table tennis is Ping-Pong.*

table tennis

tack (tak) *n.* a very short, sharp nail: *A tack is used to fasten paper to a bulletin board.* —*v.* to fasten with tacks. **tacking. tacked.**

tackle (tak′ əl) *n.* the equipment you need to go fishing, such as rods, hooks, and lines. —*v.* **1.** to deal with a big or difficult task: *The children tackled the job of weeding the garden.* **2.** in football, to bring an opponent down to the ground: *He fell heavily when he was tackled.* **tackling. tackled.**

tact (takt) *n.* an ability to speak carefully, so that nobody will be upset by what you say: *It is usually a good idea to use tact if you are talking to someone who is angry.*

tactful (takt′ fəl) *adj.* being careful about what you say, so that nobody will be upset: *My friend asked me if I liked her new haircut. I tried to be tactful and said that it looked easy to care for.* —**tactfully** *adv.*

tadpole (tad′ pōl) *n.* a young frog or toad: *A tadpole looks like a tiny, plump fish.*

> The first part of the word **tadpole**, "tad," is just another way of saying toad. "Poll" is an old word for head. Because baby toads seem to have such big heads, people called them "toad-heads," or tadpoles.

taffy, toffee (taf′ ē, tof′ ē) *n.* a chewy candy made with brown sugar and butter.

tag (tag) *n.* **1.** a label: *a price tag.* **2.** a children's game in which one person who is "it" chases after the others until he or she touches one. —*v.* **1.** to put a label on something. **2.** to touch someone in the game of tag. **3.** in baseball, to put a base runner out by touching him or her with the ball. **tagging. tagged.**

tail (tāl) *n.* **1.** the part at the back end of an animal that sticks out and can move: *Birds, fish, reptiles, and most mammals have tails.* **2.** something like an animal's tail: *a comet's tail.* **3.** the side of a coin that does not have the head on it. —*v.* to follow: *The police tailed the car.* **tailing. tailed.**

tailor (tā′ lər) *n.* a person who makes or repairs clothes, especially suits. —*v.* **1.** to make or alter clothing to fit an individual person. **2.** to do something to suit a particular purpose: *We tailored our vacation to what we enjoy doing most—swimming and hiking.* **tailoring. tailored.**

take (tāk) *v.* **1.** to get hold of or to receive: *Take my hand. Take this present.* **2.** to carry with you: *I took along an umbrella.* **3.** to do or make something: *to take a photo.* **4.** to ride on: *Alex takes the school bus.* **5.** to select: *Take a seat.* **6.** to bring into your body: *Take a deep breath, and then take your medicine.* **taking. took.** she has **taken.**

take aback to startle: *I was taken aback by his anger.*

take care of to care for a person or animal: *I took care of the injured bird until it was well enough to fly.*

take off **1.** to fly: *Our airplane takes off at 1:30 p.m.* **2.** to leave quickly: *I'm taking off now. Bye!*

take over **1.** to take or seize control: *The hijackers took over the airplane.* **2.** to continue a task that someone else has started: *I need a rest—will you take over painting the wall?*

take part to be involved in: *She took part in the school play.*

take place to happen; to occur: *When did the accident take place?*

take your time not to hurry.

takeoff (tāk′ of′) *n.* the action of leaving the ground and going up in the air: *The airplane waited on the runway, ready for takeoff.*

takeout (tak′ owt′) *adj.* having to do with food bought at a restaurant and taken home to eat: *a takeout Chinese dinner.*

tale (tāl) *n.* a story, true or made-up.

talent (tal′ ənt) *n.* a natural ability to do something: *Aaron has a real talent for acting.*

talented (tal′ ən təd) *adj.* having a talent: *She is a talented writer.*

talk (tok) *n.* **1.** a chat: *I had a long talk with my best friend.* **2.** a speech: *The speaker gave a talk on birds that live in this area.* —*v.* **1.** to say words; to speak. **2.** to chat or discuss: *We talked about our summer holidays.* **talking. talked.**

talkative (tok′ ə tiv) *adj.* talking a great deal: *She became quite talkative when I asked her to tell me about her new kitten.* —**talkatively** *adv.*

tall (tol) *adj.* **1.** very high: *a tall tower; a taller one; the tallest tower in the world.* **2.** having a certain height: *How tall are you now?*

talon (tal′ ən) *n.* the claw of a bird of prey.

tame (tām) *adj.* not wild; living with people as a pet: *a tame rabbit.* —**tamely** *adv.* —*v.* to train a wild animal to live with people: *The cowgirl tamed the wild horse so that she could ride it.* **taming. tamed.**

tamper (tam′ pər) *v.* to meddle or bother in a way that makes things worse: *They tampered with the tape recorder and broke it.* **tampering. tampered.**

tan (tan) *n.* **1.** a light brown colour. **2.** a golden-brown colour that a person with pale skin becomes when he or she spends a long time in the sun. —*adj.* having the colour of tan. —*v.* **1.** (for your skin) to turn brown from being in the sun. **2.** to make animal hides into leather by soaking them in an acid. **tanning. tanned.**

tangerine (tan′ jə rēn′) *n.* a juicy citrus fruit, rather like an orange, but smaller.

Tangerines were first exported to Europe from Tangier in Morocco, a country in North Africa. The city of Tangier has given us the name of this delicious, juicy fruit.

tangle (tang′ gəl) *v.* to become twisted or knotted together: *The strong wind has tangled her long hair.* **tangling. tangled.** (*opp.* **untangle.**)

tank (tangk) *n.* **1.** a large container that holds liquid or gas. **2.** an enclosed, powerful vehicle with guns attached to it: *Tanks are used by armies for combat purposes.*

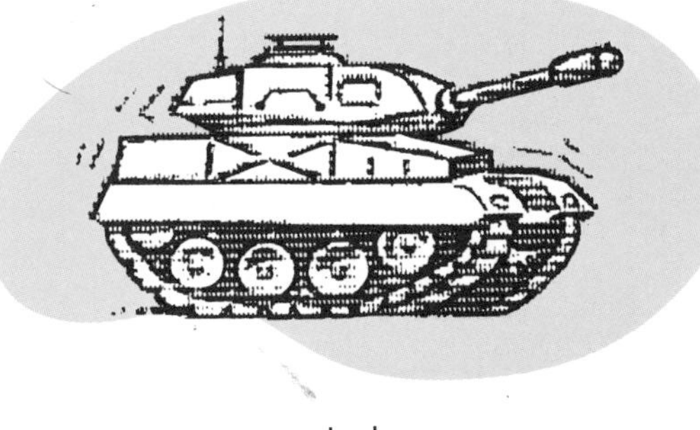

tank

tanker (tang′ kər) *n.* **1.** a large ship used to carry coal, oil, or other cargo. **2.** a large truck used to carry milk or other liquids.

tantrum (tan′ trəm) *n.* a noisy display of bad temper: *When she didn't get what she wanted, the toddler had a tantrum.*

tap (tap) *n.* a device for turning gas or water on or off: *the bathtub tap.* —*v.* **1.** to knock lightly: *She tapped on the door.* **2.** to make a hole in something so that liquid comes out: *to tap maple trees for sap.* **tapping. tapped.**

tap dance a type of dancing in which the dancer wears special shoes to make loud, fast taps on the floor.

tape (tāp) *n.* **1.** a thin, plastic strip with one sticky side. **2.** a thin, narrow strip of plastic film, used for recording sounds or pictures. —*v.* **1.** to stick or seal with tape: *Laura taped the pictures into her scrapbook.* **2.** to record sounds or pictures on a strip of film: *I taped my speech and listened to it several times to hear what it sounded like.* **taping. taped.**

tape measure a long, narrow strip of cloth, plastic, or metal, marked in centimetres or inches: *Tape measures are used to measure length or distance.*

tape recorder a machine that records sounds on a plastic magnetic tape, which can be played back later.

tar (tȧr) *n.* a thick, black, sticky substance, used to cover roads and sometimes to waterproof wood. —*v.* to cover with tar. **tarring. tarred.**

tarantula (tə ran′ chə lə) *n.* a large, hairy spider: *A tarantula can give a painful bite, but it is usually not serious.*

target (tȧr′ gət) *n.* an object or a goal to aim at: *Kit shot the arrow into the centre of the target.*

tarnish (tȧr′ nish) *v.* to lose shine and become dull, as some metals do: *Silver tarnishes easily.* **tarnishing. tarnished.**

tart (tȧrt) *n.* a small pie of fruit, custard, or some other filling. —*adj.* sharp or sour in taste: *a tart green apple.* —**tartly** *adv.*

task (task) *n.* a single job to be done: *My brother has the task of clearing out the shed.*

taste (tāst) *n.* **1.** one of the five senses—the ability to notice flavours in the mouth. **2.** the flavour of the food you eat: *a sweet taste; a sour taste.* **3.** a feeling about what will look right or wrong: *My brother shows good taste in the clothes he wears.* —*v.* **1.** to eat or drink a little of something to try its flavour: *Nadia tasted the soup and liked it.* **2.** to have a certain flavour: *This hamburger tastes spicy.* **tasting. tasted.**

tasty (tās′ tē) *adj.* having a good flavour: *a tasty strawberry; a tastier one; the tastiest strawberry of all.*

tattered (tat′ ərd) *adj.* torn; ragged: *The beggar wore a tattered old coat.*

tattletale (tat′ əl tāl′) *n.* a person who tells the secrets of other people or spreads rumours.

tattoo (ta tü′) *n.* a coloured picture pricked into the skin, using needles and permanent dye. *pl.* **tattoos.** —*v.* to prick a tattoo into the skin. **tattooing. tattooed.**

taught (tot) see **teach**.

taunt (tont) *n.* a hurtful remark. —*v.* to tease in a hurtful manner; to jeer: *the crowd taunted the visiting team at the ballgame.*

taut (tot) *adj.* pulled very tight: *a taut rope.* —**tautly** *adv.*

tax (taks) *n.* money that people pay to the government for roads, education, health care, and other public services. *pl.* **taxes.** —*v.* **1.** to put a tax on: *to tax cigarettes.* **2.** to put a heavy strain on someone: *Carrying this heavy box up four flights of stairs taxed my strength.* **taxing. taxed.**

taxi (tak′ sē) *n.* a car and driver that you hire; you pay for the distance that the driver takes you. *pl.* **taxis.** —*v.* (for an airplane) to move slowly over a surface: *the plane taxied along the runway.* **taxiing** or **taxying. taxied.** it **taxis.**

tea (tē) *n.* a drink made by pouring boiling water over dried tea leaves: *Tea plants grow in China, India, Sri Lanka, and other countries.*

teach (tēch) *v.* to show people how to do things or to give them knowledge; to give lessons. **teaching. taught.**

teacher (tēch′ ər) *n.* a person who teaches, usually in a school.

teacup (tē′ kup) *n.* a small cup with a handle, used for drinking tea: *A teacup rests on a saucer.*

team (tēm) *n.* **1.** a group of people playing or working together, often in a game: *a volleyball team.* **2.** a group of animals working together: *a team of huskies pulling a sled.* —*v.* (used with **up**) to join with other people in a game or work: *We need one more player to team up with us.* **teaming. teamed.**

teammate (tēm′ māt′) *n.* a member of the same team as a player: *My teammate helped me score the winning goal for our team.* *pl.* **teammates.**

teamwork (tēm′ wůrk′) *n.* working together: *Thanks to teamwork, the school play was a great success.*

teapot (tē′ pot′) *n.* a china pot in which tea is made; it has a handle and a spout.

teapot

tear (tēr) *n.* a drop of salty water coming from your eye.

tear (ter) *n.* a ripped spot: *Please sew the tear on my jacket.* —*v.* **1.** to rip: *I tore my sleeve.* **2.** to pull into pieces: *We tore the paper into strips.* **tearing. tore.** I have **torn.**

tease (tēz) *n.* a person who bothers someone in a playful way: *Don't be such a tease because it upsets your little brother.* —*v.* to bother or make fun of in a playful way: *Don't tease the dog. He may bite you.* **teasing. teased.**

teaspoon (tē′ spūn) *n.* **1.** a small spoon used for eating and stirring. **2.** a unit of measurement used in cooking: *A teaspoon equals 5 mL.*

technical (tek′ nə kəl) *adj.* having to do with a special skill, especially related to mechanics or technology: *The instructions for how to program the VCR are very technical.* —**technically** *adv.*

technique (tek nēk′) *n.* a style or way of doing something: *The dentist has a new technique for protecting teeth from decay.*

technological (tek nə loj′ ə kəl) *adj.* having to do with technology. —**technologically** *adv.*

technology (tek nol′ ə jē) *n.* the practical ways of using scientific knowledge to make products: *I wish that I understood the technology that makes my computer work.*

teem (tēm) *v.* **1.** to pour heavily: *The rain teemed for hours.* **2.** to be crowded with: *The swamp was teeming with mosquitoes.* **teeming. teemed.**

teen (tēn) *n.* short for **teenager**.

teenager (tēn′ āj′ ər) *n.* a person who is between 13 and 19 years of age.

teeny (tē′ nē) *adj.* tiny: *a teeny baby; a teenier baby; the teeniest baby in the crib.*

teepee (tē′ pē) see **tepee**.

teeth (tēTH) plural of **tooth**.

teethe (tēth) *v.* (for a baby) to be getting the first teeth: *Some babies have very sore gums when they are teething.* **teething. teethed.**

tele– is a prefix meaning "far": a "telephone" lets you talk to someone far away; a "telescope" makes faraway objects appear closer.

telephone (tel′ ə fōn′) *n.* an instrument that lets you speak to anyone else who has a telephone by sending your voice along electric wires. —*v.* to call someone by dialing a telephone. **telephoning. telephoned.**

telescope (tel′ ə skōp′) *n.* a tube with glass lenses that make distant objects look closer and larger.

televise (tel′ ə vīz) *v.* to broadcast by television. **televising. televised.**

television (tel′ ə vizh′ ən) *n.* a machine that receives electric signals and turns them into pictures and sound.

tell (tel) *v.* to give information or a story by talking: *Tell me the news.* **telling. told.**

teller (tel′ ər) *n.* **1.** a person who tells a story. **2.** a person who helps you in a bank.

temper (tem′ pər) *n.* the mood you are in: *When you are in a bad temper, it means that you are angry or annoyed about something.*
lose your temper to become very angry.

temperamental (temp rə men′ təl) *adj.* easily upset; moody: *It is sometimes hard to deal with a temperamental person.*

temperature (tem′ pər ə chər *or* tem′ prə chər) *n.* how hot or cold something is, especially the air: *What is the temperature outside?*

temple (tem′ pəl) *n.* **1.** a building for prayer and worship. **2.** the flat part on either side of your forehead.

temporary (tem′ pə rer′ ē) *adj.* for a short time; not permanent: *This will be my temporary desk.* —**temporarily** *adv.*

tempt (tempt) *v.* **1.** to try to make someone do something, usually something that is foolish or wrong: *I was tempted to spend all my money on candy.* **2.** to attract strongly: *The chocolate cake is tempting everyone in the room.* **tempting. tempted.**

temptation (tem tā′ shən) *n.* the act of tempting, or something that tempts: *The weekend trip you suggest is a temptation, but I have to stay home and write my essay.*

ten (ten) *n., adj.* one more than nine: 10.

tenant (ten′ ənt) *n.* a person who pays money to live in an apartment or building that belongs to someone else.

tend (tend) *v.* **1.** to care for: *to tend cattle.* **2.** to be likely to: *My friends tell me I tend to speak too fast.* **tending. tended.**

tendency (ten′ dən sē) *n.* a habit; a natural way of doing things; or a thing that is likely to happen: *The model car has a tendency to curve to the right. pl.* **tendencies.**

tender (ten′ dər) *adj.* **1.** soft; not tough: *tender meat.* **2.** gentle; loving: *a tender smile.* **3.** sore: *My sprained ankle feels tender.* —**tenderly** *adv.*

tendon (ten′ dən) *n.* a tough tissue of the body that joins the bones to the muscles.

tennis (ten′ is) *n.* a game in which one or two players on each side of a net hit a ball back and forth, using a racquet.

tense (tens) *n.* the form of a verb that shows when the action takes place: *The past tense of "see" is "saw." —adj.* not relaxed: *He was very tense before skating in front of the crowd.* —**tensely** *adv.*

tension (ten′ shən) *n.* **1.** a feeling that you cannot relax: *The arena was filled with tension during the final seconds of the tied hockey game.* **2.** tightness: *The tension caused the rope to break.*

tent (tent) *n.* a canvas or nylon shelter, held up by poles.

tent

tentacle (ten′ tə kəl) *n.* a leg or feeler of some animals: *An octopus has tentacles.*

tepee, teepee (tē′ pē) *n.* a cone-shaped tent made of poles covered with animal skins, once used by aboriginal peoples on the North American plains.

term (tûrm) *n.* **1.** a certain period of time: *a school term.* **2.** part of a contract or agreement: *A term in our lease says we can't have pets.* **3.** a word or words with special meaning: *The manual lists computer terms.*

terminal (tûr′ mə nəl) *n.* **1.** the building from which a railway, truck, bus, or airplane trip starts or ends. **2.** the place where information can be put in or taken out of the computer's memory.

termite (tûr′ mīt) *n.* a small, ant-like insect that eats wood: *Termites are very harmful to buildings and trees.*

terrarium (tər er′ ē əm) *n.* a glass or plastic container in which to grow plants.

terrestrial (tə res′ trē əl) *adj.* having to do with land or the earth, not with water or air, or the sun, moon, and stars.

terrible (ter′ ə bəl) *adj.* awful; causing fear: *a terrible accident.* —**terribly** *adv.*

terrier (ter′ ē ər) *n.* a type of dog once used for chasing animals out of their holes: *Most terriers are small, with short legs and shaggy hair.*

The **terrier** gets its name from the French word *terre,* meaning "earth" or "ground." Hunters used these dogs to dig up the tunnels of small animals such as rabbits.

terrific (tə rif′ ik) *adj.* very good or great: *a terrific hockey game; a terrific memory.* —**terrifically** *adv.*

terrify (ter′ ə fī′) *v.* to cause great fear: *The children were terrified of the bull.* **terrifying. terrified.** it **terrifies.**

territory (ter′ ə tôr′ ē) *n.* a large area of land: *The pioneers explored new territory.* *pl.* **territories.**

terror (ter′ ər) *n.* great fear; panic.

test (test) *n.* **1.** an examination: *She practised for her driving test.* **2.** an experiment; a trial: *We conducted a test in science class to see which substances would dissolve in water. —v.* **1.** to find out how much someone knows: *The teacher tested the class in math.* **2.** to try out: *The driver tested his brakes.* **testing. tested.**

testify (tes′ tə fī′) *v.* in a court of law, to give evidence or to tell what happened: *The witness testified that she saw the car hit the rail.* **testifying. testified.** she **testifies.**

text (tekst) *n.* **1.** the main amount of reading material in a book: *The book has 100 pages of text and 20 pages of pictures.* **2.** short for **textbook**.

textbook (tekst′ bu̇k) *n.* a book used for study by students.

texture (teks′ chůr) *n.* the feel or look or something: *Sandpaper has a rough texture.*

than (THan) *conj.* compared to: *She is older than I am.*

Be careful not to mix up **than** with "then"; "than" is used to compare things.

thank (thangk) *v.* to say how grateful you are for something: *Julie thanked her aunt for the present.* **thanking. thanked.**

thank you an expression showing how grateful you are for something.

thankful (thangk′ fəl) *adj.* grateful; pleased: *We are thankful that no one was hurt.* (*opp.* **unthankful.**) —**thankfully** *adv.*

thanks (thangks) *n., pl.* thank you.

that (THat) *adj.* being over there: *That flower is beautiful. pl.* **those.** —*pron.* **1.** the one over there: *That is our neighbour's house.* **2.** the one which: *the house that we live in. pl.* **those.** —*conj.* a word used to connect two parts of a sentence: *I know that they are coming to visit.*

that's (THats) a short form (contraction) of **that is.**

thaw (tho) *n.* the melting of ice and snow in mild weather: *a spring thaw.* —*v.* to become unfrozen or to melt: *The frozen turkey thawed in the refrigerator.* **thawing. thawed.**

the (THē *or* THə) *article* "a certain one" or "certain ones": *The girls are swimming.*

theatre, theater (thē′ ə tər) *n.* a building where plays are acted or movies are shown.

theatrical (thē at′ rə kəl) *adj.* **1.** having to do with the theatre. **2.** using showy gestures: *a theatrical performance.* —**theatrically** *adv.*

theft (theft) *n.* the act of stealing: *Two people were arrested for the theft of the car.*

their (THer) *adj.* belonging to them: *their project.*

theirs (THerz) *pron.* the one belonging to them: *The project is theirs.*

Be careful not to mix up **theirs** with "there's"; "there's" is short for there is.

them (THem) *pron.* the form of **they** that is used as the object of a verb or preposition: *Tom and Fatima are my friends. I like them.*

theme (thēm) *n.* the main topic or subject: *Friendship is the theme of my report.*

themselves (THem selvz′) *pron.* them alone: *They have only themselves to blame for the accident.*

Themselves is used when the subject and object of a verb are the same: *The two players hurt themselves in the ballgame.*

then (THen) *adv.* **1.** at that time: *We lived in the country then. Now we live in the city.* **2.** next: *Let's play a game, and then have a snack.* **3.** therefore; for that reason: *If you study hard for a test, then you should do well.*

theory (thē′ ə rē *or* thēr′ ē) *n.* an explanation, based on thought or ideas, for how things behave in nature or for something that has happened: *the theory of gravity. pl.* **theories.**

there (THer) *adv.* **1.** in that place: *I saw your book over there.* **2.** to that place: *They went there for the holidays.*

therefore (THer′ fôr) *adv.* for that reason; because of that: *He felt ill; therefore, he went to bed.*

there's (THerz) a short form (contraction) of **there is.**

Be careful not to mix up **there's** with "theirs": *There's the lake. That dog is theirs.*

thermal (thůr′ məl) *adj.* involving heat: *Thermal underwear will keep you warm in very cold weather.* —**thermally** *adv.*

thermometer (thür mom′ ə tər) *n.* an instrument that measures temperature in degrees.

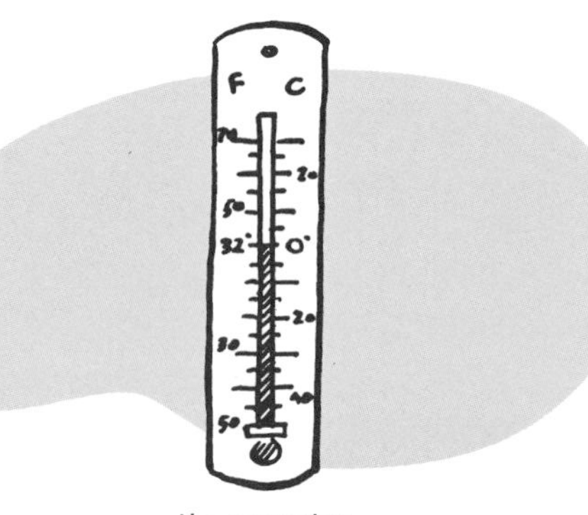
thermometer

thesaurus (thə sȯr′ əs) *n.* a kind of dictionary that lists synonyms (words that have almost the same meaning): *My thesaurus shows me that some other words that mean "angry" are "upset," "annoyed," and "furious." pl.* **thesauri** (thə sȯr ī) or **thesauruses.**

these (THēz) plural of **this**.

they (THā) *n.* the persons, animals, or things being talked about: ***They** is the plural form of **he, she,** or **it**.*

they'd (THād) a short form (contraction) of **they had** or **they would**.

they'll (THāl) a short form (contraction) of **they will**.

they're (THer) a short form (contraction) of **they are**.

they've (THāv) a short form (contraction) of **they have**.

thick (thik) *adj.* **1.** measuring a lot from side to side; not thin: *a thick slice of bread.* **2.** not watery: *thick soup.* **3.** hard to see through: *thick fog.* —**thickly** *adv.*

thicken (thik′ ən) *v.* to make thick or thicker: *A sauce can be thickened with flour.* **thickening. thickened.**

thief (thēf) *n.* a person who steals. *pl.* **thieves.**

thigh (thī) *n.* the part of your leg between the knee and hip.

thimble (thim′ bəl) *n.* a small metal or plastic cap, worn to protect the end of your finger when sewing.

thin (thin) *adj.* measuring a little from side to side; not thick; slender; slim: *a thin slice of bread; a thinner slice; the thinnest slice of all.* —**thinly** *adv.*

thing (thing) *n.* **1.** anything that can be seen or touched, but is not alive. **2.** anything that can be done, thought, or felt: *I went to my room to think things over.*

think (thingk) *v.* **1.** to use your mind: *I was thinking about what he said.* **2.** to have an opinion: *I think they are telling the truth.* **thinking. thought** (thot).

third (thürd) *n.* the one following the second: *I was third in the race.*
—*adj.* following second: *I was in third place.*

thirst (thürst) *n.* a dry feeling in your throat that tells you that you want to drink.

thirsty (thürs′ tē) *adj.* needing to drink: *a thirsty baby; a thirstier one; the thirstiest baby in the nursery.* —**thirstily** *adv.*

thirteen (thür′ tēn) *n., adj.* ten more than three: 13.

thirty (thür′ tē) *n., adj.* ten times three: 30.

this (THis) *adj.* being the person, thing, or idea already talked about: *This shirt is my favourite. pl.* **these.** —*pron.* some person, thing, or idea already talked about: *Is this your room? pl.* **these.**

thistle (this′ əl) *n.* a prickly plant.

thong (thong) *n.* **1.** a narrow strip of material, usually leather. **2.** a sandal held onto your foot by a narrow piece of leather or plastic that fits between your toes.

thorn (thȯrn) *n.* a sharp point on the sides of a stem or branch: *A rose stem has thorns that can prick your skin if you touch them.*

thorough (thůr′ ō) *adj.* **1.** done properly and carefully: *a thorough piece of work.* **2.** complete: *You need a thorough rest.* —**thoroughly** *adv.*

those (THōs) plural of **that**.

though (THō) *conj.* in spite of the fact that: *We went to the game, even though it was late.*

thought (thot) *n.* **1.** the process of thinking. **2.** what is in your mind when thinking: *Denise gave a lot of thought to the holiday.* **3.** an idea or an opinion: *What are your thoughts on this subject?* —*v.* see **think**.

thoughtful (thot′ fəl) *adj.* **1.** thinking deeply: *Tom was very thoughtful after talking to his mother.* **2.** thinking of others; kind: *It was very thoughtful of you to help me.* —**thoughtfully** *adv.*

thoughtless (thot′ ləs) *adj.* careless; not thinking about other people or things: *It was thoughtless of them not to phone to say they would be late.* —**thoughtlessly** *adv.*

thousand (thow′ zənd) *n., adj.* ten times one hundred: 1000.

thrash (thrash) *v.* **1.** to give a person or animal a beating. **2.** to move wildly: *The frightened dolphin thrashed around in the net.* **thrashing. thrashed.**

thread (thred) *n.* a very thin string of cotton, silk, or other material used in sewing. —*v.* to put thread through the eye, or hole, of a needle. **threading. threaded.**

threat (thret) *n.* a warning that harm, danger, or punishment may be coming.

threaten (thret′ ən) *v.* to make threats against someone. **threatening. threatened.**

three (thrē) *n., adj.* one more than two: 3.

thresh (thresh) *v.* to separate the grain from the husk of corn, wheat, oats, or barley. **threshing. threshed.**

thresher (thresh′ ər) *n.* a machine that threshes.

threw (thrū) see **throw**.

thrifty (thrif′ tē) *adj.* careful about the way you use money: *thrifty shoppers; thriftier ones; the thriftiest shoppers of all.*

thrill (thril) *n.* a feeling or shiver of excitement: *the thrill of riding a roller coaster.* —*v.* **1.** to give a thrill to: *The tightrope walker thrilled the crowd.* **2.** to please very much: *Our parents were thrilled by the wonderful presents we gave them for their anniversary.* **thrilling. thrilled.**

thrilling (thril′ ing) *adj.* causing thrills or great happiness: *The air show was a thrilling event.*

thrive (thrīv) *v.* to grow in a healthy way: *The flowers thrived after I put fertilizer in the soil.* **thriving. thrived.**

throat (thrōt) *n.* the inside of your neck, used for swallowing food, breathing, and making some sounds for talking.

throb (throb) *v.* to beat or pound, the way your heart does. **throbbing. throbbed.**

throne (thrōn) *n.* a special chair on which a king or queen sits during certain ceremonies.

throne

throttle (throt′ əl) *n.* a valve that controls the flow of fuel to an engine. —*v.* to choke someone: *The bully threatened to throttle me.* **throttling. throttled.**

through (thrū) *prep.* **1.** from the beginning to the end of: *The movie was long, but we sat through it all.* **2.** in one end and out the other: *The train went through the tunnel.*

3. moving in: *The ball flew through the air.* —*adj.* finished: *Are you through with my book?*

throughout (thrū owt′) *prep.* everywhere; all over: *There is water throughout the basement.*

throw (thrō) *n.* a pitch or toss of a ball or another object: *That was a good throw!* —*v.* to use your hand and arm to send a ball or another object through the air: *Throw the ball to me.* **throwing. threw** (thrū). I have **thrown** (thrōn).

throw out to put in the garbage.

throw up to vomit.

thrust (thrust) *v.* to push hard and quickly: *The farmer thrust the fork into the hay.* **thrusting. thrust.**

thumb (thum) *n.* the short, thicker finger that is separated from your other four fingers.

thumbtack (thum′ tak) *n.* a tack with a large, flat top that can be pushed into a surface with your thumb.

thump (thump) *n.* a dull, heavy sound: *He jumped off the porch and landed with a thump.* —*v.* to hit something so that you make a dull, heavy sound: *Christine thumped the table loudly.* **thumping. thumped.**

thunder (thun′ dər) *n.* the loud, rumbling noise that follows lightning in a storm. —*v.* to make a loud, rumbling noise: *The jet plane thundered over our heads.* **thundering. thundered.**

Thursday (thůrz′ dā *or* thůrz′ dē) *n.* the fifth day of the week.

tick (tik) *n.* **1.** the clicking sound that a clock makes. **2.** a mark (✔) that shows something is correct or has been counted. —*v.* to make clicking sounds, as a clock does. **ticking. ticked.**

ticket (tik′ ət) *n.* **1.** a small piece of paper or a card that shows that a fee has been paid to see a movie or a game, travel on a train, go to a concert, and so on: *José bought two tickets for the movie.* **2.** a ticket that orders someone to pay a fine: *a traffic ticket.* **3.** a label showing the price of something. —*v.* to put a ticket on something: *The police officer ticketed the car.* **ticketing. ticketed.**

tickle (tik′ əl) *v.* to touch someone's body lightly with your fingers to make him or her giggle and laugh. **tickling. tickled.**

tidal (tīd′ əl) *adj.* related to or having to do with tides: *tidal waters.*

tidal wave a powerful ocean wave, caused by an underground earthquake.

tidbit (tid′ bit) *n.* a small snack or piece of food.

tide (tīd) *n.* the regular rise and fall of the ocean that usually happens twice a day.

tidy (tī′ dē) *adj.* neat, with everything in order: *a tidy desk; a tidier one; the tidiest desk in the classoom.* (*opp.* **untidy.**) —**tidily** *adv.*

tie (tī) *n.* **1.** a long strip of cloth that is tied around the neck and hangs down the front of a shirt. **2.** an even score in a game, contest, or election; a draw. —*v.* **1.** to fasten two or more things together with string or a rope: *I tied the pile of newspapers with string.* **2.** to make a knot in: *to tie shoelaces.* **3.** to be even in a game: *The two teams tied, with a score of one goal each.* **tying. tied.** she **ties.**

tier (tēr) *n.* a series of rows or layers that are placed behind or above one another: *The wedding cake has three tiers.*

tiger (tī′ gər) *n.* a large wild cat of India and other parts of Asia: *A tiger has orangy-yellow fur with large black stripes.*

tight (tīt) *adj.* **1.** fitting very closely: *a tight shoe.* **2.** firmly fastened or stretched: *a tight knot.* —**tightly** *adv.*

tightrope (tīt′ rōp′) *n.* a rope, stretched tightly and placed high above the ground, that acrobats perform on.

tights (tīts) *n. pl.* a thin, tight-fitting covering for the body, from the shoulders or the waist down: *Dancers and acrobats often wear tights.*

tile (tīl) *n.* a hard flat piece of plastic, baked clay, or other material, used to cover floors or walls. —*v.* to put tiles into place: *My parents tiled the basement floor.* **tiling. tiled.**

till (til) *n.* a drawer in which money is kept. —*prep.* until: *We waited for him until noon, but then we had to leave.* —*conj.* until: *Wait here till I come back.* —*v.* to plough the land. **tilling. tilled.**

tilt (tilt) *v.* to lean to one side; to slant: *My desk tilts to one end, so my pencil keeps rolling off.* **tilting. tilted.**

timber (tim′ bər) *n.* **1.** large trees in a forest. **2.** wood used for building.

time (tīm) *n.* **1.** the passing seconds, minutes, hours, days, weeks, months, years, and so on: *Time includes the past, the present, and the future.* **2.** a certain length of time: *It is a long time since I saw my cousin.* **3.** a certain moment of the day, as shown on a clock: *What time is it?* **4.** an experience: *We had a good time at the party.* —*v.* to measure how fast something happens: *I timed my sister during her practice: she ran the race in one minute and twenty-one seconds.* **timing. timed.**

for the time being for now.

from time to time occasionally; once in a while.

in no time very quickly: *The ambulance arrived in no time.*

on time at the correct time: *I arrived on time, but my friend was late.*

timeless (tīm′ ləs) *adj.* lasting forever; eternal: *The plays of Shakespeare are timeless.* —**timelessly** *adv.*

time-out (tīm′ owt′) *n.* a brief rest given to a team or player in a game.

times (tīmz) *prep.* multiplied by: *12 times 3 equals 36.*

timetable (tīm′ tā′ bəl) *n.* a list showing the time that events are planned to happen: *According to the timetable, the train should have been here five minutes ago.*

timid (tim′ id) *adj.* shy; nervous; afraid. —**timidly** *adv.*

tin (tin) *n.* **1.** a silver-coloured metal that does not rust easily. **2.** a can: *a sardine tin.*

tingle (ting′ gəl) *v.* to have a prickly feeling on the skin, from fear or excitement. **tingling. tingled.**

tinsel (tin′ səl) *n.* small strips of metal foil, used for decorating.

tiny (tī′ nē) *adj.* very small: *a tiny mouse; a tinier mouse; the tiniest mouse in the cage.*

tip (tip) *n.* **1.** a small or pointed end: *a finger tip.* **2.** extra money given for a service: *My parents gave the server a tip.* **3.** a piece of helpful information; a suggestion: *Alex gave me some useful tips on cooking eggs.* —*v.* **1.** to tilt or turn: *The baby tipped over the bottle of milk.* **2.** to give extra money for a service: *She tipped the taxi driver for getting her there on time.* **tipping. tipped.**

tiptoe (tip′ tō) *v.* to walk quietly on the tips of your toes: *Dad tiptoed into the sleeping baby's room.* **tiptoeing. tiptoed.** she **tiptoes.**

tire (tīr) *n.* a band of rubber or plastic that fits around the wheel of a car, bicycle, or other vehicle. —*v.* **1.** to become worn-out from activity: *After hiking six kilometres, we were tired and took a rest.* **2.** to be bored: *I'm tired of playing this game. Let's do something else.* **tiring. tired.**

tired (tīrd) *adj.* wanting to rest or sleep.

tissue (tish′ ū) *n.* **1.** a thin, soft piece of paper, used to blow your nose and to absorb moisture. **2.** a group of similar cells that together form some part of an animal or plant: *muscle tissue.*

title (tī′ təl) *n.* **1.** the name of anything, such as a book, movie, or song. **2.** a word placed before or after a person's name to show importance or rank: *"Doctor" and "Sir" are titles.*

to (tū) *prep.* **1.** in the direction of: *Look to the left.* **2.** as far as: *Go to the store.* **3.** until: *Our practice is from two to three o'clock.* **4.** into the condition of: *They went to sleep.*

toad (tōd) *n.* an amphibian that looks like a frog, but lives mostly on land and has rough, dry skin: *Toads return to water to produce their young.*

toad

toadstool (tōd′ stūl) *n.* a poisonous mushroom.

toast (tōst) *n.* bread that is made crisp and brown by heating. —*v.* to make bread or another food crisp and brown with heat: *to toast marshmallows.* **toasting. toasted.**

toaster (tōs′ tər) *n.* an electrical appliance used to toast bread.

tobacco (tə bak′ ō) *n.* a plant whose dried leaves are used for smoking in cigarettes, pipes, or cigars.

toboggan (tə bog′ ən) *n.* a long, flat sleigh without runners. —*v.* to slide down a snowy hill on a toboggan. **tobogganing. tobogganed.**

today (tə dā′) *n.* the present day: *Today is my birthday.* —*adv.* on this day: *Our class is going to the museum today.*

toddler (tod′ lər) *n.* a small child just learning to walk.

toe (tō) *n.* one of the five end parts of your foot.

toffee (tof′ ē) see **taffy**.

together (tə geTH′ ər) *adv.* with each other: *They went together for a swim.*

toil (toil) *n.* hard work. —*v.* to do hard work: *The workers toiled in the fields all day.* **toiling. toiled.**

toilet (toil′ ət) *n.* a bowl containing water, used for flushing away body wastes.

told (tōld) see **tell**.

tolerant (tol′ ər ənt) *adj.* **1.** able to put up with something that may be annoying or difficult: *He is very tolerant of the barking dog next door.* **2.** respecting other people, their beliefs and customs; not prejudiced. —**tolerantly** *adv.*

tolerate (tol′ ər āt) *v.* to be able to put up with something that may be annoying or difficult: *I can tolerate the cold, but the hot weather bothers me.* **tolerating. tolerated.**

toll (tōl) *n.* a tax paid for the right to use something: *We pay a toll of one dollar when we drive across the bridge.*

tomato (tə mā′ tō *or* tə mo′ tō) *n.* a red, round, juicy fruit, eaten raw in salads and used in cooking. *pl.* **tomatoes.**

tomb (tūm) *n.* a grave or building in which the dead are buried.

tombstone (tūm′ stōn) *n.* a stone or marker over a grave.

tomorrow (tə mȯr′ ō) *n.* the day after today: *Tomorrow will be a nice day.* —*adv.* on the next day: *We have a spelling test tomorrow.*

ton (tun) *n.* a former standard unit for measuring mass or weight, equal to 907 kg.

tone (tōn) *n.* **1.** a musical sound. **2.** the sound of someone's voice: *Mother spoke in an angry tone.* **3.** a shade of colour: *That is a nice tone of red.*

tongue (tung) *n.* the soft, movable muscle in your mouth, used for tasting, licking, and making sounds in talking.

hold your tongue to keep from saying something or to be quiet.

tongue-tied (tung′ tīd′) *adj.* not able to speak because of shyness or embarrassment.

tonight (tə nīt′) *n.* this night: *Tonight is New Year's Eve.* —*adv.* on this night: *We are having a party tonight to celebrate.*

tonne (tun) *n.* a metric unit for measuring mass or weight; t is the symbol. 1 t = 1000 kg.

tonsil (ton′ səl) *n.* one of two small oval pieces of flesh in the back of your throat.

too (tū) *adv.* **1.** also; as well: *I am going out, and Denise is coming too.* **2.** more than enough: *I think I've eaten too much chocolate.*

took (tůk) see **take**.

tool (tūl) *n.* any object that helps you to do work: *Hammers, saws, and axes are tools.*

tooth (tūth) *n.* **1.** one of the white bony parts in your mouth, used for biting and chewing. **2.** something like a tooth: *the teeth of a comb. pl.* **teeth.**

toothache (tūth′ āk′) *n.* a pain in a tooth.

toothbrush (tūth′ brush′) *n.* a small brush on a long handle, used to clean teeth. *pl.* **toothbrushes.**

toothpaste (tūth′ pāst′) *n.* a flavoured paste for cleaning the teeth.

toothpick (tůth′ pik′) *n.* a small pointed sliver of wood, used to clean food stuck between the teeth.

top (top) *n.* **1.** the highest point or part: *the top of a hill.* **2.** the upper side: *the top of a box.* **3.** a toy which can be made to spin. —*v.* to reach and pass an amount: *The crowd topped a thousand people.* **topping. topped.**

topic (top′ ik) *n.* what is being talked or written about; a subject: *The topic of my speech is "My Most Embarrassing Experience."*

topping (top′ ing) *n.* a sauce or other trimming placed on food to add flavour: *a topping of chocolate sauce for an ice-cream sundae.*

topple (top′ əl) *v.* to fall down: *The fence post toppled over.* **toppling. toppled.**

toque (tūk) see **tuque**.

torch (tȯrch) *n.* a kind of light that has a flame at one end and can be carried by the other end. *pl.* **torches.**

tore, torn (tȯr, tȯrn) see **tear** (verb).

torment (tȯr ment′) *v.* to make someone suffer: *Don't torment your little sister; you're upsetting her!* **tormenting. tormented.**

torn (tȯrn) *adj.* ripped; having a tear.

tornado (tȯr nā′ dō) *n.* a very violent wind, shaped like a funnel, that whirls around at a high speed and can cause great damage. *pl.* **tornadoes.**

tornado

tortoise (tȯr′ təs) *n.* a large turtle that lives on land.

torture (tôr′ chər) *n.* the act of greatly hurting someone as punishment or to get a confession. —*v.* to use torture on someone. **torturing. tortured.**

toss (tos) *n.* a light throw. *pl.* **tosses.** —*v.* **1.** to throw up into the air or across the air: *I tossed the beach ball over the net to my friend.* **2.** to roll around: *He tossed in bed for two hours before falling asleep.* **tossing. tossed.**

tot (tot) *n.* a very young child.

total (tō′ təl) *n.* the whole amount when two or more numbers are added: *The total of 3 plus 5 plus 1 is 9.* —*adj.* entire: *What is the total amount on the bill?*

totally (tō′ təl ē) *adv.* completely: *I am going to bed because I am totally exhausted.*

totem pole (tō′ təm pōl′) *n.* a tall, wooden pole with many carvings on it, made by aboriginal peoples of the Pacific Coast.

touch (tuch) *n.* one of the five senses—the ability to feel with your body, especially the finger tips: *By touch, you can tell how hard, soft, rough, smooth, hot, or cold something is.* *pl.* **touches.** —*v.* **1.** to feel with your finger tips or some other part of your body. **2.** to be against: *The back of the chair touches the wall.* **3.** to make someone feel tender emotion: *Your kind words touched us.* **touching. touched.**

in touch communicating often with someone by visiting, phoning, or sending letters: *Even after our family moved, I kept in touch with my best friend.*

touchdown (tuch′ down) *n.* in football, a score made by getting the ball across the other team's goal line.

touching (tuch′ ing) *adj.* making someone feel tender or sympathetic: *a touching story about a lost cat that found its way home.* —**touchingly** *adv.*

tough (tuf) *adj.* **1.** strong and not easy to bend or break: *a tough piece of rubber.* **2.** hard to chew: *tough meat.* **3.** hard; difficult: *a tough problem in arithmetic.* —**toughly** *adv.*

tour (tūr) *n.* a pleasure trip, sometimes led by a guide. —*v.* to travel from place to place: *Lee's family will tour France next summer.* **touring. toured.**

tourist (tūr′ ist) *n.* a person on holiday who travels to see different places and things.

tournament (tůr′ nə mənt) *n.* a contest among several players or teams: *a tennis tournament.*

tow (tō) *v.* to pull or drag something with a rope: *The car broke down, and a truck towed it away.* **towing. towed.**

toward, towards (tə wȯrd′ *or* tȯrd, tə wȯrdz′ *or* tȯrds,) *prep.* in the direction of: *They walked toward the village.*

towel (tow′ əl) *n.* a heavy cloth or paper that is used for drying or wiping something.

tower (tow′ ər) *n.* a tall and narrow building or part of a building: *The CN Tower in Toronto is 553.33 m high.* —*v.* to rise higher or taller than others: *My uncle towers over my father.* **towering. towered.**

town (town) *n.* a large area of houses, stores, businesses, schools, churches, and so on: *A town is larger than a village and smaller than a city.*

out of town away in another place: *My older brother went out of town for the weekend.*

township (town′ ship) *n.* part of a county that has some powers of government.

toxic (tok′ sik) *adj.* containing a substance that can harm or kill a person; poisonous.

toy (toi) *n.* a thing to play with. —*v.* to play with: *She toyed with her ring.* **toying. toyed.**

trace (trās) *n.* **1.** a sign or evidence of the presence of something from the past. *They found traces of an ancient city.* **2.** a small amount left behind: *There is a trace of grease on the glass.* —*v.* **1.** to copy a picture by placing transparent paper on top and drawing over the lines that show through. **2.** to find someone or something, by following clues left behind: *We traced the cookies by following the trail of crumbs.* **tracing. traced.**

track (trak) *n.* **1.** the set of metal rails a train travels along. **2.** marks on the ground left by something moving: *the tracks of a bear in the snow.* **3.** the course followed by runners in a race.

keep track to follow the activities or progress of something: *We kept track of the team when they were home and when they were away.*

track down to find someone or something by carefully following clues and signs: *After going to several libraries, I finally tracked down the book I wanted.*

track and field sports events that are held on a running track and field, usually outdoors.

The events include running races, hurdles, long jump, high jump, javelin throwing, and many other activities.

tractor (trak′ tər) *n.* a machine with wheels and a powerful engine that is used on farms for pulling a plough or heavy loads.

> **Tractor** comes from the Latin word *tractus,* meaning to drag or pull: *A farmer's tractor is used to pull a plough.*

trade (trād) *n.* **1.** the business of buying and selling: *Canada has much trade with foreign countries.* **2.** a job needing the use of tools: *the trade of being a carpenter.* —*v.* to give one thing in exchange for something else: *Katya traded books with Sam.* **trading. traded.**

tradition (trə dish′ ən) *n.* activities, beliefs, or customs passed on from one generation to another: *Having a picnic in July is a tradition in our family.*

traditional (trə dish′ ən əl) *adj.* passed on by tradition. —**traditionally** *adv.*

traffic (traf′ ik) *n.* the movement of cars, buses, and trucks along roads.

tragedy (traj′ ə dē) *n.* a very sad story or event. *pl.* **tragedies.**

tragic (traj′ ik) *adj.* very sad or terrible: *The story has a tragic ending.* —**tragically** *adv.*

trail (trāl) *n.* **1.** marks on the ground, showing which way some animal or person has gone. **2.** a rough path. —*v.* to follow behind or to follow a trail: *Our team trailed by one point.* **trailing. trailed.**

trailer (trāl′ ər) *n.* a vehicle that is pulled by another vehicle: *Some trailers are for people to live in. Others are used to carry goods.*

train (trān) *n.* railway cars connected together. —*v.* **1.** to teach a skill: *Ms. Wong trains dogs.* **2.** to practise for something: *Lisa is training to be a dancer.* **training. trained.**

training (trān′ ing) *n.* the process of learning a special skill: *I am in training for the swimming finals.*

trait (trāt) *n.* a certain feature or quality that a person has: *Two of his good traits are his kindness and sense of humour.*

traitor (trā′ tər) *n.* someone who works against his or her country or friends.

tramp (tramp) *n.* a poor person who has no home. —*v.* **1.** to walk heavily. **2.** to go for a trip on foot; to hike. **tramping. tramped.**

trample (tram′ pəl) *v.* to walk heavily all over something. **trampling. trampled.**

trampoline (tram′ pə lēn′) *n.* a piece of canvas held to a frame by strong strings, used to jump on: *The gymnast bounced up and down on the trampoline, doing flips and turns.*

tranquil (trang′ kwəl) *adj.* peaceful and relaxing: *In the evening, the lake is very tranquil.* —**tranquilly** *adv.*

> **trans–** is a prefix meaning "through," "across," "beyond," or "change": *the Trans-Canada Highway extends through or across the country.* "Transport" means to carry across; "transparent" means clear, a state that lets you see beyond or through; "transform" means to change form or shape.

transfer (trans′ fər) *n.* a ticket that lets you change from one bus, subway train, or streetcar to another without having to pay more money. —*v.* to move something or somebody to another place: *My sister's company transferred her to another city.* **transferring. transferred.**

transform (trans fȯrm′) *v.* to change the form, appearance, or structure of something: *The prince was transformed into a frog.* **transforming. transformed.**

translate (tranz lāt′ *or* trans lāt′) *v.* to put words into another language. **translating. translated.**

translation (tranz lā′ shən *or* trans lā′ shən) *n.* a changing of words into another language: *Your translation of the French story into English is very good.*

transmit (tranz mit′) *v.* **1.** to send a message, especially by radio or TV: *The signal that this station transmits can be picked up 200 km away.* **2.** to spread a disease to others. **transmitting. transmitted.**

transparent (trans per′ ənt) *adj.* clear; able to be seen through: *Glass is transparent.* —**transparently** *adv.*

transplant (trans plant′) *v.* to take a plant from one place and put it into another: *My mother transplanted the seedlings from the pots to the garden.* **transplanting. transplanted.**

transport (trans′ pórt) *n.* a large truck, plane, or ship used for carrying goods.

transport (trans pórt′) *v.* to carry goods from one place to another. **transporting. transported.**

transportation (trans′ pər tā′ shən) *n.* the act of moving someone or something from one place to another.

trap (trap) *n.* a box or other device for catching birds or animals: *The mouse escaped from the trap.* —*v.* to catch with a trap. **trapping. trapped.**

trapeze (trə pēz′) *n.* a swinging bar held by two ropes, usually used by acrobats at a circus performance.

trapeze

trapper (trap′ ər) *n.* someone who makes a living by trapping animals to sell their fur.

trash (trash) *n.* garbage.

travel (tra′ vəl) *n.* the going from one place to another by car, train, airplane, or any other form of transportation. —*v.* to go on a trip. **travelling. travelled.**

traveller, traveler (trav′ əl ər) *n.* someone who travels.

trawl (trol) *n.* a net dragged along the bottom of the ocean. —*v.* to fish with such a net. **trawling. trawled.**

trawler (tro′ lər) *n.* a ship used for ocean fishing.

tray (trā) *n.* a flat piece of wood, plastic, or metal used to carry things: *a tea tray.*

tread (tred) *n.* **1.** the sound of a heavy step: *the tread of soldiers' boots.* **2.** the deep grooves in a car tire. —*v.* to step heavily; to tramp. **treading. treaded.**

treason (trē′ zən) *n.* helping the enemy: *The spy was guilty of treason.*

treasure (trezh′ ər) *n.* something very valuable; great riches: *The pirates hid their treasure on the island.* —*v.* to value very highly: *We treasure our friendship.* **treasuring. treasured.**

treasurer (trezh′ ər ər) *n.* the person in charge of the money of a business or club.

treat (trēt) *n.* **1.** something special that is good to eat, such as candy: *The children were given treats on Hallowe'en.* **2.** any special, pleasing thing: *We were taken to the zoo as a treat.* —*v.* **1.** to give someone a special and pleasant thing or time: *My father treated us to lemonade.* **2.** to behave toward: *How do you treat a new student?* **3.** to give medical attention to: *The nurse treated my cut immediately.* **treating. treated.**

treatment (trēt′ mənt) *n.* **1.** behaviour toward someone or something. **2.** a way of behaving toward someone or something: *The umpire gave both teams fair treatment.*

treaty (trē′ tē) *n.* an agreement made between two or more people, groups, cities, countries, and so on: *a peace treaty; a treaty between an aboriginal nation and the government. pl.* **treaties.**

tree (trē) *n.* a large, tall plant with a woody trunk, branches, and leaves.

trek (trek) *n.* a long journey. *—v.* to go on a long journey or to hike: *We trekked through the Rockies last summer.* **trekking. trekked.**

tremble (trem′ bəl) *v.* to shake or shiver with fear, excitement, or cold. **trembling. trembled.**

tremendous (trə men′ dəs) *adj.* huge; enormous: *a tremendous elephant.* —**tremendously** *adv.*

trench (trench) *n.* a long, narrow, deep ditch dug in the ground. *pl.* **trenches.**

trespass (tres′ pas *or* tres′ pəs) *v.* to go on someone's property without permission. **trespassing. trespassed.**

trial (trī′ əl) *n.* the hearing of a case before a judge in a court of law.

triangle (trī′ ang′ gəl) *n.* **1.** a flat shape with three sides and three angles. **2.** a percussion musical instrument made from a steel rod bent into the shape of a triangle.

triangular (trī ang′ gyə lər) *adj.* having the shape of a triangle.

tribe (trīb) *n.* a group of people who have the same customs and leaders.

trick (trik) *n.* **1.** a clever act: *The monkey was doing all kinds of tricks.* **2.** an action that fools people: *a magic trick. —v.* to fool; to cheat: *He tricked me into going to his house for my surprise party.* **tricking. tricked.**

trickle (trik′ əl) *n.* a small flow of liquid: *Only a trickle of water came out of the tap. —v.* to flow in drops or a small stream: *The water trickled over my hands.* **trickling. trickled.**

tricky (trik′ ē) *adj.* hard to deal with or solve: *a tricky riddle; a trickier riddle; the trickiest riddle of all.*

tricycle (trī′ sə kəl) *n.* a small vehicle with three wheels, ridden by small children.

tried, tries (trīd, trīz) see **try.**

trigger (trig′ ər) *n.* a small lever on a gun or pistol that is pulled to make it fire. *—v.* to set off; to begin: *The gunshot triggered the race.* **triggering. triggered.**

trill (tril) *n.* a vibrating sound produced by the voice. *—v.* to make a trill: *I like to hear the birds trill.* **trilling. trilled.**

trim (trim) *adj.* **1.** neat and tidy. **2.** a cutting of the hair. —**trimly** *adv. —v.* to make something neat by clipping it: *to trim a hedge.* **trimming. trimmed.**

trimmings (trim′ ingz) *n. pl.* extra things that come with the main part: *I like turkey and all the trimmings, especially cranberry sauce.*

trinket (tring′ kət) *n.* a small piece of jewellery or an ornament that has very little value.

trio (trē′ ō) *n.* a group of three singers or musicians. *pl.* **trios.**

trip (trip) *n.* a short or long journey: *a trip to the zoo. —v.* to catch your foot on something and almost fall; to stumble: *She tripped on the mat, fell down the stairs, and broke her leg.* **tripping. tripped.**

triple (trip′ əl) *adj.* three times as much: *a triple helping of cake. —v.* to multiply by three: *When you triple the number 2, you get 6.* **tripling. tripled.**

triplet (trip′ lət) *n.* one of three children born at the same time to the same mother.

tripod (trī′ pod) *n.* a stand or other object that has three legs: *Tripods are often used to support cameras.*

triumph (trī′ umf) *n.* a great victory or success: *Our play was a triumph!*

trivia (triv′ ē ə) *n.* information that is not very important, but is often interesting.

In Latin, **trivia** means three roads. Many years ago, people would gather where these roads met and gossip or talk about unimportant things.

trivial (triv′ ē əl) *adj.* not important: *The colour of the hero's socks is a trivial matter.*

trolley (trol′ ē) *n.* a streetcar or a bus that is powered by electricity. *pl.* **trolleys.**

trolley

trombone (trom′ bōn *or* trom bōn′) *n.* a brass musical instrument: *A trombone is like a large trumpet with a sliding, U-shaped tube that moves back and forth.*

troop (trūp) *n.* a group of soldiers or Scouts.

trophy (trō′ fē) *n.* a large, shiny metal cup or other object given as a prize to the winner of a contest. *pl.* **trophies.**

tropical (trop′ ə kəl) *adj.* having to do with the tropics.

tropics (trop′ iks) *n. pl.* the hot regions of the earth near the equator.

trot (trot) *n.* a light, gentle run of a horse. —*v.* (for a horse) to run lightly: *The horse trotted to the fence.* **trotting. trotted.**

trouble (trub′ əl) *n.* a difficult situation that causes worry; a problem: *The trouble with our house is that it is too small for our family.* —*v.* to disturb or worry: *Does the noise trouble you?* **troubling. troubled.**

trough (trof) *n.* a long, narrow, open box that holds water or food for animals.

trousers (trow′ zərz) *n. pl.* a pair of long pants.

trout (trowt) *n.* a kind of fish that lives in fresh water. *pl.* **trout.**

truck (truk) *n.* a large vehicle that carries heavy loads. —*v.* to carry heavy loads in a truck: *Fresh vegetables and fruits are trucked from the country to the city.* **trucking. trucked.**

true (trū) *adj.* **1.** real; not made up: *The story I told you is true.* (*opp.* **untrue.**) **2.** right; correct: *It is true that the sun rises in the east.* **3.** loyal: *Kim is a true friend.*

truly (trū′ lē) *adv.* really; honestly: *I am truly sorry I can't come to your party.*

trumpet (trum′ pət) *n.* a brass musical instrument, with a curving tube that widens at the end.

trunk (trungk) *n.* **1.** the main part of a tree. **2.** the main part of your body. **3.** a big, heavy box or chest, used for storing or carrying belongings. **4.** the long nose of an elephant. **5.** a space at the back of a car for carrying luggage and other things.

trust (trust) *n.* belief that a person is honest and reliable: *I have complete trust in my best friend.* —*v.* to believe and have faith in someone: *Can I trust you to look after my dog when I go away?* **trusting. trusted.**

truth (trūth) *n.* what is true and real: *It is the truth that I was sick yesterday.*

truthful (trūth′ fəl) *adj.* telling the truth; not lying. —**truthfully** *adv.*

try (trī) *n.* an attempt: *You made a good try at clearing the high jump. pl.* **tries.** —*v.* **1.** to aim at doing something; to attempt: *I tried to climb the tree.* **2.** to judge someone in a court of law: *The suspect was tried before a judge and jury.* **3.** to test something to see if it works: *We will try your new idea.* **trying. tried.** he **tries.**

try on to wear something to see how it fits and looks: *I tried on the shoes before I bought them.*

try out to use something to see how it works: *We tried out the computer before we bought it.*

T-shirt (tē′ shu̇rt) *n.* a sports shirt with short sleeves: *When placed flat, a T-shirt looks like the letter T.*

tub (tub) *n.* **1.** a large container for holding bath water: *a bathtub.* **2.** a round container for holding soft foods or materials: *a tub of yogurt.*

tuba (tū′ bə *or* tyū′ bə) *n.* a large, brass musical instrument that produces very deep sounds.

tuba

tube (tūb *or* tyūb) *n.* **1.** a thin pipe for holding or carrying liquids or gases. **2.** a soft container used for holding toothpaste or other products.

tuck (tuk) *n.* a fold in cloth. —*v.* to fold away, wrap up, or cover up: *I tucked the ends of my shirt into my pants.* **tucking. tucked.**

Tuesday (tūz′ dā *or* tyūz′ dā, tūz′dē *or* tyūz′ dē) *n.* the third day of the week.

tug (tug) *n.* **1.** a sharp pull. **2.** short for **tugboat**. —*v.* to pull sharply: *The puppy tugged at my sock to get my attention.* **tugging. tugged.**

tugboat (tug′ bōt′) *n.* a small, powerful boat used for towing and pushing large ships in and out of a harbour.

tug-of-war (tug′ əv wȯr′) *n.* a contest between two teams pulling a rope in opposite directions, each trying to pull the other over a line marked between them.

tuition (tyū ish′ ən *or* tū ish′ ən) *n.* a fee paid for a private school, music lessons, or university courses.

tulip (tū′ lip *or* tyū′ lip) *n.* a colourful flower that grows from a bulb and is shaped like a cup.

tumble (tum′ bəl) *n.* the act of falling down and rolling over: *She took a tumble when she tripped on the rope.* —*v.* to fall down and roll over: *I nearly tumbled down the stairs.* **tumbling. tumbled.**

tumour, tumor (tyū′ mər *or* tū′ mər) *n.* a growth or swelling on or in the body that is not normal: *Some tumours are not harmful, but many are.*

tuna (tū′ nə *or* tyū′ nə) *n.* a large ocean fish that is caught for food.

tundra (tun′ drə) *n.* a large area of flat, treeless land in the Arctic: *The ground beneath the tundra is always frozen.*

tune (tūn *or* tyūn) *n.* a set of notes that make up a song or other piece of music. —*v.* **1.** to adjust a radio dial to receive the correct channel: *I tuned into my favourite rock-music station.* **2.** to adjust the sound of a musical instrument. **tuning. tuned.**

tunnel (tun′ əl) *n.* a passage dug under the ground, under a river, or through a mountain. —*v.* to dig a tunnel: *The workers tunnelled through the mountain.* **tunnelling. tunnelled.**

tuque, toque (tūk *or* tyūk) *n.* a close-fitting, knitted cap, usually made of wool.

turban (tu̇r′ bən) *n.* a long scarf that is wound around the head or around a small cap.

turf (tu̇rf) *n.* a top layer of soil with grass growing on it.

turkey (tu̇r′ kē) *n.* a large North American bird that is raised for food. *pl.* **turkeys.**

turn (tůrn) *n.* **1.** a movement around in a circle. **2.** a change of direction: *a left turn.* **3.** a time or chance to do something: *It is my turn.* —*v.* **1.** to move something in a circular motion: *She turned the handle.* **2.** to change direction: *Turn right at the stop sign.* **3.** to change: *The snow turned to slush.* **turning. turned.**

turn off to shut off a machine, a light, and so on.

turnip (tůr′ nip) *n.* a large, round, white root used as a vegetable.

turnstile (tůrn′ stīl′) *n.* a kind of gate that lets people through one at a time: *I went through the turnstile into the amusement park.*

turpentine (tůr′ pən tīn′) *n.* an oil from pine trees, used as a solvent or thinner for paints and varnishes.

turquoise (tůr′ kwoiz) *n.* **1.** a precious stone with a greenish-blue colour. **2.** a greenish-blue colour. —*adj.* having such a colour.

turtle (tůr′ təl) *n.* a reptile that lives on land or in the sea; it has a hard shell, and moves very slowly.

tusk (tusk) *n.* one of two very long, large teeth that stick out from the mouth of an elephant, walrus, and some other animals.

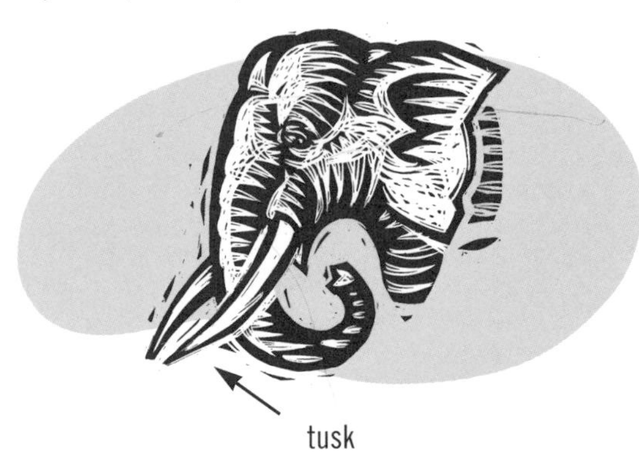

tuxedo (tuk sē′ dō) *n.* a special suit worn on formal occasions. *pl.* **tuxedos.**

TV (tē′ vē′) *n.* television.

tweezers (twē′ zərz) *n. pl.* a small tool used for pulling out or grasping small things.

twelve (twelv) *n., adj.* one more than eleven: 12.

twenty (twen′ tē) *n., adj.* ten times two: 20.

twice (twīs) *adv.* two times.

twig (twig) *n.* a very small branch on a tree or bush.

twilight (twī′ līt′) *n.* the faint light just before sunrise or just after sunset.

twin (twin) *n.* one of two children born at the same time to the same mother.

twine (twīn) *n.* a strong, heavy string.

twinkle (twing′ kəl) *n.* a sparkle: *I saw a twinkle in her eye.* —*v.* to sparkle. **twinkling. twinkled.**

twirl (twůrl) *n.* a spinning motion. —*v.* to spin around quickly: *The ballet dancer twirled on the tips of her toes.* **twirling. twirled.**

twist (twist) *n.* a winding or turning around; a spiral: *Give the bottle cap a twist.* —*v.* **1.** to wind or turn: *Twist open the jar.* **2.** to bend and change the shape of something: *I twisted the wire into a ring.* **twisting. twisted.**

twitch (twich) *n.* a small jerk in a part of your body: *I have a twitch in my eye.* *pl.* **twitches.** —*v.* to jerk slightly: *The rabbit twitched its nose.* **twitching. twitched.**

two (tū) *n., adj.* one added to one: 2.

tying (tī′ ing) see **tie.**

type (tīp) *n.* **1.** a kind; a sort: *What type of computer are you using in class?* **2.** printed letters. —*v.* to punch the keys on a typewriter or computer. **typing. typed.**

typhoon (tī fūn′) *n.* a powerful storm, much like a hurricane.

typical (tip′ ə kəl) *adj.* usual; common; what you would expect: *Quince is a typical dog—he loves to go for walks and catch sticks.* (*opp.* **atypical.**) —**typically** *adv.*

typo (tī′ pō) *n.* a mistake in a printed word: *Correct all the typos in your work before you hand it in.* *pl.* **typos.**

udder (ud′ ər) *n.* the part of the body of a female cow, sheep, or goat where the milk is stored.

udder

UFO short for **unidentified flying object**; a thing seen flying in the sky that cannot be identified: *Some people who saw the UFO thought it was an alien spaceship.*

ugly (ug′ lē) *adj.* not nice to look at; not pretty: *an ugly picture; an uglier one; the ugliest picture on the wall.*

ukulele (yū′ kə lā′ lē) *n.* a small guitar that has four strings.

ultimate (ul′ tə mət) *n.* the last thing, and sometimes the best. —*adj.* the last and sometimes the best: *The goalie made the ultimate save, allowing her team to win.* —**ultimately** *adv.*

ultraviolet rays (ul′ trə vī′ ə lət rāz′) invisible rays from the sun that cause you to tan and burn.

umbilical cord (um bil′ ə kəl kôrd) a tube that carries food and oxygen from a mother to her unborn baby: *When a baby is born, the umbilical cord is cut.*

umbrella (um brel′ ə) *n.* a thin steel frame covered with waterproof material, used for protection from the rain or sun.

umpire (um′ pīr) *n.* a person who makes sure that the rules of a game are followed. —*v.* to act as an umpire: *Will you umpire our ballgame?* **umpiring. umpired.**

un– is a prefix meaning "not" or "the opposite of": "unable" means not able; "unfold" means to open out something that is folded.

unable (un ā′ bəl) *adj.* not able: *Kenji was unable to go to school because he was sick.*

unanimous (yū nan′ ə məs) *adj.* agreed to by everybody: *It was a unanimous decision to go to Prince Edward Island for our holiday.* —**unanimously** *adv.*

unbelievable (un′ bə lē′ və bəl) *adj.* impossible to believe: *an unbelievable story about dragons.* —**unbelievably** *adv.*

uncertain (un sûr′ tən) *adj.* not certain; not sure: *Linda was uncertain about which way to go.*

uncle (ung′ kəl) *n.* a brother of your father or mother; the husband of your aunt.

uncomfortable (un kum′ fər tə bəl) *adj.* not comfortable. —**uncomfortably** *adv.*

unconscious (un kon′ shəs) *adj.* **1.** not conscious; knocked out. **2.** not aware: *She is unconscious that she has made a mistake.* —**unconsciously** *adv.*

uncover (un kuv′ ər) *v.* **1.** to take a cover or wrapping off. **2.** to reveal: *to uncover a secret plan.* **uncovering. uncovered.**

undecided (un′ di sīd′ id) *adj.* **1.** not settled: *The championship remained undecided because the game ended in a tie.* **2.** not certain: *We were undecided about what we wanted for lunch.*

under (un′ dər) *prep.* **1.** below; beneath: *The swimmer dived under the water.* **2.** lower than: *Everything in the store is under five dollars.*

under– is a prefix meaning "below" or "lower than": "underline" means to draw a line below; "underwater" means beneath the surface of the water.

underground (un′ dər grownd′) *adj.* located under the ground's surface: *an underground tunnel.*

underline (un′ dər līn′) *n.* a line drawn under some writing. *—v.* to draw a line under some writing. **underlining. underlined.**

underneath (un′ dər nēth′) *prep.* directly under: *I found my shoes underneath the table.*

understand (un′ dər stand′) *v.* **1.** to get the meaning of: *I understood the secret message.* **2.** to know what someone is feeling or trying to say. **understanding. understood.**

understanding (un′ dər stand′ ing) *n.* knowledge: *She has a good understanding of three languages. —adj.* having sympathy or kind feelings: *The counsellor is a very understanding person.*

undertaker (un′ dər tāk′ ər) *n.* a person whose job is to arrange funerals.

underwater (un′ dər wo′ tər) *adj.* found, growing, or used below the surface of the water: *underwater plants. —adv.* below the surface of the water: *to swim underwater.*

undo (un dü′) *v.* to unfasten: *Jimmy undid the buttons of his coat.* **undoing. undid.** he has **undone.** he **undoes.**

undress (un dres′) *v.* to take off your clothes. **undressing. undressed.**

uneasy (un ē′ zē) *adj.* feeling worried that something is wrong or may go wrong: *We feel uneasy about leaving our cat with a stranger for two weeks.* —**uneasily** *adv.*

unemployed (un′ em ploid′) *adj.* out of work; not having a job.

uneven (un ē′ vən) *adj.* **1.** not level or straight: *an uneven road.* **2.** not equal: *The game was uneven because they had two more players than we had.* **3.** odd; numbers that cannot be divided by two. —**unevenly** *adv.*

unexpected (un′ eks pek′ tid) *adj.* not expected; coming as a surprise: *an unexpected visit.* —**unexpectedly** *adv.*

unfair (un fer′) *adj.* not right or honest. —**unfairly** *adv.*

unfamiliar (un fə mil′ yər) *adj.* not familiar or known to you; strange: *an unfamiliar language.*

unfasten (un fas′ ən) *v.* to undo or open: *to unfasten a seat belt.* **unfastening. unfastened.**

unforgettable (un′ fər get′ ə bəl) *adj.* impossible to forget: *an unforgettable holiday.* —**unforgettably** *adv.*

unfortunate (un fȯr′ chə nət) *adj.* not having good fortune or luck: *an unfortunate accident.* —**unfortunately** *adv.*

unhappy (un hap′ ē) *adj.* not happy; sad. —**unhappily** *adv.*

unicorn (yü′ nə kȯrn′) *n.* an imaginary creature that looks like a horse with a long, straight horn on its forehead.

unicorn

unidentified (un′ ī den′ ti fīd′) *adj.* not recognized; not known: *an unidentified flying object.*

uniform (yü′ ni fȯrm′) *n.* an outfit worn to show that a person belongs to a particular group: *a school uniform; a police uniform. —adj.* **1.** all alike: *eggs of uniform size.* **2.** never changing: *She drove at a uniform speed on the highway.* —**uniformly** *adv.*

union (yün′ yən) *n.* **1.** a joining together: *A marriage is a union of two people.* **2.** a group of workers who join together to make sure that they are all treated fairly by the people who employ them.

unique (yü nēk′) *adj.* one of a kind: *The bracelet I bought at the craft sale is unique.* —**uniquely** *adv.*

unit (yü′ nit) *n.* **1.** a single thing, person, or group: *a unit of soldiers.* **2.** an amount used for measuring: *The metre is a unit of length.*

unite (yü nīt′) *v.* to join together: *The teams united to form a league.* **uniting. united.**

universal (yü nə vůr′ səl) *adj.* having to do with or shared by everyone around the world: *Laughter is universal.* —**universally** *adv.*

universe (yü′ nə vůrs) *n.* everything that exists, including all space and all matter.

university (yü′ nə vůr′ sə tē) *n.* a school of advanced learning that some people attend after high school: *Many kinds of courses are taught at a university. pl.* **universities.**

unknown (un nōn′) *adj.* not known; strange: *Many deep parts of the ocean are unknown to us.*

unlawful (un lo′ fəl) *adj.* against the law; illegal. —**unlawfully** *adv.*

unless (un les′) *conj.* except if: *I shall not go unless you come too.*

unlike (un līk′) *prep.* not like; different from: *Unlike my sister, I like vegetables.*

unlikely (un līk′ lē) *adj.* probably not going to happen: *It is unlikely to rain today.*

unlock (un lok′) *v.* to open a lock by using a key or combination number. **unlocking. unlocked.**

unlucky (un luk′ ē) *adj.* having bad luck or causing bad luck: *an unlucky man; an unlucky number.*

unnecessary (un nes′ ə ser′ ē) *adj.* not necessary or needed: *The sun is shining today; it's unnecessary to take an umbrella.* —**unnecessarily** *adv.*

unpleasant (un plez′ ənt) *adj.* not nice: *an unpleasant smell.* —**unpleasantly** *adv.*

unpopular (un pop′ yə lər) *adj.* not liked by many people: *He is an unpopular student.*

unsafe (un sāf′) *adj.* not safe: *It is unsafe to ride a bike with a flat tire.* —**unsafely** *adv.*

unsuccessful (un′ sək ses′ fəl) *adj.* not successful. —**unsuccessfully** *adv.*

untidy (un tī′ dē) *adj.* not tidy; messy. —**untidily** *adv.*

untie (un tī′) *v.* to undo something that has been tied. **untying. untied.**

until (un til′) *conj.* **1.** up to the time when: *Stay here until I come back.* **2.** before: *Don't start until everyone arrives.*

unusual (un yü′ zhü əl) *adj.* **1.** not usual: *So much rain is unusual for this time of year.* **2.** strange; rare. —**unusually** *adv.*

unwrap (un rap′) *v.* to take the wrapping off: *to unwrap a package.* **unwrapping. unwrapped.**

up (up) *prep.* from a lower to a higher place: *We walked up the hill.* —*adj.* awake and on your feet: *The children aren't up yet.* —*adv.* **1.** at or to a higher place: *Look up in the sky.* **2.** at an end or all spent: *I've used up all the film in the camera.*

upon (ə pon′) *prep.* on: *My little sister stood upon a chair to reach the shelf.*

upper (up′ ər) *adj.* higher: *the upper lip of your mouth.*

upset (up set′) *v.* **1.** to knock over: *I upset the jug of milk.* **2.** to disturb: *The bad news upset us.* **3.** to make sick: *The second milkshake upset my stomach.* **4.** to win a game unexpectedly: *The team in last place upset the first-place team.* **upsetting. upset.**

upside-down (up′ sīd′ down′) *adj., adv.* with the bottom at the top: *Nobody realized that the painting was hanging upside-down.*

upstairs (up′ sterz′) *adv.* on a higher floor.

up-to-date (up′ tü dāt′) *adj.* the newest or the most recent: *We need an up-to-date version of this computer program.*

upward, upwards (up′ wərd, up′ wərdz) *adv.* toward a higher place: *The weather balloon drifted upward until it was far above the clouds.*

uranium (yü rā′ nē əm) *n.* a silver-white metal that is much heavier than lead: *Uranium is radioactive and is used to make nuclear energy.*

Uranus (yür′ ə nəs *or* yü rā′ nəs) *n.* one of the planets of our solar system: *Uranus is the seventh planet from the sun.*

urban (ėr′ bən) *adj.* having to do with the city, not the country: *Most of the children in my class come from urban areas.*

urge (ėrj) *n.* a sudden strong wish to do something: *Zack had an urge to go swimming.* —*v.* to try to get someone to do something; to persuade; to encourage. **urging. urged.**

urgent (ėr′ jənt) *adj.* needing immediate attention or action: *The police received an urgent call for help.* —**urgently** *adv.*

urine (yür′ ən) *n.* liquid waste that comes out of your body when you go to the toilet.

us (us) *pron.* me and others. This is the form of **we** that is used as the object of a verb or preposition: *Please help us.*

usage (yüs′ əj) *n.* the way a word is used: *A noun and a verb have different usages.*

use (yüs) *n.* **1.** the power of using: *When I fractured my arm, I lost the use of it for a month.* **2.** usefulness: *There's no use in phoning them—everyone is away.*

use (yüz) *v.* to put something to work to help you: *I use a computer to write stories.* **using. used.**

used (yüzd) *adj.* not new: *My bicycle is used. My cousin gave it to me when she got a new one.*

useful (yüs′ fəl) *adj.* helpful: *a useful idea.*

useless (yüs′ ləs) *adj.* not useful: *The knife is so dull that it is useless for cutting.*

user (yü′ zər) *n.* a person who uses something, especially a machine.

usual (yü′ zhü əl) *adj.* common and expected; typical; normal: *Snow is usual for this time of year.* (*opp.* **unusual.**) —**usually** *adv.*

utensil (yü ten′ səl) *n.* a tool that is used for eating or cooking: *Forks, knives, spoons, pots, and pans are utensils.*

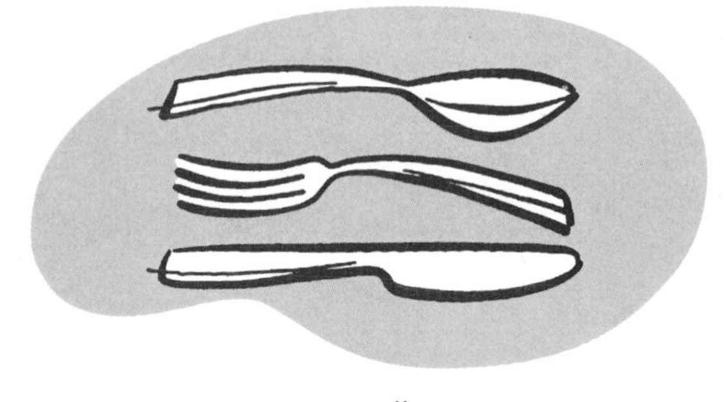

utensil

utter (ut′ ər) *adj.* complete; total: *To my utter surprise, he arrived on horseback.* —*v.* to speak: *She never uttered a word about her sickness.* **uttering. uttered.**

vacant (vā′ kənt) *adj.* **1.** empty; not occupied: *No one lives in that vacant house.* **2.** blank; without expression: *a vacant stare.* —**vacantly** *adv.*

vacation (vā kā′ shən) *n.* a holiday: *They left for their summer vacation yesterday.*

vaccinate (vak′ sə nāt′) *v.* to inject with a vaccine. **vaccinating. vaccinated.**

vaccination (vak′ sə nā′ shən) *n.* an injection of a vaccine into the body.

vaccine (vak′ sēn *or* vak sēn′) *n.* a preparation made from weakened germs that cause a disease: *Vaccines are injected into the body to help protect a person against some diseases, such as polio and flu.*

vacuum (vak′ yūm) *n.* **1.** an empty space with nothing in it, not even air. **2.** a vacuum cleaner. —*v.* to clean with a vacuum cleaner. **vacuuming. vacuumed.**

vacuum cleaner a machine that sucks up dirt from carpets, sofas, and other surfaces.

vague (vāg) *adj.* not clear: *His directions were vague, and we got lost.* —**vaguely** *adv.*

vain (vān) *adj.* **1.** having too high an opinion of yourself: *My brother is very vain about his looks.* **2.** useless; not successful: *The runner made a vain attempt to break the record.* —**vainly** *adv.*

in vain without success: *Our team tried in vain to win the game.*

valentine (val′ ən tīn′) *n.* a greeting card or gift that you give to someone you like or love on Valentine's Day, February 14.

valiant (val′ yənt) *adj.* brave: *a valiant knight.* —**valiantly** *adv.*

valid (val′ əd) *adj.* **1.** legal: *Your driver's licence is valid for one more month.* **2.** sensible, based on facts: *Can you give me a valid reason why we need another phone?*

valley (val′ ē) *n.* the low land between hills or mountains. *pl.* **valleys.**

valour, valor (val′ ər) *n.* bravery or courage in battle.

valuable (val′ yū ə bəl *or* val′ yə bəl) *adj.* having great value: *A diamond ring is valuable. He is a valuable member of the team.*

value (val′ yū) *n.* **1.** how much money something is worth: *What is the value of your ring?* **2.** the worth or importance of something: *Your friendship is of great value to me.* —*v.* to think highly of. **valuing. valued.**

valve (valv) *n.* a movable part in a pipe that controls the flow of liquid or gas.

vampire (vam′ pīr) *n.* an imaginary dead creature who comes back to life at night and sucks blood from people as they sleep.

van (van) *n.* a closed truck for carrying goods or passengers.

vandal (van′ dəl) *n.* someone who damages or destroys other people's property.

vane (vān) *n.* **1.** a metal pointer that swings when the wind blows it: *A weather vane shows the direction from which the wind is blowing.* **2.** a flat or curved metal blade that turns.

vane

vanilla (və nil′ ə) *n.* a flavouring used in candy, cake, and other sweet foods.

vanish (van′ ish) *v.* to disappear; to suddenly go out of sight: *The magician made the scarf vanish.* **vanishing. vanished.**

vapour, vapor (vā′ pər) *n.* **1.** tiny drops of water in the air, such as steam from boiling water. **2.** a gas formed from a liquid or a solid.

variation (var′ ē ā′ shən) *n.* **1.** a different form of something: *This story is a variation of one I already know.* **2.** change: *There is no variation in the patient's condition.*

variety (və rī′ ə tē) *n.* **1.** a number of different kinds; assortment: *The library carries a variety of books.*

various (ver′ ē əs) *adj.* different; several: *Various events are held at the civic centre.*

vary (ver′ ē *or* var′ ē) *v.* to change or make different: *The temperature varies between day and night.* **varying. varied.** it **varies.**

vase (vāz *or* voz) *n.* a tall, open container for holding flowers.

vast (vast) *adj.* huge in size or amount: *A prairie is a vast area of flat land.* —**vastly** *adv.*

vat (vat) *n.* a large tank for storing liquids.

vault (volt) *n.* a safe place used to store money or other valuable things. —*v.* to leap over an obstacle, using a pole or your hands. **vaulting. vaulted.**

VCR short for **videocassette recorder**.

veal (vēl) *n.* the meat of a calf.

veer (vēr) *v.* to change direction suddenly; to swerve: *The car veered to the right to avoid an accident.* **veering. veered.**

vegetable (vej′ tə bəl *or* vej′ ə tə bəl) *n.* a part of a plant used for food: *Celery, peas, beans, and carrots are vegetables.*

vegetarian (vej′ ə ter′ ē ən) *n.* a person who does not eat meat or fish.

vegetation (vej′ ə tā′ shən) *n.* plant life: *What kind of vegetation grows in your area?*

vehicle (vē′ ə kəl) *n.* anything used to move people or goods around, especially over land or in space: *Cars, trucks, bicycles, trains, wagons, and space shuttles are vehicles.*

veil (vāl) *n.* a thin piece of cloth worn to protect or hide the face.

vein (vān) *n.* one of the thin, long tubes in the body that carries blood to the heart.

velvet (vel′ vət) *n.* a kind of cloth that has short, soft, smooth fibres on one side.

> **Velvet** comes from the Latin word *villus,* meaning "hairy" or "shaggy."

velvety (vel′ və tē) *adj.* smooth and soft like velvet: *Our teacher has a velvety voice.*

vengeance (ven′ jəns) *n.* the act of getting even for some wrong or harm that was done to you; revenge; punishment.

venison (ven′ ə sən) *n.* the meat of a deer.

venom (ven′ əm) *n.* the poison of some snakes and spiders.

venomous (ven′ ə məs) *adj.* poisonous.

vent, ventilator (vent, ven′ tə lā′ tər) *n.* an opening through which gas or smoke can escape or air can enter.

ventilation (ven tə lā′ shən) *n.* the supply and moving around of fresh air: *We opened the windows to give the room some ventilation.*

ventriloquist (ven tril′ ə kwist) *n.* a performer who is able to make his or her voice sound like it is coming from somewhere else.

venture (ven′ chər) *v.* to take a risk in doing something or going somewhere: *The explorers ventured into the long, dark cave.* **venturing. ventured.**

Venus (vē′ nəs) *n.* **1.** in ancient times, the Roman goddess of love. **2.** one of the planets of our solar system: *Venus is the second closest planet to the sun.*

verandah, veranda (və ran′ də) *n.* a porch with a roof, joined to a house.

verb (vůrb) *n.* a word that shows action or a condition of being: *She has the ball. It rained yesterday.* In these sentences, the verbs are *has* and *rained.*

verbal (vůr′ bəl) *adj.* expressed in spoken, not written, words: *His verbal skills are very good.* —**verbally** *adv.*

verdict (vůr′ dikt) *n.* the decision of a jury at the end of a trial: *A jury must decide if the verdict is "guilty" or "not guilty."*

verify (ver′ ə fī) *v.* to make sure that something is correct: *Before we print the story in the newspaper, we must verify the facts.* **verifying. verified.** she **verifies.**

versatile (vůr′ sə tīl) *adj.* able to do many kinds of things well: *She is a versatile performer who sings, dances, and acts.*

verse (vůrs) *n.* **1.** poetry: *A poet writes verse.* **2.** a group of lines in a poem.

version (vůr′ zhən) *n.* a description of something from one person's point of view: *Each witness gave a different version of how the accident happened.*

vertebrate (vůr′ tə brāt′) *n.* any type of animal that has a backbone.

vertical (vůr′ ti kəl) *adj.* straight up and down: *A vertical line is drawn from top to bottom.* —**vertically** *adv.*

very (ver′ ē) *adv.* extremely: *He is a very good singer and a very bad dancer.*

vessel (ves′ əl) *n.* **1.** a ship or large boat. **2.** a vein or an artery: *a blood vessel.*

vest (vest) *n.* a sleeveless garment worn over a shirt or blouse.

veterinarian (vet′ ər ə ner′ ē ən) *n.* a doctor who treats animals.

veteran (vet′ ər ən) *n.* **1.** a person who has served in the armed forces. **2.** a person who has a lot of experience in something.

via (vē′ ə *or* vī′ ə) *prep.* by way of, or passing through: *The train travels from Ottawa to Quebec City, via Montreal.*

viaduct (vī′ ə dukt′) a long bridge over a valley or railway.

viaduct

vibrate (vī′ brāt′) *v.* to move back and forth very fast; to quiver: *When you pluck a guitar string, it vibrates.* **vibrating. vibrated.**

> **vice–** is a prefix meaning "second in importance": a vice-president takes over when the president is away or can't perform his or her duties.

vice versa (vī′ sə vůr′ sə *or* vīs ver′ sə) a Latin phrase meaning "the other way around": *I'll help you and vice versa. (and you will help me)*

vicious (vish′ əs) *adj.* cruel and violent: *a vicious crime.* —**viciously** *adv.*

vicinity (və sin′ ə tē) *n.* the area around you; the neighbourhood: *There is a post office in the vicinity of our house. pl.* **vicinities.**

victim (vik′ təm) *n.* a person who is harmed or killed by another person, a disease, an accident, and so on: *a victim of a crime.*

victor (vik′ tər) *n.* the winner of a battle, contest, or game.

victorious (vik to′ rē əs) *adj.* being the winner. —**victoriously** *adv.*

victory (vik′ tə rē) *n.* a win in a battle, contest, or game. *pl.* **victories.**

video (vid′ ē ō) *n.* **1.** the visual part of a TV program or movie. *pl.* **videos. 2.** short for **videocassette.**

videocassette (vid′ ē ō kə′ set′) *n.* a plastic case that holds magnetic tape on which a TV show or movie can be recorded.

videocassette recorder, VCR *n.* a machine that records TV programs on a tape.

videotape (vid′ ē ō tāp′) *n.* a magnetic tape used to record moving pictures and sound. —*v.* to make a videotape. **videotaping. videotaped.**

view (vyū) *n.* **1.** everything that you can see from one place: *We had a good view of the ocean from our room.* **2.** an opinion. —*v.* to look at or watch: *I viewed some slides of my friend's trip.* **viewing. viewed.**

viewpoint (vyū′ point′) *n.* an attitude: *We asked all the students in our grade for their viewpoint on the subject.*

vigour, vigor (vig′ ər) *n.* energy and strength: *We climbed the hill with vigour.*

vile (vīl) *adj.* **1.** evil. **2.** disgusting; bad: *vile weather.*

village (vil′ əj) *n.* a small group of houses and stores: *A village is smaller than a town.*

villain (vil′ ən) *n.* a wicked person: *The villain in the story tried to steal the money.*

vine (vīn) *n.* a plant whose stems creep along the ground or climb a wall or stick: *Grapes and melons grow on vines.*

vinegar (vin′ ə gər) *n.* a sour liquid used to flavour or preserve food such as pickles.

vineyard (vin′ yərd) *n.* a large piece of land where grapes are grown.

vinyl (vī′ nil) *n.* a tough plastic used for making floor polishes, table tops, raincoats, and other things.

violence (vī′ ə ləns) *n.* great physical force causing harm or damage.

violent (vī′ ə lənt) *adj.* very rough and causing harm or damage: *a violent storm; a violent person.* —**violently** *adv.*

violet (vī′ ə lət) *n.* **1.** a small plant with blue, purple, or white flowers. **2.** a blue-purple colour. —*adj.* having this colour.

violin (vī′ ə lin′) *n.* a musical instrument made of wood; it has four strings and is played with a bow.

violin

violinist (vī′ ə lin′ ist) *n.* a person who plays the violin.

virtual (vůr′ chū əl) *adj.* practically, but not actually, real: *Although I have seen her several times, she is still a virtual stranger to me.* —**virtually** *adv.*

virtual reality (vůr′ chū əl rē al′ ə te) a computer program that imitates the sights, sounds, and sensations of a real experience.

virus (vī′ rəs) *n.* a tiny living thing that causes disease; a kind of germ. *pl.* **viruses.**

visa (vē′ zə) *n.* a special stamp or document in a passport to show that the holder has permission to visit a particular country.

vise (vīs) *n.* a tool with two metal jaws that can be closed to hold something tightly.

visible (viz′ ə bəl) *adj.* able to be seen: *The night is clear, and many stars are visible.* (*opp.* **invisible.**) —**visibly** *adv.*

vision (vizh′ ən) *n.* **1.** the ability to see; sight. **2.** a picture in your mind or a dream: *I had visions of being rich.*

visual (vizh′ yū əl) *adj.* having to do with sight and seeing: *Painting and sculpture are called visual arts.* —**visually** *adv.*

visit (viz′ it) *n.* a time spent with someone: *My grandparents' visit from Jamaica was too short.* —*v.* to go see someone or something: *We visited the zoo.* **visiting. visited.**

visitor (viz′ ə tər) *n.* someone who visits you; a guest.

vital (vī′ təl) *adj.* **1.** having to do with life. **2.** necessary for life: *Food is vital for all animals.* **3.** full of life and energy: *a vital person.* **4.** very important: *It is vital that all the players attend the practice.* —**vitally** *adv.*

vitamin (vī′ tə min) *n.* a substance that is needed for good health, found in many foods.

vivid (viv′ id) *adj.* **1.** brightly coloured: *The tulips were a vivid red.* **2.** creating strong pictures in the mind: *a vivid description.* —**vividly** *adv.*

vocabulary (vō kab′ yə ler′ ē) *n.* **1.** all the words you know: *Emanuel has a large vocabulary and he writes good stories.* **2.** all the words in a language. *pl.* **vocabularies.**

vocal (vō′ kəl) *adj.* **1.** having to do with the voice. **2.** giving your opinion: *The fans were vocal in their praise.* —**vocally** *adv.*

voice (vois) *n.* the sound coming from your throat when you speak or sing.

volcanic (vol kan′ ik) *adj.* having to do with a volcano: *volcanic ash.*

volcano (vol kā′ nō) *n.* an opening in the earth's surface through which very hot lava, gases, and ashes pour out. *pl.* **volcanoes.**

The word **volcano** comes from *Vulcan,* the ancient Roman god of fire. Vulcan kept his metal workshop in the pit of a volcano.

volleyball (vol′ ē bol′) *n.* **1.** a game in which two teams, standing on either side of a net, hit a large ball back and forth with their hands. **2.** the ball used in this game.

volume (vol′ yūm) *n.* **1.** a book, or one of a set of books or magazines. **2.** loudness: *Please lower the volume of the radio.* **3.** the amount of space that an object fills.

voluntary (vol′ ən ter′ ē) *adj.* done because you want to, and not because you must.

volunteer (vol′ ən tēr′) *n.* someone who offers to help without being asked, or who works without being paid. —*v.* to offer your help without being asked or without being paid. **volunteering. volunteered.**

vomit (vom′ it) *v.* to bring up matter from the stomach through the mouth; to throw up. **vomiting. vomited.**

vote (vōt) *n.* a choice made in an election: *Amanda got the most votes for class president.* —*v.* to cast a vote. **voting. voted.**

vow (vow) *n.* a serious promise: *wedding vows.* —*v.* to make a vow: *He vowed not to tell my secret.* **vowing. vowed.**

vowel (vow′ əl) *n.* any of the letters a, e, i, o, u, and sometimes y.

voyage (voi′ əj) *n.* a long trip or journey by water, through the air, or through space.

voyageur (voi′ ə zhůr′) *n.* in earlier days, a boatman, usually a French Canadian, who carried furs and other supplies for fur-trading companies in Canada.

vulgar (vul′ gər) *adj.* very rude: *Using swear words is vulgar.*

vulture (vul′ chər) *n.* a large bird that has dark feathers and a bald head and neck: *Vultures do not kill; they feed on animals that are already dead.*

vulture

waddle (wod′ əl) *n.* a walk with short steps and swaying from side to side: *The ducks walked with a waddle.* —*v.* to walk in such a way, as a duck does. **waddling. waddled.**

wade (wād) *v.* to walk through shallow water. **wading. waded.**

waffle (wof′ əl) *n.* a light, crisp cake made from a batter, usually eaten with butter and syrup: *A waffle is cooked in a waffle iron, which presses a pattern of small squares on each side.*

wag (wag) *n.* a quick, side-to-side motion: *a wag of the dog's tail.* —*v.* to move quickly from side to side: *The dog wagged its tail.* **wagging. wagged.**

wage (wāj) *n.* money that is paid to someone for working, especially on an hourly or daily basis. —*v.* to take part in: *to wage war.* **waging. waged.**

wagon (wag′ ən) *n.* **1.** a vehicle pulled by horses and used for carrying heavy loads: *a hay wagon.* **2.** a small, low cart with four wheels and a handle for children to pull.

wail (wāl) *n.* a long, loud cry, often from sadness or pain: *the wail of a lost child.* —*v.* to make such a cry. **wailing. wailed.**

waist (wāst) *n.* the middle part of your body, between the ribs and hips.

wait (wāt) *n.* the act of staying in one place until something happens or someone comes: *We had a long wait for the bus.* —*v.* to stay in one place until something happens or someone comes: *We waited a long time for our friends to arrive.* **waiting. waited.**

wake (wāk) *v.* **1.** to make someone stop sleeping: *Father woke us in time for school.* **2.** to stop sleeping: *Beth woke up early.* **waking. woke** or **waked.** I have **woken.**

walk (wok) *n.* a trip on foot: *We went for a walk in the park.* —*v.* to go on foot: *We walked to the store.* **walking. walked.**

wall (wol) *n.* **1.** the side of a building or room that joins the floor to the ceiling and separates one space from another. **2.** a solid fence made of brick, stone, or wood, used as protection or to keep people or animals out: *the Great Wall of China.*

wallet (wol′ ət) *n.* a small, flat case that folds in half and is used to carry money, cards, photos, and so on.

wallow (wol′ ō) *v.* to lie and roll around in mud or water, as pigs and other animals do. **wallowing. wallowed.**

wallpaper (wol′ pā′ pər) *n.* large strips of paper, often with a pattern, that are used to decorate the walls of a room.

walnut (wol′ nut) *n.* **1.** a hard, round nut with a hard, crinkled shell. **2.** the tree that produces this nut. **3.** the wood of the walnut tree, often used to make furniture.

walrus (wol′ rəs) *n.* a large sea mammal, something like a seal, that has two long tusks and a thick layer of blubber. *pl.* **walruses.**

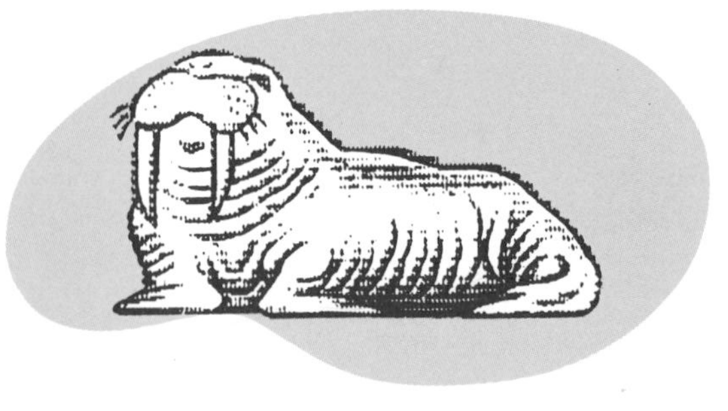

walrus

The name **walrus** comes from an old Norwegian word *hvalros,* meaning "whale-horse." This is what people thought a walrus looked like.

waltz (woltz) *n.* **1.** a graceful dance with a gliding and whirling motion: *A waltz is danced by a couple.* **2.** music for a waltz. *pl.* **waltzes.** —*v.* to dance a waltz. **waltzing. waltzed.**

wand (wond) *n.* a thin rod: *a magician's magic wand.*

wander (won′ dər) *v.* to move from one place to another, with no particular purpose or place to get to: *We wandered through the shopping mall.* **wandering. wandered.**

wane (wān) *v.* to become smaller, dimmer, less bright, less important: *The full moon waned to a thin crescent.* **waning. waned.**

want (wont) *v.* to wish to have or to do: *My sister wants a new pair of skis for her birthday in January.* **wanting. wanted.**

war (wȯr) *n.* a long fight, with weapons and soldiers, between countries or groups of people.

warble (wȯr′ bəl) *n.* the singing of some birds, with repeated sounds and trills. —*v.* to sing sweetly, as some birds do: *The choir warbled a folk song.* **warbling. warbled.**

ward (wȯrd) *n.* **1.** a large room for several patients in a hospital. **2.** a district of a city or town where a person lives and votes. **3.** a person cared for by a legal guardian.

warden (wȯr′ dən) *n.* **1.** a person in charge of a prison. **2.** a person who looks after large parks and wilderness areas.

wardrobe (wȯrd′ rōb) *n.* **1.** a supply of clothes. **2.** a closet or piece of furniture in which clothes are hung on hangers.

warehouse (wer′ hows′) *n.* a large building where goods are stored: *a furniture warehouse.*

warm (wȯrm) *adj.* **1.** slightly hot: *a warm bath.* **2.** friendly and caring: *He is a warm person.* **3.** enthusiastic: *The winning team received a warm welcome when they went home.* —**warmly** *adv.* —*v.* to make or become warm: *This hot soup will warm you.* **warming. warmed.**

warm-blooded (wȯrm′ blud′ əd) *adj.* having a warm body temperature that stays about the same whether the surrounding temperature goes up or down: *Mammals and birds are warm-blooded; fish and reptiles are cold-blooded.*

warm-hearted (wȯrm′ hȧr′ təd) *adj.* kind and affectionate: *a warm-hearted person.*

warmth (wȯrmth) *n.* the condition or feeling of being warm.

warn (wȯrn) *v.* to tell someone about possible or coming danger: *Juan warned Max to stay off the thin ice.* **warning. warned.**

warning (wȯr′ ning) *n.* something that tells of possible danger: *A lighthouse is a warning to ships that they are close to the shore.*

warp (wȯrp) *n.* a bend or a twist in something: *a warp in a piece of wood.* —*v.* to bend or twist out of shape: *The heat warped the wood.* **warping. warped.**

warrant (wȯr′ ənt) *n.* an official paper that gives an order: *The police had a warrant to search the house.*

warranty (wȯr′ ən tē) *n.* a written promise to fix or replace something if anything goes wrong with it within a certain period of time: *Our new VCR has a three-year warranty.* *pl.* **warranties.**

warrior (wȯr′ ē ər) *n.* a person who fights in battles; a soldier.

wart (wȯrt) *n.* a small, hard lump that can grow on the skin: *Warts are caused by a virus.*

wary (wer′ ē) *adj.* cautious, careful, and suspicious: *I'm wary of that promise—it sounds too good to be true.* —**warily** *adv.*

was (wuz *or* woz) *v.* a form of the verb **be** in the past tense; used with "I," "he," "she," "it," a name, or any other singular noun: *I was going to sleep. She was on holiday.*

wash (wosh) *n.* **1.** the act of cleaning: *The car needs a wash.* **2.** a load of clean or dirty laundry. *pl.* **washes.** —*v.* to clean with water and sometimes soap. **washing. washed.**

washer (wosh′ ər) *n.* **1.** a washing machine. **2.** a flat metal or rubber ring placed between a nut and bolt.

washing machine a machine for washing dirty clothes.

wasn't (wuz′ ənt) a short form (contraction) of **was not**.

wasp (wosp) *n.* a flying insect that has a narrow waist, black and yellow stripes, and a sharp sting.

wasp

waste (wāst) *n.* **1.** a poor use of something, or the use of more than you need: *The meeting was a waste of time because nobody was there.* **2.** garbage; anything that you do not need any more. —*v.* to use more money, time, material, or energy than you need: *I always turn off the light whenever I leave a room, so that I don't waste electricity.* **wasting. wasted.**

wasteful (wāst′ fəl) *adj.* using or spending too much. —**wastefully** *adv.*

watch (woch) *n.* a small clock, usually worn on the wrist. *pl.* **watches.** —*v.* **1.** to look at in a steady or careful way: *We watched the wild birds with binoculars.* **2.** to wait and look for: *Watch for my signal.* **3.** to guard: *Watch our luggage in the airport.* **watching. watched.**

water (wo′ tər) *n.* the colourless liquid that fills the oceans, lakes, and rivers and falls from clouds as rain. —*v.* to supply water to: *to water plants.* **watering. watered.**

watercolour, watercolor (wo′ tər kul′ ər) *n.* **1.** a type of paint that is mixed with water, not oil. **2.** a painting made with this paint.

waterfall (wo′ tər fol′) *n.* a stream of water falling from a high place.

waterfall

watermelon (wo′ tər mel′ ən) *n.* a very large, juicy fruit that has sweet, pink flesh and a thick, green rind.

waterproof (wo′ tər prūf′) *adj.* not letting water pass through: *a waterproof coat.* —*v.* to put a coating on something so that water cannot pass through: *to waterproof winter boots.* **waterproofing. waterproofed.**

water-ski (wo′ tər skē′) *v.* to glide over water on one or two water skis while being towed along by a rope attached to a motorboat. **water-skiing. water-skied.** she **water-skis.**

wave (wāv) *n.* **1.** an up-and-down movement on water. **2.** a gesture with the hand and arm, up and down or from side to side. **3.** a vibration that carries sound, heat, light, or energy, and moves in the pattern of a wave: *radio waves.* —*v.* to move up and down or from side to side: *to wave your hand; to wave a flag.* **waving. waved.**

wavy (wāv′ ē) *adj.* looking like waves: *wavy hair; wavier hair; the waviest hair of all.*

wax (waks) *n.* **1.** a solid, yellow substance made by bees. **2.** any substance that resembles this: *furniture wax. pl.* **waxes.** —*v.* **1.** to rub wax on something, as when polishing furniture. **2.** (for the moon) to become round and full: *The moon waxes and wanes.* **waxing. waxed.**

way (wā) *n.* **1.** a road or path: *That isn't the right way.* **2.** a direction: *Which way is south?* **3.** how to do something; a manner; a method: *This is the way to knead bread dough.*

we (wē) *pron. pl.* you and I, and anyone else who is speaking or writing. **We** is used as the subject of a verb: *We went to the movies.*

weak (wēk) *adj.* **1.** not strong or powerful: *a weak link in a chain.* **2.** feeble: *weak from illness.* —**weakly** *adv.*

weakness (wēk′ nəs) *n.* **1.** a lack of strength or power: *a weakness in my arm.* **2.** a liking for something: *I have a weakness for chocolate. pl.* **weaknesses.**

wealth (welth) *n.* a great deal of money or valuable things.

wealthy (wel′ thē) *adj.* having a lot of money; rich: *a wealthy family; a wealthier family; the wealthiest family in town.*

weapon (wep′ ən) *n.* a tool or anything else used for fighting or hunting.

wear (wer) *v.* **1.** to put on your body: *Marie wore her new dress and earrings.* **2.** to become thin and damaged from much use: *The middle of the hall rug has become worn.* **wearing. wore.** I have **worn.**

wear away to become slowly damaged or destroyed: *The rain is causing the metal pipe to rust and wear away.*

wear off to stop having an effect: *As the cold medicine wore off, my nose started running again.*

wear out **1.** to make very tired: *Their long arguments wear me out.* **2.** to become thin and damaged from much use: *When my jeans wore out at the knees, I covered the holes with patches.*

weary (wēr′ ē) *adj.* very tired; worn out: *a weary workhorse; a wearier one; the weariest workhorse on the farm.* —**wearily** *adv.*

weasel (wē′ zəl) *n.* a small wild mammal with a long, slender body and short legs.

weather (weTH′ ər) *n.* what it is like outside: *Weather is usually wet or dry, hot or cold, sunny or cloudy, windy or still.*

> Be careful not to mix up **weather** with "whether"; "whether" means if.

weave (wēv) *v.* to make cloth by passing threads over and under one another. **weaving. wove.** I have **woven.**

web (web) *n.* **1.** a net of sticky threads spun by a spider to catch flying insects. **2.** the skin joining the toes of some water birds and some animals, such as ducks, geese, and otters.

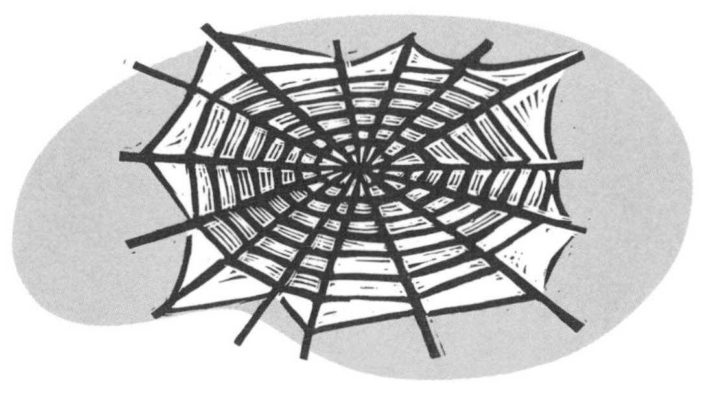

web

wed (wed) *v.* to marry. **wedding. wedded.**

we'd (wēd) a contraction (short form) of **we had** or **we would**.

wedding (wed′ ing) *n.* the occasion when two people are married.

wedge (wej) *n.* a piece of wood, cheese, pie, and so on that is thin at one end and wider at the other.

Wednesday (wenz′ dā *or* wenz′ dē) *n.* the fourth day of the week.

weed (wēd) *n.* any wild plant that grows in places where it is not wanted and is hard to get rid of. —*v.* to take out the weeds from an area: *to weed a lawn.* **weeding. weeded.**

week (wēk) *n.* a period of seven days, beginning with Sunday and ending with Saturday.

weekday (wēk′ dā) *n.* any day of the week except Saturday and Sunday: *People usually work or go to school on weekdays.*

weekend (wēk′ end) *n.* Saturday and Sunday: *Many people don't work or go to school on the weekend.*

weekly (wēk′ lē) *adj.* coming out or happening every week: *a weekly meeting.* —*adv.* once a week: *The magazine comes out weekly.*

weep (wēp) *v.* to shed tears. **weeping. wept.**

weigh (wā) *v.* to find the mass or weight of a person or thing by using a scale. **weighing. weighed.**

weight (wāt) *n.* **1.** how heavy a person or thing is. **2.** something heavy: *A metal weight keeps papers from blowing off a desk.*

weird (wērd) *adj.* very strange; eerie: *We heard weird noises coming from the attic.* —**weirdly** *adv.*

welcome (wel′ kəm) *n.* a friendly greeting: *Our new neighbours gave us a warm welcome.* —*adj.* received gladly: *Your suggestions are welcome.* —*v.* **1.** to greet in a friendly, warm way: *We welcomed our friends at the bus station.* **2.** to receive gladly: *I welcome your suggestions.* **welcoming. welcomed.**

weld (weld) *v.* to join two pieces of metal together by melting them with a very hot flame: *The mechanic welded a new steel panel to the side of the car.* **welding. welded.**

welfare (wel′ fer) *n.* **1.** health and happiness: *My parents are concerned about my uncle's welfare now that he has lost his job.* **2.** money or other help provided by the government to people in need.

well (wel) *n.* a hole drilled in the ground to get water or oil. —*adj.* healthy; not sick: *Last week I had a cold, but I am well now.* —*adv.* **1.** in a good way: *You did this work well.* **2.** in a close way: *I know her well.* —*interj.* a word that expresses surprise or a pause while you are thinking: *Well, I don't know.*

we'll (wēl) a short form (contraction) of **we will** or **we shall**.

well-done (wel′ dun′) *adj.* completely cooked; not rare: *This steak is well-done.*

well-known (wel′ nōn′) *adj.* famous.

went (went) see **go**.

wept (wept) see **weep**.

were (wûr) *v.* a form of the verb **be** in the past tense; used with "you," "we," "they," and plural nouns: *The children were going to sleep. You were there. We were lucky.*

we're (wēr) a short form (contraction) of **we are**.

weren't (wûrnt *or* wûr′ ənt) a short form (contraction) of **were not**.

west (west) *n.* the direction in which the sun sets; opposite to east. —*adv.* to the west: *The pioneers went west.*

western (wes′ tərn) *adj.* in or of the west: *British Columbia is a western province.*

westward, westwards (west′ wərd, west′ wərdz) *adv.* toward or facing the west: *We looked westward at the setting sun.*

wet (wet) *adj.* **1.** covered or soaked with water: *a wet towel; a wetter one; the wettest towel in the bathroom.* **2.** rainy: *a wet day.* —*v.* to make wet. **wetting. wetted.**

we've (wēv) a short form (contraction) of **we have**.

whack (hwak *or* wak) *n.* a hit or blow that makes a loud smacking sound: *She hit the ball with a whack.* —*v.* to hit with a loud, smacking sound. **whacking. whacked.**

whale (hwāl *or* wāl) *n.* a very large ocean animal that has a body like a fish but is really a mammal: *Whales breathe air.*

wharf (hwôrf *or* wôrf) *n.* a landing place for boats or ships; a large pier. *pl.* **wharves** or **wharfs.**

what (hwut *or* wut) *adj.* which: *What time is it?* —*pron.* **1.** which thing, activity, and so on: *What are you doing?* **2.** the thing that: *He doesn't know what is in the box.*

whatever (hwut ev′ ər *or* wut ev′ ər) *pron.* no matter what: *I will do whatever I can to help.*

what's (hwuts *or* wuts) a short form (contraction) of **what is** or **what has**.

wheat (hwēt *or* wēt) *n.* a grain that looks like tall grass; it turns yellow when ripe: *The kernels of wheat are ground to make flour.*

wheel (hwēl *or* wēl) *n.* a round frame or disk made of metal, plastic, rubber, wood, and so on that turns around on an axle. —*v.* to push on wheels: *He wheeled the shopping cart.* **wheeling. wheeled.**

wheelbarrow (hwēl′ bar′ ō *or* wēl′ bar′ ō) *n.* a small cart with one wheel and two handles: *A wheelbarrow is pushed by hand and is used to carry heavy loads.*

wheelbarrow

wheelchair (hwēl′ cher *or* wēl′ cher) *n.* a chair on wheels, used by people who cannot walk or who are sick.

when (hwen *or* wen) *adv.* at what time: *When did the game begin?* —*conj.* at the time: *Not many people were left when we arrived late at the party.*

whenever (hwen ev′ ər *or* wen ev′ ər) *conj.* at any time that: *We shall go whenever you are ready.*

where (hwer *or* wer) *adv.* in or to what place: *Where is my pen?* —*conj.* in the place that: *We shall stop where we can rest.*

wherever (hwer ev′ ər *or* wer ev′ ər) *adv.* in any place that: *My dog goes wherever I go.*

whether (hweTH′ ər *or* weTH′ ər) *conj.* if. "Whether" is often used with "or" to show a choice: *I don't know whether to go or stay.*

which (hwich *or* wich) *adj.* what (one among several ones): *Which car in the parking lot is yours?* —*pron.* **1.** what one among several ones: *Which is yours?* **2.** the one that: *His coat, which is blue and has a hood, is in the closet.* **3.** that: *The house, which we were interested in buying, is no longer for sale.*

while (hwīl *or* wīl) *n.* a period of time: *a short while; a long while.* —*conj.* during the time that: *I read while the bread was baking.*

whimper (hwim′ pər *or* wim′ pər) *n.* a soft, sad cry. —*v.* to make such a cry: *We heard the puppy whimpering outside.* **whimpering. whimpered.**

whine (hwīn *or* wīn) *n.* a long, complaining cry, or a noise like it: *the whine of an electric saw.* —*v.* to make such a cry; to complain. **whining. whined.**

whip (hwip *or* wip) *n.* a long piece of rope or leather joined to a handle and used for hitting or beating. —*v.* **1.** to hit with a whip. **2.** to beat very fast and hard into a foam: *to whip cream.* **whipping. whipped.**

whirl (hwûrl *or* hwûrl) *n.* a quick spin. —*v.* to spin around quickly. **whirling. whirled.**

whiskers (hwis′ kərz *or* wis′ kərz) *n. pl.* **1.** the stiff hair that grows on the lower part of a man's face. **2.** the stiff hair at each side of the nose and mouth of some animals: *Cats have whiskers.*

whisper (hwis′ pər *or* wis′ pər) *n.* a word or words spoken very softly. —*v.* to speak very softly: *Nadia whispered the secret into my ear.* **whispering. whispered.**

whistle (hwis′ əl *or* wis′ əl) *n.* **1.** a clear, sharp sound made by making your lips into an "O" and blowing through them. **2.** a small pipe that makes such a sound: *The referee blew the whistle.* —*v.* to make a high, sharp sound by blowing through your lips or using a whistle. **whistling. whistled.**

white (hwīt *or* wīt) *n.* **1.** the colour of snow, opposite to black. **2.** the almost clear and colourless part of an egg around the yolk. *—adj.* having the colour of snow.

who (hū) *pron.* **1.** which person or persons: *Who left the message?* **2.** the person or persons that: *The girl who won the science fair is my cousin.*

whoever (hū ev′ ər) *pron.* any person that: *Whoever borrows a book from the library should return it.*

whole (hōl) *adj.* complete; entire: *The whole school had a holiday.*

wholesome (hōl′ sum) *adj.* healthy, or good for your health: *a wholesome meal.*

whole-wheat (hōl′ hwēt′ *or* hōl′ wēt′) *adj.* made from the whole wheat kernel: *Whole-wheat bread is made from whole-wheat flour.*

whom (hūm) *pron.* the form of **who** that is used as the object of a verb or preposition: *Whom did you phone?*

who's (hūz) a short form (contraction) of **who is** or **who has**.

Be careful not to mix up **who's** with **whose**: ***Who's*** *that girl?* ***Whose*** *homework is this?*

whose (hūz) *pron.* **1.** to whom it belongs: *Whose hat is this?* **2.** of whom or of which: *We saw the car whose driver caused an accident.*

why (hwī *or* wī) *adv.* for what reason: *Why didn't you tell me? —conj.* the reason for which: *He is on a diet; that's why he has lost weight.*

wick (wik) *n.* a string in a candle or oil lamp that is lighted to cause the candle or lamp to burn.

wicked (wik′ əd) *adj.* very bad: *We read about a wicked magician.* —**wickedly** *adv.*

wide (wīd) *adj.* measuring from side to side; broad; not narrow: *The St. Lawrence is a wide river. —adv.* completely: *The window is wide open.*

widely (wīd′ lē) *adv.* to a great degree: *a widely known poet.*

widen (wī′ dən) *v.* to make or become wider: *Workers widened the tunnel.* **widening. widened.**

widow (wid′ ō) *n.* a woman whose husband has died and who has not married again.

widower (wid′ ō ər) *n.* a man whose wife has died and who has not married again.

width (width) *n.* how wide something is, measured from side to side.

wiener (wē′ nər) *n.* a reddish-coloured sausage, usually made of beef and pork.

wife (wīf) *n.* the woman to whom a husband is married. *pl.* **wives.**

wig (wig) *n.* a cap of fake or real hair worn on the head, often over your own hair.

wiggle (wig′ əl) *v.* to move with short, quick movements from side to side: *to wiggle your ears.* **wiggling. wiggled.**

wigwam (wig′ wom) *n.* a dwelling in which some North American aboriginal peoples used to live: *A wigwam is shaped like a cone and made from poles covered with bark or animal skins.*

wigwam

wild (wīld) *adj.* **1.** living in nature; not tame: *wild animals.* **2.** not calm and not controlled: *a wild crowd; a wild storm.* —**wildly** *adv.*

wilderness (wil′ dər nəs) *n.* an area of nature where no people live; the natural environment.

wildlife (wīld′ līf′) *n.* the animals and birds that live in an area: *the wildlife of the Arctic.*

will (wil) *n.* **1.** the power of your mind to choose and decide what to do: *the will to win a game.* **2.** a written document in which a person says who is to have his or her money and property after he or she dies. —*v.* a helping (auxiliary) verb placed before another verb to show: **1.** a future action or event: *The team will play next week.* **2.** a polite request: *Please will you help me?* **3.** an intention: *I will give you my help.* **4.** an order: *You will do as I say.* **would.**

willing (wil′ ing) *adj.* glad and ready to do something: *I am willing to help you rake the leaves.* (*opp.* **unwilling.**) —**willingly** *adv.*

willow (wil′ ō) *n.* a tree with narrow leaves and long, thin branches that bend easily.

willpower (wil′ pow′ ər) *n.* the strength of your will; your ability to control your actions: *It took a lot of willpower for me to walk past the bakery without going inside.*

wilt (wilt) *v.* to become dry and limp from lack of water: *The plant is wilting because nobody watered it.* **wilting. wilted.**

win (win) *n.* a victory in a game, contest, or fight. —*v.* **1.** to be first in a game, contest, or fight: *to win a hockey game.* **2.** to earn by hard work: *She won praise for her fine acting.* **winning. won.**

wind (wind) *n.* air that is moving.

wind (wīnd) *v.* **1.** to wrap or twist around something: *to wind a long bandage around an ankle.* **2.** to curve in one direction and then another; to twist: *The path winds through the woods.* **3.** to tighten the spring of a watch or clock. **winding. wound.** (*opp.* **unwind.**)

wind instrument a musical instrument played by blowing air into it: *The recorder, flute, and trumpet are wind instruments.*

windmill (wind′ mil′) *n.* a mill or machine with vanes that are turned by the wind: *Windmills are used to grind grain into flour, to pump water, and to produce energy.*

windmill

window (win′ dō) *n.* **1.** an opening in the wall of a building or vehicle that lets in light or air: *Windows are usually covered with glass.* **2.** on a computer screen, the area where a program shows information.

windshield (wind′ shēld′) *n.* the broad glass or plastic screen in a vehicle that protects the driver from wind and rain.

windsurfing (wind′ sûrf′ ing) *n.* a sport in which a person stands on a large board with a sail attached to it and glides across the water: *You need a good wind and good balance for windsurfing.*

windy (wind′ ē) *adj.* having much wind: *a windy day; a windier day; the windiest day of all.*

wine (wīn) *n.* an alcoholic drink made from the juice of grapes or other fruit.

wing (wing) *n.* **1.** one of two body parts that a bird, bat, or insect uses for flying. **2.** a flat, narrow stretch of metal on either side of an airplane that helps keep it in the air when flying. **3.** a part that sticks out from the main part of a building. **4. wings** the area on either side of a stage that the audience cannot see.

wink (wingk) *n.* a quick closing and opening of one eye, often as a friendly signal. —*v.* to close and open an eye quickly. **winking. winked.**

winner (win′ ər) *n.* a team or person who wins something.

winter (win′ tər) *n.* the season after autumn.

wipe (wīp) *v.* to clean or dry by rubbing with a cloth or on a mat: *Wipe your feet before you come into the house.* **wiping. wiped.**

wipe out to destroy completely: *The forest fire wiped out many trees and animals.*

wire (wīr) *n.* a metal thread that usually bends easily. —*v.* to put in wires for electricity: *The electrician wired the new house.* **wiring. wired.**

wisdom (wiz′ dəm) *n.* knowledge and good judgment, often gained from experience: *My grandparents have much wisdom.*

wise (wīz) *adj.* **1.** having much knowledge and good sense, gained from experience: *a wise person.* **2.** showing good judgment: *a wise decision.* —**wisely** *adv.*

wish (wish) *n.* a strong desire or hope for something: *My wish for a sunny weekend came true.* —*pl.* **wishes.** —*v.* **1.** to want something very much. **2.** to say what you hope for: *I wish you good luck.* **wishing. wished.**

wistful (wist′ fəl) *adj.* full of sad longing: *a wistful child in a toy store.* —**wistfully** *adv.*

with (with) *prep.* **1.** in the company of: *Joyce walked with Ben.* **2.** having: *My cousin is the girl with dark hair.* **3.** because of: *We shouted with happiness.* **4.** using: *Marla hit the ball with the bat.* **5.** against: *Don't fight with them.*

withdraw (with′ dro) *v.* **1.** to move out: *The soldiers withdrew from the city.* **2.** to take back something you said, gave, or offered: *Freida is withdrawing her offer to coach the team.* **3.** to take out: *to withdraw money from the bank.* **withdrawing. withdrew.** I have **withdrawn.**

wither (wiᴛʜ′ ər) *v.* to dry up and shrivel: *The plants withered under the hot sun.* **withering. withered.**

within (with in′) *prep.* inside of: *The box on the shelf was within Jim's reach.*

without (with owt′) *prep.* not having: *I left the library without borrowing any books.*

witness (wit′ nəs) *n.* **1.** someone who saw something happen: *a witness to an accident.* **2.** in a court of law, a person who is asked to tell what he or she saw. *pl.* **witnesses.** —*v.* to see something happen: *We witnessed the accident.* **witnessing. witnessed.**

wives (wīvz) plural of **wife**.

woe (wō) *n.* great sorrow or trouble. —**woeful** *adj.*

wok (wok) *n.* a deep frying pan, shaped like a bowl: *A wok is often used to cook Chinese food.*

woke, woken (wōk, wō′ kən) see **wake**.

wolf (wu̇lf) *n.* a wild mammal, usually grey, that is closely related to dogs. *pl.* **wolves.**

wolverine (wu̇l′ vər ēn′) *n.* a dark brown mammal that looks like a large weasel and lives in cold, northern regions.

wolverine

woman (wu̇m′ ən) *n.* an adult female human being. *pl.* **women** (wim′ in).

won (wun) see **win**.

wonder (wun′ dər) *n.* **1.** a surprising, unusual, and often splendid thing: *Niagara Falls is one of the world's great wonders.* **2.** a feeling of amazement: *We watched in wonder as the magician did her tricks.* —*v.* to be curious about: *I wonder who lives in that big house.* **wondering. wondered.**

wonderful (wun′ dər fəl) *adj.* **1.** causing wonder; amazing; marvellous: *a wonderful sunset.* **2.** giving a lot of pleasure: *a wonderful party.* —**wonderfully** *adv.*

won't (wōnt) a contraction (short form) of **will not.**

wood (wu̇d) *n.* the hard part, underneath the bark, that makes up the trunk and branches of a tree: *Wood can be made into many things, such as furniture.*

wooden (wu̇d′ ən) *adj.* made of wood.

woodpecker (wu̇d′ pek′ ər) *n.* a bird that has a strong, pointed bill: *A woodpecker taps on trees to get at the insects under the bark.*

woods (wu̇dz) *n. pl.* a forest; a large number of trees growing together.

wool (wu̇l) *n.* **1.** the thick hair of sheep and some other animals. **2.** thread, yarn, or cloth made from this hair.

woollen, woolen (wu̇l′ ən) *adj.* made of wool.

word (wu̇rd) *n.* **1.** a sound or group of sounds that mean something when spoken, written, or read. **2.** a promise: *I give you my word.*

wore (wȯr) see **wear.**

work (wu̇rk) *n.* **1.** something that a person does to earn money; a job. **2.** an activity that uses effort: *Growing crops is hard work.* **3.** something done or made by someone: *a work of art.* —*v.* **1.** to do work for pay: *My grandmother works as a librarian.* **2.** to do or make something through effort: *We worked on our project after school.* **3.** to run or operate: *The radio does not work.* **working. worked.**

worker (wu̇r′ kər) *n.* a person who works.

workshop (wu̇rk′ shop) *n.* a place where work is done by hand or by machine.

world (wu̇rld) *n.* **1.** the earth and all the people, animals, and plants living on it. **2.** a special part of the earth: *the animal world.* **3.** any special interest: *the world of computers.* **4.** another planet in space.

worm (wu̇rm) *n.* a small crawling animal with a long, soft body and no legs.

worn (wȯrn) see **wear.**

worry (wu̇r′ ē) *n.* a troubled feeling. *pl.* **worries.** —*v.* to feel troubled about something bad that may happen or may have happened: *I was worried about our dog because he wasn't eating very much.* **worrying. worried.** he **worries.**

worse (wu̇rs) *adj.* more than bad: *Sabina's cold is bad. Tomas's is even worse.*

worship (wu̇r′ ship) *n.* prayers and praise given to a god. —*v.* to show respect and love for a god. **worshipping. worshipped.**

worst (wu̇rst) *adj.* the most harmful, painful, unattractive, evil, and so on: *The orange team is bad. The blue team is worse. The green team is the worst of all.*

worth (wu̇rth) *n.* value or importance: *You cannot measure the worth of friendship.* —*adj.* **1.** equal in value to: *The ring is worth five dollars.* **2.** good enough for: *This book is worth reading.*

worthless (wu̇rth′ ləs) *adj.* not worth anything; not useful or valuable.

worthwhile (wu̇rth′ hwīl *or* wu̇rth′ wīl) *adj.* worth spending time or money on: *Volunteer work is a worthwhile activity.*

would (wu̇d) see **will.**

wouldn't (wu̇d′ ənt) short for **would not.**

wound (wūnd) *n.* an injury caused by a knife, a gun, and so on. —*v.* to injure with a knife, gun, and so on. **wounding. wounded.**

wound (wownd) see **wind** (verb).

wove, woven (wōv, wō′ vən) see **weave.**

wrap (rap) *v.* to put paper or cloth tightly all around something: *to wrap a present.* **wrapping. wrapped.**

wreath (rēath) *n.* a large ring of flowers, branches, and other decorations twisted together.

wreath

wreck (rek) *n.* something destroyed, such as a crashed airplane. —*v.* to damage badly, ruin, destroy: *The hurricane wrecked many houses.* **wrecking. wrecked.**

wren (ren) *n.* a small songbird that eats insects.

wrench (rench) *n.* **1.** a tool that is used to twist something such as nuts and bolts. **2.** a sharp pull or twist. *pl.* **wrenches.** —*v.* to pull or twist hard: *I wrenched a muscle in my arm.* **wrenching. wrenched.**

wrestle (res′ əl) *v.* to struggle with someone and force him or her to the ground without hitting with the hand. **wrestling. wrestled.**

wrestling (res′ ling) *n.* a sport in which two people use their arms, bodies, and legs to try to force each other to the ground.

wriggle (rig′ əl) *v.* **1.** to twist and turn. **2.** to move by twisting and turning: *The skunk wriggled through a hole in the fence.* **wriggling. wriggled.**

wring (ring) *v.* to twist and squeeze tightly: *I wrung my wet bathing suit until it stopped dripping.* **wringing. wrung.**

wrinkle (ring′ kəl) *n.* a crease in cloth or on the skin. —*v.* to become creased. **wrinkling. wrinkled.**

wrist (rist) *n.* the joint between your hand and elbow.

write (rīt) *v.* **1.** to put words, numbers, or other symbols down on paper, on a board, or on a computer screen, so that people can read them. **2.** to create a story, poem, or other written piece. **writing. wrote.** I have **written.**

writer (rīt′ ər) *n.* **1.** person who writes books, stories, poems, and so on as a job. **2.** a person who writes somethng.

writing (rīt′ ing) *n.* **1.** the act of making words with pen, pencil, chalk, a computer keyboard, and so on. **2.** any written work: *The teacher asked us to choose our best piece of writing to include in a class magazine.*

written (rit′ ən) see **write**.

wrong (rong) *adj.* **1.** not true or correct: *a wrong answer.* **2.** not right, good, or fair: *It is wrong to steal.* **3.** not working as it should be: *Something is wrong with the computer.*

wrote (rōt) see **write**.

wrung (rung) see **wring**.

X (eks) *n.* **1.** the twenty-fourth letter of the alphabet. **2.** an unidentified person or thing: *Mr. X; Ms. X.* **3.** a marker: *X marks where we are on this map.* **4.** the Roman numeral meaning 10. *pl.* **Xs** or **X's.**

xebec (zē′ bek′) *n.* a small sailing ship that has three masts and is used on the Mediterranean Sea.

xenophile (zē′ nə fīl′) *n.* a person who likes and enjoys things and people from other countries.

xenophobe (zē′ nə fōb′) *n.* a person who dislikes or is afraid of things and especially people from other countries.

xenophobia (zē′ nə fō′ bē ə) *n.* a dislike or fear of things and people from countries or cultures other than your own.

In ancient Greek, *xenos* means "stranger" and "guest," *philos* means "loving," and *phobos* means "fearing." Can you see how the words **xenophile**, **xenophobe**, and **xenophobia** were formed?

xerography (zi rog′ rə fē) *n.* the process by which photocopies are made: *An electric charge makes a dry powder stick to a blank piece of paper in exactly the same shapes as the printing on the page being copied. Heat then melts the powder onto the paper and the photocopy is done.*

X-ray (eks′ rā′) *n.* a picture taken of the inside of your body using **X-rays**, special rays that pass through the soft parts of your body: *The doctor looked at an X-ray of the broken bone in my arm.*

X's and O's (eks′ əs ənd ōz′) *n.* a game in which two players take turns marking crosses or circles on a drawing of nine squares; the game ends when there are three of the same marks in a row. Also called tick-tack-toe.

xylem (zī′ ləm) *n.* the woody part of a plant stem that carries water up from the roots and into the leaves.

xylophone (zī′ lə fōn′) *n.* a musical percussion instrument made of wooden or metal bars of different lengths. The bars are tapped with a pair of small wooden hammers to create musical notes.

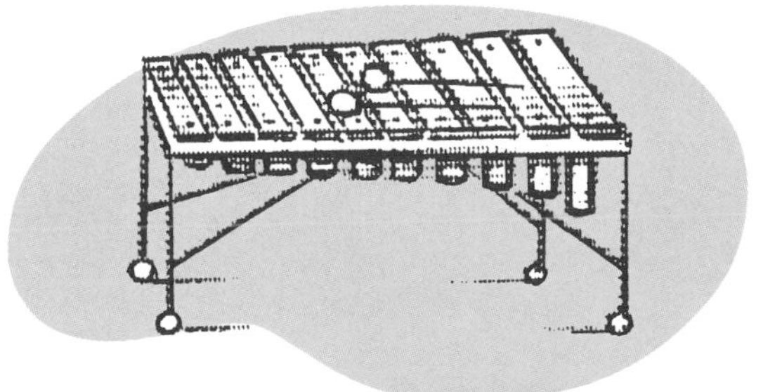

xylophone

In ancient Greek, *xylon* means "wood" and *phone* means "sound." Say the words together and you'll hear how we get the word **xylophone**.

yacht (yot) *n.* **1.** a sailing boat, often used for racing. **2.** a small ship used for pleasure trips.

yak (yak) *n.* a long-haired mammal that lives in Asia: *Yaks are related to cattle and buffalo.* —*v.* (*slang*) to talk or chat a lot. **yakking. yakked.**

yak

yam (yam) *n.* a thick root, used for food: *Yams grow in warm places and are similar to potatoes.*

yank (yangk) *n.* a sudden, hard pull: *Ben gave a yank on the rope.* —*v.* to give such a pull. **yanking. yanked.**

Yankee (yang′ kē) *n.* **1.** an American from the northern states of the United States. **2.** any American.

yap (yap) *n.* a short, high bark of a small dog. —*v.* to make such a noise. **yapping. yapped.**

yard (yȧrd) *n.* **1.** an area of ground next to or around a house, school, or other building. **2.** a unit for measuring length, equal to a little less than one metre.

yarn (yȧrn) *n.* **1.** thick thread used in knitting or weaving. **2.** a long, made-up adventure story: *The old sailor told the children yarns about his adventures on the sea.*

yawn (yon) *n.* a slow, deep breath with your mouth wide open, taken in because you are tired or bored. —*v.* to take a yawn. **yawning. yawned.**

year (yēr) *n.* a long measure of time equal to one complete revolution of the earth around the sun: *A year is 365 days (366 days in a leap year), 52 weeks, or 12 months long.*

yearbook (yēr′ bu̇k′) *n.* a book published every year that includes information about the past year: *Our school yearbook contains written compositions and drawings by students, photos of sports events, and information about each grade.*

yearling (yēr′ ling *or* yu̇r′ ling) *n.* an animal, such as a horse, that is one year old.

yearly (yēr′ lē) *adv.* once a year: *The circus comes to town yearly.* —*adj.* happening every year: *We take our yearly holiday in July.*

yearn (yu̇rn) *v.* to wish for something very much; to long: *He yearns to get a position on the team.* **yearning. yearned.**

yeast (yēst) *n.* a yellow substance made up of small fungus cells. Yeast is used to make dough rise when making bread. It is also used to make beer and other alcoholic drinks.

yell (yel) *n.* a loud shout. —*v.* to shout very loudly. **yelling. yelled.**

yellow (yel′ ō) *n.* the colour of a lemon, an egg yolk, or a dandelion. —*adj.* having such a colour.

yelp (yelp) *n.* a quick bark or cry of pain. —*v.* to make such a bark or cry: *I yelped when I stubbed my toe.* **yelping. yelped.**

yes (yes) *adv.* the opposite of no; it means "That is right," "I agree," "I will do it."

yesterday (yes′ tər dā′ *or* yes′ tər dē) *n.* the day before today; the day just past:

Yesterday was my birthday. —*adv.* on the day before today: *We went to the lake yesterday.*

yet (yet) *adv.* **1.** up to now: *I have not read the book yet.* **2.** still: *They may yet arrive.* **3.** at this time: *Don't start yet.* —*conj.* but: *It is sunny, yet it may rain later.*

yield (yēld) *n.* an amount that is produced: *The farmer got a good yield of corn this year.* —*v.* **1.** to produce: *The orchard yields much fruit.* **2.** to give way to someone or something: *The car yielded to the truck.* **yielding. yielded.**

yodel (yō′ dəl) *v.* to sing or call with very high and low notes: *People living in the Swiss mountains used to yodel as a way to call to each other across a valley.* **yodelling. yodelled.**

yogurt (yō′ gürt) *n.* a thick, creamy food made from milk and often sweetened with honey or fruit.

yoke (yōk) *n.* a wooden frame fastened around the necks of two work animals to enable them to work together as they pull a plough or a wagon.

yoke

yolk (yōk) *n.* the yellow, round part of an egg.

yonder (yon′ dər) *adj.* over there: *Look at yonder valley.*

yore (yȯr) *n.* long ago: *days of yore.*

you (yü) *pron.* the person or persons you are speaking or writing to. **You** is used both as the subject of a verb and as the object of a verb or preposition: *You invited me to your party. I gave my present to you.*

you'd (yüd) a short form (contraction) of **you had** or **you would**.

you'll (yül) a short form (contraction) of **you will**.

young (yung) *n.* **1.** the babies or young animals of an adult animal: *The mother bird looked for worms for her young.* **2.** young people; youth. —*adj.* in the early part of life; not old.

youngster (yung′ stər) *n.* a young boy or girl; a child.

your (yȯr) *adj.* belonging to you: *Is this your hat?*

you're (yȯr *or* yər) a short form (contraction) of **you are**.

Be careful not to mix up **your** with **you're**. You're stands for "you are," while your means "belonging to you."

yours (yȯrz) *pron.* the one belonging to you: *That isn't my hat; it's yours.*

yourself (yȯr self′ *or* yər self′) *pron.* your self alone. "Yourself" is used when the subject and object of a verb are the same: *Can you see yourself? pl.* **yourselves.**

youth (yüth) *n.* **1.** the time between being a child and being an adult: *In her youth, my mother was a track-and-field athlete.* **2.** a young person. *pl.* **youth** or **youths.**

youthful (yüth′ fəl) *adj.* **1.** seeming to be young in the way you look or act: *My grandparents have a youthful sense of humour; they enjoy the movie comedies that we do.*

you've (yüv) a short form (contraction) of **you have**.

yo-yo (yō′ yō) *n.* a small toy, like a spool, that is spun up and down on a string. *pl.* **yo-yos.**

yummy (yum′ ē) *adj.* (*informal*) delicious.

Appendix

Provinces, Territories, and Capitals of Canada

The capital of Canada is Ottawa, Ontario.

Provinces (from west to east)	*Abbreviations*	*Capitals*
British Columbia	BC	Victoria
Alberta	AB	Edmonton
Saskatchewan	SK	Regina
Manitoba	MB	Winnipeg
Ontario	ON	Toronto
Québec	QC	Québec City
New Brunswick	NB	Fredericton
Nova Scotia	NS	Halifax
Prince Edward Island	PE	Charlottetown
Newfoundland	NF	St. John's
Territories		
Yukon	YT	Whitehorse
Northwest Territories	NT	Yellowknife

Days and Months

There are 7 days in a week. There are 52 weeks, or 365 days, in a year. Every fourth year, called a leap year, has 366 days. (The extra day is added to the end of February.) There are 12 months in a year.

Days of the Week
Sunday (Sun.)
Monday (Mon.)
Tuesday (Tues.)
Wednesday (Wed.)
Thursday (Thurs.)
Friday (Fri.)
Saturday (Sat.)

Months	*Number of Days*
January (Jan.)	31
February (Feb.)	28 (29 in a leap year)
March (Mar.)	31
April (Apr.)	30
May (May)	31
June (Jun.)	30
July (Jul.)	31
August (Aug.)	31
September (Sept.)	30
October (Oct.)	31
November (Nov.)	30
December (Dec.)	31

Numbers

Numerals	*Cardinal*	*Ordinal*
1	one	first
2	two	second
3	three	third
4	four	fourth
5	five	fifth
6	six	sixth
7	seven	seventh
8	eight	eighth
9	nine	ninth
10	ten	tenth
11	eleven	eleventh
12	twelve	twelfth
13	thirteen	thirteenth
14	fourteen	fourteenth
15	fifteen	fifteenth
16	sixteen	sixteenth
17	seventeen	seventeenth
18	eighteen	eighteenth
19	nineteen	nineteenth
20	twenty	twentieth
30	thirty	thirtieth
40	forty	fortieth
50	fifty	fiftieth
60	sixty	sixtieth
70	seventy	seventieth
80	eighty	eightieth
90	ninety	ninetieth
100	one hundred	hundredth
1000	one thousand	thousandth
1 000 000	one million	millionth
1 000 000 000	one billion	billionth

Writing out other numbers
The number "twenty-one" comes after "twenty." "Twenty-first" comes after "twentieth." When writing out numbers like these, use a hyphen between the first and second part of the number.

Metric Symbols

Symbol	*Meaning*
mm	millimetre
cm	centimetre
m	metre
km	kilometre
s	second
min	minute
h	hour
d	day
a	year
km/h	kilometres per hour
mL	millilitre
L	litre
kL	kilolitre
mg	milligram
g	gram
kg	kilogram
t	tonne
cm^2	square centimetre
m^2	square metre
km^2	square kilometre
ha	hectare
cm^3	cubic centimetre
m^3	cubic metre
°C	degrees Celsius

Some Holidays and Special Days

New Year's Day	*January 1*
Solnal (Korean New Year)	*January 1*
Epiphany (Christian)	*January 6*
Ukrainian Christmas	*January 7*
Iroquois Midwinter Festival (New Year)	*Eight days in January*
Burns Night (Scottish)	*January 25*
Chinese New Year	*During first moon in late January or February*
Black History Month	*Month of February*
Carnival, Mardi Gras (Christian)	*Several days or weeks leading up to Lent*
Ash Wednesday (Christian)	*First day of Lent (between February 3 and March 5)*
Valentine's Day	*February 14*
Shiva Ratri (Hindu)	*Mid-February*
Purim (Jewish)	*One day in February or March*
St. Patrick's Day (Irish)	*March 17*
Now Ruz (West Asian New Year)	*March 20 or 21*
Passover (Jewish)	*Eight days in March or April*
Good Friday (Christian)	*Friday before Easter Sunday*
Easter Sunday (Christian)	*Between March 22 and April 20 (First Sunday following the full moon that is on or just after March 21)*
April Fool's Day	*April 1*
Hana Matsuri (Buddha Day—Buddhist)	*April 8*
Baisakhi (Solar New Year—Sikh, Hindu, Buddhist, Jain)	*April 13 or 14*
Toonik Tyme (Inuit)	*Third weekend in April*
Earth Day	*April 22*
St. George's Day (Greek and Coptic Orthodox)	*April 23*
Mother's Day	*Second Sunday in May*
Wesak (Buddha's Birthday—Buddhist)	*Around second Sunday in May*
Victoria Day	*Monday before May 24*
Father's Day	*Third Sunday in June*
St-Jean Baptiste Day (Canada: QC)	*June 24*
Canada Day	*July 1*
Obon (Japanese)	*July 15*

Sun Dance (First Nations)	*Various dates in the summer*
Civic Day (Canada: NWT, BC, SK, MB, ON, NB)	*First Monday in August*
Labour Day	*First Monday in September*
Chinese Mid-Autumn (Moon) Festival	*Full moon in September*
Rosh Hashana (Jewish New Year)	*Full moon in late September or early October*
Yom Kippur (Jewish)	*Late September or October*
Navaratri (Hindu)	*Nine nights in September or October*
Canadian Thanksgiving	*Second Monday in October*
Oktoberfest (German)	*Some time in October*
Hallowe'en	*October 31*
All Saint's Day (Christian)	*November 1*
Divali (Festival of Lights—Hindu)	*Late October or November*
American Thanksgiving	*Fourth Thursday in November*
Remembrance Day	*November 11*
Hanukkah or Chanukah (Jewish)	*Eight nights in late November or December*
Christmas (Christian)	*December 25*
Boxing Day	*December 26*
Kwanzaa (Black heritage celebration)	*December 26 to January 1*

Muslim Holidays*

Ramadan (Month of Fasting)	*Ninth month of the Muslim calendar*
Eed-ul-Fitr	*Three-day festival at the end of Ramadan*
Eed-ul-Adha (Feast of Sacrifice)	*Tenth day of the twelfth month*
Ras Al-Sana (New Year's Day)	*First day of the Muslim calendar*

* ***Note:*** Since all of the Muslim holidays are on different dates every year, they are listed separately.

Punctuation

Punctuation Mark	*Usage*	*Example*
Apostrophe (')	1. Replaces the missing letters in a contraction (short form) of a word. 2. Shows possession — • singular: • plural:	*do not = don't* *she will = she'll* *the dog's tail* *the bees' hive*
Colon (:)	1. Introduces a list, an example, or sometimes a quotation. 2. Used after the name of the person to whom a business letter is addressed.	*We put everything we needed in the picnic basket: plates, glasses, cutlery, napkins, a blanket, and the food.* *Dear Ms. Taylor:* *Dear Mr. Wong:*
Comma (,)	1. Indicates a pause in a sentence. 2. Shows different parts of a list. 3. Used before and after quotation marks. 4. Used after the name of a person being spoken to. 5. Used after the name of the person to whom a friendly letter is addressed, and in the closing of *all* letters.	*It started raining, so the baseball game was postponed.* *We are having salad, tacos, and refried beans for dinner.* *She exclaimed, "I can't wait for the weekend!"* *"Neither can I," he echoed.* *Ravi, may I please borrow a pencil?* *Dear Cory,* *Yours truly,*

Exclamation mark **(!)**	Used at the end of a sentence to show great feeling, such as joy, surprise, excitement, or anger.	*Hurray!* *Look out! There's danger ahead!*
Period **(.)**	1. Used at the end of a sentence that is a statement or command. 2. Used to show an abbreviation.	*Sam swims every day.* *Shut the window.* *Dr. Izso* *Byward St.*
Question mark **(?)**	Used at the end of a sentence that asks a question.	*What is your name?* *Where are they going?*
Quotation marks **(" ")**	1. Used to show the beginning and end of the exact words spoken by a person. 2. Used to set words apart or draw attention to them for some reason.	*The umpire called, "Strike three!"* *Do you know the difference between "council" and "counsel"?*
Semicolon **(;)**	Used to separate the parts of a complicated sentence or a complicated list.	*My knapsack contains two pairs of jeans; three shirts, one with long sleeves; four pairs of wool socks; two pairs of boots, one waterproof; and one sweater.*

Pronunciation

Pronunciation is given (in brackets) for all the words in this dictionary. The letters and signs are pronounced as in the examples below.

Vowel Sounds

a	as in **a**nd, b**a**d, s**a**ng
ā	as in f**a**ce, **a**ble, m**ai**l
ȧ	as in **a**rt, c**a**r, he**a**rt
e	as in b**e**nd, h**ea**d, wh**e**n
ē	as in b**e**, b**ee**, **ea**t
ə	as in met**a**l, brok**e**n, penc**i**l, bac**o**n, circ**u**s (ə is an unstressed syllable called a schwa)
i	as in **i**f, s**i**t, w**i**ll
ī	as in **I**, f**i**ne, b**y**
o	as in **o**n, p**o**t, p**aw**
ō	as in r**o**pe, s**oa**p, **ow**n
ȯ	as in **o**rder, ab**oa**rd, c**o**re
u	as in **u**p, **o**ther, s**u**ng
ū	as in r**u**de, c**oo**l, bl**ew**, sh**oe**
u̇	as in f**u**ll, c**oo**k, f**u**r, sear**ch**

Consonant Sounds

th	as in **th**ing, bo**th**
TH	as in o**th**er, **th**an
zh	as in mea**s**ure, vi**si**on

Stress Marks

′	main stress
′	secondary stress

Stress marks appear after the syllables that are pronounced with the most force. The pronunciation for "basketball" (bas**′** kət bol′) shows that the first and last syllables are both stressed, but the first syllable is stressed the most.

Abbreviations

The following abbreviations, or short forms, are used in this dictionary.

adj.	adjective
adv.	adverb
conj.	conjunction
fem.	feminine
interj.	interjection
masc.	masculine
n.	noun
opp.	opposite
pl.	plural
prep.	preposition
pron.	pronoun
sing.	singular
v.	verb